ARCHETYPE
FANTASY
PSYCHEDELIC
SPECIAL EFFECTS
NONSENSE AND HUMOUR
SYMBOLIC DESIGN
PROGRAMMATIC WORKS
ILLUSTRATIONS
TRANSFORMED WORKS
MODERNISM
NUDE
ANIMAL HISTORY ON COVER ARTS
PORTRAITS
LETTERING
EXOTICISM AND RACISM
JAZZ MODE
SLEEVE VARIATIONS
RECORD LABELS

A

SIDE 2
STEREO 331/3
ISBN4-7661-1268-7
MADE IN JAPAN

In Search of the Lost Record

British Album Cover Art of 50's to 80's

MATSUI Takumi

In Search of the Lost Record
British Album Cover Art of 50's to 80's
By MATSUI Takumi

First edition published in October 2001

Coordinator: MURAMATSU chie (Remington Corporation)
Photographer: HIROSE masatoshi
Translation from Japanese: YOSHIDA kaori, HAGIHARA yumiko
Editor: MURAMATSU chie
URATA yoshihiro (Graphic-sha Publishing Co., Ltd.)
Designer: TERAI keiji

Printed by DAI NIPPON PRINTING CO., LTD
Published by Graphic-sha Publishing Co., Ltd.

Special thanks to ASAI tamotsu, KOYAMA tetsuto, MIYAWAKI hiroshi and YOKOYAMA shigeru for the loan of their valuable collections.

Graphic-sha Publishing Co., Ltd.
1-9-12 Kudankita Chiyoda-ku Tokyo, 102-0073, Japan
PHONE 81 (3) 3263-4579
FAX 81 (3) 5275-3579
URL http://www.graphicsha.co.jp

まえがき

アナログ・レコードは、過渡期の音楽媒体である。第二次世界大戦後、SP(スタンダード・プレイング・レコード)はLP(ロング・プレイング・レコード)に取って変わられた。しかし、そのLPも、CD、あるいはMDといったデジタル媒体によって、ほぼ完全に駆逐された。いまでは、ネット配信という音楽の供給手段も、着実に需要を伸ばしつつある。

こうした進化における最大のお題目は、いかに記憶容量を大きく、反面、いかに容器を小さくするかであった。かさばって、保管もめんどうなアナログ・レコードは、いつか滅びゆく運命だったのである。昔の作品が聴きたいのなら、再発CDで十分こと足りてしまうだろう。

けれども、そうしたアナログ特有のサイズが、かえって斬新なアートを生み出していたのも事実である。レコードが誕生したばかりの頃、それはあくまで補助的な手段とみなされていたはずだ。音楽の最大の聴きどころは、生演奏にあった。それが60年代になると、録音技術が進化を遂げ、テープの大幅な編集や加工が可能となり、レコードがたんなる生演奏の再生手段から、レコーディング・スタジオでしか作れない実験的な音を収めたアート作品へと、劇的に変化していく。

そして、レコードのアート性は、当然、人々の目をパッケージ・デザインにも向けさせることとなり、"カヴァー・アート(あるいはジャケット・アート)"という概念を生み出した。60年代末から70年代初頭のサイケデリック芸術やプログレッシヴ・ロックの実験主義は、そんなカヴァー・アートの隆盛に、さらに拍車をかける結果となった。

とりわけ、LPレコードにおいては、30センチ四方の大きなサイズ、ジャケットに使われる厚紙の質感、ヴィニール・ディスクならではの重量感といった特性が、最大限に生かされた。それが、正方形のシングル・ジャケットだけでなく、見開きじゃケットや変型ジャケットなどの大胆な発想に結びつき、レコード作品のアート性を、よりいっそう高める結果となったのである。アナログ・レコードのジャケットがCDやMDほどの視認性しかなかったら、果たしてあれほどまでに多彩なヴィジュアル作家たちの発表の場たり得たかどうか。これもまた、負の要素もまた可なり、という、ひとつの典型例といえるのではないだろうか。

本書はいわば、アナログ・レコードのアルバム・カヴァーを、ヴィジュアル・アートの視点で捉え、一冊にまとめたものである。もちろん、アルバム・カヴァーをアートと捉える視点は、イギリスだけを対象にしたものではないが、なんといってもこの国は、キーフやヒプノシス、ロジャー・ディーンをはじめとする、イギリスならではのセンスを感じさせるヴィジュアル作家たちを数多く輩出している。また、とくに60年代後半から70年代初頭にかけての英国盤には、他国盤にはない艶やかな発色があって、そうした印刷の美しさも、コレクター市場で人気を呼ぶ一因となっているようだ。

したがって本書にも、その年代の英国アナログ盤が、もっとも多く収録されている。印刷の美しさと紙ジャケットの質感が織りなす独特の風合いをできるだけリアルに再現できるよう、カメラマンの広瀬雅敏氏には無理をいって、ひとつひとつのジャケットにきちんと影をつけて撮影してもらった。読者には、どうかそのあたりの努力も汲み取っていただきたい。

ただし、どうしてもセレクションに偏りが出てしまうのだけは、やむを得ない。個人の収蔵には限界があるし、選択基準はあくまでも主観によるものだからだ。とはいえ、結局のところ、誰がどうセレクトしようとも、多少の違いはあろうとも、レコード・ジャケットの魅力自体は、少しも揺らぐことがないはずである。ということは、本当は誰が著者であろうとかまわなかったのだ!

本書のタイトル『失われたレコードを求めて』は、ブリティッシュ・ロック・ファンにはお馴染み、ムーディー・ブルースが68年に発表したアルバム『失われたコードを求めて(In Search of the Lost Chord)』のもじりである。もはや失われゆく文化遺産であるアナログ・レコードへの哀惜の意を込めてというには、あまりにもベタだが、気軽に楽しめる本にしたかったので、こんなシャレを思いついた。

introduction

Analog records transformed music. Soon after World War II, standard-playing records (SP) were replaced by long-playing record (LP). Similarly, LP records have been rendered obsolete by new digital media, such as compact discs (CD) and mini discs (MD). The Internet is yet another new medium for the distribution of music. Evolution in such media is driven forward by the motto "large capacity in a small package". The comparative bulk of the analog record, and its fragility, meant its inevitable extinction. For listeners who want to hear old recordings, a CD reissue is more than sufficient. Yet, the distinct size of the analog record produced an entire genre of innovative record jacket art. The artwork of these protective records sleeve has always been regarded as a vital compliment to the record from its very introduction into the market. Up until the 60's live performance was the best way to hear music. However, there was a development in recording techniques and also editing and tape processing became possible, thereby changing the record. It was no longer a mere copy of a live performance. Along with experimentation possible only in the recording studio, the record itself became a work of art. Therefore the artistic value of the record itself altered the new way in which the record's package design was seen and "cover art" (or "jacket art") was born. The boom in psychedelic art and the progressive art experimentation of the late 60's and early 70's further propelled the new appreciation of cover art.

The LP record jacket provided a good canvas to ignite the artist's imagination. The surface was a large 30 x 30 cm area, the paper was thick, and the weight of the vinyl record gave the total package a tangible feel. Soon, the simple form of the jacket evolved and there appeared gatefold jackets or special, custom sleeves in a colorful variety. Undoubtedly, these elements complemented the artistic aura of the record and the music itself. If the LP record had been as small as CDs or MDs, would these visual artists have been able to create as freely as they actually did on the LP jackets?

This book is a compilation of analog record jackets, collected and arranged as independent works of visual art. Considering analog record cover art as visual art is not something that is limited to British records. However, the United Kingdom had a lot of visual artists such as Keef or Roger Dean who had a distinctly "British" visual sense. Records made in the United Kingdom from the late 60's to the early 70's are especially adored by collectors, mainly because of the beauty and excellence in printing, which was rarely found in the products of other countries during those days. Therefore, the majority of the sleeves contained in this book are analog records made in the United Kingdom. In order to reproduce the beauty of the printing and the texture of the original jacket paper, I asked photographer Mr. Hirose to capture the subtle shades of each and every jacket. The superlative reproductions in this volume are thanks to him.

Another difficulty I faced was the selection of items. The limitations of my personal collection was confounded by the criterion for selection, which is solely my own judgement. In the end, however, it doesn't really matter who is the judge. The record jackets and their beauty definitely do the talking themselves.

The title of this book, In Search for the Lost Record, is a rather obvious pun that pays tribute to "In Search of the Lost Chord" (1968) by the fantastic Moody Blues. This book is dedicated to the analog record, a cultural property on its way to extinction.

contents

index

E

F

G

H

I

J

K

L

M

N

O

P

Q

R

S

T

U, V, W, X, Y, Z

A

SIDE 2

STEREO 331/3
ISBN4-7661-1268-7
MADE IN JAPAN

In Search of the Lost Record

British Album Cover Art of 50's to 80's

MATSUI Takumi

 PRODUCED AND MANUFACTURED BY GRAPHIC-SHA, INC.

archetype
イギリスの原風景

THE BEATLES:PLEASE PLEASE ME / PARLOPHONE PMC1202 (1963)
Photo/ Angus McBean

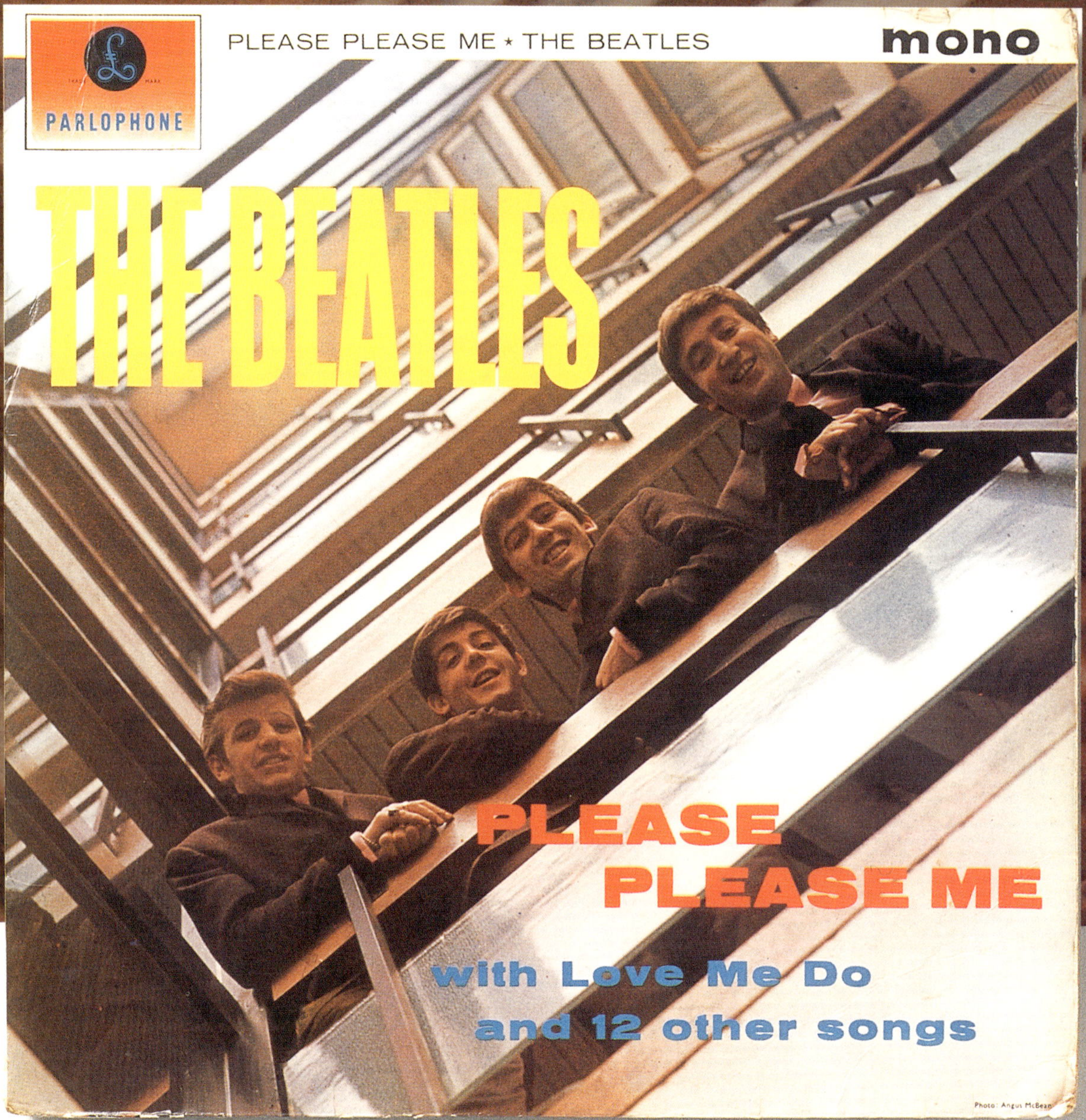

London and the Country
ロンドンと田園

イギリス人が自国の景観を好み、それを芸術に移し変えたいと願う気持ちを強く持っていることは、マーガレット・ドラブルがその著書『風景のイギリス文学』でも指摘するとおりだろう。ミルトンが詠った楽園のヴィジョンや、カンスタブルが描いた風景画は、恵み豊かな、実在する牧歌的な田園風景だった。また賛美の対象はかならずしも美しい風景だけでなく、過酷な巡礼地や荒涼としたニュータウンのこともあれば、まるで街全体が骨董市のようなロンドンの下町だったりすることもある。

近頃は“グローバル化”が著しく、こうした情趣を味わう機会もめっきり減ったように思うけれど、60〜70年代のロンドンやイギリスを描いたアルバム・ジャケットには、この種の伝統がまだまだ根強く残っていることを感じさせるものが多い。あの時代のブリティッシュ・ロックを懐かしむ人々のなかには、そうした残像をまぶたの裏に焼きつかせ、いまもその音の向こうに、レンガと石畳で茶色にくすんだロンドンや、神秘の謎に包まれた聖地や、短い夏を惜しむ田園地方を思い描いている人も多いのではないだろうか。

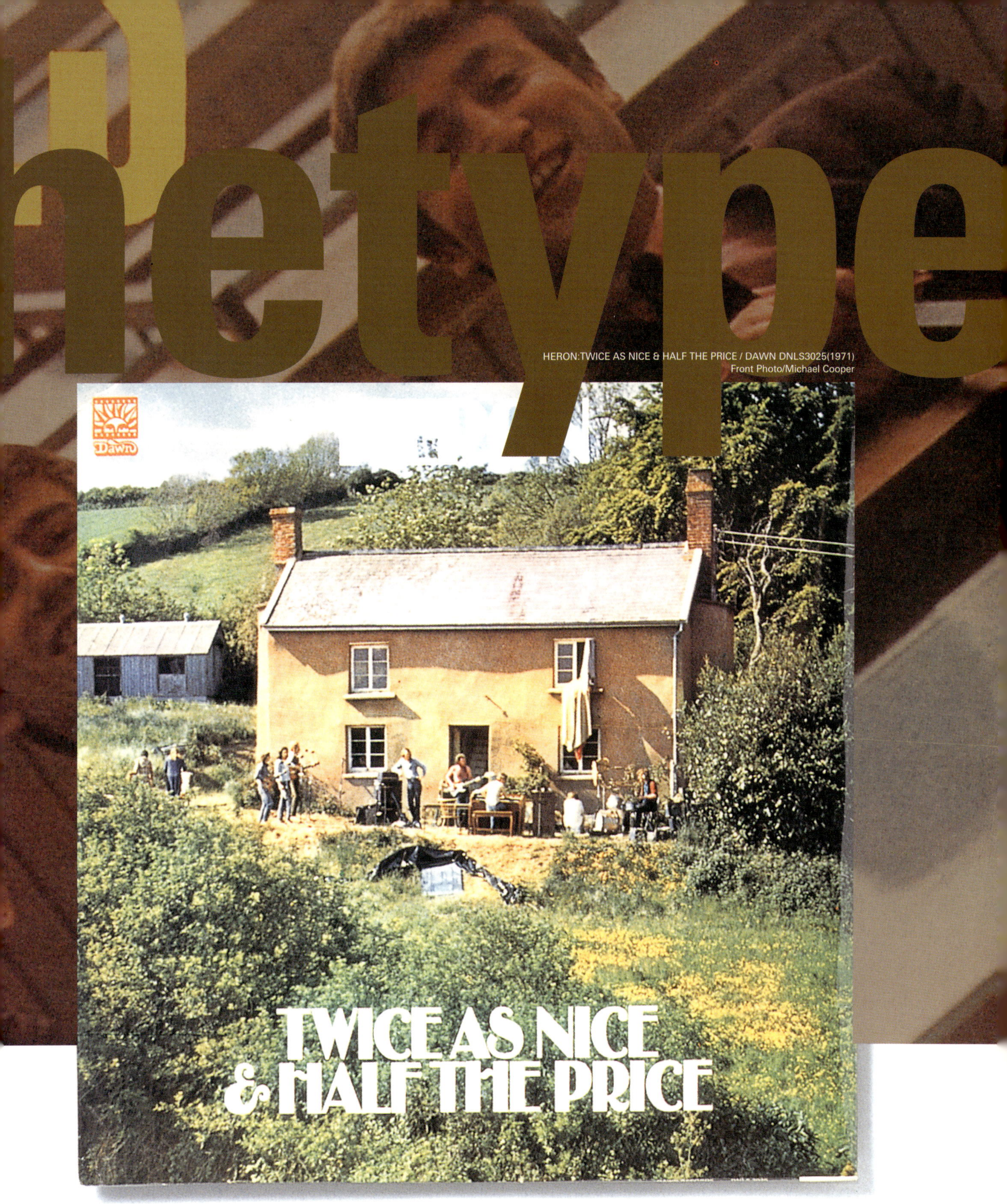

HERON:TWICE AS NICE & HALF THE PRICE / DAWN DNLS3025(1971)
Front Photo/Michael Cooper

As Margaret Drabble pointed out by in A Writer's Britain: Landscape in Literature, the British adore the landscape of their own country and have always enjoyed representing its beauty in their arts. The Elysium envisioned by Milton, for example, or the landscape paintings by John Constable, were based on existing scenery in the idyllic English countryside—rich and abundant in its beauty. There were also scenes that were far from idyllic. London, and its surrounding environ, was sometimes rendered in wild and cruel manners. The whole town, being a sort of an antique market, also received lavish admiration.

Sadly, with the advent of globalization, there are ever fewer opportunities to appreciate such scenic beauty in Britain today. However, album sleeves from the 60's to the 70's portraying scenes of London or elsewhere in Britain demonstrated that the tradition of representing the British landscape had continued. I imagine there is a common association of British Rock from this period with visions of the British landscape. Perhaps what comes to mind is a glimpse of London's bricks and pavement in brownish haze, the Holy Land in its mystic enigma, or it could be the brief splendor of the country side in the summertime.

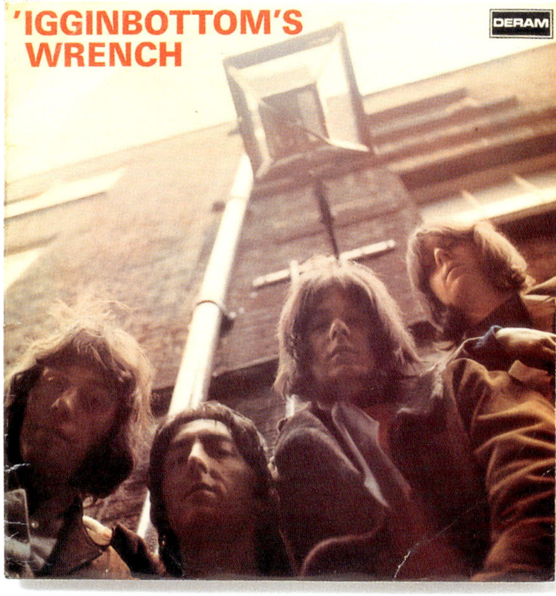

IGGINBOTTOM:IGGINBOTTOM'S WRENCH/DERAM SML1051(1969)
Photo/Terence Freeman

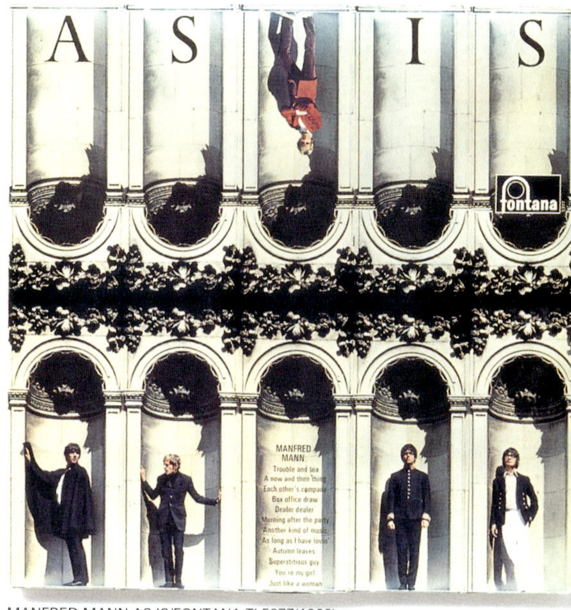

MANFRED MANN:AS IS/FONTANA TL5377(1966)
Designed the Cover/Klaus Voormann

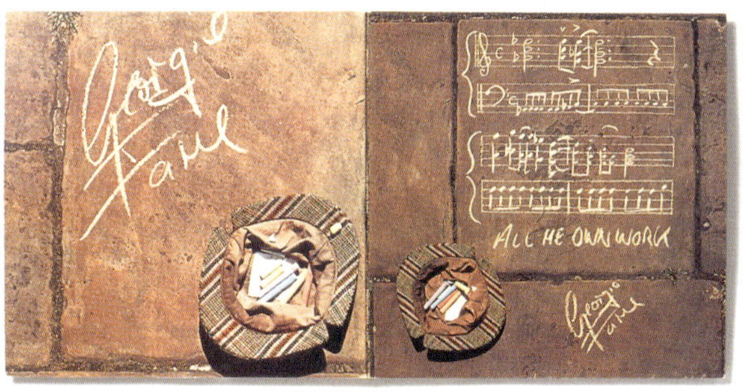

GEORGIE FAME:ALL ME OWN WORK/REPRISE K44183(1972)
Sleeve Design/Georgie Fame,Michael O'Neill,Colin Green
Photography by Christopher Thynne

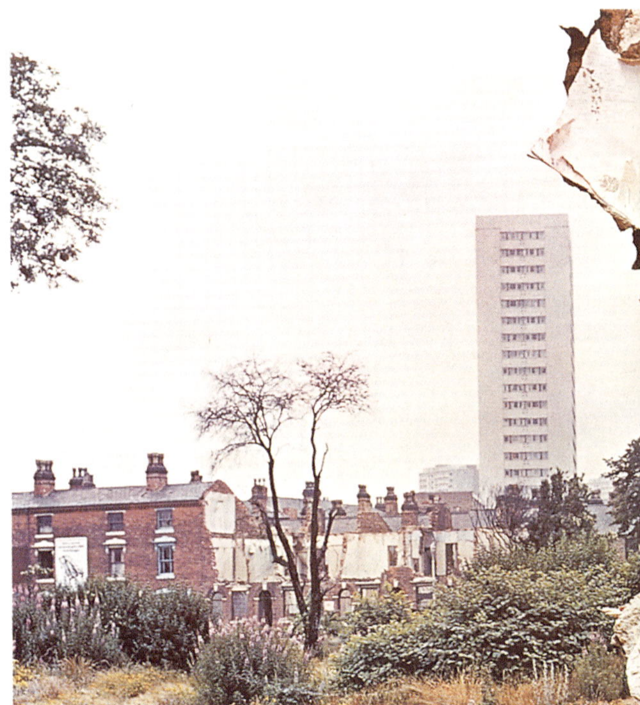

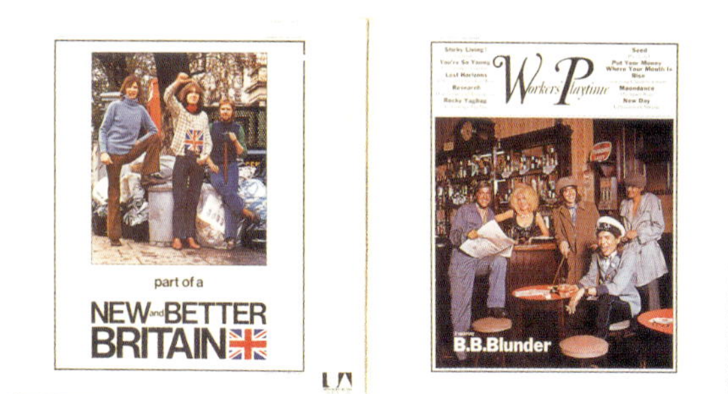

B.B.BLUNDER:WORKERS' PLAYTIME/UNITED ARTISTS UAG29156(1971)
Album Cover Conceived and Directed by Peter Swales&Kevin Wastlake
Design by Keith Davis&Grahame Berny
Front and Back Cover Photos by Keith Morris

LED ZEPPELIN:FOUR SYMBOLS/ATLANTIC 2401 012(1971)
Deisgn Co-ordination/Graphreaks

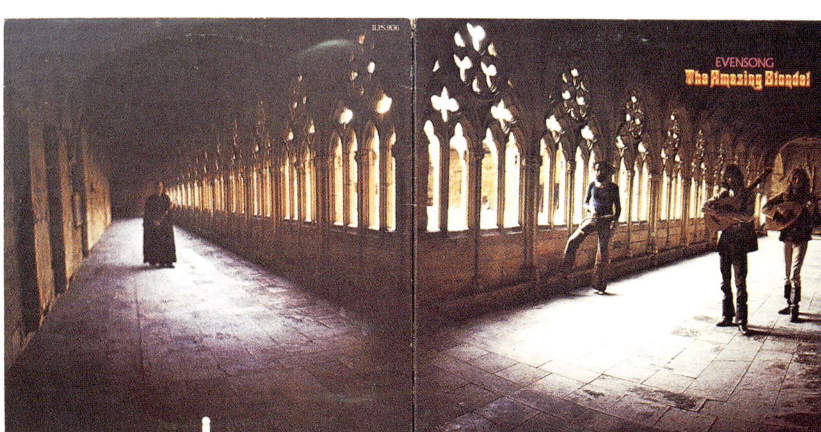

THE AMAZING BLONDEL:EVENSONG/
ISLAND ILPS9136(1970)
Photography/ Shepard Sherbell

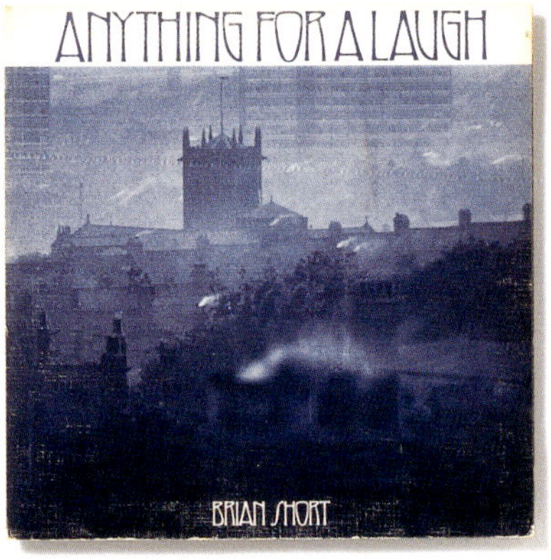

BRIAN SHORT:ANYTHING FOR A LAUGH/
TRANSATLANTIC TRA245(1971)
Album Design and Photo of Tyneside by Ian Vincentini

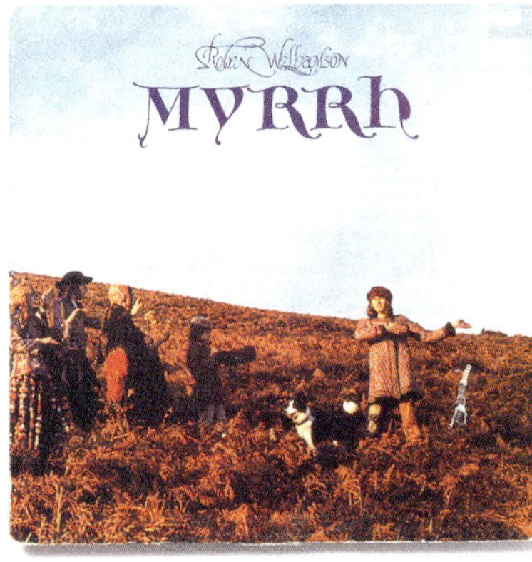

ROBIN WILLIAMSON:MYRRTH/ISLAND HELP2(1972)

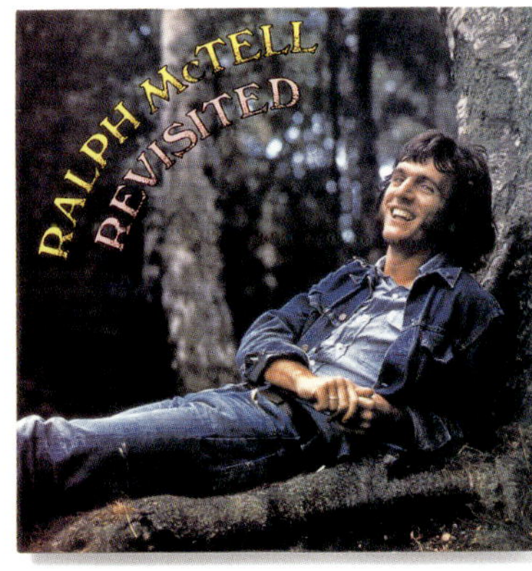

RALPH McTELL:REVISTED/TRANSATLANTIC TRA227(1970)
Sleeve Design/Rainbow
Photography/Keith Morris

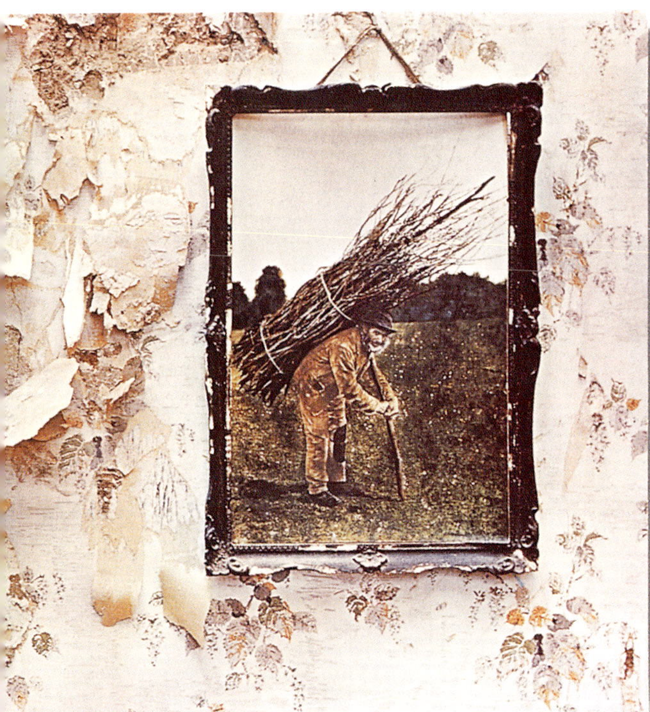

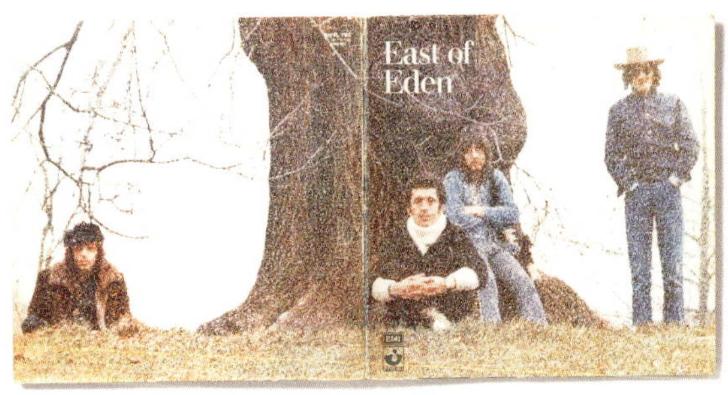

EAST OF EDEN:EAST OF EDEN/HARVEST SHVL 792(1971)
Cover Design and Photos by Hipgnosis

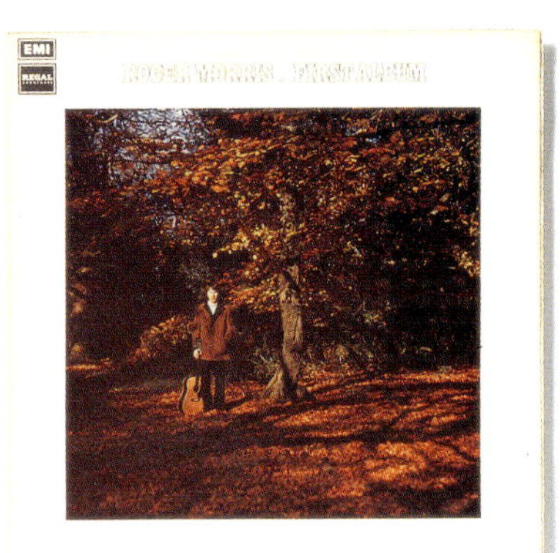

ROGER MORRIS:FIRST ALBUM/
EMI SRZA8509 (1972)
Sleeve Design and Photography by Gerard Kelly

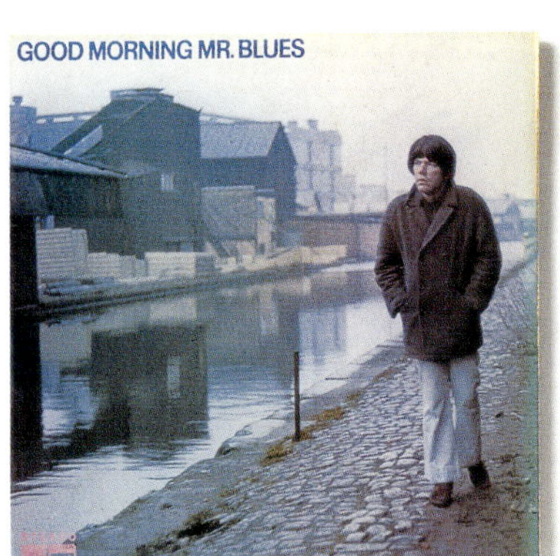

DAVE PEACE QUARTET:GOOD MORNING MR.BLUES/
SAGA FID2155(1969)
Potographed by Simon Livingstone

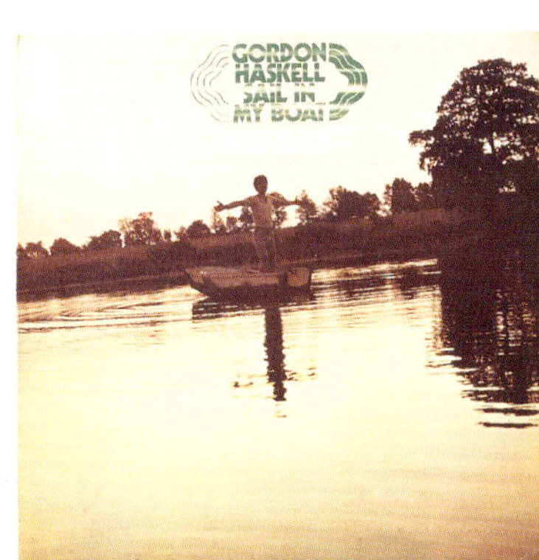

GORDON HASKEL:SAIL IN MY BOAT/CBS 63741(1969)
Photography by Nicholas Wright
Sleeve Design by John Hays

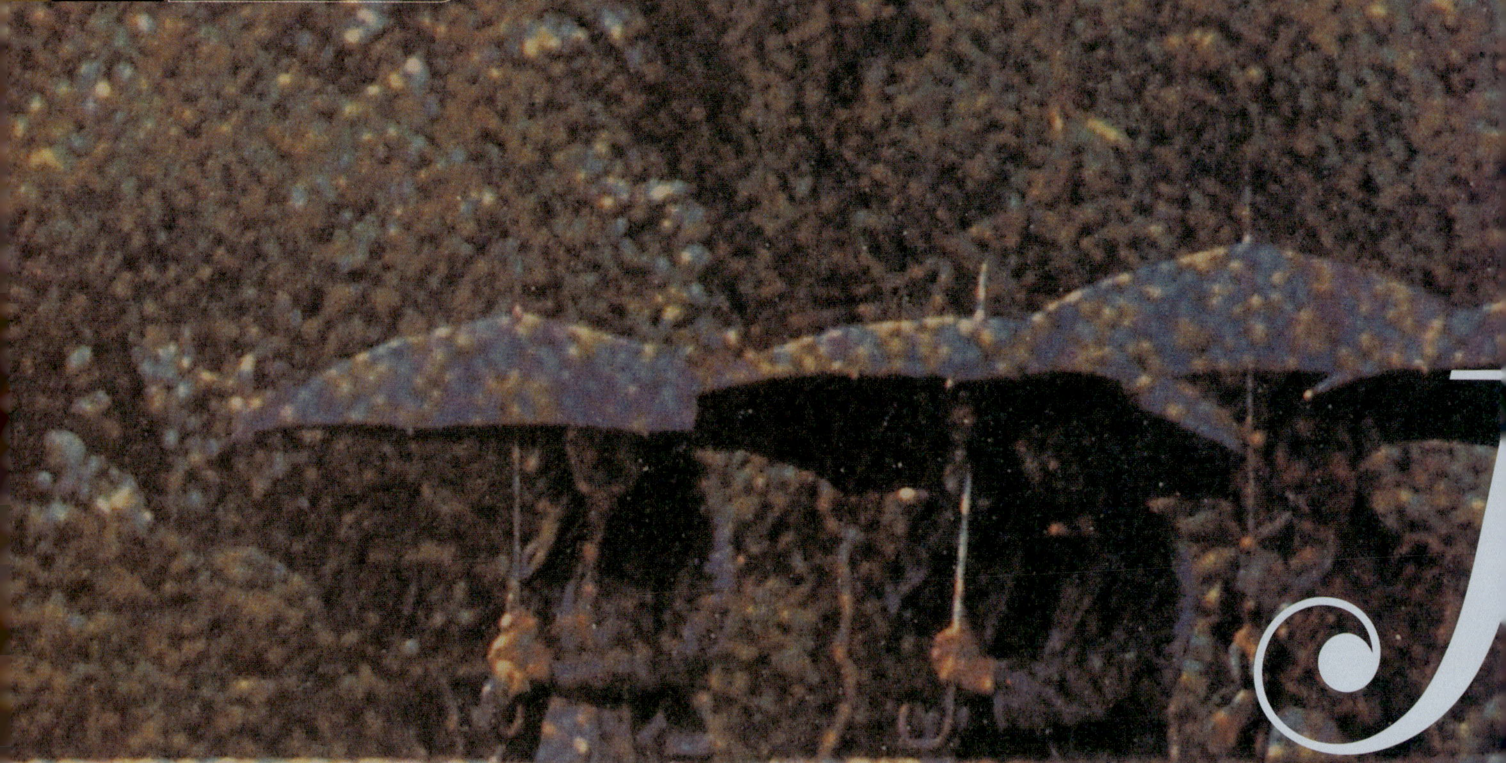

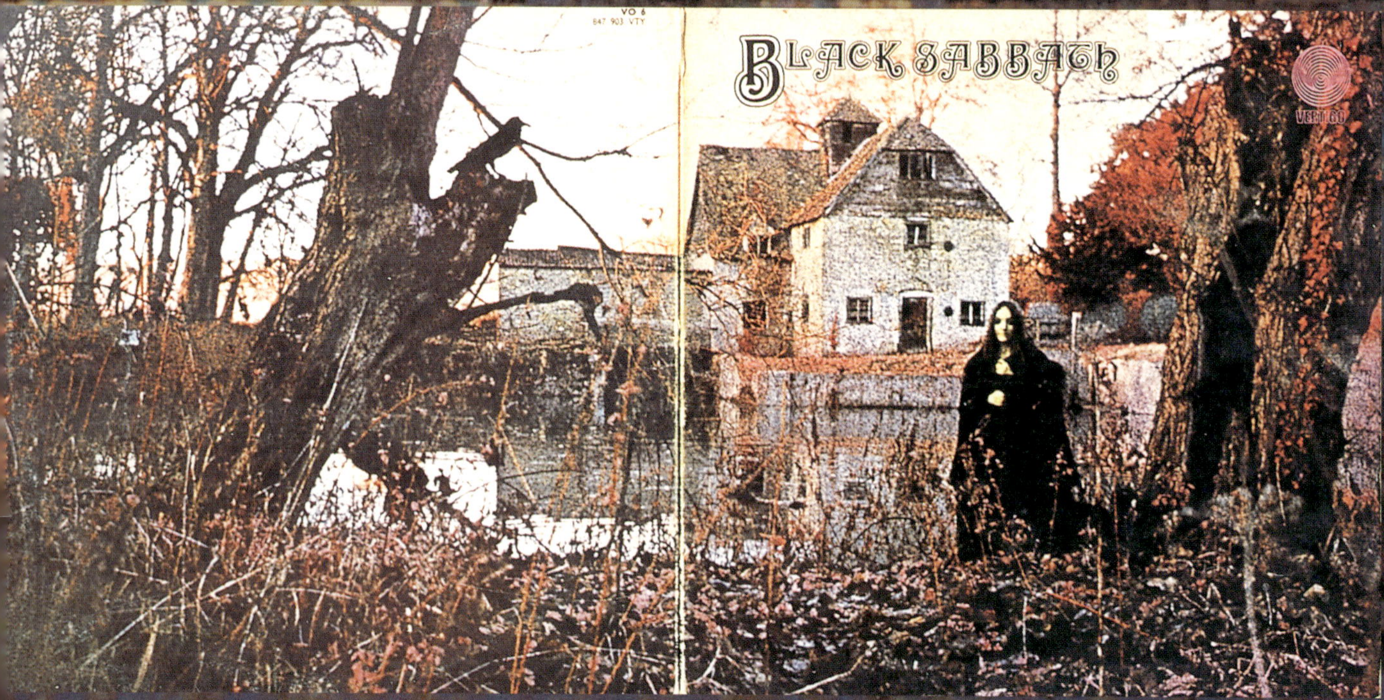

BLACK SABBATH:BLACK SABBATH/VERTIGO VO6(1970)*front and back
Album Designed and Photographed by Keef

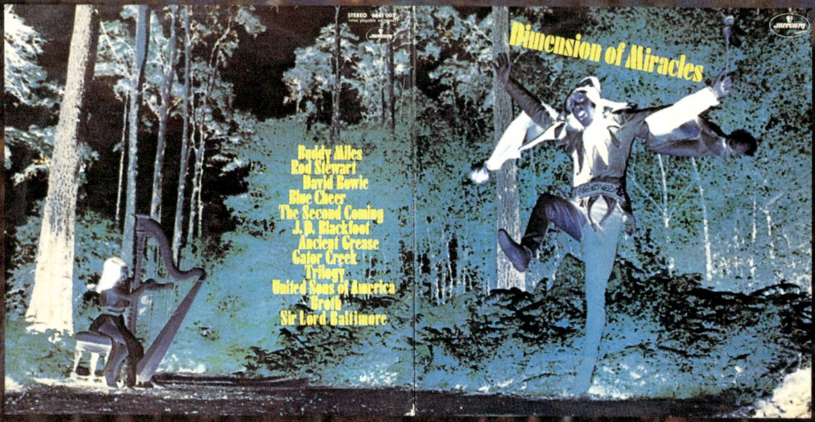

VARIOUS ARTISTS:DIMENSION OF MIRACLES/
MERCURY 6641 005(1971)*front and back
Photographs by Marcus Keef

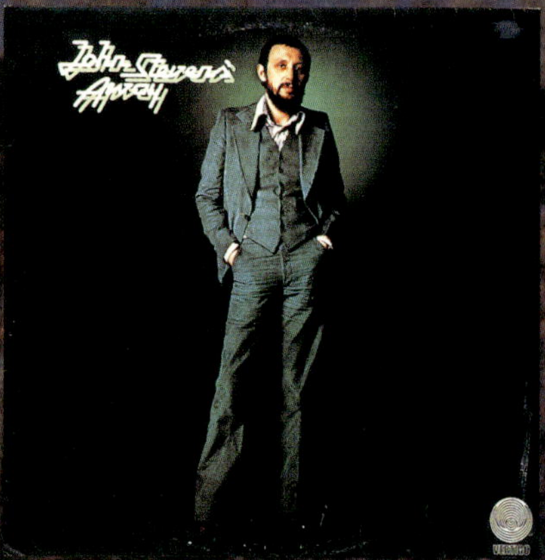

JOHN STEVENS' AWAY:JOHN STEVENS' AWAY/
VERTIGO 6360131
Front Photography/Keef
Design/Brian Palmer

① NUCLEUS:UNDER THE SUN/
VERTIGO 6360 110(1974)
Sleeve Design/Keef

② STATUS QUO:ON THE LEVEL/
VERTIGO 9102 002()
Photo/Keef
Art Direction/Jack Wood

Keef

キーフ

マーカス・キーフは本名をキース・マクミランといい、70年代の半ば頃からミュージック・ヴィデオのディレクターとして活躍しているが、それ以前には主にヴァーティゴ、ネオン、ネペンサといったブリティッシュ・プログレッシヴ系レーベルでカヴァー・アートを担当するフォトグラファー兼デザイナーだった。彼の作品づくりの特色となっているのは、マンフレッド・マン・チャプター・スリー『ヴォリューム2』やブラック・サバスに代表される赤外線フィルムの使用、直接フィルムに彩色するなどの手法による独特の色彩感と構図、あるいはクレシダ『アサイラム』や『ヴァーティゴ・アニュアル』にみられるような"死"を暗示させる被写体の道具立てである。そして、感度の低いフィルムに収めたこれらの情景をさらに大きく引き伸ばし、淡く翳りのある色調とすることで、キーフのデザインするアルバム・カヴァーは、コラージュ多用型のヒプノシスとも異なるプレモダンな凄惨さを見る者に印象づけている。そこに我々が、音楽との相乗効果で、大量消費と能率主義を基盤に置いたアメリカ社会とは対称的な、イギリスの精神風土を感じ取っていることはまちがいない。
もちろん、実写とはいえ特殊な撮影技術が用いられた作品群が、常識的な意味での原風景と呼べるものでないことは明らかだ。が、我々がキーフのアルバム・カヴァーを通して見ているのは、心象風景のなかに浮かび上がるイメージの原型としてのイギリスなのである。

Marcus Keef (born Keith McMillan) has been directing music videos since the mid-70's. Before that he was a photographer and designer of album sleeves mainly for British Progressive Rock labels, such as Vertigo, Neon and Nepentha.

What characterized his work was the use of infrared films, best typified by "Volume 2" by Manfred Man Chapter Three or Black Sabbath albums. Also, his unique method of painting directly onto the film created a particular color scheme and composition. Furthermore, his choice of subject was often associated with death, as with "Asylum" or "Vertigo Annual" by Cressida. By enlarging photographs taken with low-sensitivity film, he evoked a palette of nuanced pastel shades. In this manner, Keef's work sometimes had a pre-modern intensity that was completely different from that of Hipgnosis, who repeatedly used collage. No doubt, listener's of music encased in one of Keef's sleeves received a message of British sensibility, which contrasted with the American culture of mass production and efficiency. Certainly, the use of special photography was not an archetype of the British landscape but in Keef's work there was a nostalgic image of the British landscape, which only existed in the mind's eye.

①
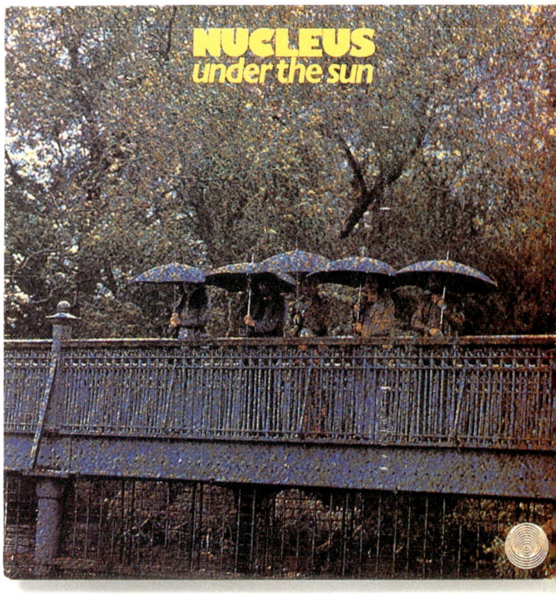

②
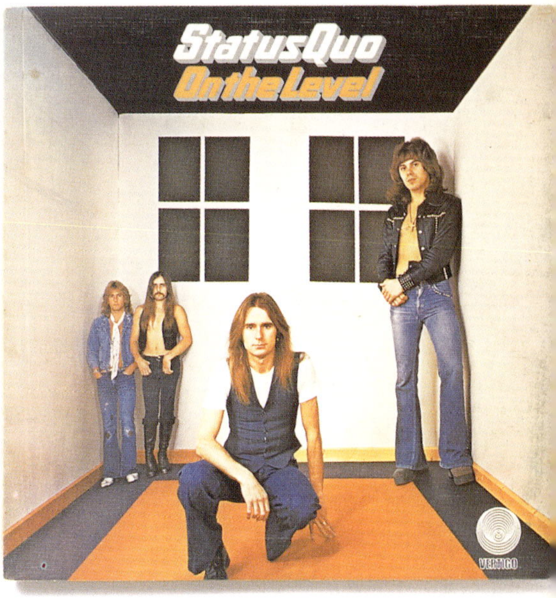

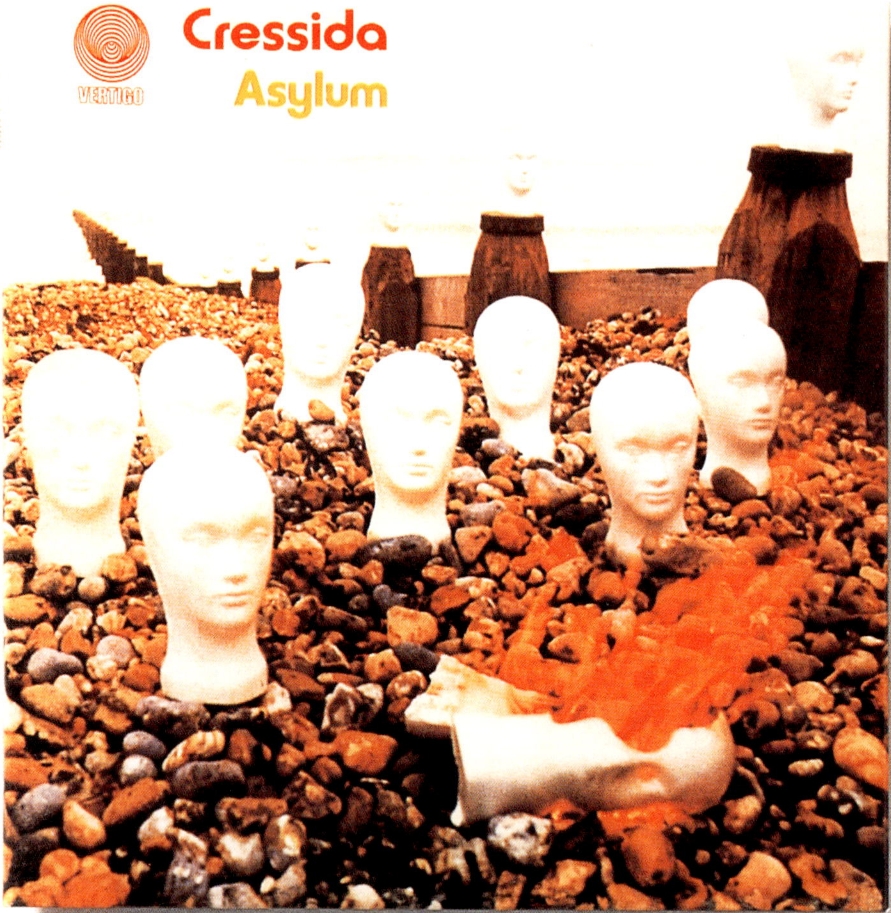

CRESSIDA:ASYLUM/VERTIGO 6360 025(1971)
Album Design by Keef

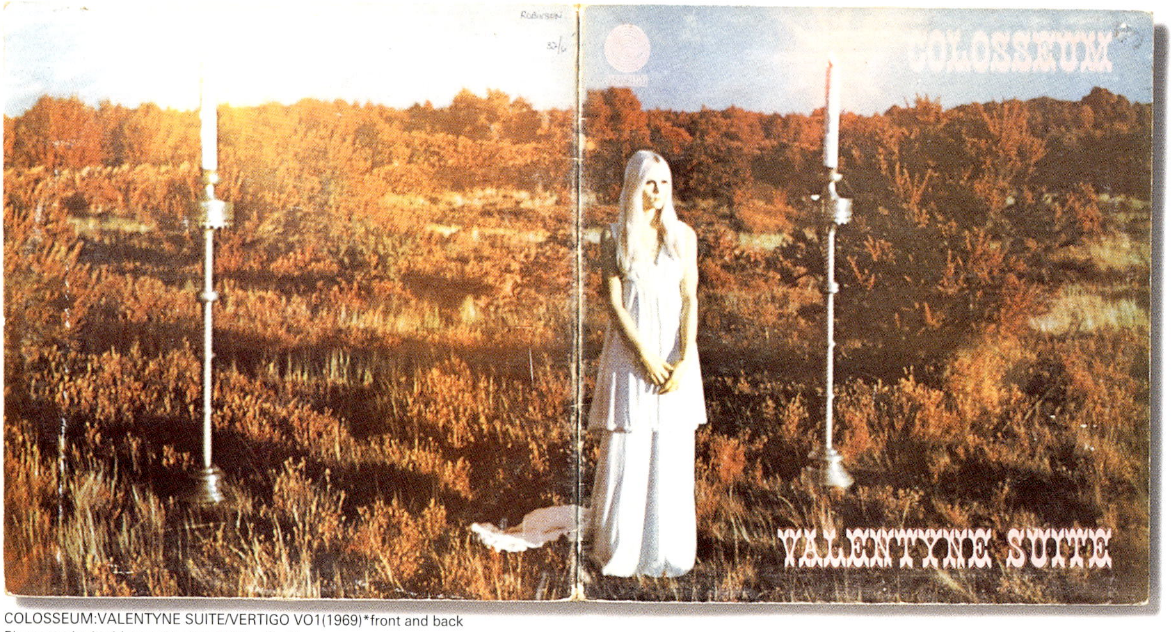

COLOSSEUM:VALENTYNE SUITE/VERTIGO VO1(1969)*front and back
Photography by Marcus Keef and Peter Smith
Cover Design/Marcus Keef
Inside Design/Linda Glover

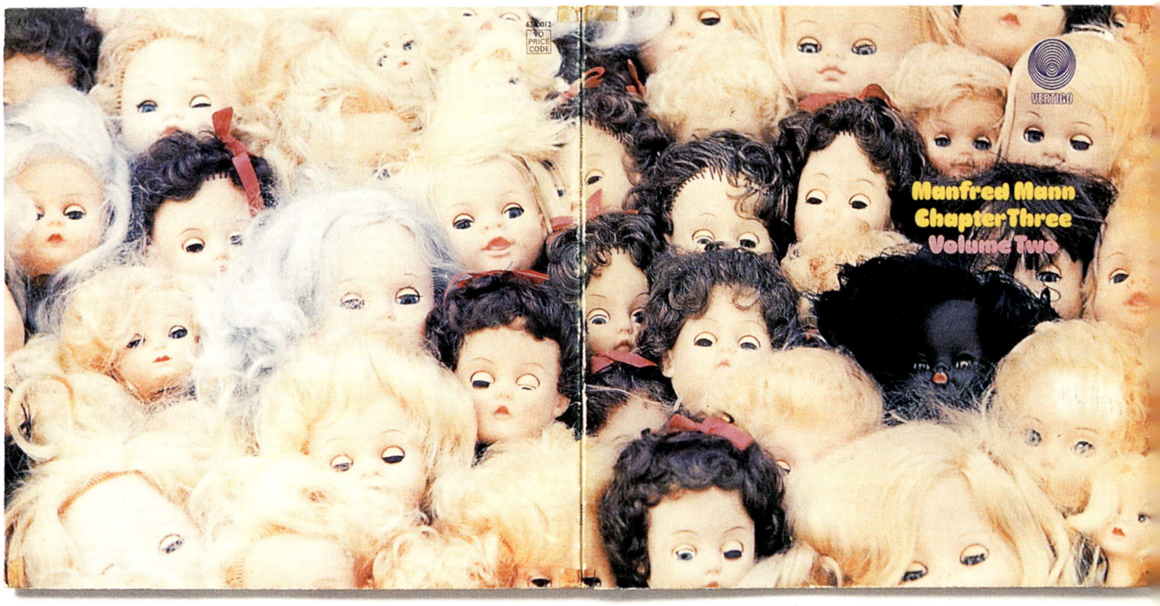

MANFRED MANN CHAPTER THREE:
VOLUME TWO/
VERTIGO 6360 012(1970)
*front and back
Album Designed
and Photographed by Keef

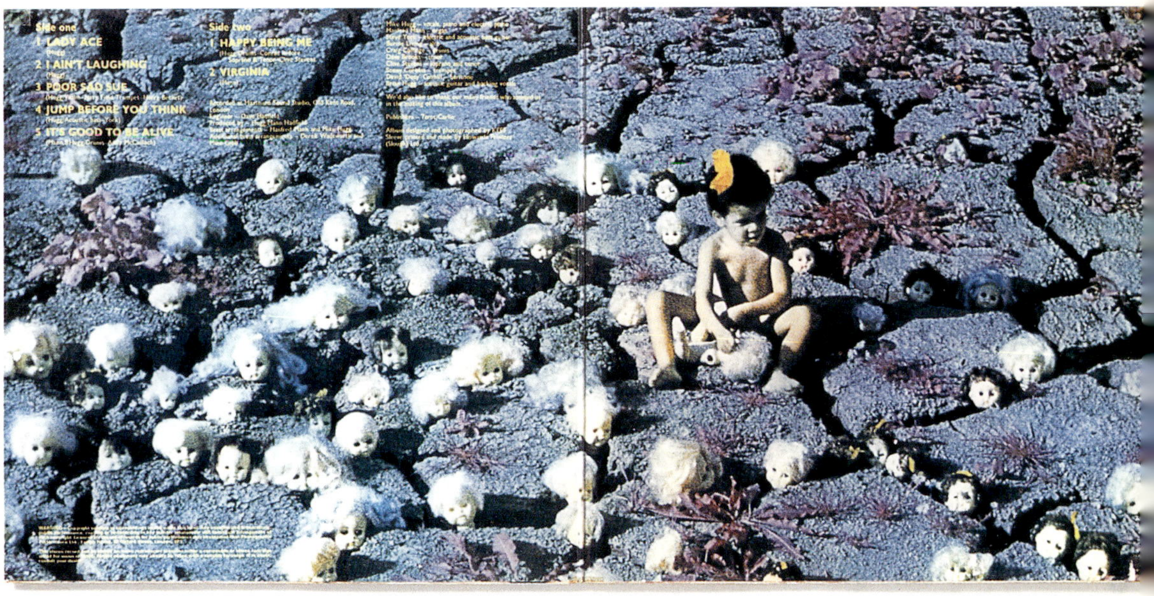

MANFRED MANN CHAPTER THREE:
VOLUME TWO/
VERTIGO 6360 012(1970)
*inner

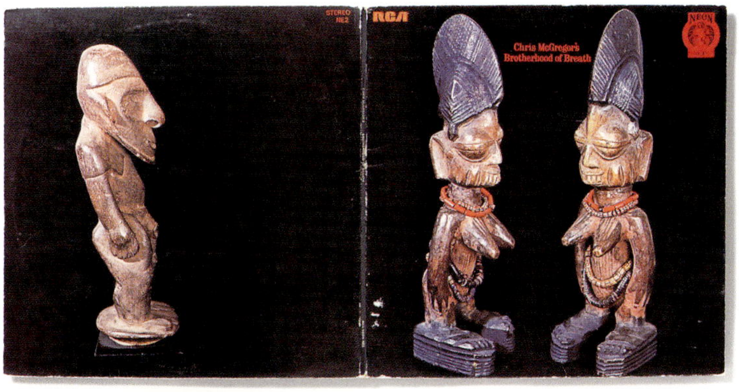

CHRIS McGREGOR'S BROTHERHOOD OF BREATH:
CHRIS McGREGOR'S BROTHERHOOD OF BREATH/
NEON NE2(1971)
*front and back
Album Designed by Keef

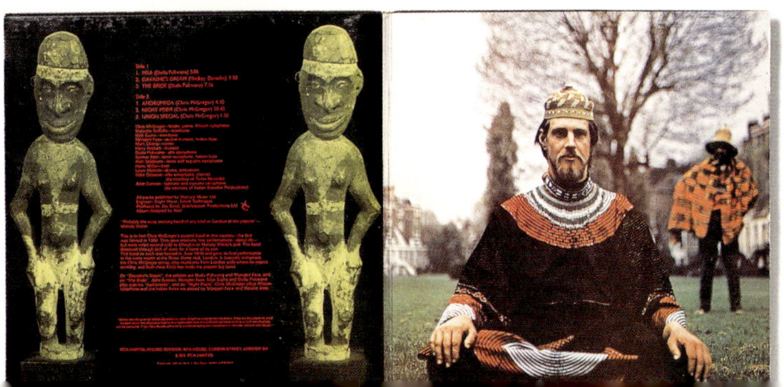

CHRIS McGREGOR'S BROTHERHOOD OF BREATH:
CHRIS McGREGOR'S BROTHERHOOD OF BREATH/
NEON NE2(1971)
*inner

FAIR WEATHER:BEGINNING FROM AN END/
NEON NE1(1971)
*front and back
Album Designed by Keef

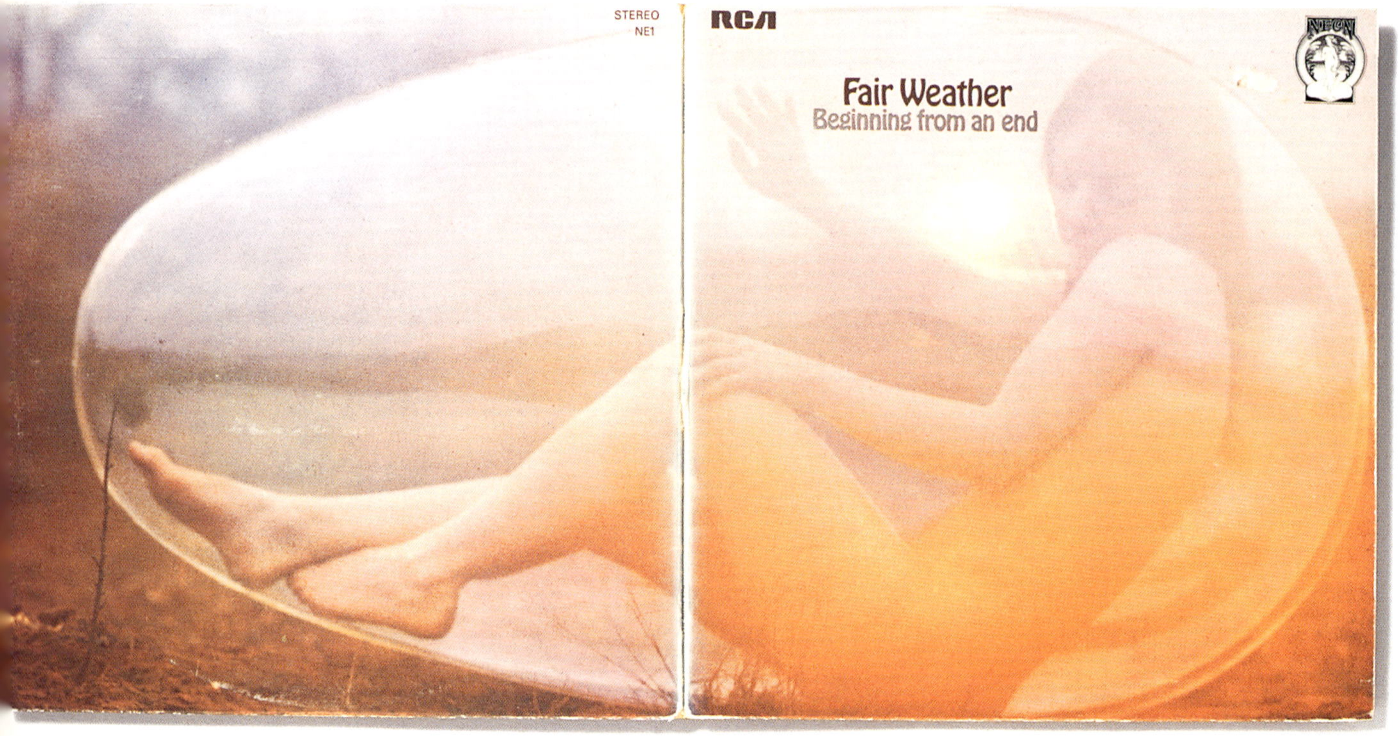

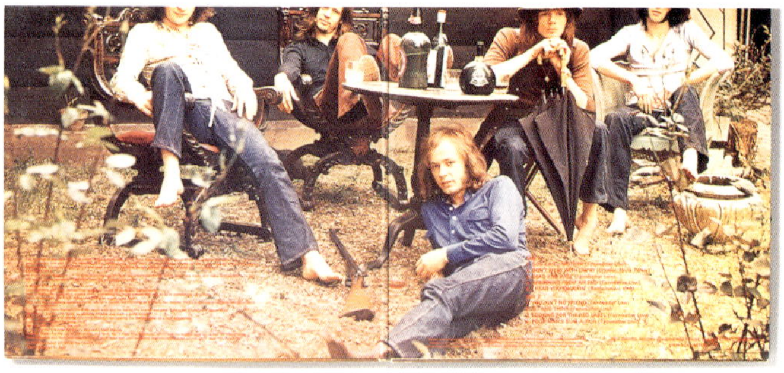

FAIR WEATHER:BEGINNING FROM AN END/
NEON NE1(1971)*inner

ROD STEWART:AN OLD RAINCOAT WON'T EVER LET YOU DOWN/
VERTIGO VO4(1970) *front and back

ROD STEWART:AN OLD RAINCOAT WON'T EVER LET YOU DOWN/
VERTIGO VO4(1970) *inner

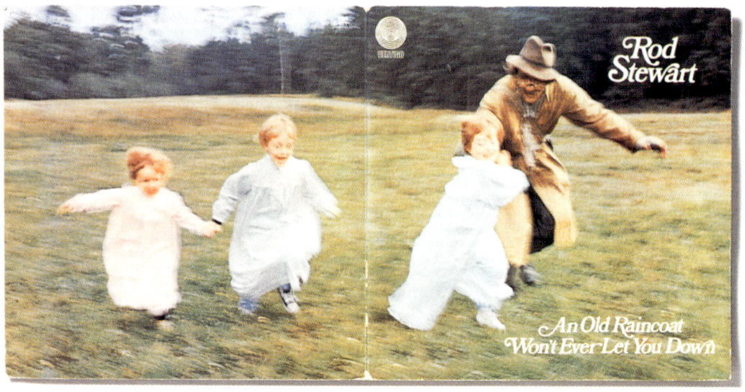

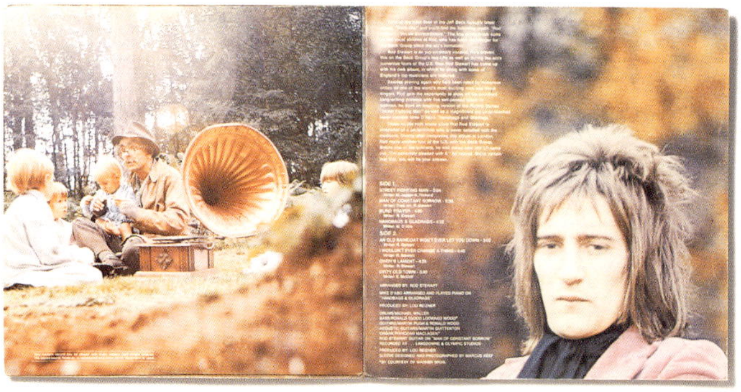

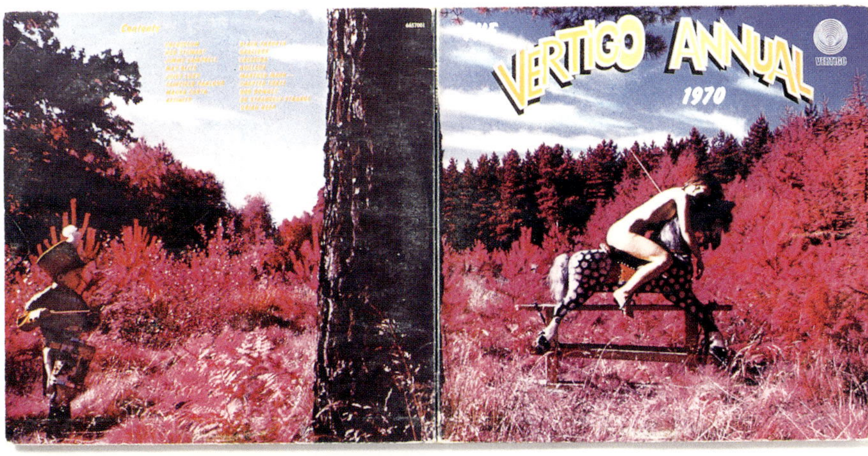

VARIOUS ARTISTS:VERTIGO ANNUAL/
VERTIGO 6657001(1970)*front and back
Type Designed by Sandy Field
Cover Designed and Photographed by Keef

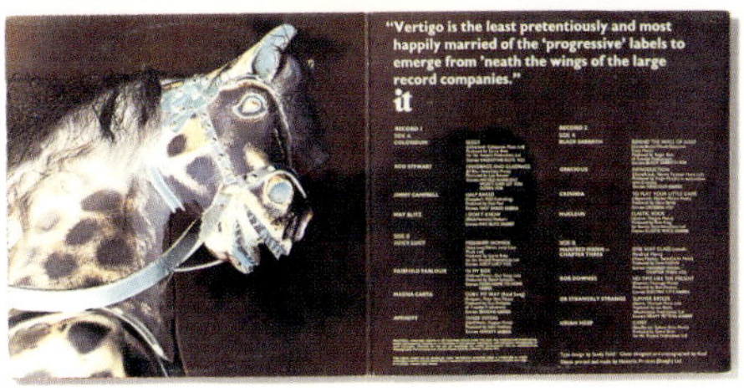

VARIOUS ARTISTS:VERTIGO ANNUAL/
VERTIGO 6657001(1970)
*inner

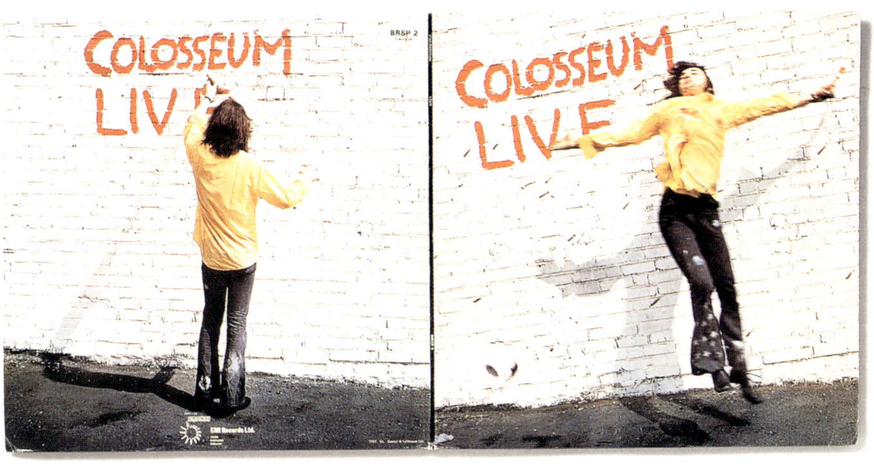

COLOSSEUM:LIVE/BRONZE BPSP2(1971)
Photography/Harry Isles and Keef
Cover Design/Keef

ROBIN LENT:SCARECROW'S JOURNEY/
NEPENTHA 6437002(1971)
Designed by Keef

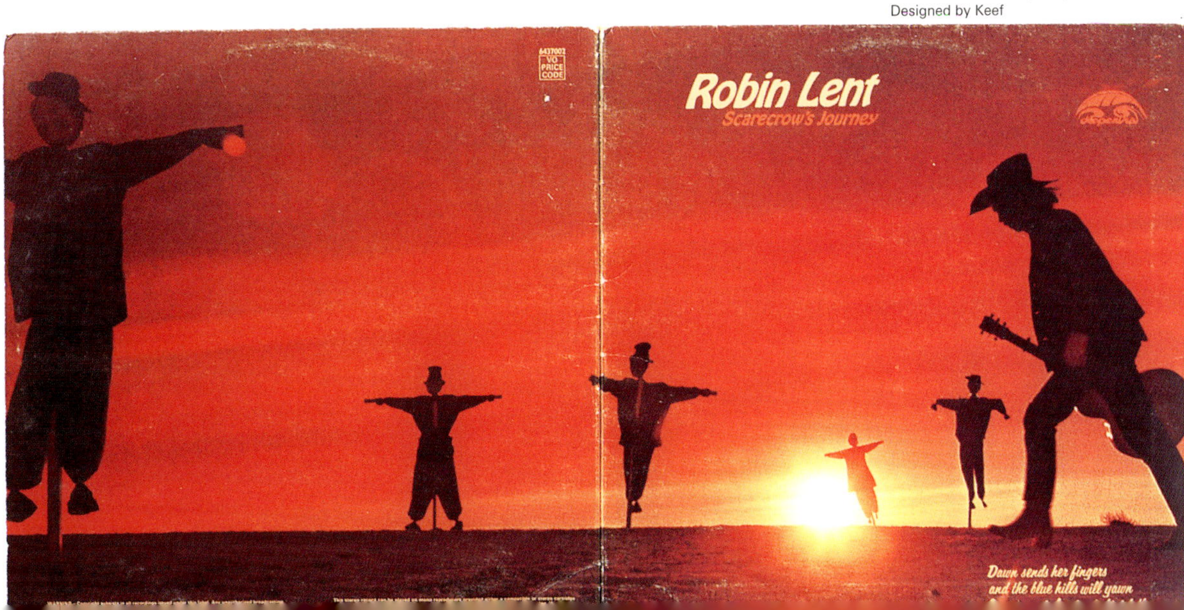

FRUUPP:THE PRINCE OF HEAVEN'S EYES/DAWN DNLH2(1974) *front and back
Art Direction by Mrtin Cropper Design Machine
Illustration by Graham Marsh
Inside Photo by Brian Lynch

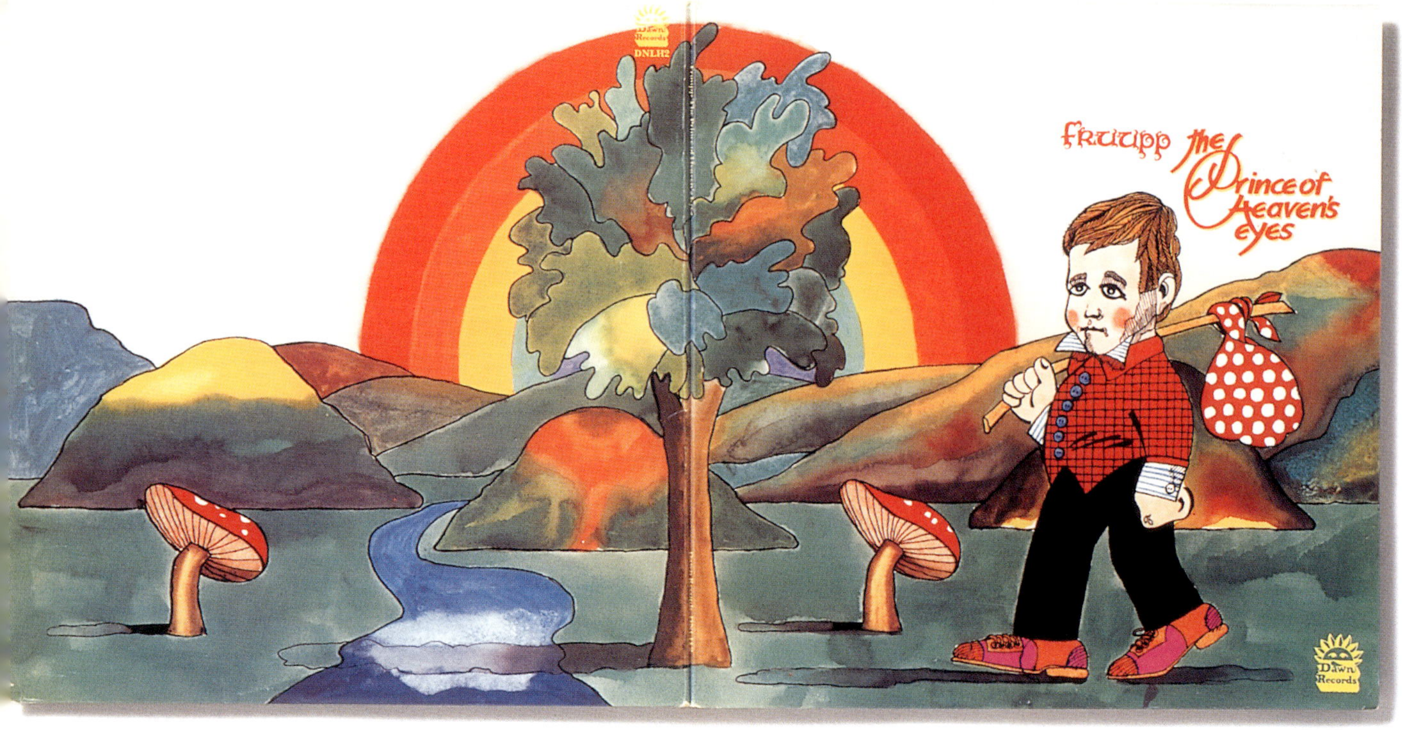

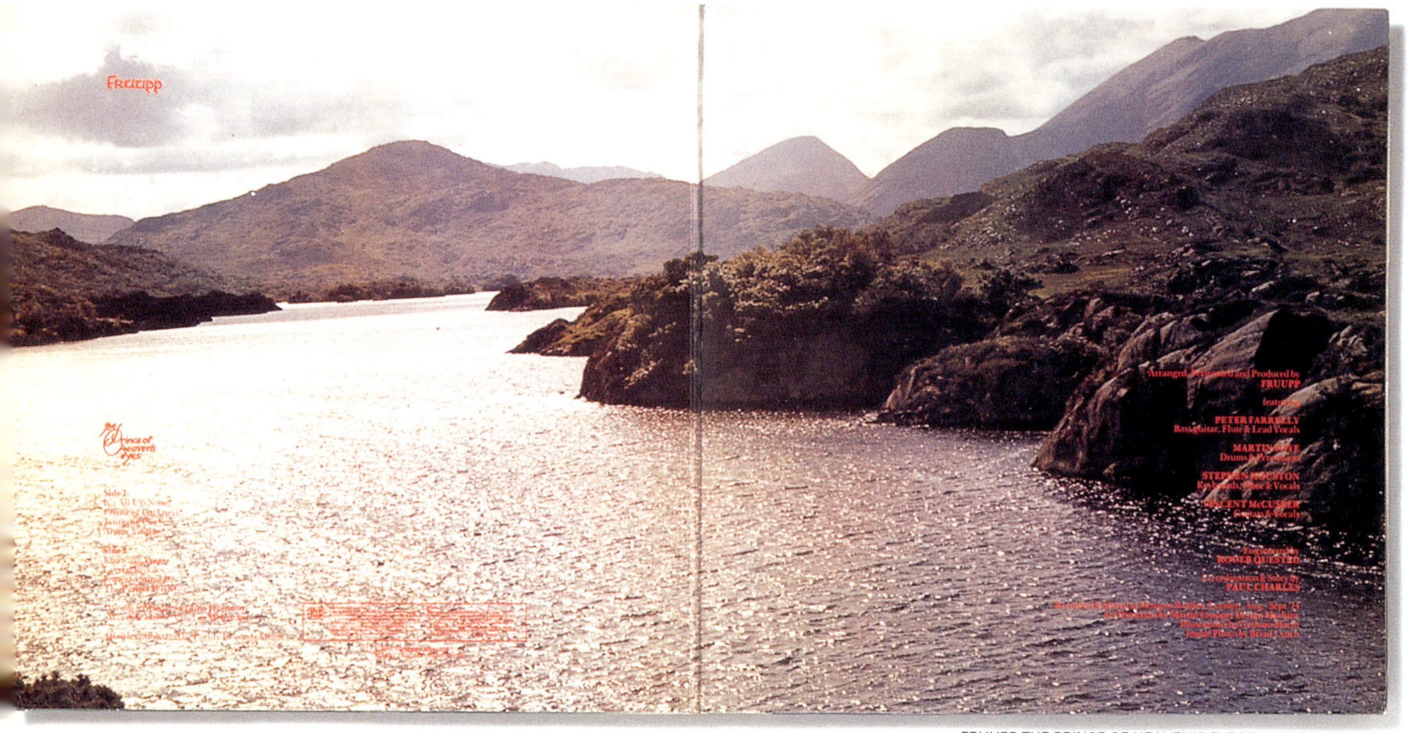

FRUUPP:THE PRINCE OF HEAVEN'S EYES/DAWN DNLH2(1974)
*inner

60年代後半から70年代にかけての英国ポピュラー音楽の功績のひとつに、イギリス伝統の音楽や文学をロックやジャズの形式のなかに消化し、これを革新的な作品にまで高めたというのがある。多くの場合、モチーフとなったのは50年代の末頃から一部の音楽家・研究家たちによって発掘・採集がすすめられてきたアイルランド、スコットランド、ウェールズ、イングランドの伝統歌であり、英雄伝説や妖精物語、おとぎばなしや滑稽譚、あるいはそれらに基づく19世紀後半以降のイギリス・ファンタジー文学であった。ロック世代にとっては、アイリッシュ文化を基盤とするフループのドラマティックな怪奇幻想趣味や、バークレイ・ジェームス・ハーヴェストの叙情的な神話物語が、北の大地に広がる妖精の国の詩的源泉に触れ、幻視の異界に遊ぶモメントとなったのである。そうしたアーティストたちは、チャールズ・キングズレイやルイス・キャロルといったファンタジー作家たちと同じかそれ以上に、重要な意味をもっていた。　幻想性に富むすぐれたカヴァー・アートがこの手のアーティストの作品のなかに多いのも特徴で、73年にデビューしたその名もずばりファンタジーのファースト・アルバム『ペイント・ア・ピクチャー』などは、その哀愁ただようブリティッシュ・サウンド以上にカヴァー・アートのすばらしさから、コレクターの間で高値で取引される幻の名盤といわれ続けてきた。

One of the remarkable achievements of British Pop Music from the late 60's to the 70's was the successful integration of traditional English music and literature with the new artistic paradigm of Rock and Jazz music, assembling disparate elements into innovative works of art. In most cases, adoption of traditional ballads and folk songs from Ireland, Scotland, Wales, and England, which had been unearthed and collected by a group of scholars and music connoisseurs since the late 50's. Heroic legends and fairy tales, folk tales and comical short anecdotes, as well as 19th century English fantasy literature based on these

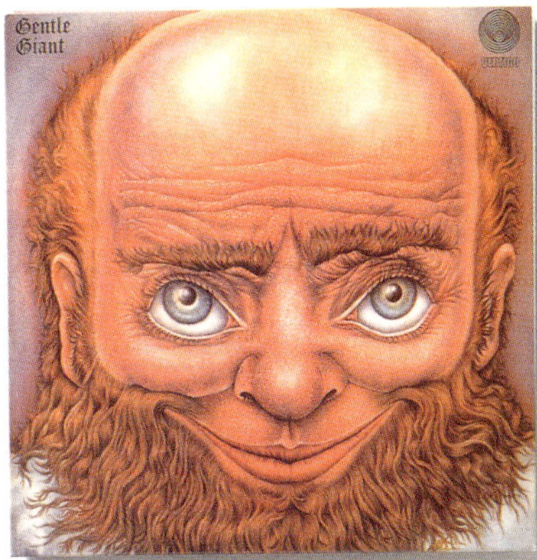

GENTLE GIANT:GENTLE GIANT/VERTIGO 6360 020(1970)
Cover Art/George Underwood

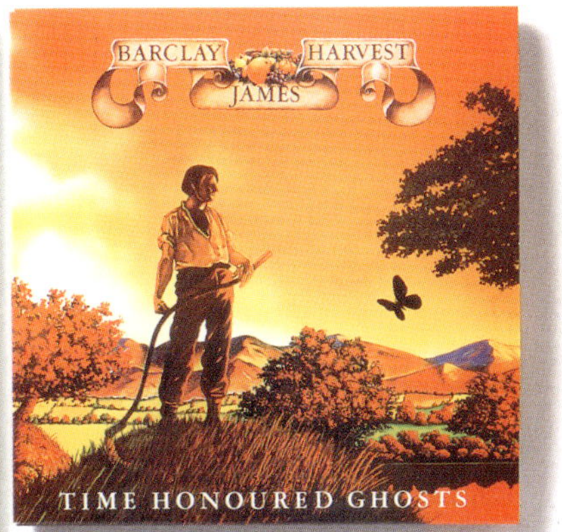

BARCLAY JAMES HARVEST:TIME HONOURED GHOSTS/
POLYDOR 2383 361(1975)
Art Direction/Paul Welch
Design,Illustration/Bill Dare

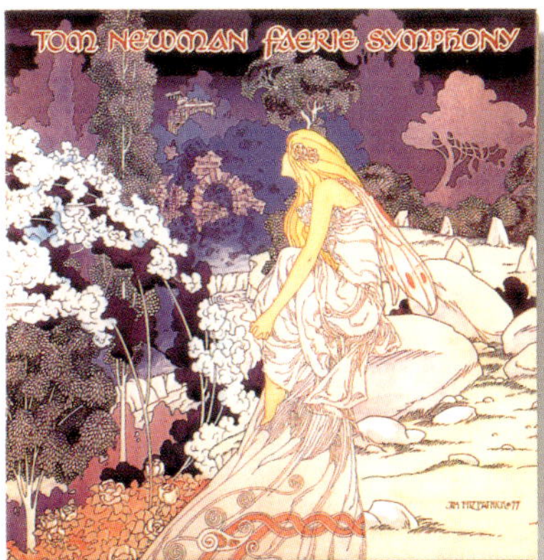

TOM NEWMAN:FAERIE SYMPHONY/
DECCA TXS123(1977)
Cover Design and Illustration/Jim Fizz Patrick

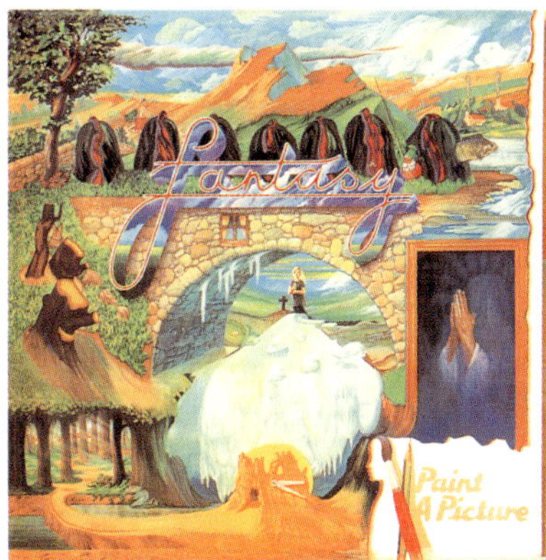

FANTASY:PAINT A PICTURE/POLYDOR 2383 246(1973)
Cover Design/Larry Learmonth
Art Direction/Ian Murray

fantasy

fantasy
ファンタジー

sources, became common sources of inspiration.

For the Rock 'n' Roll generation, fanatasy literature rooted in Irish culture or Barkley James Harvest's romantic myths were as important as, or even more important, than the works of Charles Kingsley or Lewis Carrol. These writings allowed artists's imaginations to dive into the source of poetry in the fairyland, northern wilderness and to take flight in the realm of the visionary. It is no surprise that the albums by these artists were often encased in fine cover art. The group Fantasy debuted in 1973 with a poignantly titled ablum "Paint a Picture". The ablum is a highly valued among collectors for its cover art rather than for the music itself.

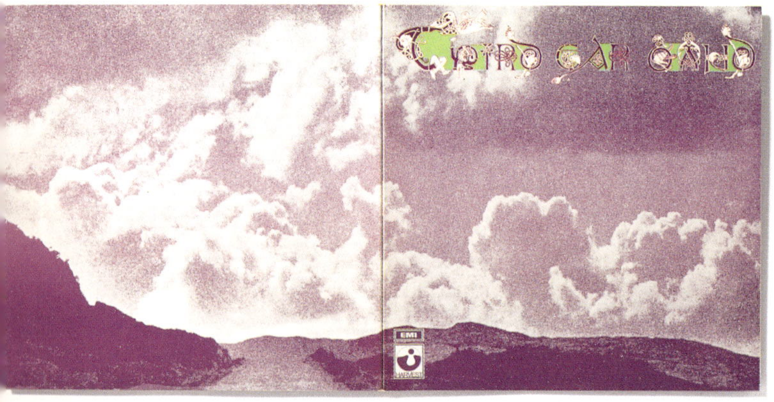
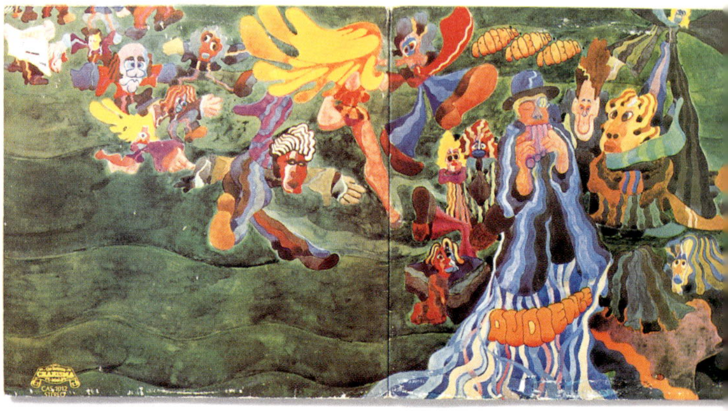
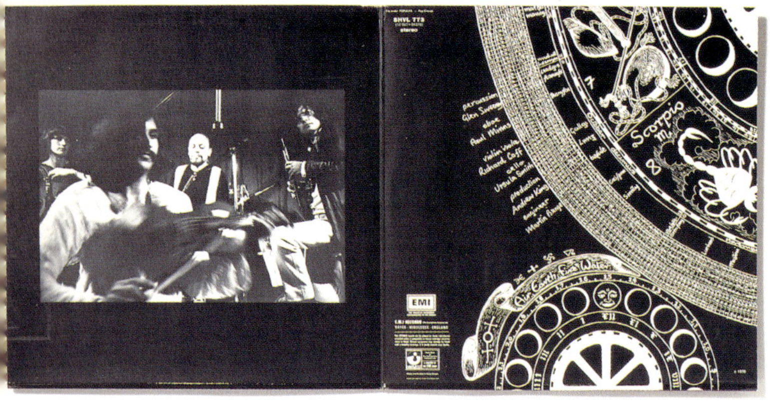
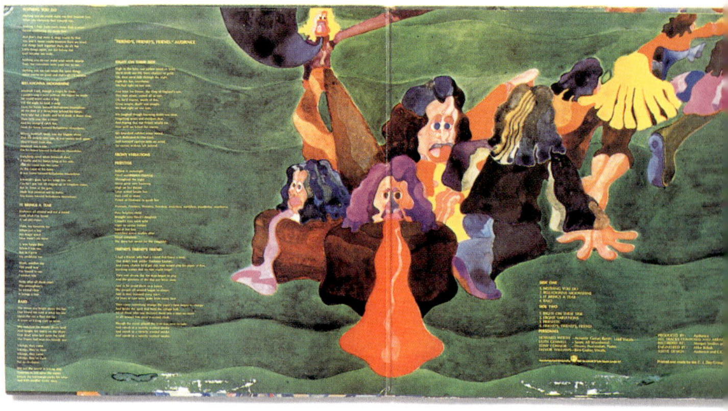

THIRD EAR BAND:THIRD EAR BAND/
HARVEST SHVL773(1970)*front and back

THIRD EAR BAND:THIRD EAR BAND/
HARVEST SHVL773(1970)*inner

AUDIENCE:FRIEND'S FRIEND'S FRIEND/
B&C CAS1012(1970)*front and back
Sleeve Design/Audience and C.C.S.

AUDIENCE:FRIEND'S FRIEND'S FRIEND/
B&C CAS1012(1970)*inner

①
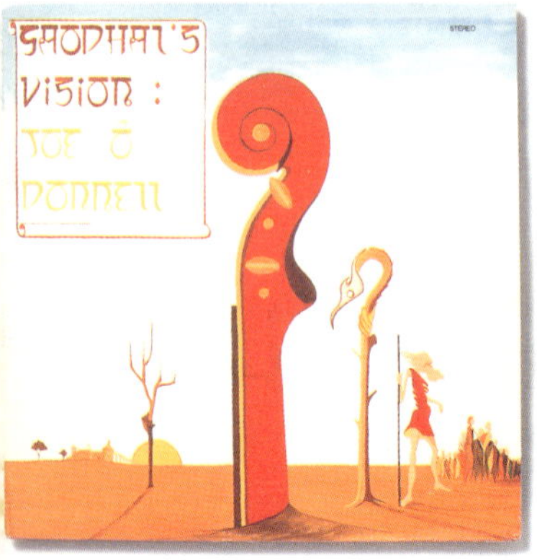

②
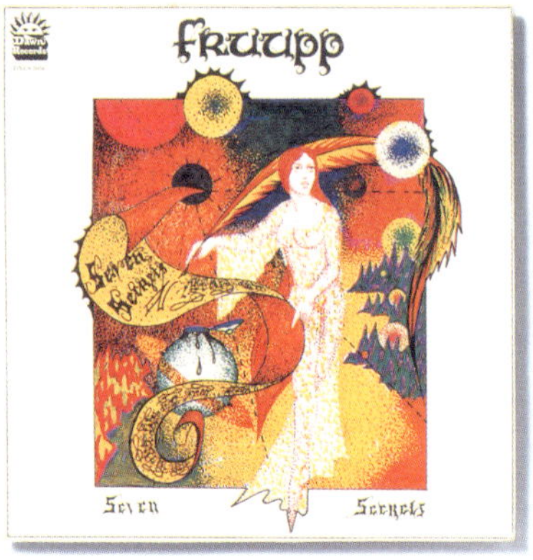

③
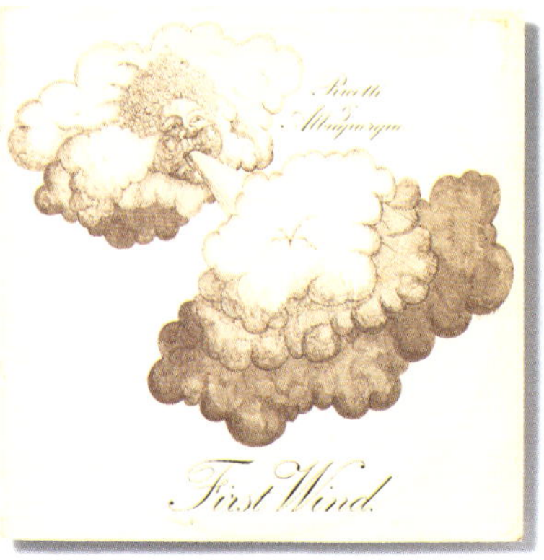

④
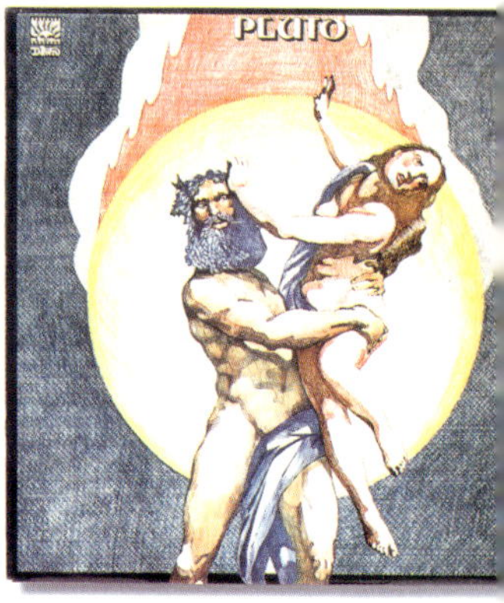

⑤
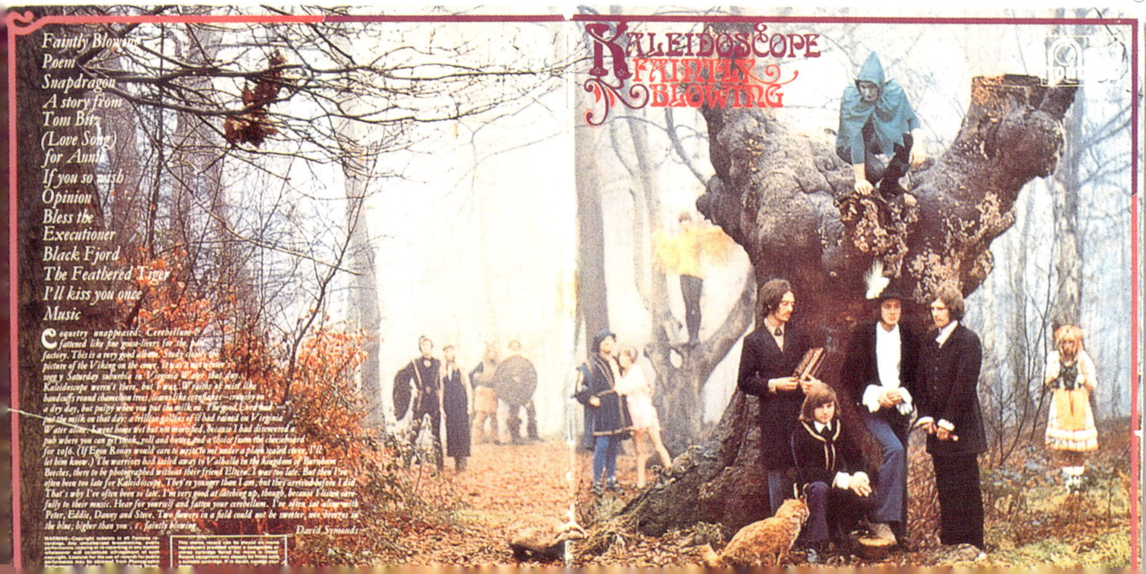

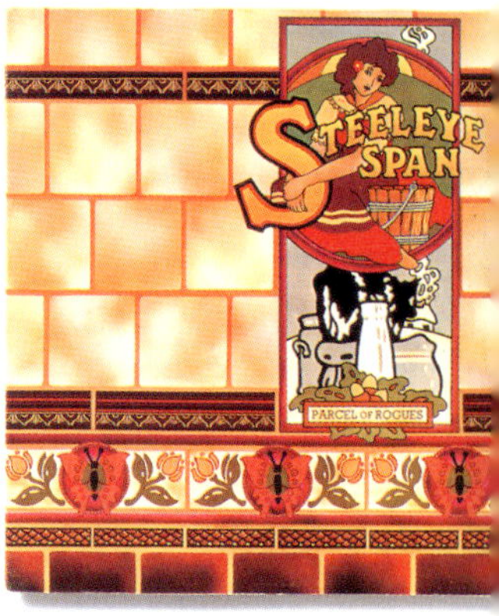

⑥

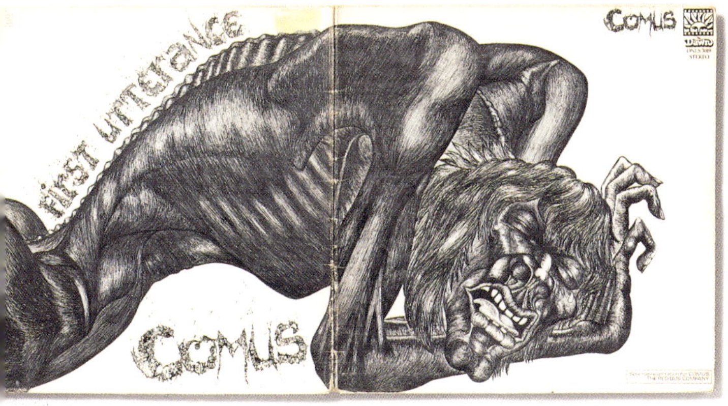

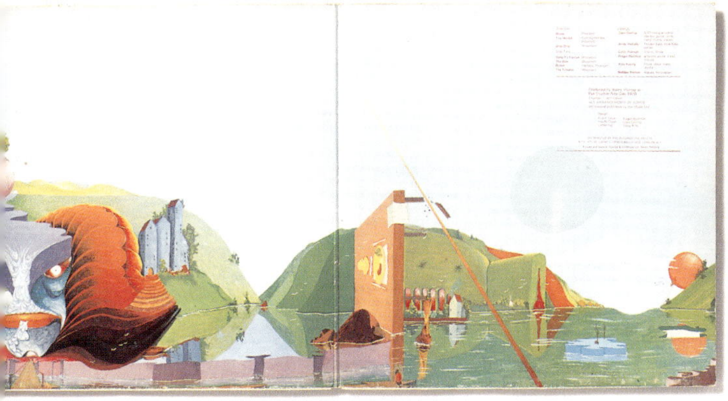

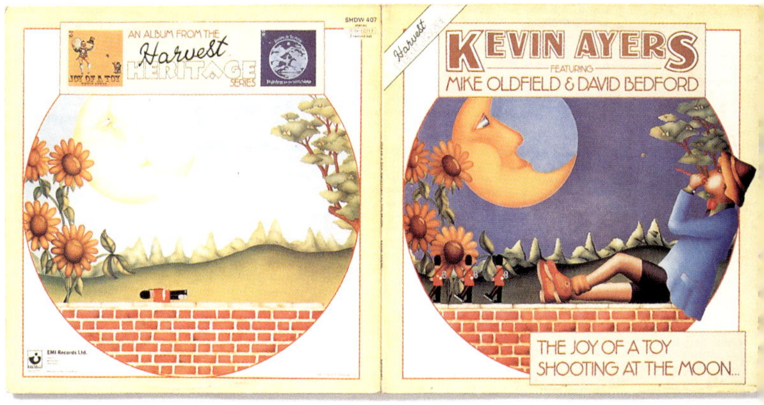

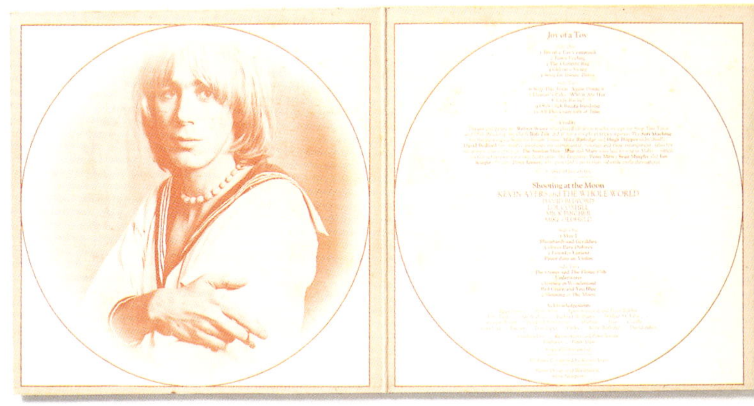

COMUS:FIRST UTTERANCE/DAWN DNLS 3019(1970) *front and back
Front Cover Design/Roger Wootton
Inside Cover/Glen Goring
Lettering/Tony Kite

COMUS:FIRST UTTERANCE/DAWN DNLS 3019(1970)*inner

KEVIN AYERS:THE JOY OF A TOY,SHOOTING AT THE MOON/
HARVEST SHDW407(1975) *front and back
Sleeve Design and Illustration/Steve Newport

KEVIN AYERS:THE JOY OF A TOY,SHOOTING AT THE MOON/
HARVEST SHDW407(1975) *inner

⑦
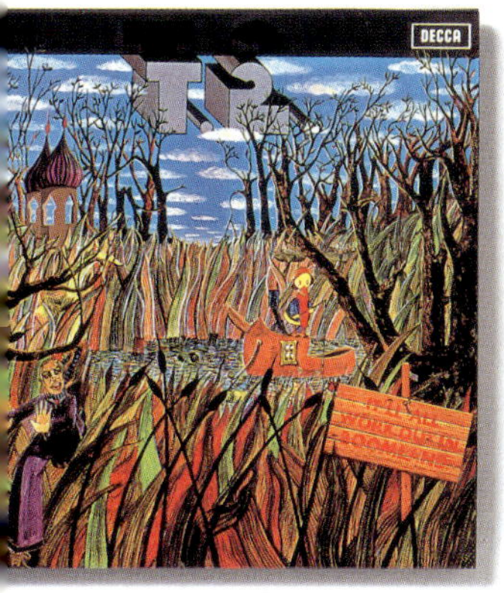

⑧
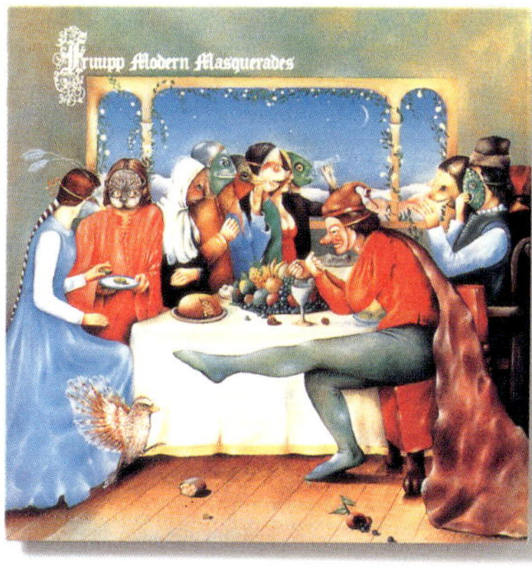

⑨
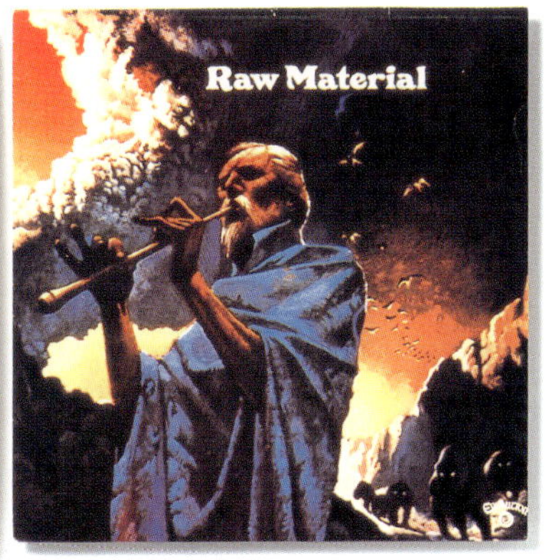

⑩
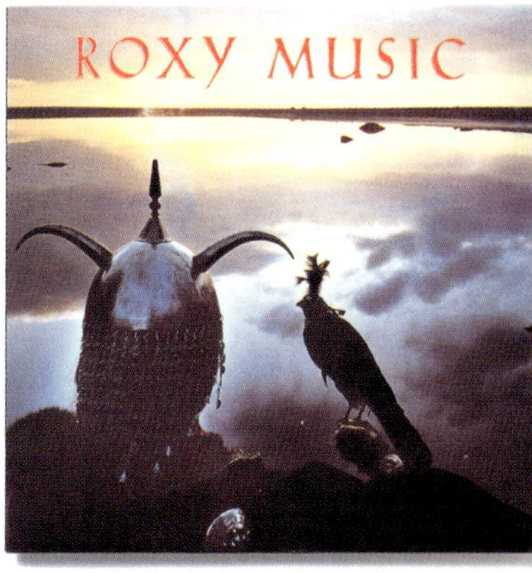

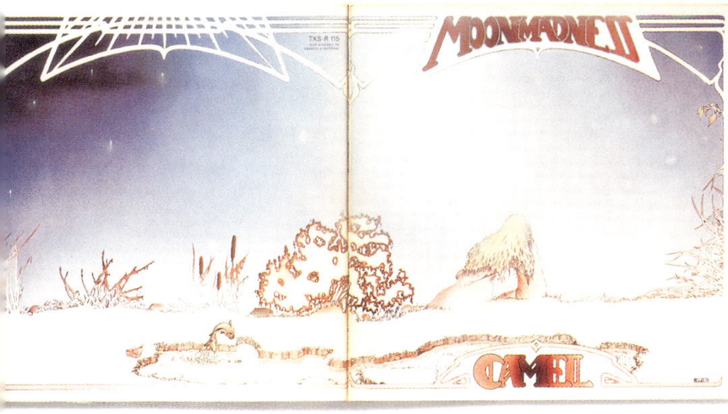

⑪

① JOE O'DONNELL:GAODHAL'S VISION/
POLYDOR 2383 465(1977)
Artwork/Marian McAllister

② FRUUPP:SEVEN SECRETS/
DAWN DNLS3058(1974)
Illustration by Peter Farrelly

③ RICOTTI&ALBUQUERQUE:FIRST WIND/
PEGASUS PEG2(1971)
Sleeve Design/Jane de Albuquerque
Illustration/Roger Knights

④ PLUTO:PLUTO/DAWN DNLS3030(1971)
Design&Art Direction/ROC Advertising

⑤ KALEIDOSCOPE:FAINTLY BLOWING/
FONTANA STL5491(1969)
Sleeve Design/Robin Nicol
Photography/Johnny Clamp

⑥ STTELEYE SPAN:PARCEL OF ROGUES/
CHRYSALIS CHR1046(1973)
Illustration and Design by
Grahame Berney of Dream Studios

⑦ FT2:IT'LL ALL WORK OUT IN BOOMLAND/
DECCA SKL5050(1970)
Illustrations/ Peter Thaine

⑧ FRUUPP:MODERN MASQUERADES/
DAWN DNLS3070(1975)
Art Direction/Martin Cropper at Design Machine

⑨ RAW MATERIAL:RAW MATERIAL/
EVOLUTION Z1006(1970)

⑩ ROXY MUSIC:AVALON/EG EGH50(1982)
Cover by Bryan Ferry, Neil Kirk,
Anthony Price and Peter Saville

⑪ CAMEL:MOONMADNESS/
DECCA TXS-R115(1976)
Sleeve Design by Field

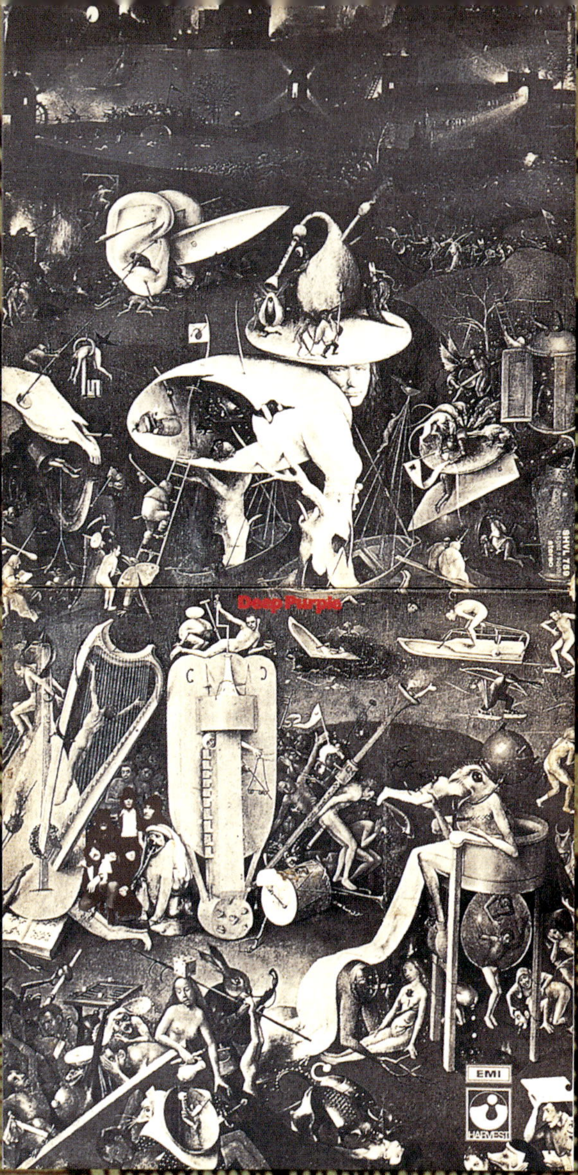

DEEP PURPLE:DEEP PURPLE/
HARVEST SHVL759(1969)
Cover Paintings by Hieronymus Bosch

fantasy

Quotations

古典の引用

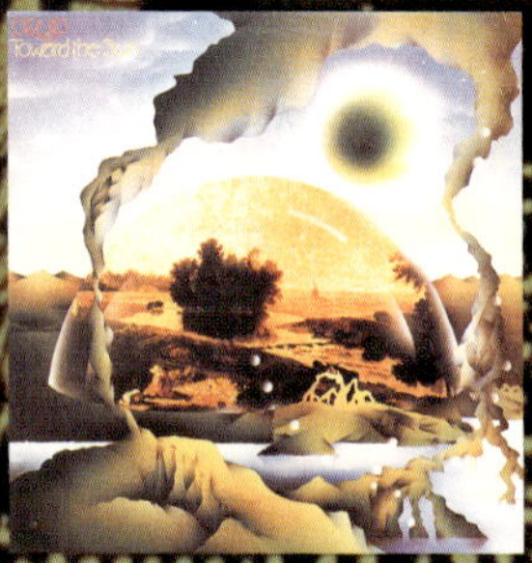
①

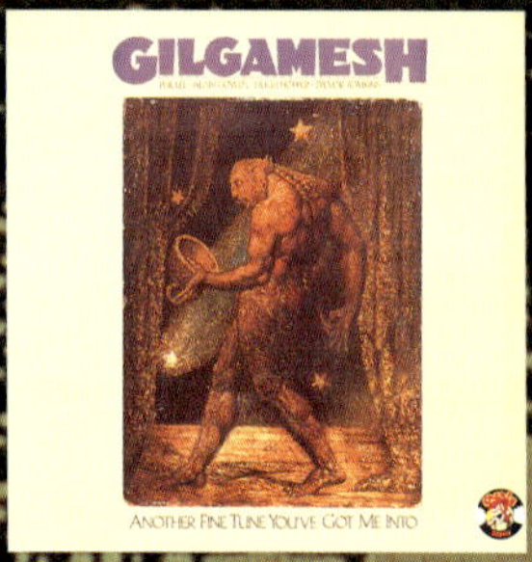

②

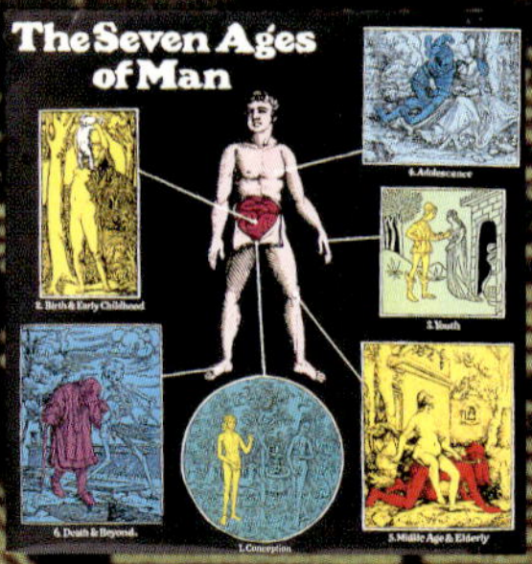

③

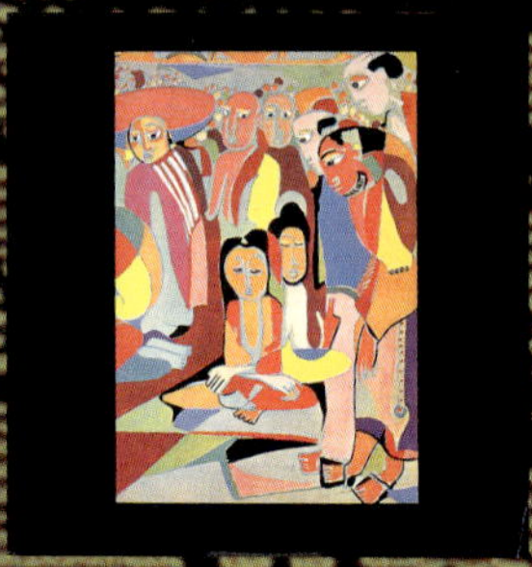
④

In Search of the Lost Record

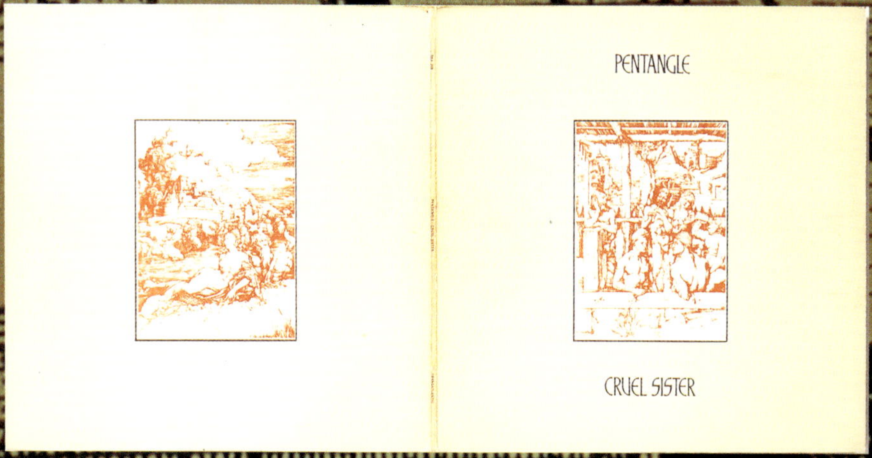

PENTAGLE:CRUEL SISTER/
TRANSATLANTIC TRA228(1970)
Sleeve Design/Hamish&Gustav

① DRUID:TOWARD THE SUN/EMI EMC 3081(1975)
Cover Design and Artwork/Adrian Sadgrove
Cover Picture Courtesy of Tate Gallery London

② GILGAMESH:
ANOTHER FINE TUNE YOU'VE GOT ME INTO/
CHARLY CRL5009(1978)
Cover Painting/The Ghost of a Fela' by William Blake,reproduced by permission of The Tate Gallery

③ THE SEVEN AGES OF MAN:
THE SEVEN AGES OF MAN/REDIFFUSION ZS115(1972)
Graphics/Steven Hill Design Services

④ BRIAN DAVISON:EVERY WITCH WAY/
CHARISMA CAS1021(1970)
Cover Painting by Nan Cuz
from the book`In the Kingdom of Mescal'

⑤ THIRD EAR BAND:ALCHEMY/
HARVEST SHVL756(1969) *front and back
Cover Design and Artwork by Dave Loxley
Photograpy by Ray Stevenson

⑥ THIRD EAR BAND:ALCHEMY/HARVEST
SHVL756(1969) *inner

⑦ JOHN RENBOURN:SHIP OF FOOLS/
RUN RIVER RRA009(1988)
Cover Painting/Bosch-Ship of Fools

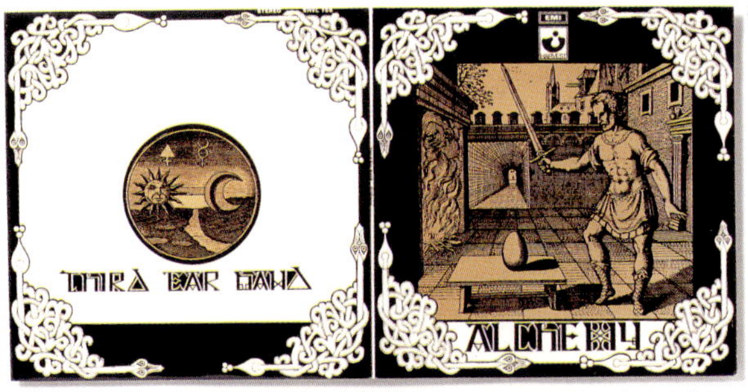

⑤

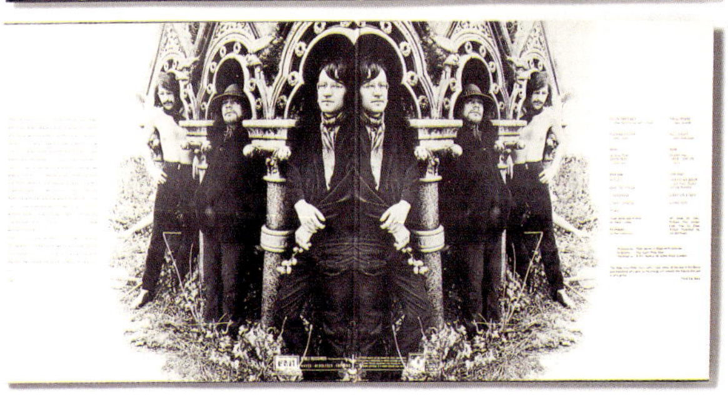

⑥

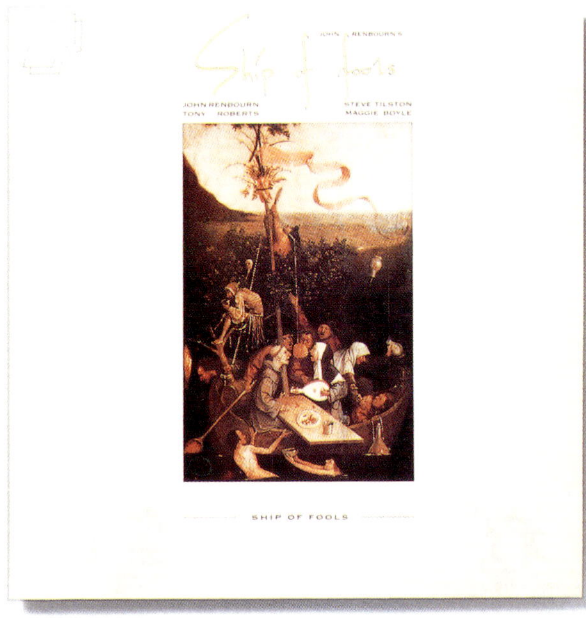

⑦

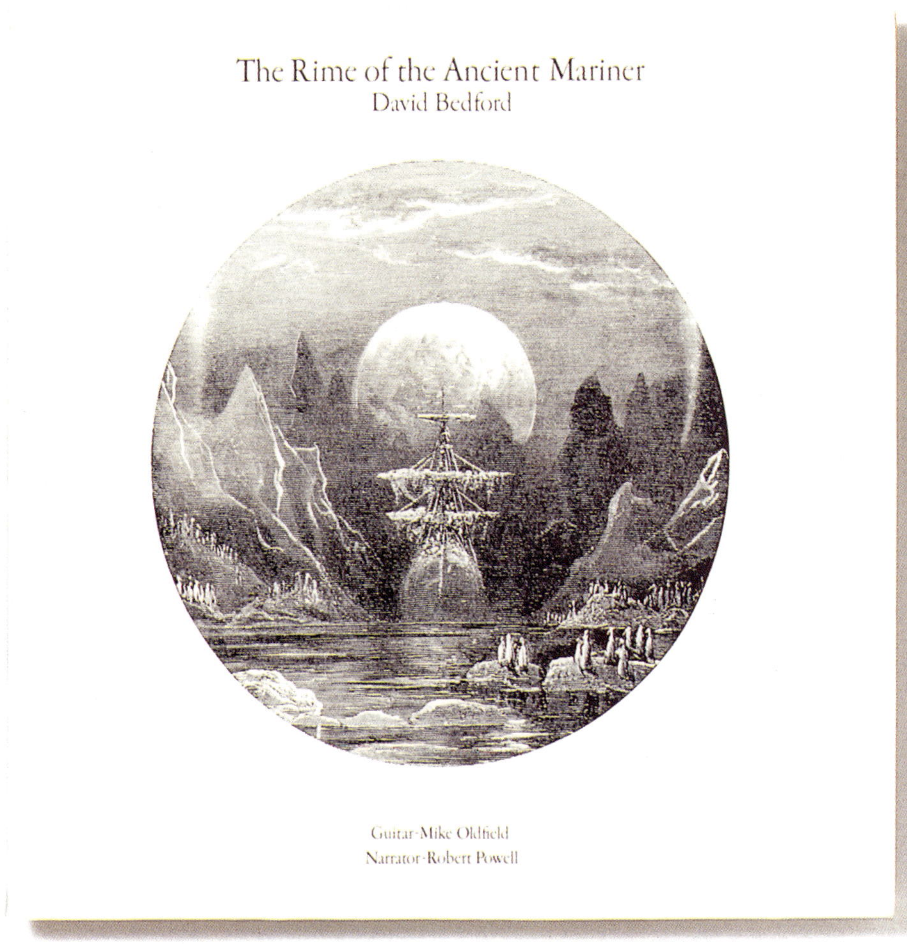

DAVID BEDFORD:THE RIME OF THE ANCIENT MARINER/
VIRGIN OVED152(1975)
Cover/Gustav Dore

psychedeli

psychedelic
サイケデリック

psychedelic
Original Psyche
オリジナルサイケ

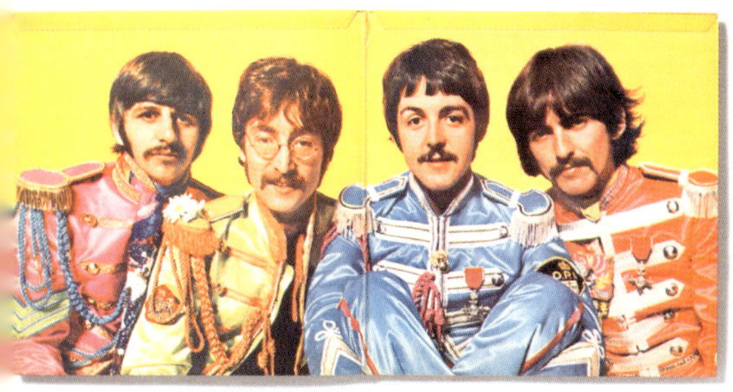

THE BEATLES:SGT.PEPPERS LONELY HEARTS CLUB BAND/
PARLOPHONE PMC7027(1967)
*inner

THE BEATLES:SGT.PEPPERS LONELY HEARTS CLUB BAND/
PARLOPHONE PMC7027(1967)
*front and back
Photographed by Michael Cooper
Wax Figures by Madame Tussauds

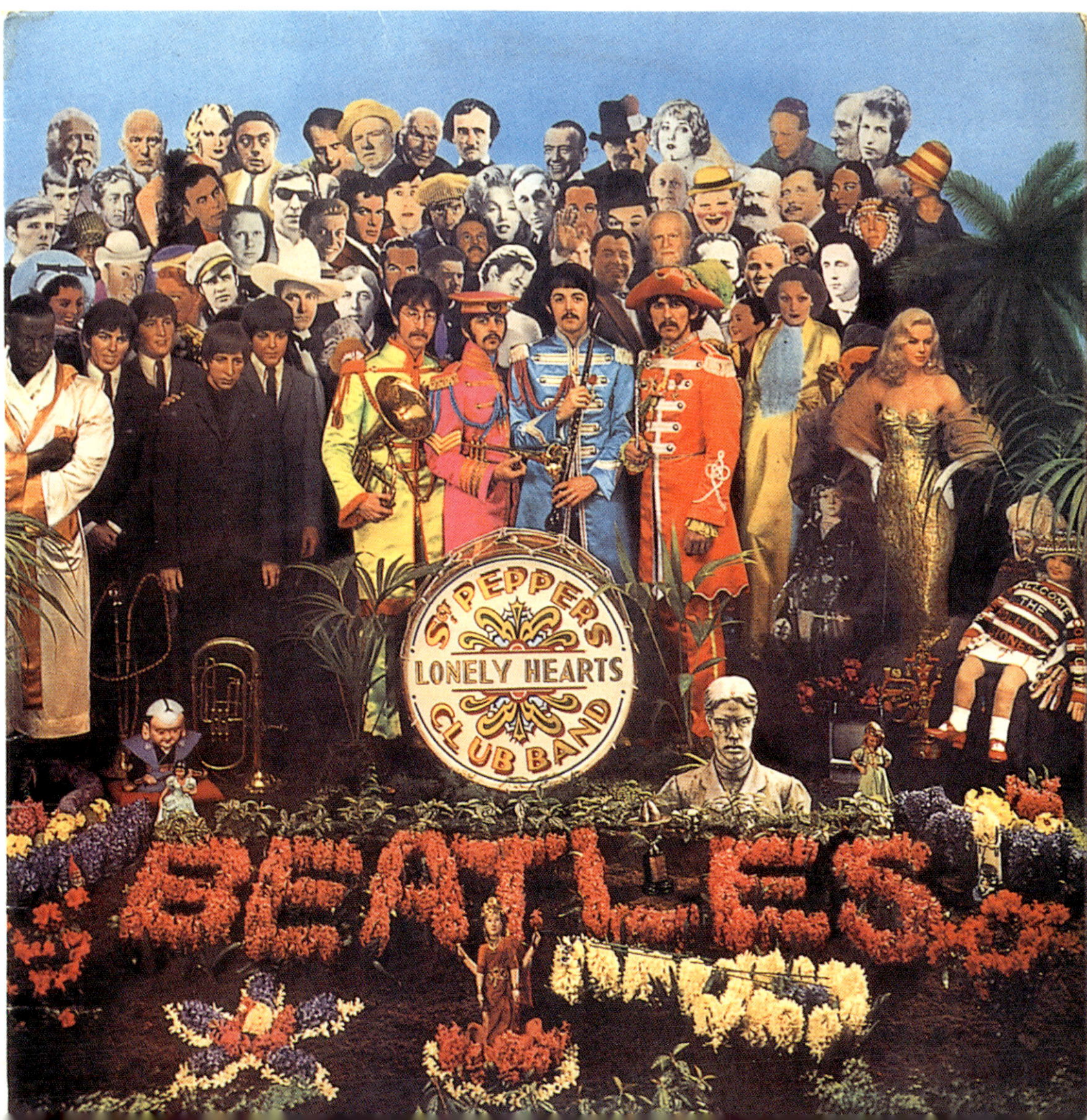

LSDやマリファナの服用による幻覚体験がサイケデリック・アートの導火線であるのは、周知の事実である。その背景には、60年代後半のベトナム反戦運動、人種解放問題といった歴史的転換点に芽生えた反権力・反知性への志向と、そこから導き出される感覚的・抽象的な創造革新への移行という大きな流れがあった。既存のアカデミズムや権威に対するカウンター作用という性格を帯びていたがゆえに、その出発点から通俗音楽、ポップ・ミュージックとの結びつきを容易なものにしていたサイケは、やがてアートと音楽が渾然となった一大ポップ・カルチャーへと裾野を広げていく。“総天然色”という言葉がピッタリのカラフルなサイケ・アルバム・ジャケットは、まさしくそんな時代の記憶を視覚的に辿ることのできる格好の素材といえる。しかしそれ以上に注目すべき点は、反知性をかかげた60年代カウンター・カルチャーのサイケにも、作品としてみれば、そこにしっかりと知的なアプローチがなされていることだ。美術であれなんであれ、どんなに画期的な概念も、構成のバランスを欠いた稚拙な表現で終わっては説得力を失ってしまう。すぐれたサイケ・アートは、そんな当たり前の事実を改めて我々に思い出させてくれる。

It is a widely known fact that psychedelic art came about from the hallucinatory effects of drugs like LSD and marijuana. The Vietnam anti-war movement and the human rights movement were contributing factors leading to the drug culture of the 60's. These social issues spurred the anti-authority and anti-intellectual spirit of this turning point in history. This grew into a bigger movement of innovation and creativity that heavily drew on sensitivity and abstractness. Since the psychedelic nature was an attack on established academics and authority, the psychedelic culture, which, from its nascence had a strong connection with generic and popular music, broadened its horizons to an entirely new popular culture in a mixture of art and music. A psychedelic album cover with a myriad of organic colors is probably the best example of the image that the psychedelic era engrained in our memories. Even though the psychedelic culture was rooted in anti-intellectualism, psychedelic art was surely handled with true intelligence. Any form of innovation in either art or music loses its persuasiveness and authority without a solid and balanced structure. A magnificent piece of psychedelic art succeeds in reminding us of this.

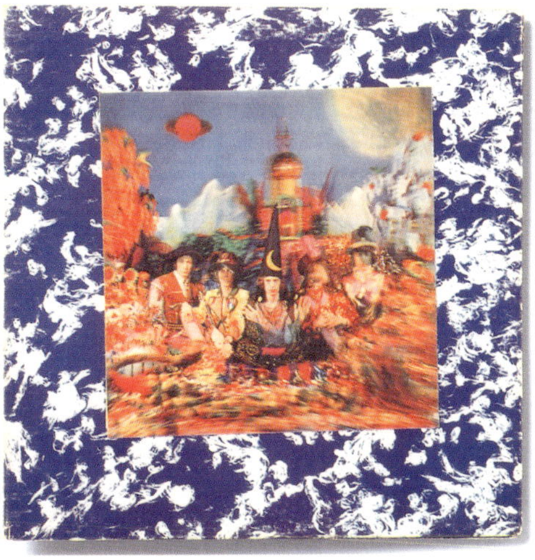

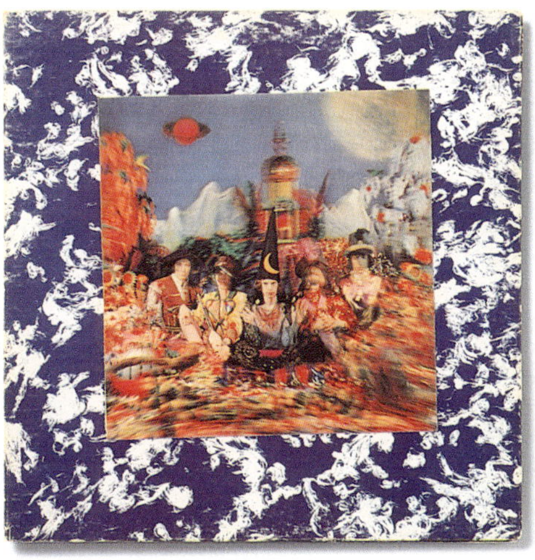

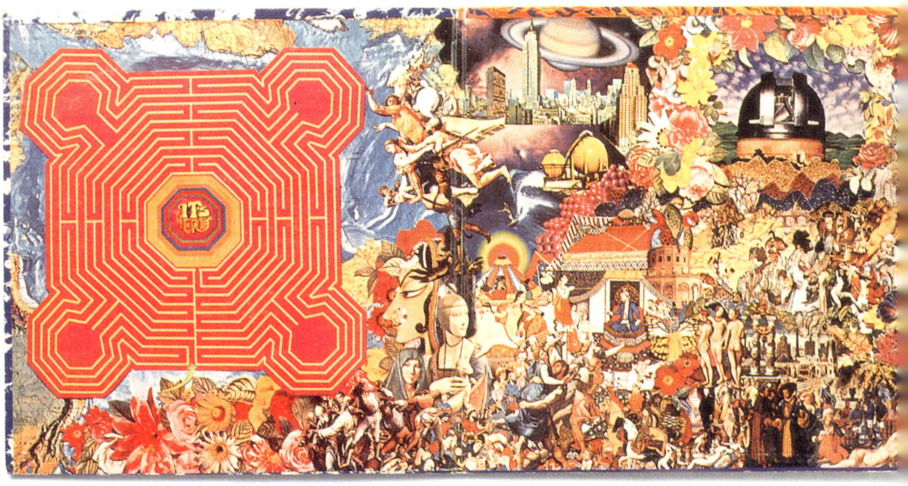

THE ROLLING STONES:THEIR SATANIC MAJESTIES REQUEST/DECCA TXS103(1967) *inner

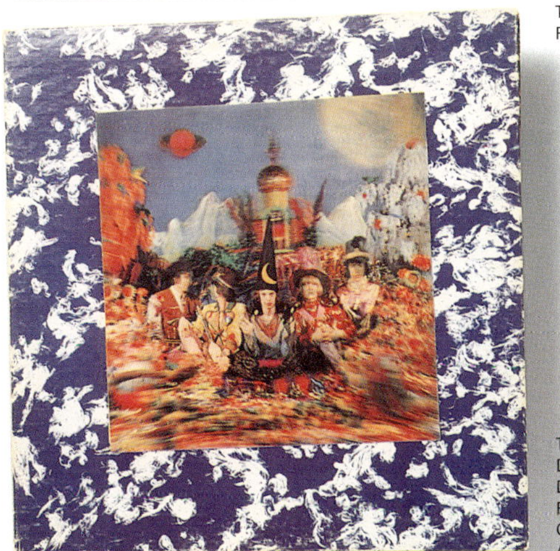

THE ROLLING STONES:THEIR SATANIC MAJESTIES REQUEST/
DECCA TXS103(1967) *front
Design&Photograph/Michael Cooper
Back Cover Illustration by Tony Meeviwiffen
Cover Photo Built by the Rolling Stones,Michael Cooper and
Artchie at Pictorial Productions

① TRAFFIC:MR.FANTASY/ISLAND ILPS9061(1967)
Photography/John Benton Harris
Sleeve Design/Chris Wood and CCS Advertising Associates

② THE MOODY BLUES:DAYS OF FUTURE PASSED/DERAM SML707(1967)
Cover Painting by David Anstey

③ DEEP PURPLE:
SHADES OF DEEP PURPLE/
PARLOPHONE PCS7055(1968)

④ PINK FLOYD:
THE PIPER AT THE GATES OF DAWN/
COLUMBIA SCX6157(1967)
Front Cover Photo/Vic Singh

⑤ THE BEATLES:YELLOW SUBMARINE/
APPLE PCS7070 (1969)

⑥ JULY:JULY/MAJOR MINOR MMLP29 (1968)
Sleeve Design by Stephen Hill

⑦ SKIP BIFFERTY:SKIP BIFFERTY/
RCA VICTOR SF7941(1968)
Cover Painting/ R.Wagner

⑧ THE MODERN JAZZ QUARTET:
UNDER THE JASMINE TREE/
APPLE APCOR4 (1968)

①
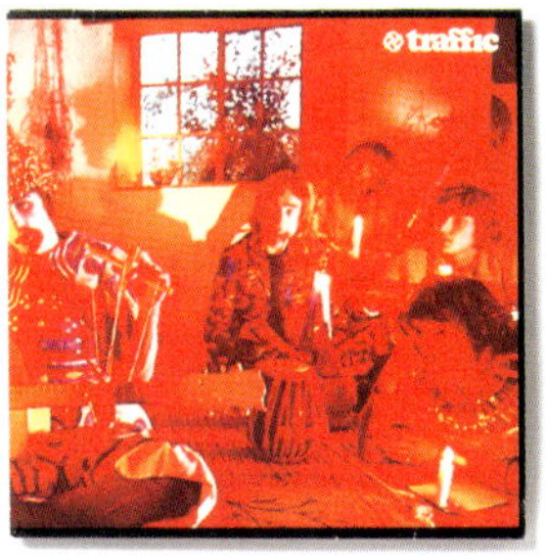

②
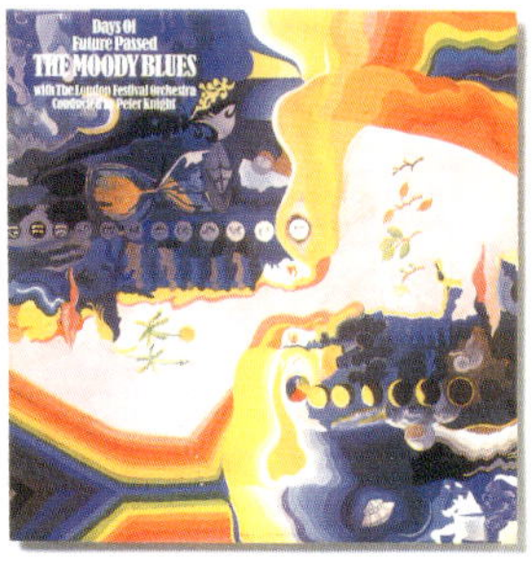

③
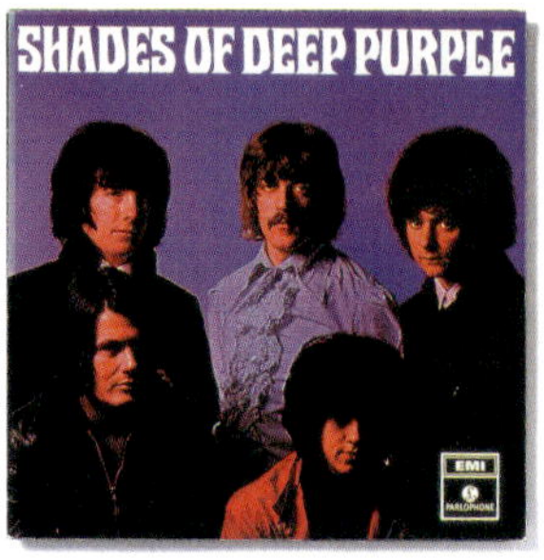

④
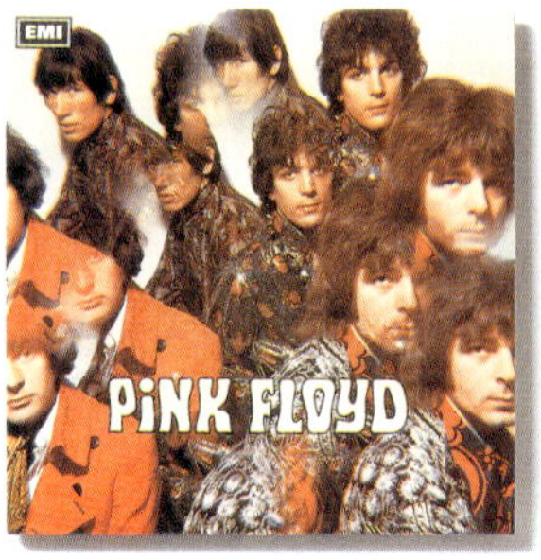

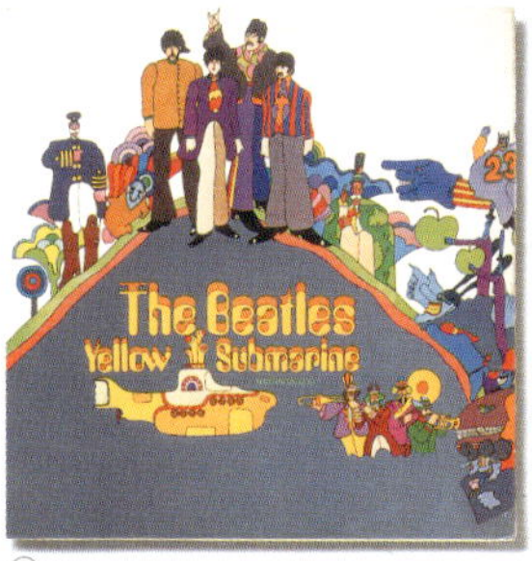

⑤

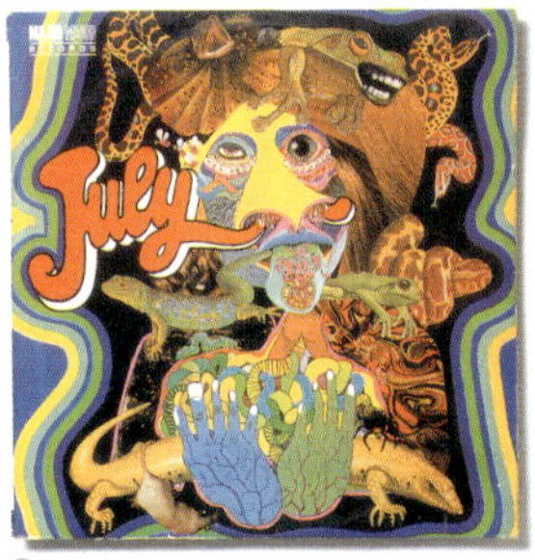

⑥

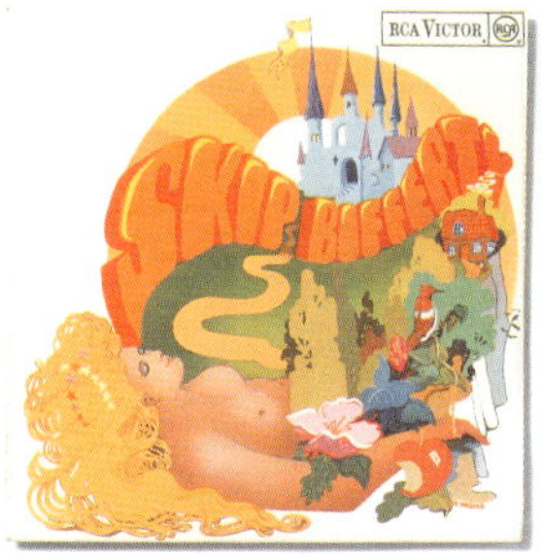

⑦

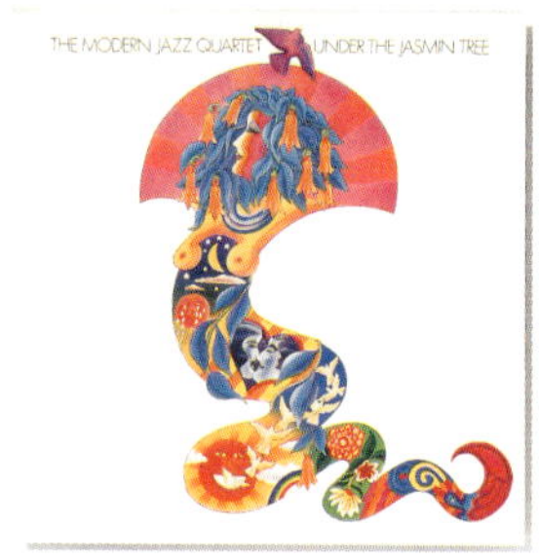

⑧

CREAM:DISRAELI GEARS/
REACTION 594 003(1966)

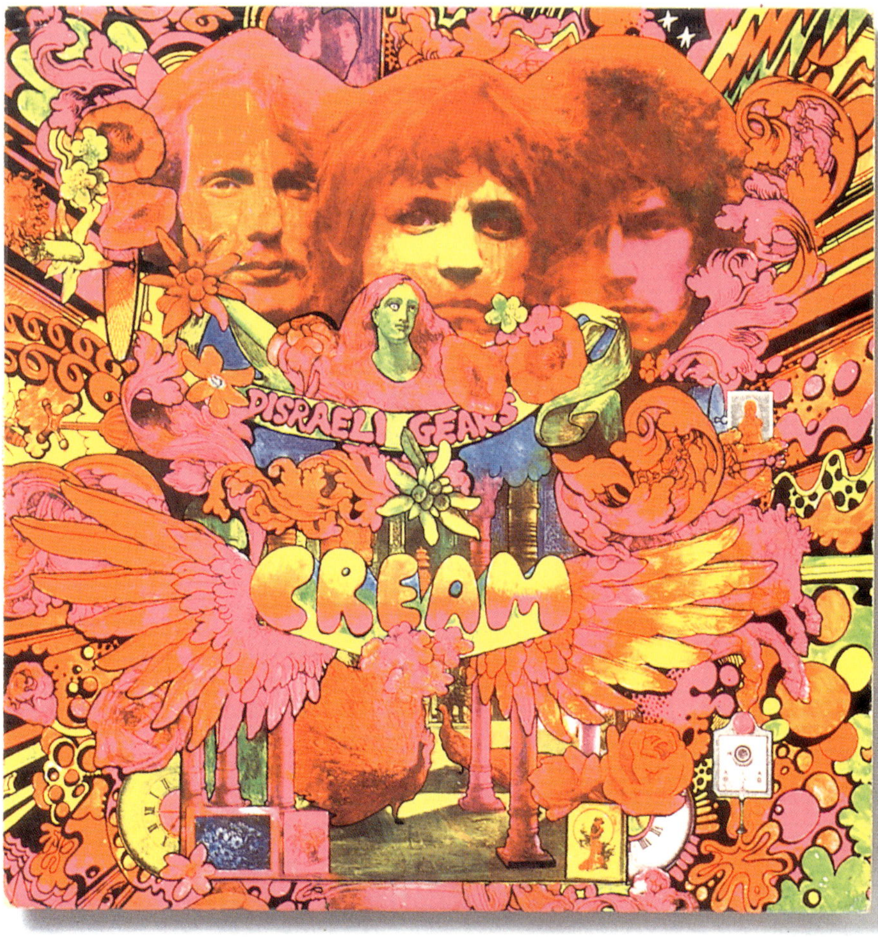

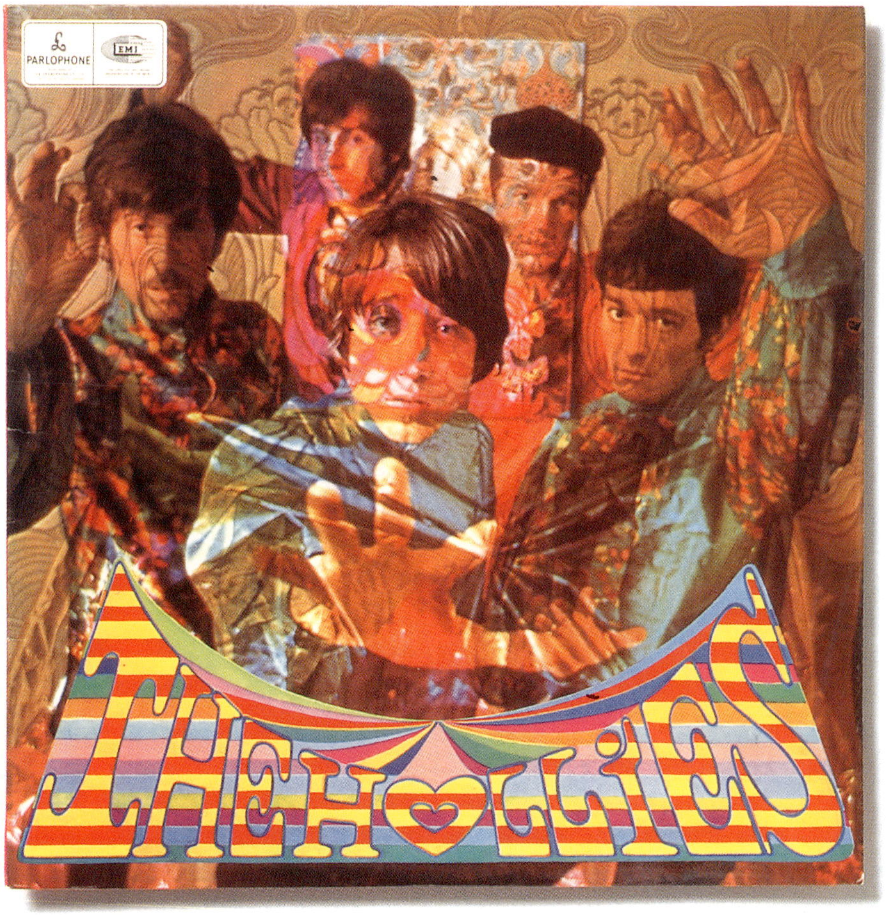

THE HOLLIES:EVOLUTION/
PARLOPHONE PMC7022 (1967)
Cover Design and Art Work / Simon & Marijke
Photographic Design(front) / Karl Ferris

⑨

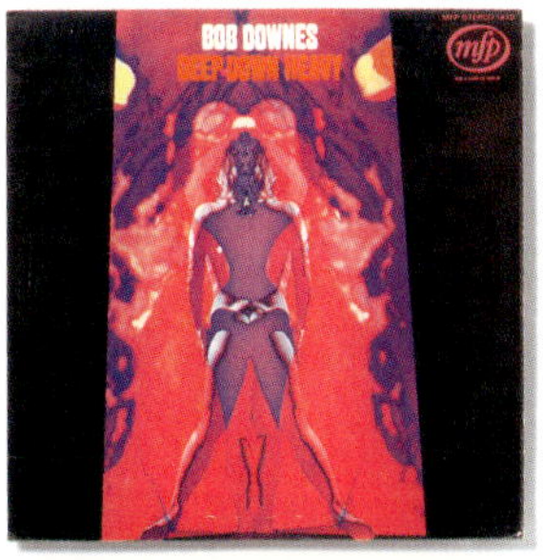

⑩

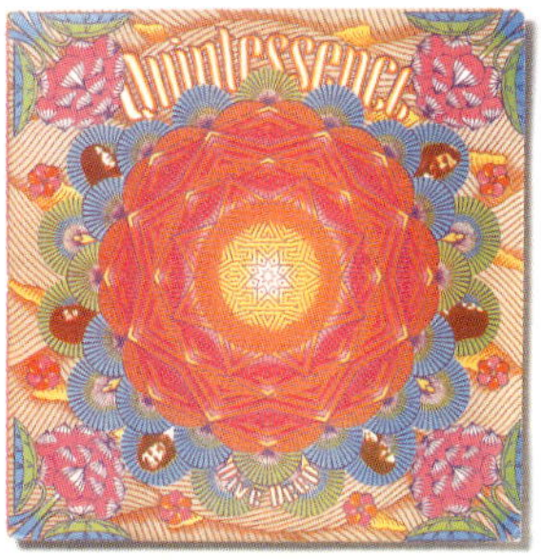

⑪

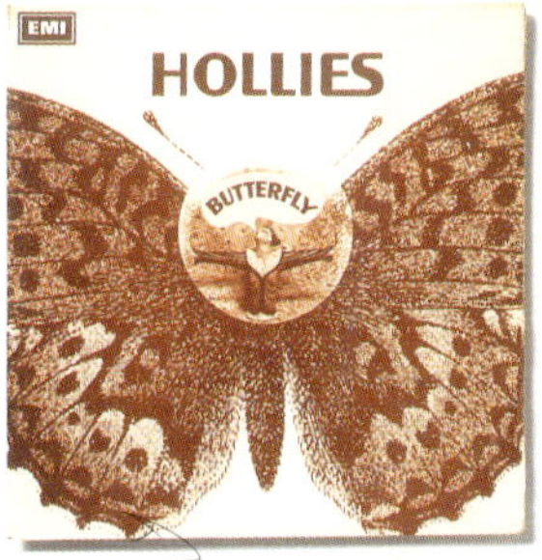

⑫

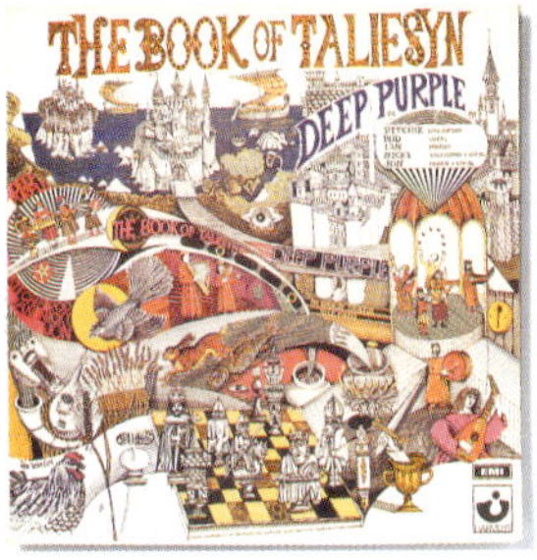

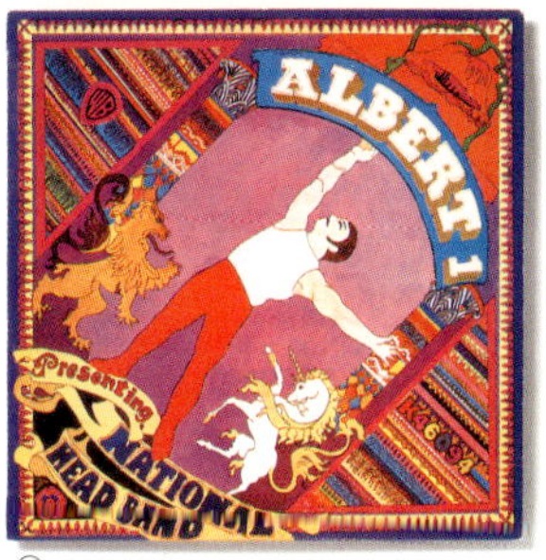

⑬

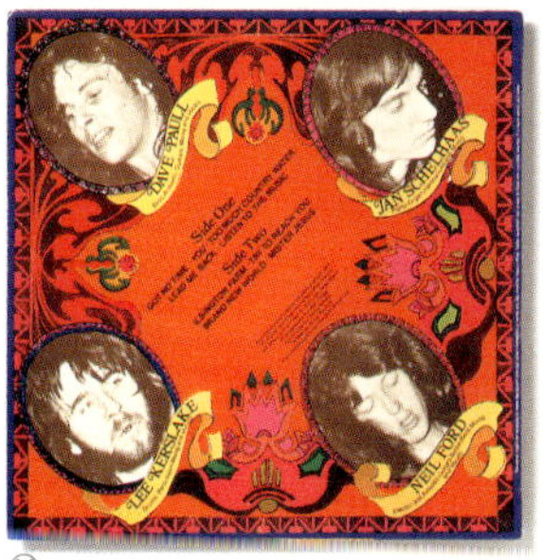

⑭

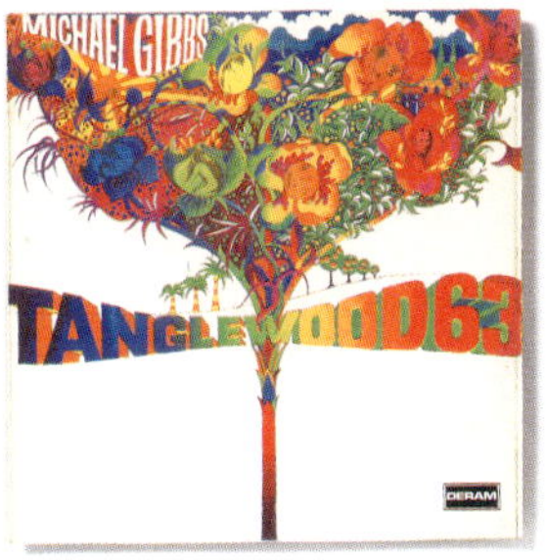

⑮

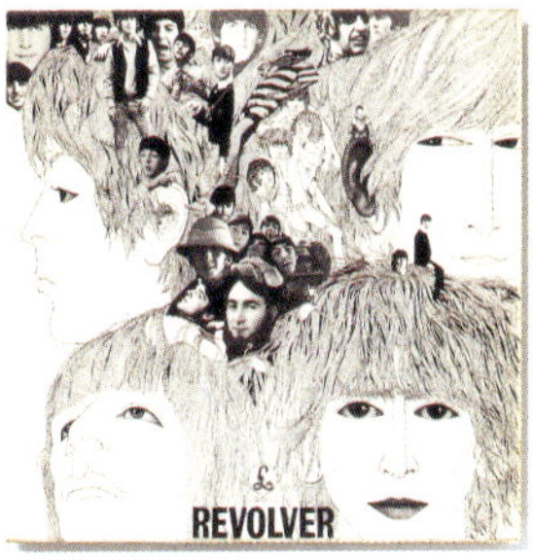

⑯

⑨ BOB DOWNES:DEEP DOWN HEAVY/
MFP 1412(1970)
Photograph/Photo Media
Sleeve Design/Jack Wood

⑩ QUINTESSENCE:DIVE DEEP/
ISLAND ILPS9143(1971)
Cover Design by Sumiko
Front Photos by Derek Davies

⑪ HOLLIES:BUTTERFLY/
PARLOPHONE PCS7039(1967)
Front Cover Design and Photographed by Tony Robins

⑫ DEEP PURPLE:THE BOOK OF TALIESYN/
HARVEST SHVL 751(1969)
Cover Painting/John Vernon Lord

⑬ NATIONAL HEAD BAND:ALBERT1/
WARNER K46094(1971) *front
Photographs Vincent Clegg
Cover Design Ginny Gillan

⑭ NATIONAL HEAD BAND:ALBERT1/
WARNER K46094(1971)*back

⑮ MICHAEL GIBBS:TANGLEWOOD63/
DERAM SML1087(1971)
Cover Picture and Design/Diz Dewhirst

⑯ THE BEATLES:REVOLVER/
PARLOPHONE PCS7009(1966)
Cover Design by Klaus Voormann

right: KILLING FLOOR:OUT OF URANUS/
PENNY FARTHING PELS511(1970) *front and back
Cover Design/Rick Breach

right below: KILLING FLOOR:OUT OF URANUS/
PENNY FARTHING PELS511(1970)*inner

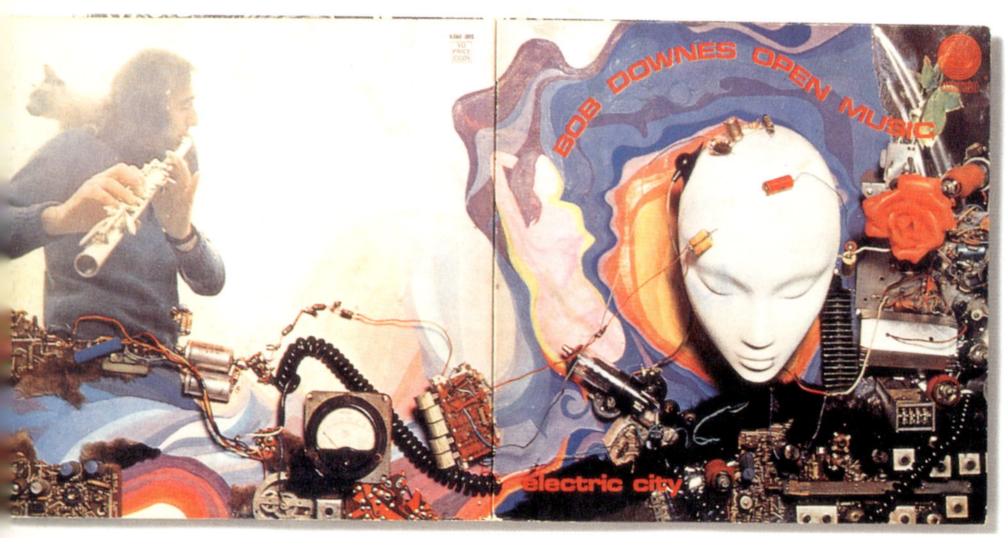

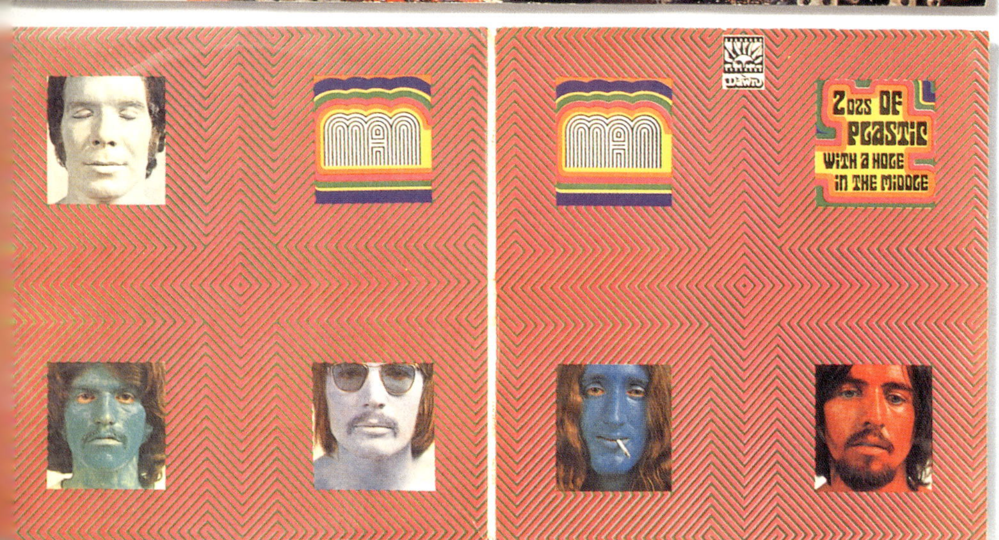

above: BOB DOWNES OPEN MUSIC:ELECTRIC CITY/
VERTIGO 6360 005(1970)
Sleeve Design/Nigel Rollings,Rob Lett
Inside and Back Cover Photographs/Jake Jackson

left: MAN:2 OZS.OF PLASTIC WITH A HOLE IN THE MIDDLE/
DAWN DNLS3003(1969)

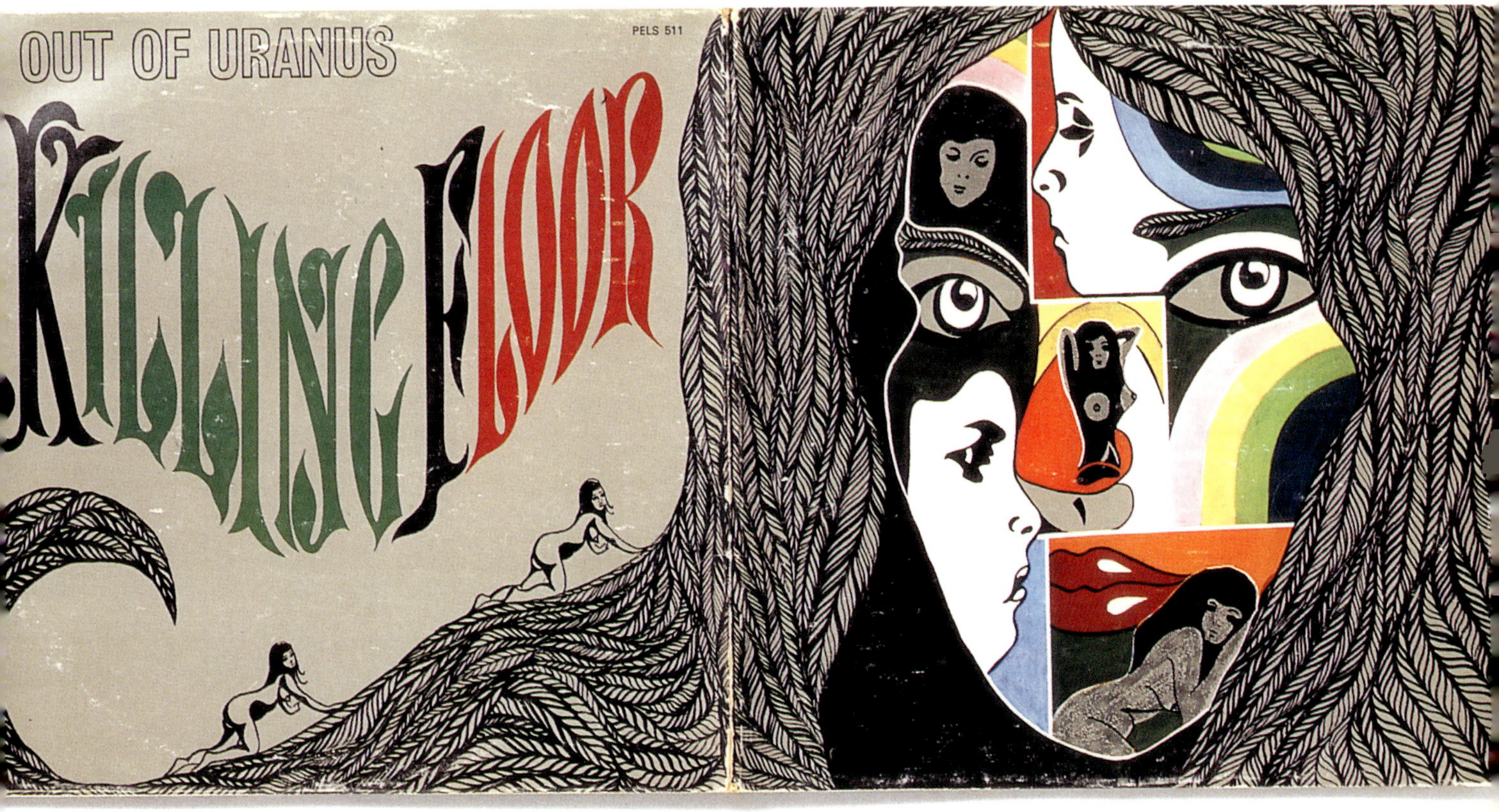
OUT OF URANUS
PELS 511
KILLING FLOOR

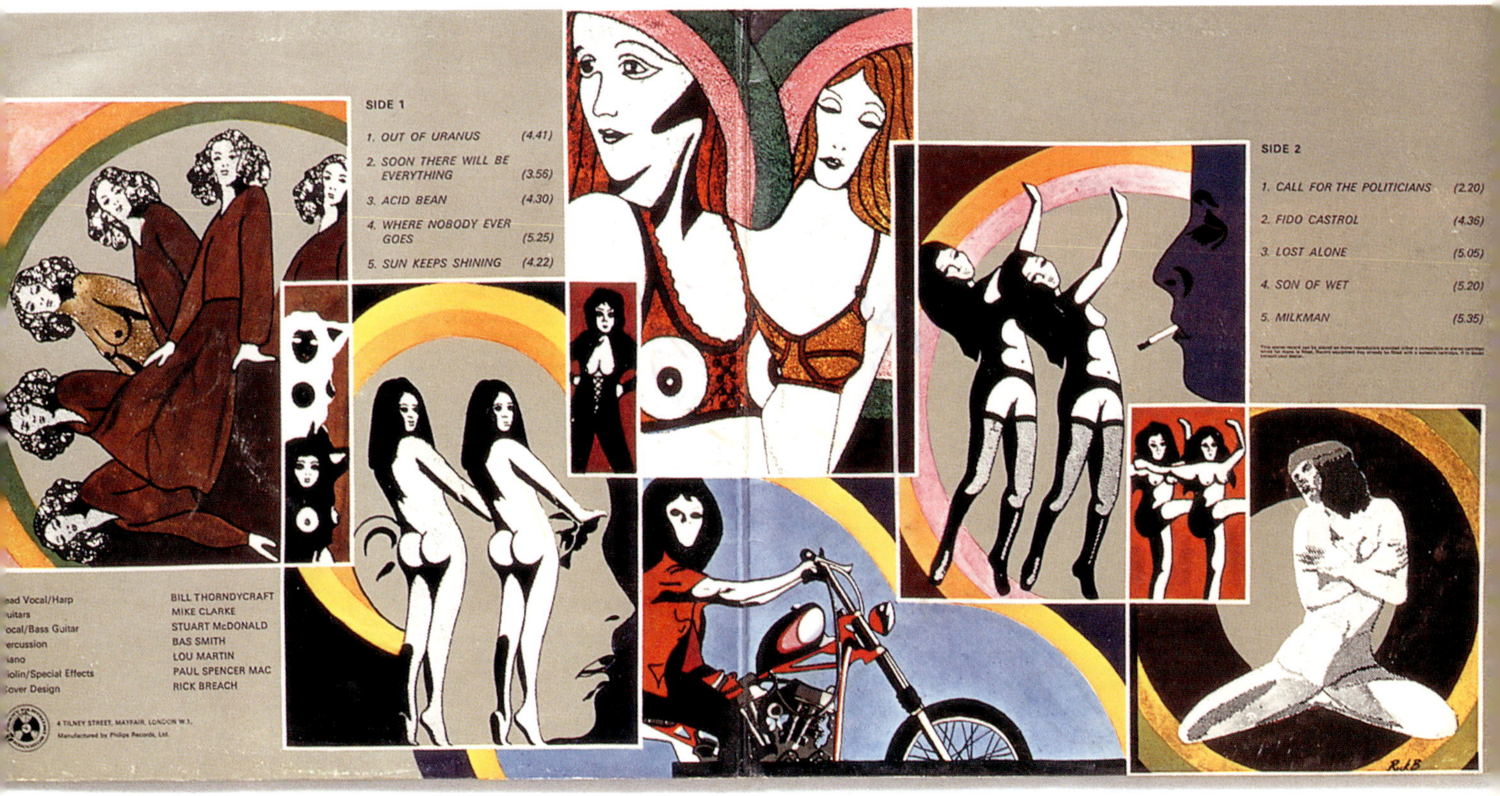
SIDE 1
1. OUT OF URANUS (4.41)
2. SOON THERE WILL BE EVERYTHING (3.56)
3. ACID BEAN (4.30)
4. WHERE NOBODY EVER GOES (5.25)
5. SUN KEEPS SHINING (4.22)
SIDE 2
1. CALL FOR THE POLITICIANS (2.20)
2. FIDO CASTROL (4.36)
3. LOST ALONE (5.05)
4. SON OF WET (5.20)
5. MILKMAN (5.35)
ead Vocal/Harp BILL THORNDYCRAFT
uitars MIKE CLARKE
ocal/Bass Guitar STUART McDONALD
ercussion BAS SMITH
iano LOU MARTIN
iolin/Special Effects PAUL SPENCER MAC
Cover Design RICK BREACH
4 TILNEY STREET, MAYFAIR, LONDON W.1.
Manufactured by Philips Records, Ltd.

psychedelic Modern Psyche サイケのモダン化

あれだけカラフルな色彩を放っていたサイケデリック・アートが70年頃を境にどこへ行ってしまったのか。その問いかけに対する答えのつもりで、「サイケのモダン化」なる項目をまとめてみた。もっと多くのサイケデリック・アルバムを参照すれば、またちがった結論が導き出されるのかもしれないが、少なくともここに集めたジャケットを眺めて気づくのは、総天然色と形容された温もりのあるデザインが、多くの場合、幾何学的なモチーフに取って代わられていることである。これをロジェ・カイヨワ風に解釈するなら、60年代のサイケと70年代以降のサイケとの関係を、古代・中世の妖精物語や19世紀の幻想怪奇譚に対する、20世紀のサイエンス・フィクション（SF）のような関係にたとえることができないだろうか。

妖精物語が原因不明の自然現象に対する不安と願望の産物であったのに対し、幻想怪奇譚は、未熟な実験科学の整合性が不可解な力の作用によって覆されたときの恐怖を描き出していた。一方、SFは、科学が急速な進歩を迎えた時代の不安を反映させている。つまり、いずれも時代の潜在的な不安から生じたジャンルだった。これが、妖精物語～幻想怪奇譚～SFの一貫性を示そうとするカイヨワの論拠である。音楽のみならず社会全体においても、テクノロジーが新たな局面を迎えつつあった70年以降、思考実験としてのサイケデリック・アートのなかにSF世界と同種の期待と不安が込められていたとしても、むしろそれは当然といえるだろう。また、そうした時代の急激な変化を目の当たりにしているからこそ我々は、XTCのメンバーが85年に変名で発表したアルバム『25 O'clock』のような古き良き時代のサイケを模したジャケットに、かえって心が和んでしまうのかもしれない。

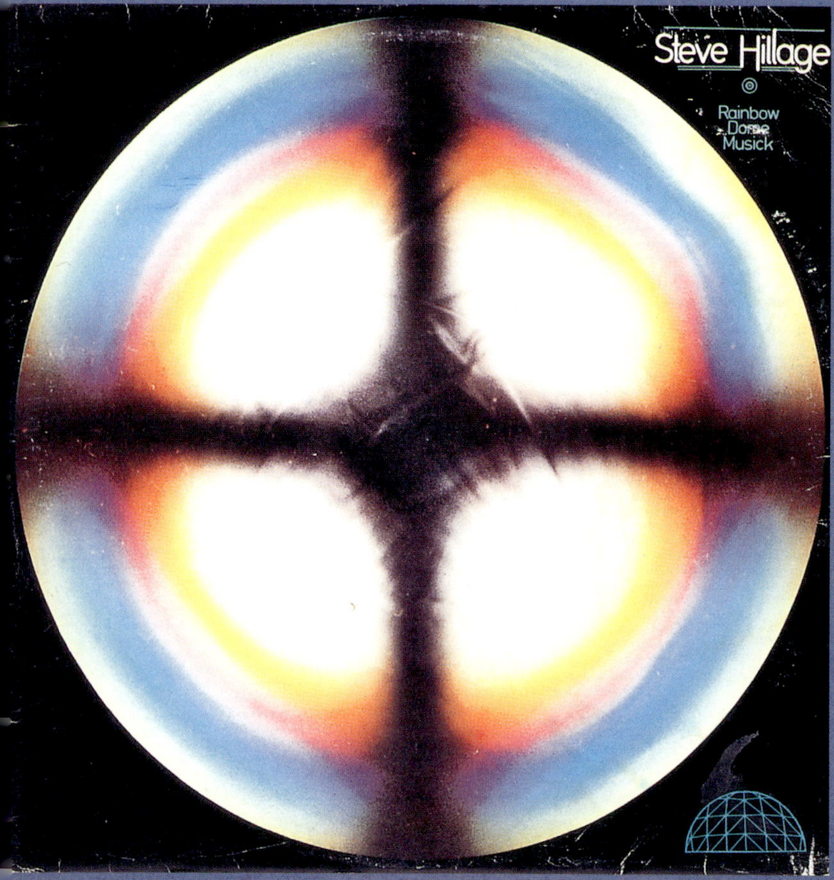

STEVE HILLAGE:RAINBOW DOME MUSICK/
VIRGIN VR1(1979)
Sleeve by Rupert Atwill/Laserphaze

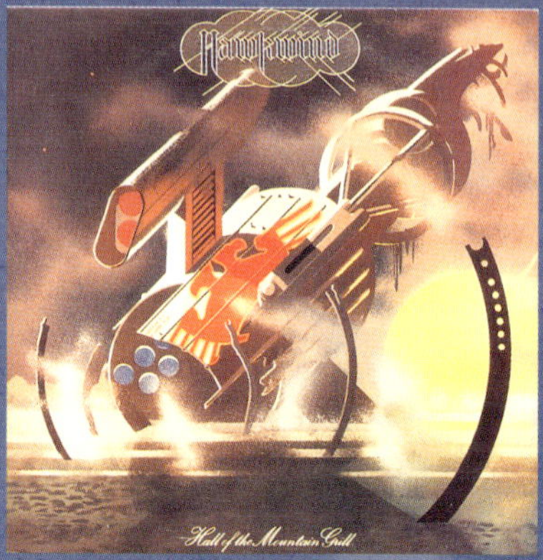

HAWKWIND:HALL OF THE MOUNTAIN GRILL
UNITED ARTISTS UAG 29672(1974)
Front Cover:Barney Bubbles

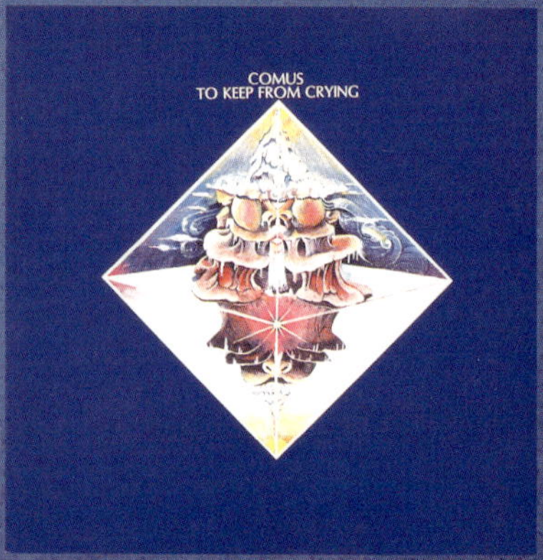

COMUS:TO KEEP FROM CRYING/
VIRGIN V2018(1974)
Cover Art/Sheira MacLurkin

In Search of the Lost Record

What happened to the brightly colored psychedelic art after the 70's? Trying to find an answer, here I have compiled a section called "Modern Psyche". Looking at a greater variety of psychedelic artwork than this might lead us to a different conclusion. But what we can discern by studying the album covers compiled here is that the once brightly colored organic designs have reverted to their geometric motifs. French intellect Roger Caillois would interpret the relationship between the psyche of the 60's and that of the 70's as similar to the relationship between medieval fairy tales or 19th century gothic tales to contemporary science fiction. While fairy tales were a product of hope or fear of an unidentified natural phenomenon, gothic fantasy tales depicted the fear that emerged when the co-ordination of primitive science experiments were overcome by some unknown force. On the other hand, science fiction literature reflects the fear of a generation facing a radical evolution in science. In short, each literary genre was born from an unconscious fear of it's generation. This is the basis of Caillois' theory, asserting the consistency in the flow of fairy tales to gothic fantasy tales and then to science fiction.

In the 70's, not only was music entering a new era but so was technology. It comes as no surprise that the same kind of anticipation mixed with fear found in science fiction novels also appeared in psychedelic art in the form of experiments with perspective and points of view. Maybe this is why the generation that had experienced this radical change first-hand tends to feel nostalgic toward psychedelic album covers of the 'good old days,' such as the album "25 O'clock"(1985), made by a member of XTC.

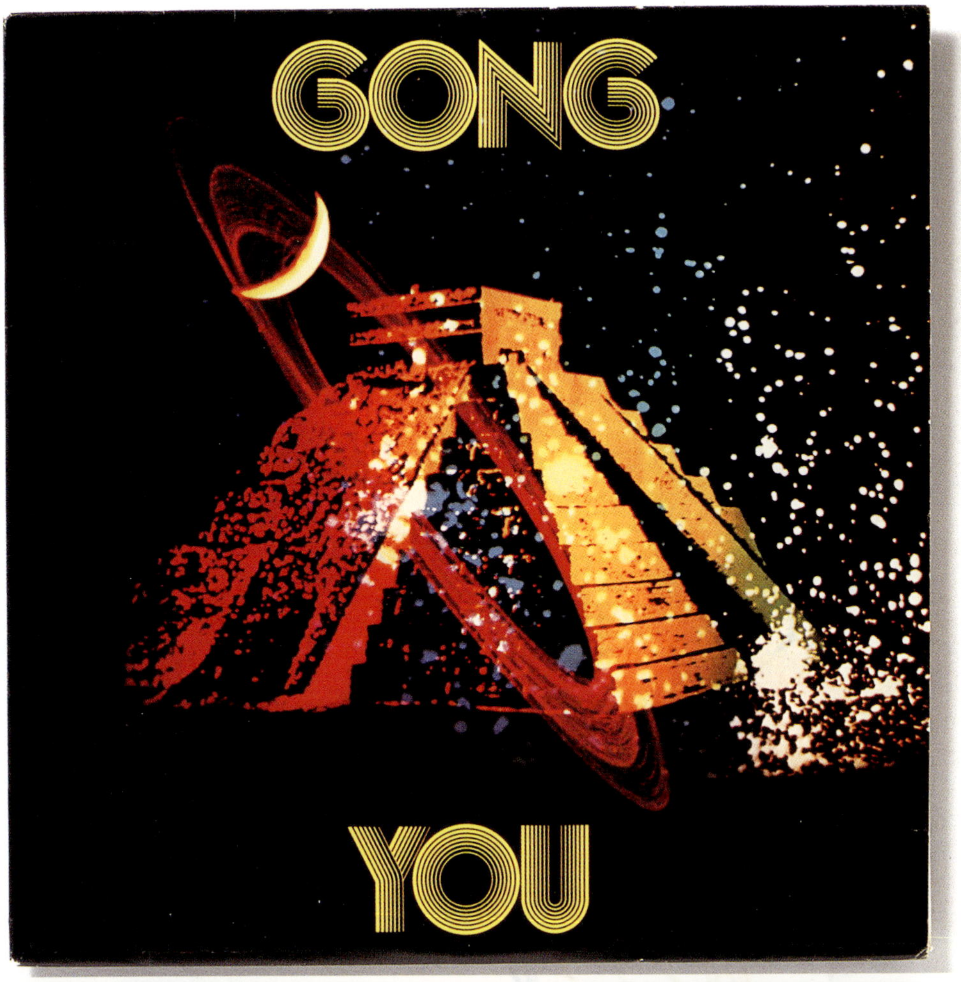

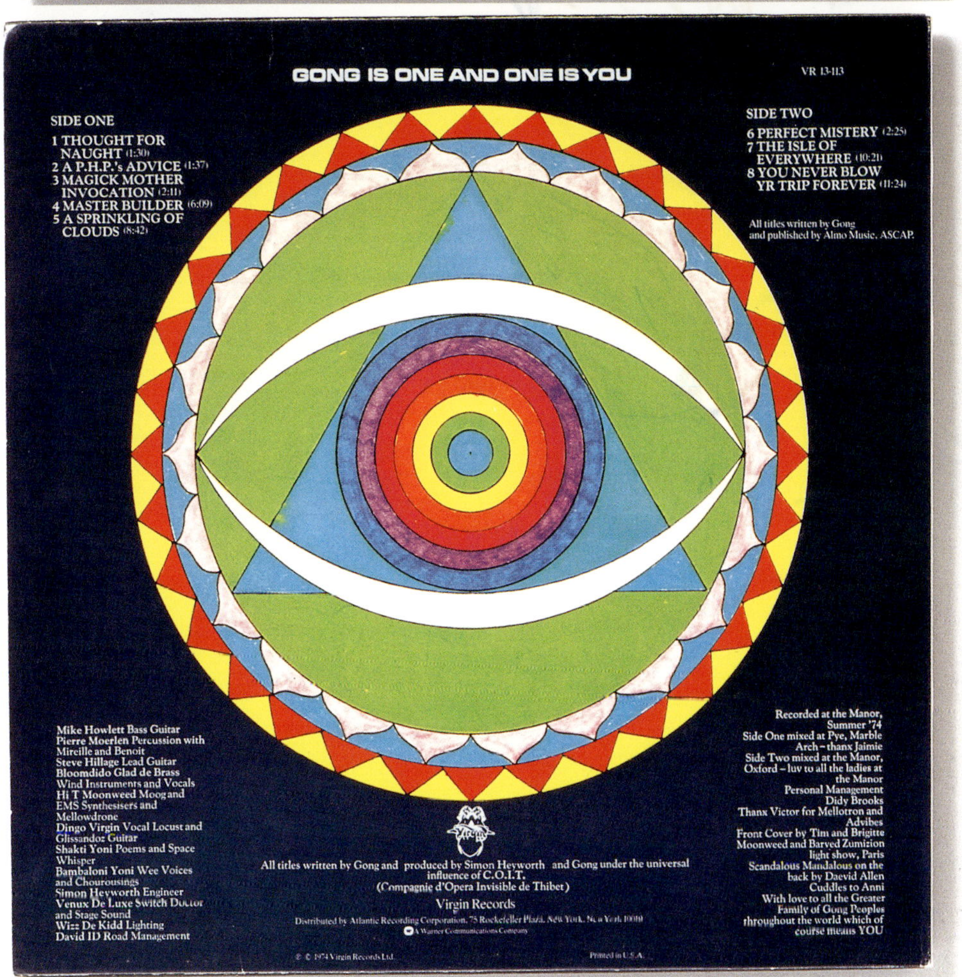

GONG:YOU/VIRGIN VR13-113(1974) *front
Front Cover by Tim and Brigitte
Back by David Allen

GONG:YOU/VIRGIN VR13-113(1974) *back

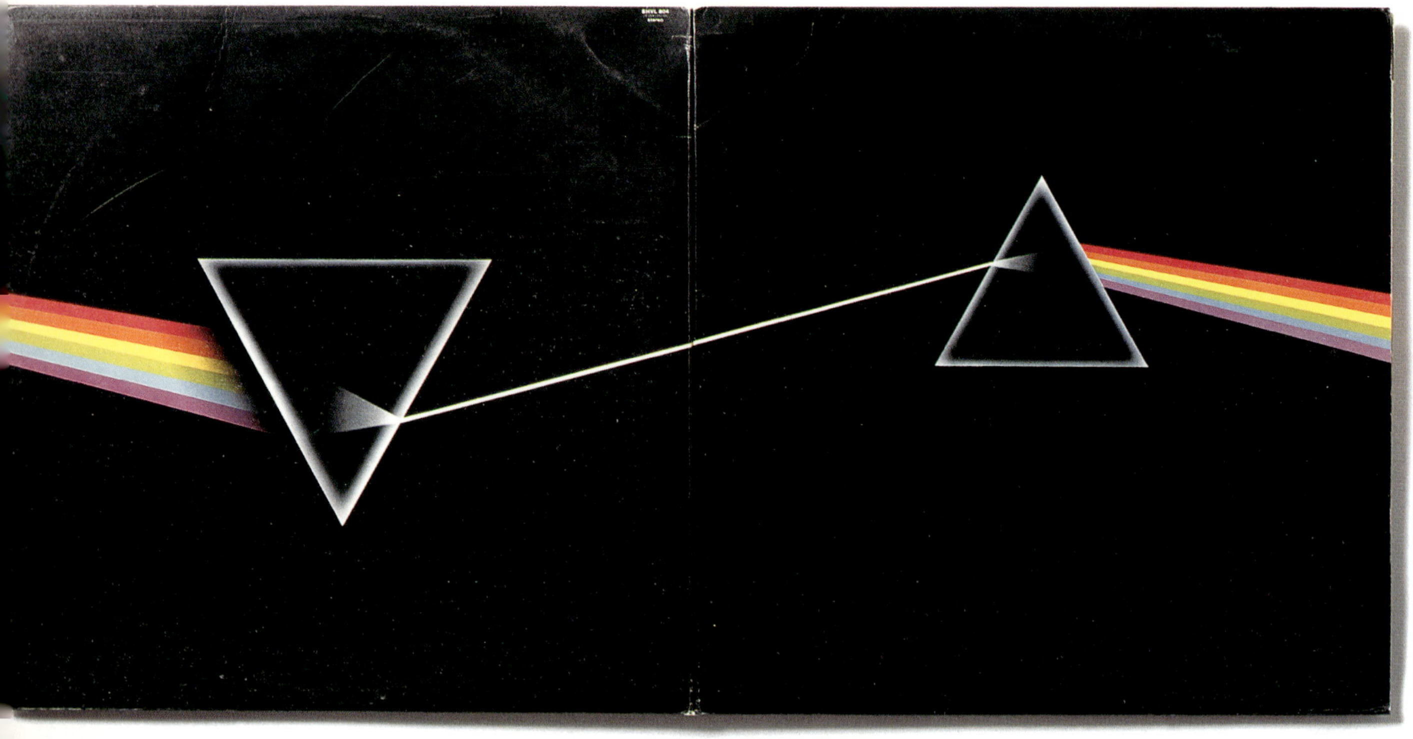

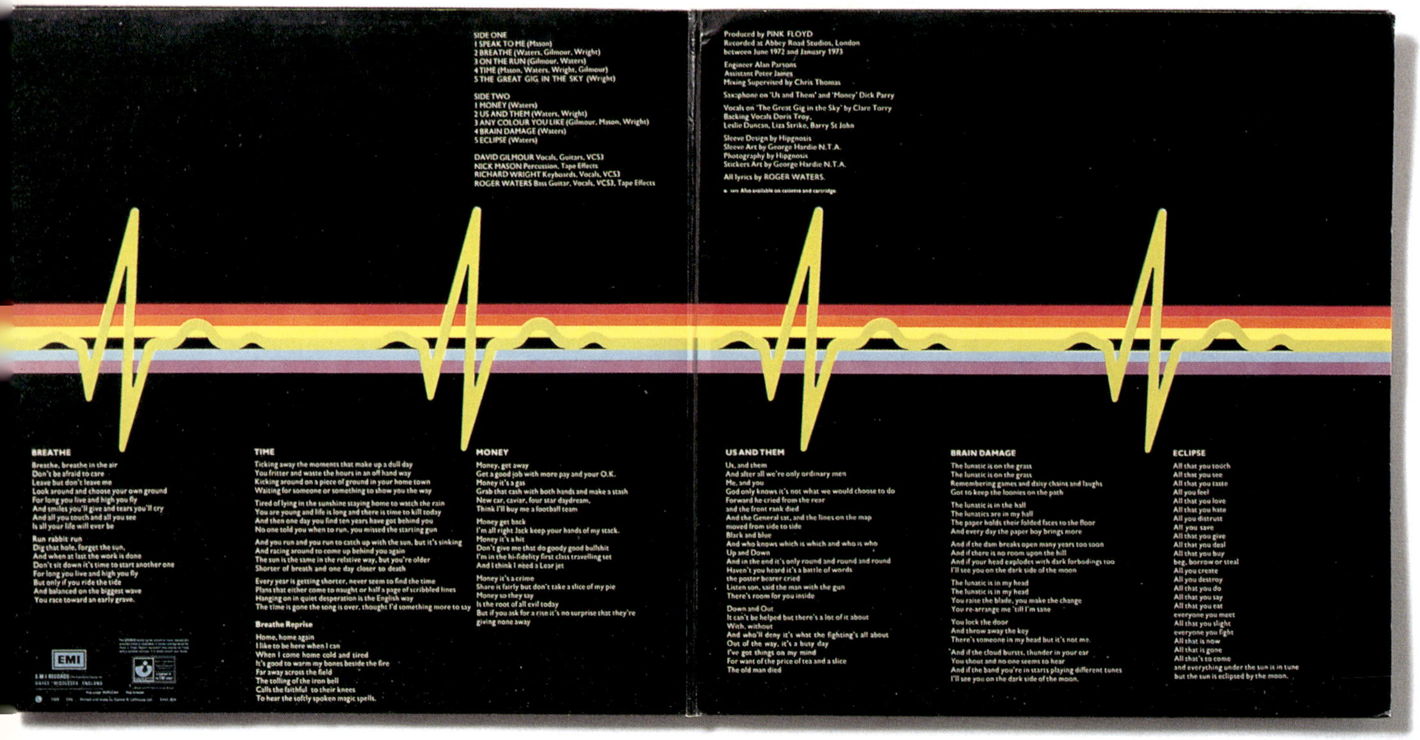

PINK FLOYD:THE DARK SIDE OF THE MOON/
HARVEST SHVL804(1973)
*front and back
Sleeve Design by Hipgnosis

PINK FLOYD:THE DARK SIDE OF THE MOON/
HARVEST SHVL804(1973)
*inner

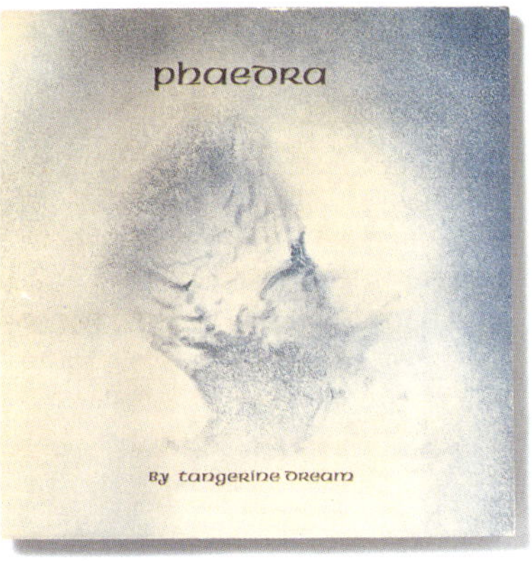

TANGERINE DREAM:PHAEDRA/
VIRGIN V2010(1974)
Sleeve Design and Cover Painting/Edgar Froese

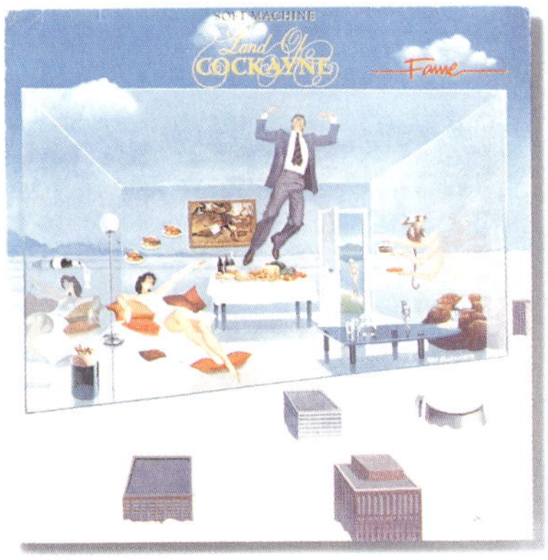

SOFT MACHINE:LAND OF COCKAYNE/
EMI EMC3348(1981)
Coverpainting/Roy Ellsworth

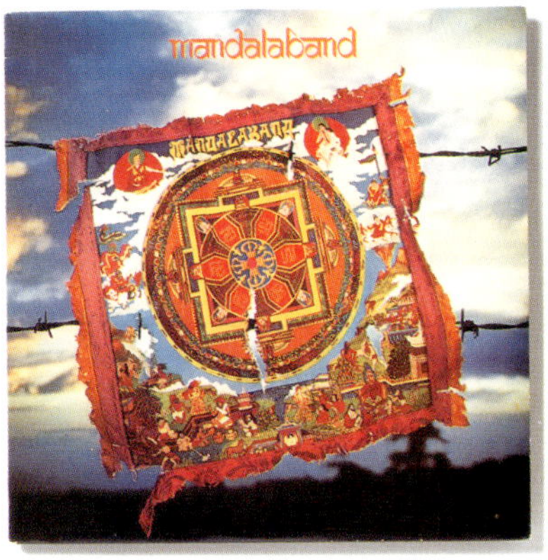

MANDALABAND:MANDALABAND/
CHRYSALIS CHR1095(1975)
Cover Photography and Concept by Trevor Key
Mandala Painting by David and Gilly Rohl

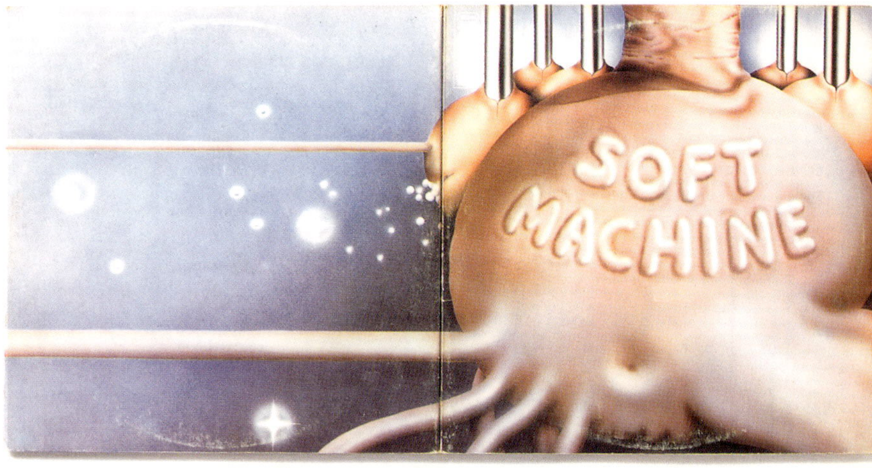

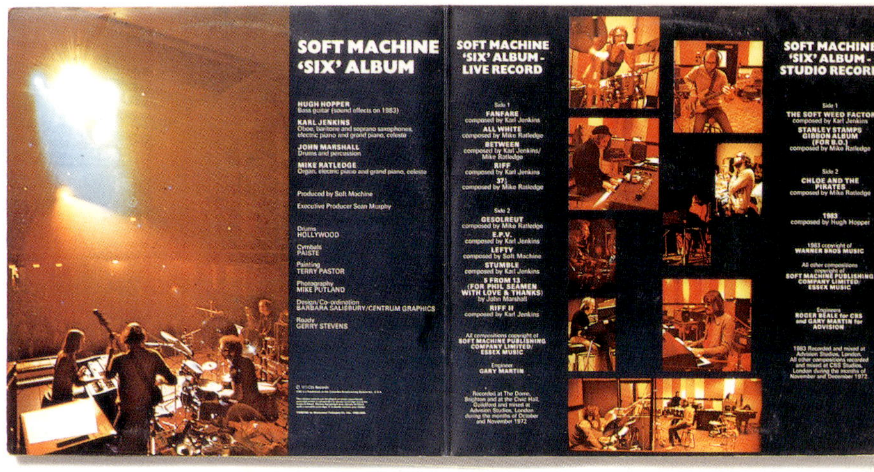

SOFT MACHINE:SIX/CBS 68214(1973) *front and back
Painting/Terry Pastor
Photograpy/Mike Putland
Design,Co-ordination/Barbara Salisbury, Centrum Graphics

SOFT MACHINE:SIX/CBS 68214(1973) *inner

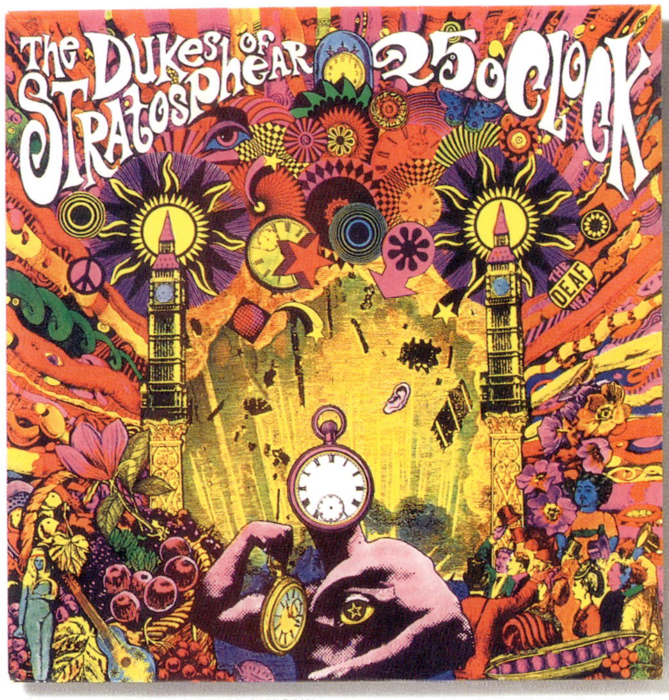

THE DUKES OF STRATOSPHEAR:25 O'CLOCK/
VIRGIN WOW1(1985)
Sleeve Art/Sir John Johns

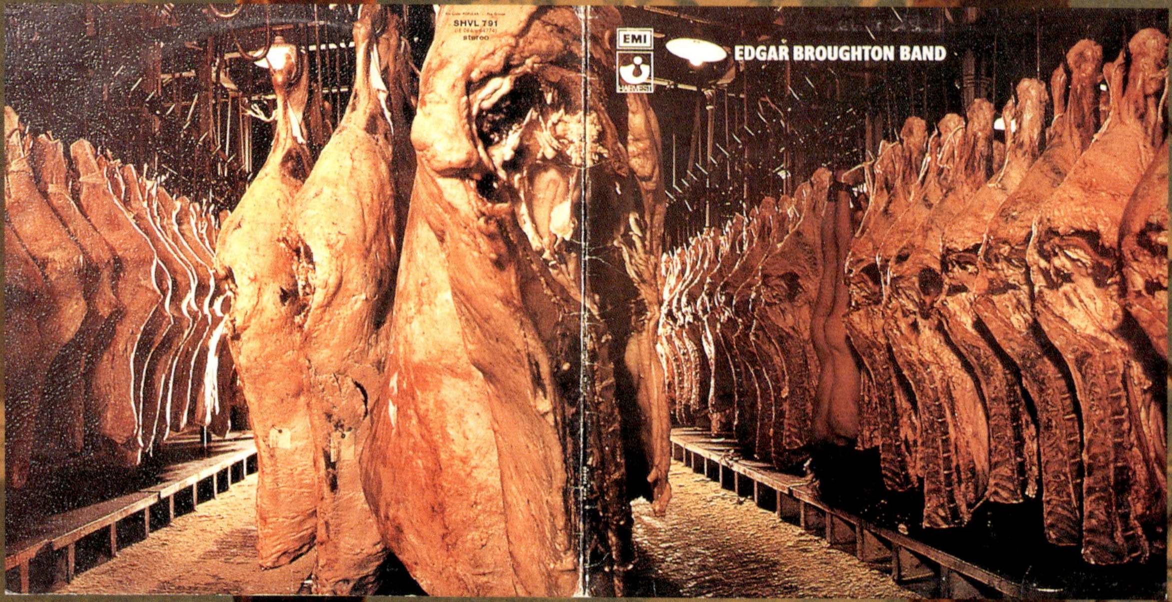

①

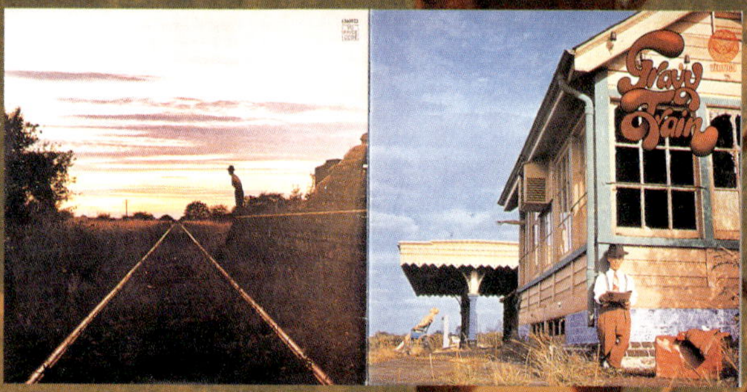

②

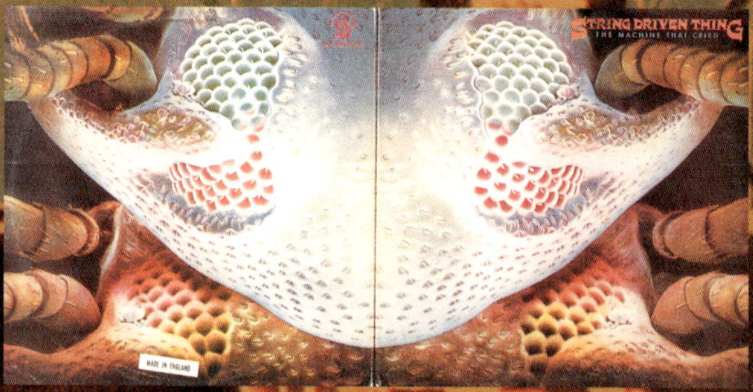

③

Hipgnosis special effects
ヒプノシス

① EDGAR BROUGHTON BAND:
EDGAR BROUGHTON BAND/
HARVEST SHVL791(1971)
Cover:Hipgnosis

② GRAVY TRAIN:GRAVY TRAIN/
VERTIGO 6360023(1970)
Cover Design and Photos by Hipgnosis

③ STRING DRIVEN THING:
THE MACHINE THAT CRIED/
CHARISMA CAS1070(1973)
Cover by Hipgnosis

special effects
特殊効果

特殊効果を駆使したアルバム・カヴァーといえば、第一にヒプノシスの名前を挙げないわけにはいかない。写真のコラージュ、イラストと写真の合成、異物を配置した特異な構図、実際に特殊メイクを施した人物の撮影など、じつは非常に幅広い手法をその都度選び出しているにもかかわらず、つねにヒプノシスらしさを見る者に印象づけてしまうところが、彼らの真骨頂だろう。それは、現実認識を撹乱するというストーム・トーガソンのヴィジョンが、一本の太い背骨のように貫かれているからにほかならない。
デザイン集団のヒプノシスが設立されたのは68年のこと。それぞれロイヤル・カレッジ・オブ・アートとロンドン・スクール・オブ・フィルム・テクニックの学生だったストーム・トーガソンとオーブリー・パウェルが中心となり、当初は本のカヴァー・デザインを手がけていたが、やがてトーガソンがピンク・フロイドの中心メンバーであるロジャー・ウォーターズと友人関係にあったのが縁となって、ピンク・フロイドのセカンド・アルバム『神秘』以降のスリーヴ・デザインを担当することになったという。ヒプノシスは83年に解散したが、その後もトーガソンはピンク・フロイド関連のCDを中心に、その他のアーティストの作品も手がける一方で、ウェブ・デザインなどにも活動の場を広げている。

special

Any discussion of special effect techniques on album covers should begin with the work of Hipgnosis. Even though they used a wide variety of techniques—photo collage, illustration mixed with photography—and a range of thematic treatments, their work was always distinctive and readily identifiable. Indeed, such a pronounced style was a key for Hipgnosis' work, which born from the unsettling visions created by Storm Thorgerson. His mastery of vision helped Hipgnosis maintain a consistency throughout their entire oeuvre. In 1968, Hipgnosis was established by Storm Thorgerson, who, at the time, was a student at the Royal College of Art, and Aubrey Powell, a student of the London School of Film. Their initial work was mainly book cover design but Thorgerson happened to be friends with Roger Waters and this connection gave them the chance to design the sleeve for "A Saucerful of Secrets," Pink Floyd's second album. Hipgnosis continued to design the band's album covers thereafter. Hipgnosis spilt up in 1983 but Thorgerson continues to design, creating CD covers for Pink Floyd releases and many other artists, while expanding into the field of website design.

④ CAPABILITY BROWN:VOICE/
CHARISMA CAS1068(1973)
Outside Cover by Hipgnosis

⑤ WILLIAM LYALL:SOLO CASTING/
EMI EMA780(1976)
Sleeve Desgin and Photographs by Hipgnosis

⑥ ROY HARPER:
FLASHES FROM THE ARCHIVES OF OBLIVION/
HARBEST SHDW 405(1974)
Sleeve Design,Continuous Argument between Roy Harper and Hipgnosis

④

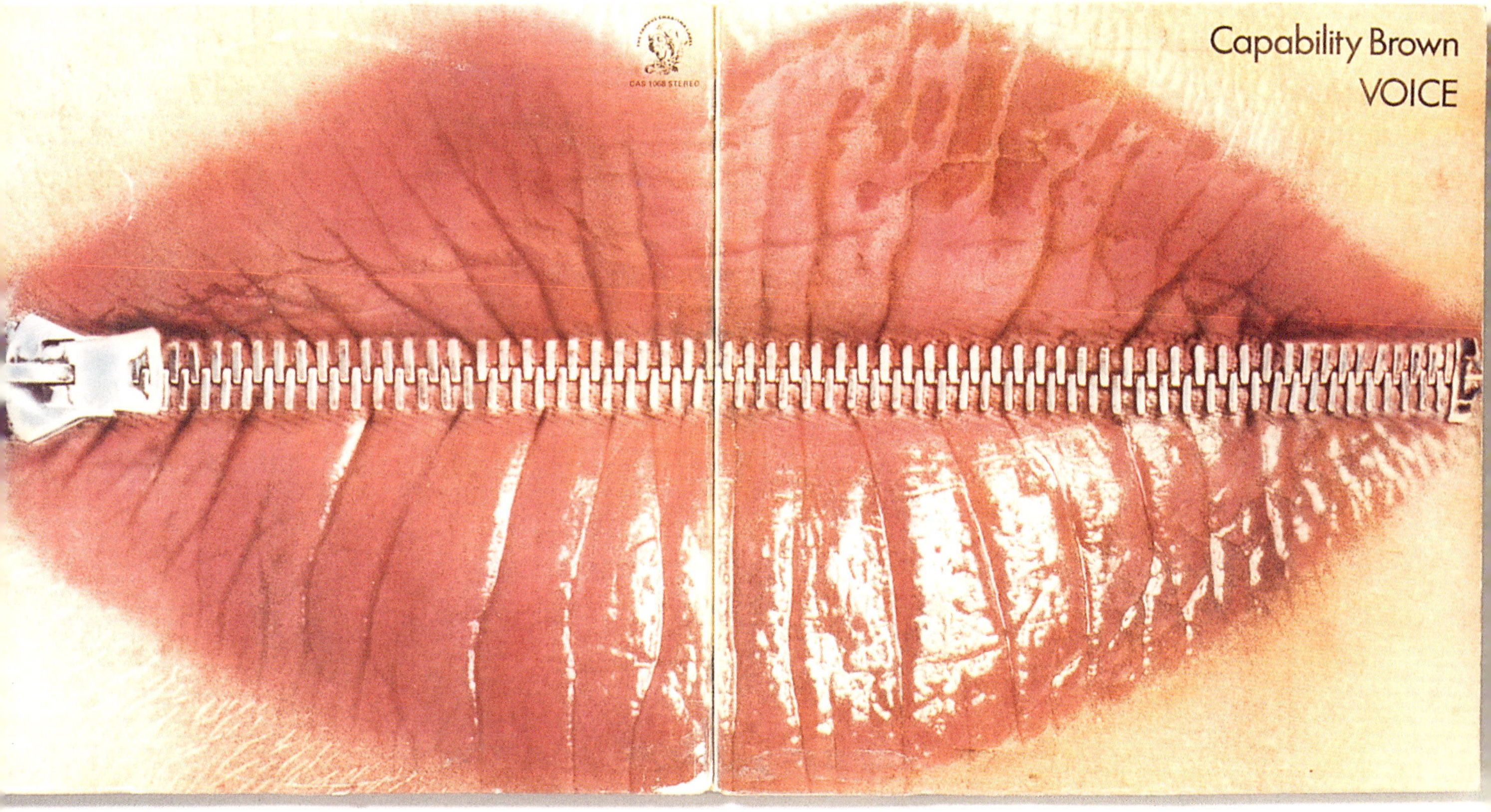

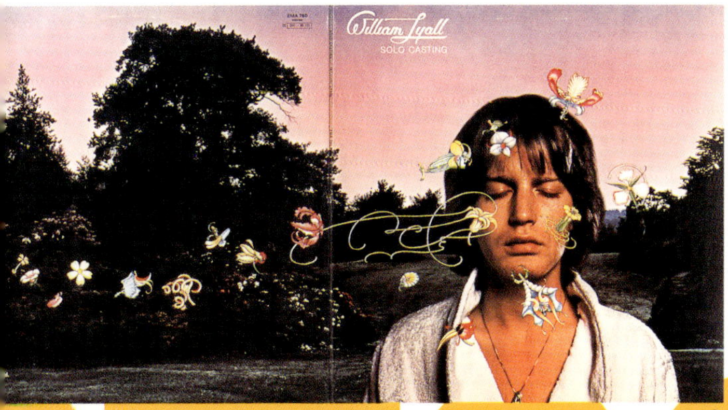

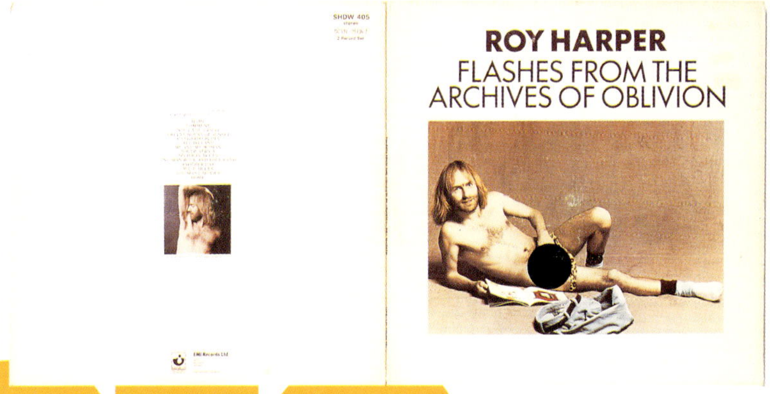

⑤ ⑥

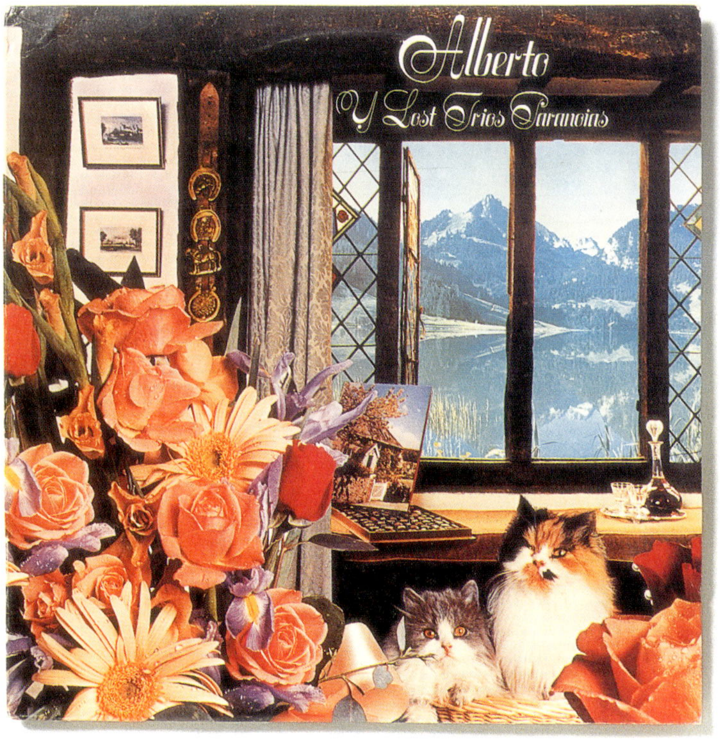

ALBERTO Y LOST TRIOS PARANOIAS:
ALBERTO Y LOST TRIOS PARANOIAS/
TRANSATLANTIC TRA316(1976)
Sleeve Design and Photos by Hipgnosis

LED ZEPPELIN:HOUSES OF THE HOLLY/
ATLANTIC K50014(1973)
*inner

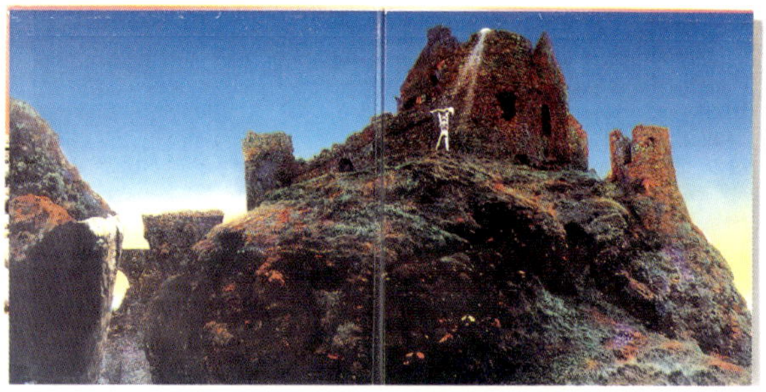

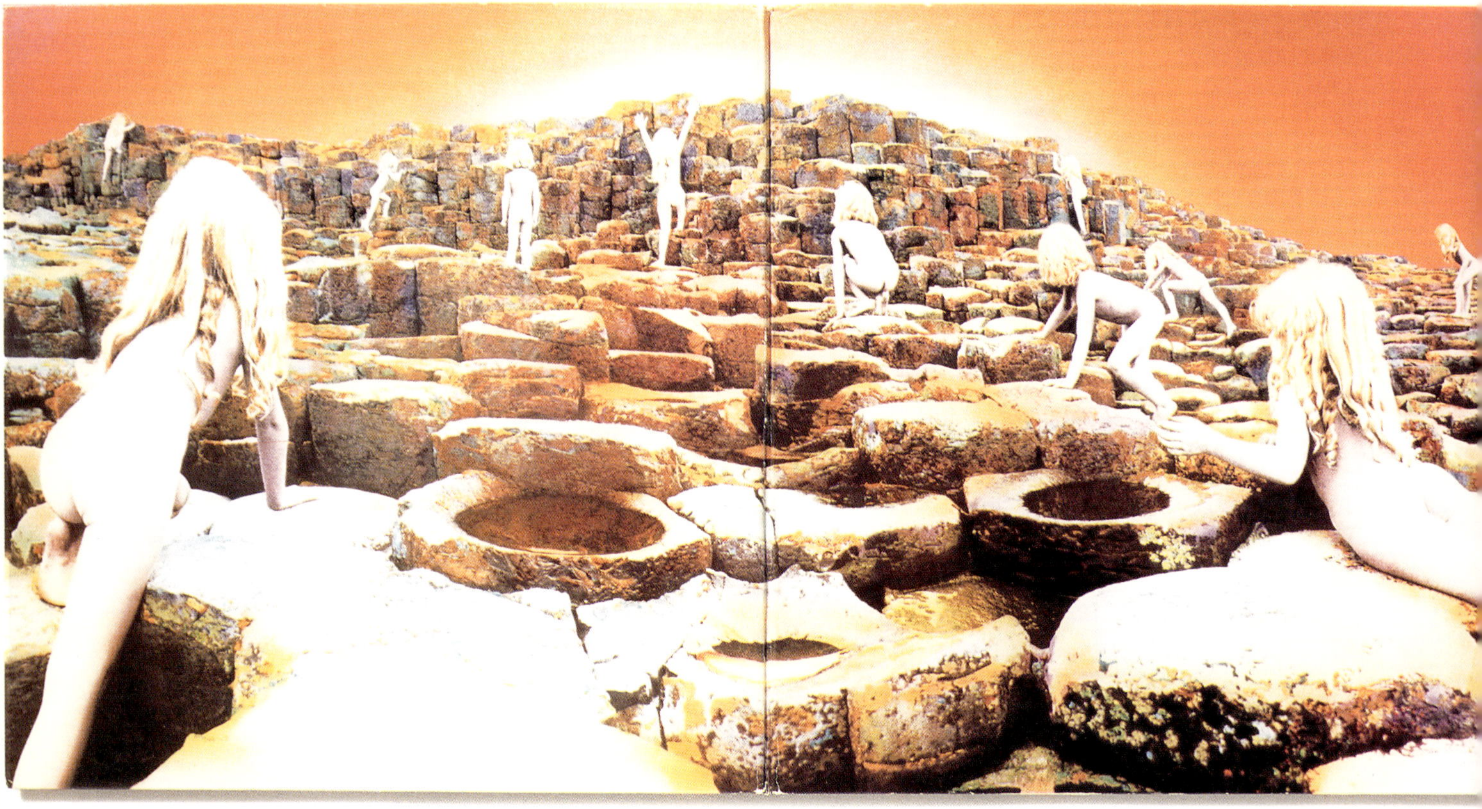

LED ZEPPELIN:HOUSES OF THE HOLLY/
ATLANTIC K50014(1973)*front and back
Sleeve by Hipgnosis

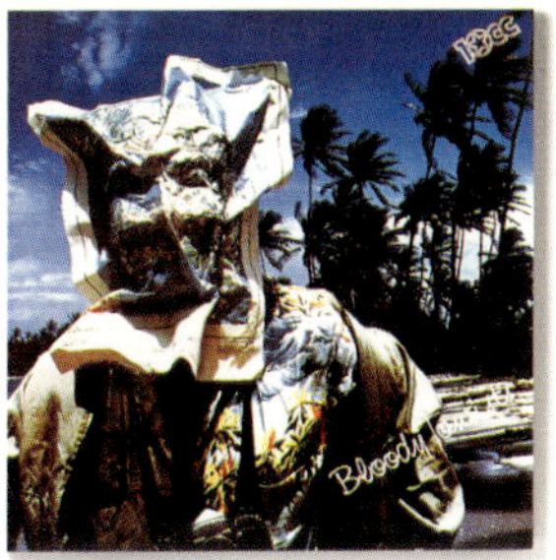

①

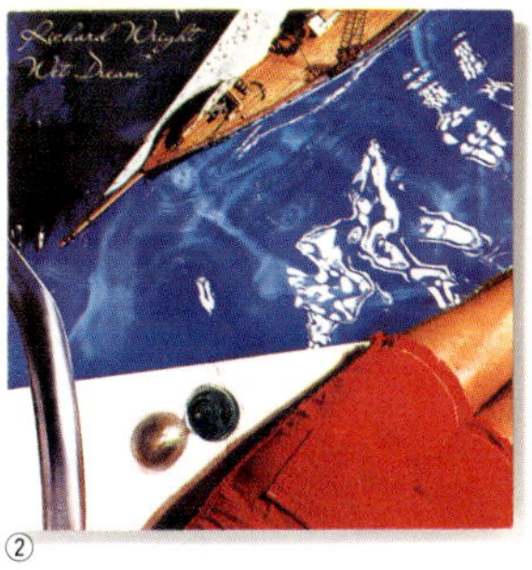

②

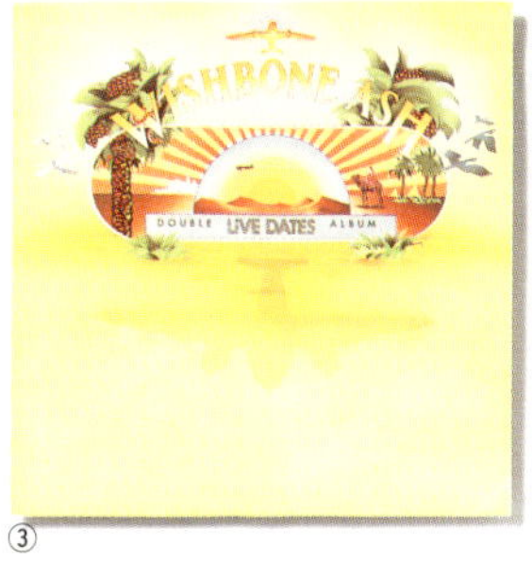

③

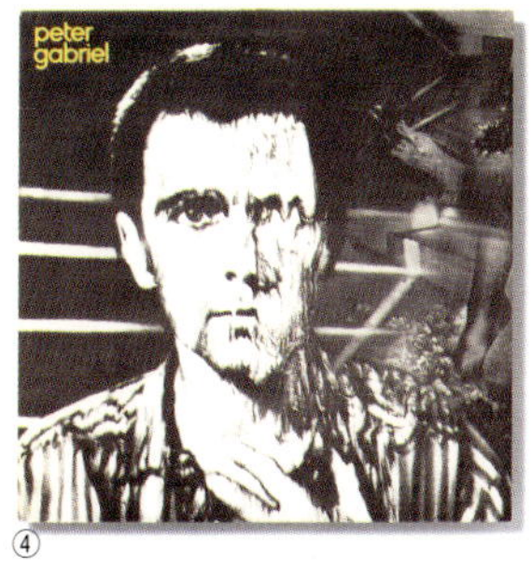

④

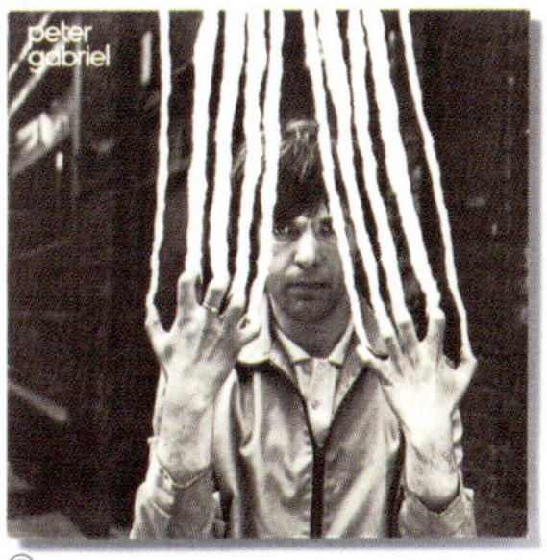

⑤

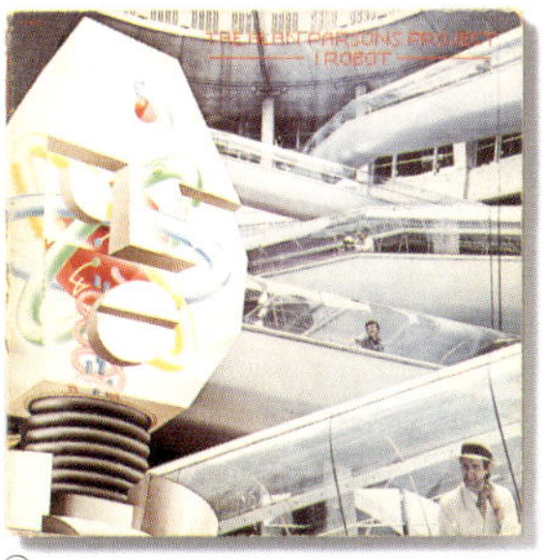

⑥

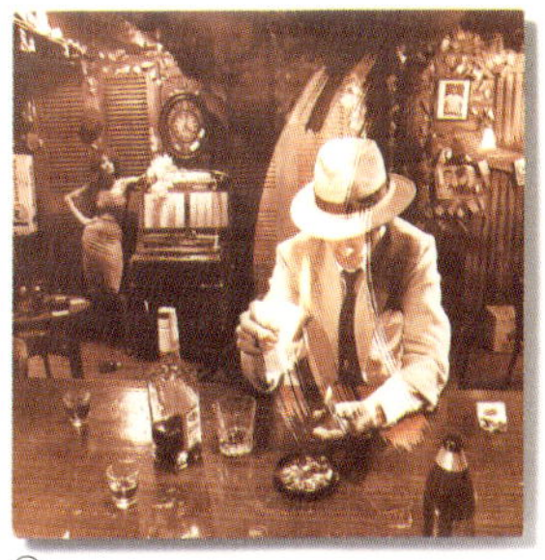

⑦

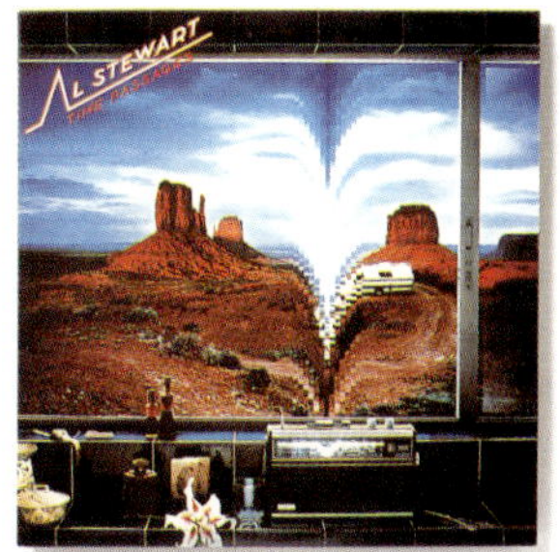

⑧

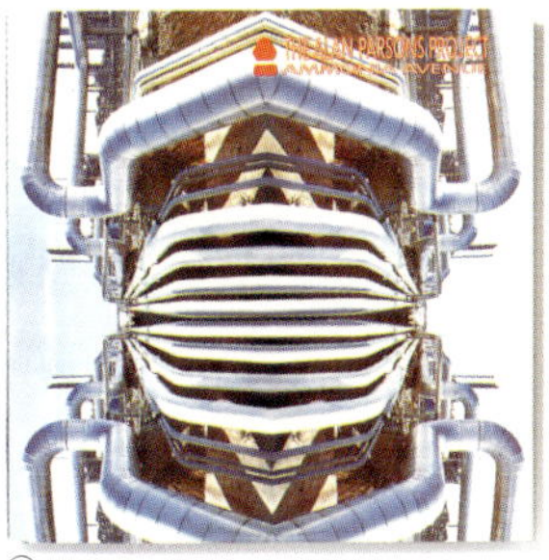

⑨

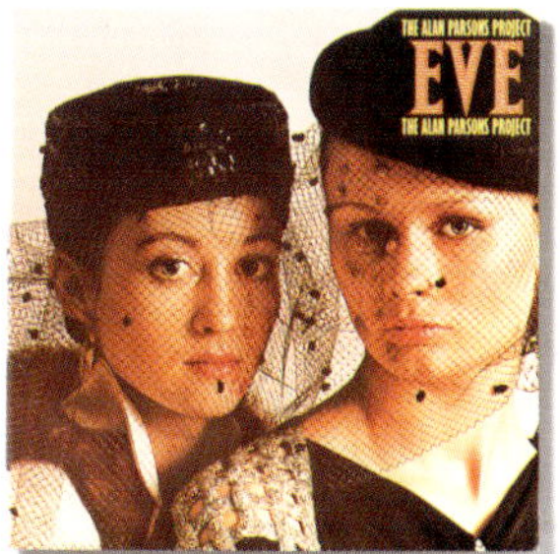

⑩

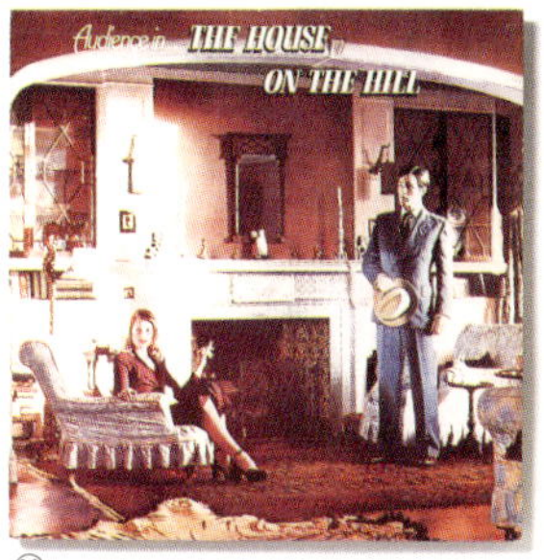

⑪

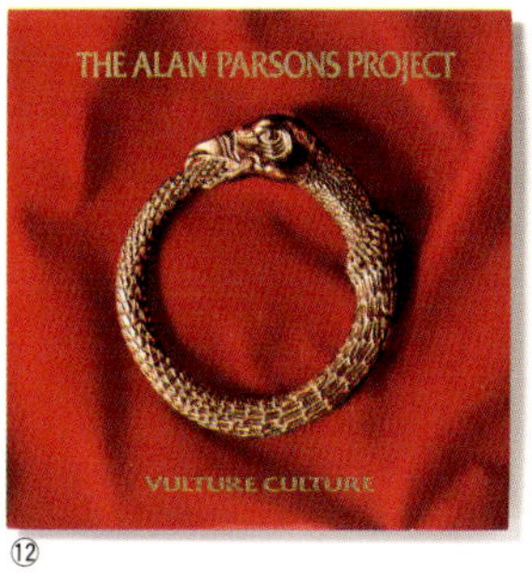

⑫

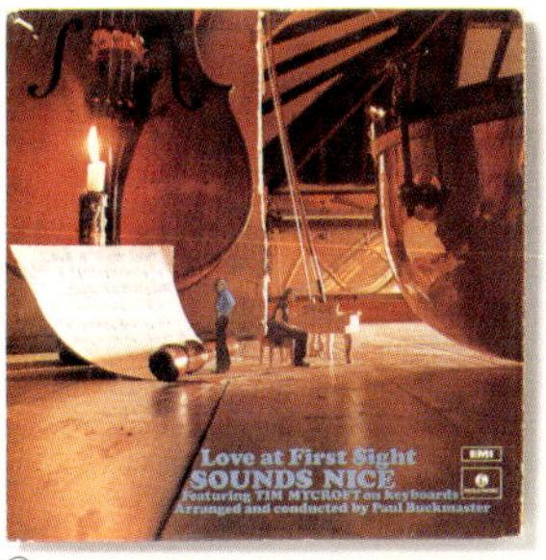

⑬

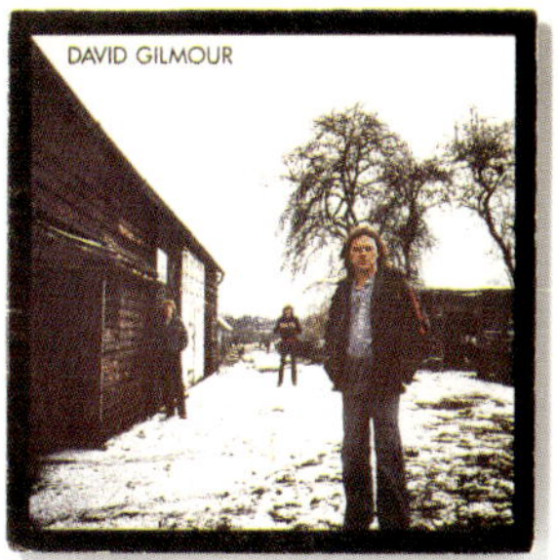

⑭

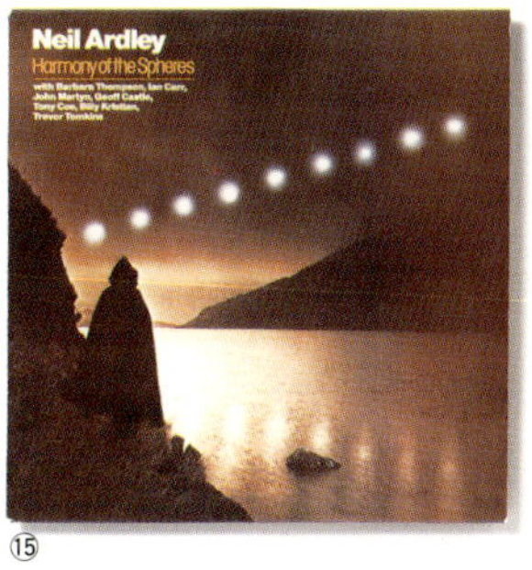

⑮

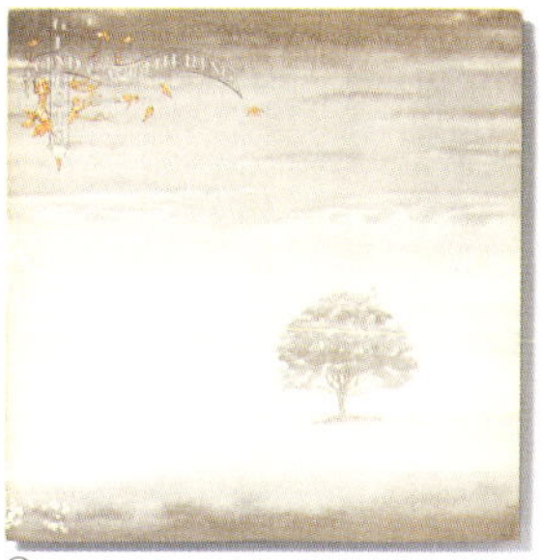

⑯

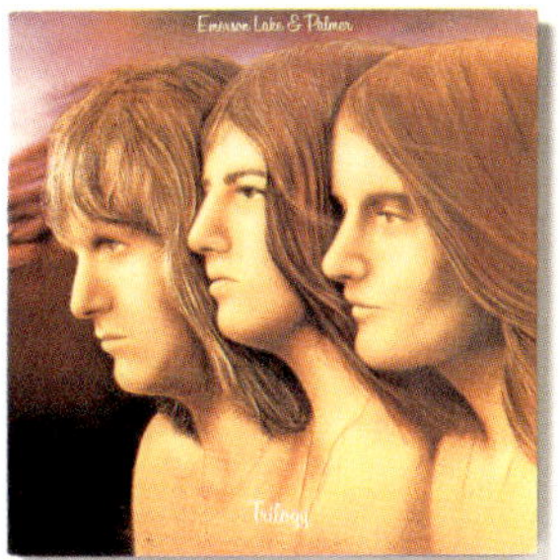

⑰

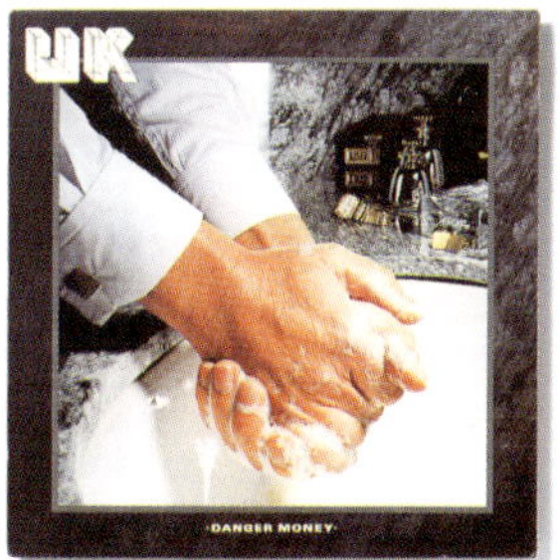

⑱

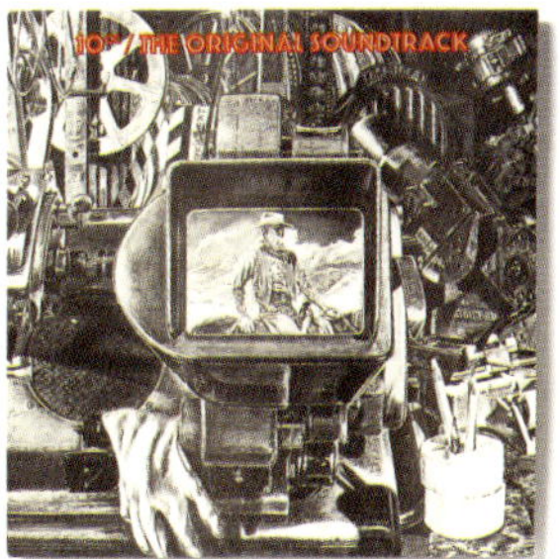

⑲

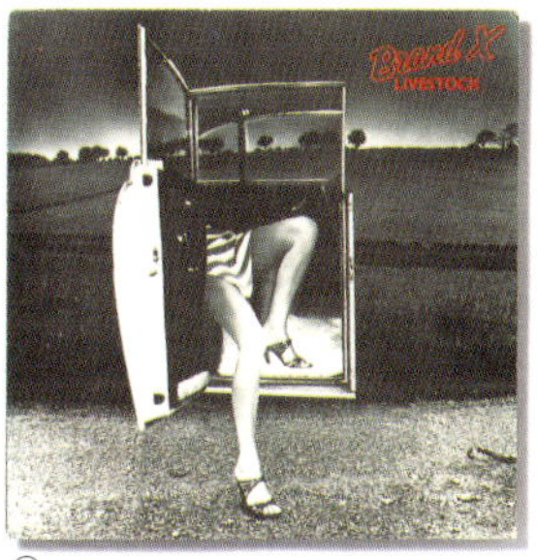

⑳

① 10cc:BLOODY TOURISTS/
Cover Design&Photo/Hipgnosis
Graphics/George Hardie

② RICHARD WRIGHT:WET DREAM/
HARVEST SHVL818(1978)
Cover Design/Hipgnosis
Cover Photos/Hipgnosis,Brimson

③ WISHBORNE ASH:LIVE DATES/
Cover Design and Concept/Hipgnosis
Drawing-Artwork/Colin Elgie

④ PETER GABRIEL:PETER GABRIEL 3/CHARISMA
CDS4019(1980)
Sleeve Design&Photo/Hipgnosis

⑤ PETER GABRIEL:PETER GABRIEL 2/
CHARISMA CDS4013(1978)
Sleeve Design&Photo/Hipgnosis

⑥ THE ALAN PARSONS PROJECT:I ROBOT/
Cover Design/Hipgnosis

⑦ LED ZEPPELIN:IN THROUGH THE OUT DOOR/
SWAN SONG SSK59410(1979)
Sleeve by Hipgnosis

⑧ AL STEWART:TIME PASSAGES/
RCA PL25173 (1978)
Cover Design/Hipgnosis

⑨ THE ALAN PARSONS PROJECT:
AMMONIA AVENUE/ARISTA 1610105 (1984)
Sleeve Design/STD

⑩ THE ALAN PARSONS PROJECT:EVE/(1979)
Cover Design/Hipgnosis

⑪ AUDIENCE:THE HOUSE ON THE HILL/
CHARISMA CAS1032(1971)
Sleeve Design and Photography by Hipgnosis

⑫ THE ALAN PARSONS PROJECT:
VULTURE CULTURE/
Cover Design/Hipgnosis

⑬ SOUNDS NICE:LOVE AT FIRST SIGHT/
PARLOPHONE PCS7089(1970)
Sleeve Design and Photographs by Hipgnosis

⑭ DAVID GILMOUR:DAVID GILMOUR/
HARVEST SHVL817(1978)
Cover Design/Hipgnosis&DAVID GILMOUR
Outer Cover Photos/Hipgnosis

⑮ NEIL ARDLEY:HARMONY OF SPHERES/
DECCA 6.23985AS(1979)
Photography by Alex Henderson, Artworks
by Richard Manning,
Art Direction by Storm Thorgerson

⑯ GENESIS:WIND&WUTHERING/
CHARISMA CDS4005(1977)
Sleeve Design/Hipgnosis,Colin Elgie

⑰ EMERSON LAKE & PALMER:TRILOGY/
ISLAND ILPS9186(1972)
Cover Design & Photography by Hipgnosis

⑱ UK:DANGER MONEY/
POLYDOR 2302 089(1978)
Cover Design/Hipgnosis

⑲ 10cc:THE ORIGINAL SOUNDTRACK/
MERCURY 9102 500(1975)
Sleeve Design/Hipgnosis
Pencil Drawing/Humphrey Ocean
Photo/Hipgnosis

⑳ BRAND X:LIVESTOCK/
CHARISMA CLASS5(1977)
Sleeve Design&Photos by Hipgnosis

LABI SIFFRE:CRYING LAUGHING LOVING LYING/
PYE NSPL28163(1972)
Sleeve Photographs/ Hipgnosis

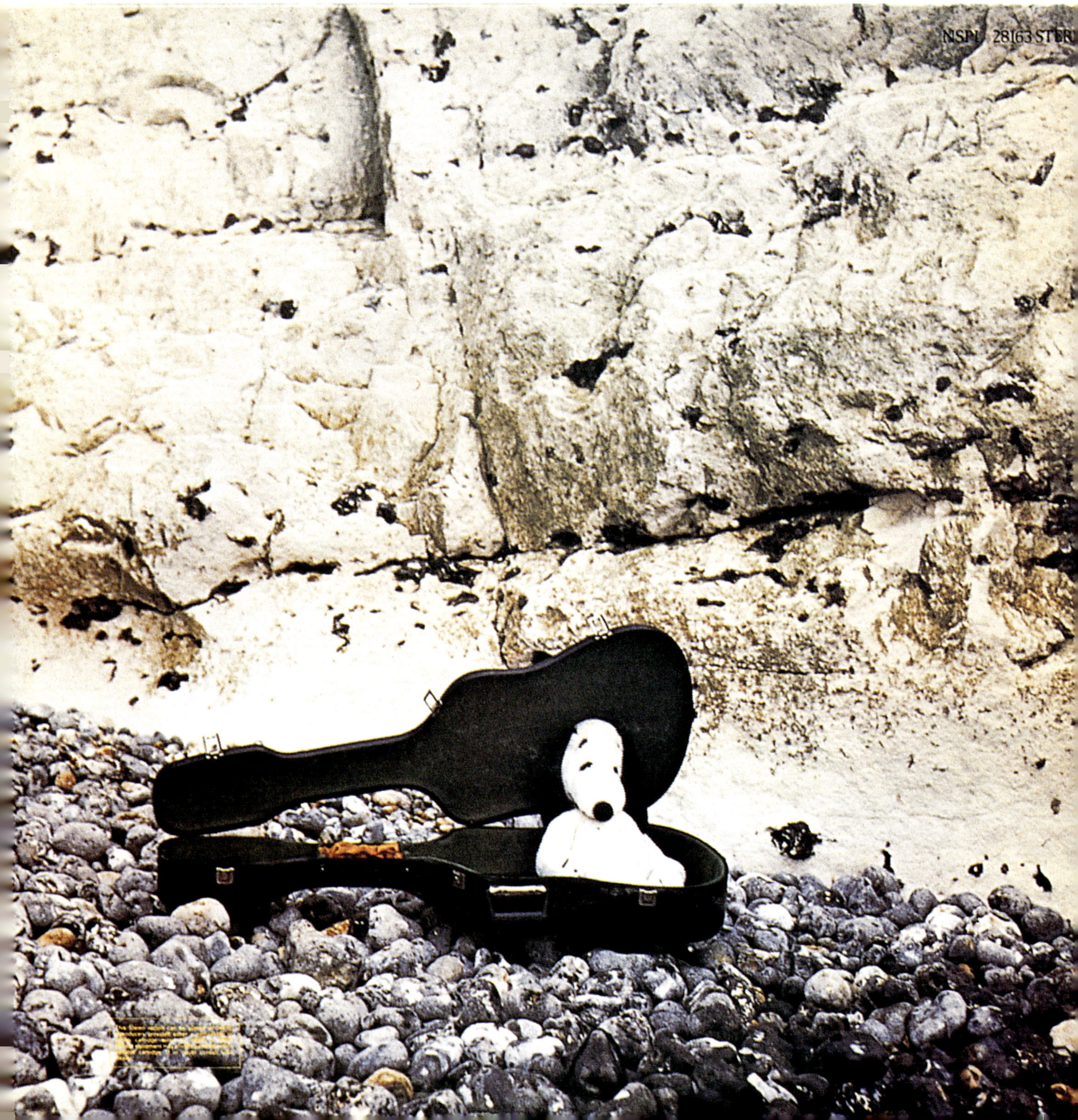

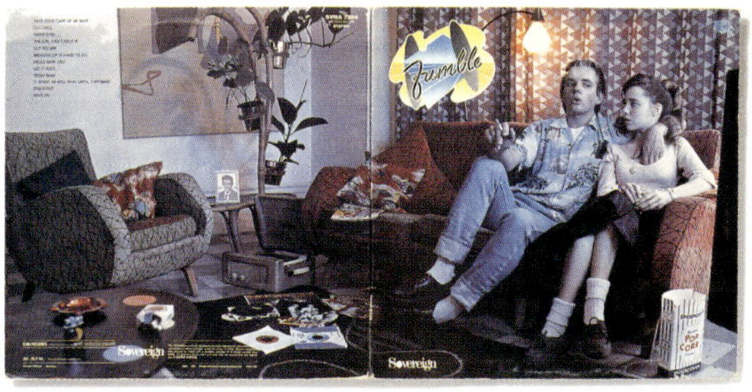

FUMBLE:FUMBLE/
SOVEREIGN SVNA7254(1972)
Cover Design and Photography:Hipgnosis

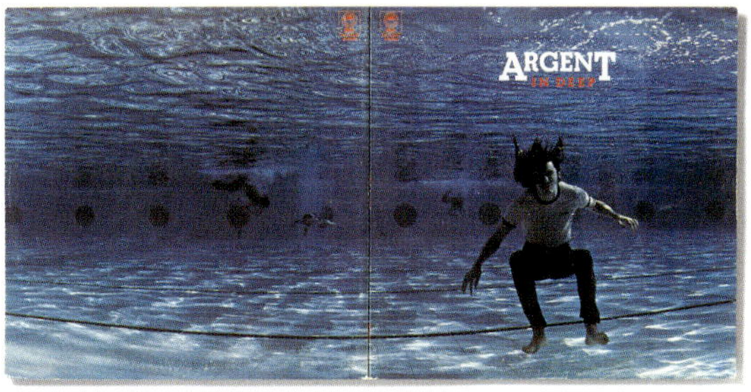

ARGENT:IN DEEP/
EPIC EPC65475(1973)
Cover Design and Photograpy by Hipgnosis

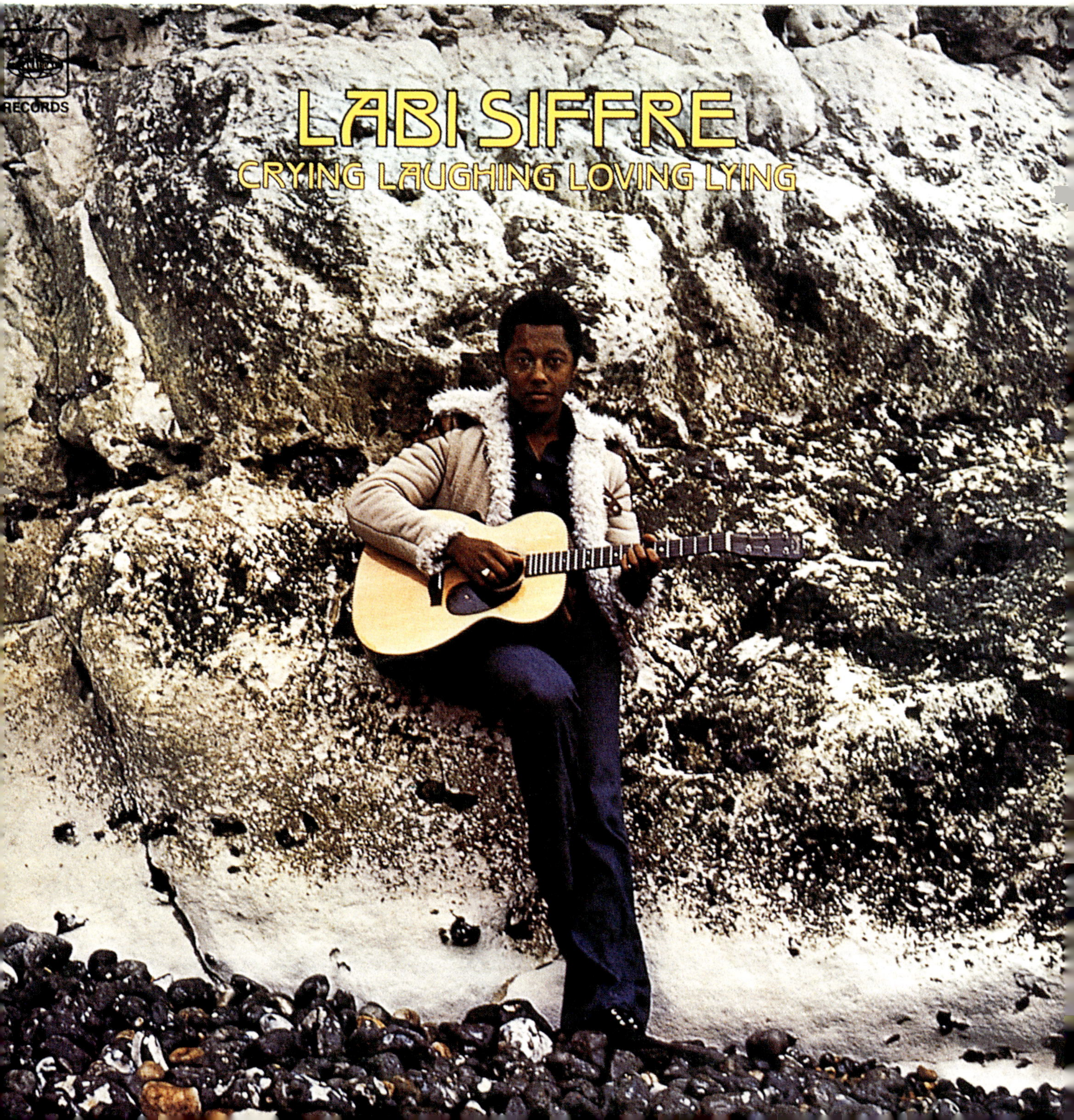

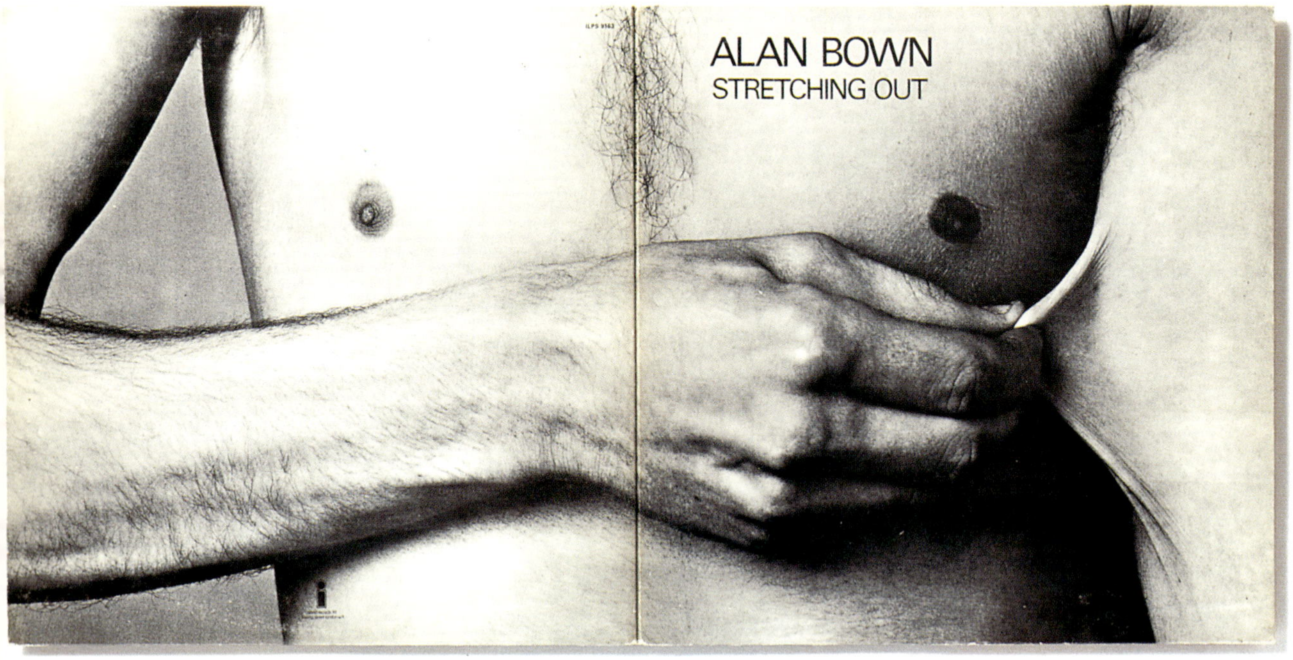

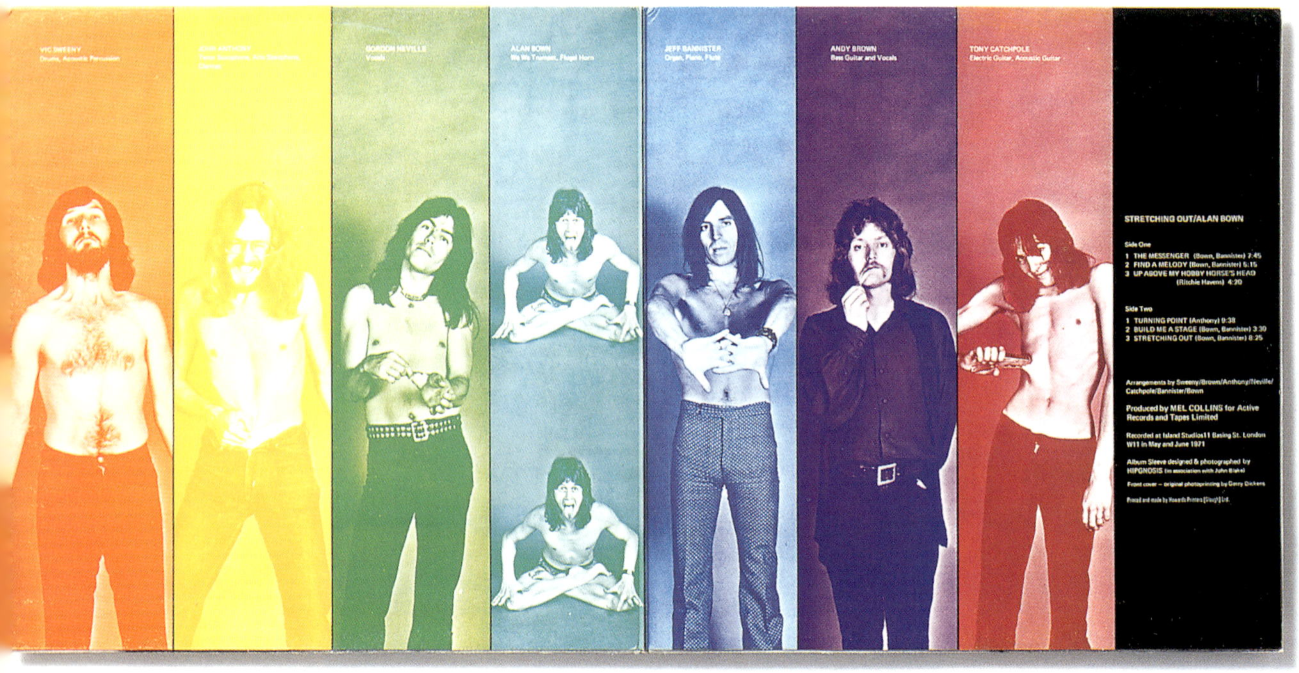

ALAN BOWN:STRETCHING OUT/ISLAND
ILPS9163(1971)*front and back
Album Sleeve Designed and Photographed by
Hipgnosis(in association with John Blake)
Front Cover-Original Photoprinting by Gerry Dickens

ALAN BOWN:STRETCHING OUT/ISLAND
ILPS9163(1971)*inner

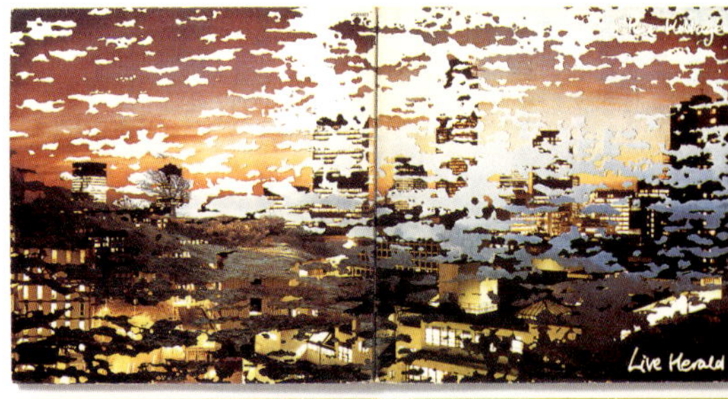

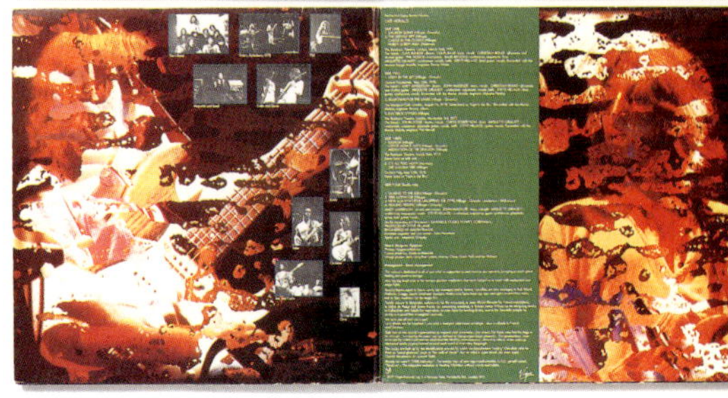

STEVE HILLAGE:LIVE HERALD/
VIRGIN VGD3502(1979)*front and back
Sleeve Design by Hipgnosis
Photos:Hipgnosis/Brimson

STEVE HILLAGE:LIVE HERALD/
VIRGIN VGD3502(1979) *inner

GENESIS:THE LAMB LIES DOWN ON
BROADWAY/CHARISMA CGS101(1974) *front and back
Sleeve Design by Hipgnosis

GENESIS:THE LAMB LIES DOWN ON
BROADWAY/CHARISMA CGS101(1974) *inner

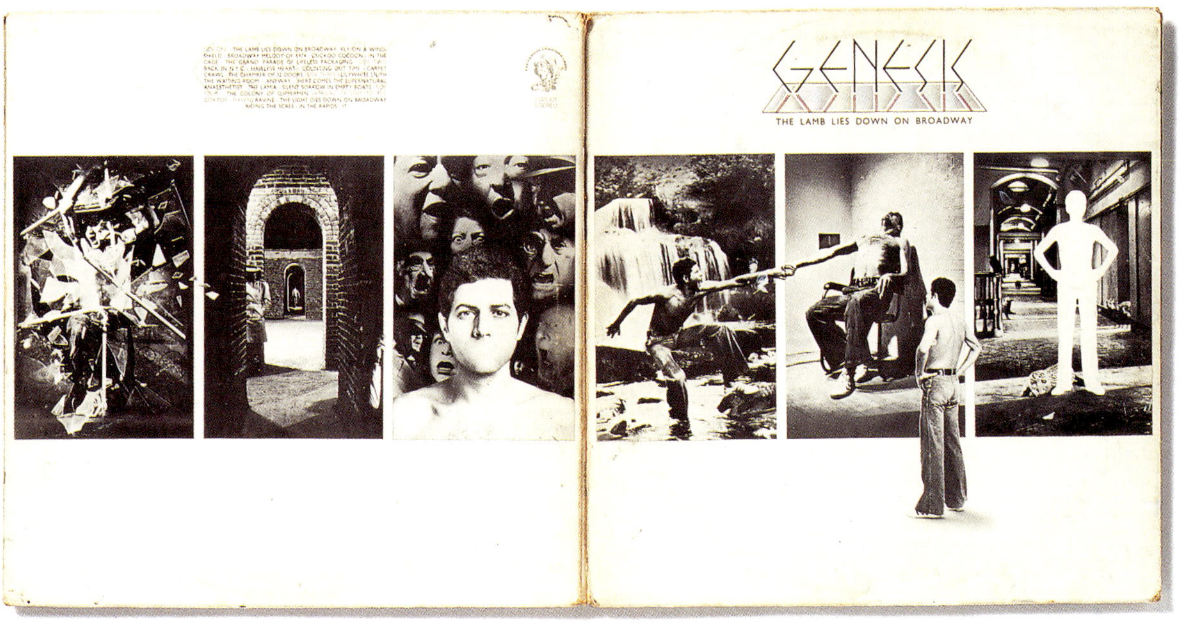

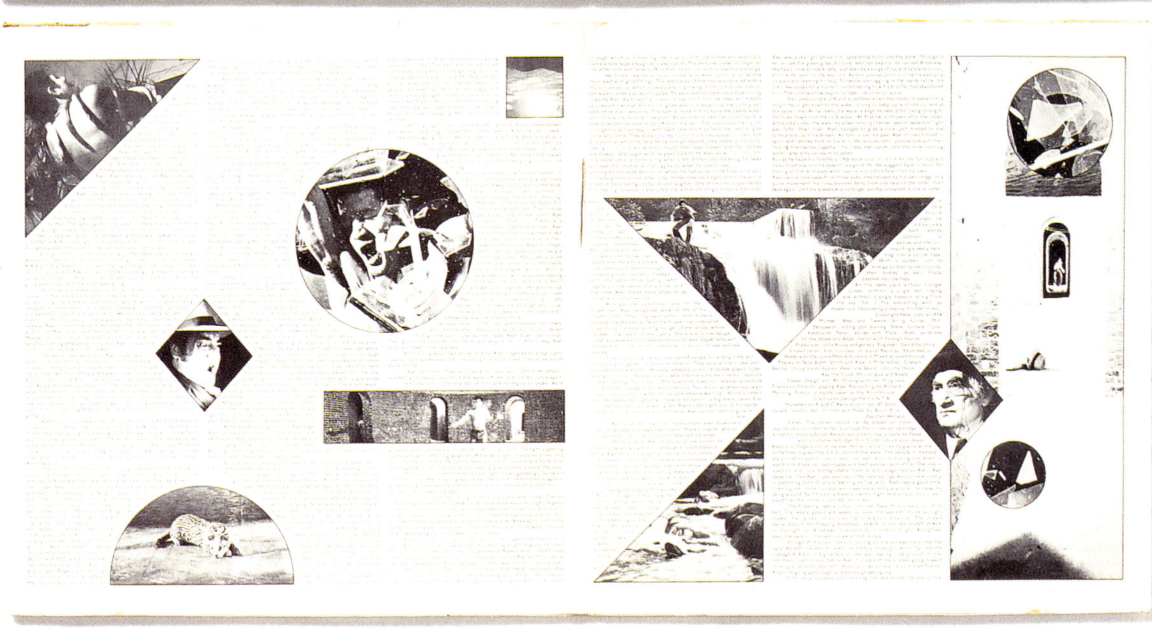

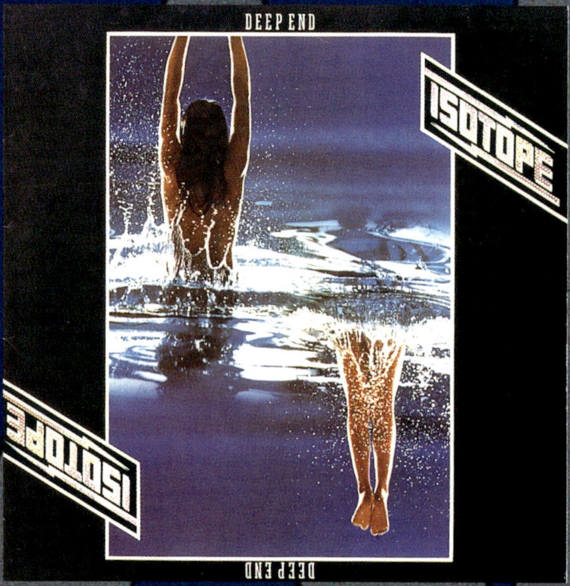

ISOTPE:DEEP END/GULL GULP1017(1976)
Sleeve Design/John Pasche.Gull Graphics
Cover Photo/Phil Jude

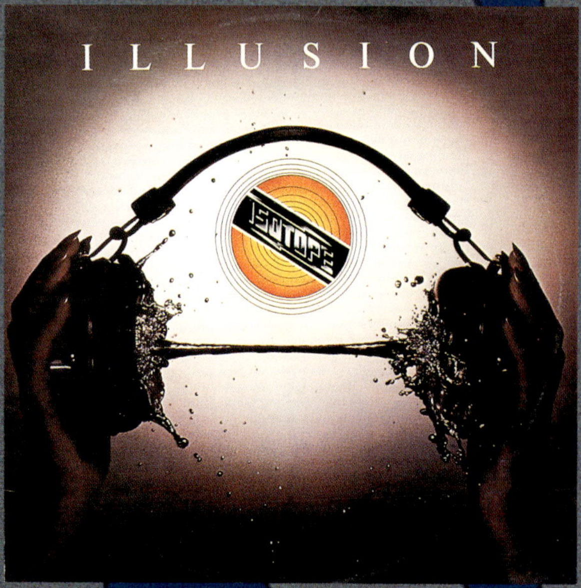

ISOTOPE:ILLUSION/GULL GULP1006(1974)
Sleeve Design/John Pasche.Gull Graphics
Front Photo/Phil Jude

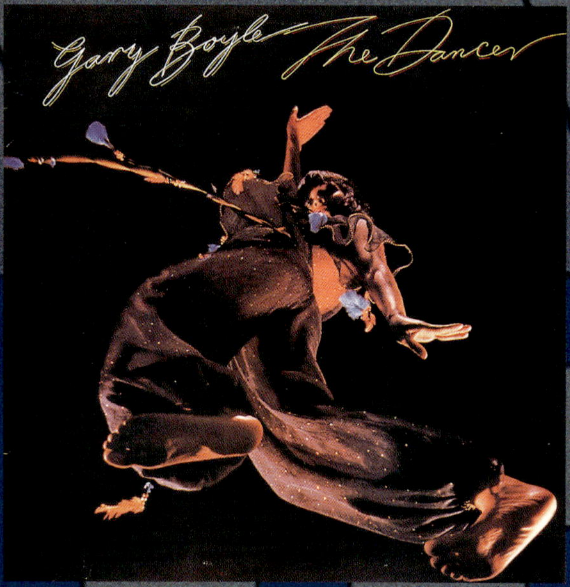

GARY BOYLE:THE DANCER/GULL GULP1020(1977)
Sleeve Design/John Pasche.Gull Graphics
Cover Photo/Phil Jude

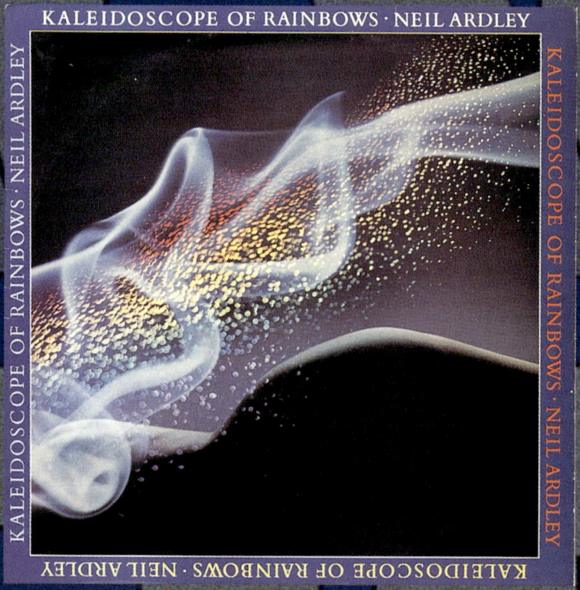

NEIL ARDLEY:KALEIDOSCOPE OF RAINBOWS/
GULL GULP1018(1975)
Sleeve Design/John Pasche.Gull Graphics
Cover Photo/Phil Jude

John Pasche
special effects

ジョン・パシェ

コラージュや超高速撮影等の特殊技法を駆使して“リアルな非現実世界”を描き出すジョン・パシェのデザイン感覚は、それが意識的であるにせよ無意識的であるにせよ、ヒプノシス登場以前と以後との落差を強く感じさせるものとなっている。ジョン・パシェは、73年に設立されたプログレッシヴ系レーベル、ガル・レコーズの系列デザイン会社ガル・グラフィックスにおける中心的デザイナー。テクニカルなミュージシャン揃いだったガルのレーベル・カラーは、瞬間的なダイナミズムを精度の高い技法でとらえる彼のデザインに負うところも大きかった。レア・バード『アズ・ユア・マインド・フライズ・バイ』はそれ以前の70年発表作品。

Whether he consciously did so or not, John Pache's use of collage and high-speed photography evoked a surrealism that demonstrated a distinct difference in sleeve art before and after Hipgnosis. Pache was the main designer at Gull Graphics, an affiliate of the progressive rock label Gull Records, which was represented by David Howell, who had worked for CBS and MCA as an A&R since the mid 60's. In fact, representing many technically superb musicians, Gull's label probably owed much of its distinctiveness in the market to Pache's design work, which excelled at capturing the dynamism of a millisecond with precision. "As Your Mind Flies By" by <Rare Bird> was released in the 70's.

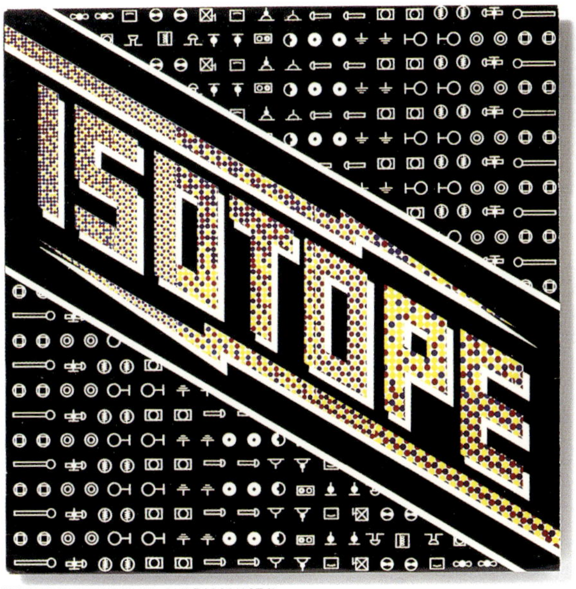

ISOTPE:ISOTOPE/GULL GULP1002(1974)
Sleeve Design/John Pasche.Gull Graphics

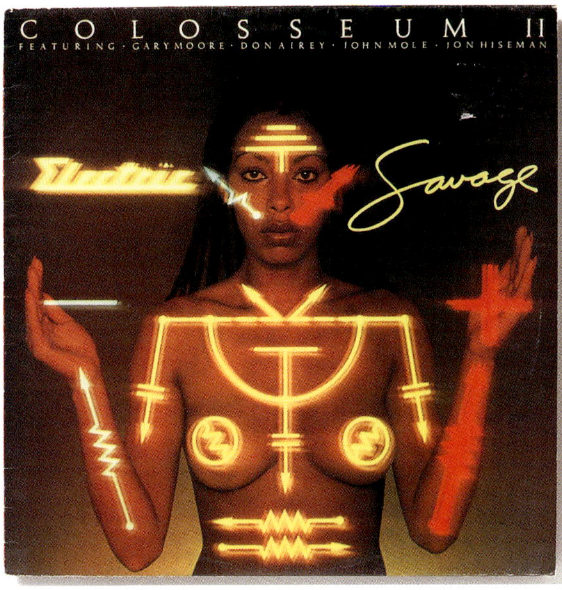

COLOSSEUM II:ELECTRIC SAVAGE/
MCA MCF2800(1977)
Sleeve Design/John Pasche.Gull Graphics
Cover Photo/Phil Jude

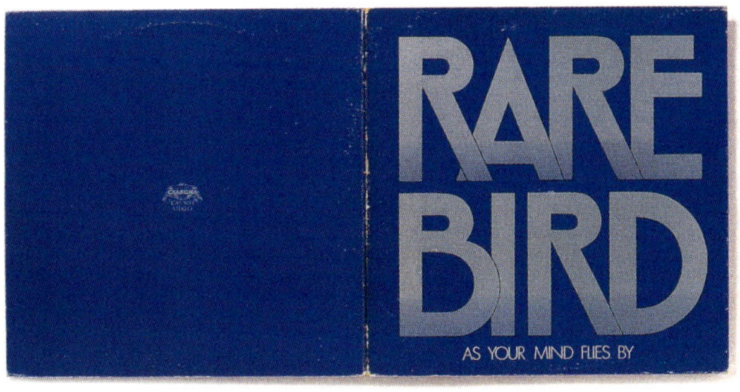

RARE BIRD:AS YOUR MIND FLIES BY/
CHARISMA CAS1011(1970)
Sleeve Design/John Pasche
Photography/Roger Brown*front and back

RARE BIRD:AS YOUR MIND FLIES BY/
CHARISMA CAS1011(1970)*inner

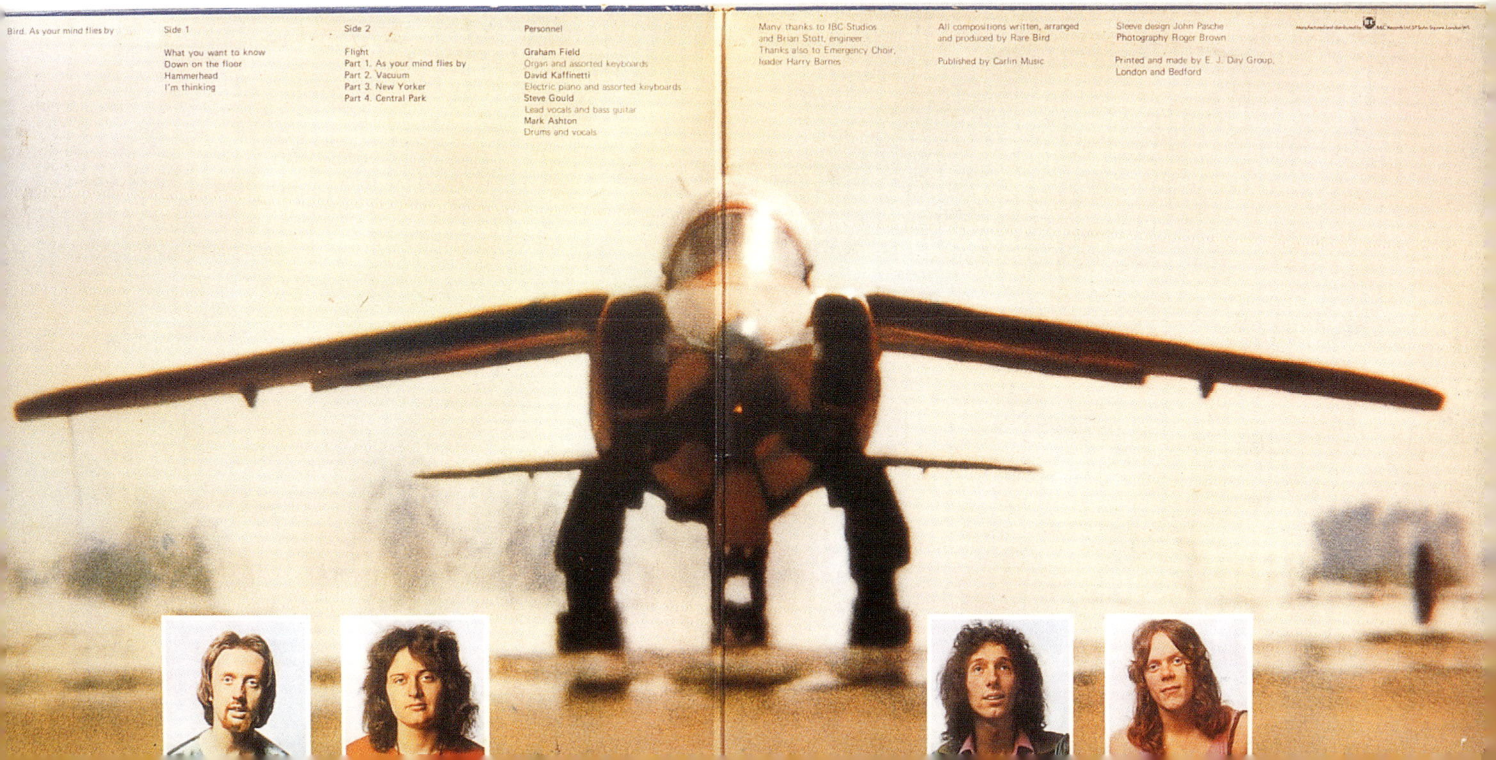

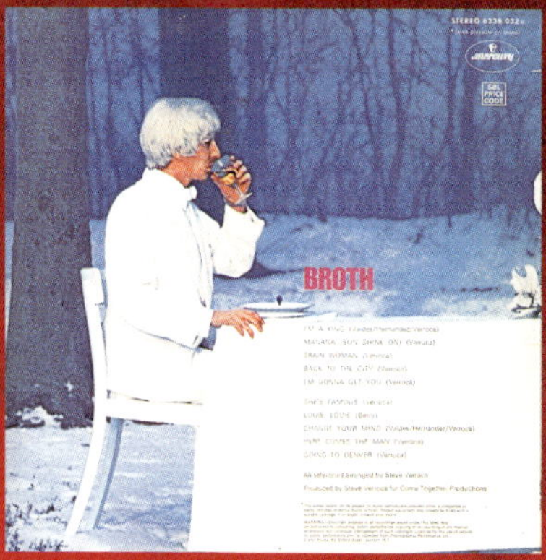

BROTH:BROTH/MERCURY 6338 032(1970)*back

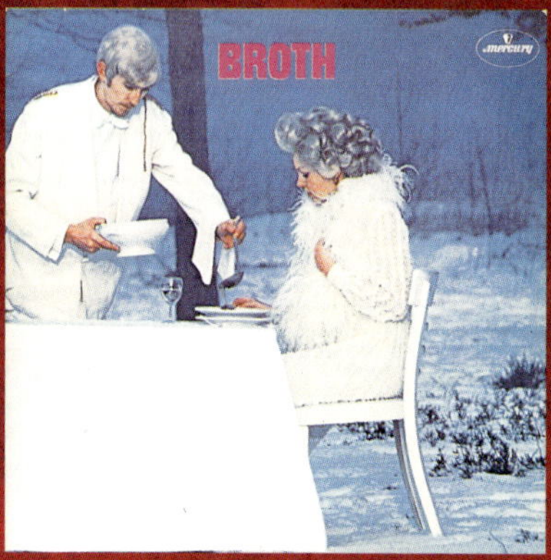

BROTH:BROTH/MERCURY 6338 032(1970)*front

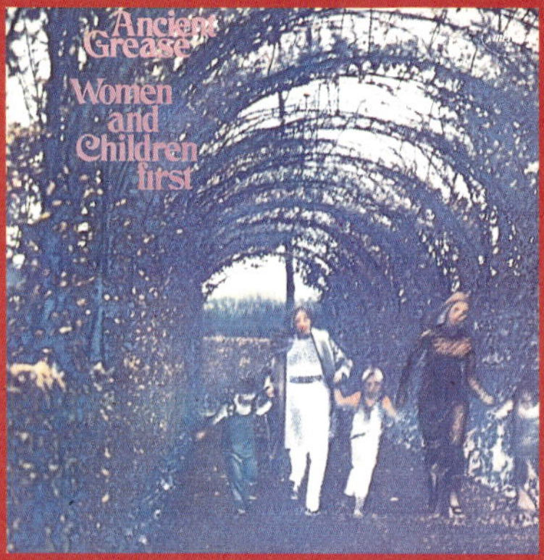

ANCIENT GREASE:WOMEN AND CHILDREN FIRST/
MERCURY 6338 033(1970)

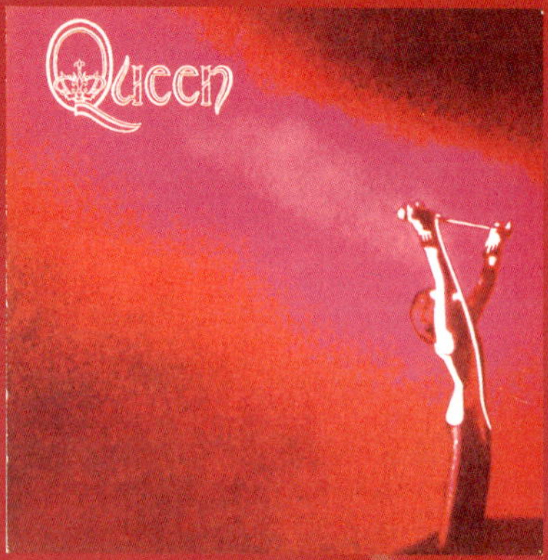

QUEEN:QUEEN/ EMI EMC3006(1973)
Photograph/Douglas Puddifoot
Cover Design/Douglas,Freddie and Brian

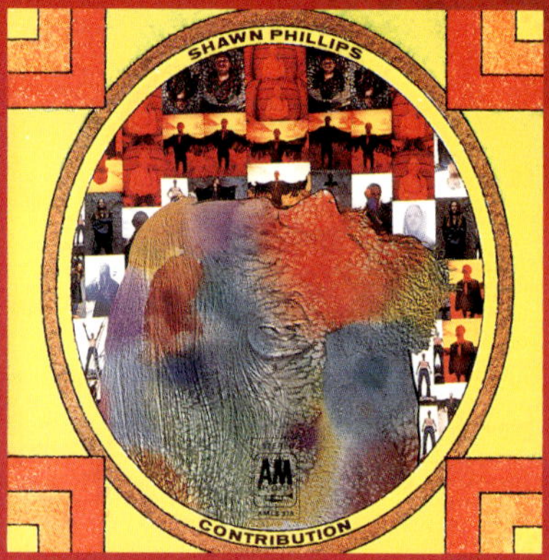

SHAWN PHILLIPS:CONTRIBUTION/
A&M AMLS978(1970)
Art Direction/Tom Wilkes
Photograpy/Jim McCrary

psychedelic

The Other Special Effects

特殊効果いろいろ

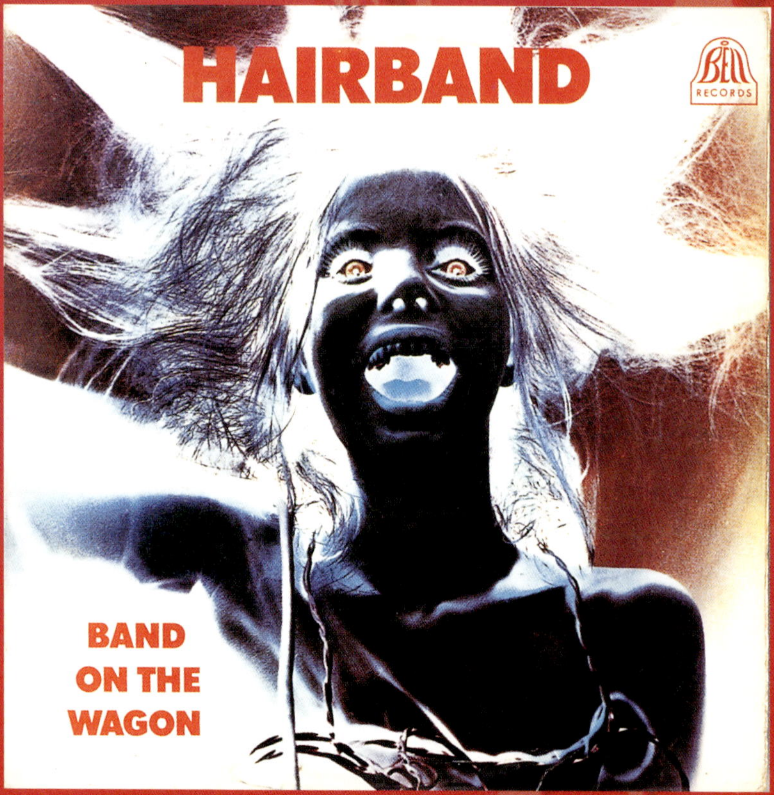

HAIRBAND:BAND ON THE WAGON/
BELL SBLL123(1969)
Cover/Trence Ibbott

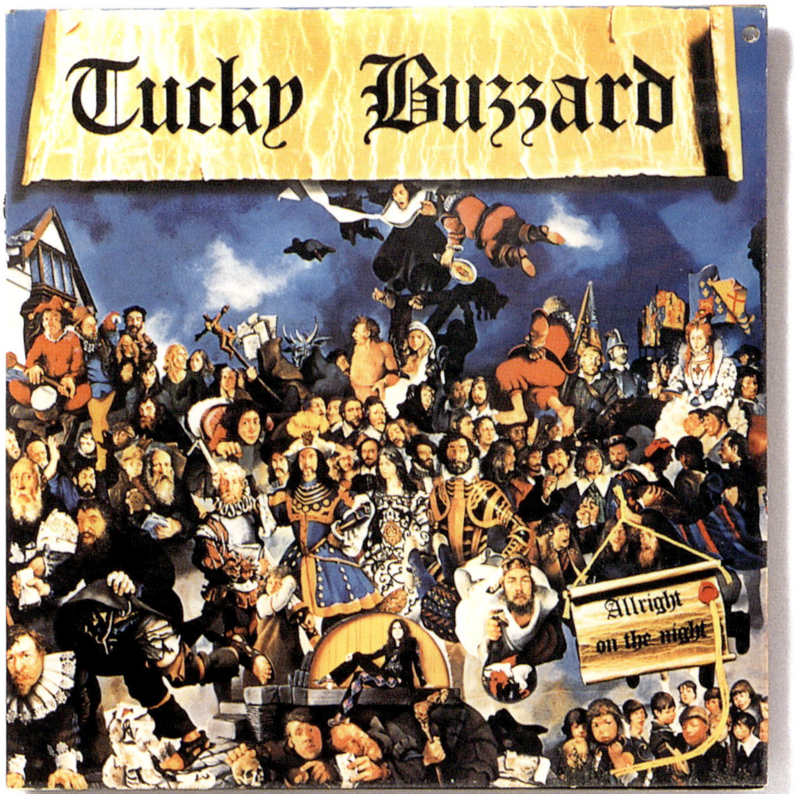

TUCKY BUZZARD:ALLRIGHT ON THE NIGHT/
PURPLE TPSA7510(1973)
Outer Sleeve Photography/Tony Whibley
Artwork/Alex Marshall

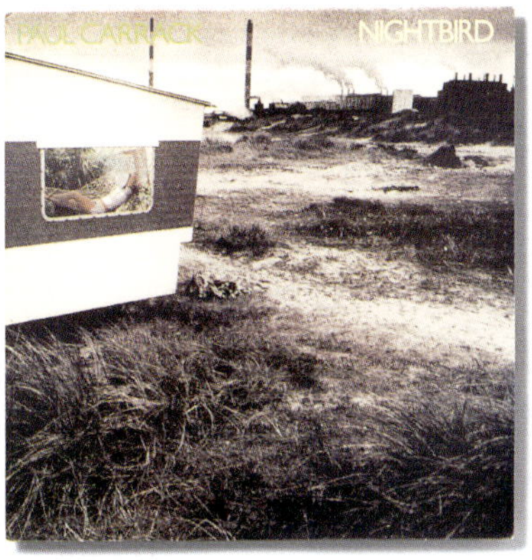

PAUL CARRACK:NIGHTBIRD/
VERTIGO 6359 016(1980)
Front Cover Black and White/Iain McKELL
Front Cover Colour/Brendan Wlash

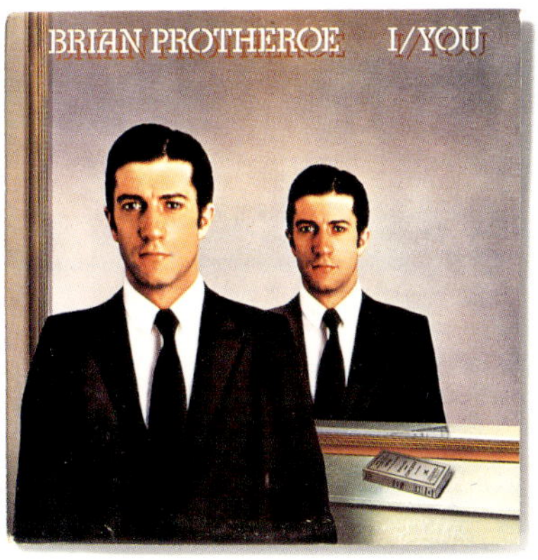

BRIAN PROTHEROE:I YOU/
CHRYSALIS CHR1108 (1976)

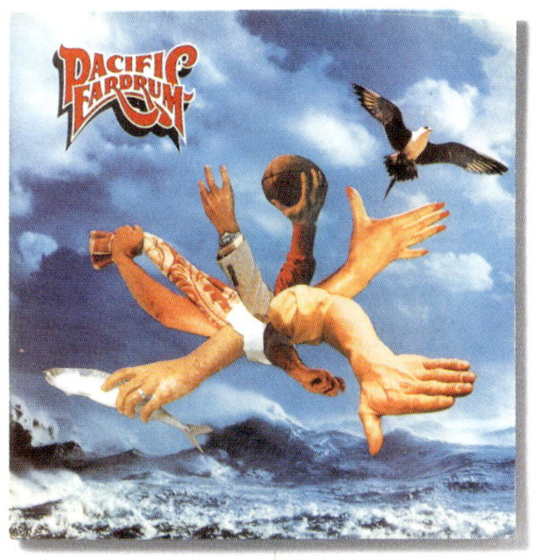

PACIFIC EARDRUM:PACIFIC EARDRUM/
CHARISMA CAS1133 (1977)
Front Cover Art Work/David Halliwell
Art and Logo/AD Design
Art Direction/Frank Sansom

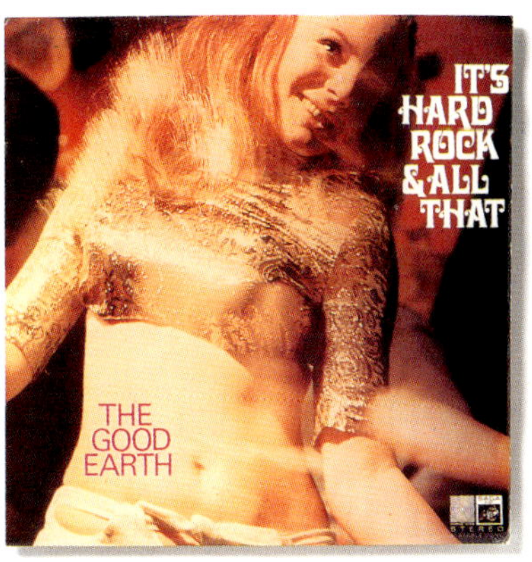

THE GOOD EARTH:IT'S HARD ROCK&ALL THAT/
SAGA FID2112

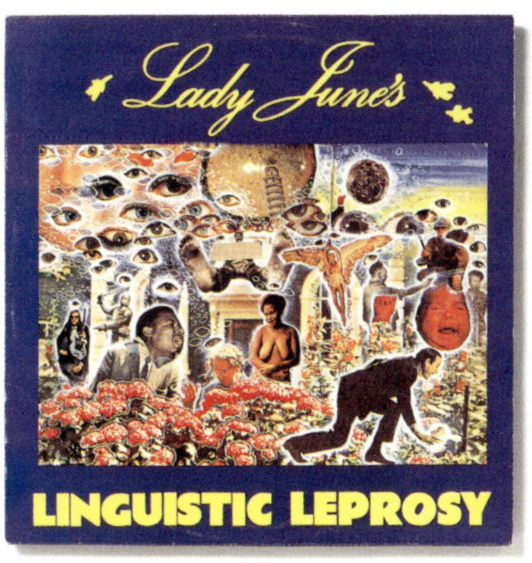

LADY JUNE:LINGUISTIC LEPROSY/
CAROLINE C1509(1974)
Cover Art/Lady June
Photograph/Trevor Key

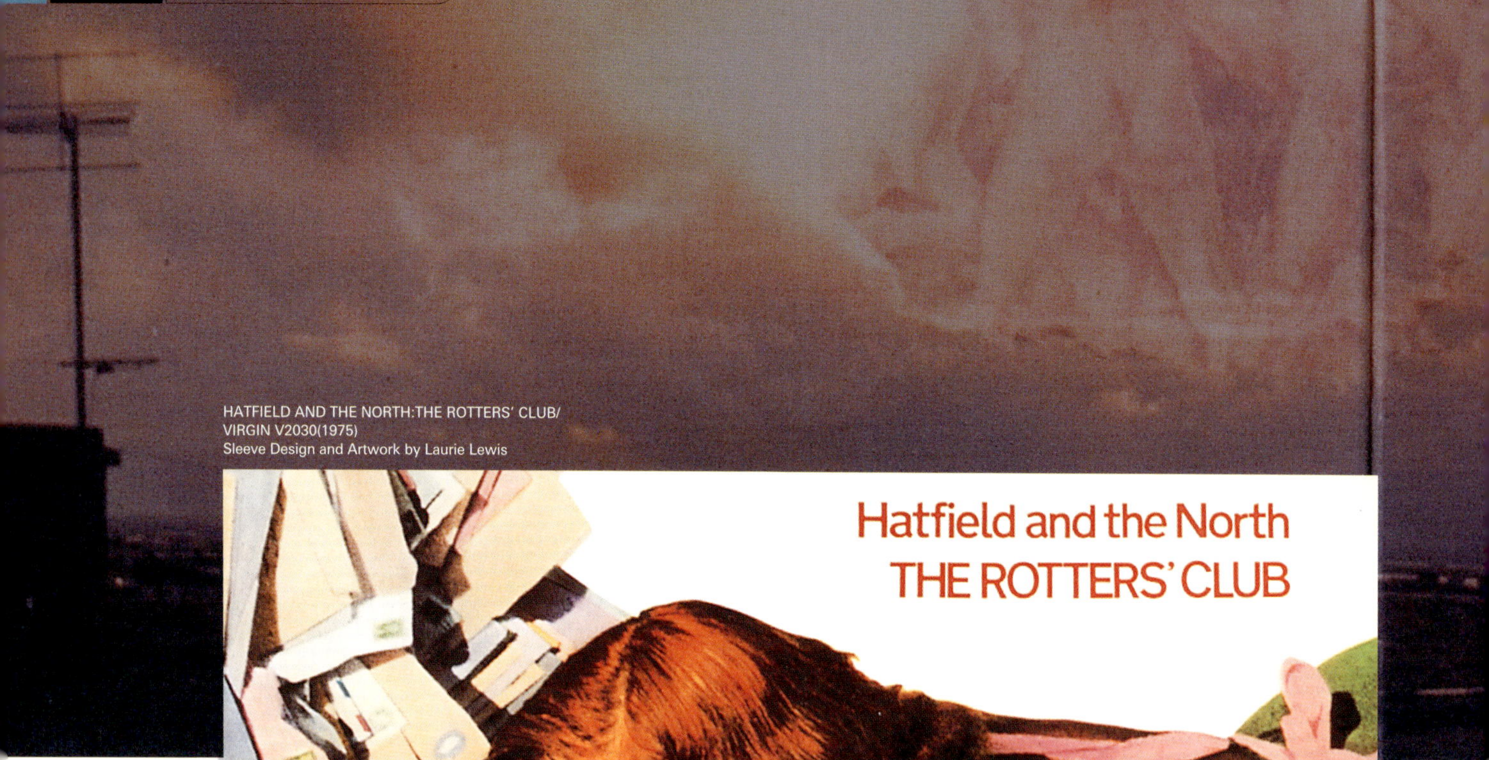

HATFIELD AND THE NORTH:THE ROTTERS' CLUB/
VIRGIN V2030(1975)
Sleeve Design and Artwork by Laurie Lewis

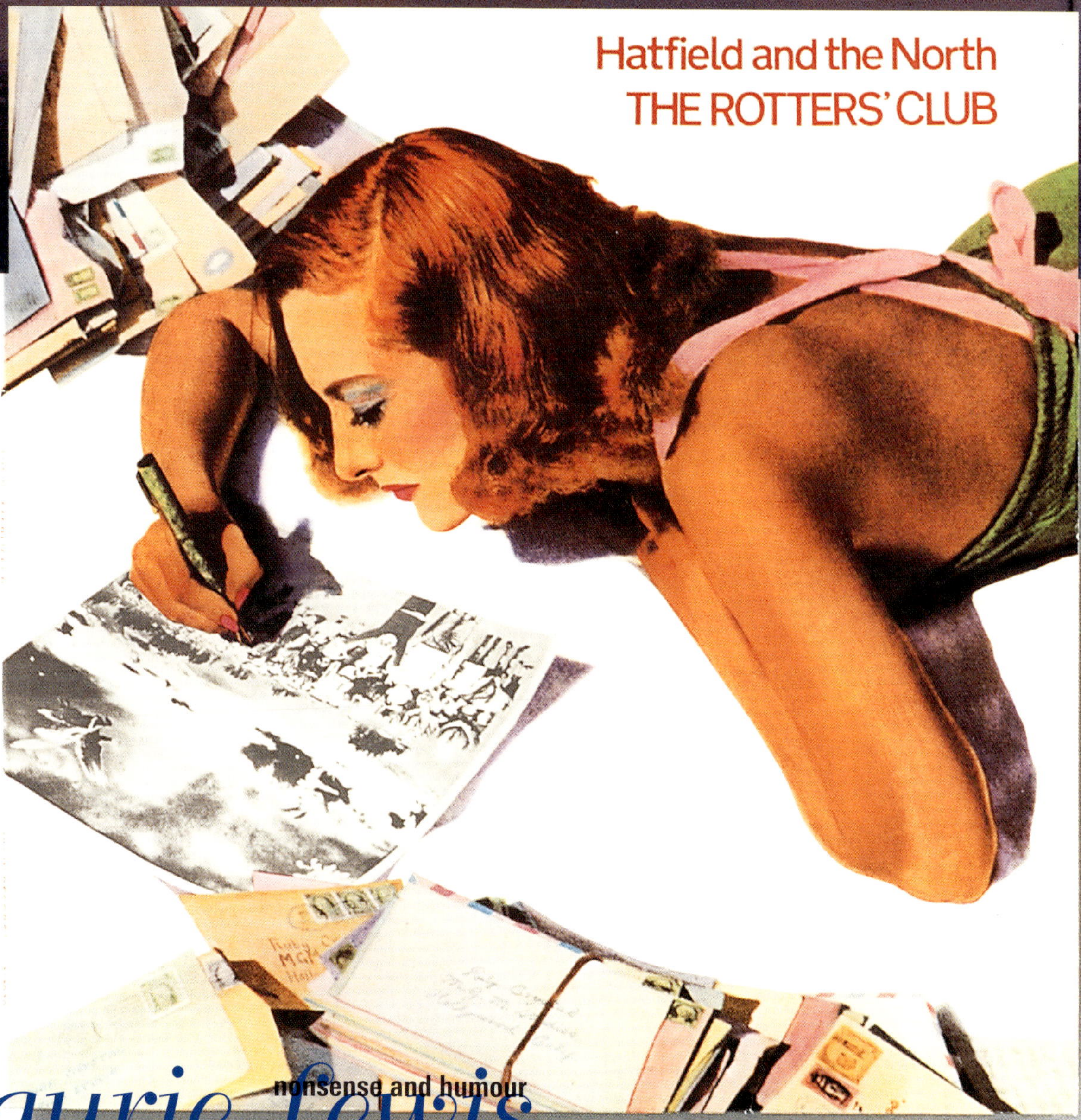

Laurie Lewis

nonsense and humour

ローリー・ルイス

nonsense and humour
ナンセンスとユーモア

nonsense and

イギリスにおけるナンセンスやユーモアの正体を、わずかな言葉で語り尽くすことはできないし、それは文字どおり、まったくもってナンセンスなこととしかいいようがない。ここはひとつ、謎の部分はそのままに、英国ユーモアの深い迷宮へと分け入ってみよう。

カンタベリーの重鎮たちが70年代結成したハットフィールド＆ザ・ノース、さらにその後継グループだったナショナル・ヘルスのカヴァー写真とデザインを手がけているのはローリー・ルイスだ。14世紀末の詩人ジェフリー・チョーサーの『カンタベリー物語』と20世紀後半のカンタベリー・ミュージックとを並べて語るのは一種の禁じ手にちがいないが、一見ナンセンスな笑いをたたえた世界のなかに、人間社会や自然に対する知的な洞察をしのばせているという点では、たしかに共通するものがあるようだ。

Though it would be impossible to succintly explain the British sense of humor, take a look at the wealth of humor present in album sleeves. Laurie Lewis was responsible for the sleeve photography and design of the albums by Hatfield and The North, and their successor National Health. It would be a great mistake to draw a comparison between The Canterbury Tales and the Canterbury

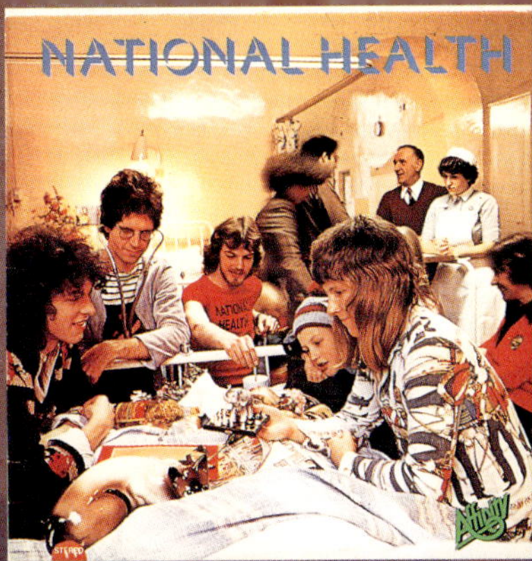

NATIONAL HEALTH:NATIONAL HEALTH/
AFFINITY AFF6(1977)
Sleeve Design by Kevin Burke
Photography by Laurie Lewis

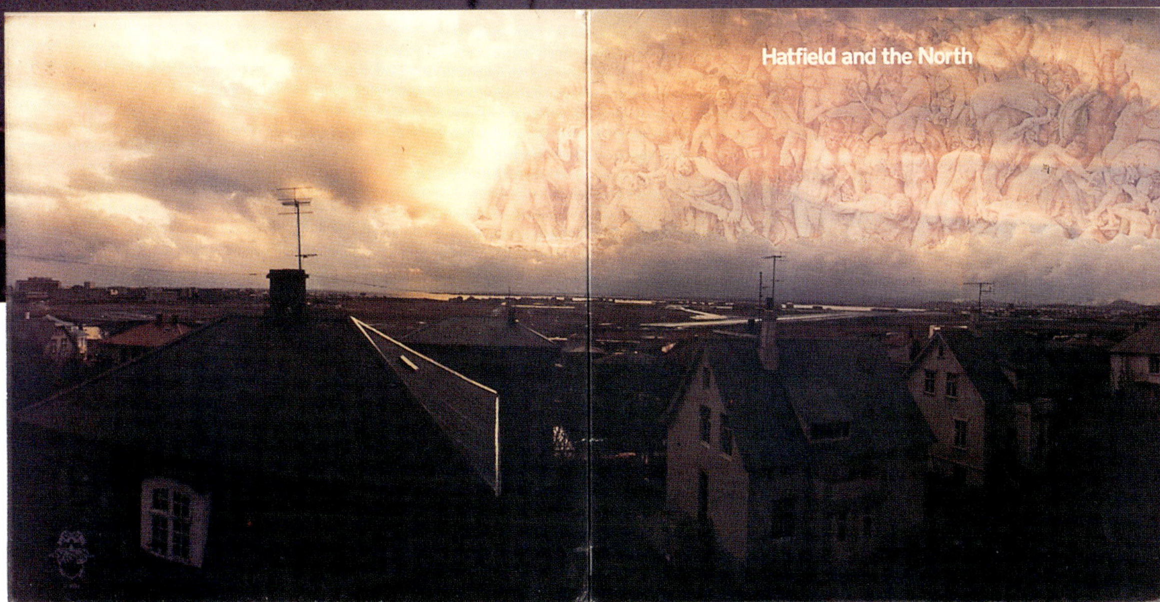

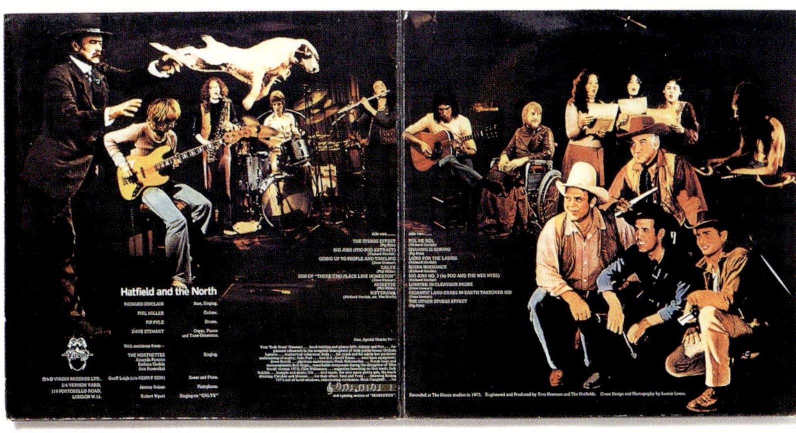

HATFIELD AND THE NORTH:HATFIELD AND THE NORTH/
VIRGIN V2008(1973) *front and back
Cover Design and Photography by Laurie Lewis

HATFIELD AND THE NORTH:HATFIELD AND THE NORTH/
VIRGIN V2008(1973) *inner

humour

music scene at the end of the last century. But there certainly was something in the shared locale, as both of these have in common satire and laughter as well as a insightful grasp of humanity and nature.

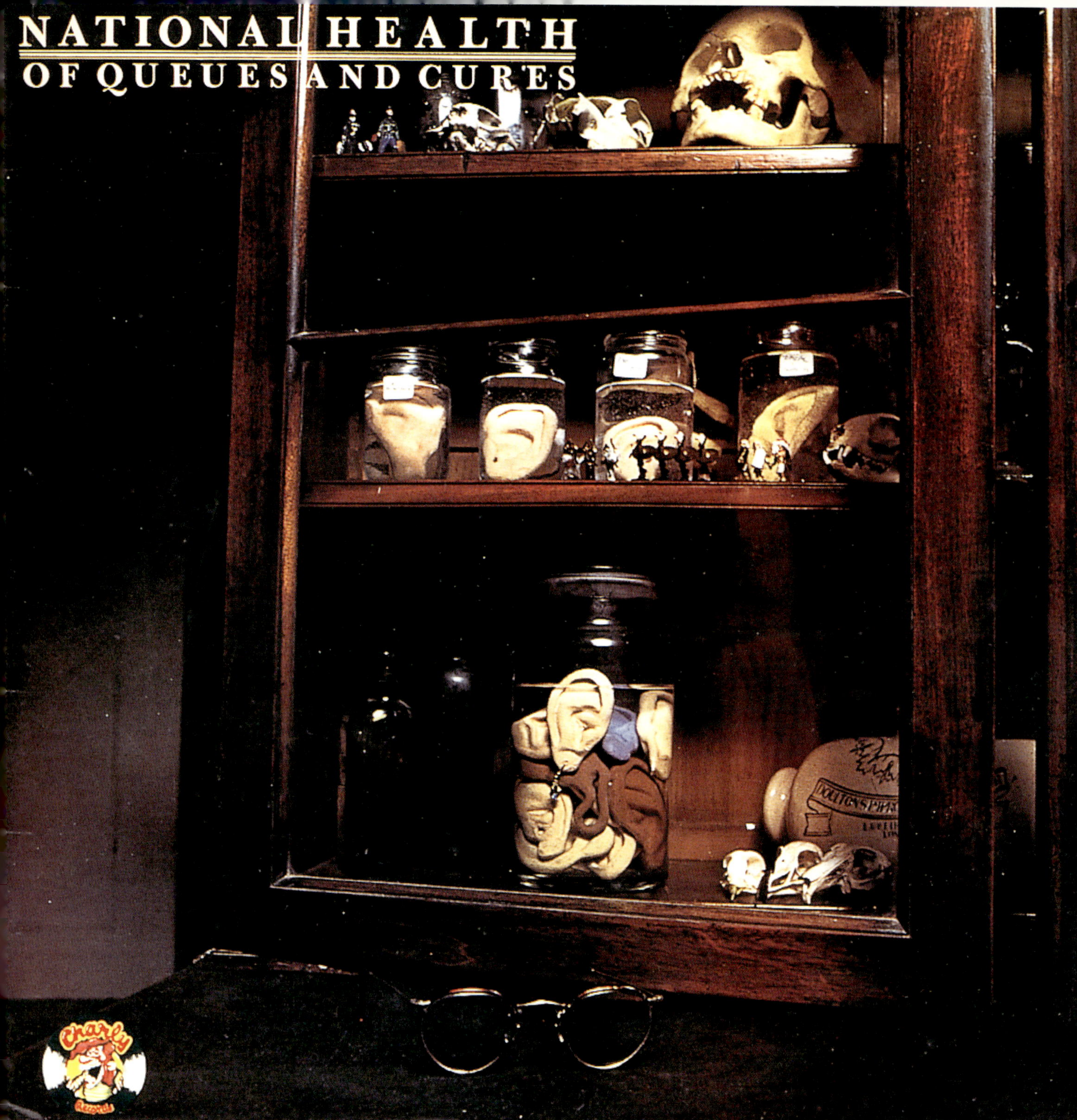

NATIONAL HEALTH:OF QUEUES AND QURES/
CHARLY CRL5010(1978)
Sleeve Design/Jill P.Mumford
Front Photo/Brian Rule

nonsense and humour

British Humour Through the Sleeves

アルバム・カヴァーで辿る英国ユーモア

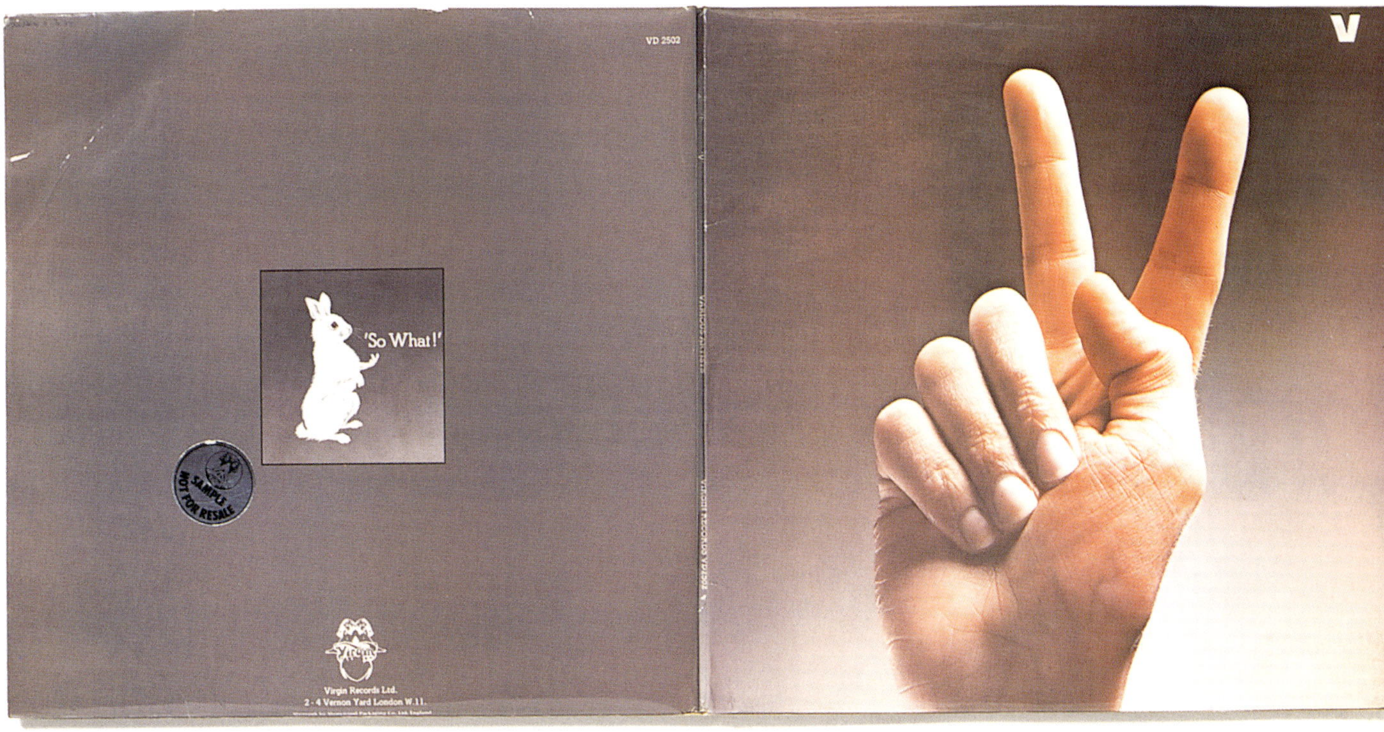

VARIOUS ARTISTS:'V'/VIRGIN VD2502(1975)
Photographs by Michael Joseph
Retouching by Michael Mann Studio
Back Cover by Hargrave Hands
Concept and Design by Trevor Key

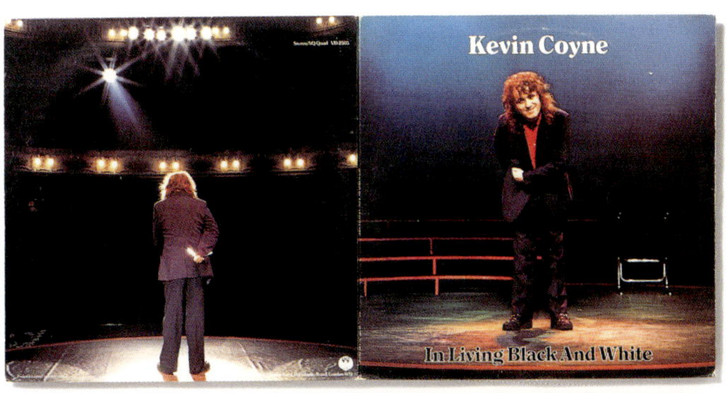

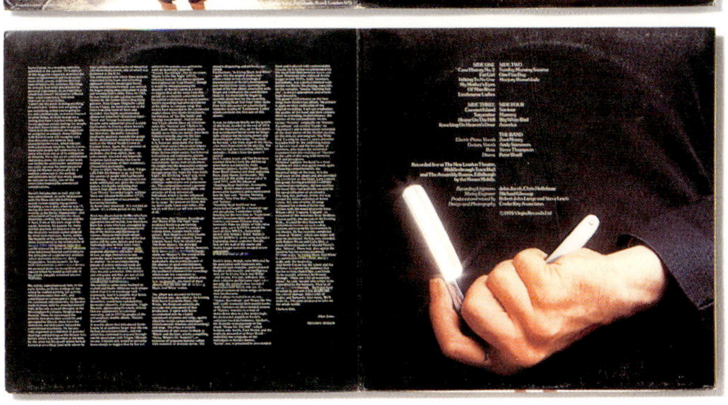

KEVIN COYNE:IN LIVING BLACK AND WHITE/
VIRGIN VD2505(1976) *front and back
Design and Photography/Cooke Key Associates

KEVIN COYNE:IN LIVING BLACK AND WHITE/
VIRGIN VD2505(1976) *inner

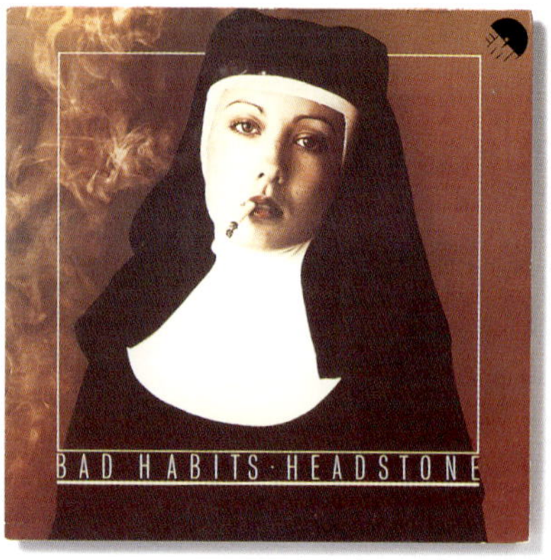

①

① BAD HABITS:HEADSTONE/EMI EMA766(1974)
Sleeve Desgin/Derek Rangecroft
Picture by James Wedge

② THE DEVIANTS:THE DEVIANTS/
TRANSATLANTIC TRA204(1969) *front

③ THE DEVIANTS:THE DEVIANTS/
TRANSATLANTIC TRA204(1969) *back

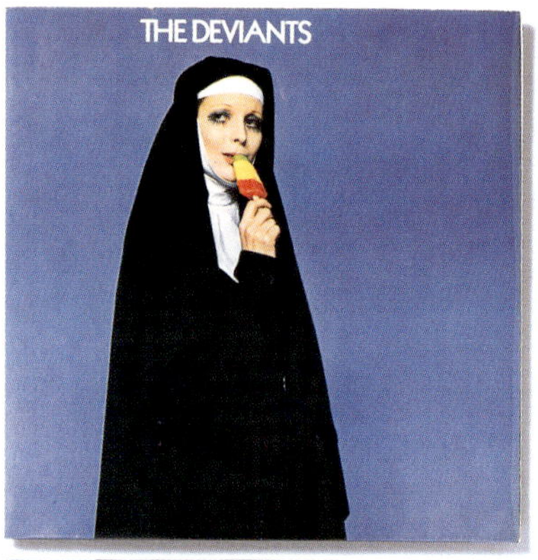

②

③

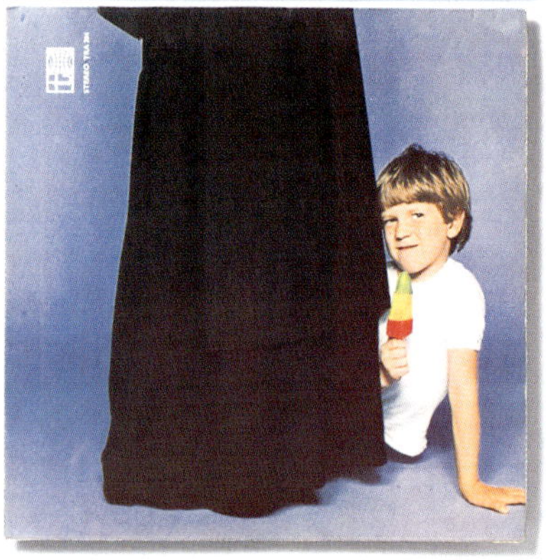

CARAVAN:FOR GIRLS WHO GROW PLUMP IN THE NIGHT/
DERAM SDL-R12(1973) *front and back
Cover Design and Photography by Mark Lawrence

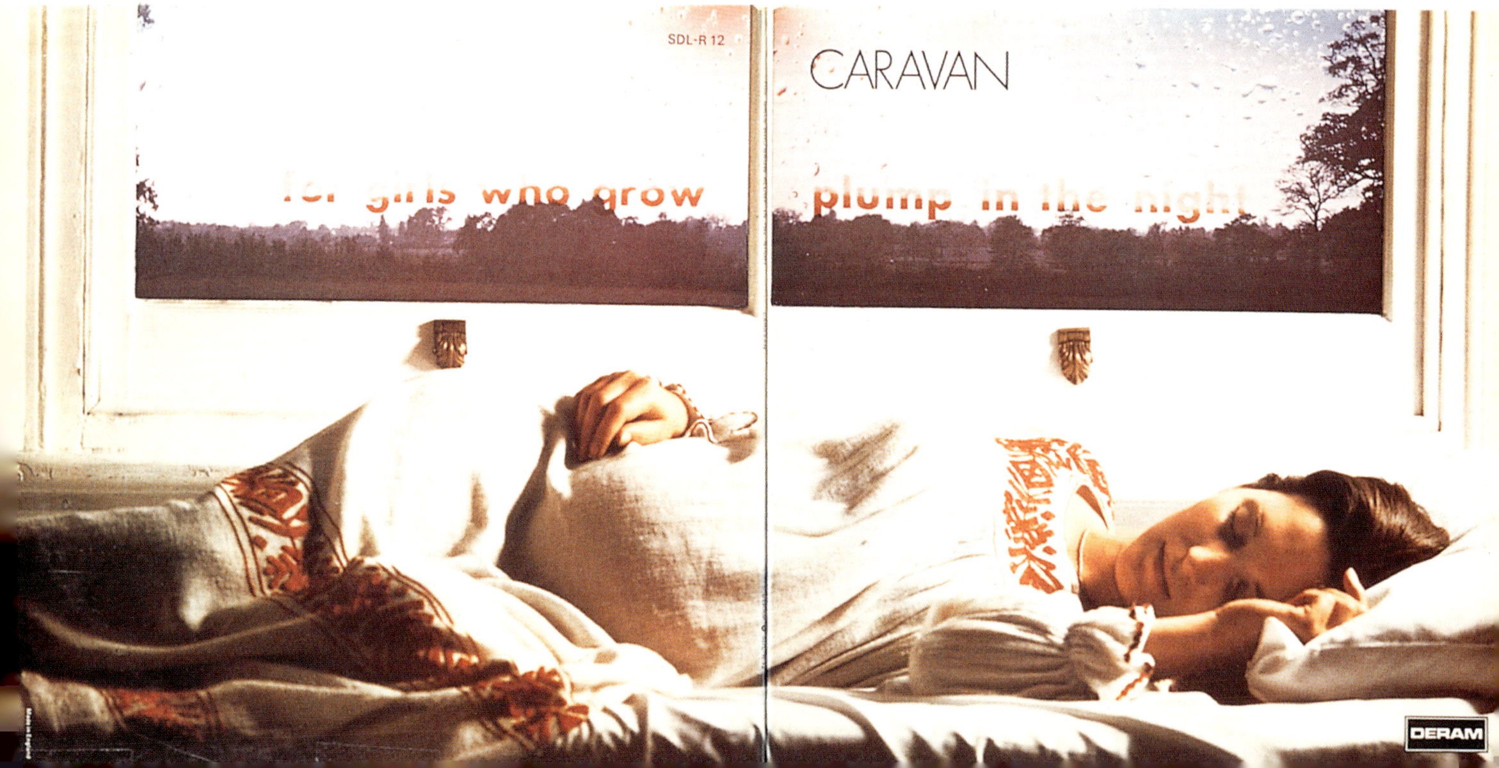

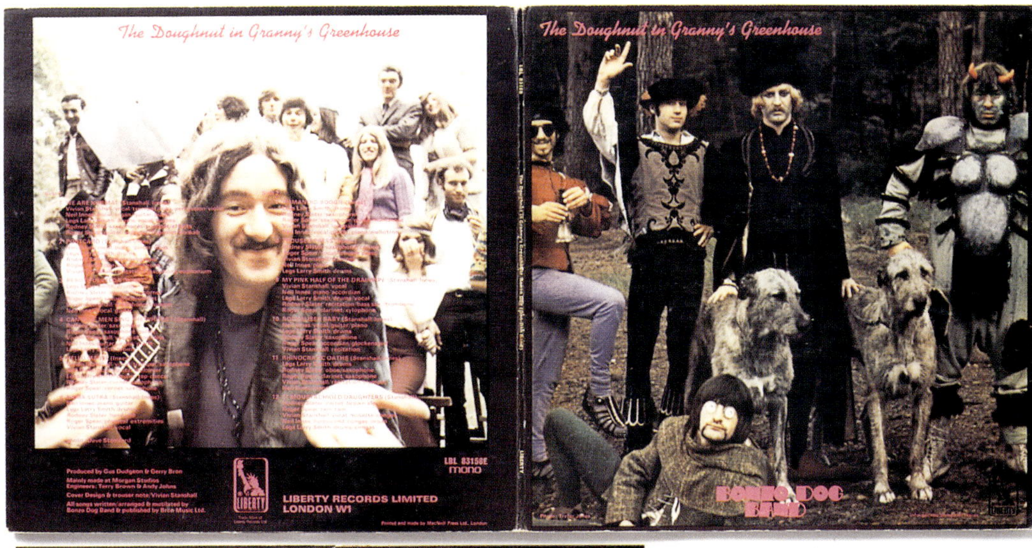

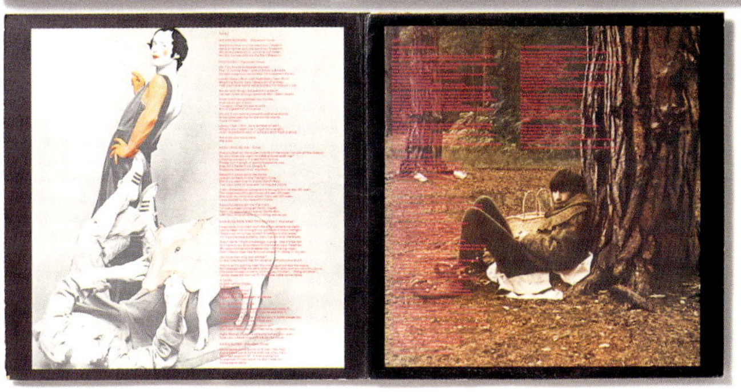

above: BONZO DOG BAND:
THE DOUGHNUT IN GRANNY'S GREENHOUSE
*front and back
Cover Design&Trouser Note/Vivian Stanshall

left: BONZO DOG BAND:
THE DOUGHNUT IN GRANNY'S GREENHOUSE
*inner

④
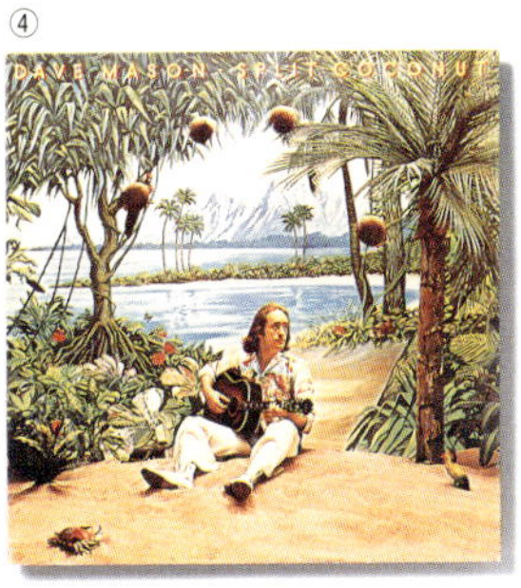

⑤
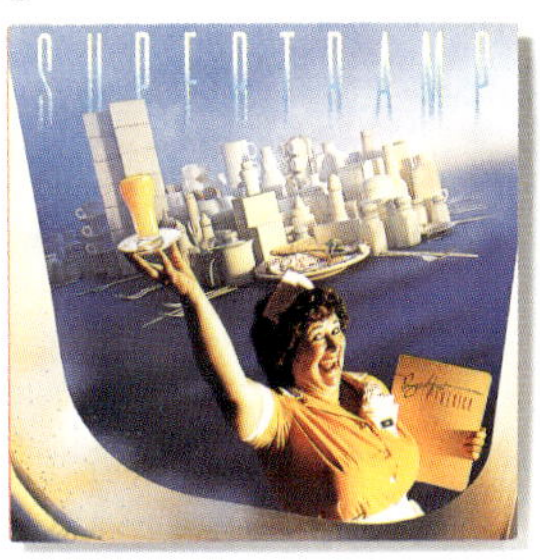

⑥
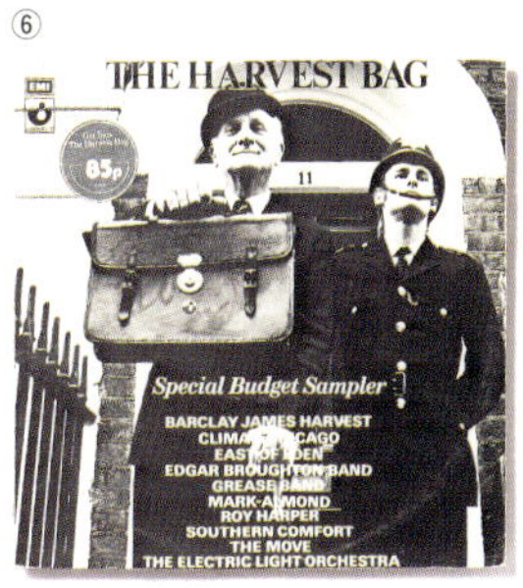

⑦
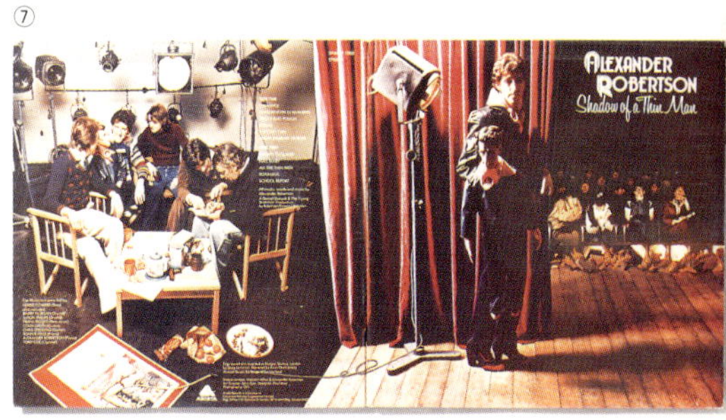

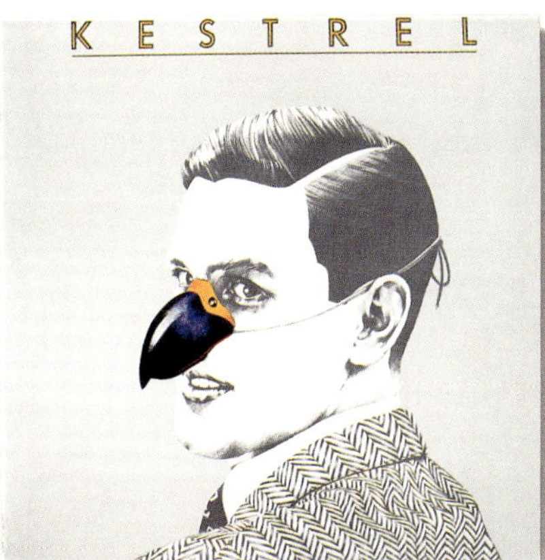

⑧

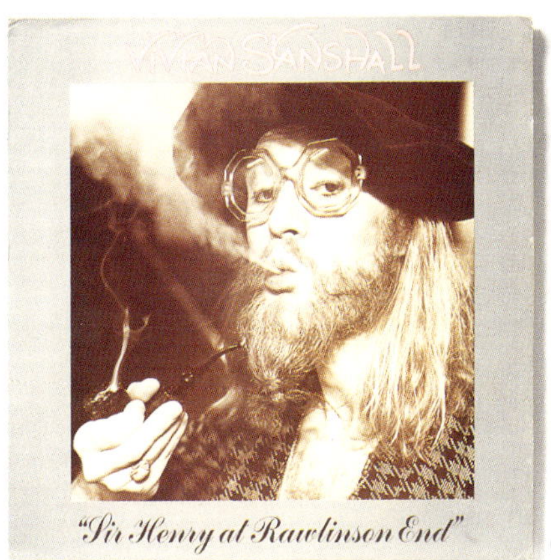

⑩

⑨
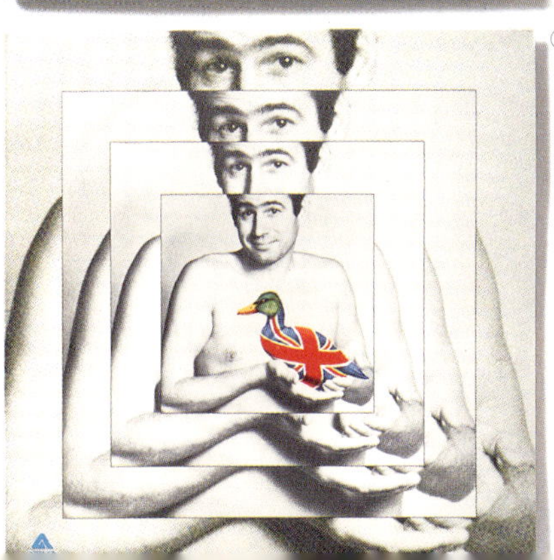

④ DAVE MASON:SPLIT COCONUT/
Illustration/Joe Garnett&Ron Kriss
Design/Ron Coro

⑤ SUPERTRAMP:BREAKFAST IN AMERICA/
A&M AMLK63708(1979)
Art Direction&Cover Concept by Mike Doud
Design by Mick Haggerty
Cover Photography by Aaron Rapoport

⑥ VARIOUS ARTISTS:THE HARVEST BAG/
HARVEST SHSS3(1971)

⑦ ALEXANDER ROBERTSON:SHADOW OF A THIN MAN/
ARISTA SPARTY1000(1977)
Sleeve Conception/Malcom Allan&Alexander Robertson
Art Director/John Dyer
Designer/Paul May
Phtography/Ollie

⑧ KESTREL:KESTREL/CUBE HIFLY19(1975)
Sleeve Design by Arty Types

⑨ NEIL INNES:TAKING OFF/
ARISTA SPARTY1004(1977)
Created by Visual Arts,London

⑩ VIVIAN STANSHALL:
SIR HENRY AT PAWLINSON END/
CHARISMA CAS1139(1978)
Photographic Work/Brian Kinchy(57Varietys Productions)
Sleeve Trouser Design/Vivian Stanshall
Lettering Design by Vivian Stanshall&Clive Hardy
Typography by Clive Hardy

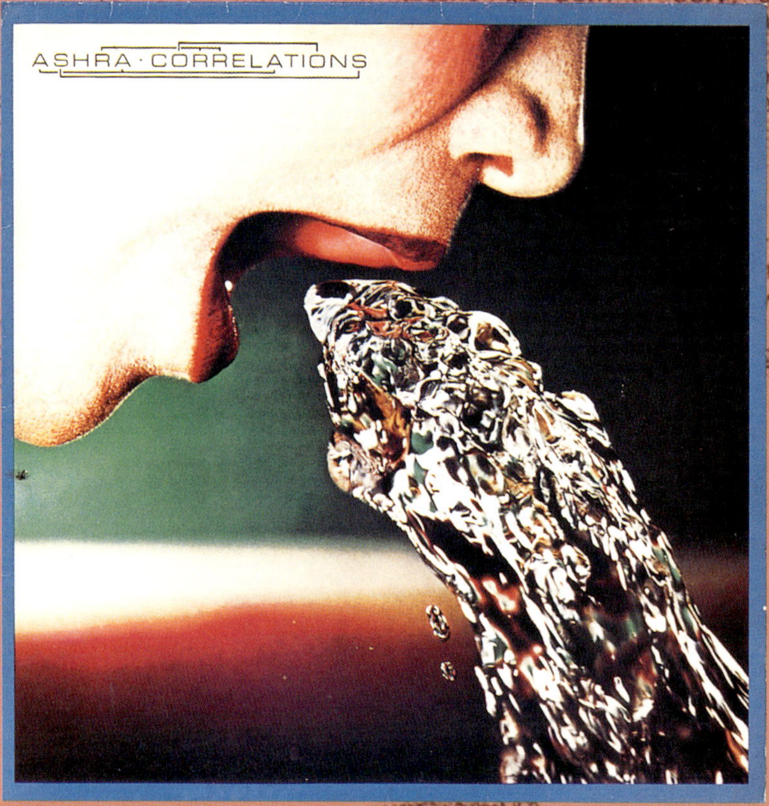

ASHRA:CORRELATIONS/
VIRGIN V2117(1979) *front
Sleeve Design & photography by Hipgnosis

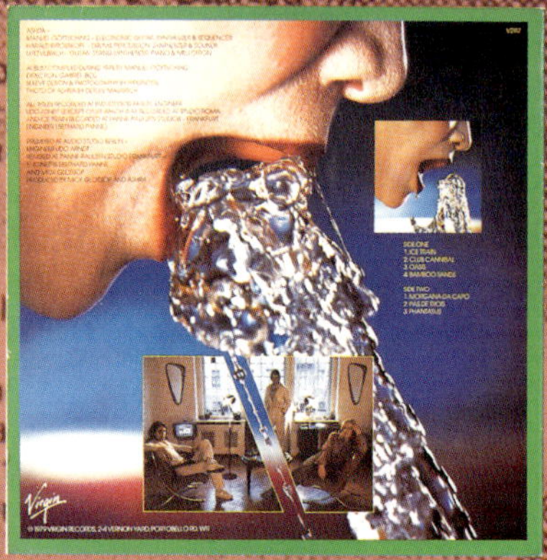

ASHRA:CORRELATIONS/VIRGIN V2117(1979) *back

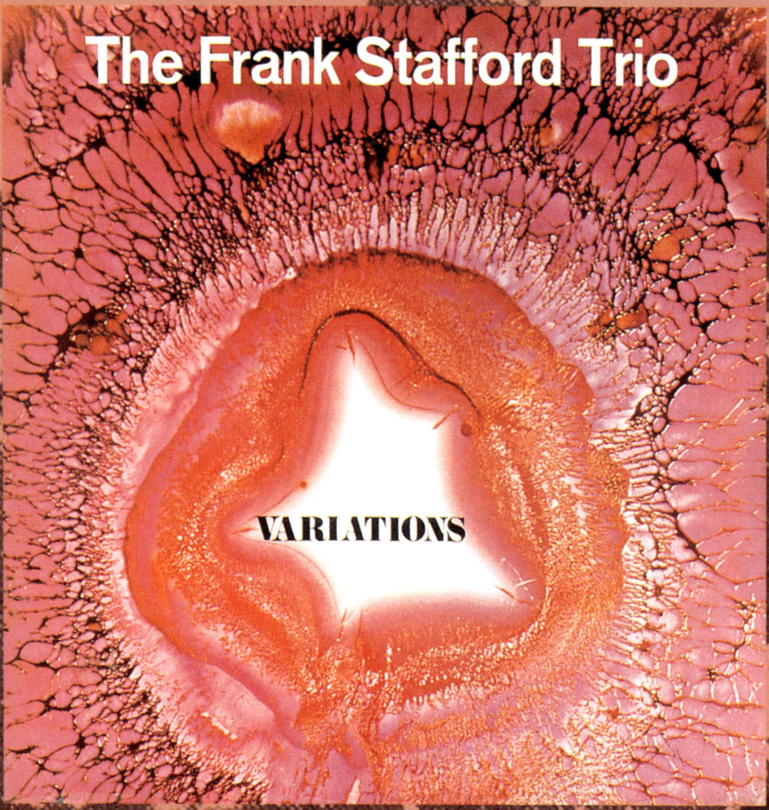

THE FRANK STAFFORD TRIO:VARIATIONS/
SAGA EROS8139(1970)

アルバム・ジャケットのもっとも重要な役割は、音楽という聴覚に訴える芸術を、視覚的に代弁または捕捉することにある。もちろん、デザイン素材は写真でもイラストでも自由自在なので、かなりの程度までリアルに視覚化することも可能だ。しかし、じつはそこにこそデザイナーやアート・ディレクターの悩みがある。いくらどんなにリアルな表現に拠って立とうとも、それが作品の本質をいい当てるとはかぎらないし、かえってイメージを狭めてしまう危険すらあるのだ。象徴的なデザインは、いわばそんなジレンマに対するひとつの解決策。「言葉で説明不能の物事を説明しようとする欲求が、隠喩と逆説とを結びつけ、謎めいた図像のなかに神秘的な解釈の余地を与えた」という意味のことを述べているのは、ウィーン生まれの美術史家E・H・ゴンブリッチだが、この種の努力は、いつの時代のあらゆる分野でも続けられているのである。たとえば、レイ・ラッセル『ドラゴン・ヒル』は、創造性あふれる即興演奏を、クールなサウンドで包み込んだ前衛ジャズ。美しい地球の青と、その後ろに広がる宇宙の茫洋たる風情との対照は、まるで具体的な根拠がないにもかかわらず、不思議とこのアルバムの本質をいい当てているような気がする。まぁ、アシュラ・テンペルの『コーリレイションズ』やフランク・スタフォード・トリオのエロチックなシンボリック・イメージがどれだけ実際の音楽に沿ったものかはわからないが、意味深長という意味での視覚効果は抜群だ。

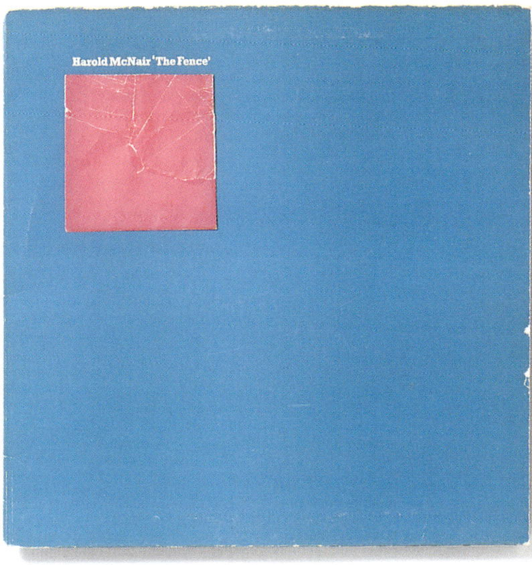

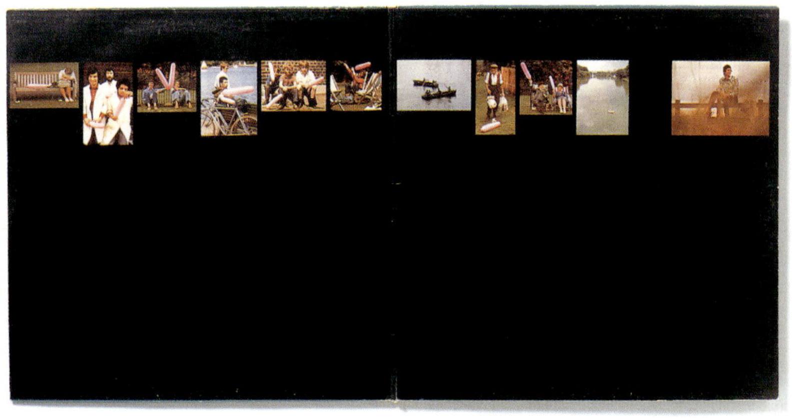

left: HAROLD McNAIR:THE FENCE/
B&C CAS1016(1970) *front
Art Direction-Design/Keith Davis,Grahame Berney
Photography/Keith Morris

above: HAROLD McNAIR:THE FENCE/B&C
CAS1016(1970) *inner

THE WORLD:LUCKY PLANET/LIBERTY
LBG83419(1970)*inner

THE WORLD:LUCKY PLANET/LIBERTY
LBG83419(1970)*front and back
Design/John Seaton

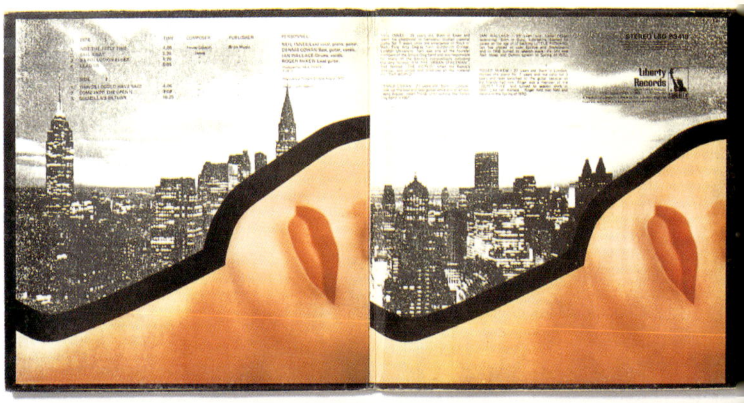

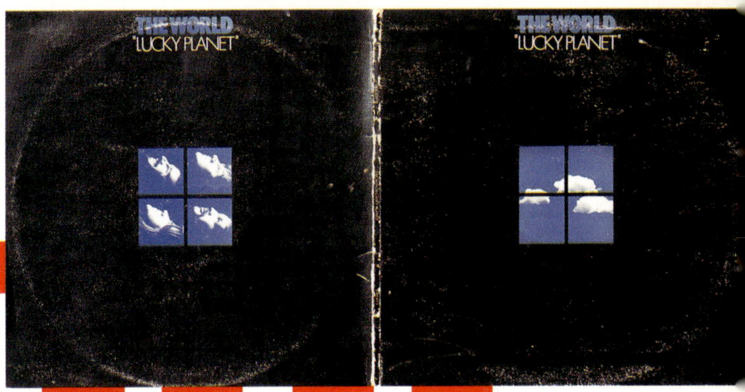

symbolic design
象徴的なデザイン

The role of an album cover is to visually represent or compliment the content of the album itself, which is an aural, not visual, medium. Surely, the design components for an album cover can range from a photograph to an illustration, enabling the designer to visually render the music. This was the main concern for the designer or art director. The designer may have been able to achieve a realistic image, but it may not have necessarily represented the essence of the music, and may have even limited the music's appreciation instead of enhancing it. One solution to the dilemma was 'symbolic design'. To paraphrase Vienna-born art historian E. H. Gombrich, the desire to explain verbally that which is inherently inexplicable in words builds a relationship between the metaphor and the paradox, making room for a mystical interpretation within a mysterious icon. This sort of effort has prevailed throughout history and in every field of art. For instance, "Dragon Hill" by Ray Russell featured avant garde Jazz with innovative Improvisation wrapped in smooth sounds. The contrast of the beautiful blue of Earth with the boundless elegance of outer space on the album's cover seems to have no apparent connection with the music. Yet, it strangely expresses the essence of the album. On the other hand, it's difficult to judge whether the erotic symbolistic image of Ash Ra Tempel's "Correlations" or of Frank Stafford Trio(?) has a direct connection to the music, even though they are somewhat profound in meaning.

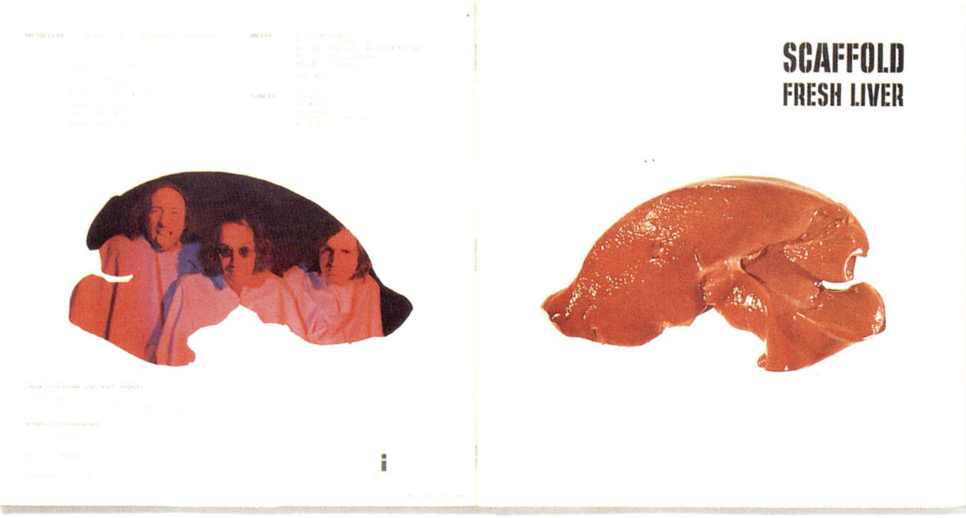

SCAFFOLD:FRESH LIVER/
ISLAND ILPS9234(1973) *front and back
Scaffold Photographs by Fin Costello
Layout etc. by Tony White+Harvey Weismuller

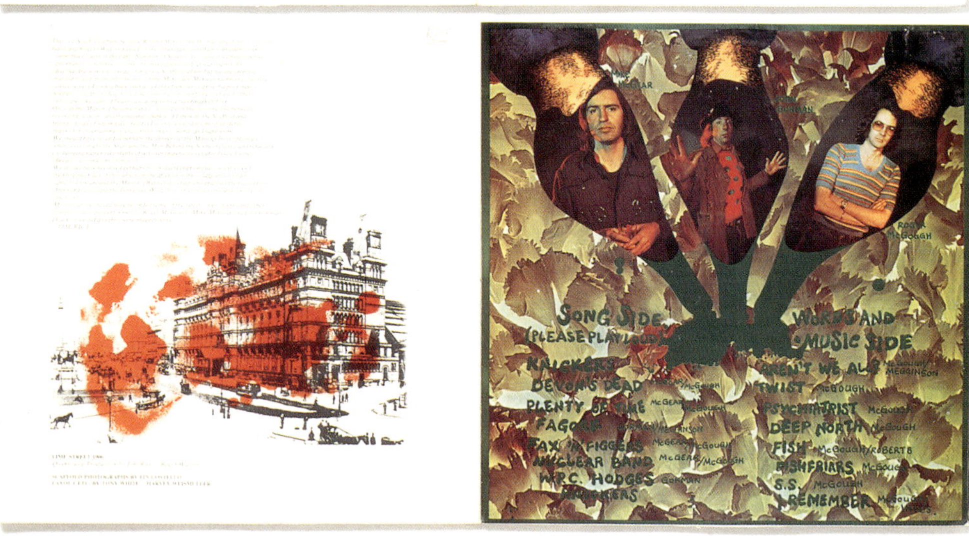

SCAFFOLD:FRESH LIVER/
ISLAND ILPS9234(1973) *inner

IAN CARR WITH NUCLEUS:SOLAR PLEXUS/
VERTIGO 6360 039(1971)*front and back
B.E.Ltd Designed the Cover

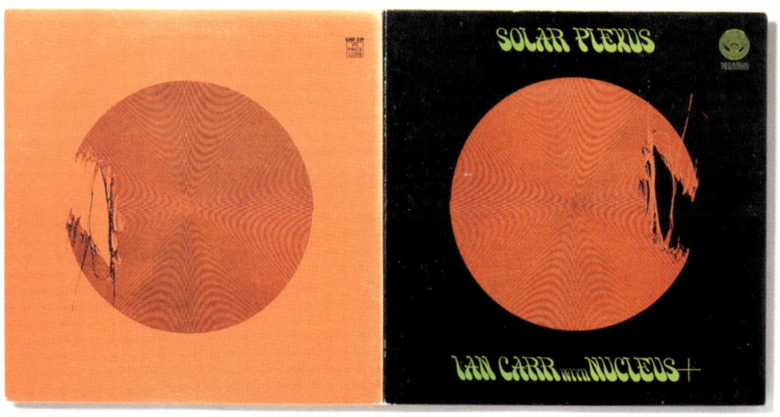

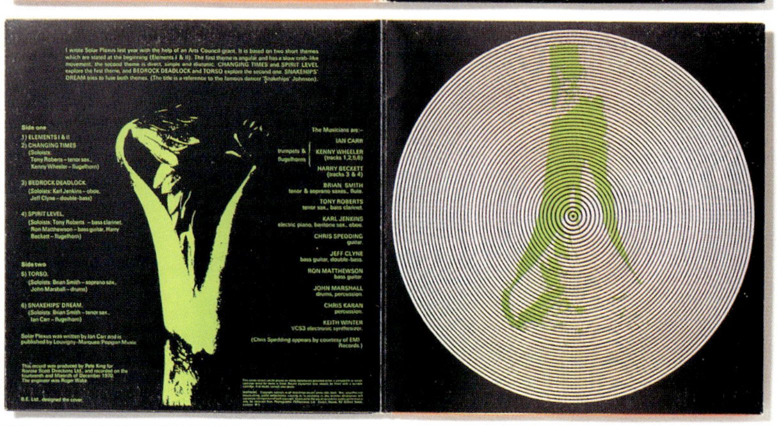

IAN CARR WITH NUCLEUS:SOLAR PLEXUS/
VERTIGO 6360 039(1971)*inner

RAY RUSSELL QUARTET:DRAGON HILL/
CBS 52663(1969)

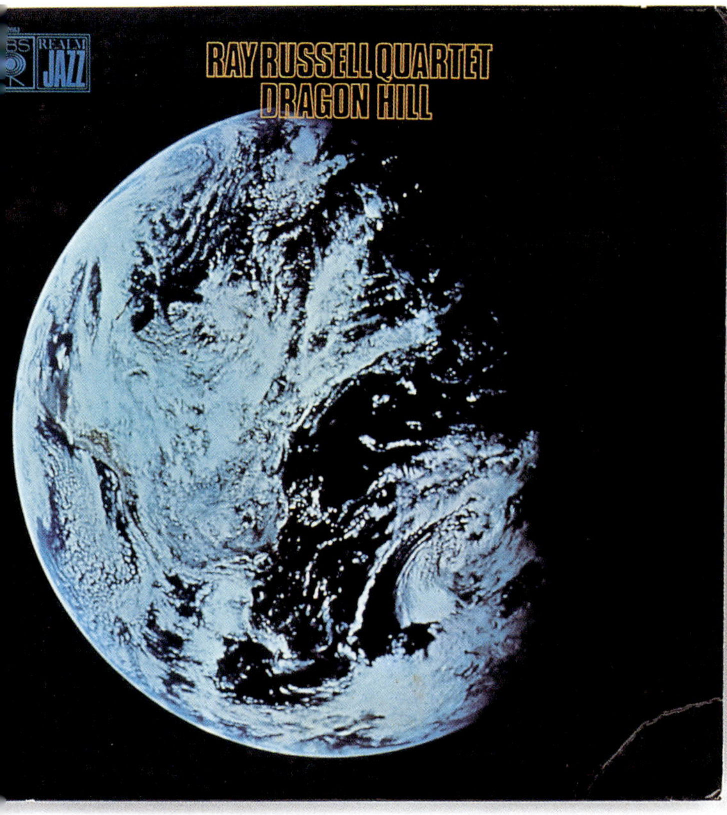

BOXER:ABSOLUTELY/EPIC EPC82151(1977)
Design&Photography/Herbert Worthington
Logo/Jack Upston

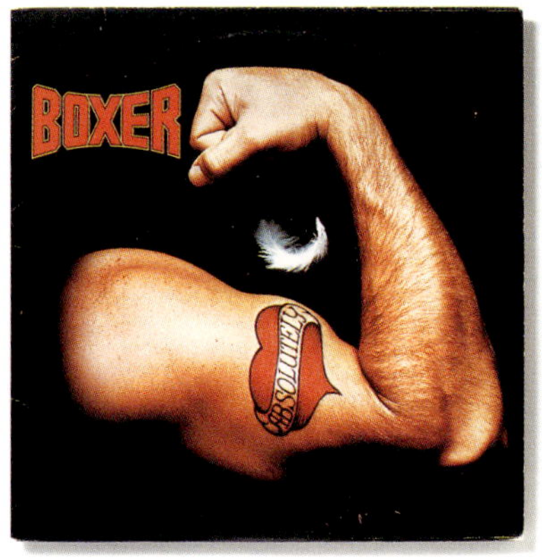

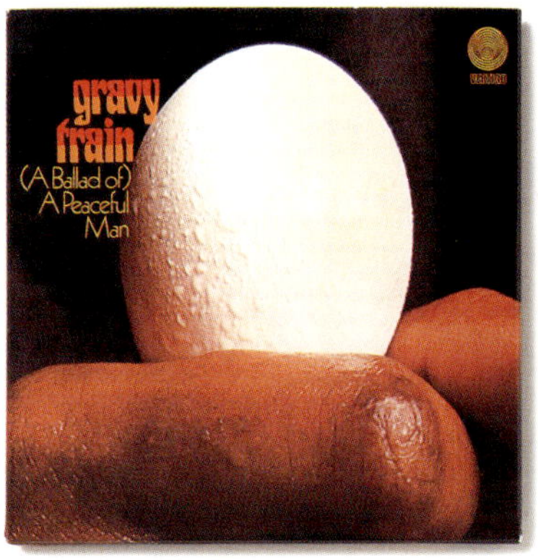

GRAVY TRAIN:A BALLD OF A PEACEFUL MAN/
VERTIGO 6360 051(1971)
Photography/Robert Lambert and Robert Le

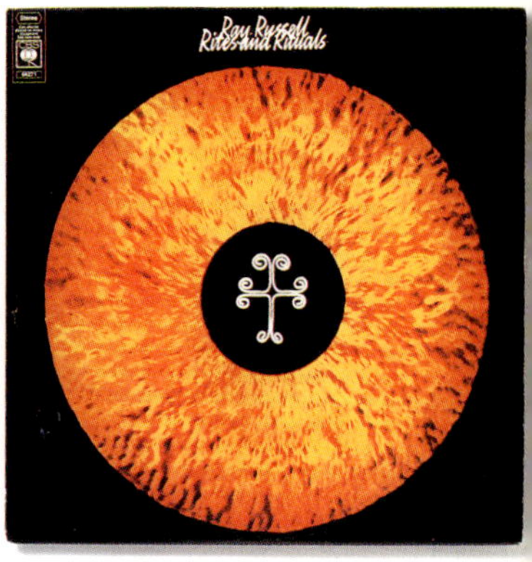

RAY RUSSELL:RITES AND RITUALS/
CBS 64271(1970)

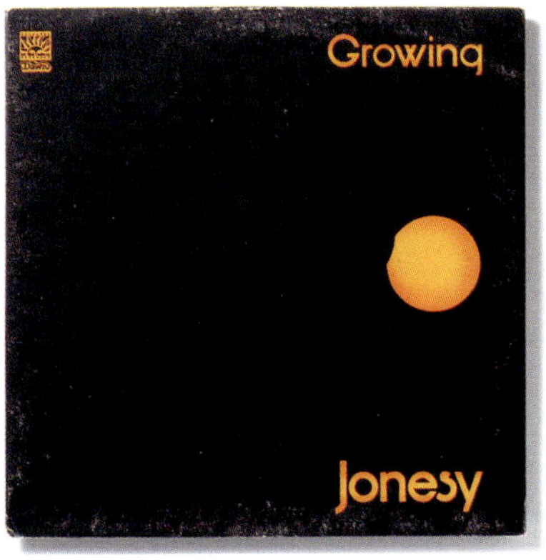

JONESY:GROWING/DAWN DNLS3055(1973)
Design/Jonesy and Martin Cropper Design Machine

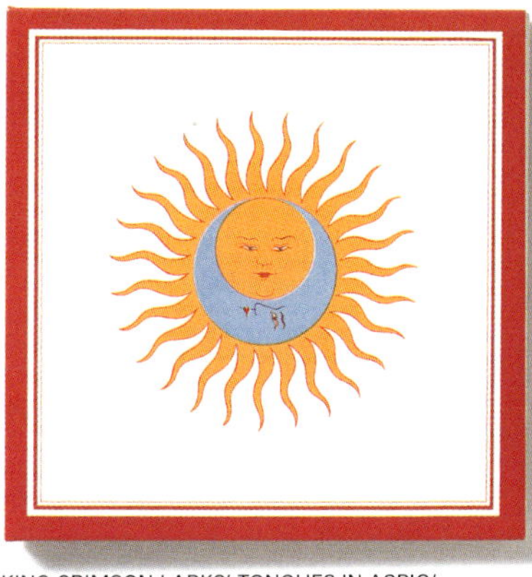

KING CRIMSON:LARKS' TONGUES IN ASPIC/
ISLAND ILPS9230(1973)
Cover Design by Tantra Designs

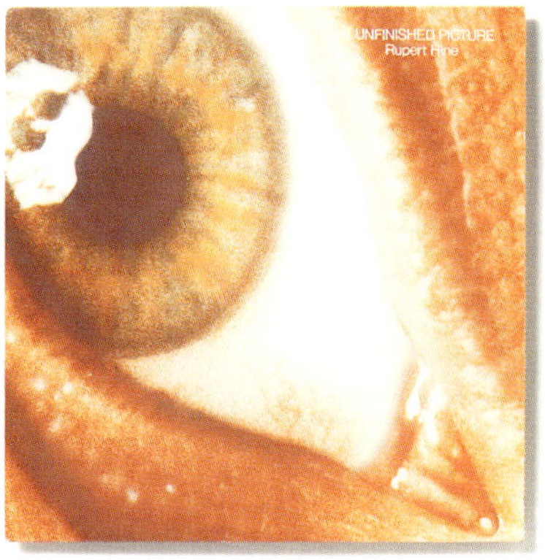

RUPERT HINE:UNFINISHED PICTURE/
PURPLE TPSA7509(1973)

In Search of the Lost Record

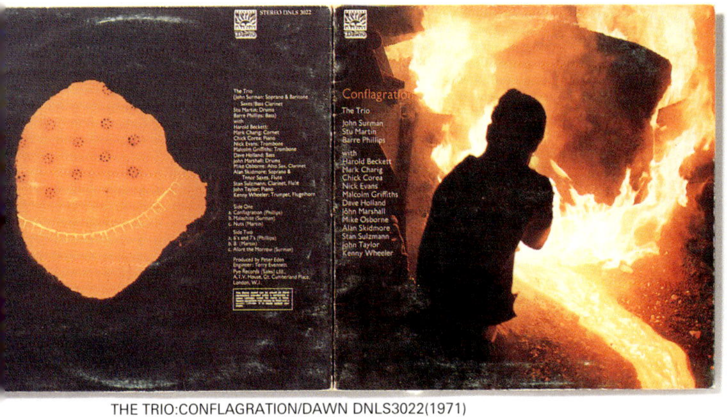

THE TRIO:CONFLAGRATION/DAWN DNLS3022(1971)

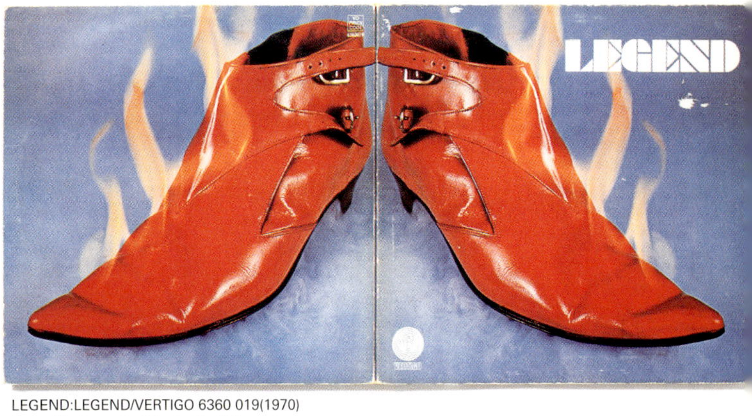

LEGEND:LEGEND/VERTIGO 6360 019(1970)
Cover Photographs&Design/Karl Stoecker

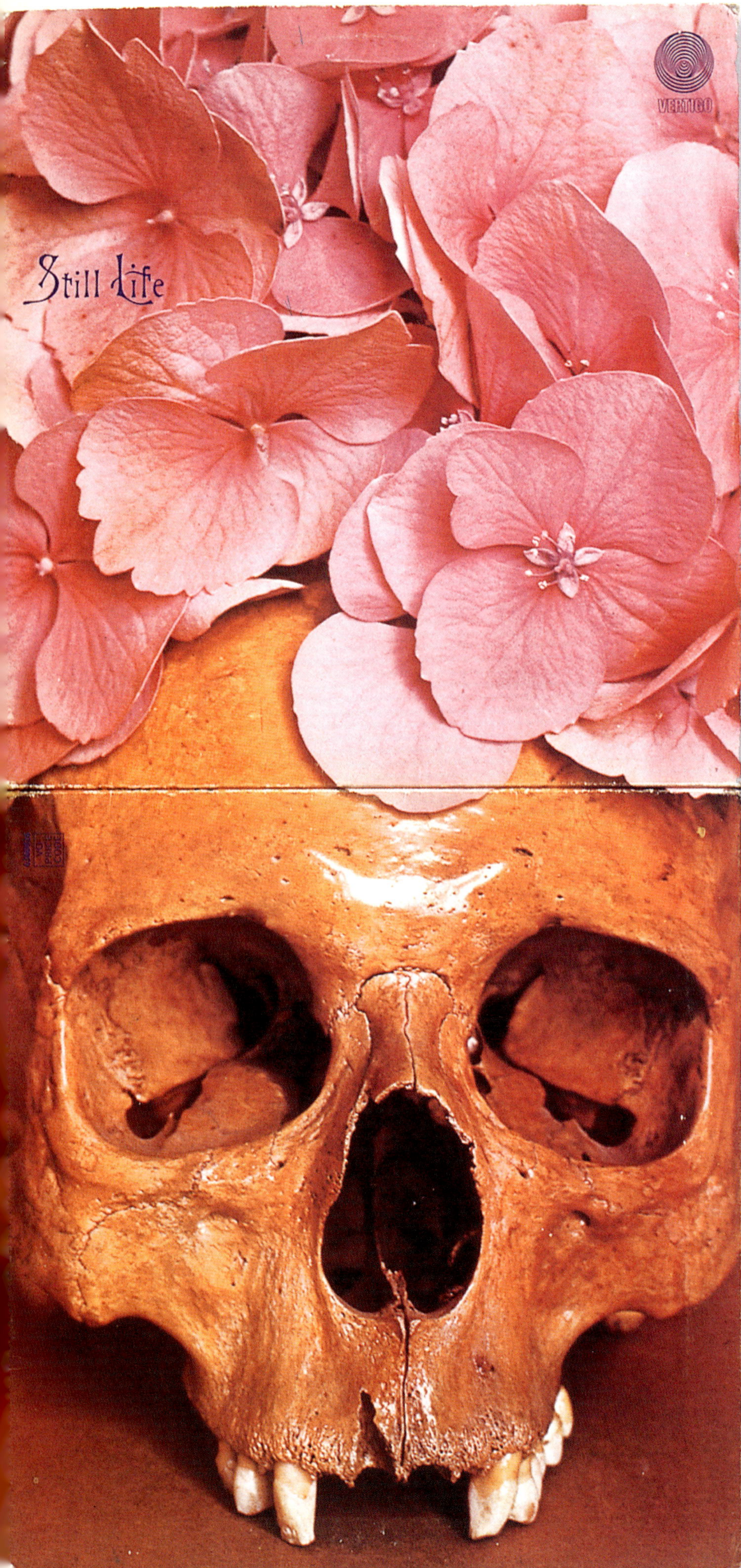

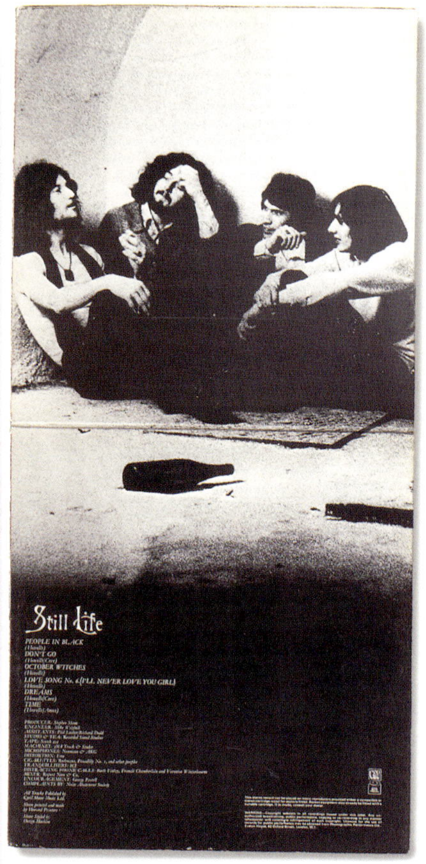

above: STILL LIFE:STILL LIFE/
VERTIGO 6360026(1971) *inner

left: STILL LIFE:STILL LIFE/
VERTIGO 6360026(1971)
Slleve Styled by Design Mchine *front and back

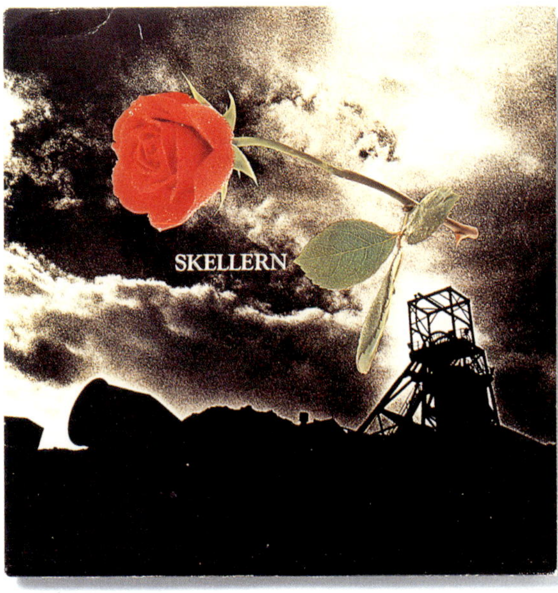

PETER SKELLERN:SKELLERN/
MERCURY 9109 701(1978)
Photography and Art Direction/ Martin Reavley

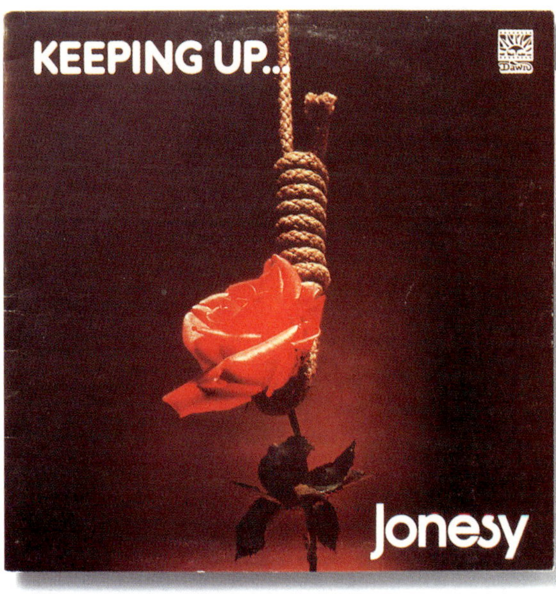

JONESY:KEEPING UP/
DAWN DNLS3048(1973)
Design/Barry White and Jonesy
Photo/Barry White

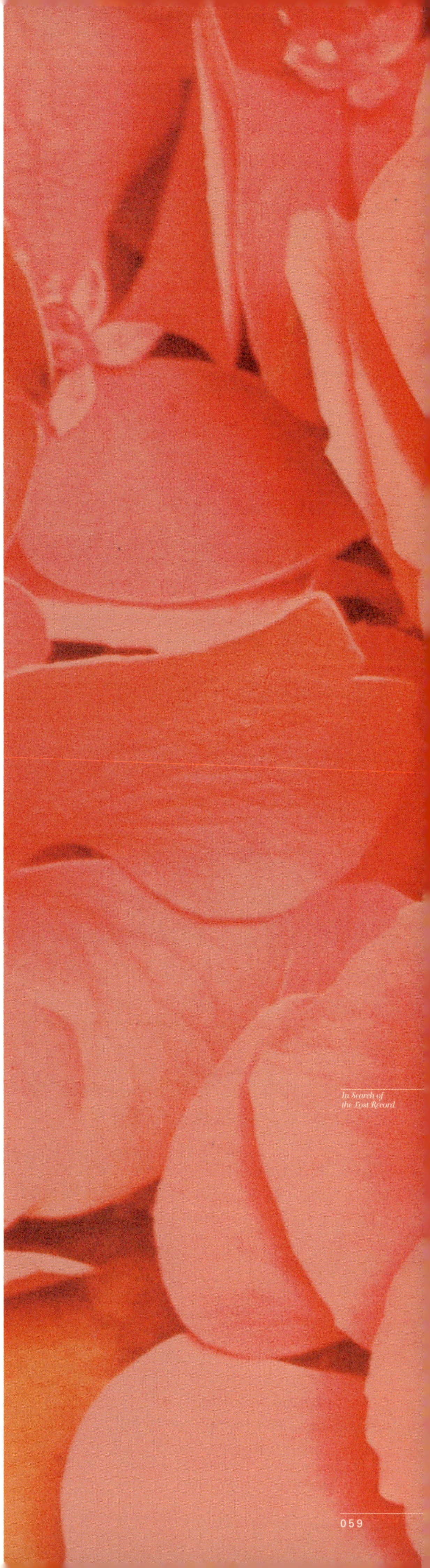

バナナというのは、かならずしもイギリスの専売特許ではない。むしろヴェルヴェット・アンダーグラウンド＆ニコによって66年に発表されたファースト・アルバム、アンディ・ウォーホルの手になるシルクスクリーン作品を用いたカヴァー・ジャケットが、多かれ少なかれ規範になっていると思われる。同作の収録曲に「ヘロイン」とあるように、バナナには麻薬を連想させるイメージがあるほか、「ペニス」「セックス」あるいは「狂人」を意味するスラングとして使われることもある。英国アンダーグラウンドにも多大な影響を与えたヴェルヴェッツの、スキャンダラスな精神と一脈通じるアーティストの作品にバナナのモチーフが登場するのも、けっして偶然などではないのだ。ただし、そんななかにも英国的なユーモアを忘れないのが彼らのいいところで、とくにケヴィン・エアーズのアルバム『Bananamour（バナナの恋人）』は、数ある英国産"バナナ・ジャケ"のなかでも秀作といえるだろう。

Banana' is not a copyright-protected word. But it's safe to consider the 1966 release of Velvet Underground and Nico's first album, with a silkscreen by Andy Warhol on the cover, to be more or less a model. As with the song "Heroin" included in this album, the banana conjures images of drugs, male genitals, sex, and lunacy. It is no coincidence that other British bands and artists with a similar, scandalous spirit of underground music used bananas as a motif. The English have never failed to incorporate a sly sense of humor. Kevin Ayers' "Bananamour" album cover is praise-worth as a superlative work among the many British "banana covers" .

symbolic design
Bananas
バナナの系譜

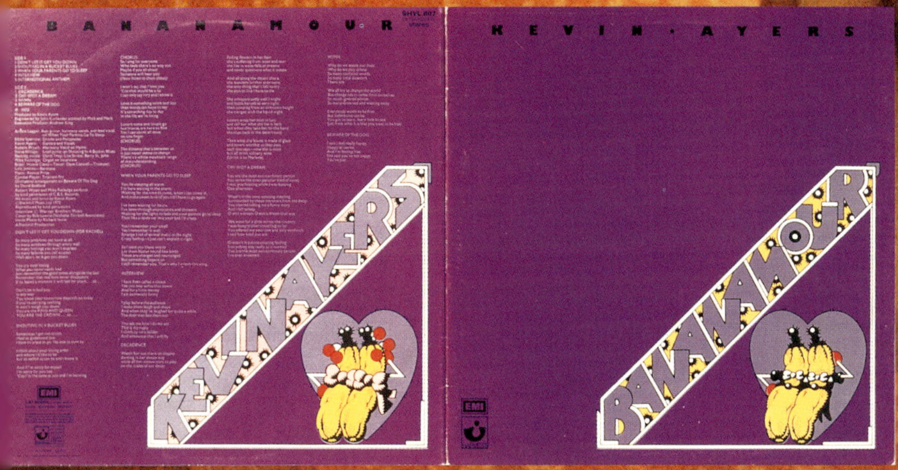

KEVIN AYERS:BANANAMOUR/
HARVEST SHVL807(1973) *front and back
Cover by Bob Lawrie(Nicholas Thirkell Associates)
Inside Photo by Richard Imrie

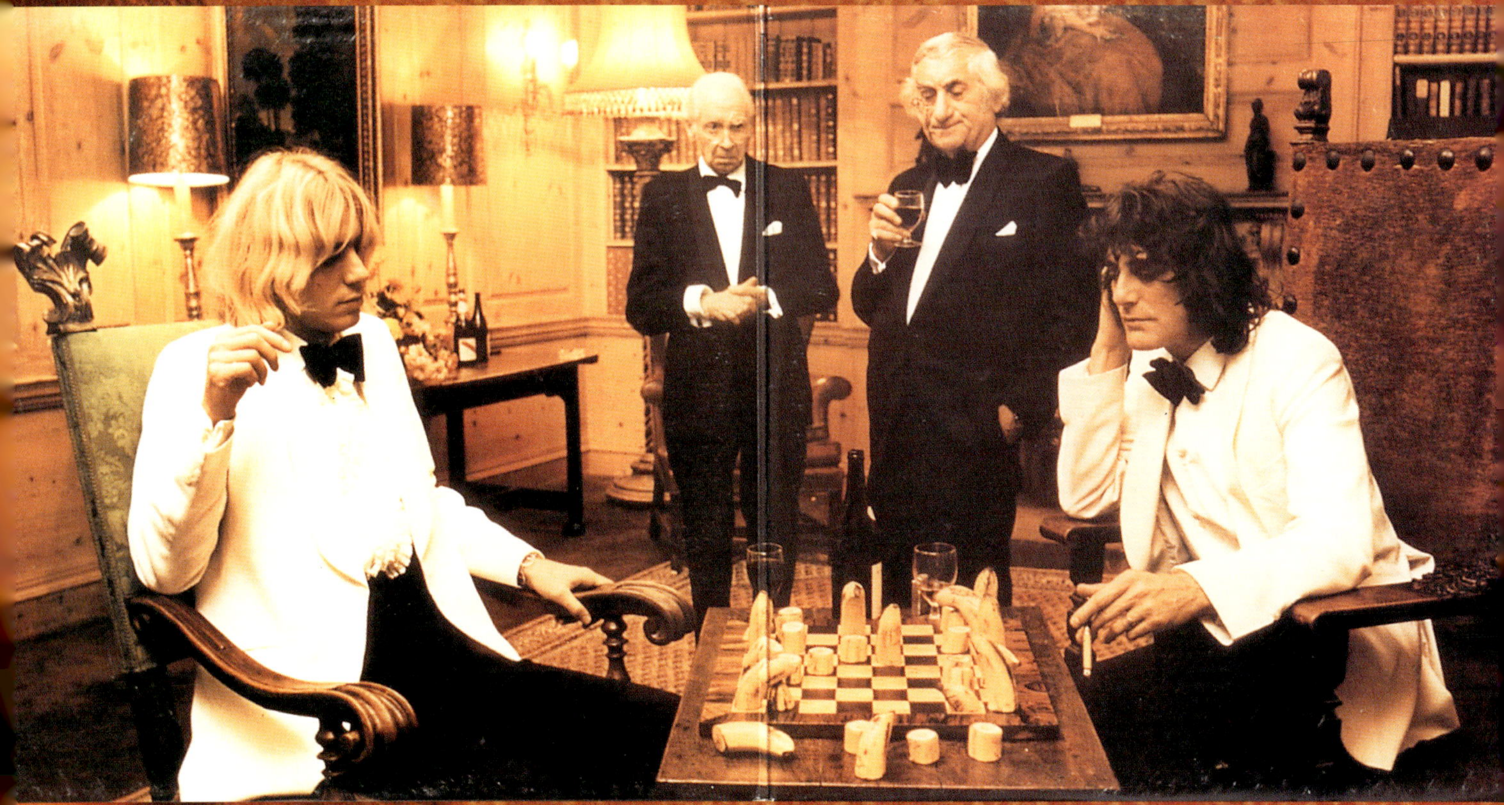

KEVIN AYERS:BANANAMOUR/
HARVEST SHVL807(1973) *inner

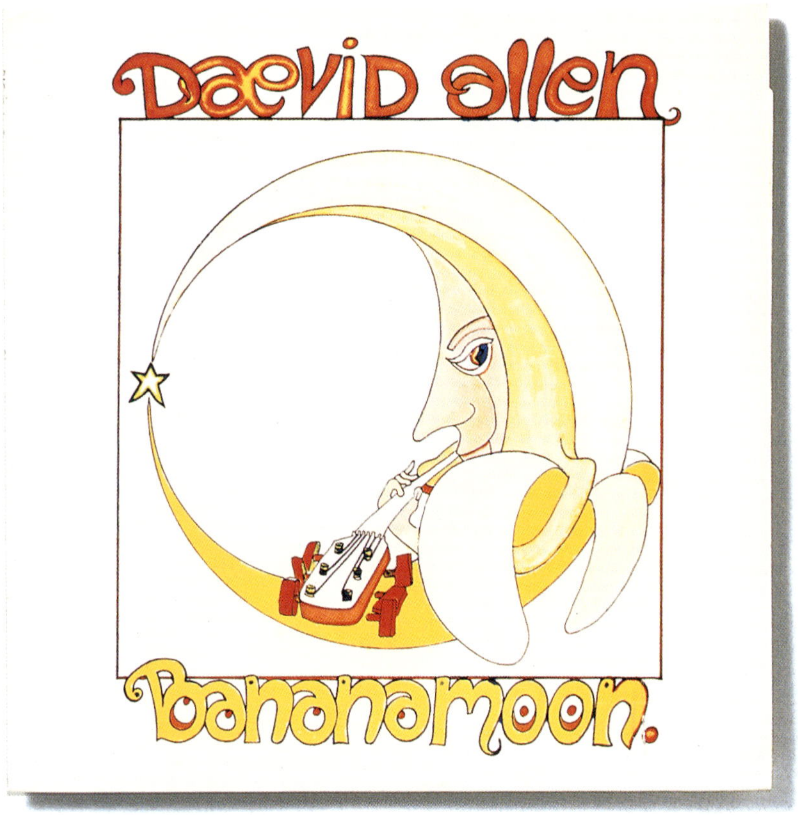

DAVID ALLEN:BANANA MOON/
CAROLINE C1512(1975)

ELECTRIC BANANA:THE SEVENTIES/
BUTT RECORDS NOTT001(1978) *front
Sleeve-Cooke Key
Photo-Brian Key

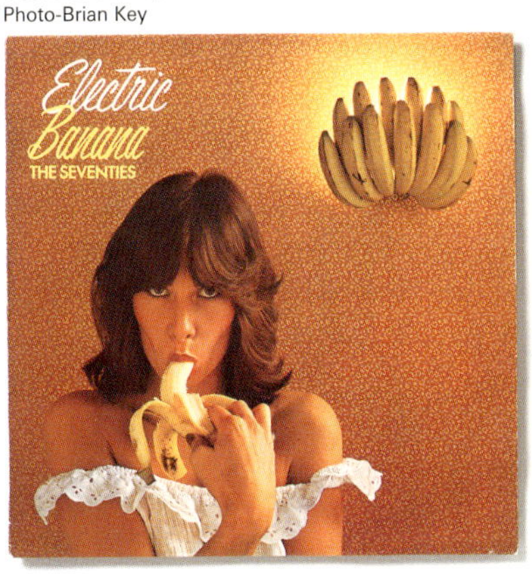

ELECTRIC BANANA:THE SEVENTIES/
BUTT RECORDS NOTT001(1978) *back

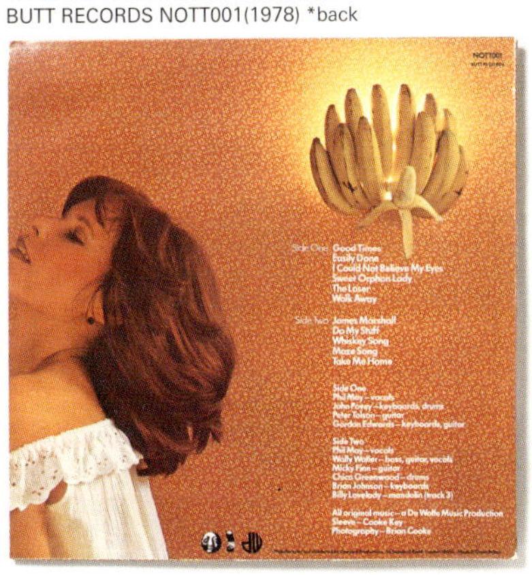

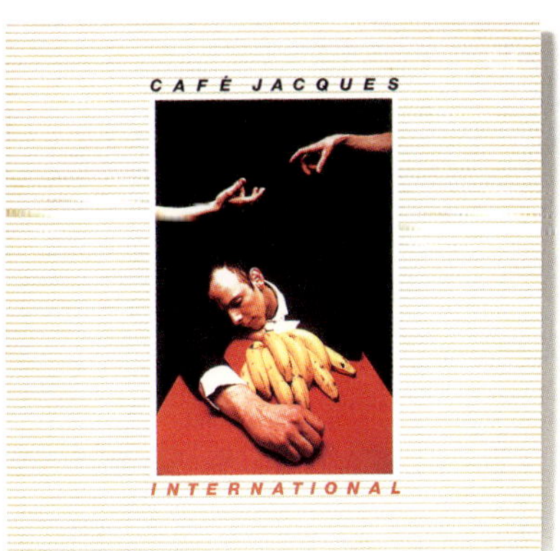

CAFE JACQUES:INTERNATIONAL
/EPIC EPC83042(1978)

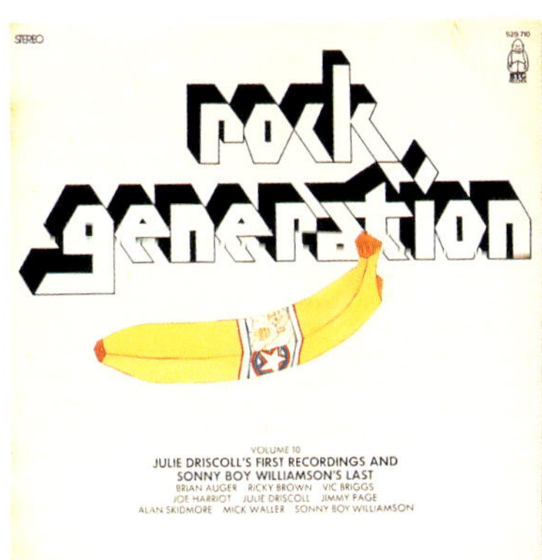

VARIOUS ARTISTS:
ROCK GENERATION VOL 10 ENGLAND 1962-1967/
BYG 529 710
Cover Design/Claude Roman

①
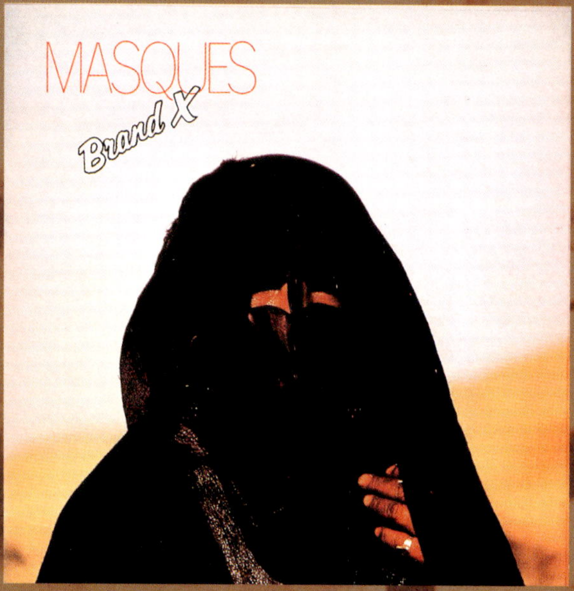

標題音楽（program music）というのがあるけれど、ようするにここに集めたのは、アルバム・タイトルを直接的に視覚化したデザイン・ワーク。象徴的なデザインとは正反対の性質をもった作品である。一見安易にはちがいないし、ともすれば陳腐とも映りかねない。しかし、それが見事にはまったときには、あたかも風刺画か一発芸のように、直截的な衝撃を見る者に与えてくれる。どうでもいいような内容を細部に至るまで真面目に視覚化していればいるほど、この種のデザインの価値は高まるように思うのだが、いかがなものだろう？

Just like the music genre called 'program music', here we have album cover designs that directly visualize the album title. These programmatic works have the exact opposite nature of symbolic designs. It's surely simple at a glance, and also risk being viewed as cheap or common-place. However, when the connection is masterfully brilliant, it gives out an instant blow like a caricature or a one-shot trick. It seems as though the more detailed visualization there is within the more meaningless or irrelevant parts increase the value of this style of design.

②
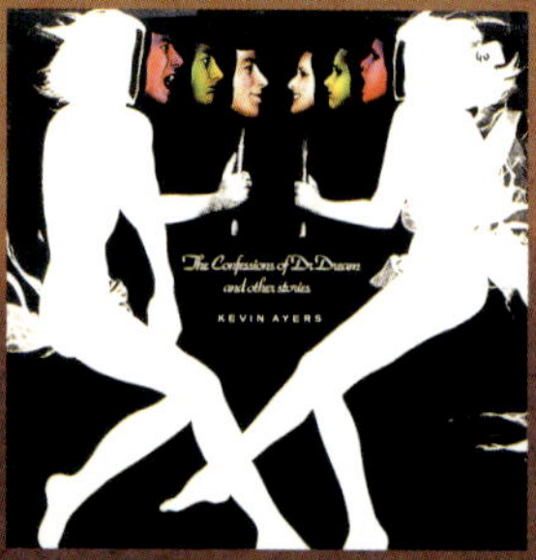

③
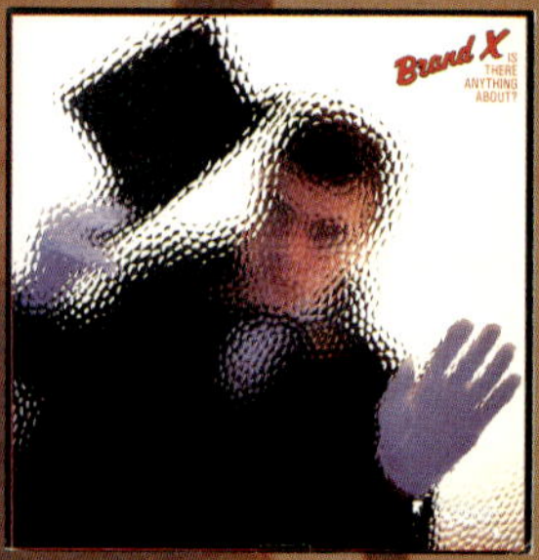

④
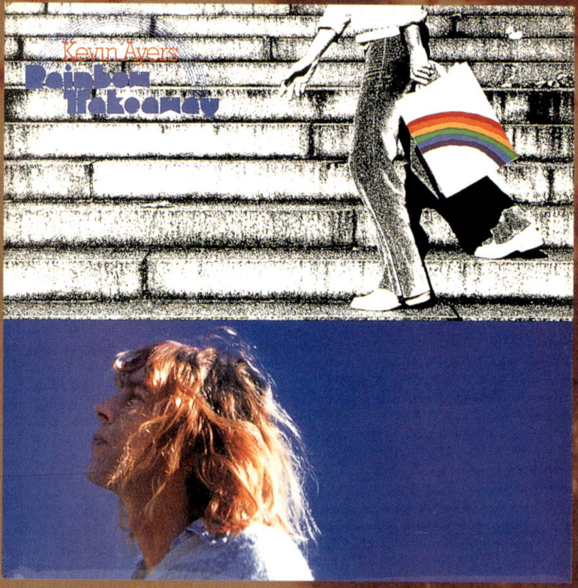

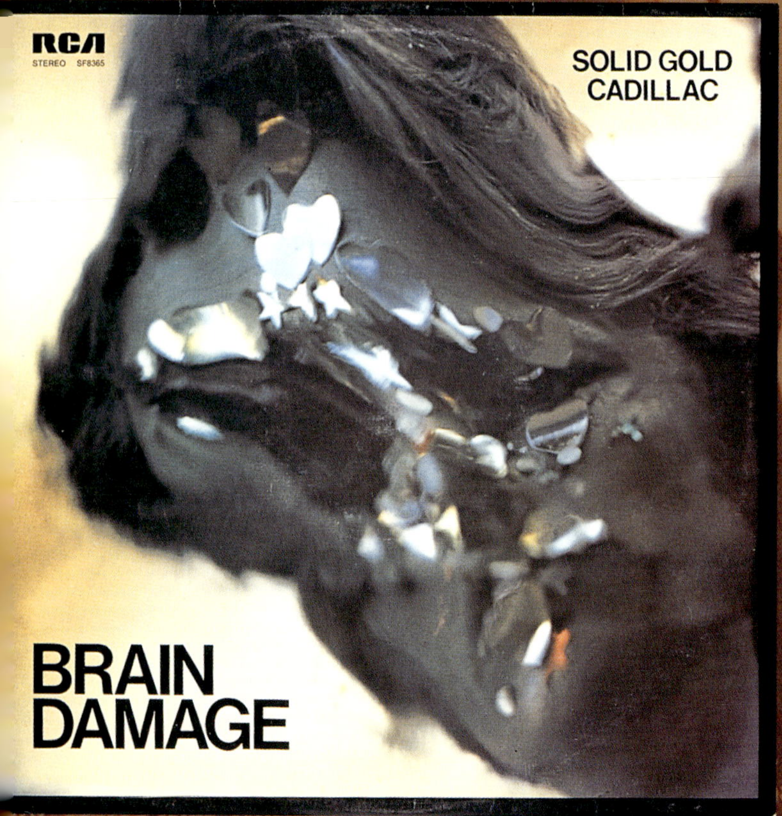

SOLID GOLD CADILLAC:BRAIN DAMAGE/
RCA SF8365(1973)
Sleeve Design and Photography by
Charles Mapelston

⑤
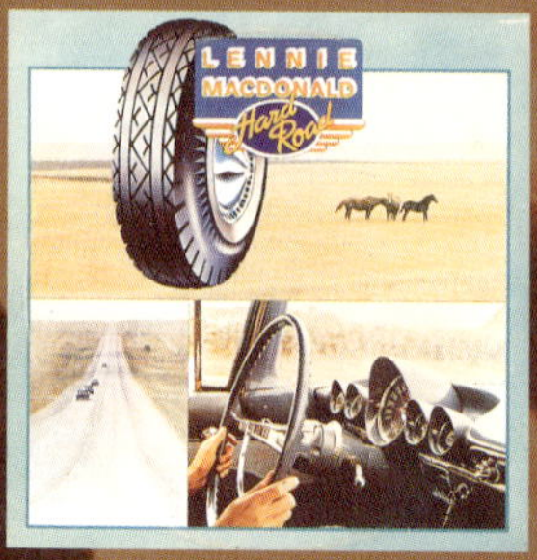

⑥
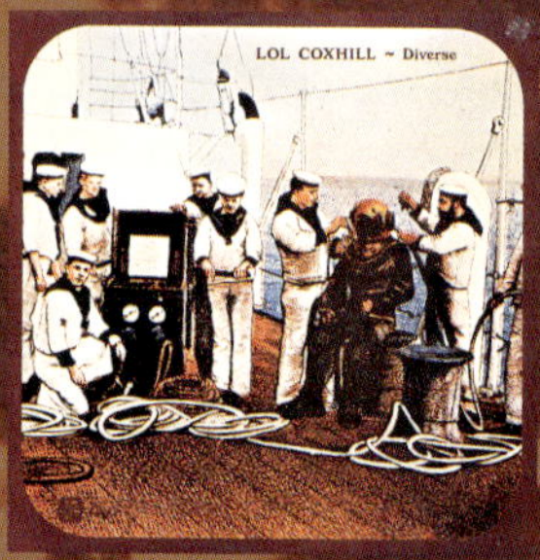

⑦
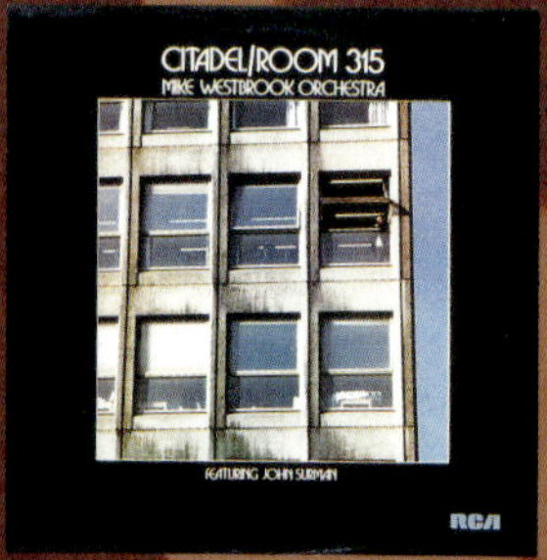

① BRAND X:MASQUES/
CHARISMA CAS1138(1978)
Sleeve Design,Front Photo/Chris Kutschera

② KEVIN AYERS:THE CONFESSIONS OF DR.DREAM AND OTHER STORIES
/ISLAND ILPS9263(1974)
Cover Designs Conceived and Comissioned by Group Five
Illustrations by James Wedge and George Smith

③ BRAND X:IS THERE ANYTHING ABOUT?/
CBS 85967(1982)
Sleeve by Bill Smith
Photography by Andrew Douglas

④ KEVIN AYERS:RAINBOW TAKE AWAY/
HARVEST SHSP4085(1978)
Photogrpahy/Peter Vernon
Artwork/Sharon Coventry
Art Direction/Brian Palmer

⑤ LENNIE MacDONALD:HARD ROAD/
ARTY 117
Sleeve Design/Paul May

⑥ LOL COXHILL:DIVERSE/
OGUN OG510(1976)
Front Cover/Victrian Lantern Slide(anon.)

⑦ MIKE WESTBROOK ORCHESTRA:CITADEL/ROOM315/RCA SF8433(1975)
photography by Kate Barnard

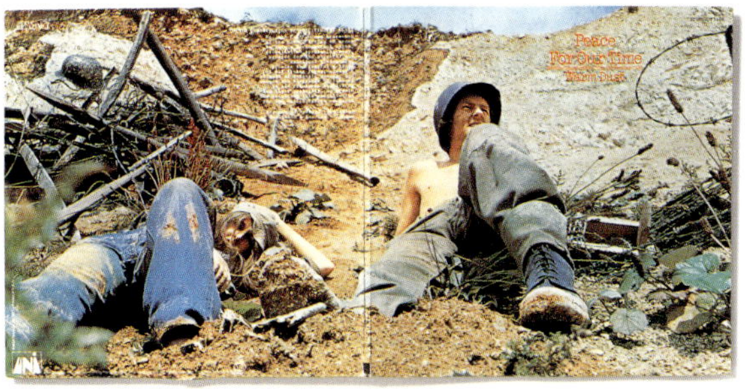

⑧

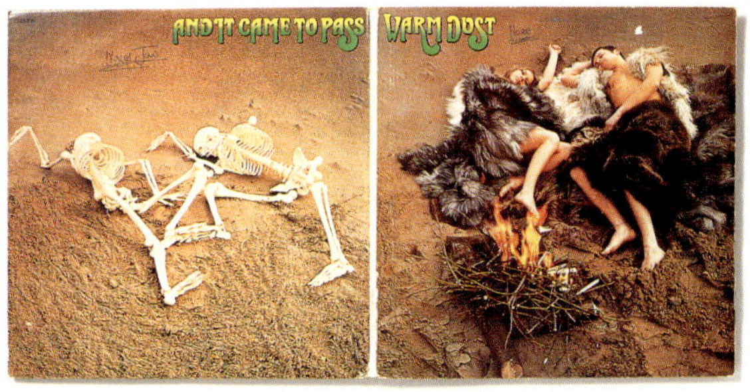

⑨

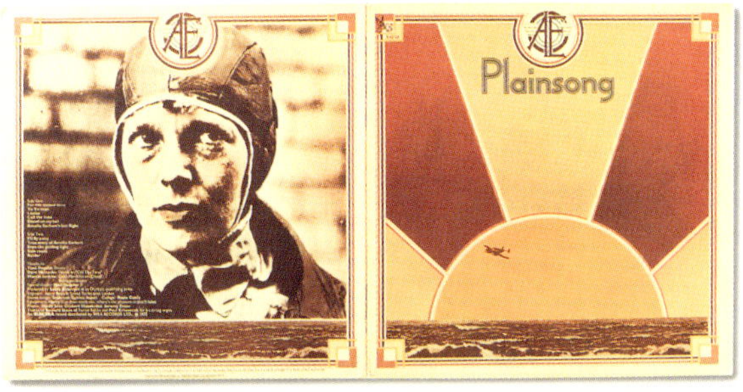

⑩

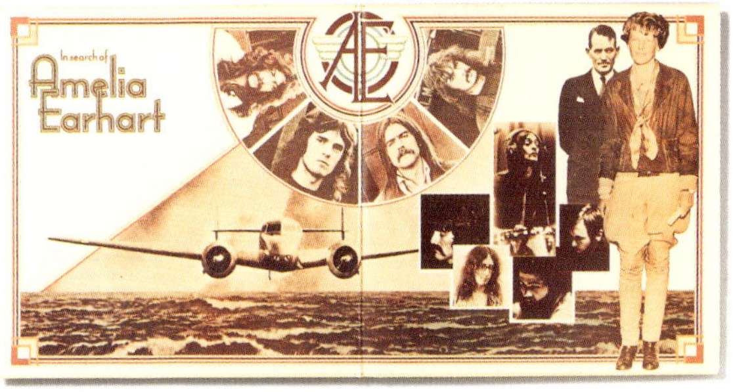

⑪

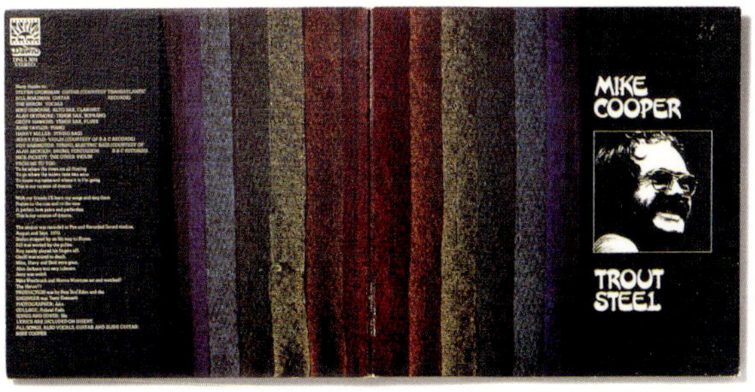

⑫

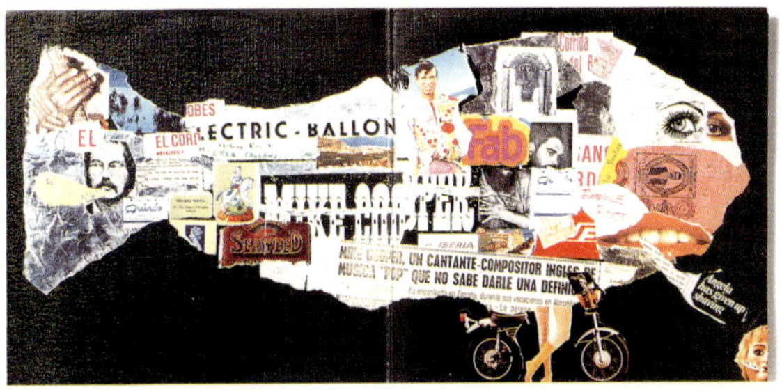

⑬

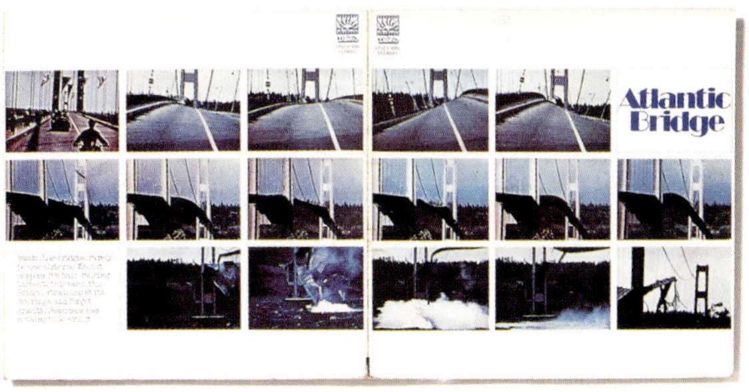

⑭

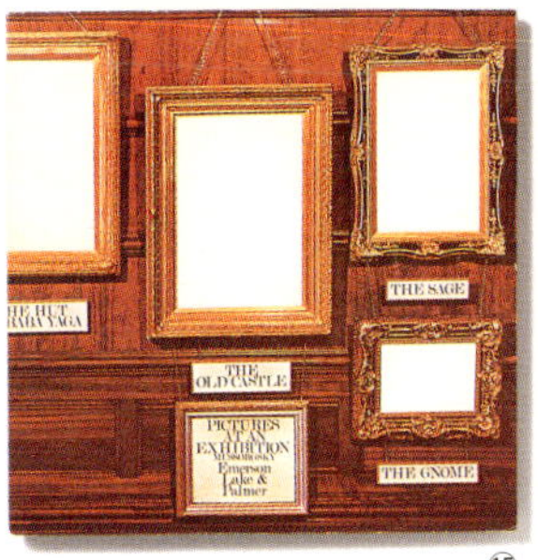

⑮

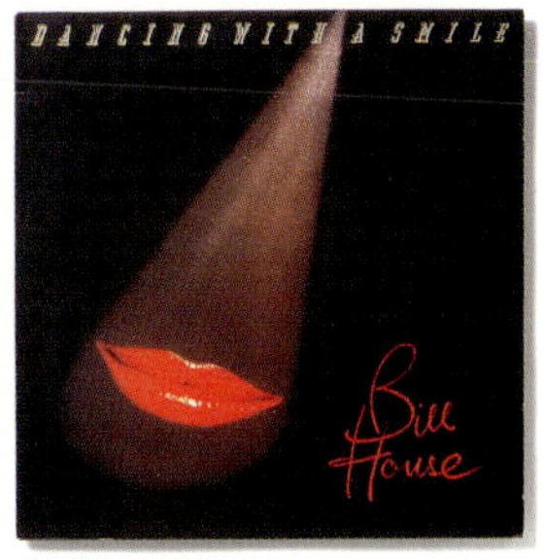

⑯

symbolic design

Programmatic Works

標題主義

⑧ WARM DUST:PEACE FOR OUR TIME/
TREND 6480 001(1971)

⑨ WARM DUST:AND IT CAME TO PASS/
TREND TNLS700(1970)

⑩ PLAIN SONG:IN SEARCH OF AMELIA EARHART/
ELEKTRA K42120(1972)*front and back
Sleeve Design/ Seabrook,Graves,Aslett
Collage/ Rosie Coole
Photo/ Harry Isles,Gijsbert Hanekroot,Jeremy Ensor

⑪ PLAIN SONG:IN SEARCH OF AMELIA EARHART/
ELEKTRA K42120(1972) *inner

⑫ MIKE COOPER:TROUT STEEL/
DAWN DNLS3011(1970) *front and back
Photographer/Jake
Collage/Roland Fade

⑬ MIKE COOPER:TROUT STEEL/DAWN
DNLS3011(1970)*inner

⑭ ATLANTIC BRIDGE:ATLANTIC BRIDGE/DAWN
DNLS3014(1970) *front and back
Sleeve Design and Art Direction/Pye Records Studios

⑮ EMERSON,LAKE&PALMER:PICTURES AT AN
EXHIBITION/ISLAND HELP1(1971)
Cover&Painting/William Neal

⑯ BILL HOUSE:DANCING WITH A SMILE/DECCA TXS-
R136

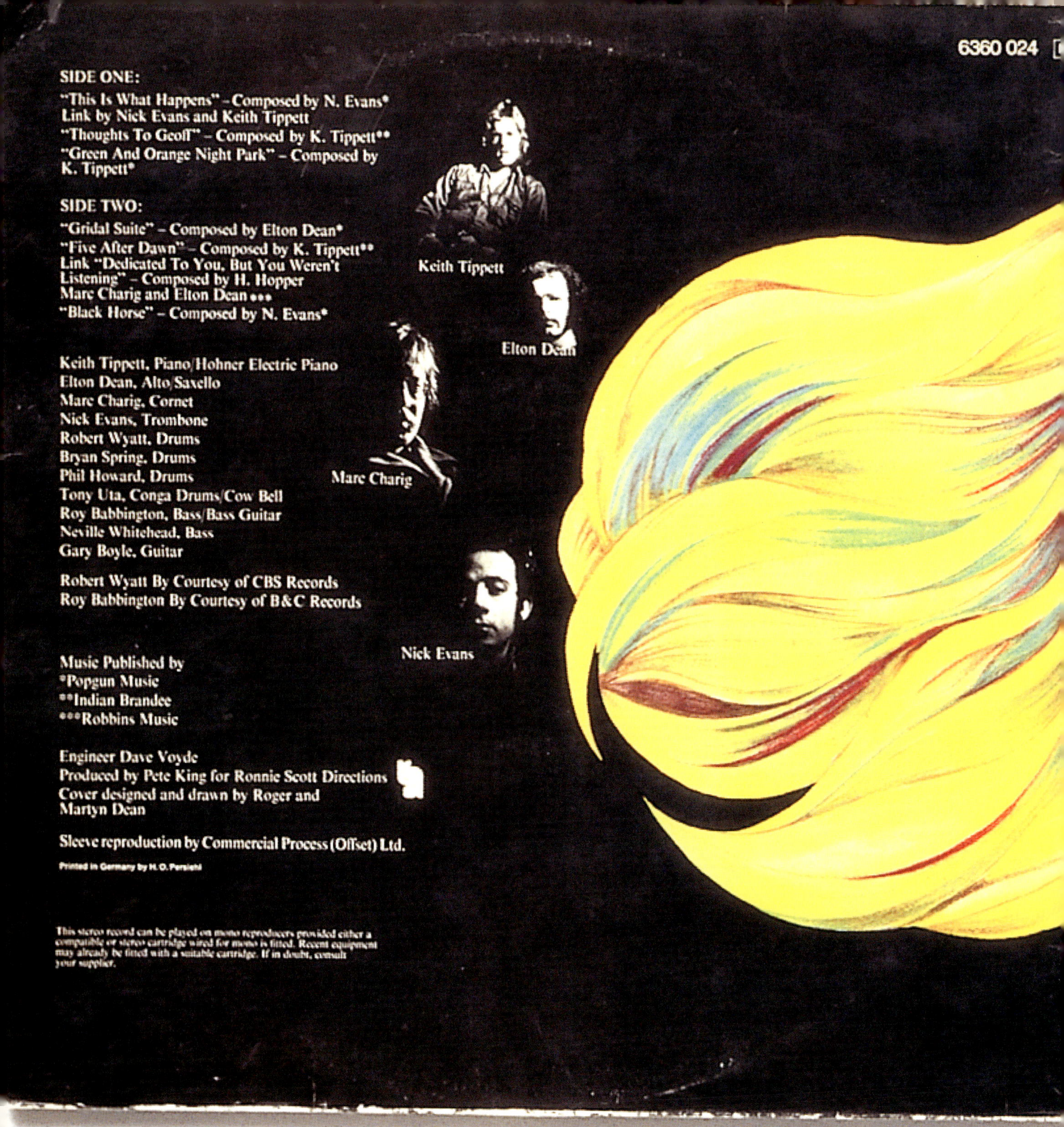

Roger Dean illustrations

ロジャー・ディーン

illustration

イラストレーション

デザイナー、写真家にとってそうだったように、イラストレーターにとってもまた、アルバム・ジャケットは重要な作品発表の場であった。その代表的な存在をひとり挙げるとすれば、なんといってもロジャー・ディーンだろう。ロジャー・ディーンは44年ケント州生まれ。61～64年、カンタベリー・スクール・オブ・アートで工業デザインを学んだ彼は、その後、ロイヤル・カレッジ・オブ・アートに進学し、在学中に"Sea Urchin"と名づけられた椅子のデザインで作家デビューを果たした。アルバム・カヴァーのイラストレーターとして、あるいはステージ・セットのデザイナーとして活躍するようになるのはこの直後のことだが、マッシュルーム型でポリエステル製のSea Urchinが、すでに後の彼の作品世界を連想させているところは興味深い。有機的なモチーフと無機的なモチーフとをリアルなタッチで融合させた独特のイラストは、どんなアーティストのアルバムに用いられていようとも、すぐにそれとわかる強烈な個性を放っている。

An album cover was a great opportunity and creative outlet for illustrators as well as designers and photographers. The illustrator that first comes to mind is certainly Roger Dean. He was born in Kent, England in 1944. After studying industrial design at the Canterbury School of Art from 1961 to 1964, he moved on to the Royal College of Art. During his student years, he made his debut as an artist with a chair design titled "Sea Urchin". Immediately after this, he started to work as an illustrator for album covers and also as a stage set

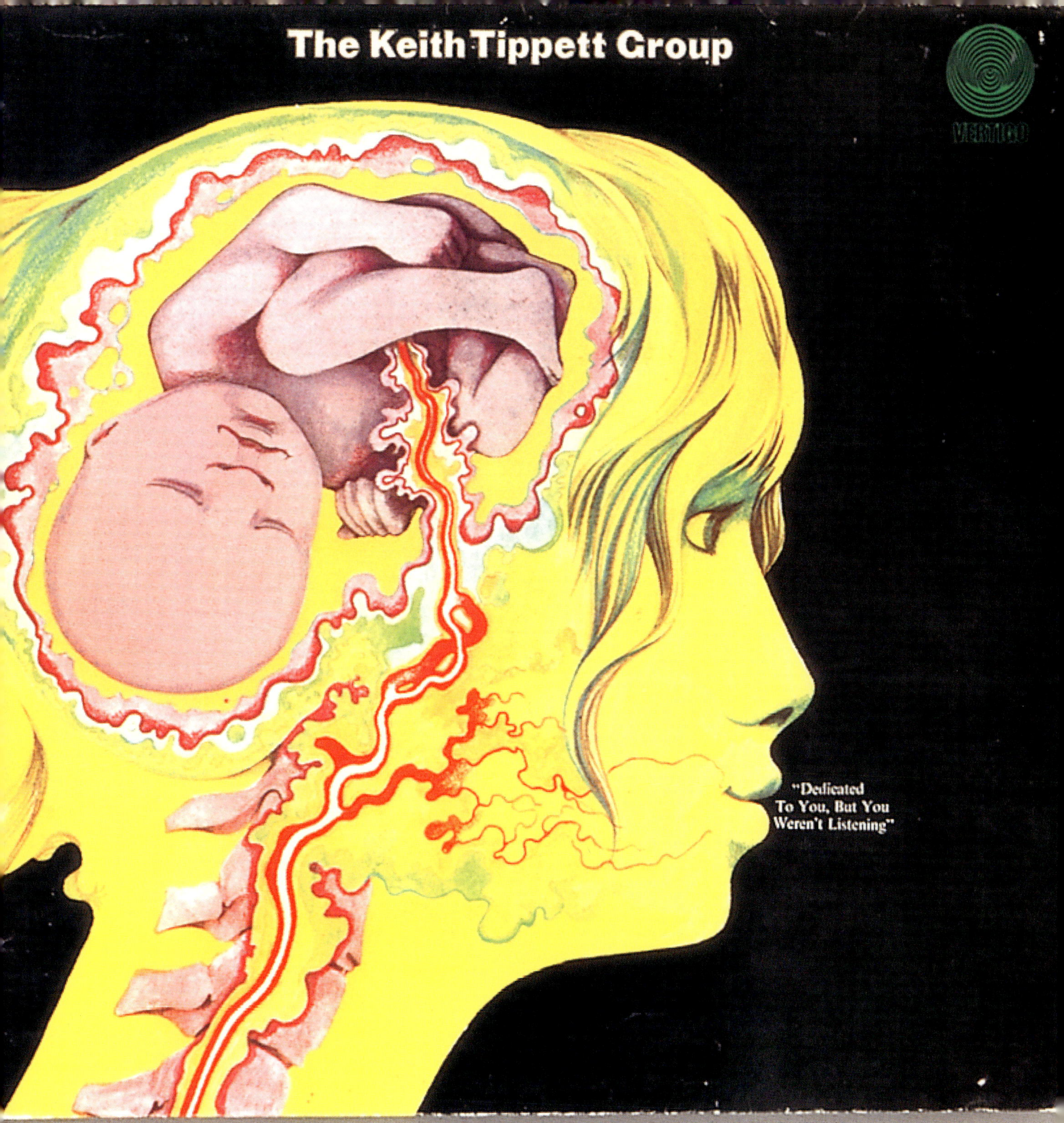

THE KEITH TIPPETT GROUP:DEDICATED TO YOU, BUT YOU WEREN'T LISTENING/
VERTIGO 6360 024(1971) *front and back
Cover Designed and drawn by Roger and Martyn Dean

ons

designer. The polyester, mushroom-shaped "Sea Urchin" became the signature design style that characterized his works thereafter. His unique illustrations, which succeeded in blending organic and inorganic motifs with a touch of realism, posseses a strong originality that made his work immediately recognizable.

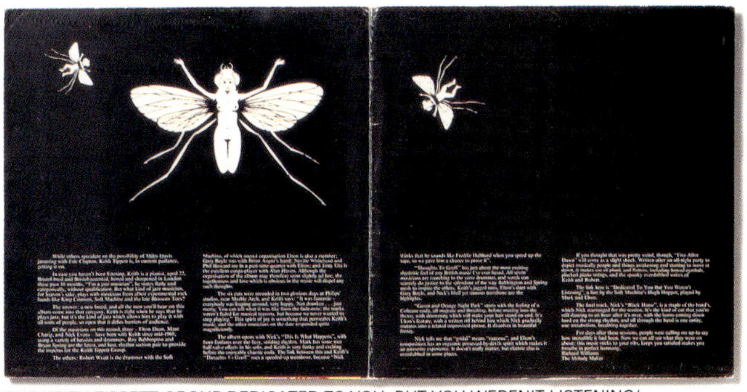

THE KEITH TIPPETT GROUP:DEDICATED TO YOU, BUT YOU WEREN'T LISTENING/
VERTIGO 6360 024(1971)*inner

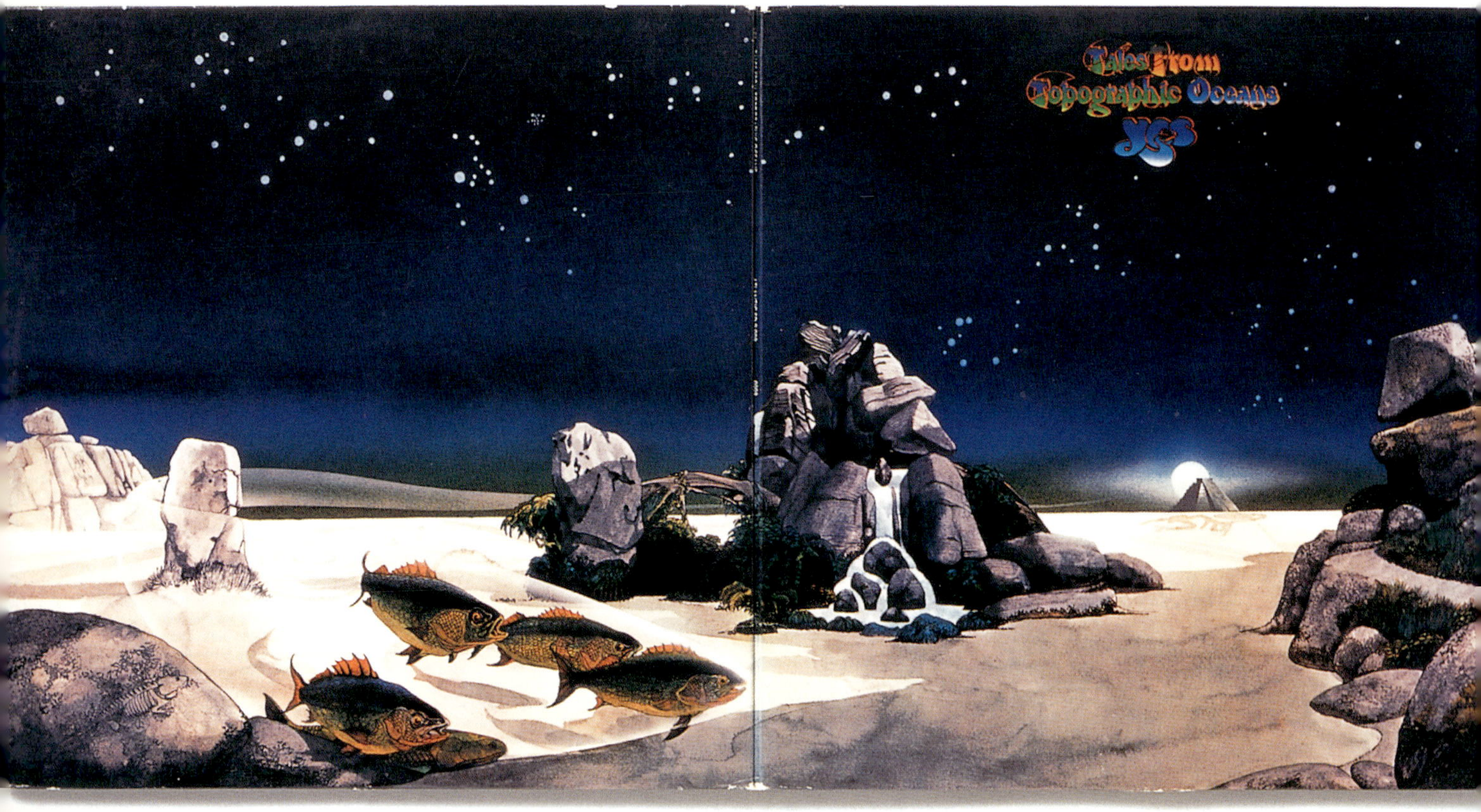

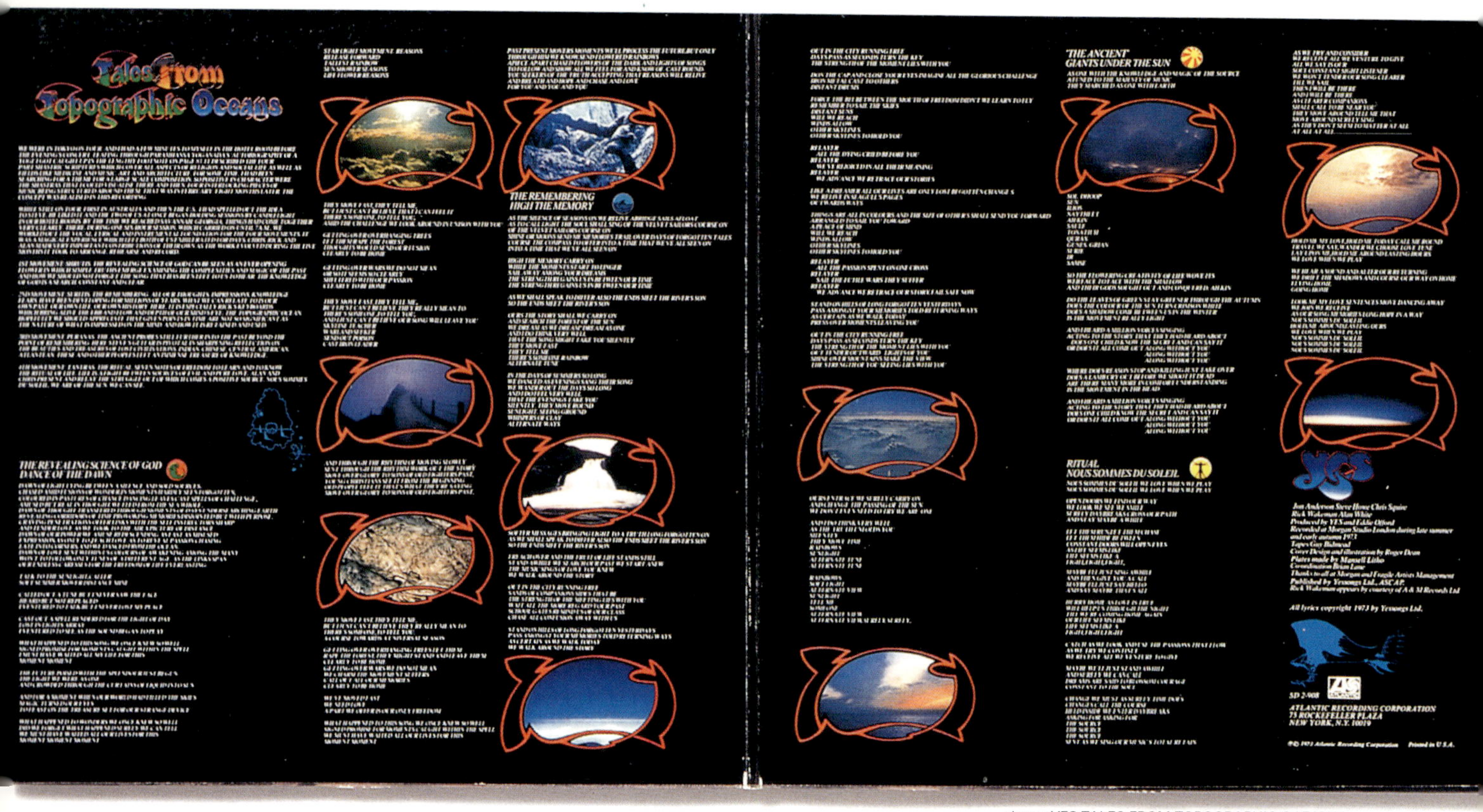

above: YES:TALES FROM TOPOGRAPHIC OCEANS/
ATLANTIC K80001(1973)*front and back
Cover Design and Illustration by Roger Dean

below: YES:TALES FROM TOPOGRAPHIC OCEANS/
ATLANTIC K80001(1973) *inner

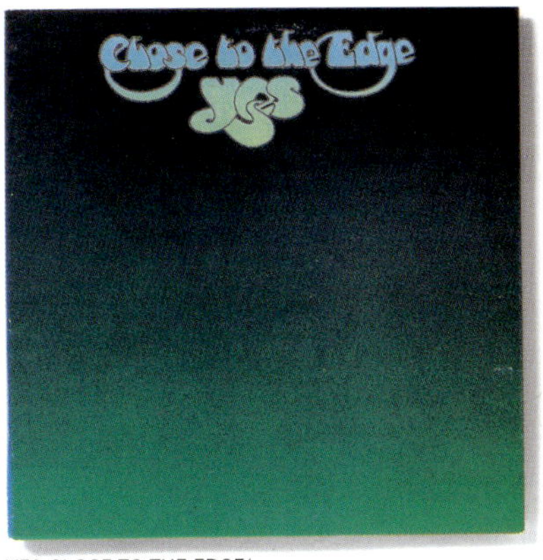

YES:CLOSE TO THE EDGE/
ATLANTIC K50012(1972)
Cover/Roger Dean
Photographs/Martin Adelman & Roger Dean

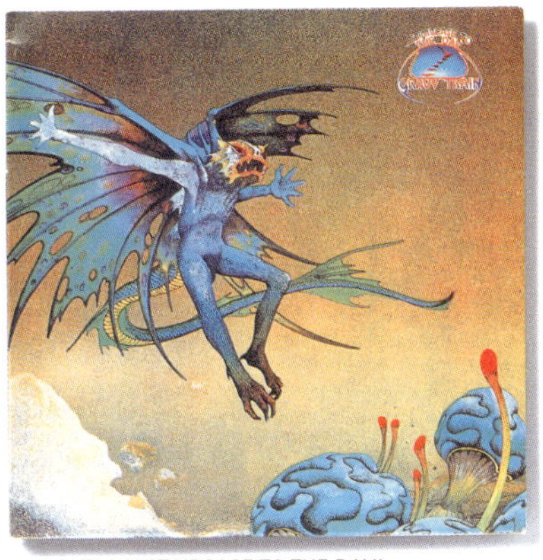

GRAVY TRAIN:STAIRCASE TO THE DAY/
DAWN DNLH1(1974)
Sleeve Design and Layout/Roger Dean

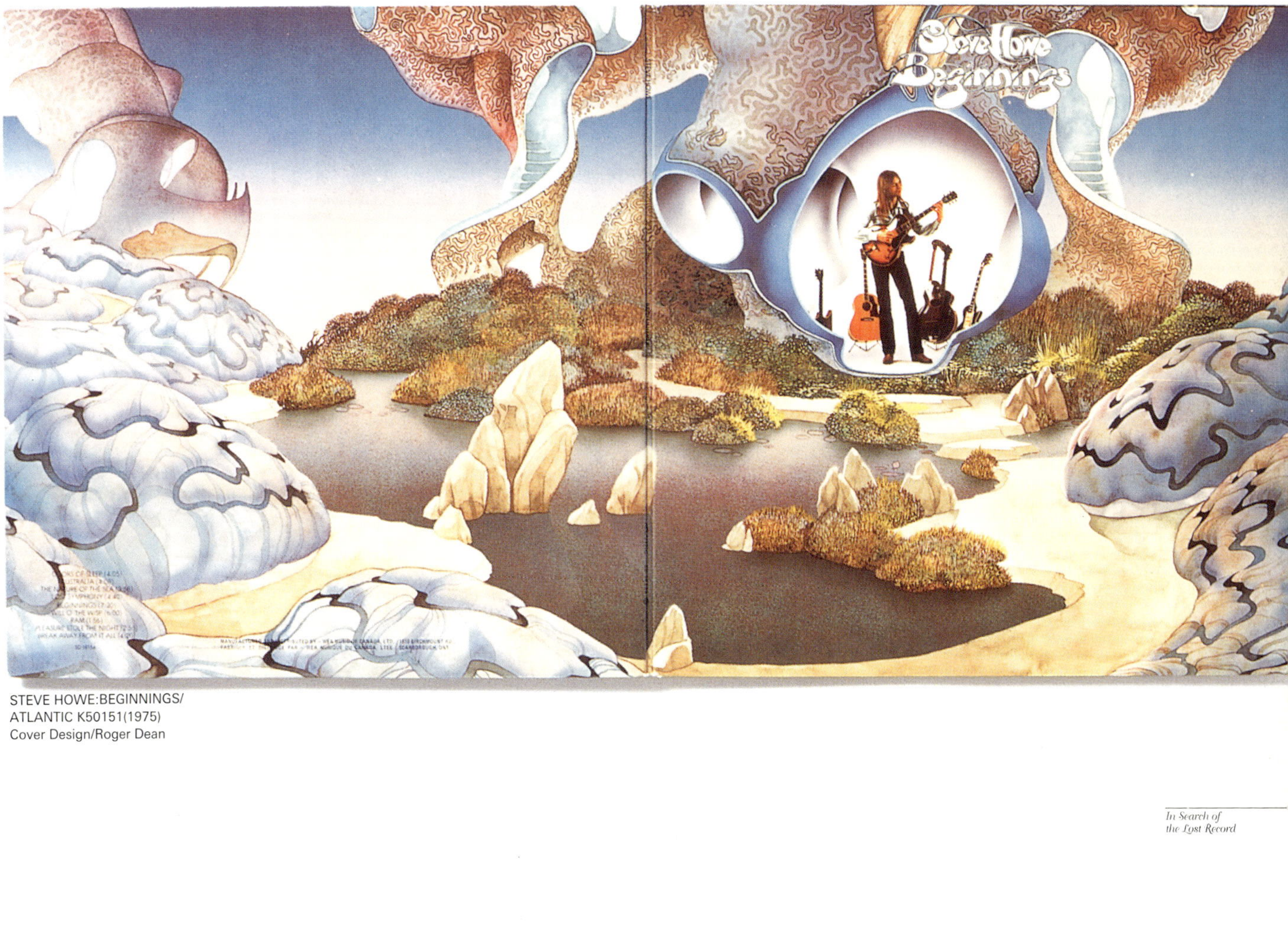

STEVE HOWE:BEGINNINGS/
ATLANTIC K50151(1975)
Cover Design/Roger Dean

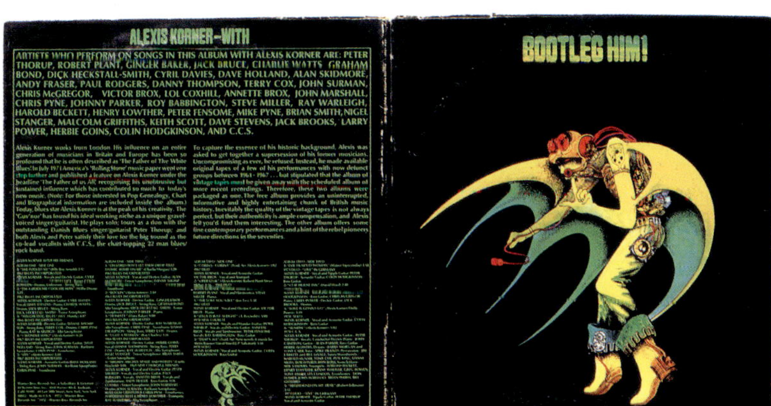

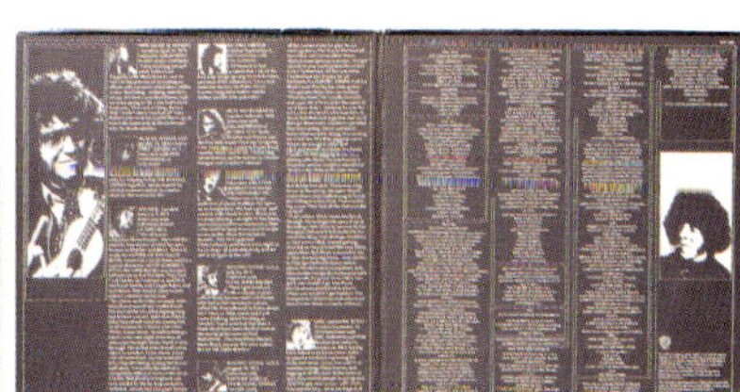

ALEXIS KORNER:BOOTLEG HIM!/
RAK SPAKSP51(1972) *front and back
Album Design:Roger Dean

ALEXIS KORNER:BOOTLEG HIM!/ RAK SPAKSP51(1972) *inner

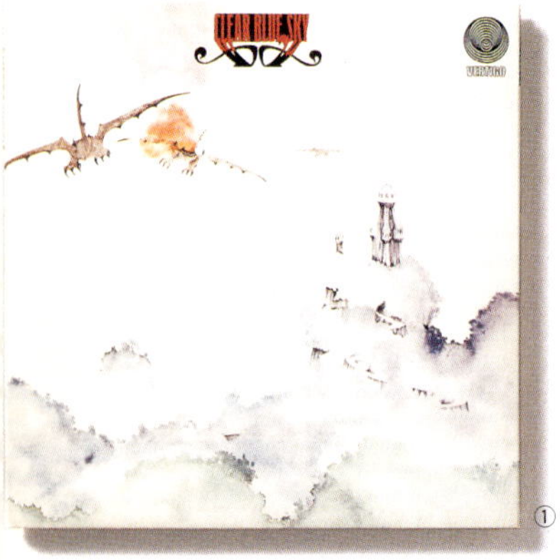

①

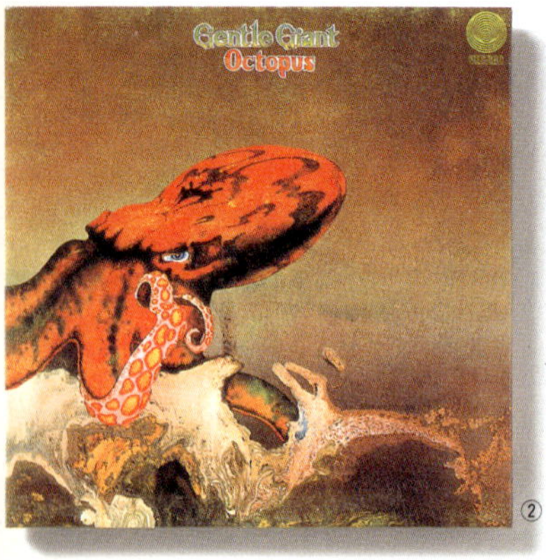

②

① CLEAR BLUE SKY:CLEAR BLUE SKY/
VERTIGO 6360 013(1971)
Designed and Drawn by Roger Dean

② GENTLE GIANT:OCTOPUS/VERTIGO 6360 080(1972)
Cover Painting/Roger Dean

③ GRAHAM COLLIER MUSIC:MOSAICS/
PHILIPS 6308051(1970)
Design/Roger Dean
Photography/Peter Sinclair and Roger Dean

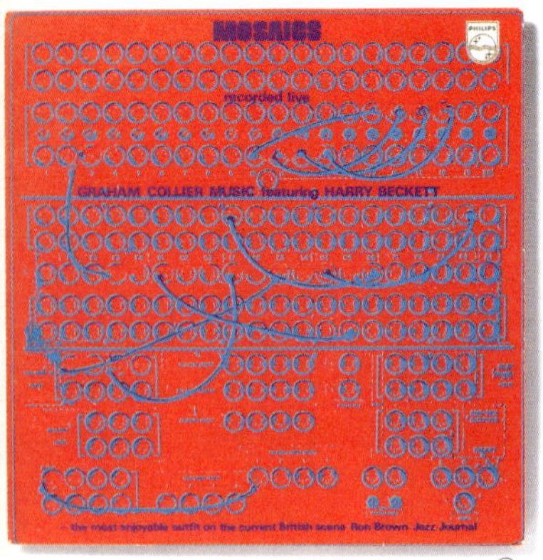

③

④

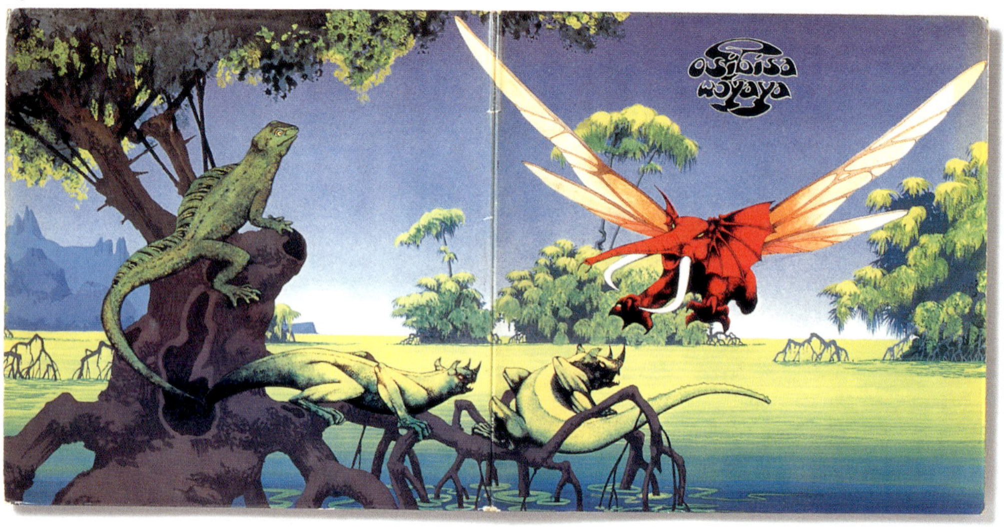

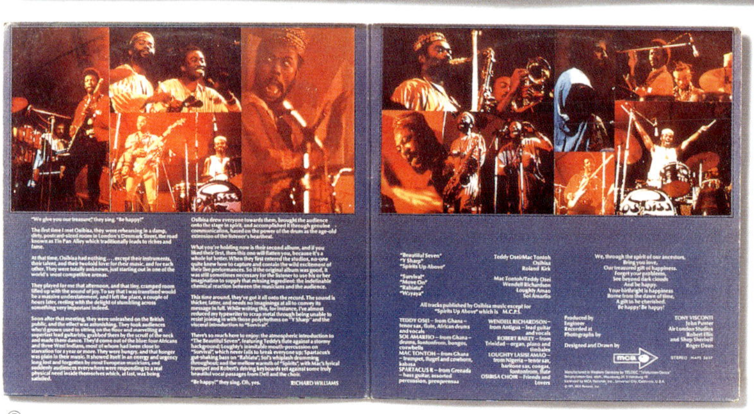

⑤

④ OSIBISA:WOYAYA/
MCA MDKS8005(1971) *front and back
Photographs by Robert Ellis and Shep Sherbell
Design & Drawn by Roger Dean

⑤ OSIBISA:WOYAYA/MCA MDKS8005(1971) *inner

where did we lose the way to do nothing?
somewhere in the childhood wood.
where has our soft-glow gone?

DONOVAN:H.M.S.DONOVAN
/DAWN DNLD4001(1971) *front and back
Art Direction by Sid Maurer
Cover Painting/Patrick

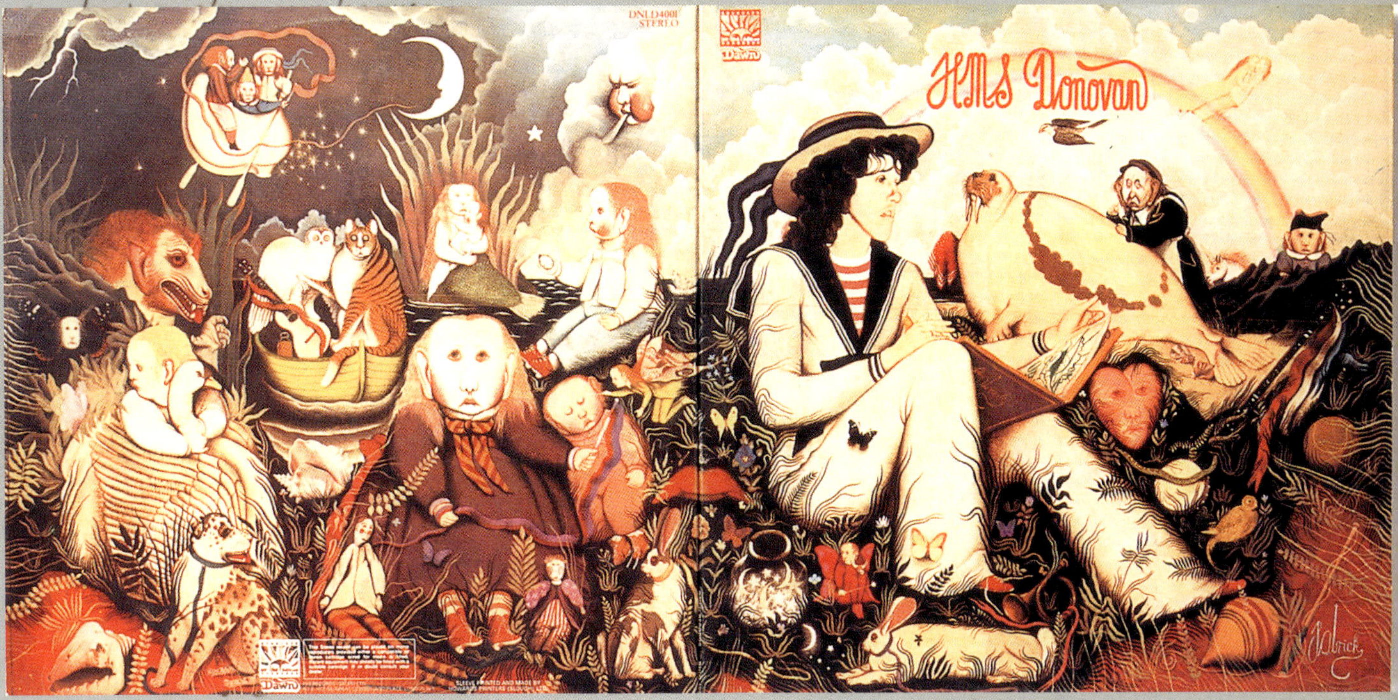

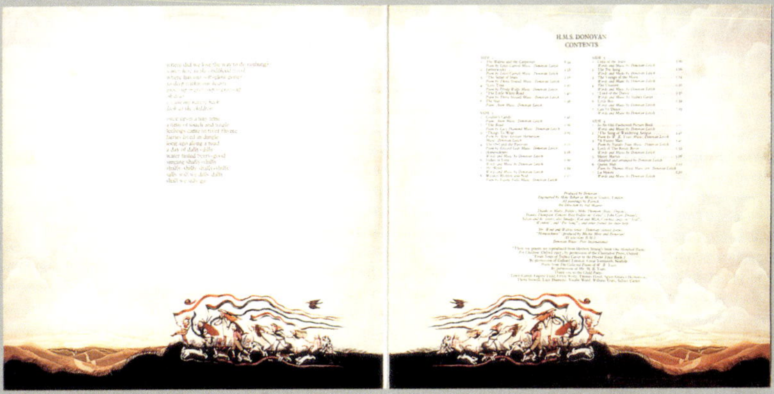

DONOVAN:H.M.S.DONOVAN/
DAWN DNLD4001(1971) *inner

illustrations

Patrick

パトリック

イギリスのファンタジーに通じる牧歌的な世界を、18世紀ヨーロッパの博物図をも想わせるような、画面の隅々まで丁寧に仕上げる細密なタッチと大胆な構図で描き出すパトリック。その音楽性との親和性からドノヴァン71年のアルバム『HMS　ドノヴァン』が傑作とされているが、ほかにも、ビートルズの編集盤『ビートルズ・バラード・ベスト20』（80年）や、イギリスの男性デュオ、スティーラーズ・ホイールの『ファーガスリー・パーク』（74年）、同じくイギリスのシンガー・ソングライター、ジェリー・ラファティの『シティ・トゥ・シティ』（78年）、『ナイト・アウル』（80年）などが有名だ。

Patrick's fine touch, detailing every inch of the canvas, and daring compositions were reminiscent of an English pastoral scene or even an 18th century European illustration. The affinity of Patrick's style with musicality lead to the creation of the album cover masterpiece for Donovan's "HMS Donovan" (1971). Other popular works include The Beatles' compilation album, "Beatles Ballads Best 20" (1980), British male duo, Stealer's Wheel's "Ferguslie Park" (1974), and Stealer's Wheel's singer-songwriter Gerry Rafferty's "City To City" (1978) and "Night Owl" (1980).

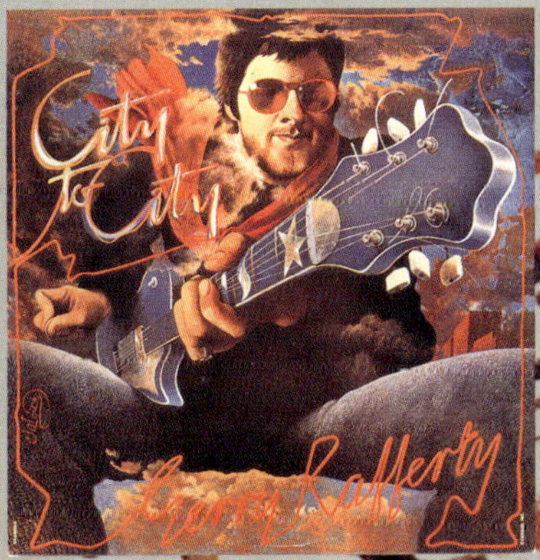

GERRY RAFFERTY:CITY TO CITY/
UNITED ARTISTS UAS30104(1978)
Cover Painted by John Patrick Byrne

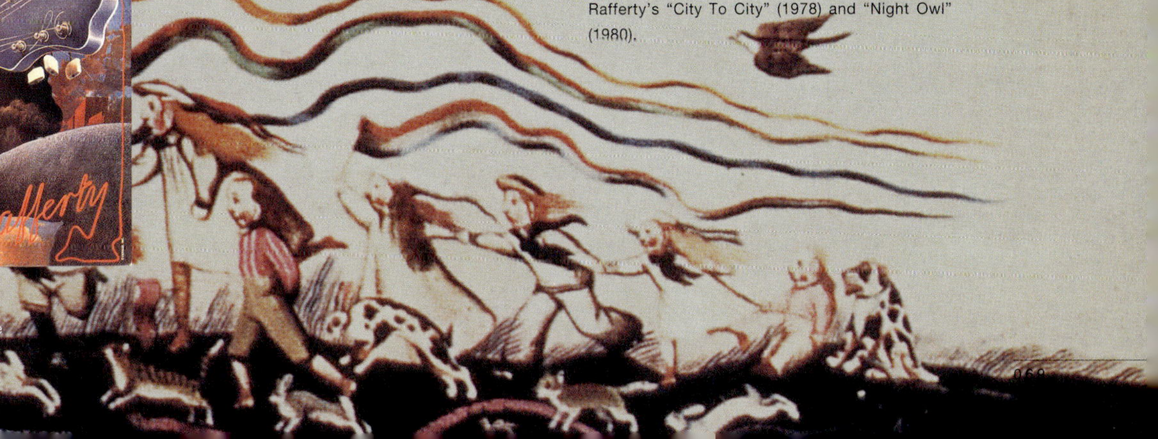

illustrations

Barry Godber

バリー・ゴッドバー

KING CRIMSON: IN THE COURT OF THE CRIMSON KING/
Island ILPS9111(1969) *front
Cover by Barry Godber

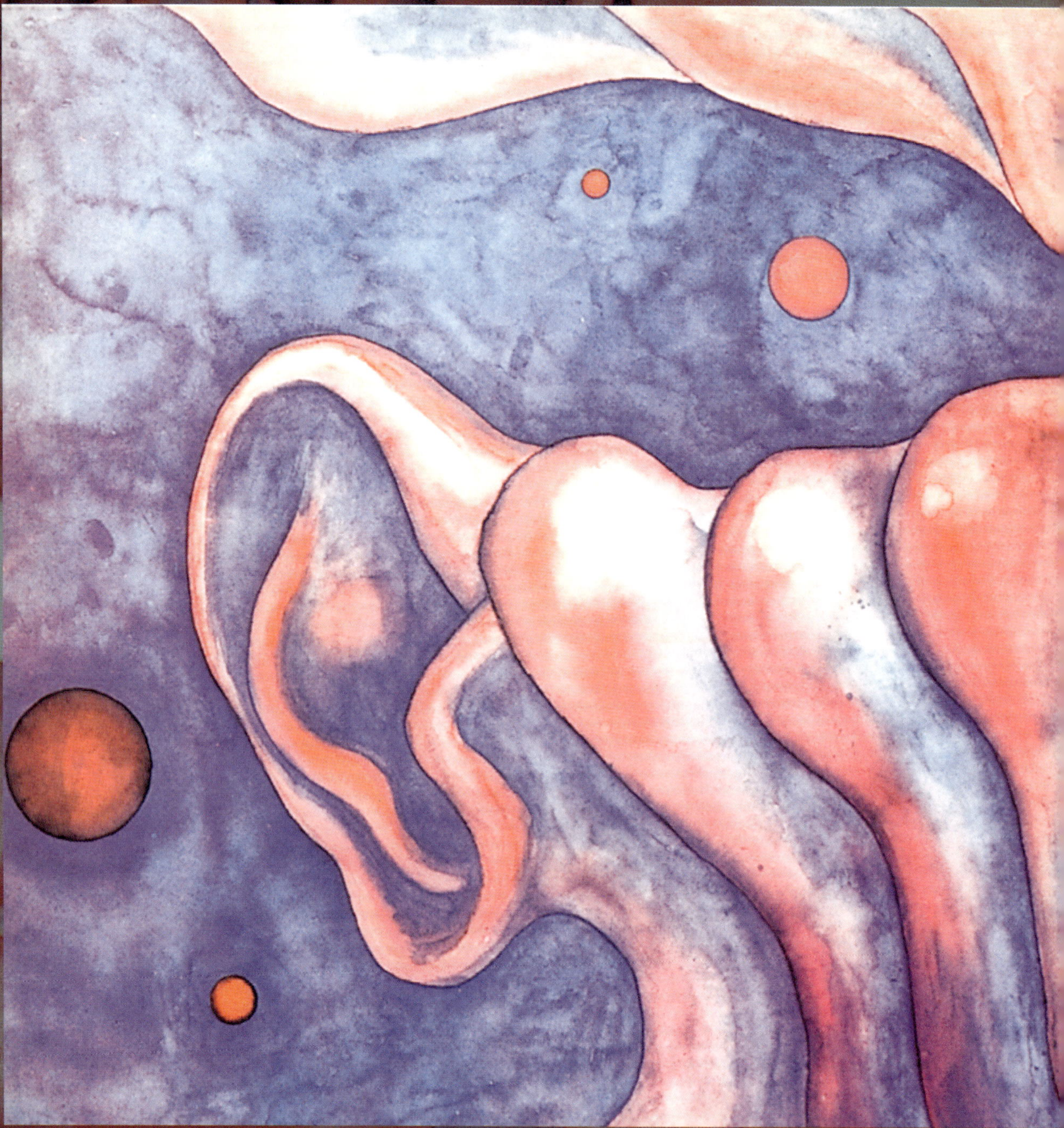

ポピュラー音楽史を語るうえで欠かすことのできないキング・クリムゾンのファースト・アルバムは、それと同時にジャケット・アートの重要性をも決定づける記念碑的な作品といえるだろう。恐怖と苦痛に歪む表ジャケットの表情と、その苦痛からの解脱を示す内ジャケットとの鮮やかな対比は、混沌としたサウンドを圧倒的な構成力でまとめあげながら、物質主義を痛烈に批判するクリムゾンのサウンドとぴったり呼応し、いまも具象的なメッセージを我々に向かって語り続けている。このイラストを描いたバリー・ゴッドバーは、もともとピート・シンフィールドがコンピューター会社で働いていたときの同僚で、当時はチェルシー・アート・スクールを卒業後、コンピューター・プログラマーをしながらアーティストとしての一歩を踏み出し始めたばかりだった。彼にジャケット・ワークの制作を依頼したのもシンフィールドで、制作に当たっては、あらかじめ録音を終えて間もないクリムゾンの曲を聴かせるなど、具体的なイメージを伝えたうえですすめられたという。見開き型のジャケット・サイズと文字位置を計算に入れながら緻密に構成されている点も、アルバムの総体的な完成度を高める結果となっている。しかし、ゴッドバーはこの作品を完成させた直後に24歳の若さで他界、彼の短い創作人生は、サイケデリックというはかない季節の終焉とともに終わりを告げる格好となった。オリジナルの水彩画は、いまもグループを率いて活動を続けるロバート・フリップが所有している。

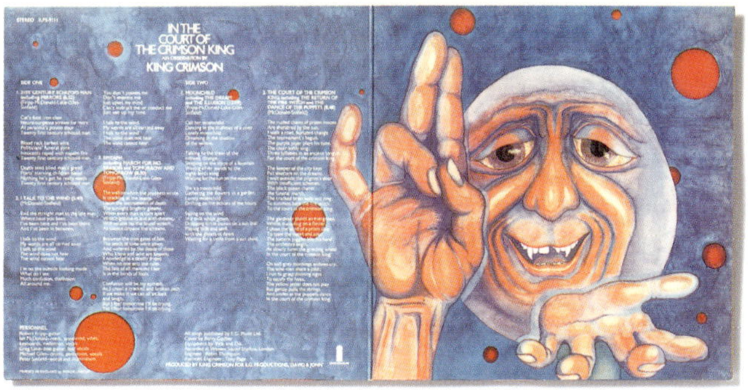

KING CRIMSON: IN THE COURT OF THE CRIMSON KING/
Island ILPS9111(1969)
*Inner

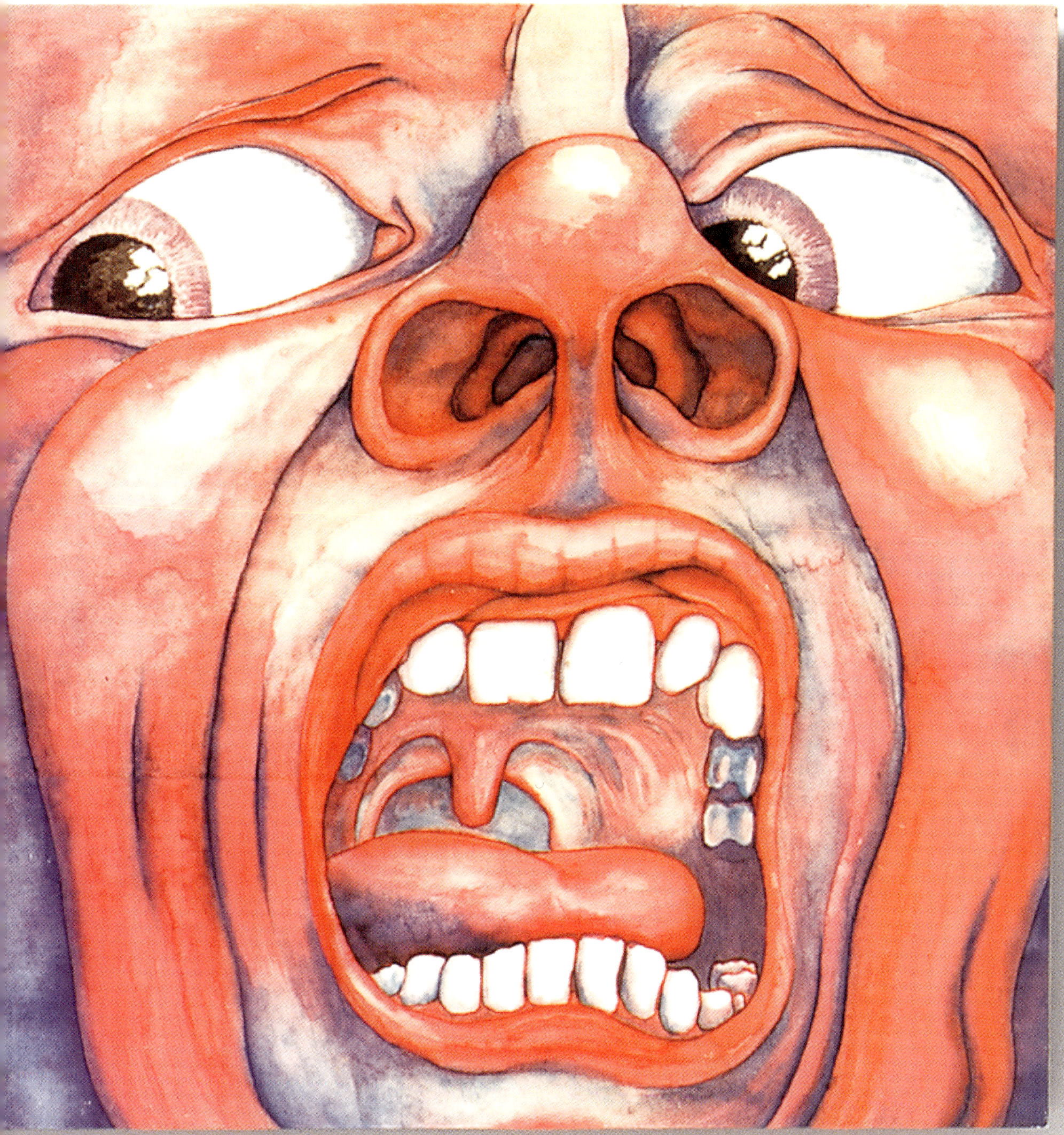

The first album by King Crimson was very important in the history of popular music. Similarly, the cover artwork for this famed album established for itself an important position in the world of album cover artwork. The sharp contrast between the front cover, an expression of fear and agony, and the inner jacket, an expression of release from pain, aptly represented King Crimson's sound, which resulted from an enormous talent of arranging and unifying a chaos of sounds while severely criticizing materialism. The artwork clearly spoke its concrete message. Barry Godber, the artist of this illustration, was originally Pete Sinfield's colleague at a computer firm. After graduating from the Chelsea Art School, Godber began his artistic career while working as a computer programmer. Sinfield approached Godber to contribute work for King Crimson's first album. Sinfield had presented Godber with a tape of the newly recorded material so that Godber will be well acquainted with the sound. The form of a gatefold cover and the meticulous positioning of the type were also salient points enhancing the overall quality of the package. Unfortunately, Godber passed away at the young age of twenty-four, right after the completion of this work. His short creative life seemed to echo with the transient season of psychedelia. The original watercolor painting of this album cover is owned by Robert Fripp, who presently still leads King Crimson.

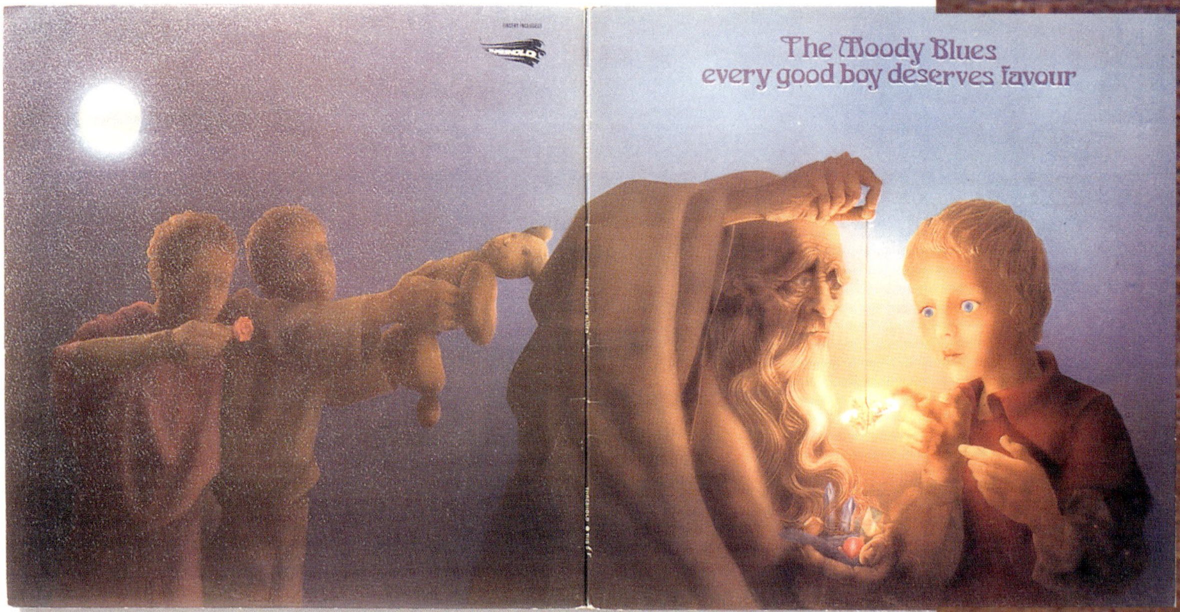

THE MOODY BLUES:EVERY GOOD BOY DESERVES FAVOUR/
THRESHOLD THS5(1971) *front and cover
Sleeve Artist/Phil Travers

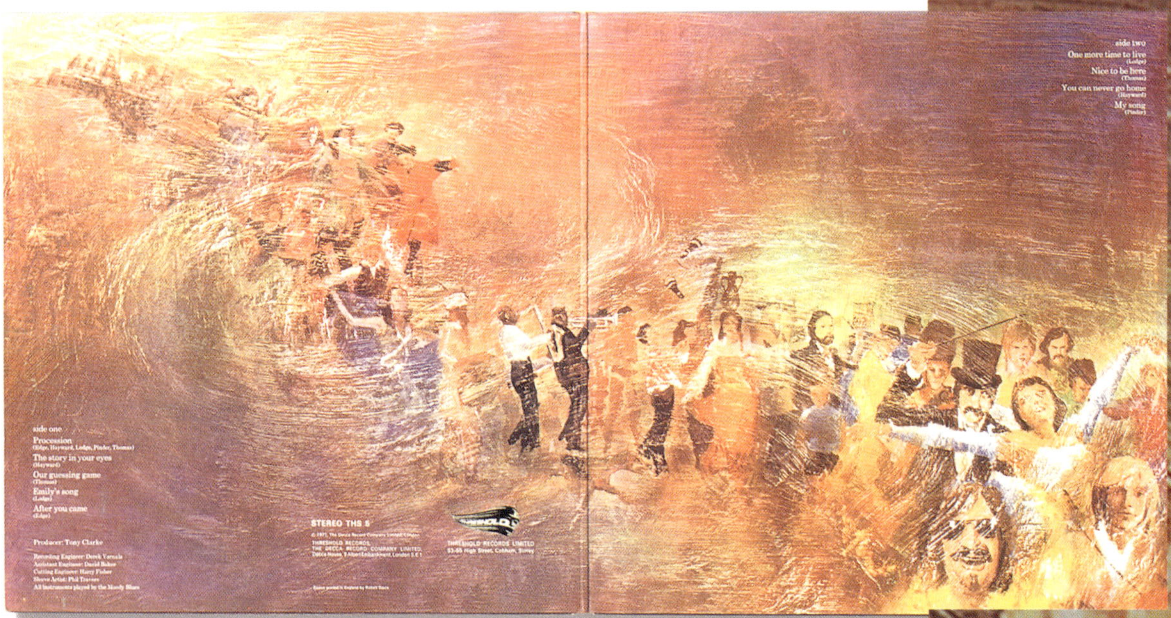

THE MOODY BLUES:EVERY GOOD BOY DESERVES FAVOUR/
THRESHOLD THS5(1971) *inner

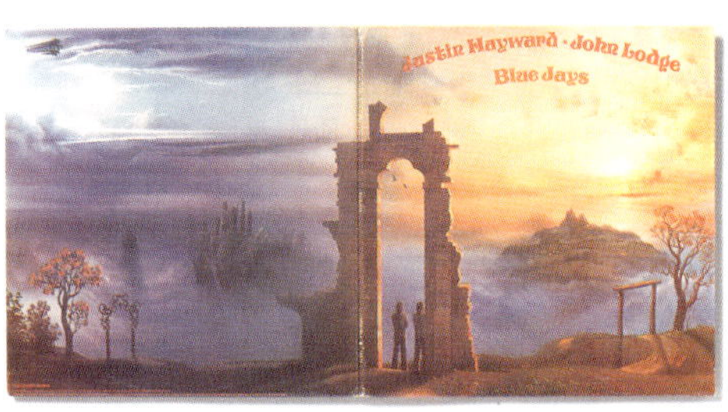

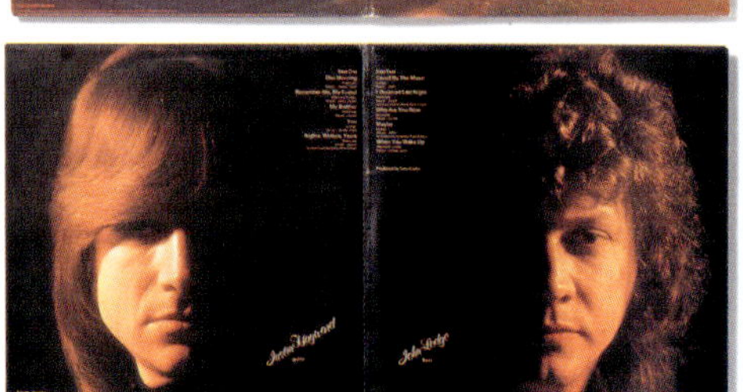

JUSTIN HAYWARD,JOHN LODGE:BLUEJAYS/
THRESHOLD THS12(1975) *front and back
Illustration and Design/Phil Travers

JUSTIN HAYWARD,JOHN LODGE:BLUEJAYS/
THRESHOLD THS12(1975) *inner

illustrations

Phil Travers
フィル・トラヴァーズ

アルバム・カヴァー・イラストにおけるフィル・トラヴァーズの仕事は、そのほとんどがムーディー・ブルース関連にかぎられている。66年までのムーディー・ブルースはR&Bを主体とするビート・バンドだったが、67年の『デイズ・オブ・フューチャー・パスト』を境にトータル・コンセプトを重視するプログレッシヴなグループへと転身する。続く『失われたコードを求めて(IN SEARCH OF THE LOST CHORD)』から72年の『セヴンス・ソジャーン』の計6作に起用されたトラヴァーズのイラストは、そんな彼らの壮大で幻想味あふれるサウンドを、視覚的に捕捉したという意味で、サウンドと同等の象徴性をそなえていた。初期ジェネシスやルネッサンスにおけるポール・ホワイトヘッド、英国ブルースの重鎮イアン・A・アンダーソンが設立したヴィレッジ・シング・レーベルにおけるロッド・マシューズの仕事にも、ちょうどそれと同じような影響力があった。

illustrations

Paul Whitehead

ポール・ホワイトヘッド

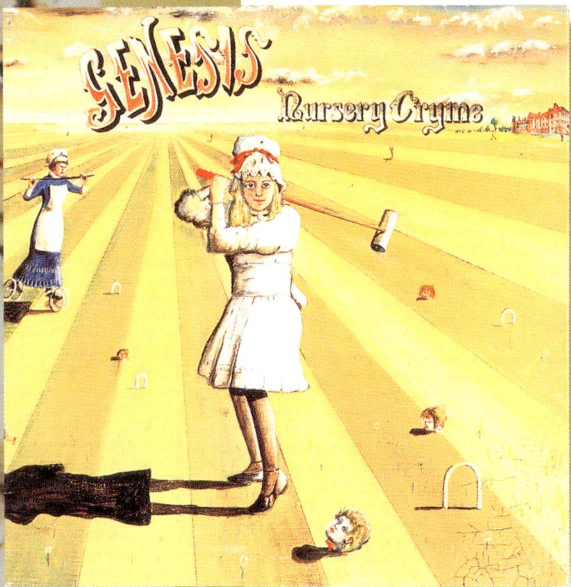

GENESIS:NURSERY CRYME/
CHARISMA CAS1052(1971)
Sleeve Design/Paul Whitehead Inspired by "The Musical Box"

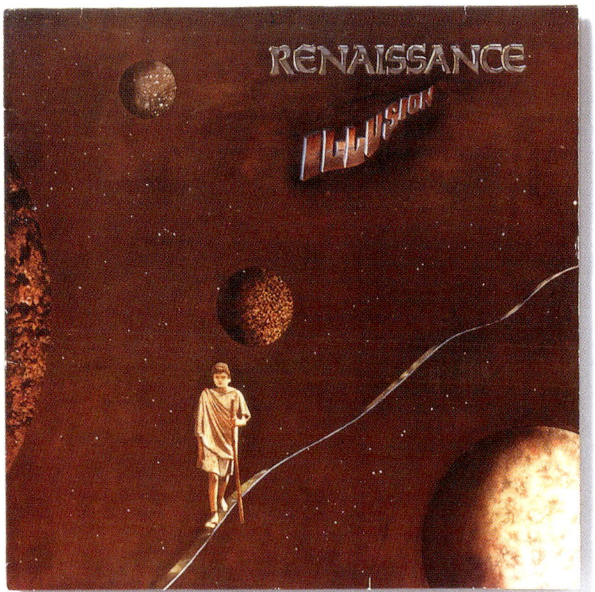

RENAISSANCE:ILLUSION/
ISLAND HELP27(1971)
Sleeve Design/Paul Whitehead

illustrations

Rod Matthews

ロッド・マシューズ

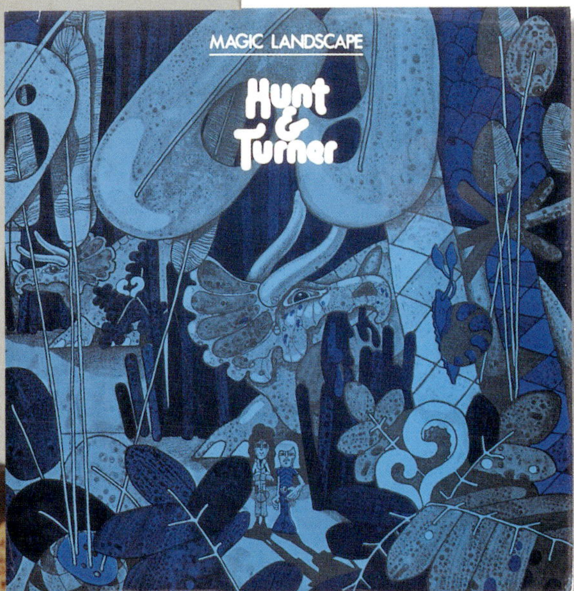

HUNT&TURNER:MAGIC LANDSCAPE/
THE VILLAGE THING VTS11(1972)
Sleeve/Rod Matthews

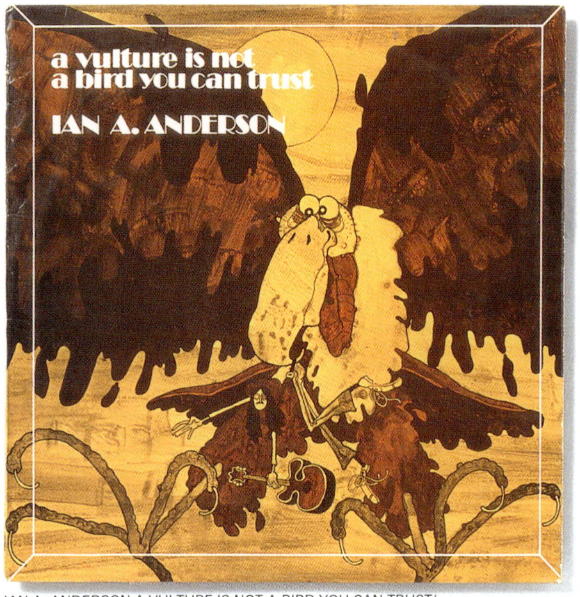

IAN A. ANDERSON:A VULTURE IS NOT A BIRD YOU CAN TRUST/
THE VILLAGE THING VTS9(1971)
Sleeve/Rod Matthews

Phil Travers's album covers illustrations were done mainly for The Moody Blues. Up until 1966, The Moody Blues was a "beat band", playing R&B standards. With "Days of Future Past" (1967), the band became an overnight success as a progressive group with a focused concept. From the succeeding "In Search of the Lost Chord" and through to "Seventh Sojourn"(1972), Travers illustrated six of the band's album sleeves. His artwork was indeed a visual complement to the magnificent sound of the band, sharing equal significance with the music. Other sleeve artists exerted the same kind of influence over music: Paul Whitehead for early Genesis and Renaissance and Rod Matthews for the Village Sing Label (launched by the British Blues magnate Ian A. Anderson).

後年、絵本作家としての地位を確立するデヴィッド・アンスティーは、ムーディー・ブルース『デイズ・オブ・フューチャー・パスト』(67年)から『ザ・ロッキー・ホラー・ショー』(73年)まで幅広いタッチの作品を残しているが、本書で積極的に取り上げるとすれば、なんといっても70年代初頭のデッカ/デラムで手がけた作品群。装飾写本の戯画や伝承童話の挿し絵を想わせる可愛らしくもグロテスクなイラストは、構図も配色もまさにアナログ・ジャケットのために用意されたとしかいいようのない絶妙さだ。マイケル・ファレルはイラストも手がけるが、デザイナーとしての仕事も多く、ニュークリアス『スネイク・ヒップス・エトセトラ』はその両方に彼の名がクレジットされた作品。

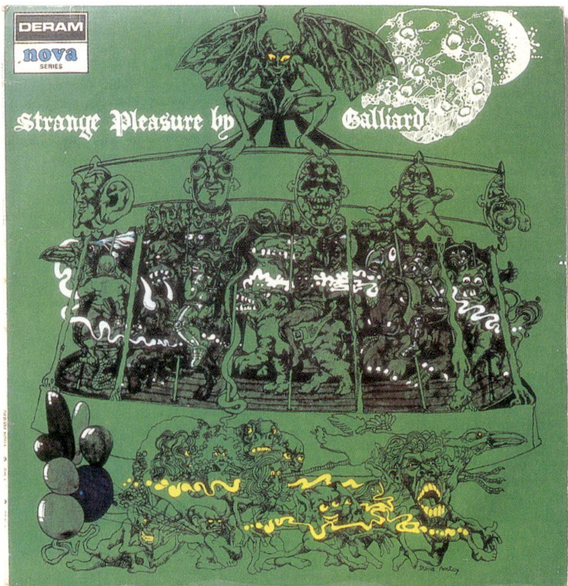

GALLIARD:STRANGE PLEASURE/
DERAM nova SDN4(1970)
Cover Painting/David Anstey

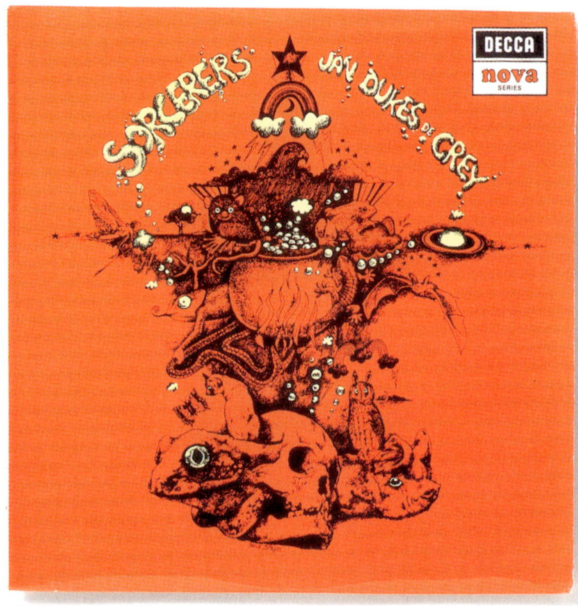

JAN DUKES DE GREY:SORCERERS/
DECCA nova SDN8(1970)
Cover Painting by David Anstey

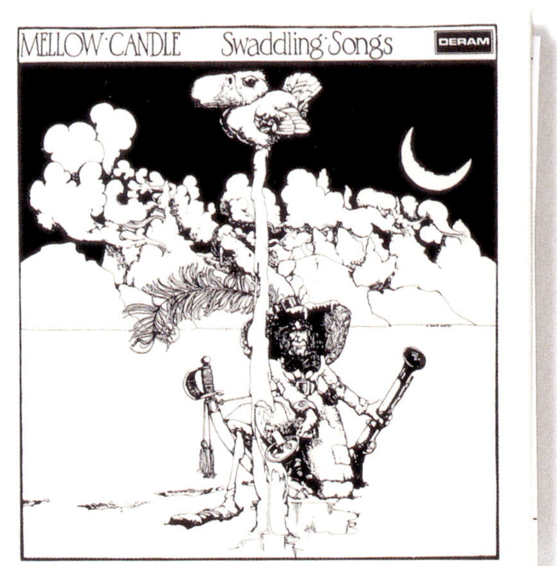

MELLOW CANDLE:SWANDING SONGS/
DERAM SDL7(1972)
Cover Painting/David Anstey

David Anstey illustrations
デヴィッド・アンスティー

David Anstey, who later became an established picture book artist, also created a variety of album sleeves, such as "Days of Future Past" (1967) and "The Rocky Horror show"(1973). In this book, however, we need to focus on the body of work done in the early 70's with Decca/Deram records. These illustrations, with their cute but strangely grotesque illustration reminiscent of decorative books or illustrated folk tales, were best suited to the analog LPs in terms of both composition and color scheme.

Michael Farrell (page 75) also did illustration, but he had a very successful career as a designer. "Snake Hip Et Cetera" by Nucleus credited him both as illustrator and designer.

illustration

Michael Farrell

マイケル・ファレル

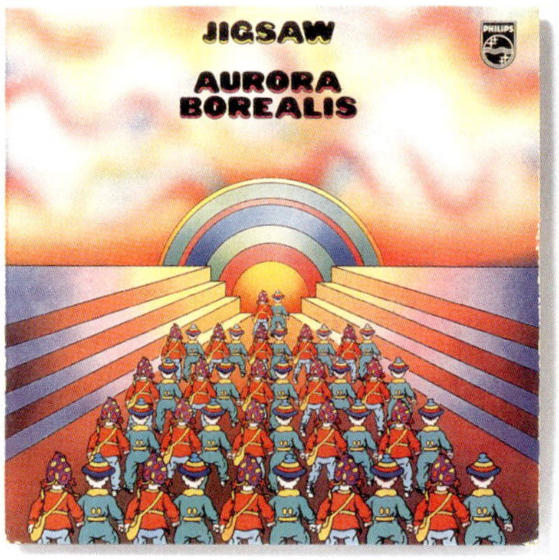

JIGSAW:AURORA BOREALIS/
PHILIPS 6308 072(1972)
Sleeve Design by Michael Farrell

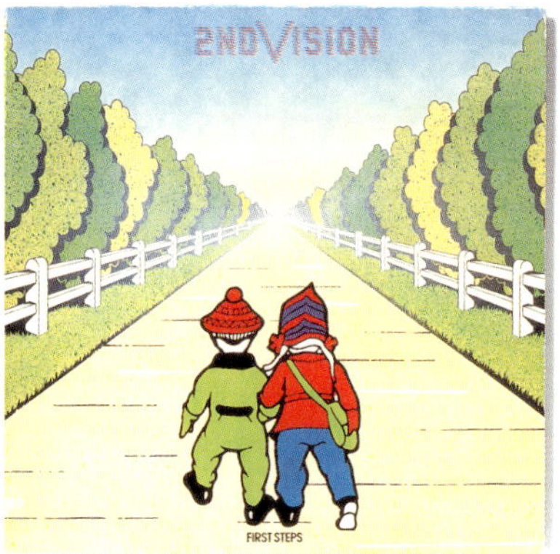

2ND VISION:FIRST STEPS/
CHRYSALIS CHR1289(1980)
Art Direction Peter Wagg
Front Cover Illustration Courtesy of Start-Rite Shoes Ltd

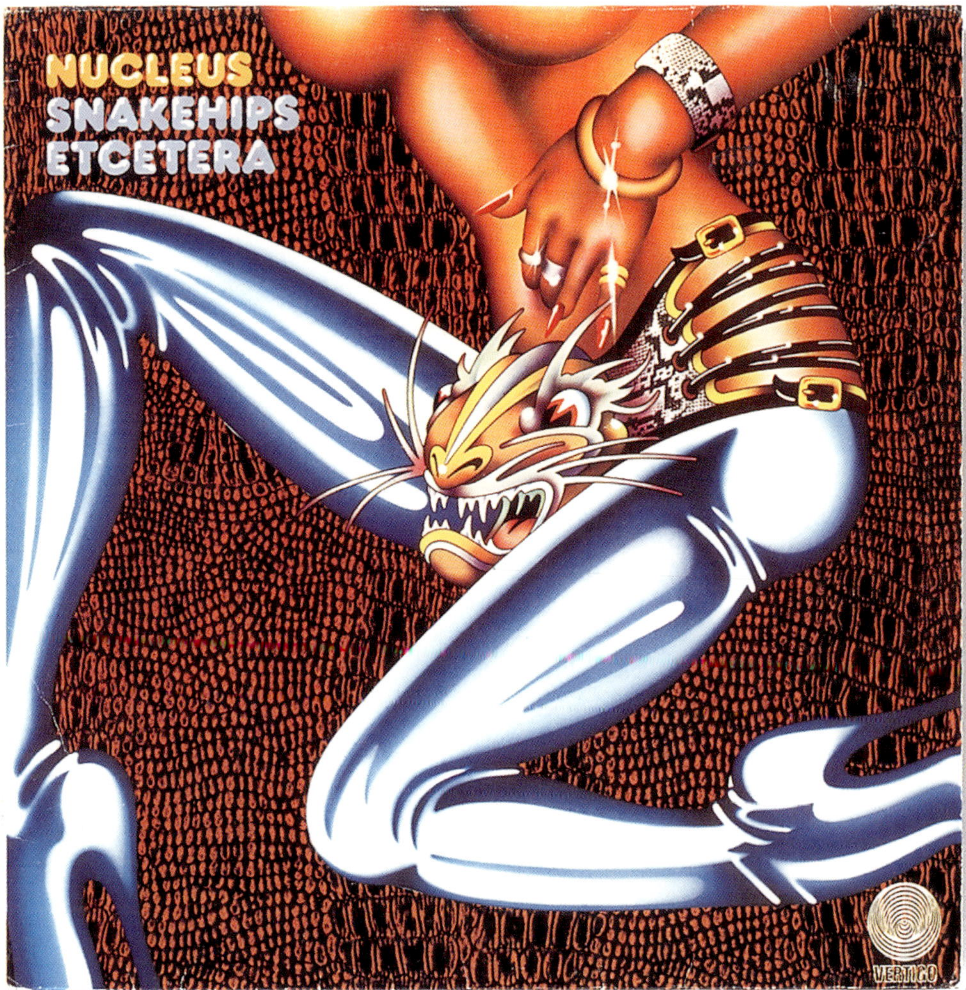

NUCLEUS:SNAKEHIPS ETCETERA/
VERTIGO 6360 119(1975)
Sleeve Design/Illustration by Michael Farrell

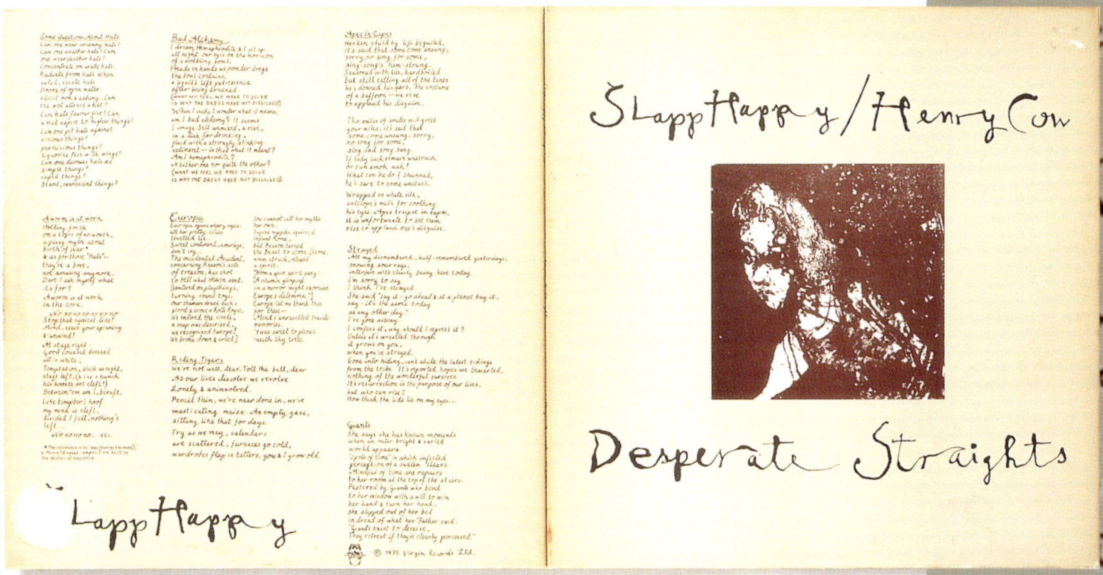

SLAPP HAPPY/HENRY COW:DESPERATE STRAIGHTS/
VIRGIN V2024(1975) *front and back
Cover&Lithograph by Peter Blegvad

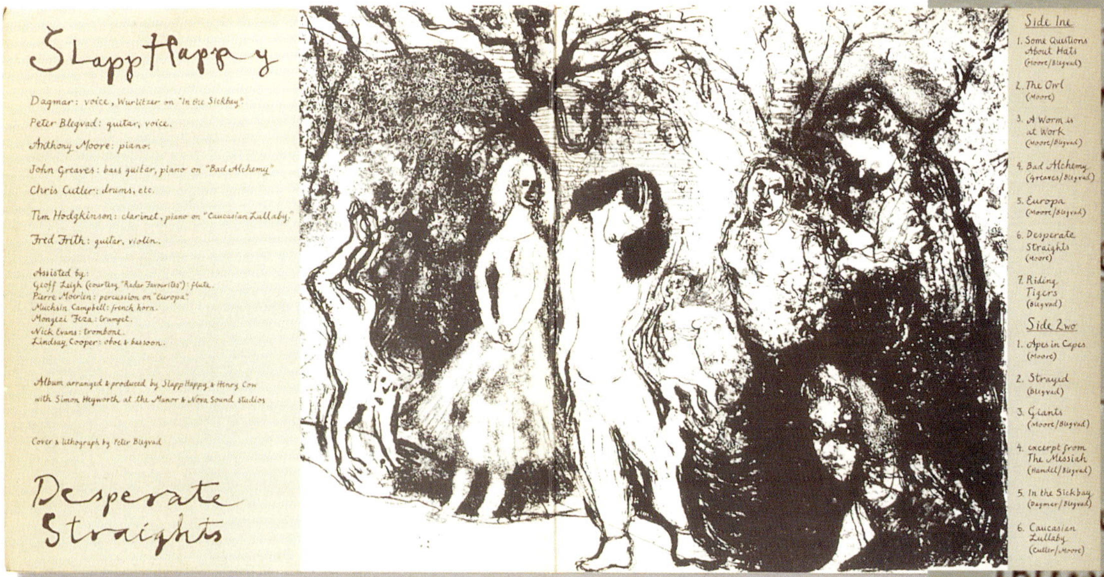

SLAPP HAPPY/HENRY COW:DESPERATE STRAIGHTS/
VIRGIN V2024(1975) *inner

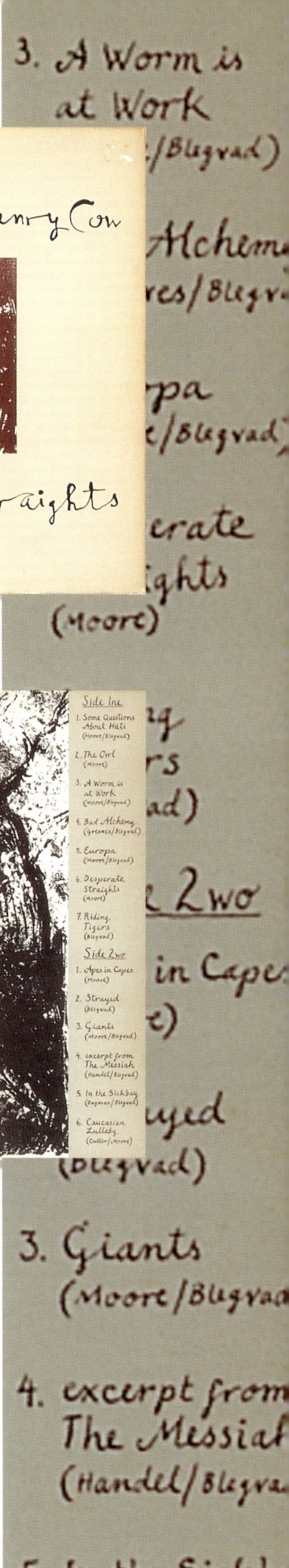

In Search of the Lost Record

Peter Blegvad illustration
ピーター・ブレグヴァド

ピーター・ブレグヴァドはもちろん鬼才ポップ集団スラップ・ハッピーのメンバーとして活躍する人物だが、そのマルチ・アーティストぶりは画業でも発揮され、英インディペンデント紙に寄稿しているマンガの連載も、すでに丸7年を数えている。どこかつかみどころのない変幻自在なスタイルが黒い底光りをみせているところは、スラップ・ハッピーやソロにおける彼の音楽性とも通じる。

ダニエル・ダックスも、80年代以降、ミュージシャン兼ヴィジュアル・アーティストとして多方面に活躍するひとり。彼女自身のソロ・アルバムでは、イングランド出身のインスタレーション作家ホリー・ワーバートンを起用し続けている。一方、キム・プーアの名は、ロック・ファンには元ジェネシスのギタリスト、スティーヴ・ハケットの奥方として有名だが、現代美術の愛好家には世界的な画家として広くその名が知られている。ブラジルに生まれ、ニューヨークでデザインを学び、晩年のダリとも親交を結んだ彼女の作風は、そのダリから"ダイアファニズム(「捉えどころのない;霊妙な」あるいは「女性避妊具」を意味するダイアファナスに由来する造語)"と評された。

A member of the wunderkind Pop group Slap Happy, Peter Blegvad was also active as an ingenious visual artist. The serial comic strip he created for The Independent will soon be in its eigth year. His lines and shapes escaped definition and pigeonholing. They exuded a black humor that was common to Slap Happy's music and his solo music. Daniel Dax was also a multi-talented; she was a musician and visual artist active from the 80's. For her own solo albums, Holly Warburton,

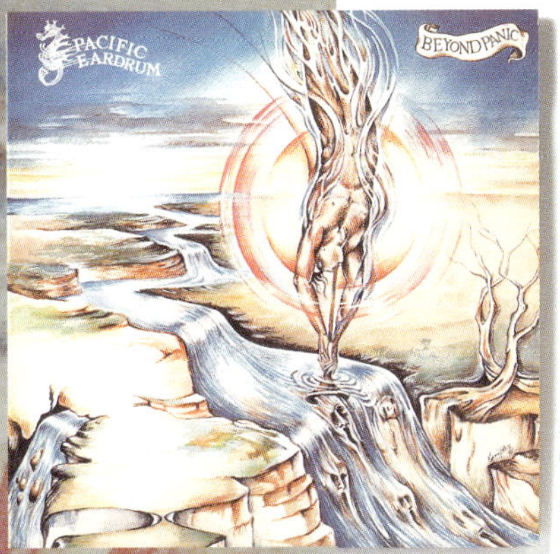

PACIFIC EARDRUM:BEYOND PANIC/CHARISMA (1978)
Front Cover Design by Kim Poor

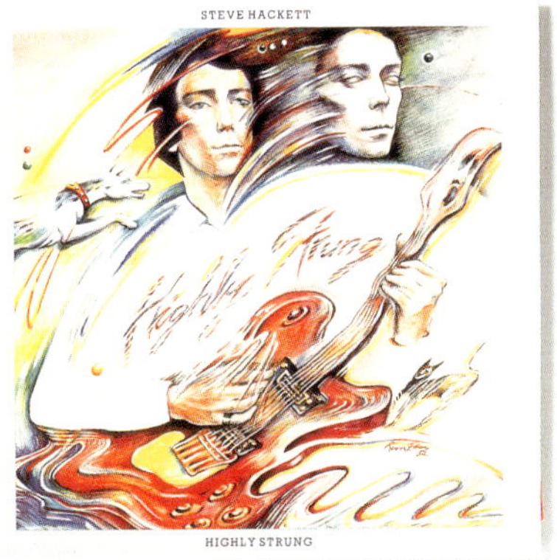

STEVE HACKETT:HIGHLY STRUNG/
CHARISMA CHC40(1983)
Front&Back Painting by Kim Poor

illustrations *Kim Poor*

キム・プーア

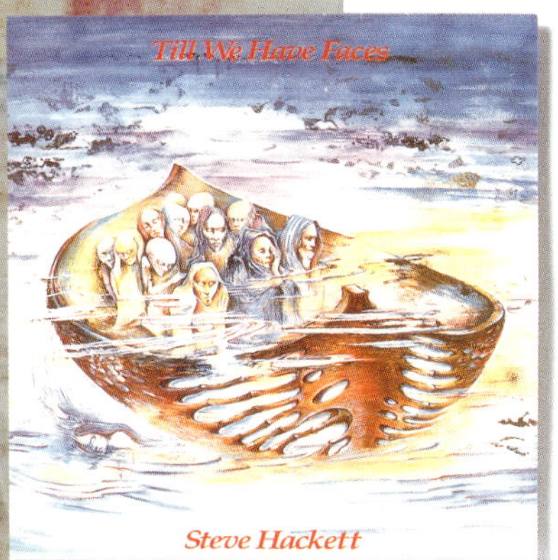

STEVE HACKETT:TILL WE HAVE FACES/
START STL11(1987)
Cover Painting by Kim Poor

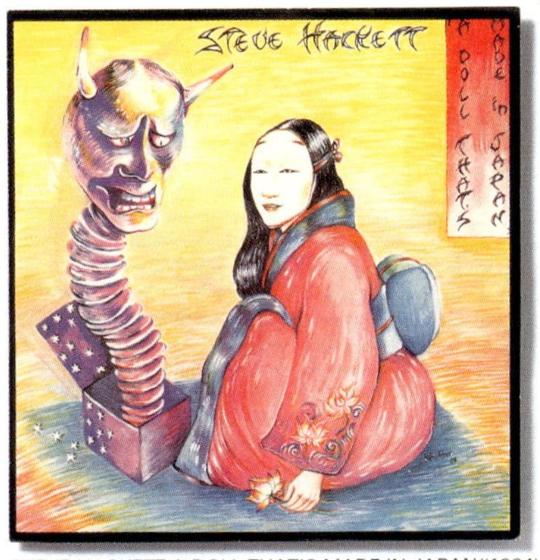

STEVE HACKETT:A DOLL THAT'S MADE IN JAPAN/(1984)
Front&Back Painting by Kim Poor

illustrations *Danielle Dax*

ダニエル・ダックス

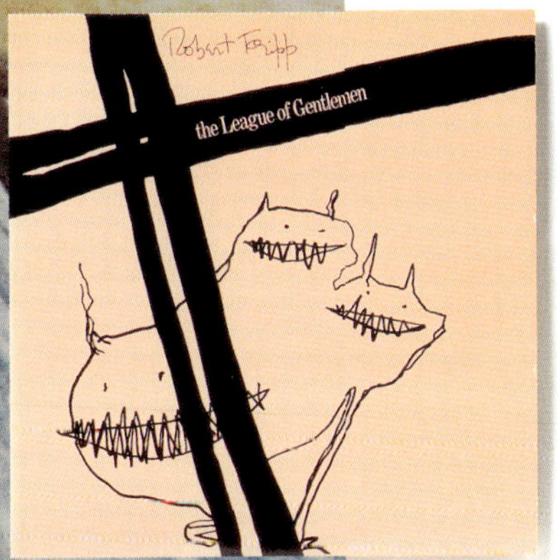

ROBERT FRIPP:THE LEAGUE OF GENTLEMEN/EG
EGED9(1981)
Cover/Danielle Dax

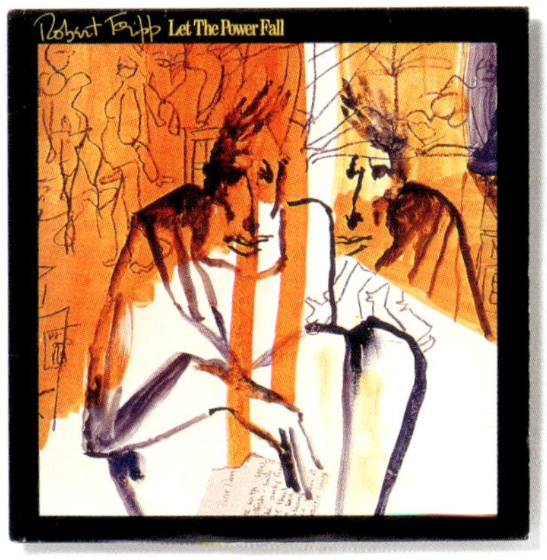

ROBERT FRIPP:LET THE POWER FALL/
EG EGED10(1981)
Cover/Danielle Dax

an installation artist from England, always served as sleeve designer. Kim Poor was known among rock fans as the wife of former Genesis guitarist Steve Hacket and as the artist of her husband's album sleeves. She now is an internationally reknowned artist. Born in Brazil, she studied design in New York and was a close friend of Salvador Dali, who, having an high opinion of her work, called it "diaphanous".

illustrations

The Other Selected Illustrations

その他のイラストレーション

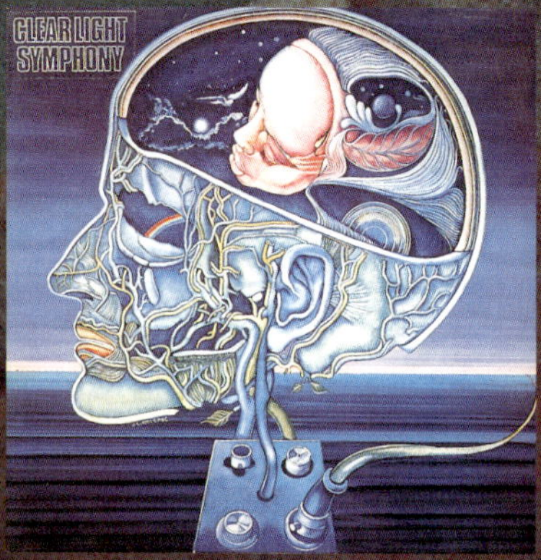

CLEARLIGHT SYMPHONY:CLEARLIGHT SYMPHONY/
VIRGIN V2029(1975)
Front Cover Painting by Jean Claude Michael
Courtesy of C.O.I.T.

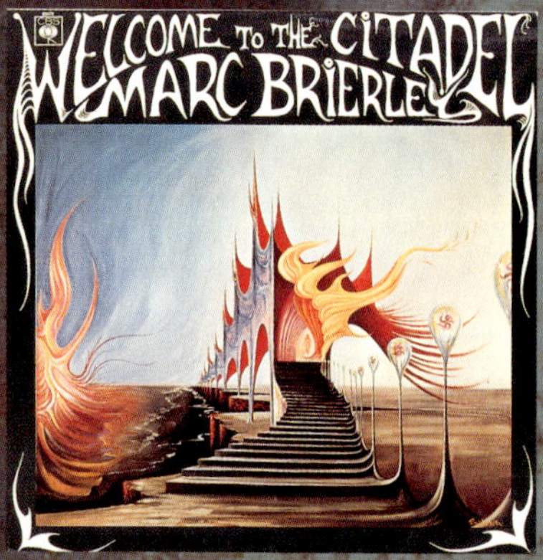

MARK BRIERLEY:WELCOME TO THE CITADEL/
CBS 63478(1968)
Cover Painting and Design/Ron Henderson

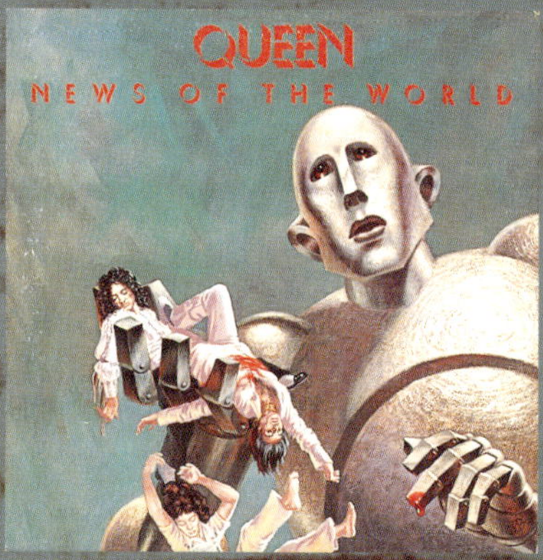

QUEEN:NEWS OF THE WORLD/EMI EMA784(1977)
Original Artwork by Frank Kelly Freas
Layout and Sleeve Co-ordination/Cream

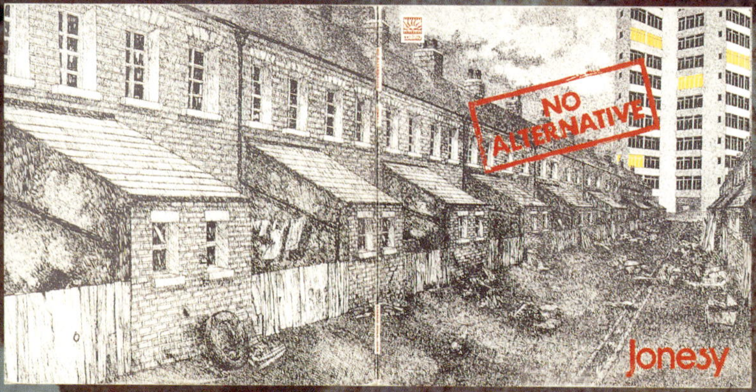

JONSEY:NO ALTERNATIVE/
DAWN DNLS3042(1972)
Cover Drawn by Allen of Allan Burrows Limited

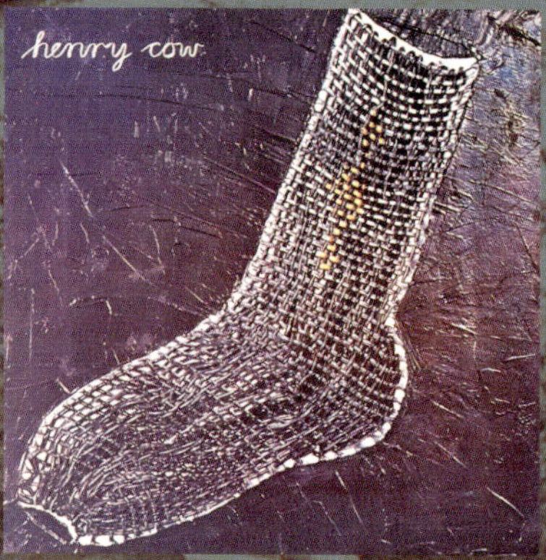

HENRY COW:UNREST/VIRGIN V2011(1974)
Cover Paintings and Inside Photograph by Ray Smith
Cover Paintings Photographed by Anne Lamberty

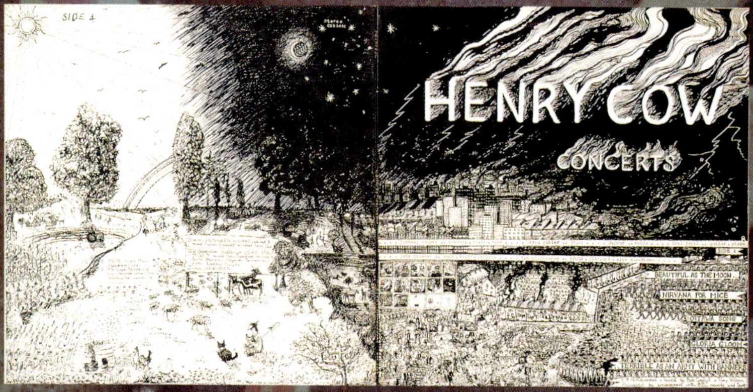

HENRY COW:CONCERTS/CAROLINE CAD3002(1975)

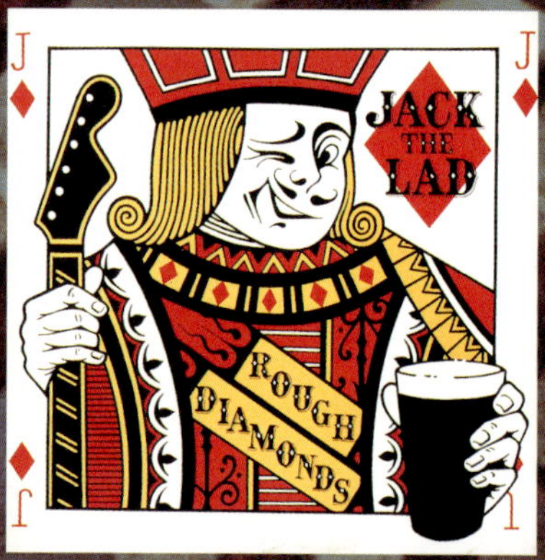

JACK THE LAD:ROUGH DIAMONDS/
CHARISMA CAS 1110(1975)
Sleeve Design/Chips and Jacka

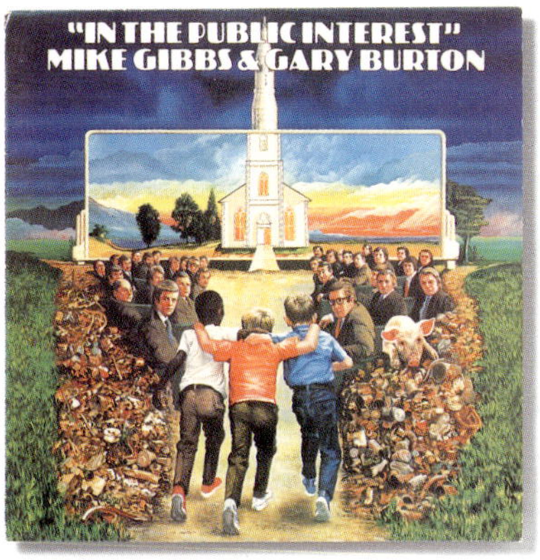

MIKE GIBBS&GARY BURTON/IN THE PUBLIC INTEREST/
POLYDOR 2383 252(1974)
Cover Design/Larry Learmonth
Art Direction/Ian Murray
Typography/John Constable

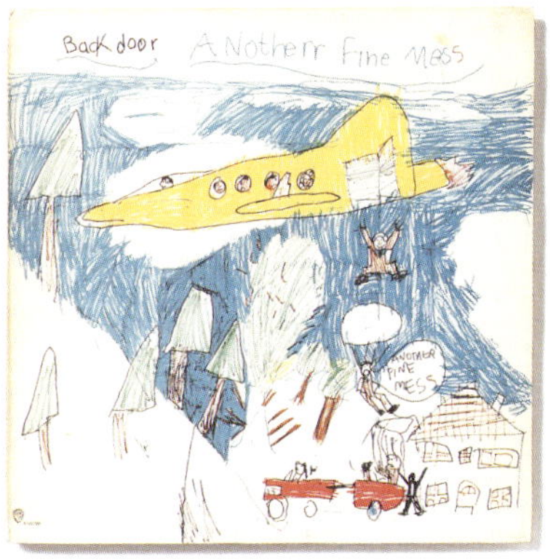

BACK DOOR:ANOTHER FINE MESS/
WARNER K56098(1975)
Sleeve Design/ Seabrook Graves Aslett
Illustrations/ Sam Learmouth

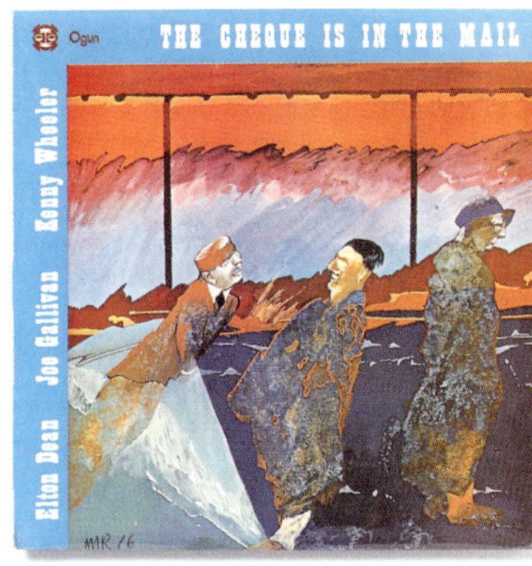

ELTON DEAN,JOE GALLIVAN,KENNY WHEELER:
THE CHEQUE IS IN THE MAIL/
OGUN OG610(1977)

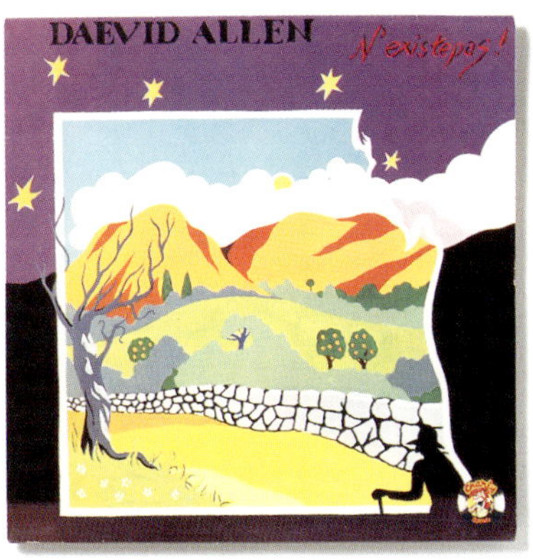

DAVID ALLEN:N'EXITE PAS!/CHARLY CRL5015(1979)

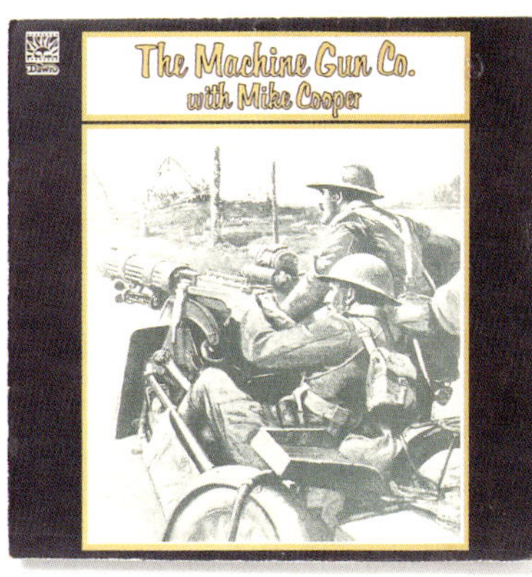

MIKE COOPER:THE MACHINE GUN CO./
DAWN DNLS3031(1972)

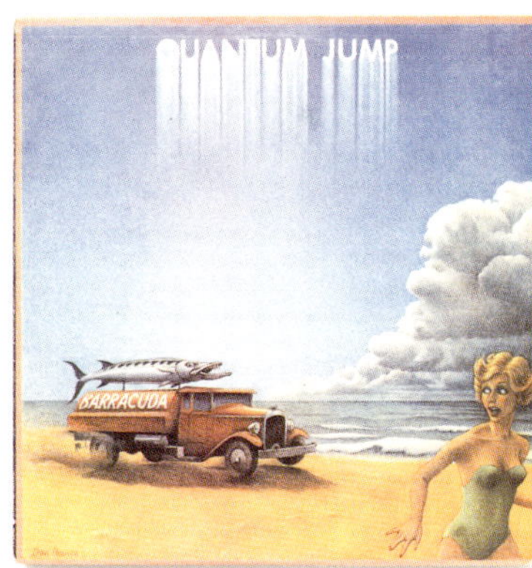

QUANTUM JUMP:BARRACDA/
ELECTRIC TRIX3(1977)
Illustration/Dan Pearce

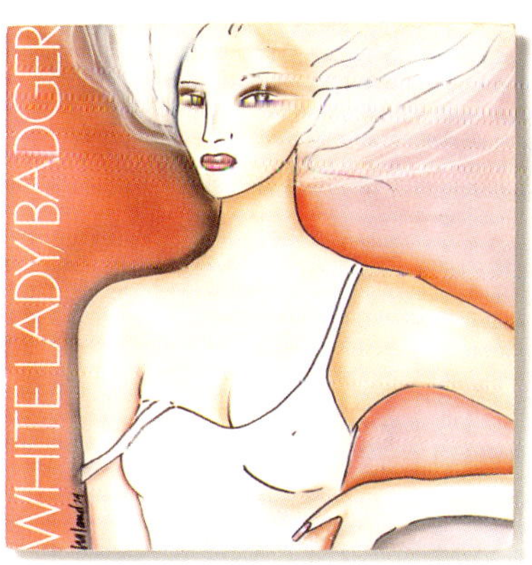

BADGER:WHITE LADY/EPIC EPC80009(1974)
Cover Art/David Croland
Design/John Berg

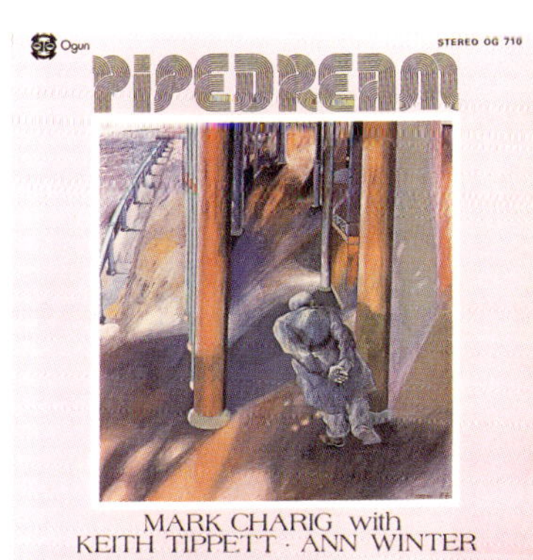

MARK CHARIG:PIPEDREAM/OGUN OG710(1977)
Front Cover Painting/Mick Rooney
Layout/Trish Rooney

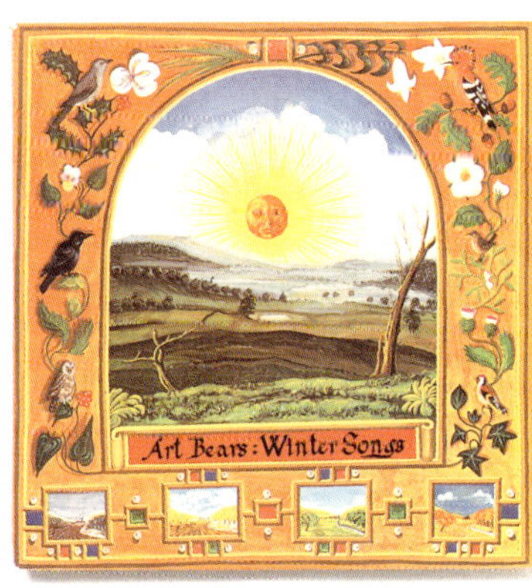

ART BEARS:WINTER SONG/RE 0618(1979)

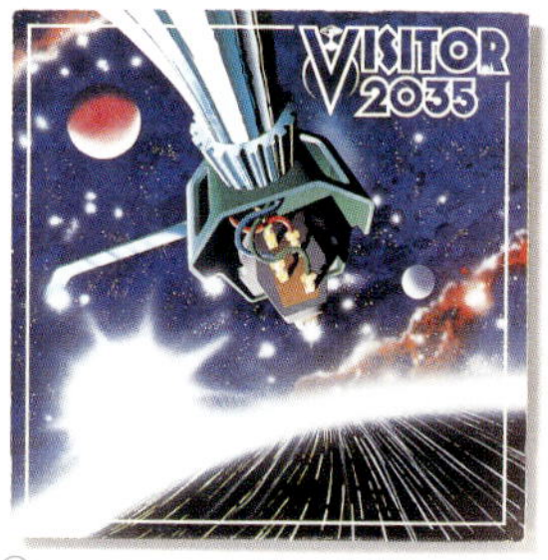

①

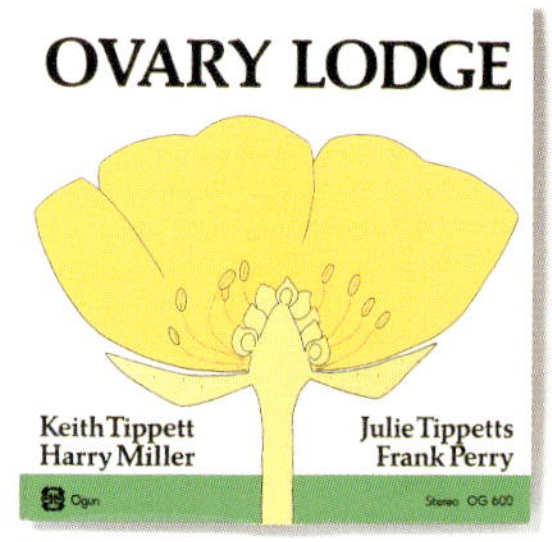

②

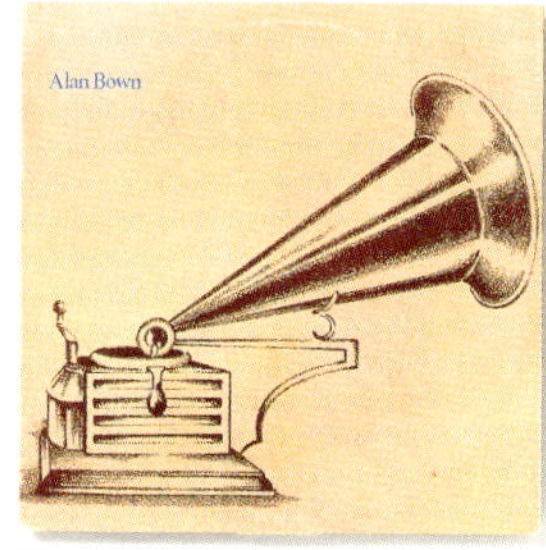

③

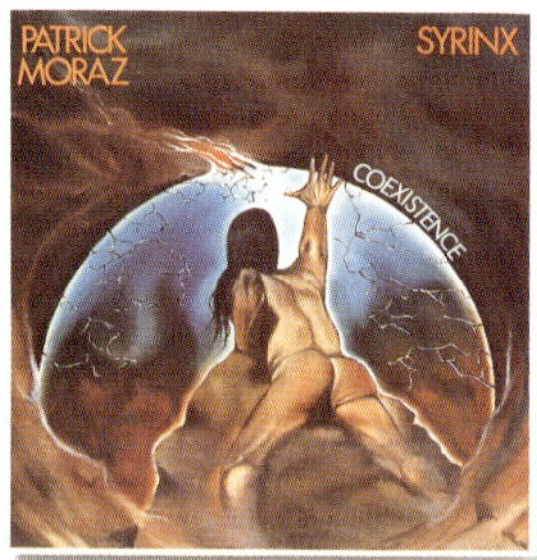

④

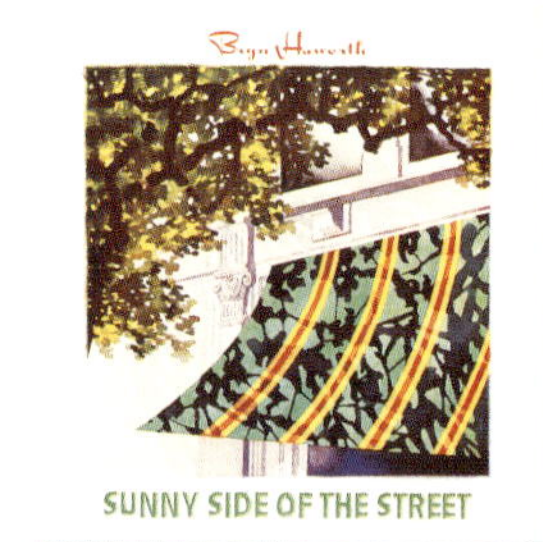

⑤

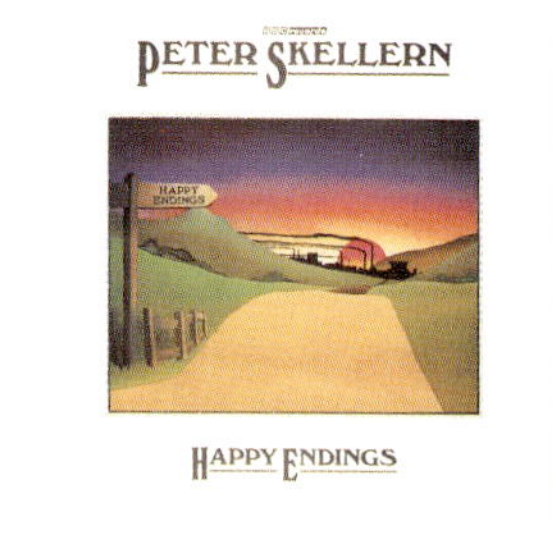

⑥

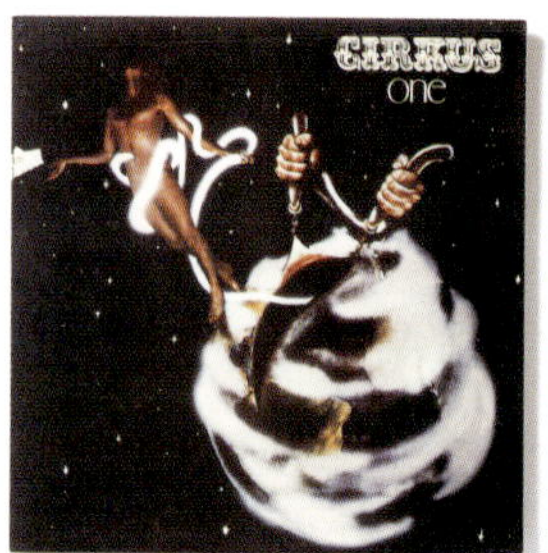

⑦

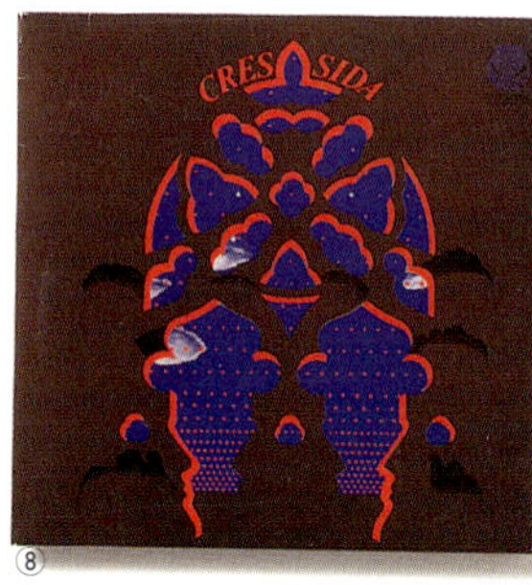

⑧

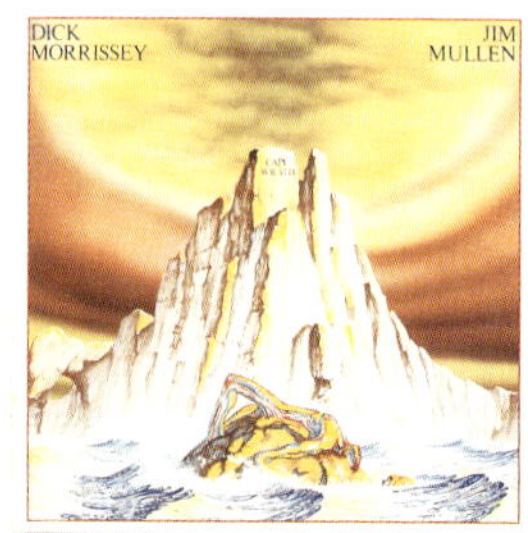

⑨

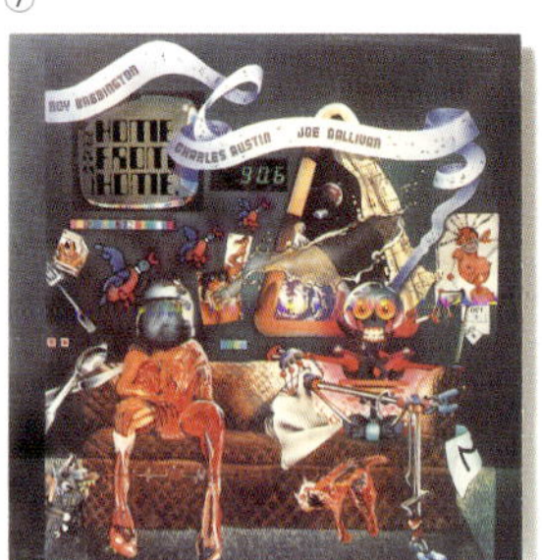
⑩

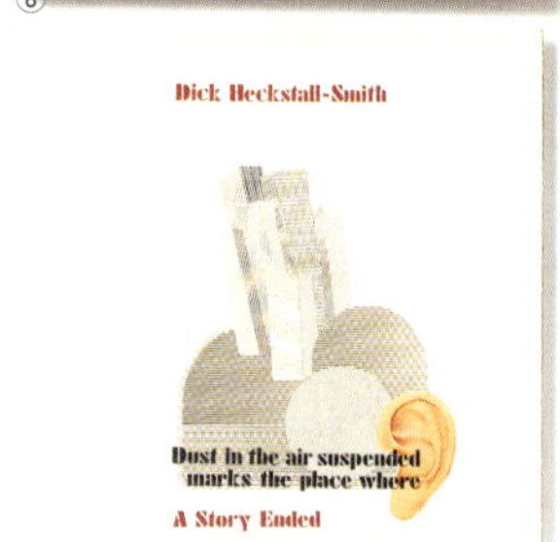

⑪

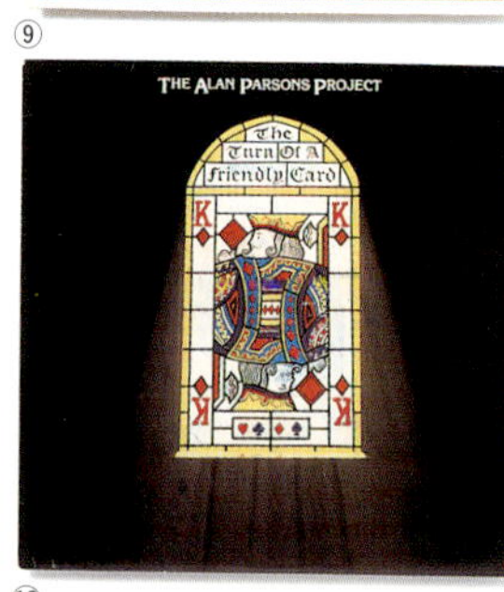

⑫

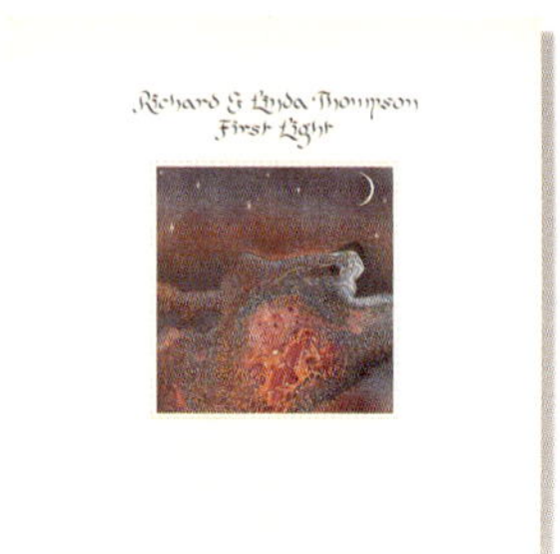
⑬

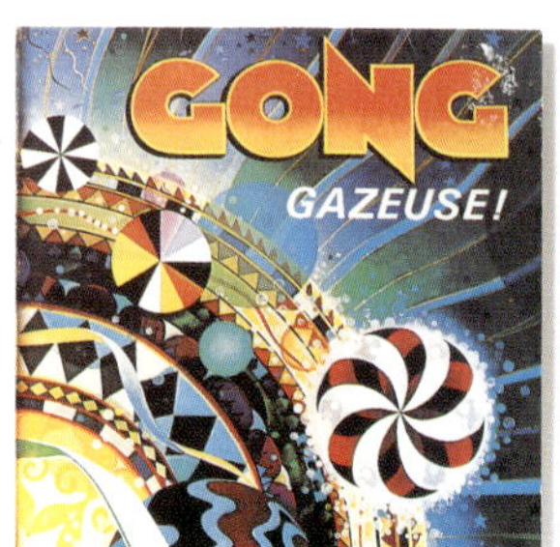

⑭

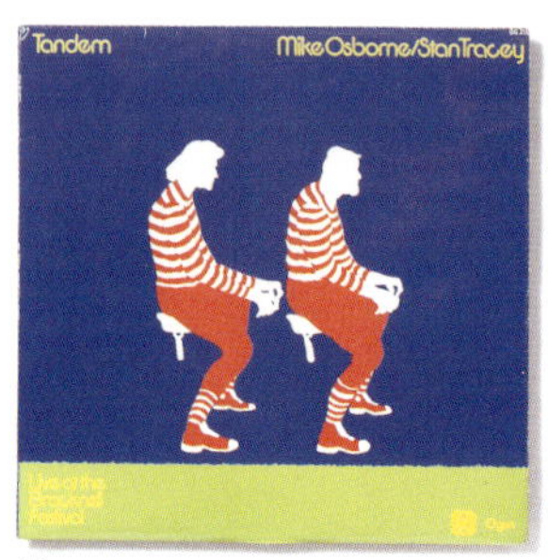

⑮

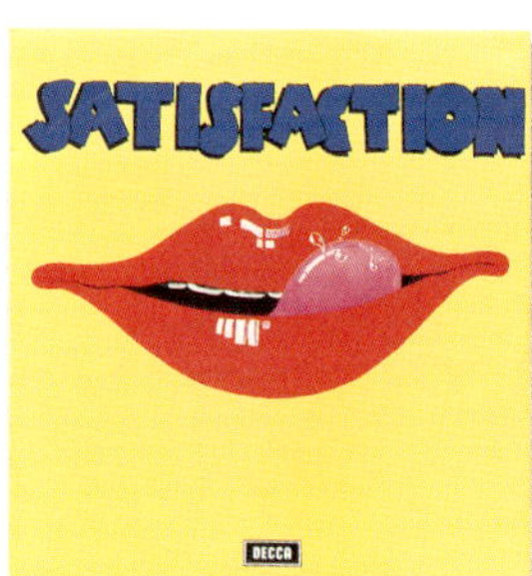

⑯

①VISITOR 2035: VISITOR 2035/
ARIOLA HANSA AHAL8003(1978)
Sleeve Design/John Andrews

②OVARY LODGE:OVARY LODGE/
OGUN OG600(1976)
Cover Design/Liz Walton

③ALAN BOWN:LISTEN/
ISLAND ILPS9131(1970)

④PATRICK MORATZ,SYRINX:
COEXISTENCE/(1980)
Illustration/Aliocha

⑤BRYN HAWORTH:SUNNY SIDE OF THE
STREET/ISLAND ILPS9332(1975)
Illustration/Tony Wright
Design/Eckford Stimpson

⑥PETER SKELLERN:HAPPY ENDINGS/
BBC REP430()
Artwork/Jean-Luke Epstein&
LolSaford(Graphyk)
Photography/Cliff Pinnock

⑦CIRKUS:ONE/RCB1(1971)
Artwork by P.Linard

⑧ CRESSIDA:CRESSIDA/ VERTIGO VO7(1970)
Designed by Teenburger

⑨DICK MORRISEY,JIM MULLEN:CAPE
WRATH/HAVEST SHSP4098(1979)
Illustration/Derek Riggs

⑩ROY BABBINGTON,CHARLES AUSTIN,
JOE GALLIVAN:HOME FROM HOME/
OGUN
OG522(1979)
Sleeve Designed by Daniel Kleinman

⑪DICK HECKSTALL-SMITH:
A STORY ENDED/BRONZE ILPS9196(1972)
Cover Design and Photography by
Christine Roche

⑫ THE ALAN PARSONS PROJECT:
THE TURN OF A FRIENDLY CARD/
ARISTA DLART1(1980)
Sleeve Concept/ Lol Cream&Kevin Godley

⑬ RICHARD&LINDA THOMPSON:FIRST LIGHT/
CHRYSALIS CHR1177(1978)
Front Cover Illustration by Adrian Day
Art Direction by Peter Wagg

⑭GONG:GAZEUSE!/VIRGIN V2074(1976)

⑮MIKE OSBORNE,STAN TRACEY:TANDEM/
OGUN OG210(1977)
Cover Design by Niklaus Troxler
Photographs by Dennis Austin and
Fred Kavalier

⑯SATISFACTION:SATISFACTION/
DECCA SKL5075(1970)

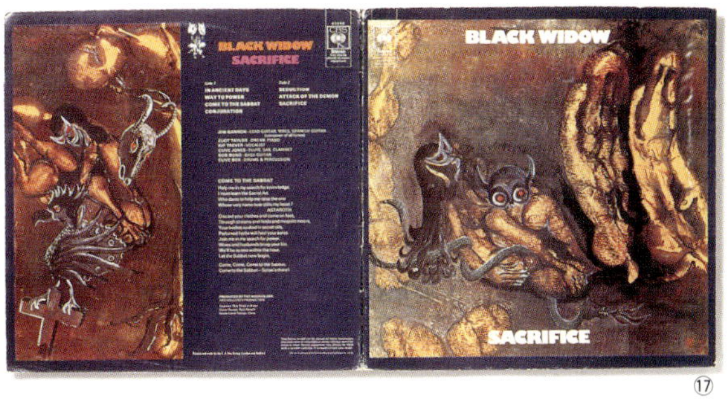

⑰

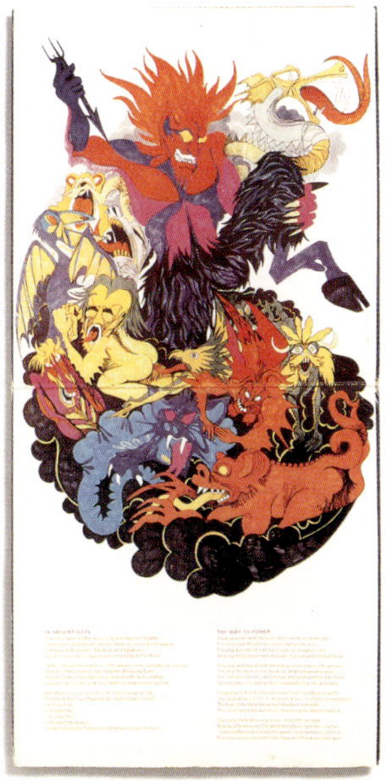

⑱

⑰ BLACK WIDOW:SACRIFICE/
CBS 63948(1970) *front and back
Cover Design/Rick Breach
Inside Cover Design/Circa

⑱ BLACK WIDOW:SACRIFICE/
CBS 63948(1970) *inner

MUNGO JERRY: YOU DON'T HAVE TO BE IN THE ARMY/
DAWN DNLS 3028 (1971)
Sleeve Design/Art Direction/Illustration/Allan Lee

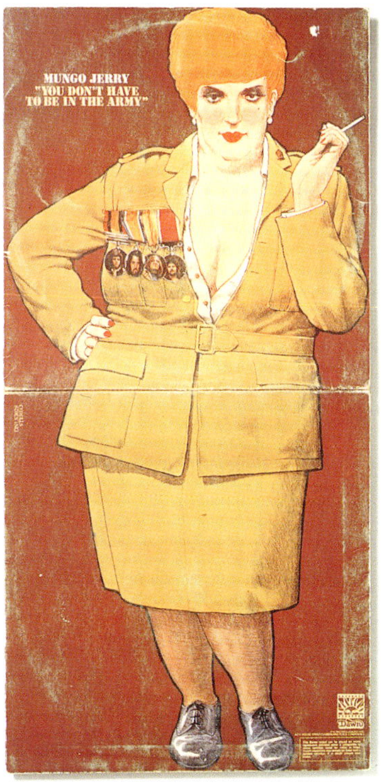

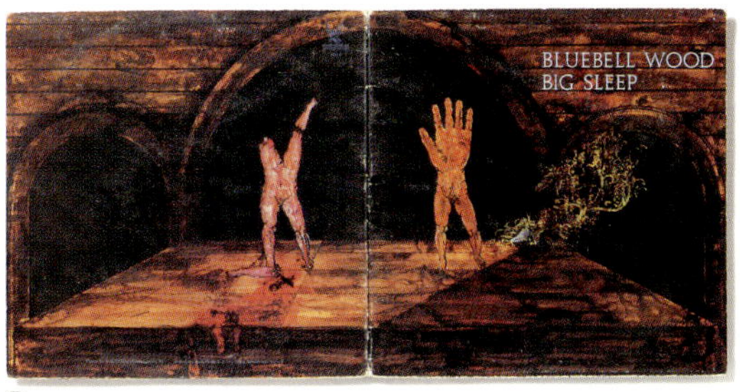

⑲

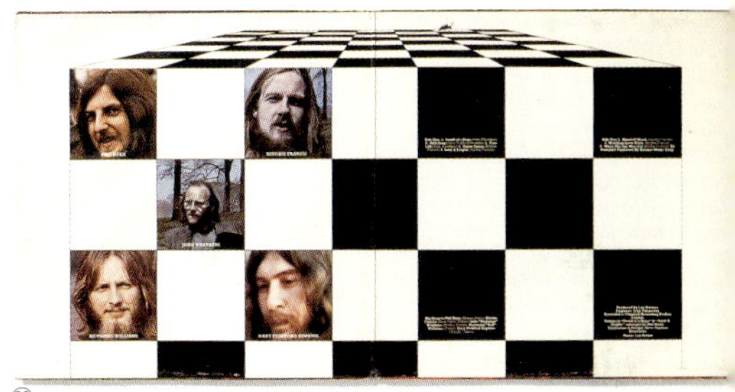

⑳

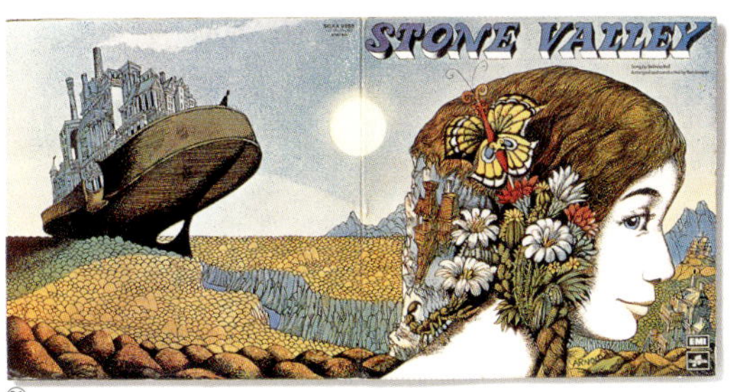

㉑

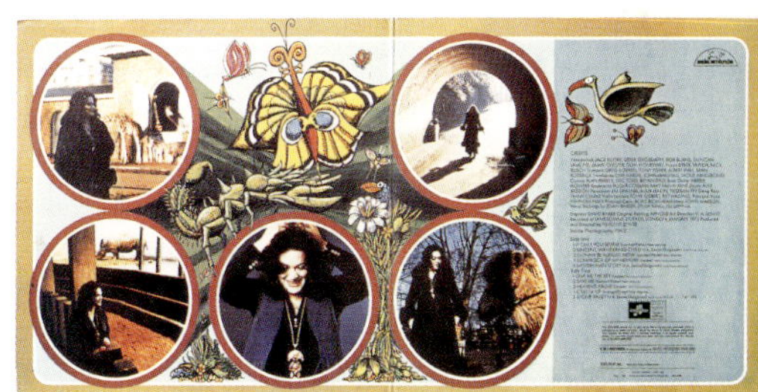

㉒

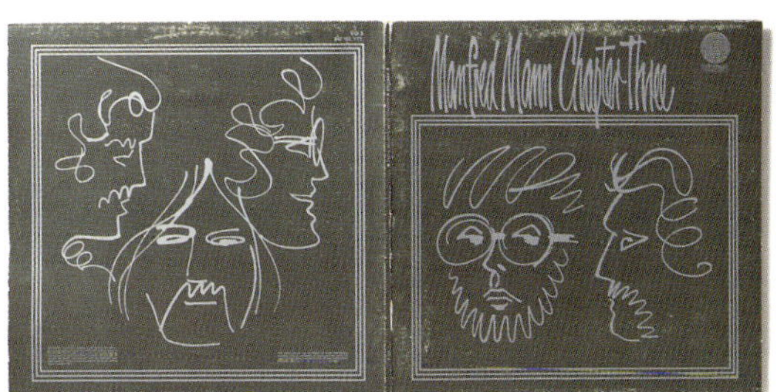

㉓

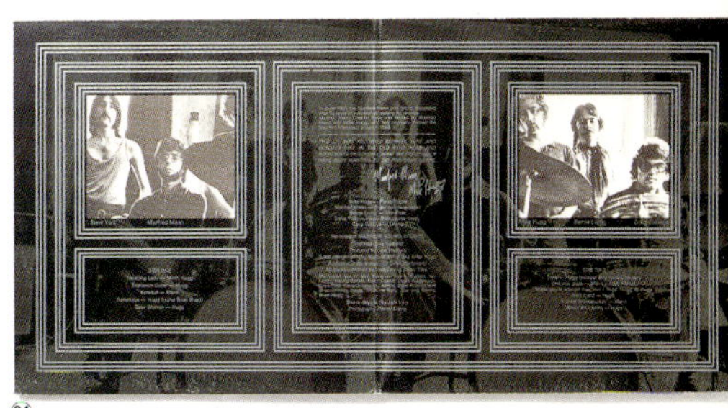

㉔

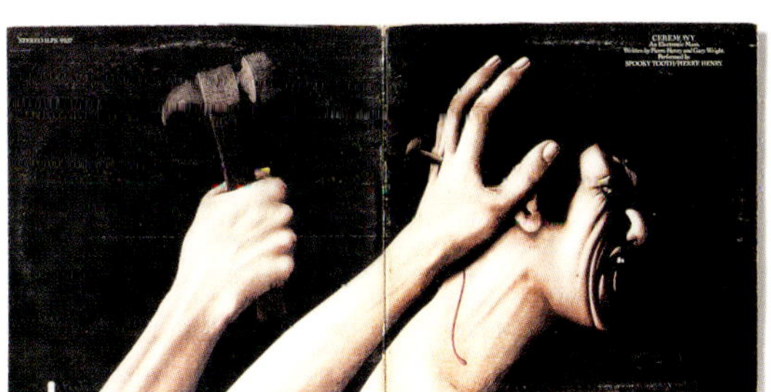

㉕

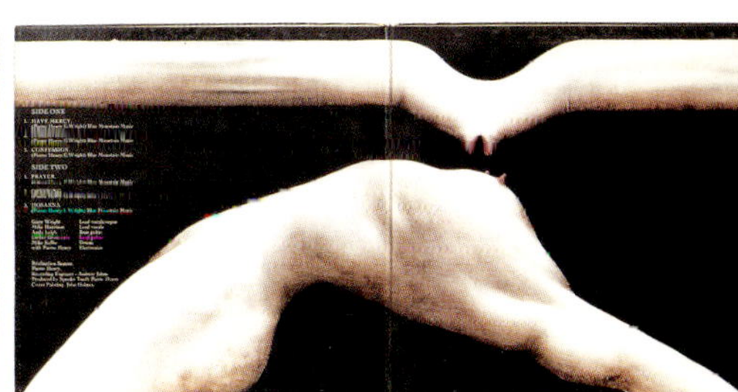

㉖

⑲ BIG SLEEP:BLUEBELL WOOD/
PEGASUS PEG4(1971)*front and back
Illustration&Design/Steve Thomas Associates
Photos/Lou Reizner

⑳ BIG SLEEP:BLUEBELL WOOD/
PEGASUS PEG4(1971)*inner

㉑ STONE VALLEY:STONE VALLEY/
EMI SCXA9255(1973)*front and back
Original Painting/Arnold Art Direction
Inside Photography/P.H.V.

㉒ STONE VALLEY:STONE VALLEY/
EMI SCXA9255(1973)*inner

㉓ MANFRED MANN CHAPTER THREE:
MANFRED MANN CHAPTER THREE/
VERTIGO VO3 (1970) *front and back
Sleeve Designed by Jack Levy
Photography/Johnny Clamp

㉔ MANFRED MANN CHAPTER THREE:MANFRED
MANN CHAPTER THREE/VERTIGO VO3
(1970)*inner

㉕ SPOOKY TOOTH:CEREMONY/
ISLAND ILPS9107(1969) *front and back
Cover Pinting/John Holmes

㉖ SPOOKY TOOTH:CEREMONY/
ISLAND ILPS9107(1969) *inner

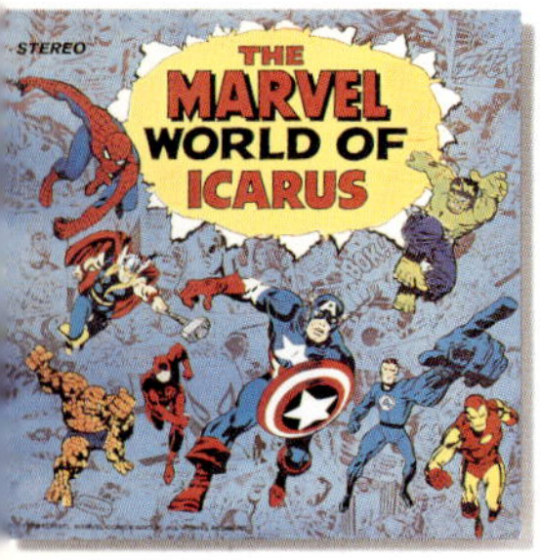

①

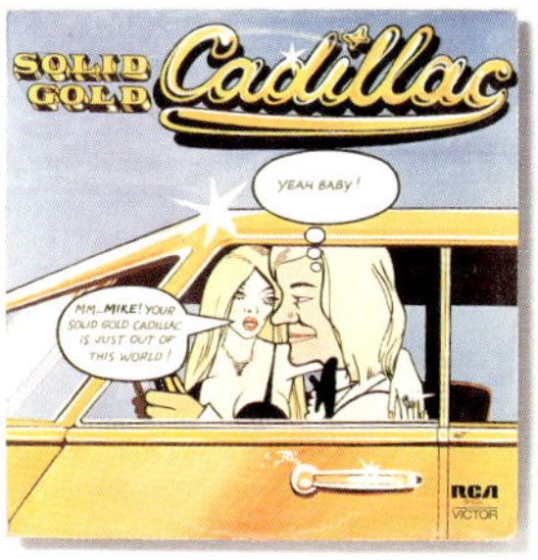

②

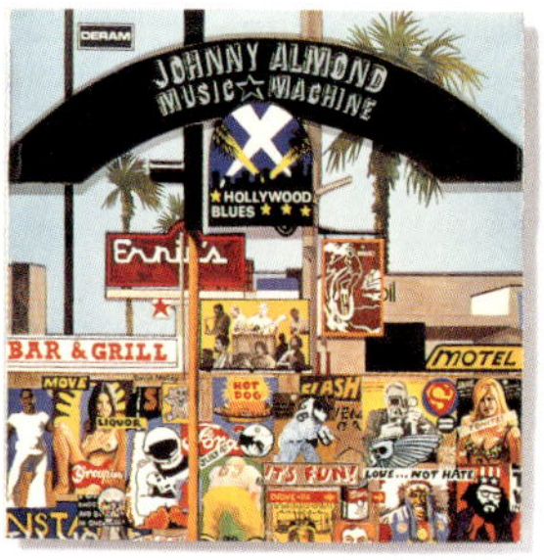

③

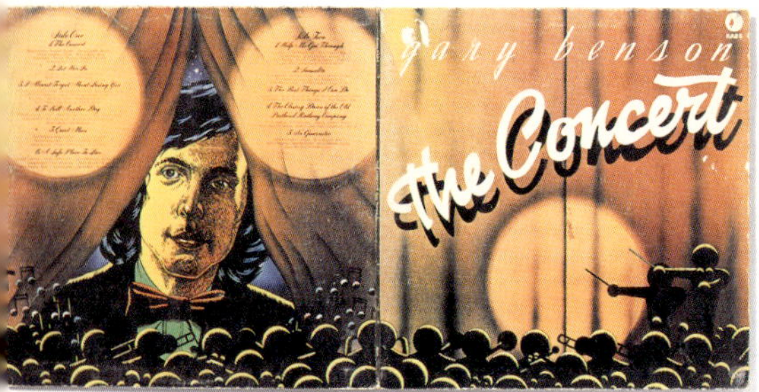

④

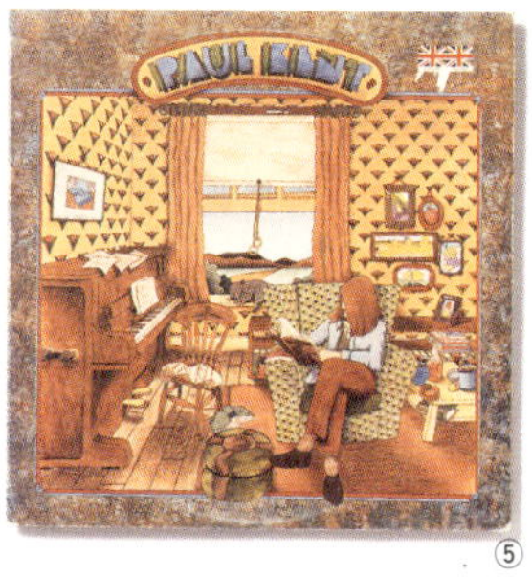

⑤

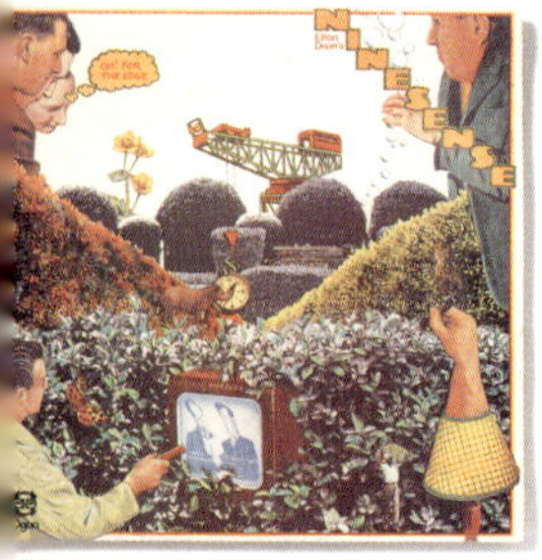

⑥

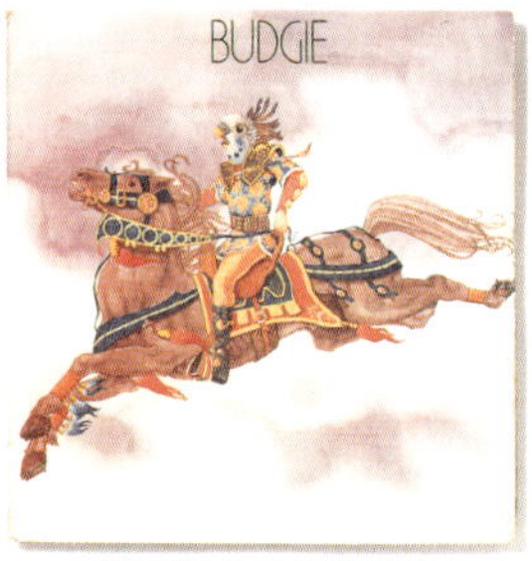

⑦

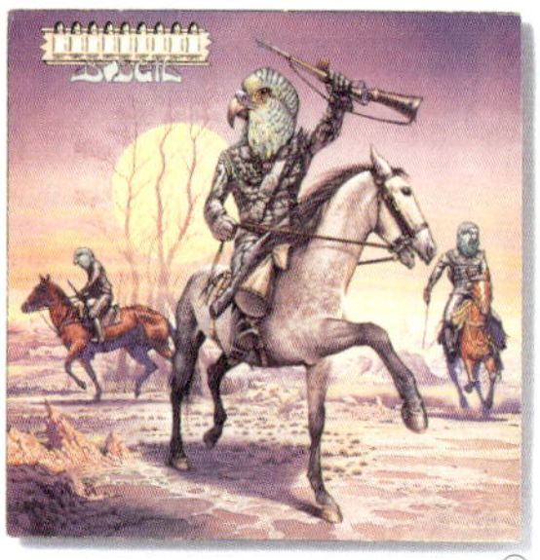

⑧

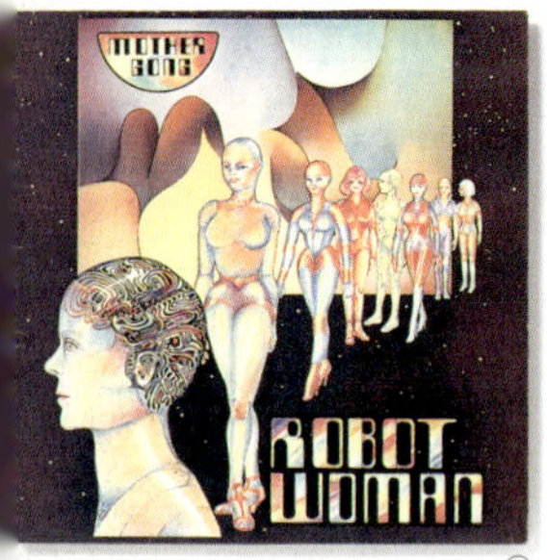

⑨

⑩

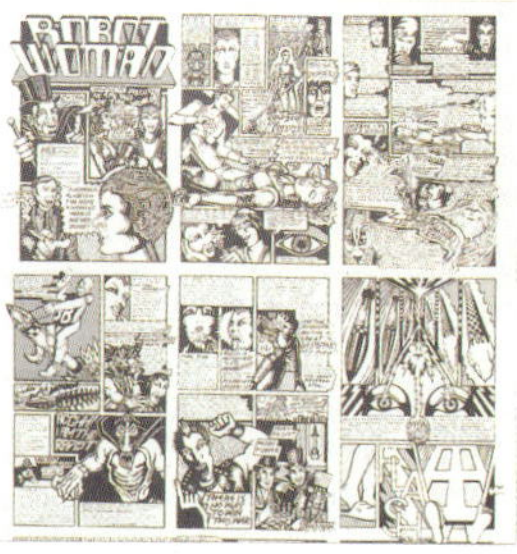

⑪

①THE MARVEL WORLD OF ICARUS:
THE MARVEL WORLD OF ICARUS/
INTERNATIONAL NSPL28161(1972)

②SOLID GOLD CADILLAC:SOLID GOLD CADILLAC/
RCA SF8311(1972)
Cover Painting by Alan Jackson

③JOHNNY ALMOND MUSIC MACHINE:
HOLYWOOD BLUES/
DERAM SML1057(1970)

④GARY BENSON:THE CONCERT/
BIRTH RAB5
Cover Design/ Mick Brownfield and Chris Angell

⑤PAUL KENT:PAUL KENT/B&C CAS 1044(1971)
Photograph/Jane Lovell
Art Direction,Illustration/Davis,Berney,Wade

⑥ELTON DEAN'S NINESENSE:OH! FOR THE EDGE/
OGUN OG900(1976)
Cover Design/Dick Whitbread

⑦BUDGIE:BUDGIE/MCA MKPS2018(1971)
Cover Painting/David Sparling

⑧BUDGIE:BANDOLIER/MCA MCF2723(1975)
Art Direction/John Pasche
Cover Illustration/Patrick Woodroffe

⑨MOTHER GONG:ROBOT WOMAN/BUTT003(1986)

⑩MOTHER GONG:ROBOT WOMAN2/
SHANGHAI HAI100(1982)
Cartoon&Cover Design/Pete Wooley

⑪MOTHER GONG:ROBOT WOMAN2/
SHANGHAI HAI100(1982)*poster

illustration Cartoons

マンガ風イラスト

SPONTANEOUS COMBUSTION:SPONTANEOUS COMBUSTION/
HARVEST SHVL801(1972) *front and back
Sleeve Design/ Paul May

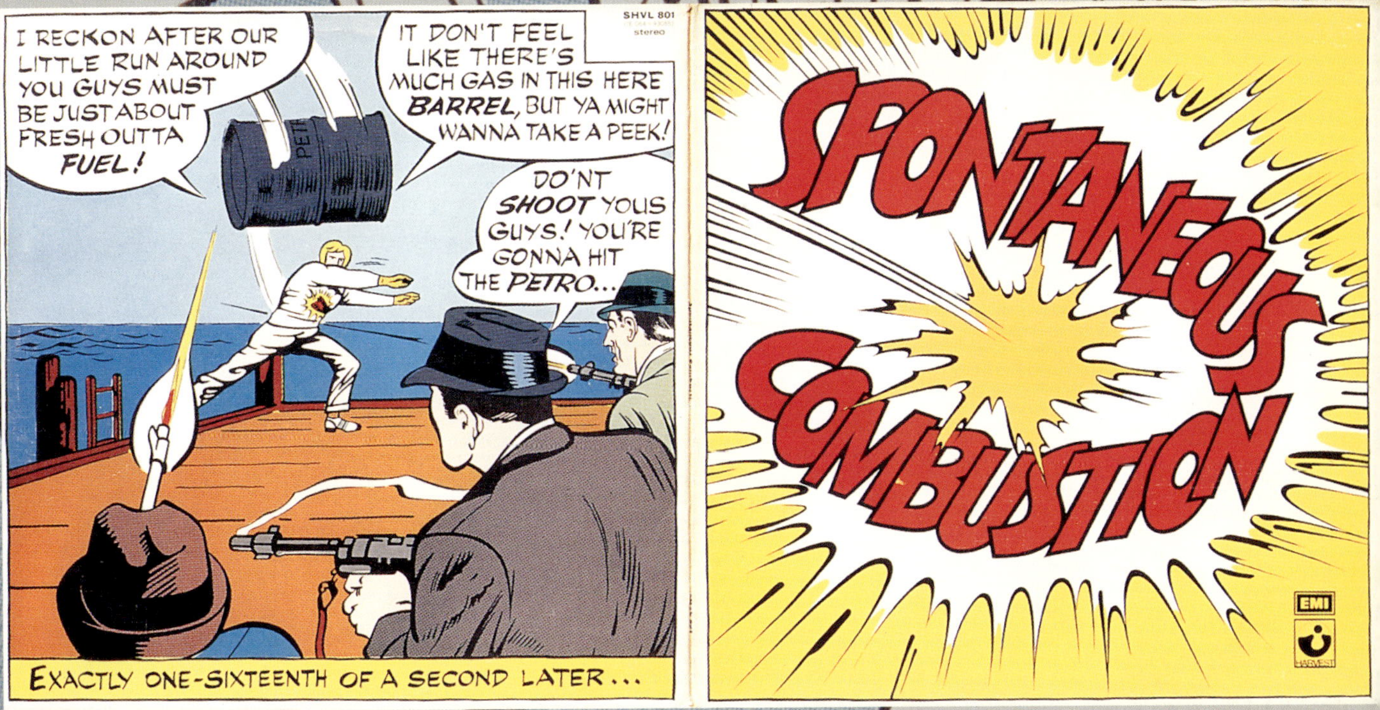

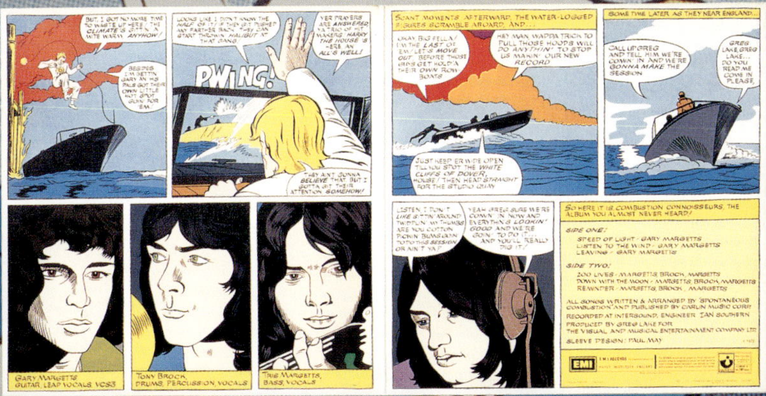

SPONTANEOUS COMBUSTION:SPONTANEOUS COMBUSTION/
HARVEST SHVL801(1972)*inner

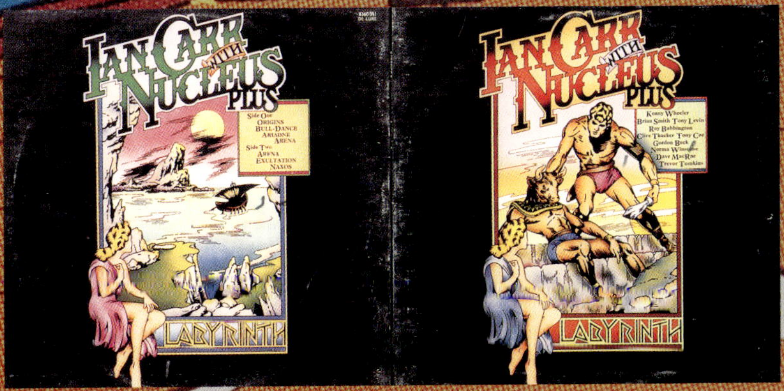

IAN CARR WITH NUCELUS:LABYRINTH/
VERTIGO 6360 091(1973) *front and back
Sleeve Design by Keith Davis of Davis,Wade

IAN CARR WITH NUCELUS:LABYRINTH/
VERTIGO 6360 091(1973) *inner

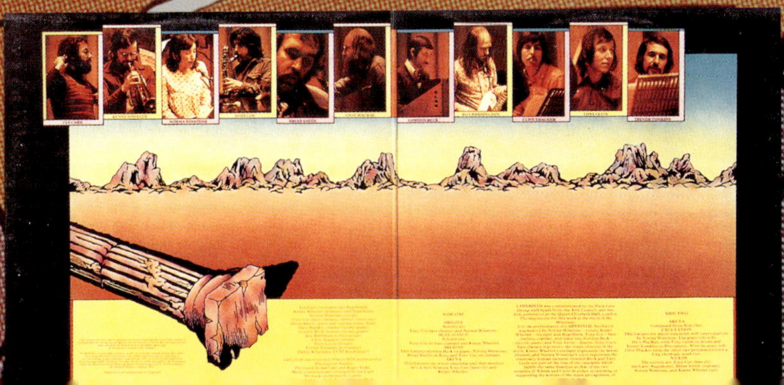

Contrast

色彩のコントラスト

① 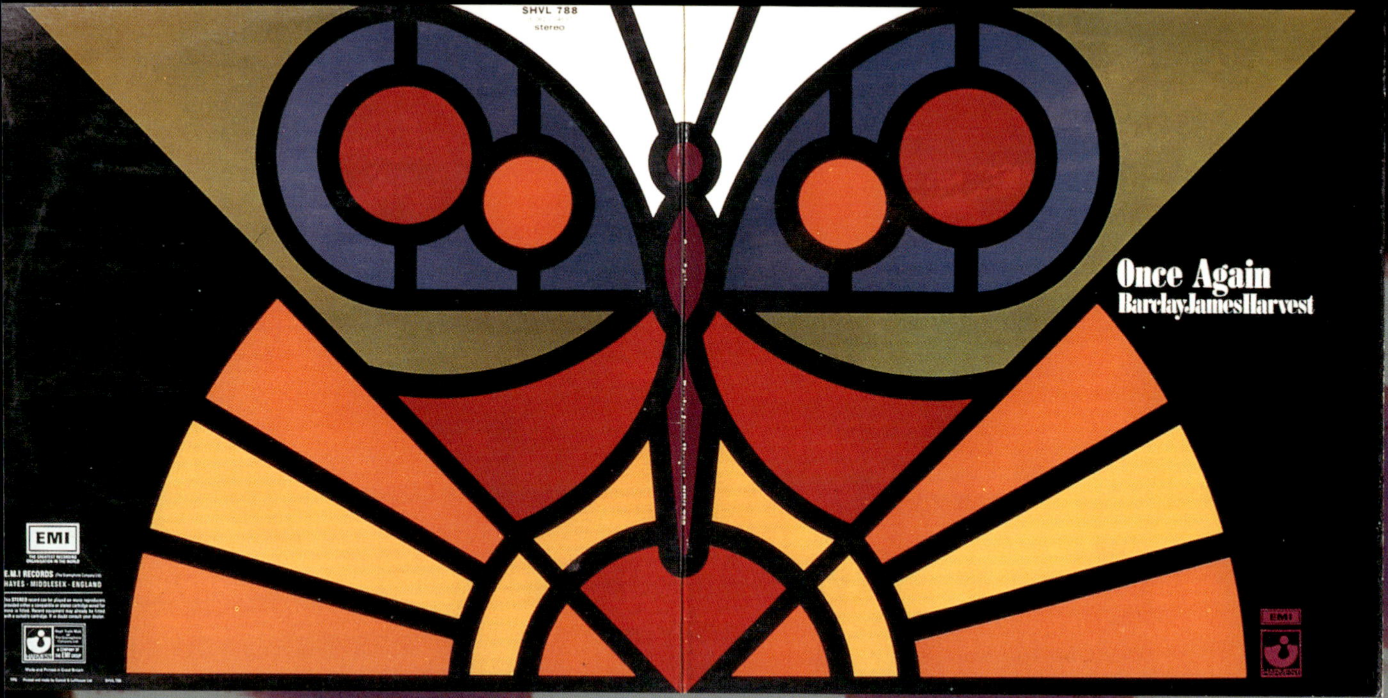

② 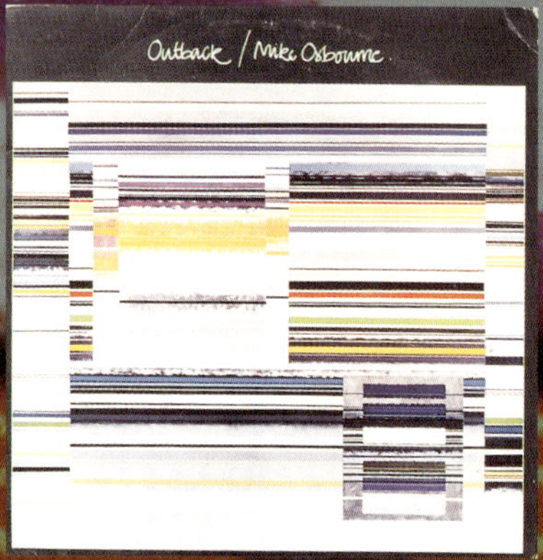

③ 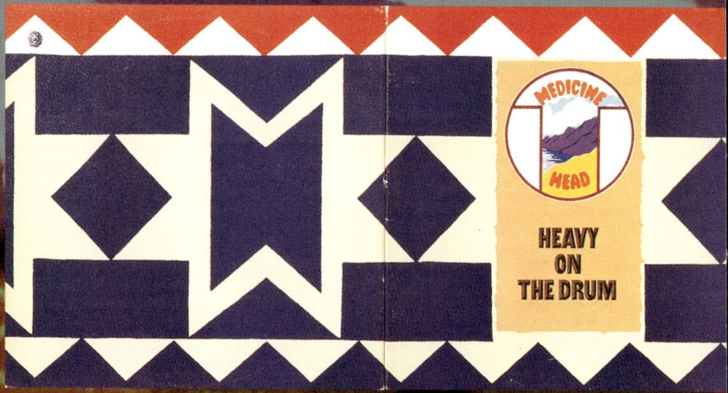

④ 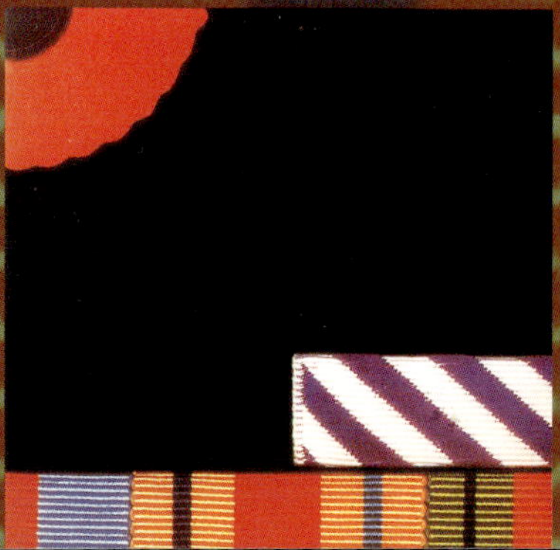

① BARCLAY JAMES HARVEST:ONCE AGAIN/
HARVEST SHVL788(1971)
Design by Latimer Reeves Published

② MIKE OSBORNE:OUTBACK/
TURTLE TUR300(1970)
Cover Painting/John Eaves

③ MEDICINE HEAD:HEAVY ON THE DRUM/
DANDELION DAN8005(1971)
Sleeve/ Forehead Designs

④ PINK FLOYD:THE FINAL CUT/
HARVEST SHPF1983(1983)
Sleeve Design/Roger Waters
Photo/Willie Christie
Artwork/Artful Dodgers

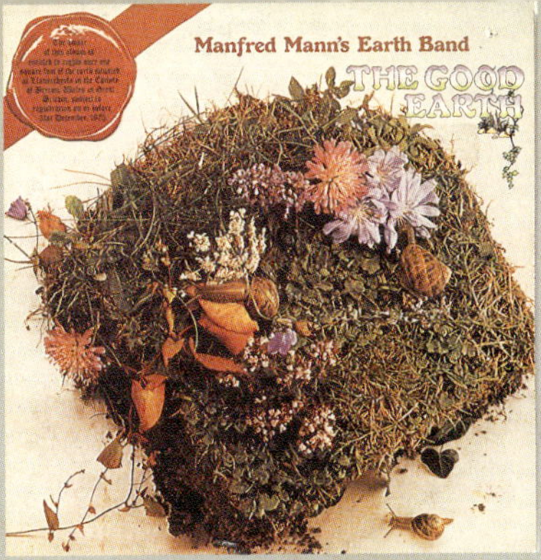

MANFRED MANN'S EARTH BAND:THE GOOD EARTH/
BRONZE ILPS9306(1974)

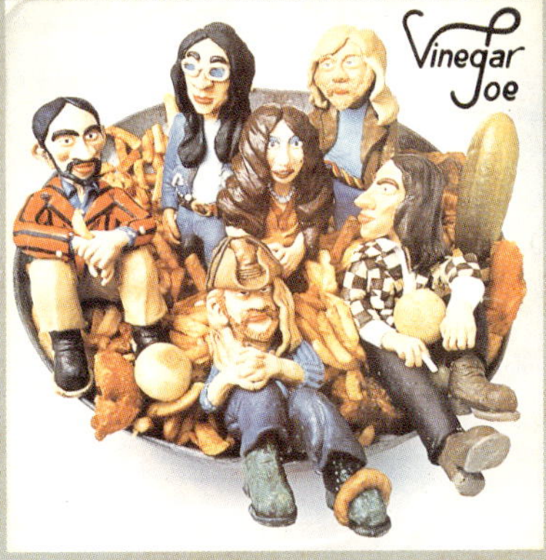

VINEGAR JOE:VINEGAR JOE/
ISLAND ILPS9183 (1972)
Photography and Cover Design/Visualeyes
Mannequins/John Padley

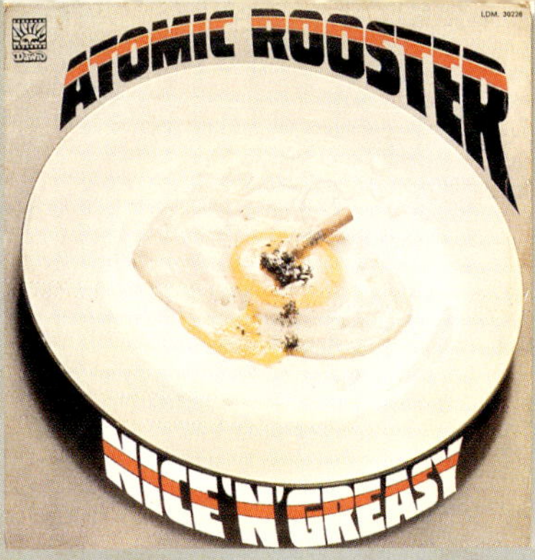

ATOMIC ROOSTER:NICE'N'GREASY/
DAWN DNLS3049(1973)
Graphics/Paul Chave

illustrations Objet
オブジェ

TEN YEARS AFTER:CRICKLEWOOD GREEN/
DERAM SML1065(1970) *inner

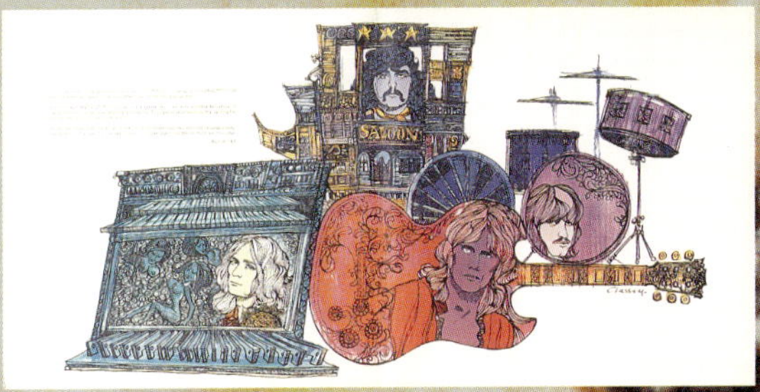

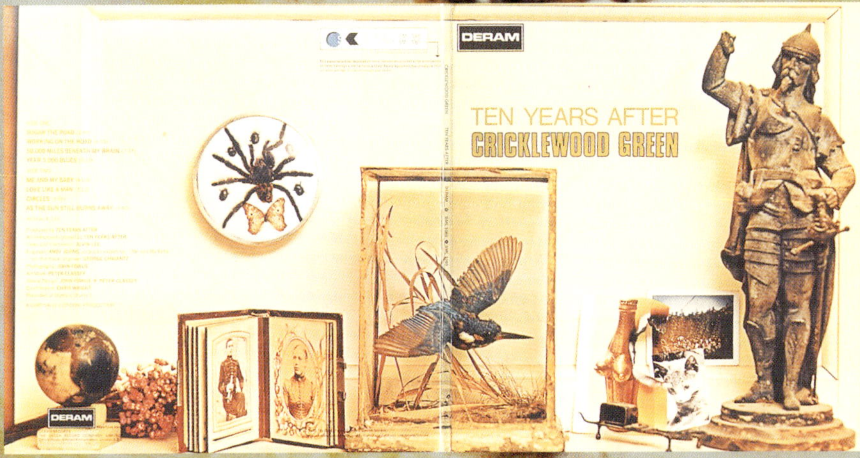

TEN YEARS AFTER:CRICKLEWOOD GREEN/
DERAM SML1065(1970)*front and back
Photography/John Fowlie
Art Work/ Peter Classey
Sleeve Design/ John Fowlie+Peter Classey

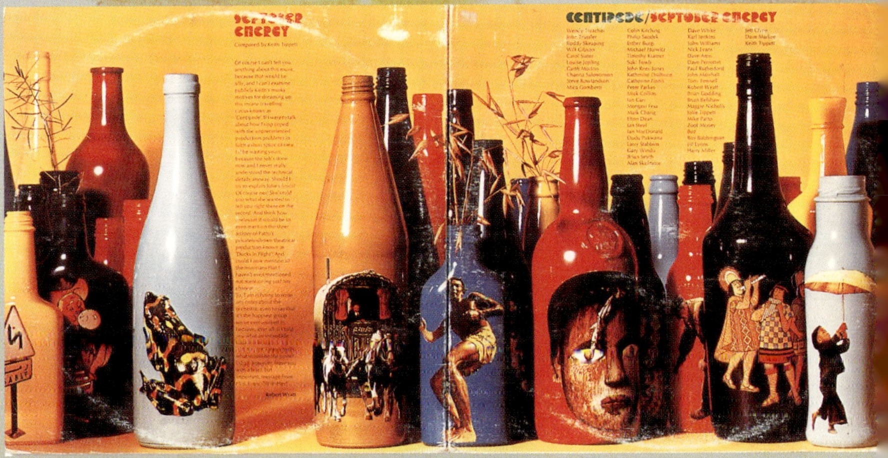

CENTIPEDE:SEPTOBER ENERGY/RCA DPS2054(1974) *front and back
Album Design by Dick Whitbread of Foster&Knowles
Cover Photograph by Martin Adelman

CENTIPEDE:SEPTOBER ENERGY/
RCA DPS2054(1974) *inner

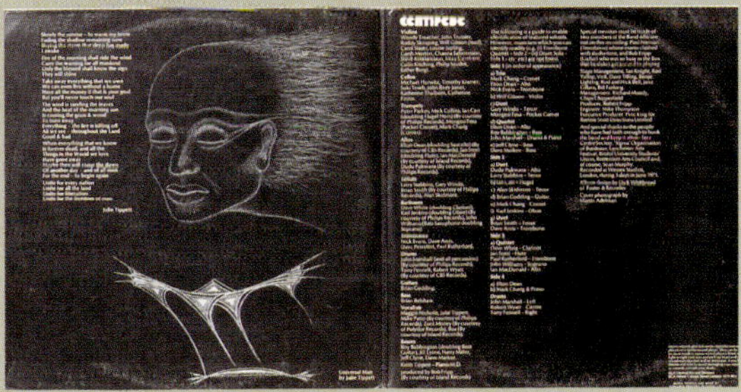

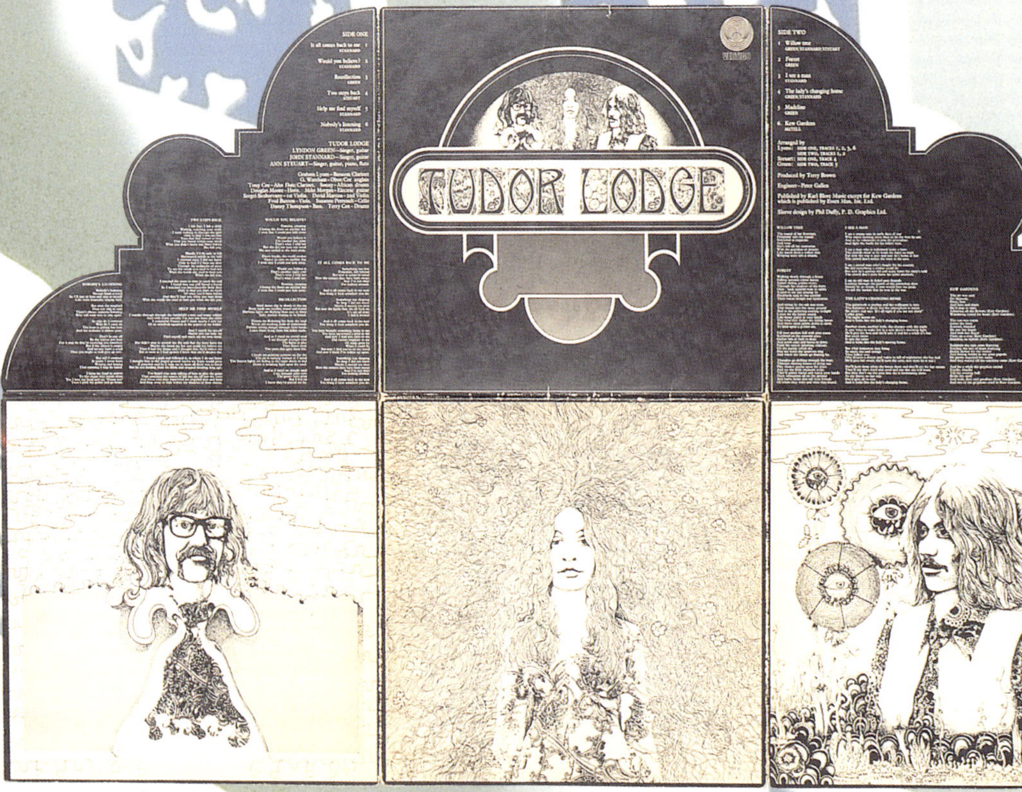

TUDOR LODGE:TUDOR LODGE/
VERTIGO 6360 043(1971)
Sleeve Design by Phil Duff,P.D.Graphics Ltd.

transformed works
変型ジャケット

レコード・ジャケットは紙でできている。その単純な事実が、逆に30センチ四方の決まり切ったかたちを大きく覆す、変型ジャケットを生みだした。p86は、イギリスの男女混成フォーク・ロック・トリオ、チューダー・ロッジの六面変型ジャケット。畳んだ状態だとふつうの正方形サイズが展開するとまったくちがった形になるというコンセプトは、味気ない正方形だからこそ、かえってその意外性が効果的なものとなる。キーフのデザインによるヘヴン『ブラス・ロック1』の十字架仕様、同じくロジャー・ディーンのイラストで飾られたドクター・ストレンジリー・ストレンジ『ヘヴィ・ペッティング』も同様のアイデアだが、後者がどういう理由からこんな不思議なかたちとなったのかは、はっきり言ってよくわからない。しかし、よくわからないところが魅力となっているのも事実である。英国を代表するジャズ・ロック・グループ、ニュークリアスの『エラスティック・ロック』やストレンジなポップ・サウンドを聴かせるラマセス『グラストップ・コフィン』のように、表ジャケットがくり抜かれ、開くと内側からまったく別のヴィジュアルが現れる形式も、プラスティック・ケースのCDではあり得ないアナログ独自の仕様といえるだろう。

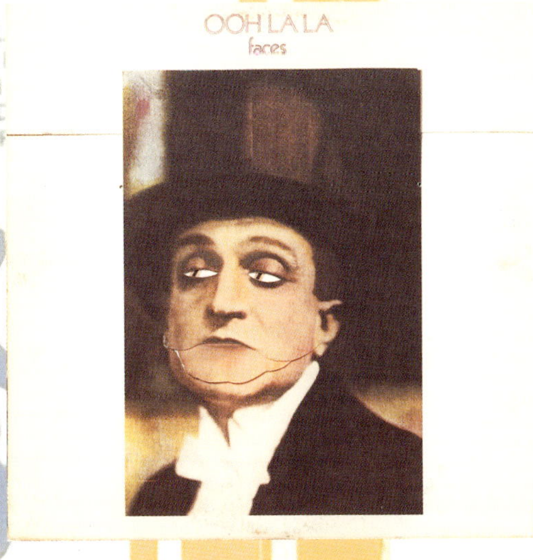

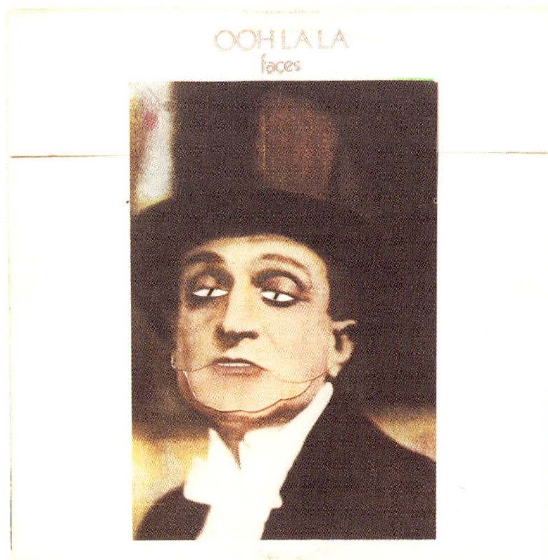

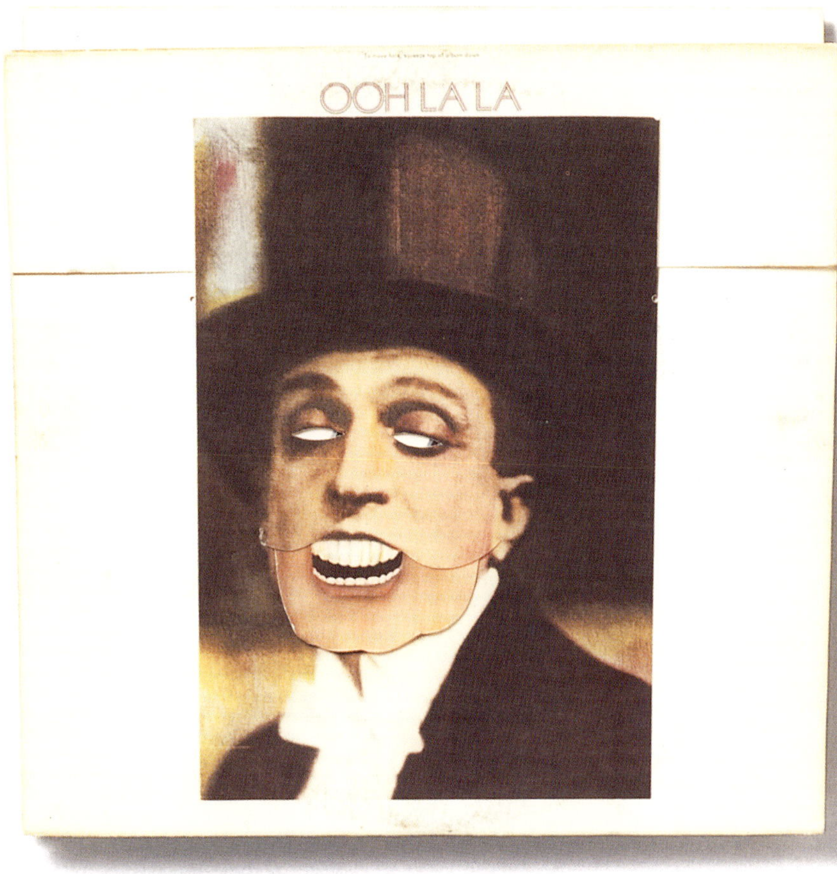

FACES:OOH LA LA/WARNER K56011(1973)
Photography by Tom Wright
Album Design by Jim Ladwig,AGI

Record jackets were made from paper generally. This simple fact itself allowed for variations of the standard 31.5 cm square album jacket. On page 86 is a six-sided album jacket by the British Folk Rock trio, Tudor Lodge. When unfolded the common, square jacket turns into a totally different shape. The effect of this design was surprising. On page 91 is the album jacket of Heaven's "Brass Rock 1", a cross-shaped jacket designed by Keef. A similar concept was used for Doctor Strangely Strange's "Heavy Petting" (page 88), which features illustration work by Roger Dean. Though it is not clear why this album had an unusual shape, its mystery was also the key. Top British Jazz Rock group Nucleus' "Elastic Rock" and avant garde Pop group Ramses' "Glasstop Coffin" took on different forms depending on which part of the front cover was cut out. When unfolded an entirely different visual popped out. This design was most effective with vinyl record jackets, something that cannot be done with the plastic case of CDs.

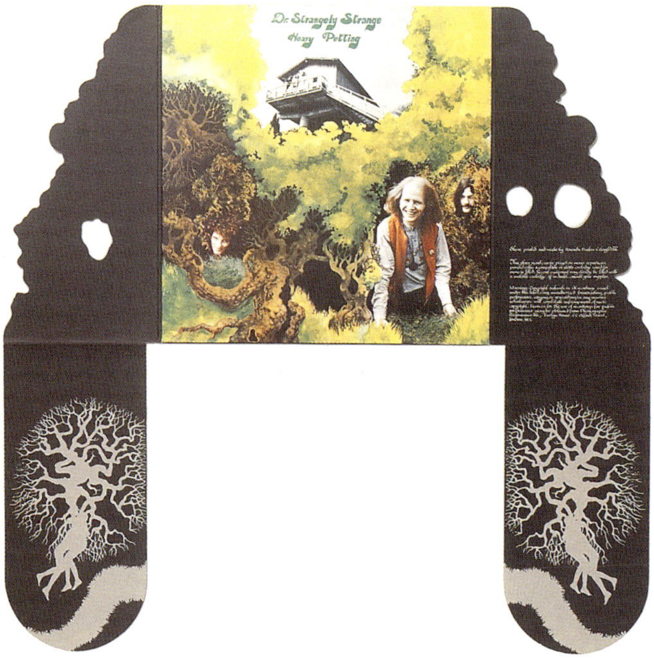

DR.STRANGELY STRANGE:HEAVY PETTING/
VERTIGO 6360 009(1970)
*unfolded(front)

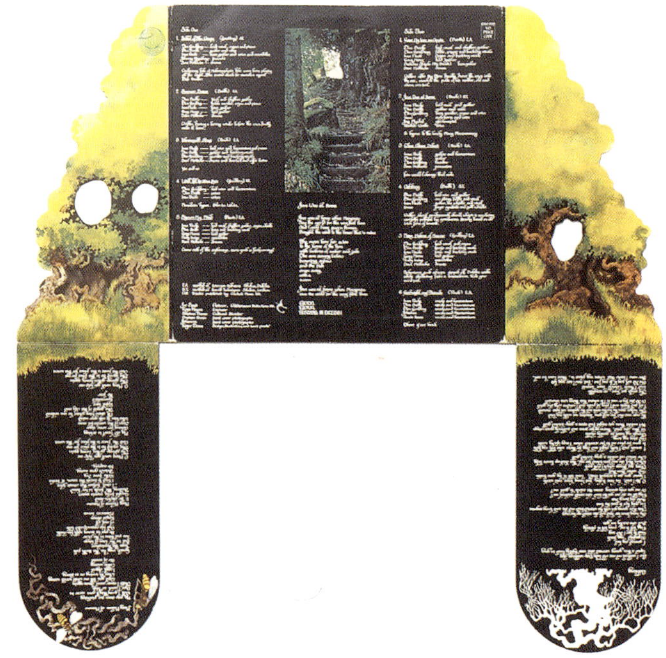

DR.STRANGELY STRANGE:HEAVY PETTING/
VERTIGO 6360 009(1970)
*unfolded(back)

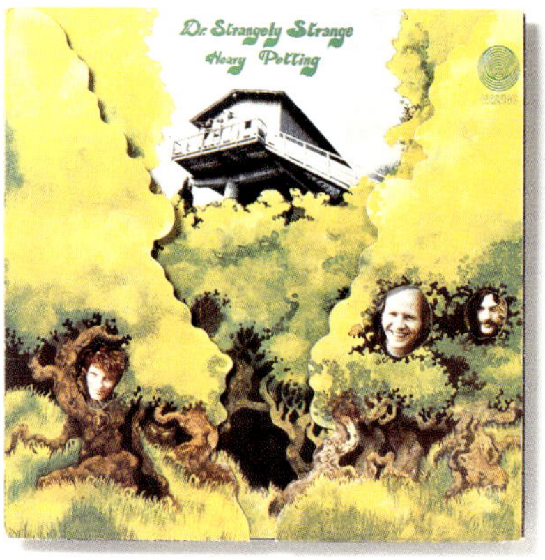

DR.STRANGELY STRANGE:HEAVY PETTING/
VERTIGO 6360 009(1970) *front
Illustration by Roger Dean

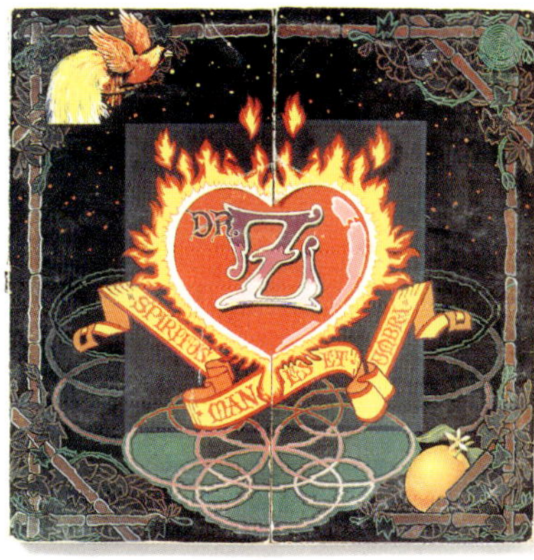

DR.Z:THREE PARTS TO MY SOUL/
VERTIGO 6360 048(1971) *front

DR.Z:THREE PARTS TO MY SOUL/
VERTIGO 6360 048(1971) *unfolded

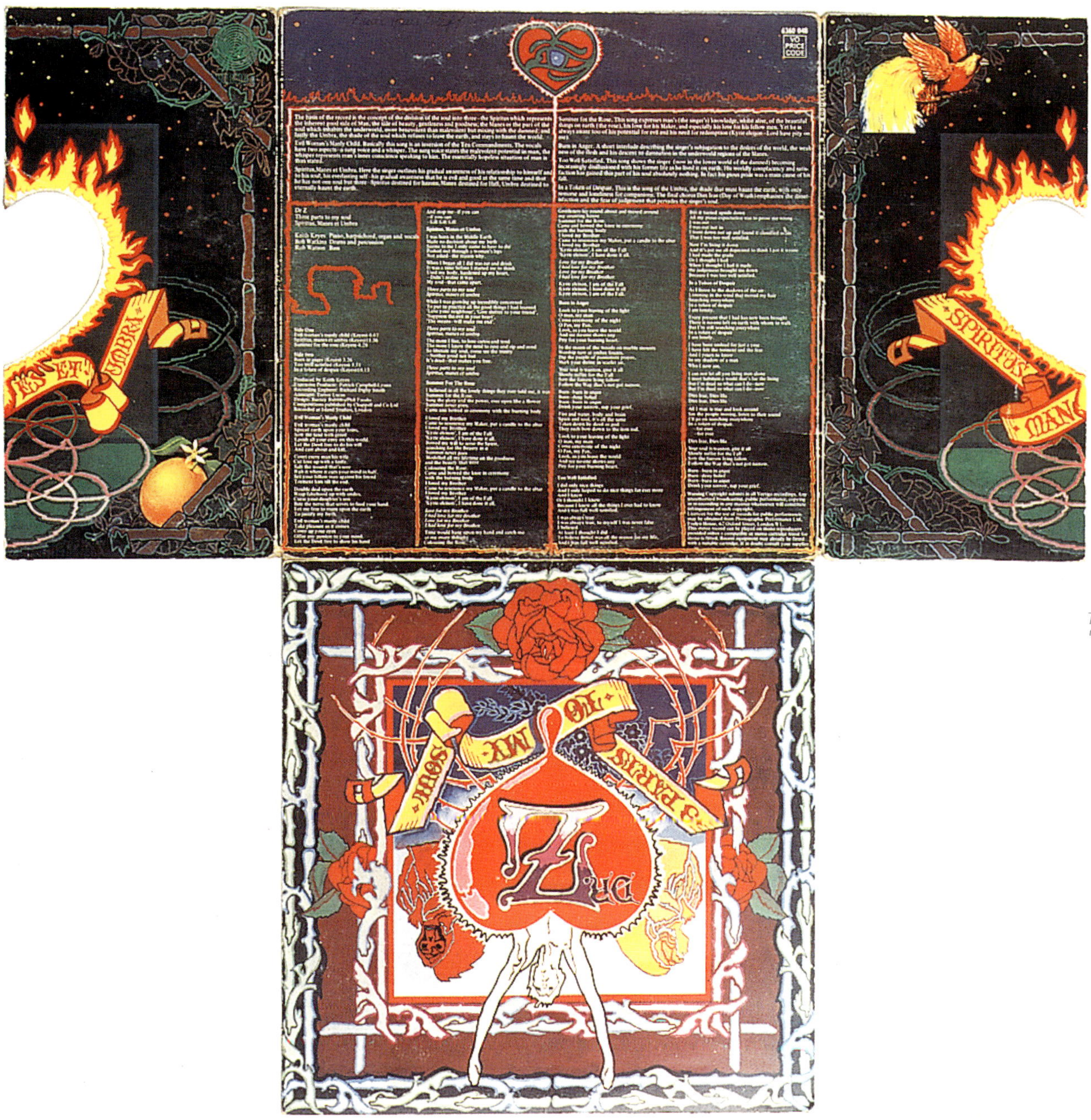

①

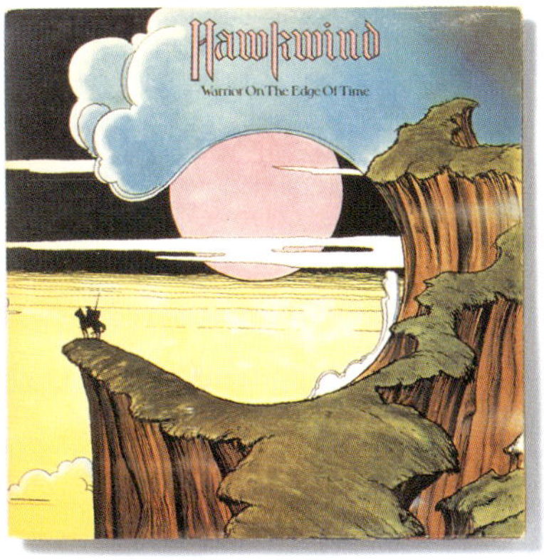

②

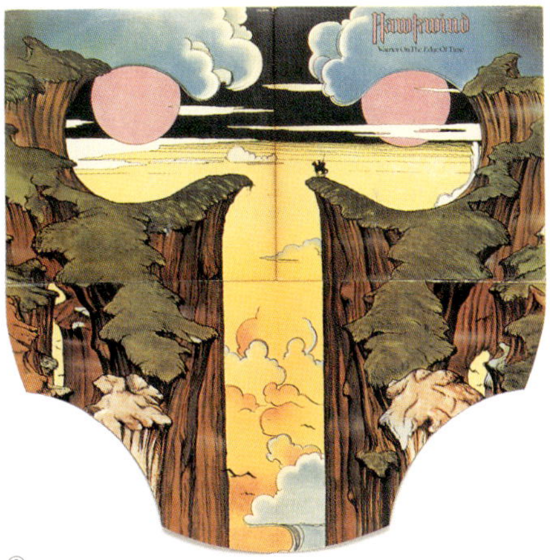

① HAWKWIND:WARRIOR ON THE EDGE OF TIME/
UNITED ARTISTS UAG29766(1975)
Photos/Doughnut
Concept&Art Direction/Comte Pierre D'auvergne,
Eddie Brash

② HAWKWIND:WARRIOR ON THE EDGE OF TIME/
UNITED ARTISTS UAG29766(1975)
*unfolded (front)

③ HAWKWIND:WARRIOR ON THE EDGE OF TIME/
UNITED ARTISTS UAG29766(1975)
*unfolded (back)

③

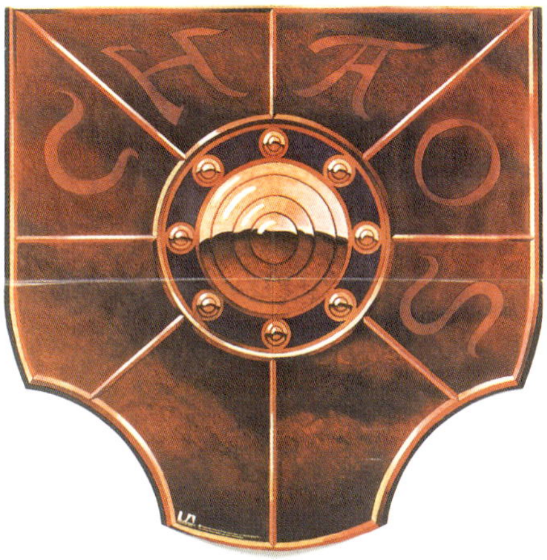

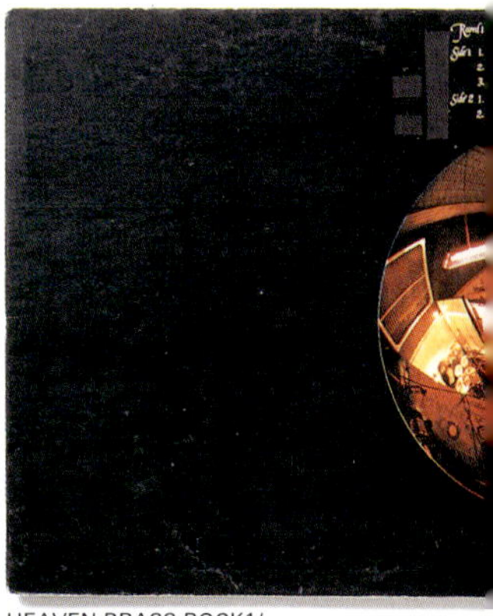

HEAVEN:BRASS ROCK1/
CBS 66293(1971) *inner

④

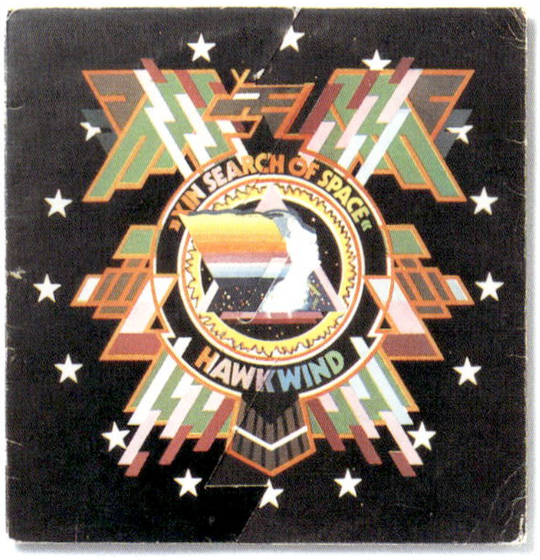

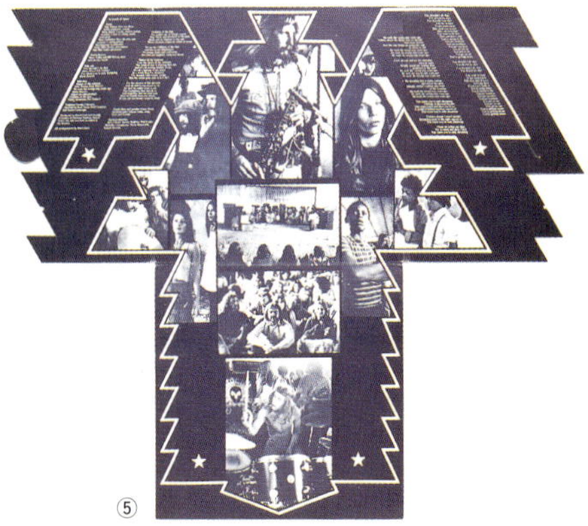

⑤

④ HAWKWIND:IN SEARCH OF SPACE/
UNITED ARTISTS UAG29202(1971)

⑤ JETHRO TULL:THICK AS A BRICK/
CHRYSALIS CHR1003(1972) *unfolded (front)

⑥

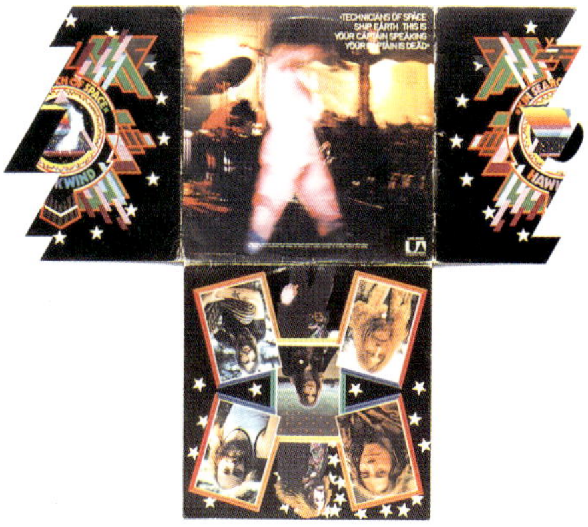

⑥ JETHRO TULL:THICK AS A BRICK/
CHRYSALIS CHR1003(1972) *unfolded *(back)

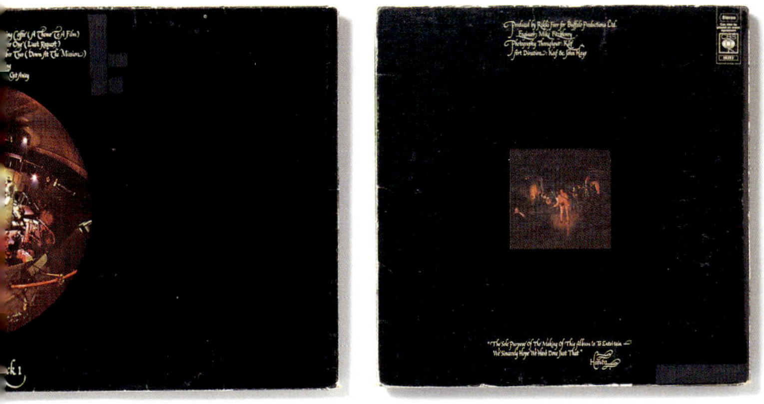

HEAVEN:BRASS ROCK1/
CBS 66293(1971)*back

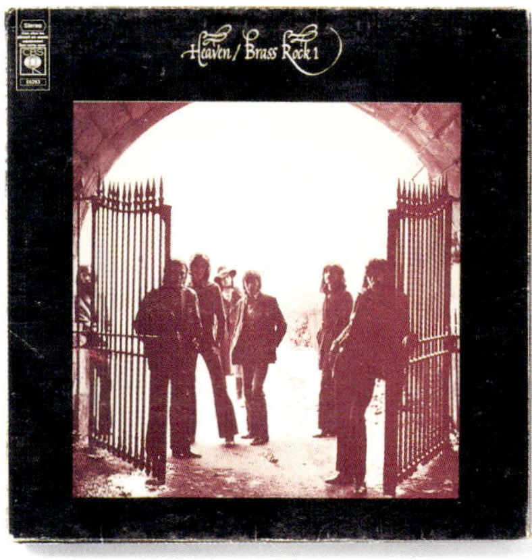

HEAVEN:BRASS ROCK1/CBS 66293(1971)*front
Photography Throughout/Keef
Art Direction/Keef&John Hays

HEAVEN:BRASS ROCK1/
CBS 66293(1971) *unfolded

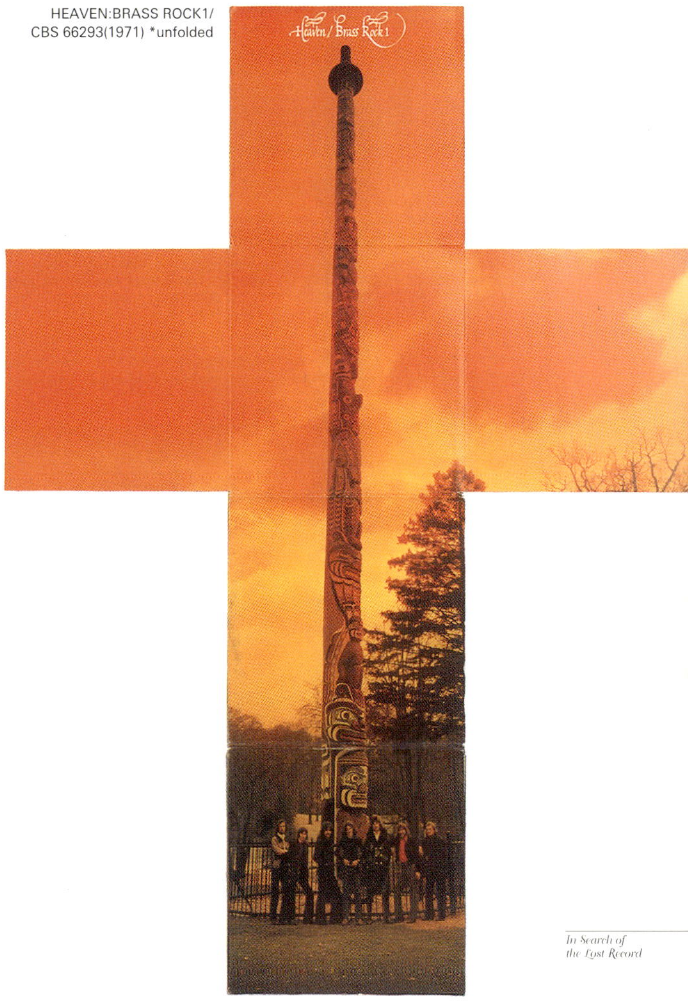

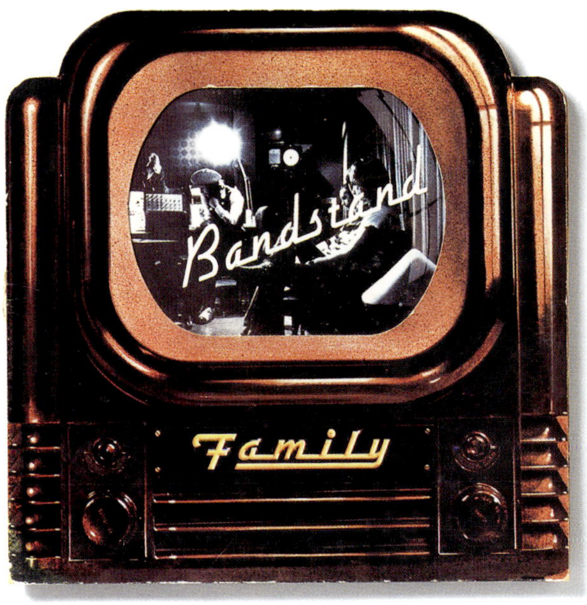

FAMILY BANDSTAND/REPRISE K54006(1972) *front
Cover Design,Conception/John Kosh
Photography,Conception/Peter Howe

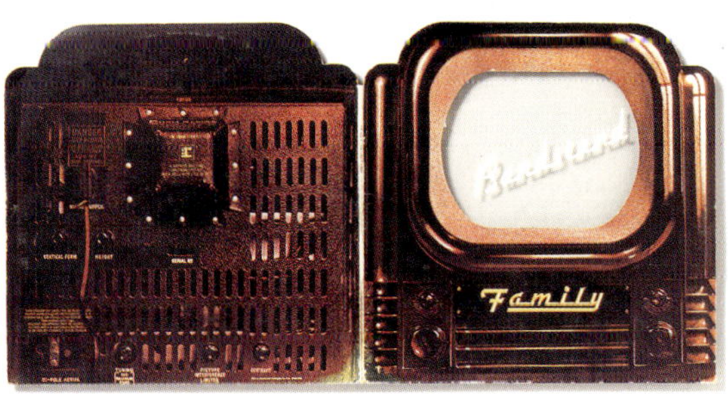

FAMILY:BANDSTAND/
REPRISE K54006(1972) *front and back

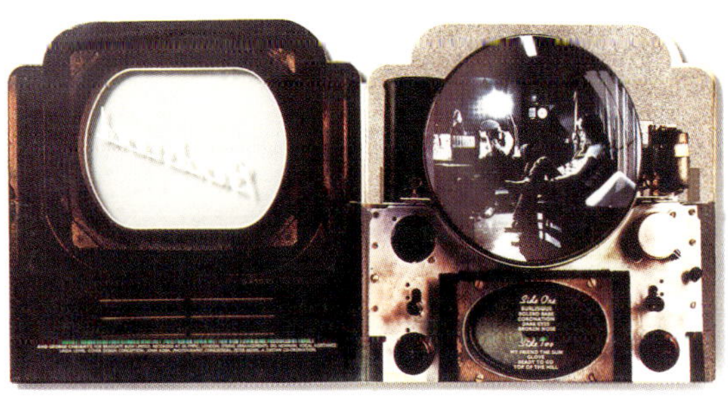

FAMILY:BANDSTAND/
REPRISE K54006(1972) *inner

①RAMASES:GLASS TOP COFFIN/
VERTIGO 6360 115(1975) *front and back
Cover Concept by Ramases
Artwork by Dave Field
Art Direction by Jack Wood

②RAMASES:GLASS TOP COFFIN/VERTIGO 6360 115(1975)*inner

③NUCLEUS:ELASTIC ROCK/
VERTIGO 6360 008(1970) *front and back
Cover Design and Illustration/Roger Dean

④NUCLEUS:ELASTIC ROCK/
VERTIGO 6360 008(1970)*inner

⑤SPLINTER:THE PLACE I LOVE/ DARK HORSE AMLH22001(1974) *front
Art Direction/ Fabio Nicoli
Design/ Jack Katz,Nick Marshall
Photography/ Terry O'Neill

⑥SPLINTER:THE PLACE I LOVE/
DARK HORSE AMLH22001(1974) *unfolded (back)

⑦SPLINTER:THE PLACE I LOVE/
DARK HORSE AMLH22001(1974) *inner

⑧SPLINTER:THE PLACE I LOVE/
DARK HORSE AMLH22001(1974) *inner

⑨ROY HARPER:LIFEMASK/HARVEST SHVL808(1973)

⑩ROY HARPER:LIFEMASK/
HARVEST SHVL808(1973) *inner

⑪JETHRO TULL:THICK AS A BRICK/
CHRYSALIS CHR1003(1972)

⑫JETHRO TULL:THICK AS A BRICK/
CHRYSALIS CHR1003(1972) *front and back

①
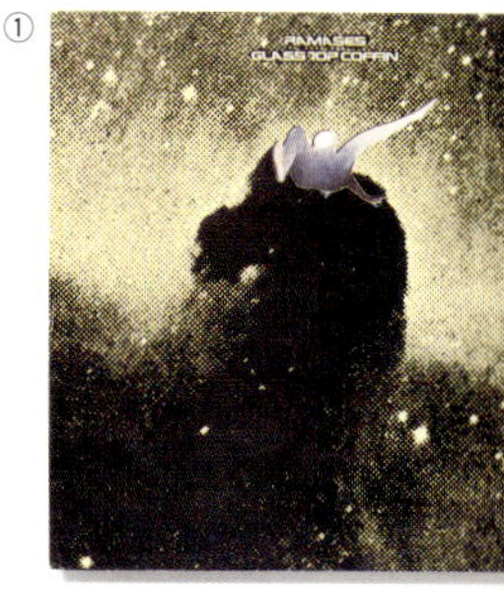

③
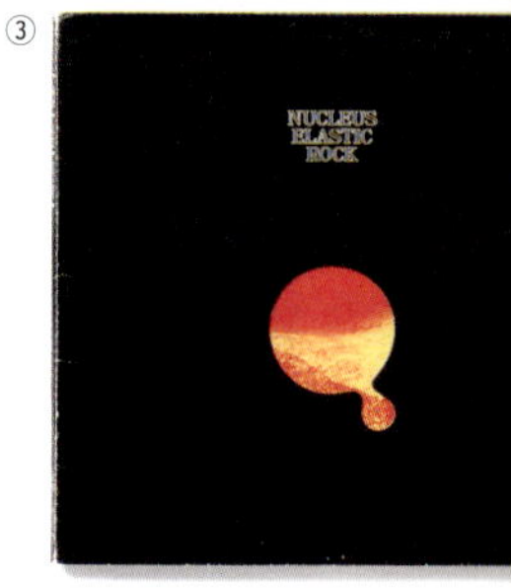

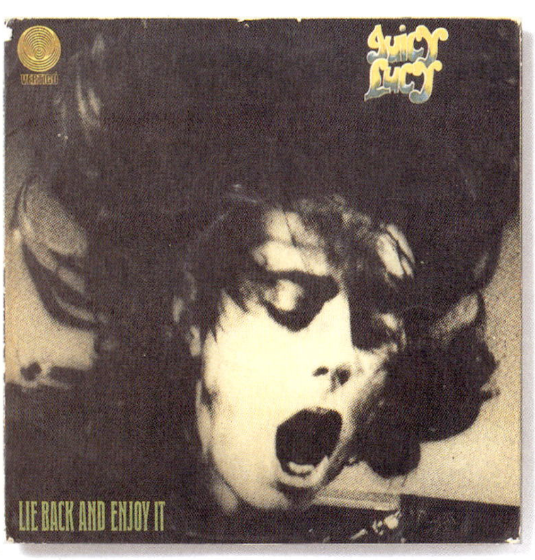

JUICY LUCY:LIE BACK AND ENJOY IT/
VERTIGO 6360 014(1970) *front
Photo/Pete Smith
Sleeve Design/Nigel Thomas

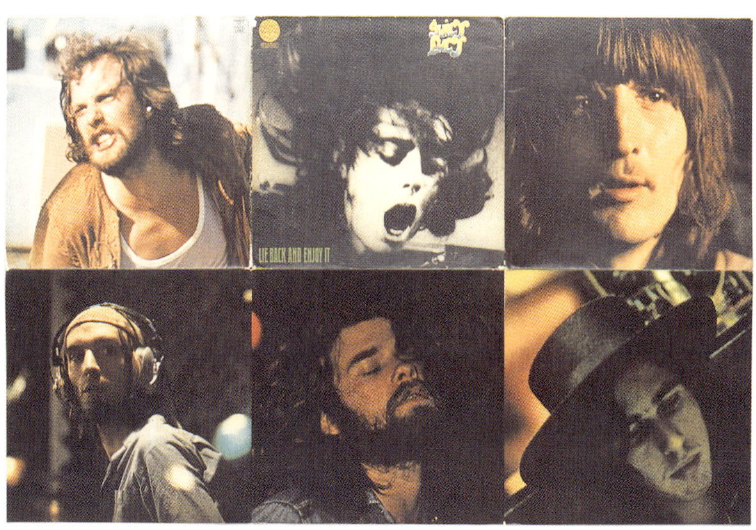

JUICY LUCY:LIE BACK AND ENJOY IT/
VERTIGO 6360 014(1970) *unfolded

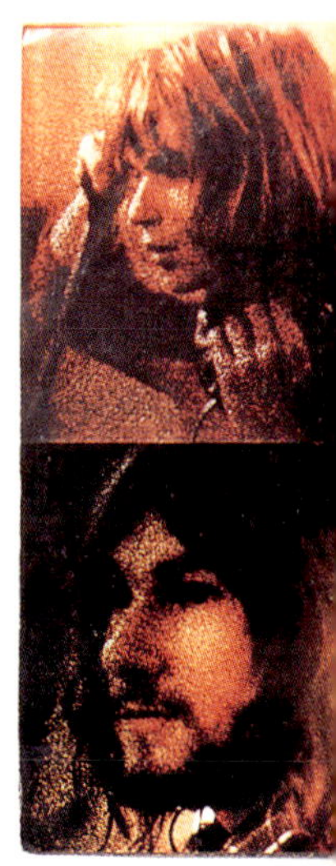

⑤

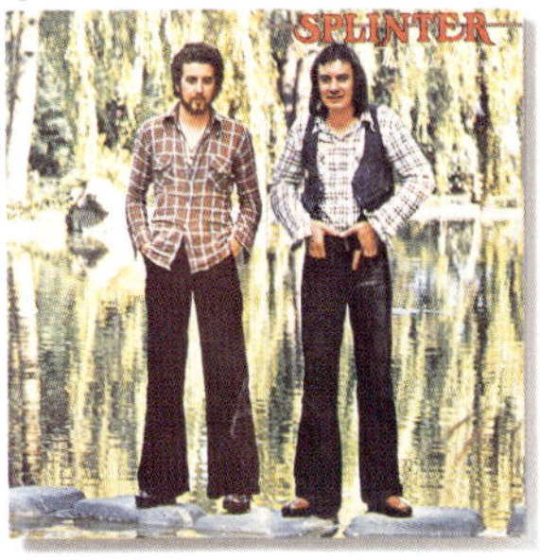

⑥

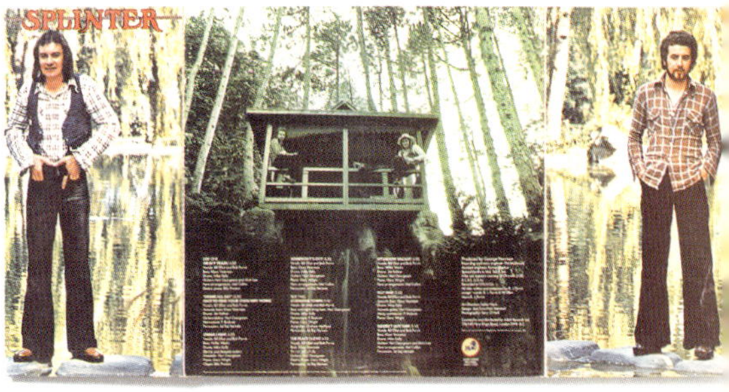

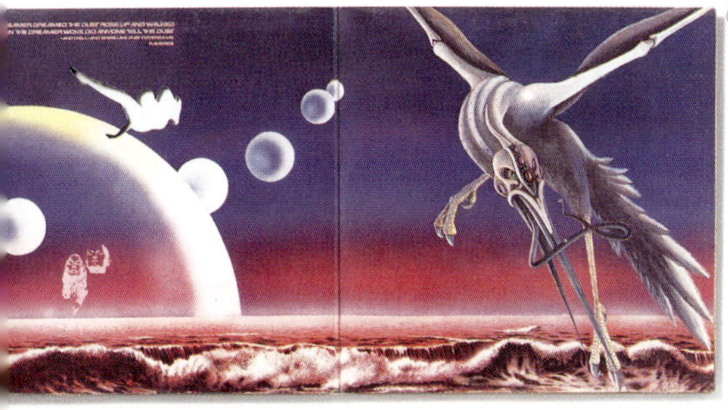

②

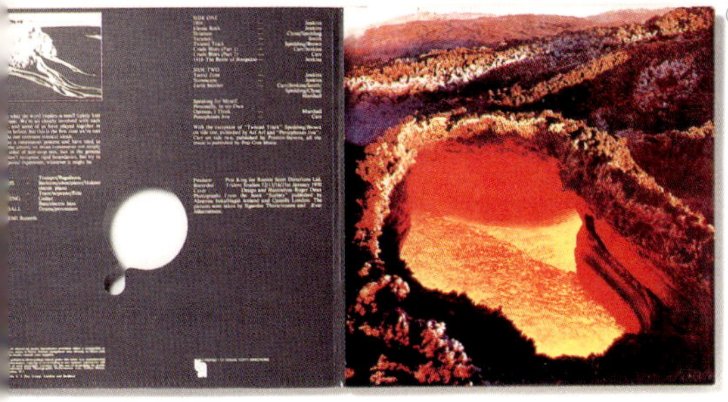

④

⑦

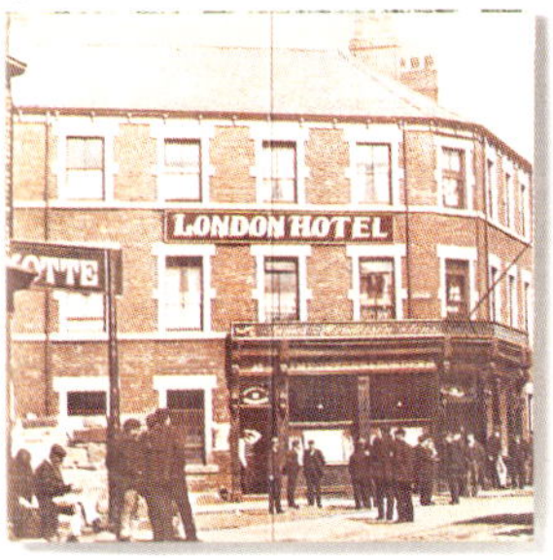

⑧

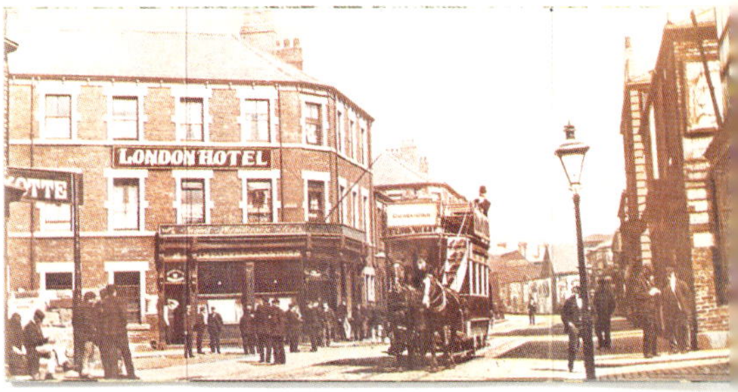

⑨

⑩

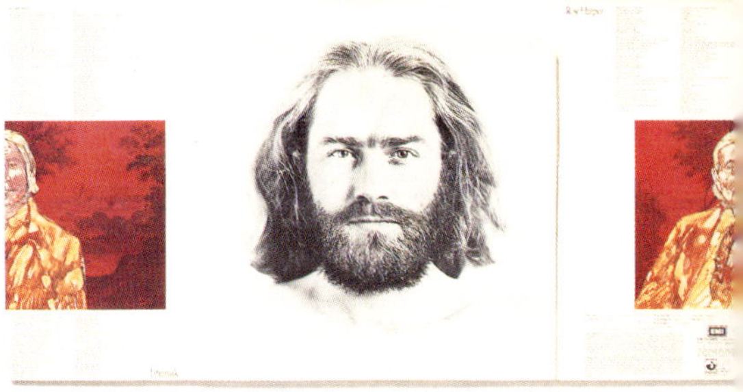

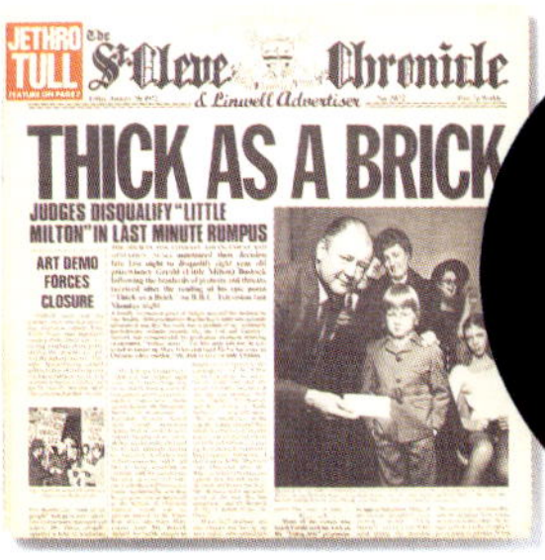

⑪

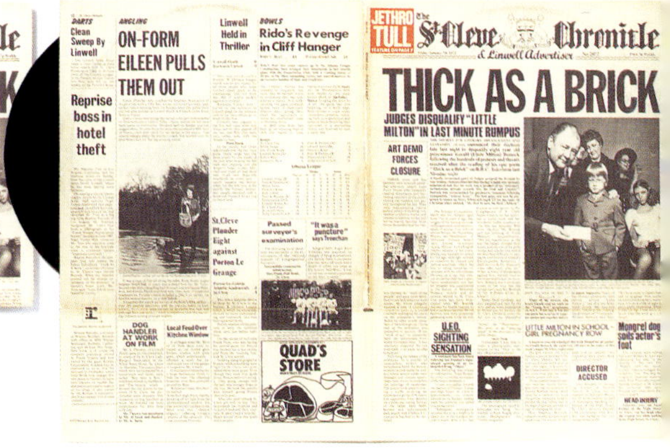

⑫

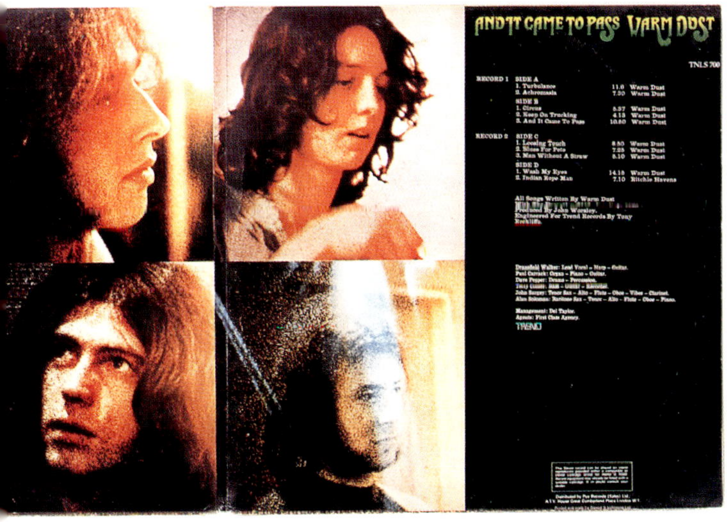

JUICY LUCY:LIE BACK AND ENJOY IT/
VERTIGO 6360 014(1970) *inner

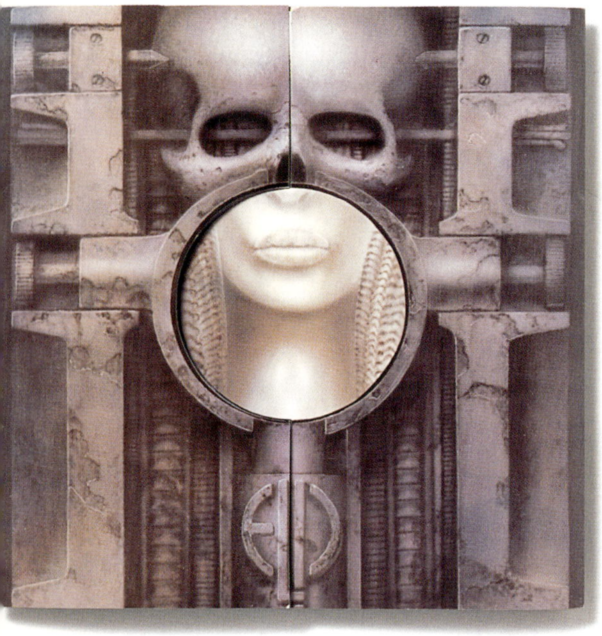

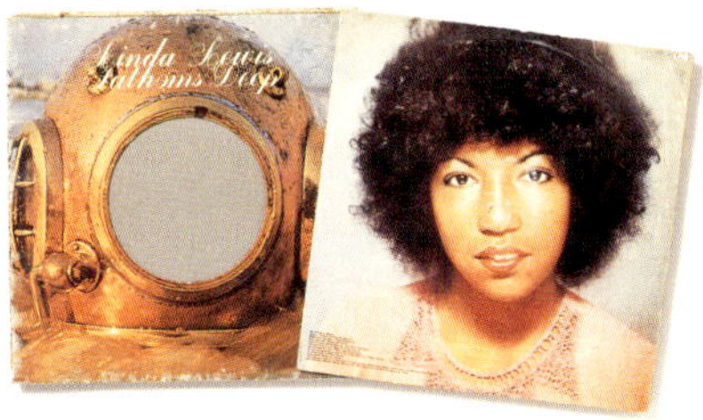

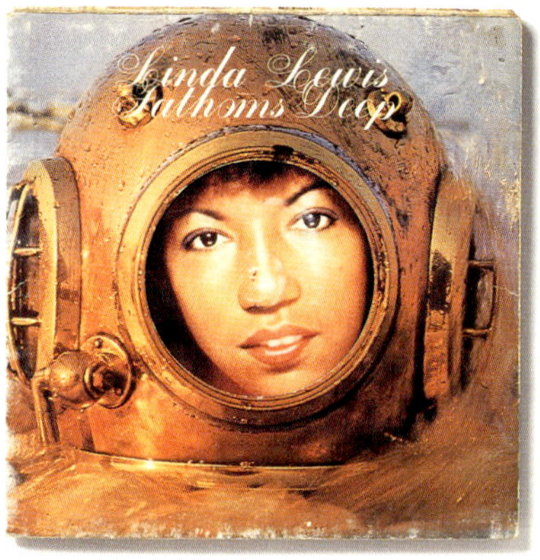

LINDA LEWIS:FATHOMS DEEP/RAFT RA48501(1973)
Cover Design&Prepared by John Kosh and Peter Howe
Photography by Peter Howe

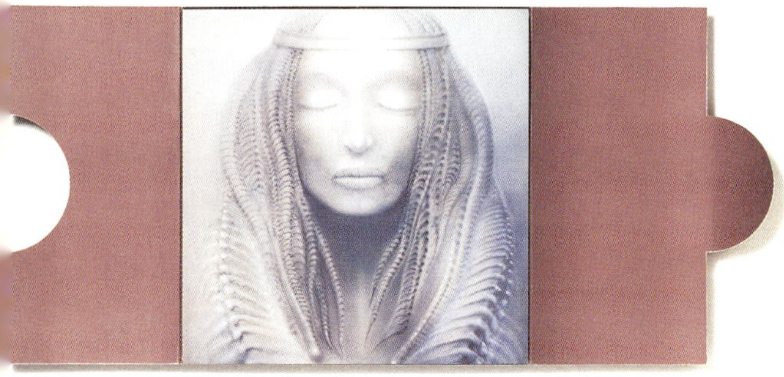

EMERSON,LAKE&PARMER:BRAIN SALAD SURGERY/
MANTICORE K53501(1973)
Design and Art Direction/Fabio Nicoli Associates
Original Cover Painting by H.R.Giger

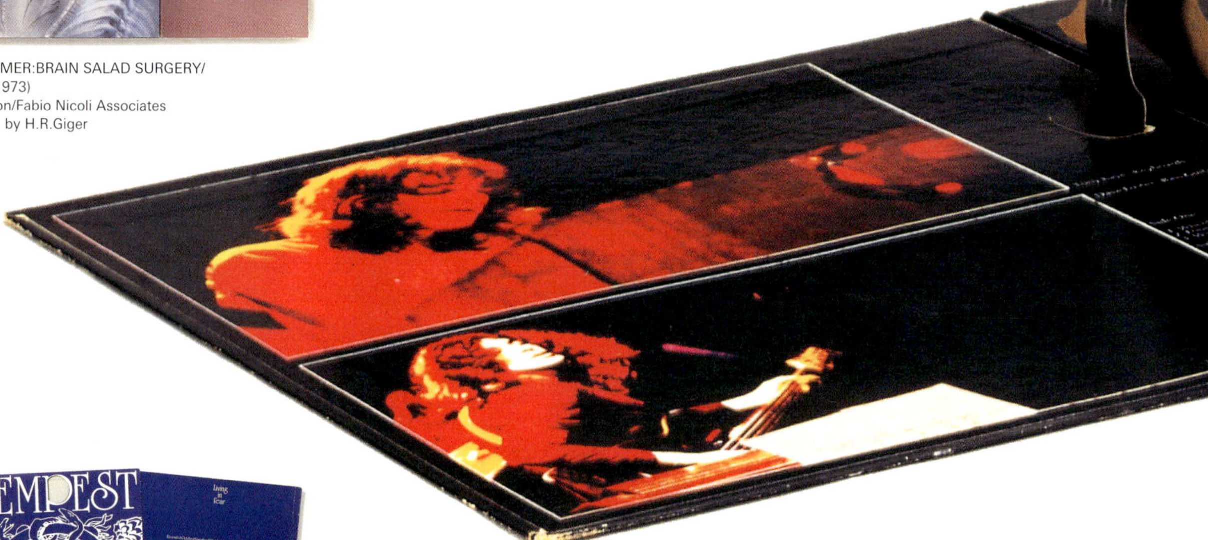

ROD STEWART:SING IT AGAIN ROD/
MERCURY 6499484(1973)
Photography/Cosimo Scianna,Emerson,Lowe and Steve Azzaro
Album Design/Shakey Pete Corriston

In Search of the Lost Record

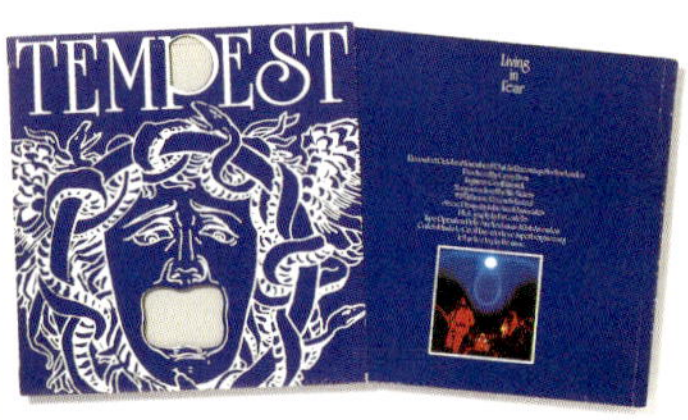

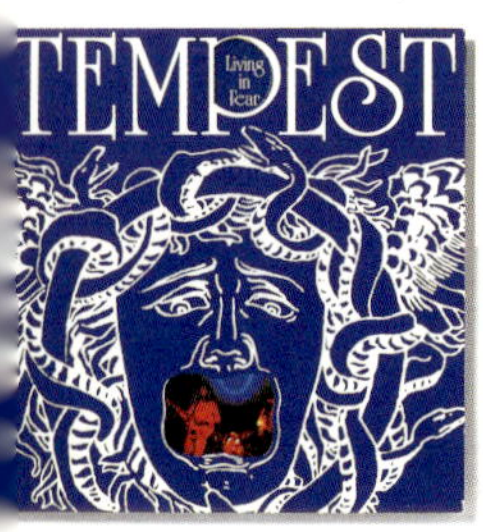

TEMPEST:LIVING IN FEAR/BRONZE ILPS9267(1974)
Sleeve Design by Fabio Nicoli Associates
Photography by Fin Costello

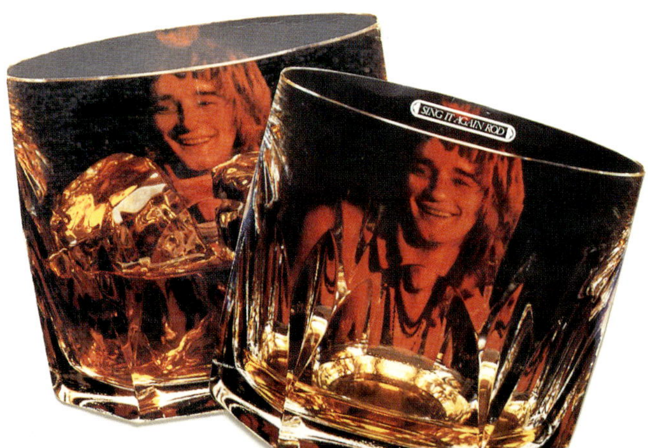

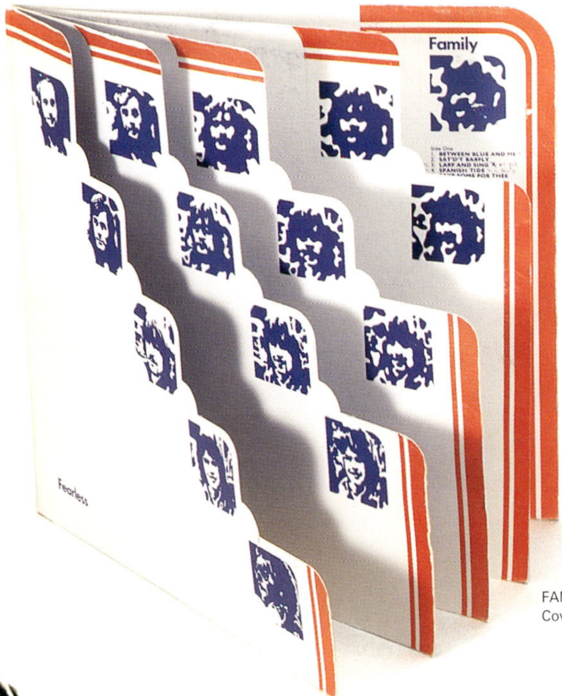

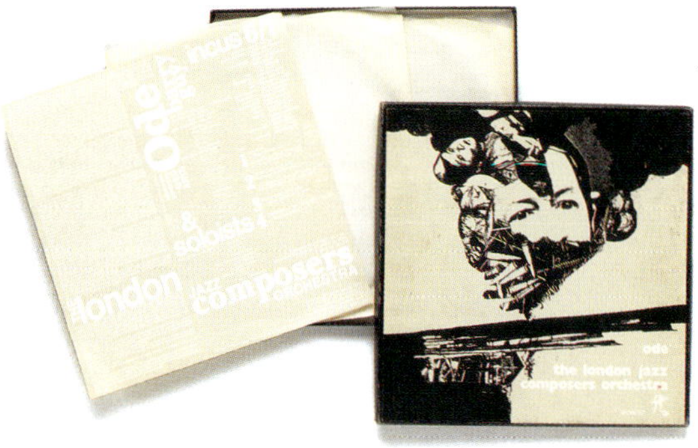

THE LONDON JAZZ COMPOSERS ORCHESTRA:ODE/
INCUS 6,7(1972)
Melancholy Departure Painted by Georgio de Chirico in 1916,
is Part VII of Ode

SOFT MACHINE:TRIPLE ECHO/
HARVEST SHTW800(1977)
Photography/Bill Richmond

FAMILY:FEARLESS/REPRISE K54003(1971)
Cover Design/John Kosh

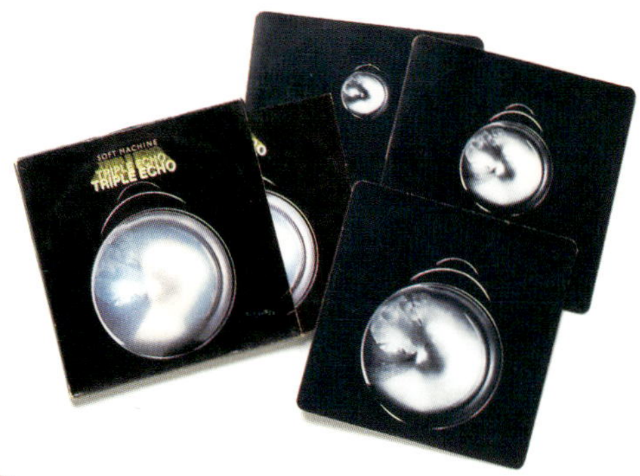

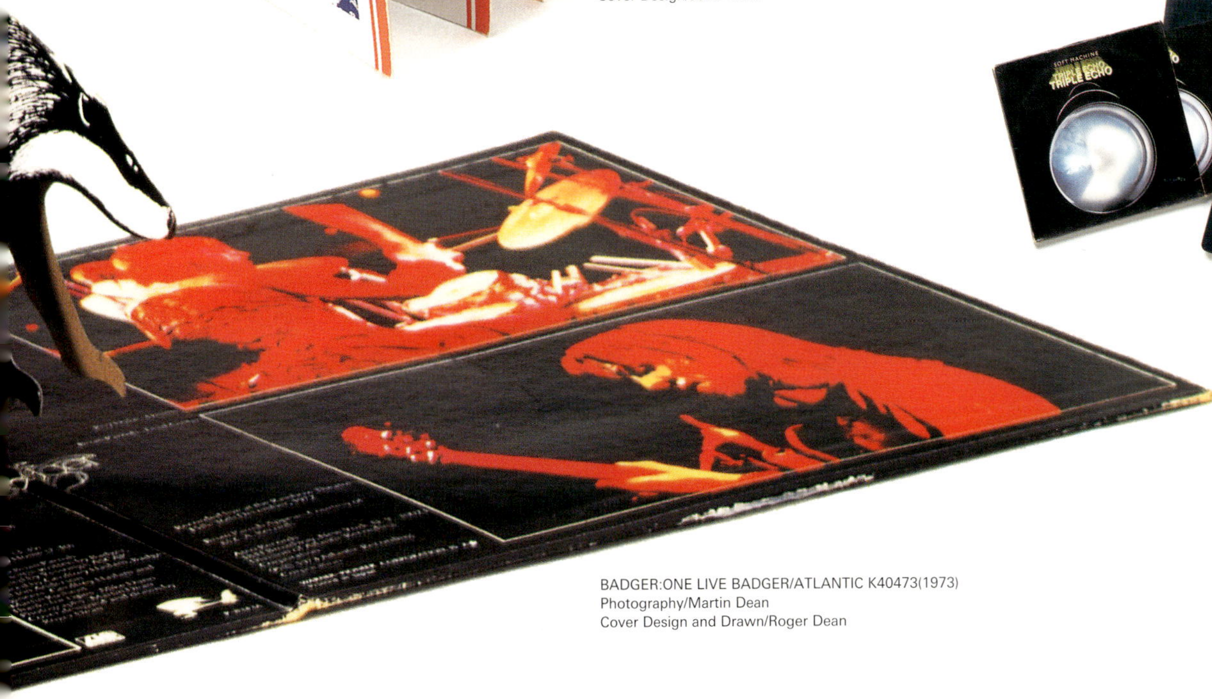

BADGER:ONE LIVE BADGER/ATLANTIC K40473(1973)
Photography/Martin Dean
Cover Design and Drawn/Roger Dean

LON&DERREK VAN EATON:BROTHER/
APPLE SAPCOR25(1973)
Cover Design by Klaus Voormann

GRIMMS:ROCKIN' DUCK/
ISLAND ILPS9248(1973)
Design/Devonshire Studios Limited

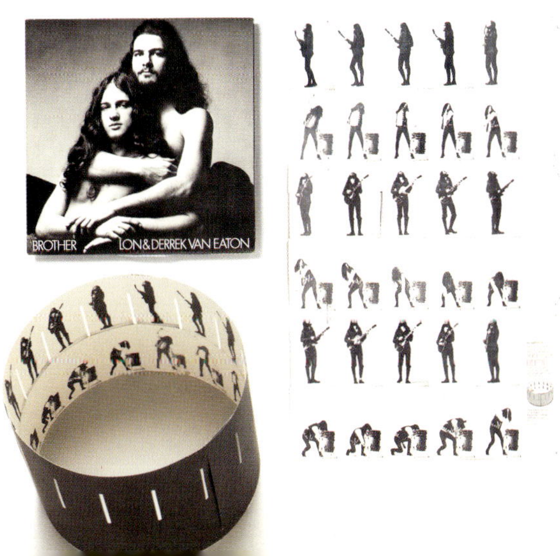

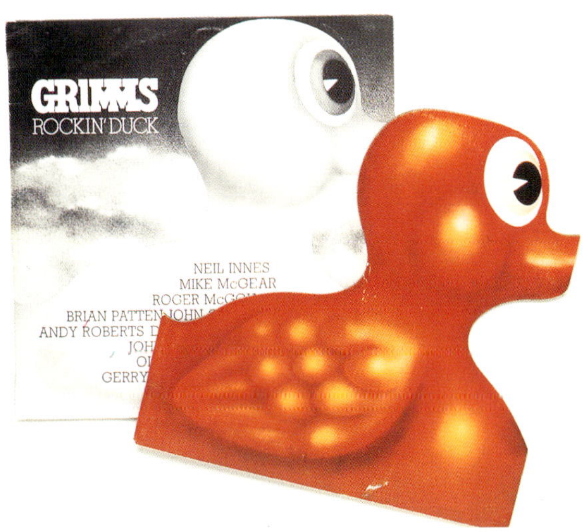

modernism
象徴的なデザイン

ROXY MUSIC:ROXY MUSIC/
ISLAND ILPS9200(1972) ®front and back
Cover Concept/Bryan Ferry
Art/Nicholas de Ville
Photography/Karl Stoecker
Artwork by C.C.S.

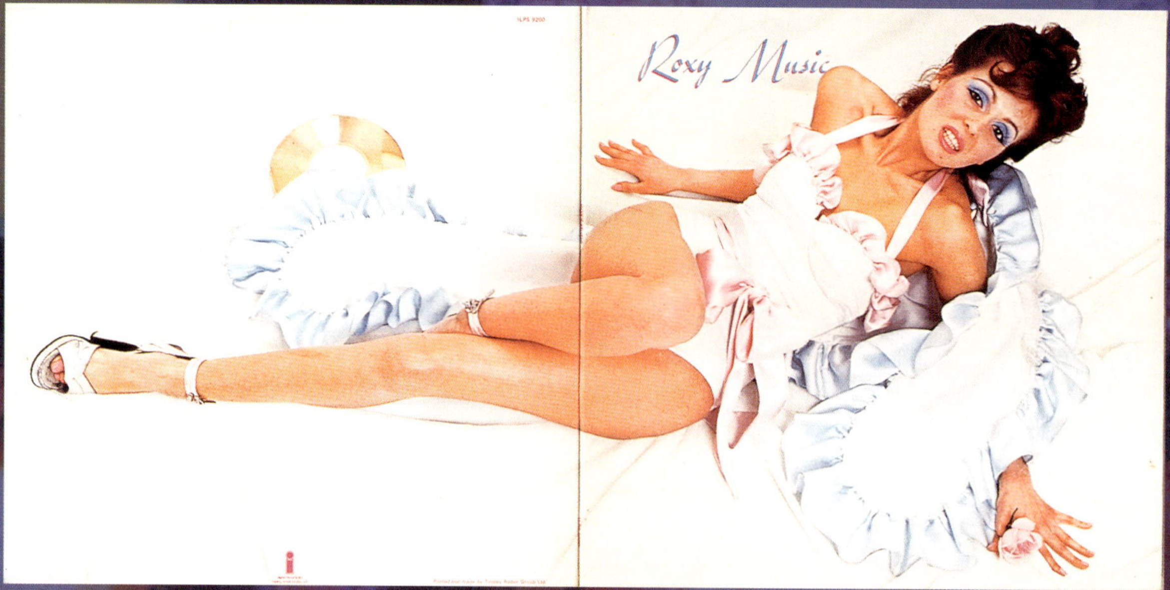

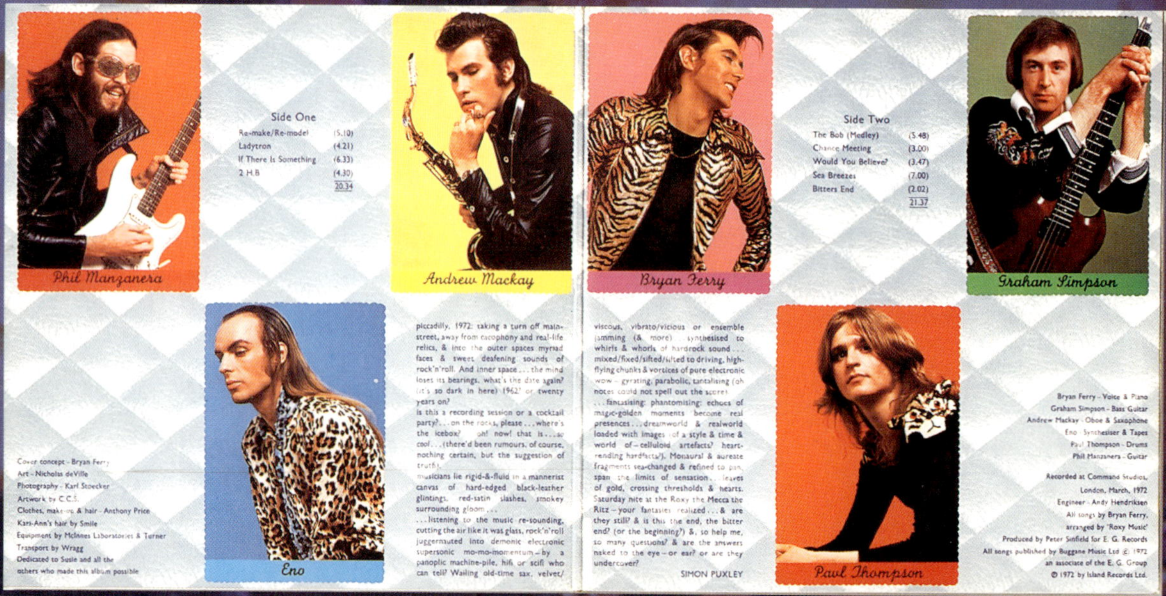

ROXY MUSIC:ROXY MUSIC/
ISLAND ILPS9200(1972) ®inner

In Search of the Lost Record

Nichoras de Ville

modernism

ニコラス・ドヴィル

サイケやプログレッシヴの爛熟と衰退に続く70年代モダン・ポップの系譜は、コスチュームからアルバム・ジャケットにいたるまで、あらゆる視覚的要素が音楽にもたらす効果を、それまで以上に計算に入れた戦略という側面をもっていた。ニコラス・ド・ヴィルが手がけたロキシー・ミュージック初期のアルバムなどは、まさにミュージシャンの音楽的ヴィジョンとキッチュな視覚イメージとが合致したモダニズム・デザインの傑作というべきだろう。そうしたエポックメイキングな事象が当時のレコード業界にどれほどの影響を及ぼしていたのか、正確に把握することは難しいけれども、少なくとも70年代に発表されたレコードの多くが、60年代のそれとはあきらかに違う"新しさ"を備えていたことだけはたしかだ。たとえばそれは、CBSの社員デザイナーだったラズロ・サボの手がけたアルバム・ジャケットなどからも明確に感じ取ることができるのである。

Compared to psychedelia and progressive music, the imagery, costumes, and cover art of Modern Pop in the 70's had a meticulously calculated strategy, greatly influencing the music's package. The early Roxy Music albums that Nicholas de Ville had designed are the best examples of the modern style of album cover design, unifying the music with a kitch visual. It's difficult to evaluate the extent to which this design style influenced the

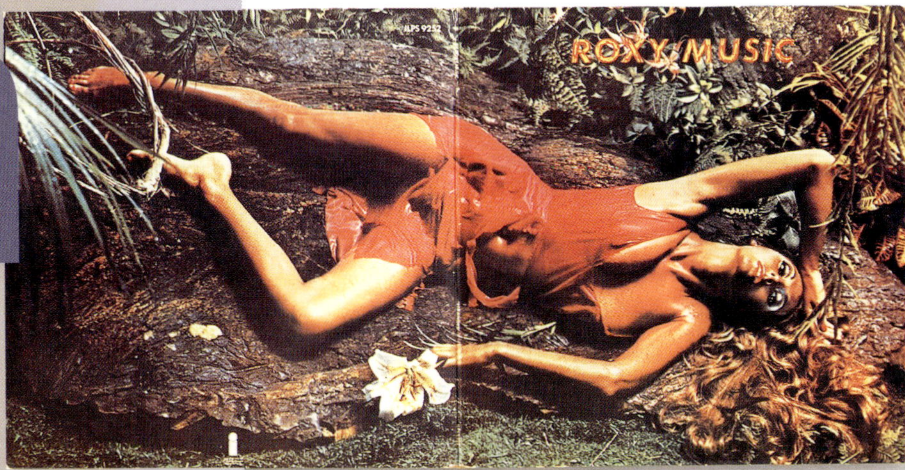

ROXY MUSIC:STLANDED/
ISLAND ILPS9252(1973) *front and back
Cover Design/Nicholas de Ville
Photography/Karl Stoecker
Artwork/Bob Bowkett C.C.S.
Cover Concept/Bryan Ferry

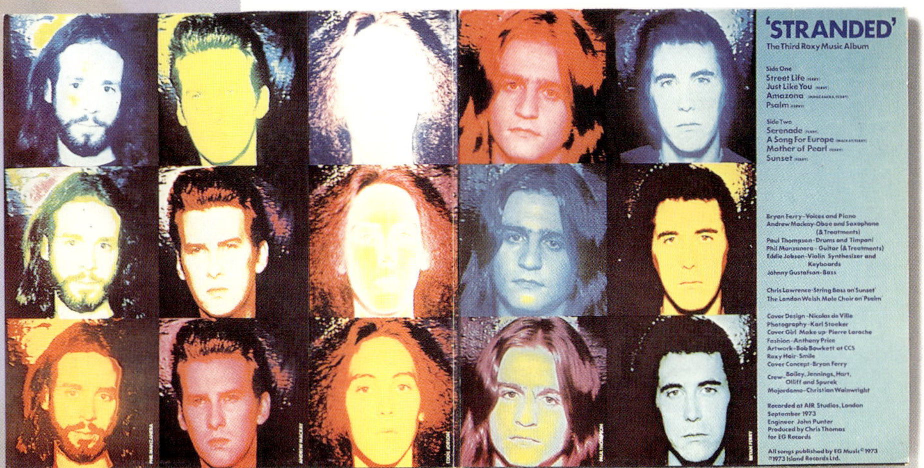

ROXY MUSIC:STLANDED/
ISLAND ILPS9252(1973) *inner

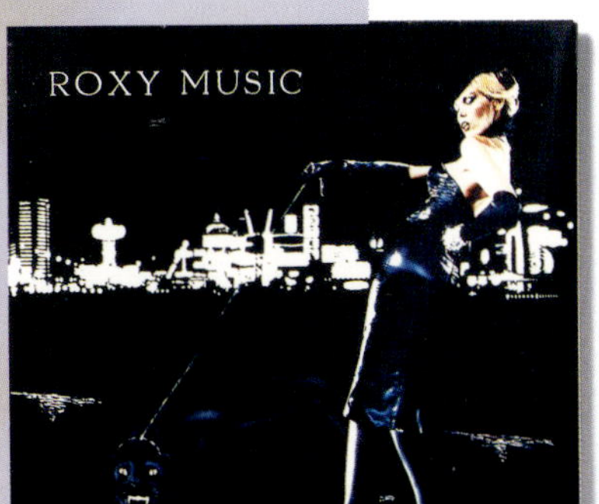

ROXY MUSIC:FOR YOUR PLEASURE/
ISLAND ILPS9232(1973)
Cover Design/Nicholas de Ville
Photography/Karl Stoecker
Artwork/C.C.S.

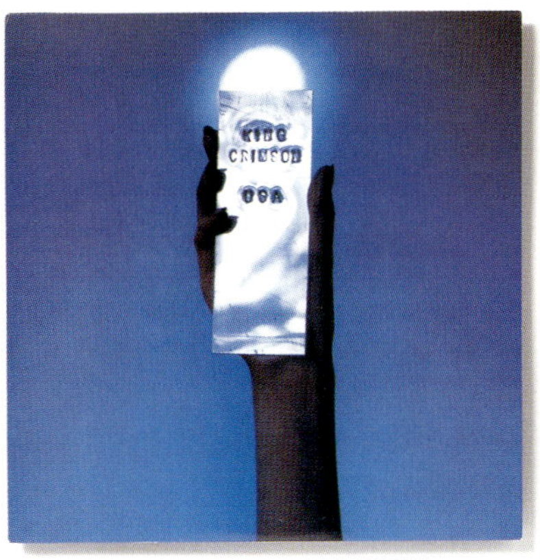

KING CRIMSON:USA/ISLAND ILPS9316(1975)
Cover/Nicholas de Ville
Typography/Bob Bowkett,C.C.S.
Photography/Willie Christie

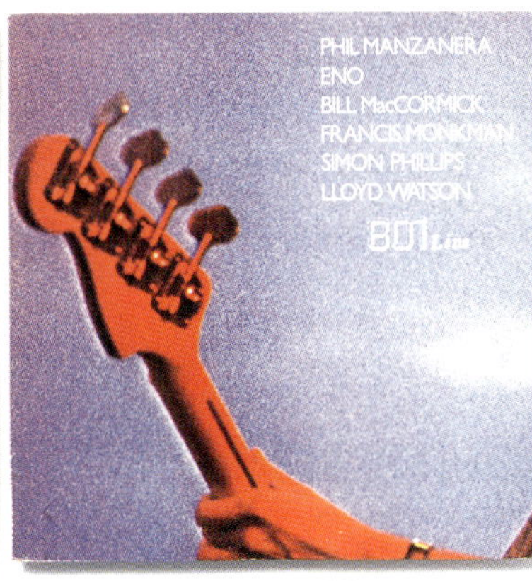

801:801 LIVE/ISLAND ILPS9444(1976)
Photography/Richard Wallis
Typography/Bob Bowkett&Nicholas de Ville

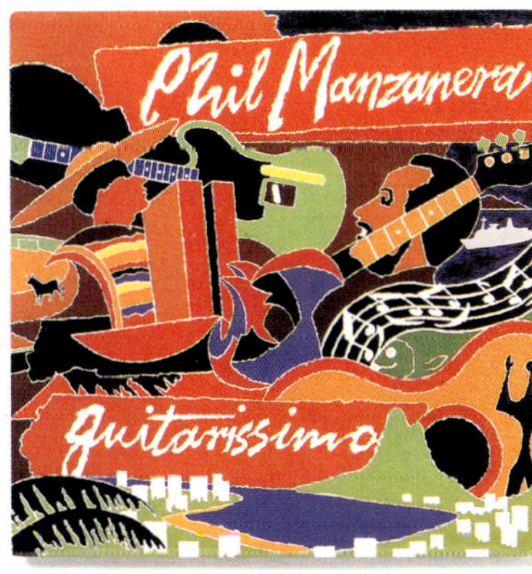

PHIL MANZANERA:GUITARISSIMO/
EG EGLP69(1991)
Cover Art Direction/Nick de Ville

music industry on the whole, but it's safe to say that many records of the 70's assumed an entirely new image compared to those of the 60's. The distinct feel of the 70's style is also clearly expressed in the cover art designs by CBS's in-house designer Roslav Szabo.

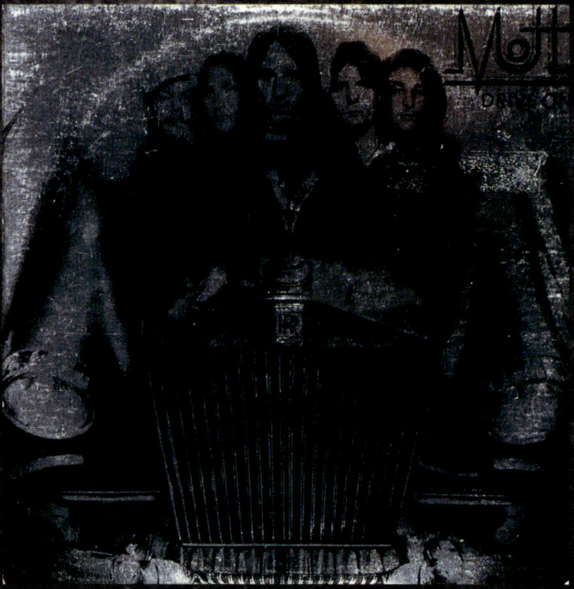

MOTT:DRIVE ON/CBS 69154(1975)
Art Direction/Roslav Szaybo
Sleeve Design/Michael Farrell
Front Cover Photo/Roger Bamber

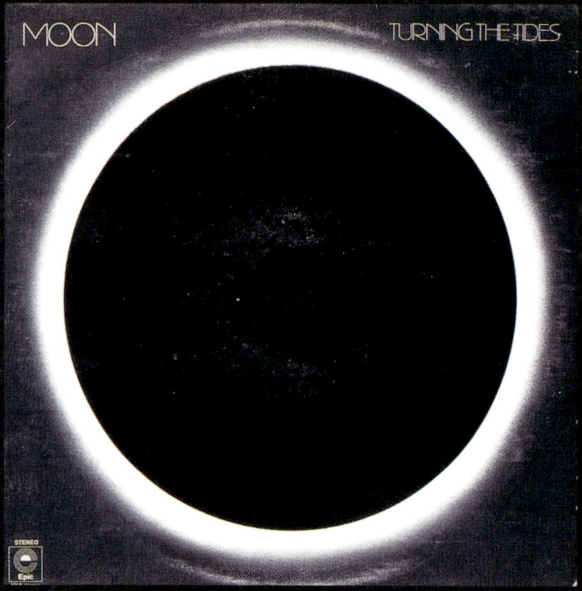

MOON:TURNING THE TIDES/EPIC EPC82084(1977)
Art Direction and Design/Roslav Szaybo
Typography/Les May

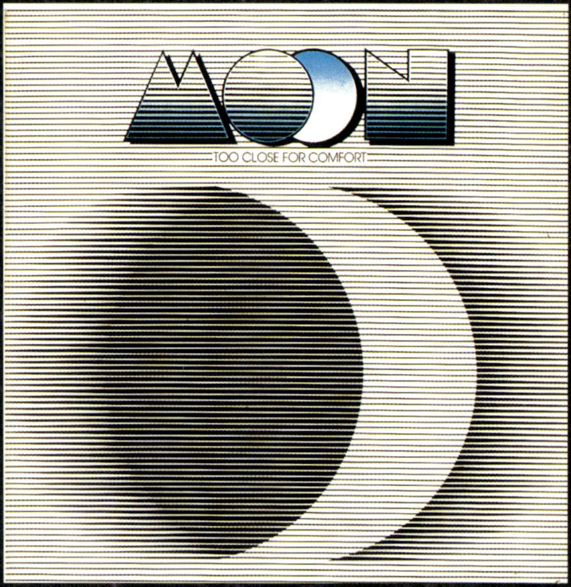

MOON:TOO CLOSE FOR COMFORT/
EPIC EPC81456(1976)
Sleeve Desin/Roslav Szaybo and Les May

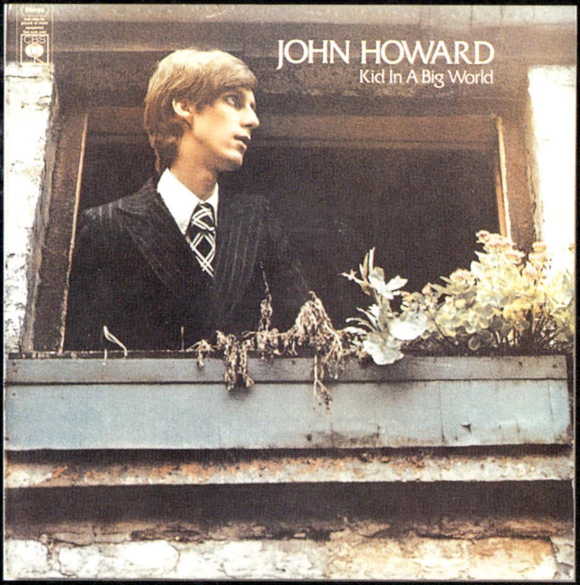

JOHN HOWARD:KID A BIG WORLD/CBS 80473()
Photo/Mike Nicholson
Cover Design/Roslav Szaybo

Roslav Szaybo

modernism

ラズロ・サボ

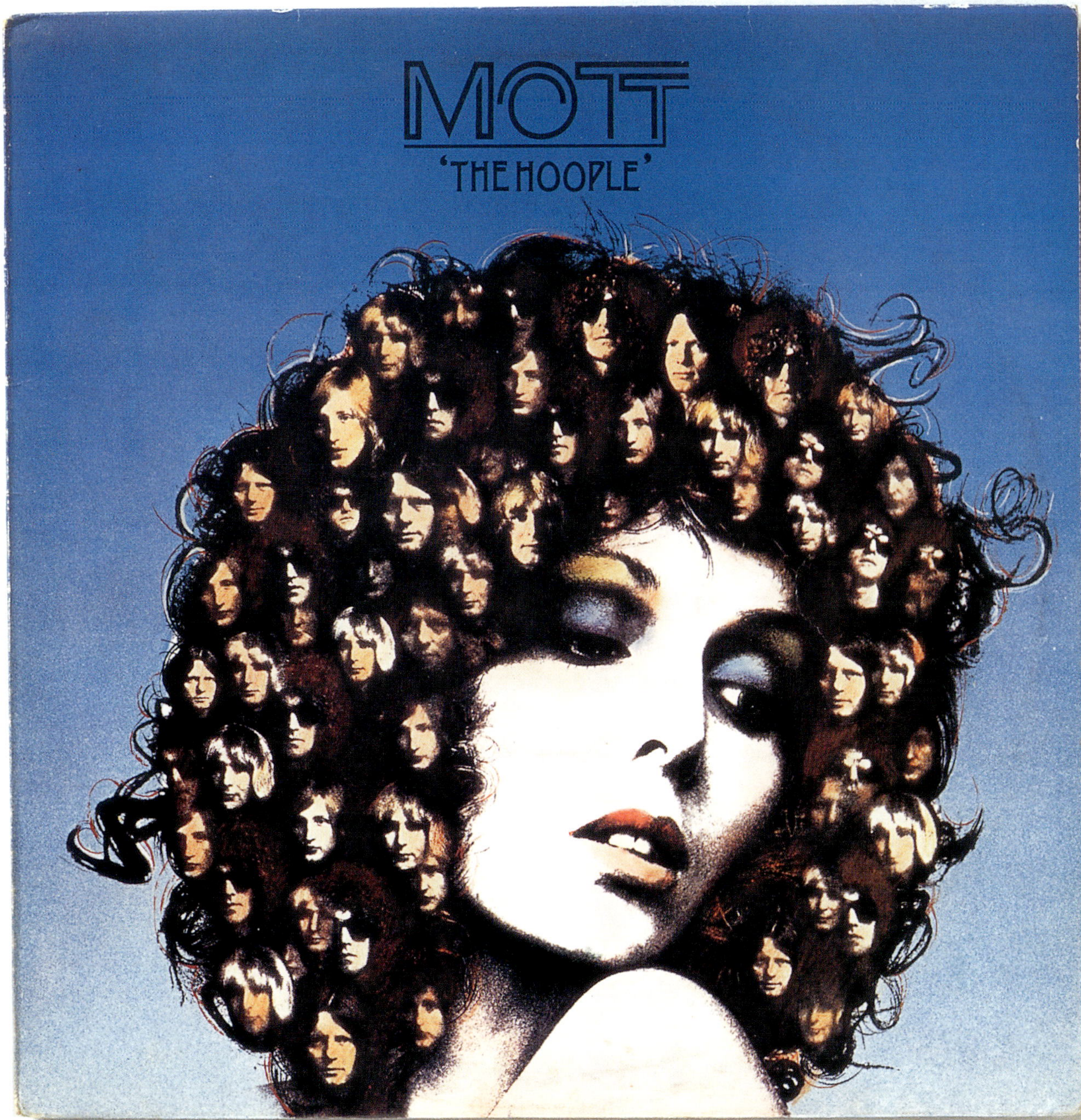

MOTT THE HOOPLE:THE HOOPLE/CBS 69062(1974)
Sleeve Concept and Design/Roslav Szaybo
Photography/John Brown

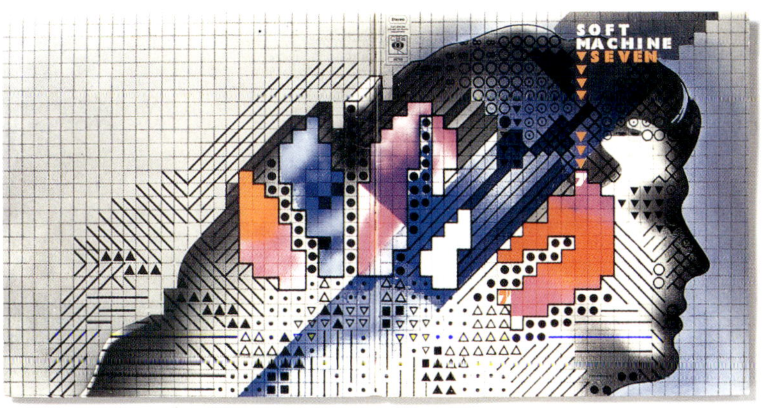

SOFT MACHINE:SEVEN/CBS 65799(1973)
Design and Art Direction/Roslav Szaybo
Photography/Tim Fulford-Brown
Inside Artwork/Simon Cantwell

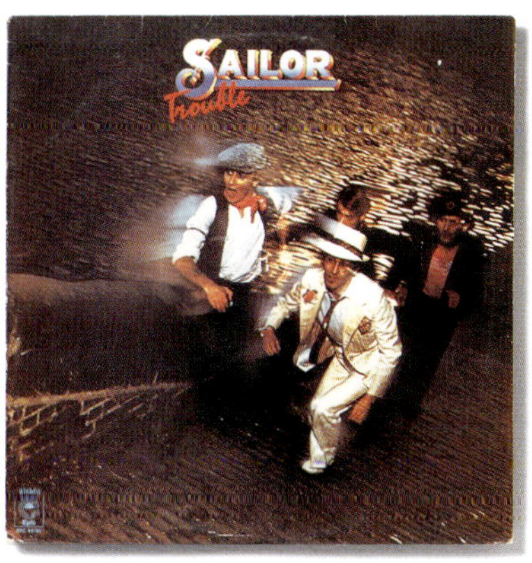

SAILOR:TROUBLE/EPIC EPC69192(1975)
Design/Roslav Szaybo
Photography/Peter Lavery

WHITE TRAILS

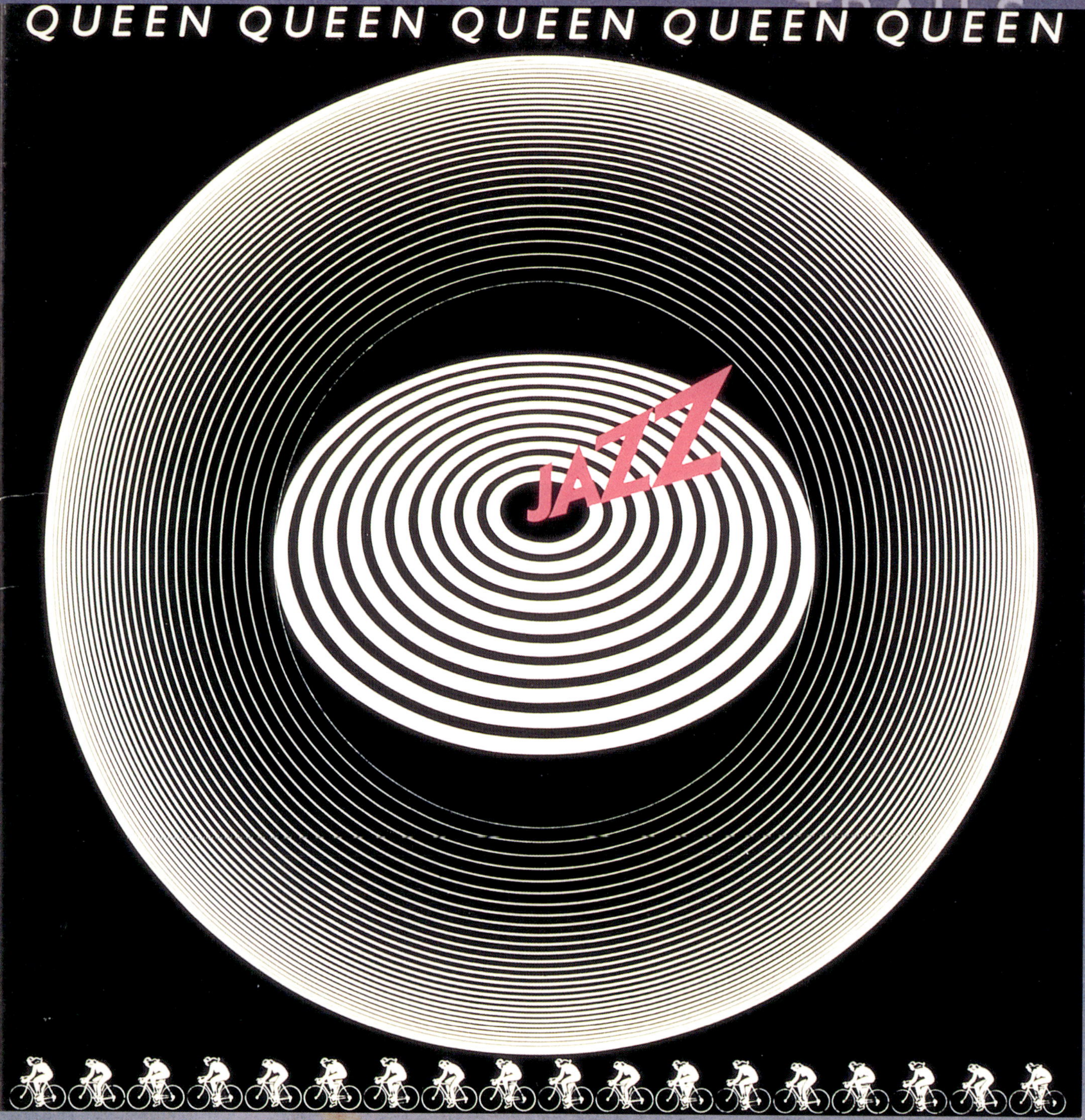

QUEEN:JAZZ/EMI EMA788(1978)
Sleeve Design by Cream

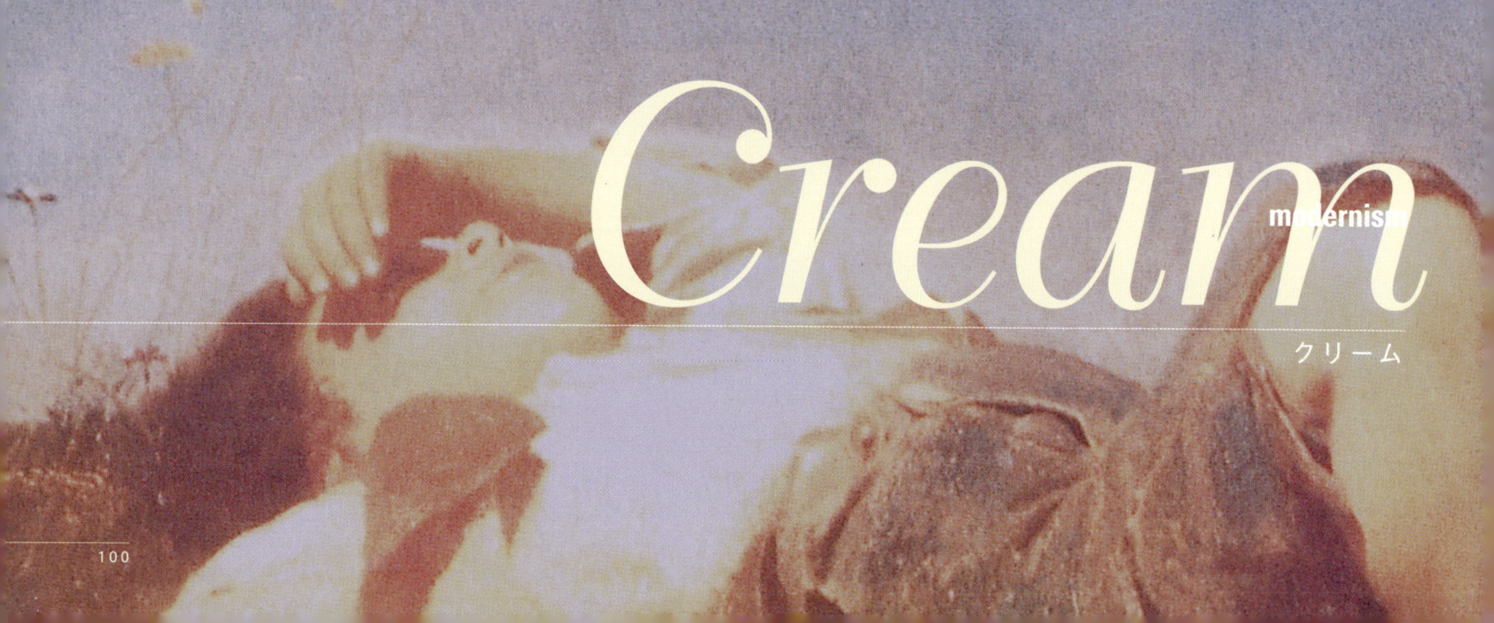

Cream

modernism

クリーム

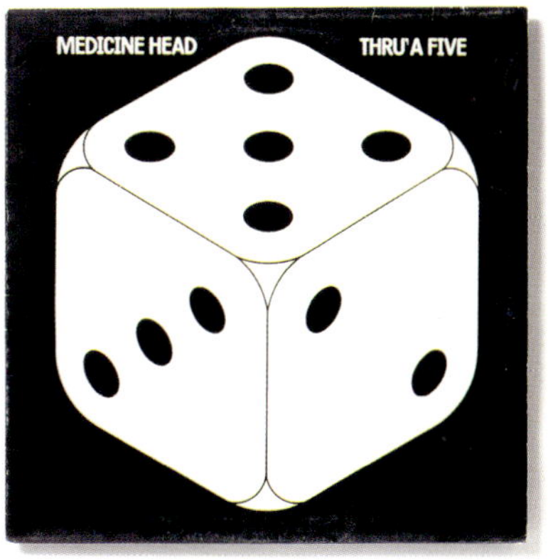

MEDICINE HEAD:THRU'A FIVE/
POLYDOR 2383 272(1974)
Cover Design Produced by Cream

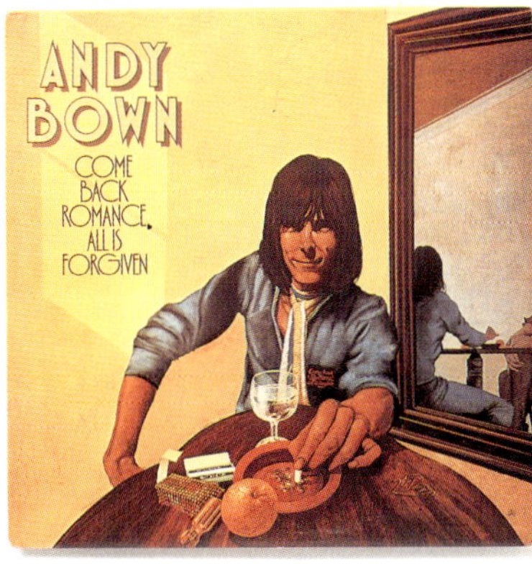

ANDY BOWN:
COME BACK ROMANCE ALL IS FORGIVEN/
EMI EMC3176(1977)
Cover Painting by Mike Francis
Design/Cream

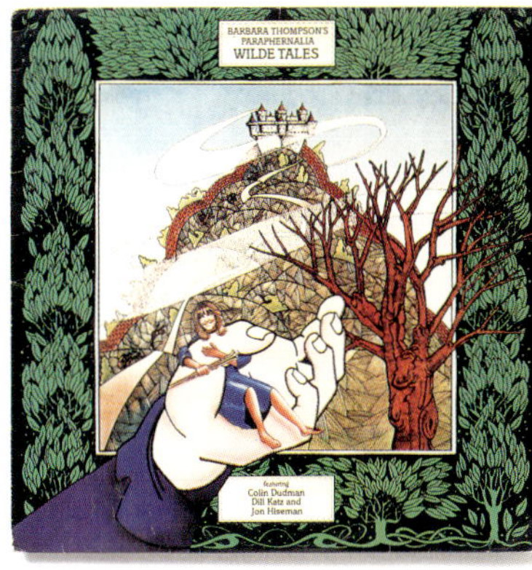

BARBARA THOMPSON'S PARAPHERNALIA:
WILDE TALES/
MCA MCF3047(1979)
Deisgn and Artwork/Cream

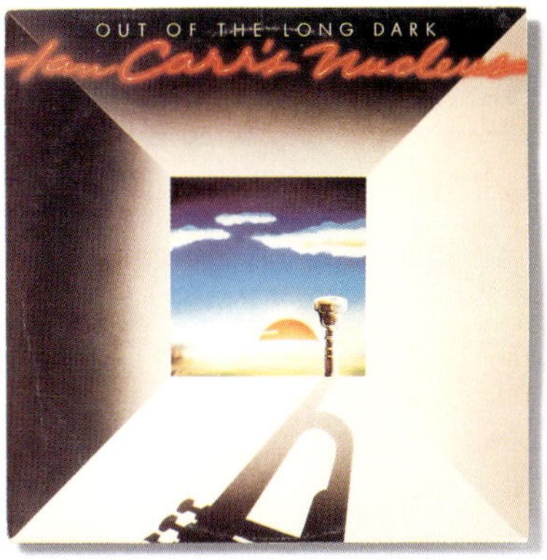

IAN CARR'S NUCLEUS:OUT OF THE LONG DARK/
CAPITOL EMI E-ST11916(1978)
Design and Art Direction/Chris Archer,Cream

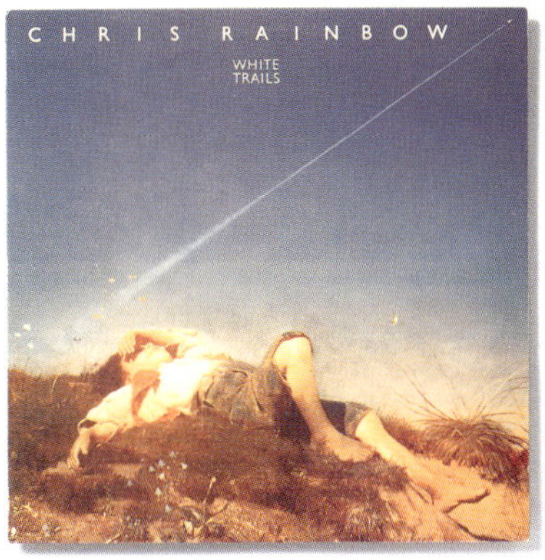

CHRIS RAINBOW:WHITE TRAILS/
EMI EMC3305(1979)
Art Work/Cream

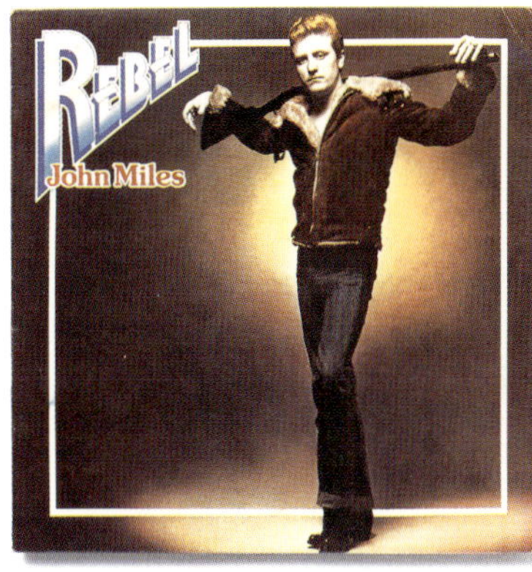

JOHN MILES:REBEL/DECCA SKL5231(1976)
Sleeve Design/Nick Nicol For Cream
Photographs and Concept/Tony O'Neill

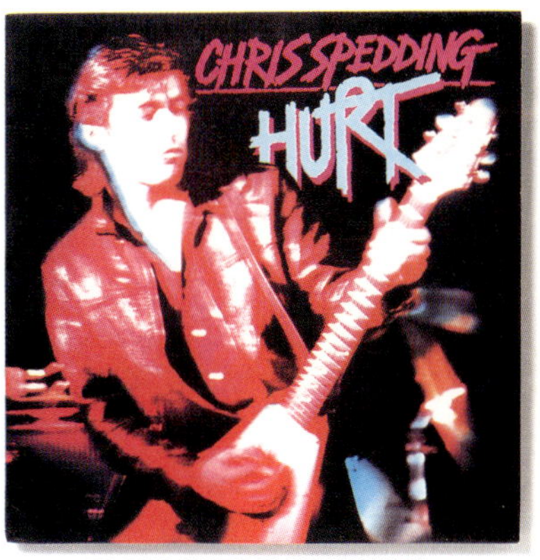

CHRIS SPEDDING:HURT/RAK SPAK529(1977)
Cover Design Produced by Cream

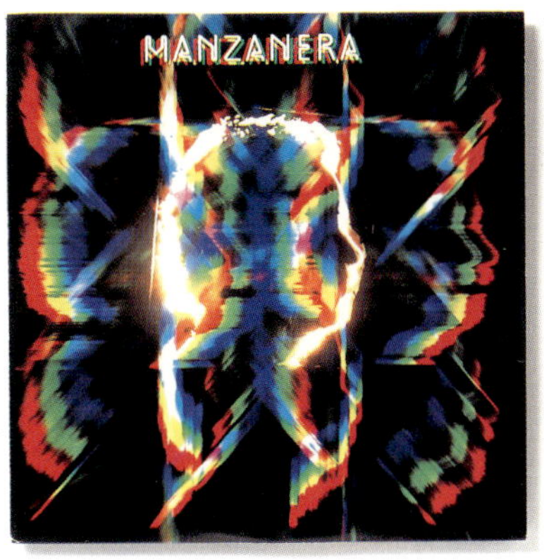

MANZANERA:K-SCOPE/POLYDOR 2302 083 (1978)
Cover Concept/Chris Hopper
Design/Cream

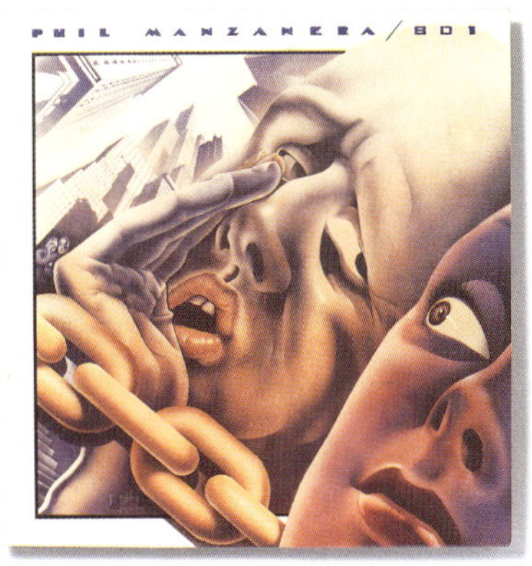

PHIL MANZANERA:LISTEN NOW/
POLYDOR 2302 074(1977)
Design and Concept Cover/Philip Castle
Artwork/Cream

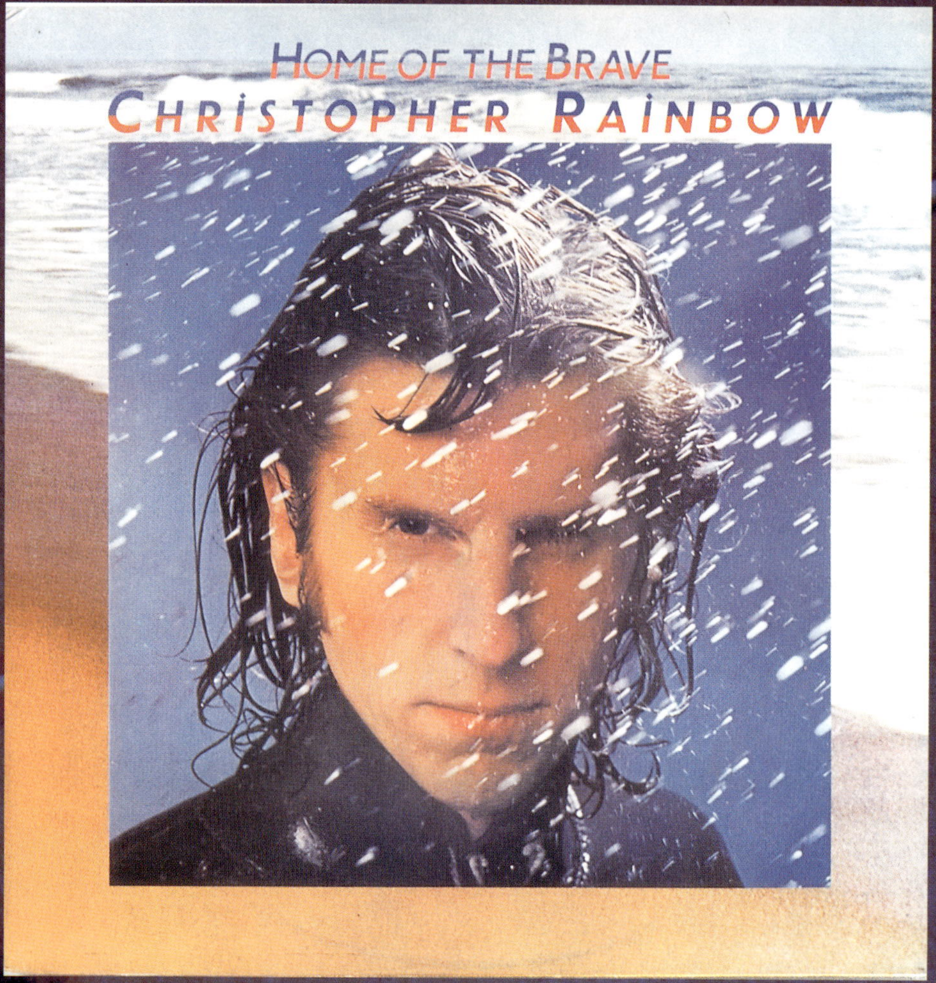

CHRISTOPHER RAINBOW:HOME OF THE BRAVE/
POLYDOR 2383 338(1975) *front
Cover Photography/Ethan A.Russell
Cover Designed&Prepared by John Kosh

CHRISTOPHER RAINBOW:HOME OF THE BRAVE/
POLYDOR 2383 338(1975) *back

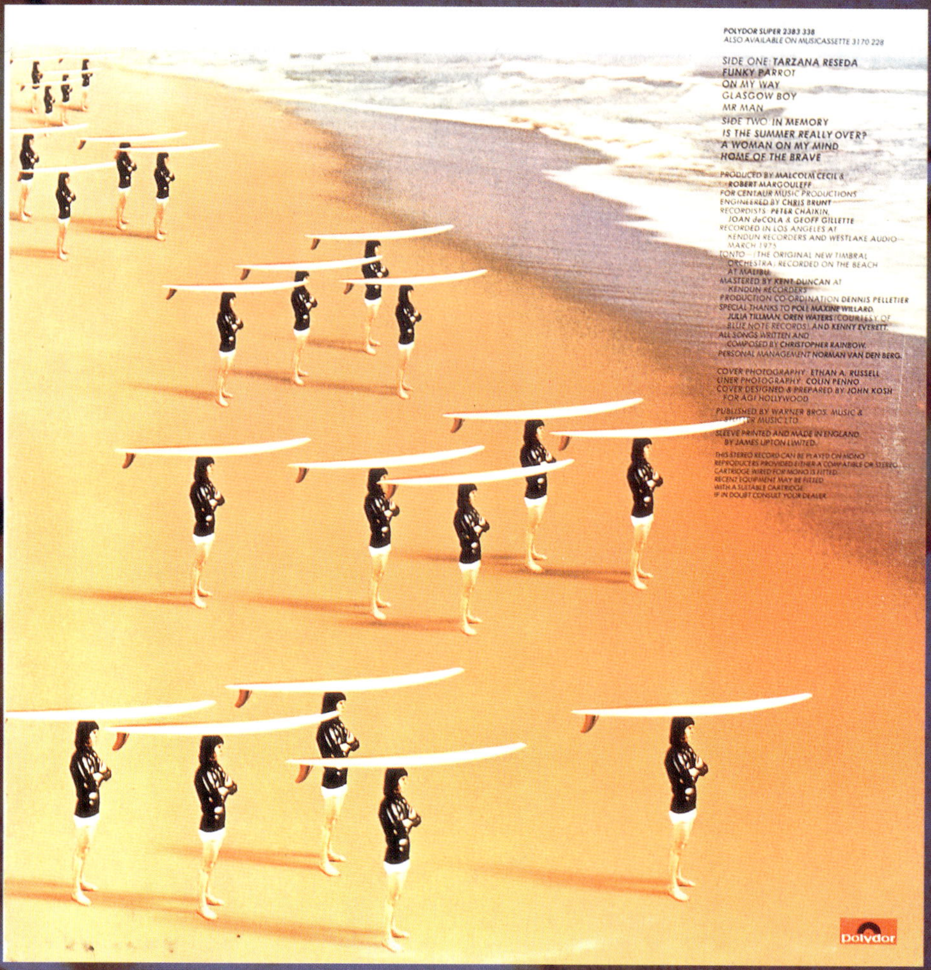

In Search of the Lost Record

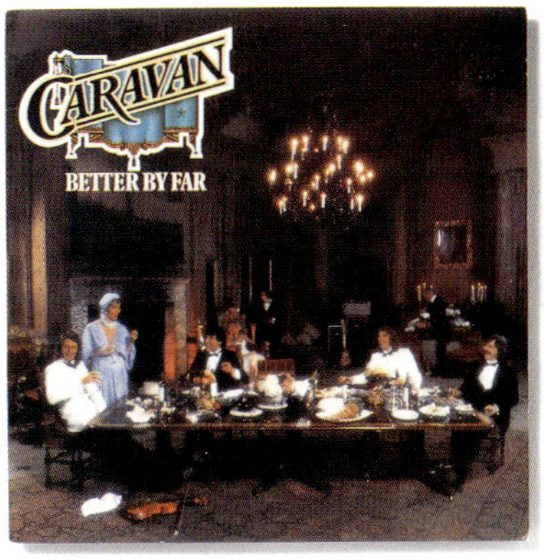

CARAVAN:BETTER BY FAR/
ARISTA SPARTY1008(1977)
Design/Bob Searles
Photography/Brian Hennessey
Art Direction/John Dyer

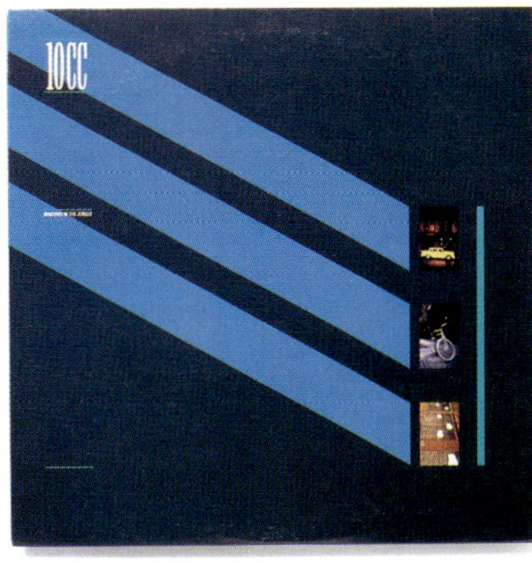

10cc:WINDOWS IN THE JUNGLE/
MERCURY MERL28(1983)
Sleeve by Std

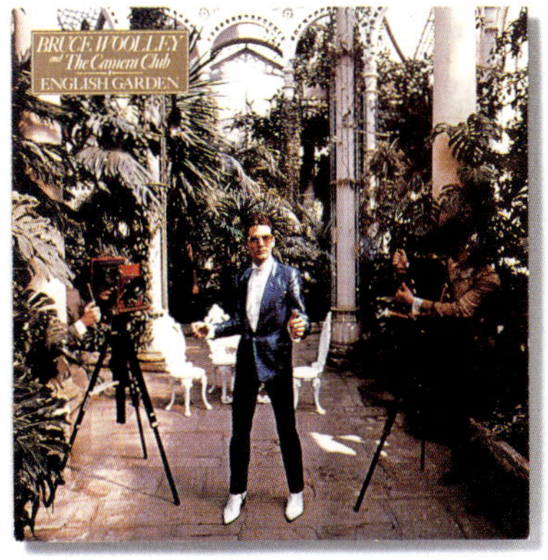

BRUCE WOOLEY AND THE CAMERA CLUB:
ENGLISHA GARDEN/EPIC EPC83893(1979)
Art Direction&Design/Nicholas Marchant
Photography/Robert Elsdale

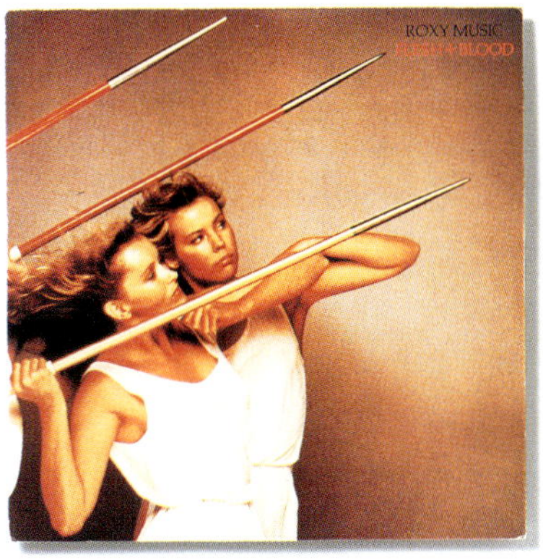

ROXY MUSIC:FLESH+BLOOD/
POLYDOR 2302 099(1980)

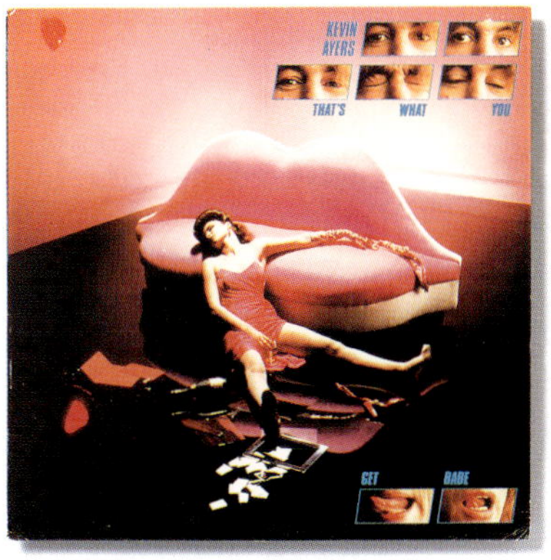

KEVIN AYERS:THAT'S WHAT YOU GET BABE/
HARVEST SHSP4106(1980)
Cover Art/Chris Morton
Photos/John Thornton

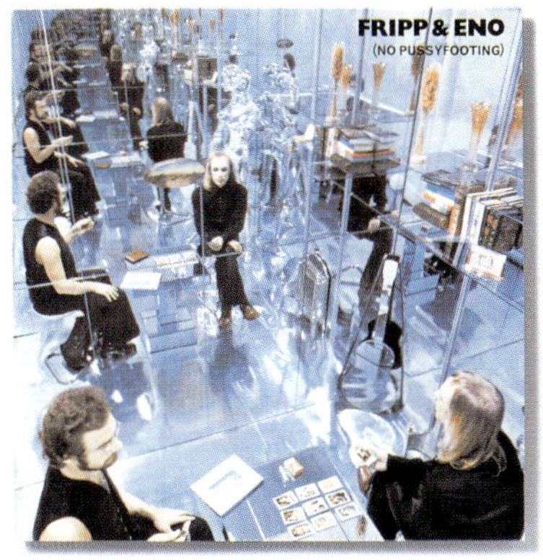

FRIPP&ENO:NO PUSSY FOOTING/ISLAND HELP16(1972)
Cover Design&Photography/Willie Christie

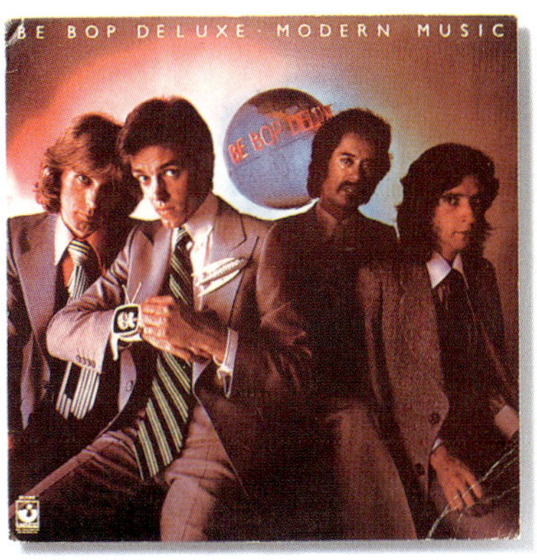

BE BOP DELUXE:MODERN MUSIC/
HARVEST SHSP40588 (1976)
Cover Photography by Roger Bamber

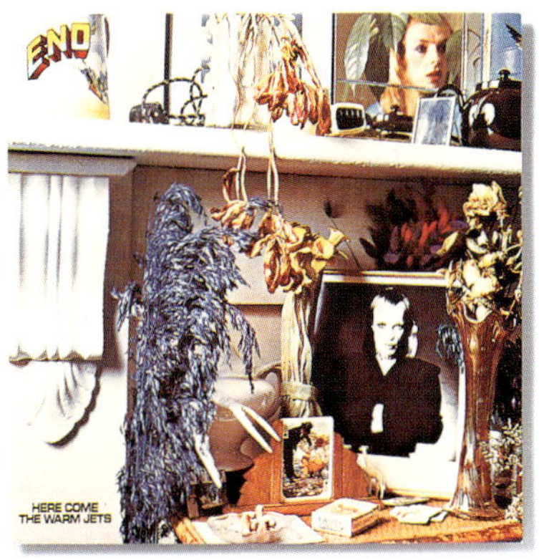

ENO:HERE COMES THE WARM JETS/
ISLAND ILPS9268 (1973)
Cover Photography/Lorenz Zatecky
Design Siper Vision/Carol McNicol
Artwork/CCS Associates

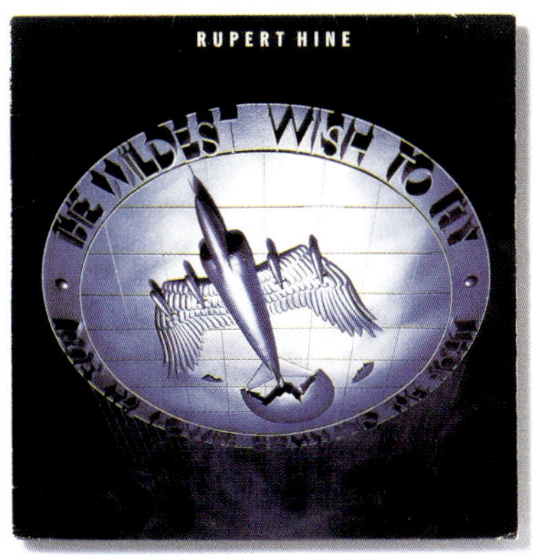

RUPERT HINE:THE WILDEST WISH TO FLY/
ISLAND ILPS9747 (1983)
Art Directon/Jeannette Obstoj

modernism

The Other Modernism Selections

その他のモダン・デザイン

nude

レコード・ジャケットにヌード。そのアイデア自体は、50年代のジャズのレコードを飾ったエロチックな女性ピンナップあたりにルーツをみることができる。無骨な男性ポートレートより、女性の柔肌の方が売り上げに貢献してくれるというわけだ。その場合、ミュージシャンのポートレートは、インナー・スリーヴや裏ジャケットに押しやられることが多かった。60～70年代のレコード・ジャケットにおけるヌードにも同じ効果をねらったものが数多く見受けられるが、性と人種の解放を掲げたラヴ＆ピースの時代にはジミ・ヘンドリクス『エレクトリック・レディランド』のように既成社会への急進的なメッセージをはらんだものもあった。いずれにしろ、ヌードが絶大な視覚的効果をもたらすものであることだけはまちがいなさそうだ。だがそれにしても、ただ一般的な美しさだけを追求したような麗しいヌードより、やつれきって体の線が崩れてしまったり露悪的だったりするハダカの方が、イギリスのアルバム・ジャケットにふさわしく思えてしまうのはなぜだろう？ そんなところからも、ひねくれ具合の激しい英国ポップ・ミュージックの本質がにじみ出ているのであろうか。

The use of nudes on album covers was rooted in 50' s jazz album covers featuring erotic female pin-up shots. The female body also does more for sales than portraits of gruff-looking men. In many cases, the musician's portraits were tucked into the inner jacket sleeve or simply moved to the back cover. In the 60's and 70's, the use of nudes was not only a sales tool but a loaded, radical protest, as with Jimi Hendrix's "Electric Ladyland", a product of the "love and peace" generation that called for the liberation of sex and racial harmony. In either case, it's unmistakable that the nude possessed an immediate and immense potency. It is curious to think why an out-of-shape model or a somewhat tacky nude felt more appropriate for British album covers than a sexy nudes with perfect forms. Perhaps the essence of the cynical British Pop music was present as well.

nude
ヌード

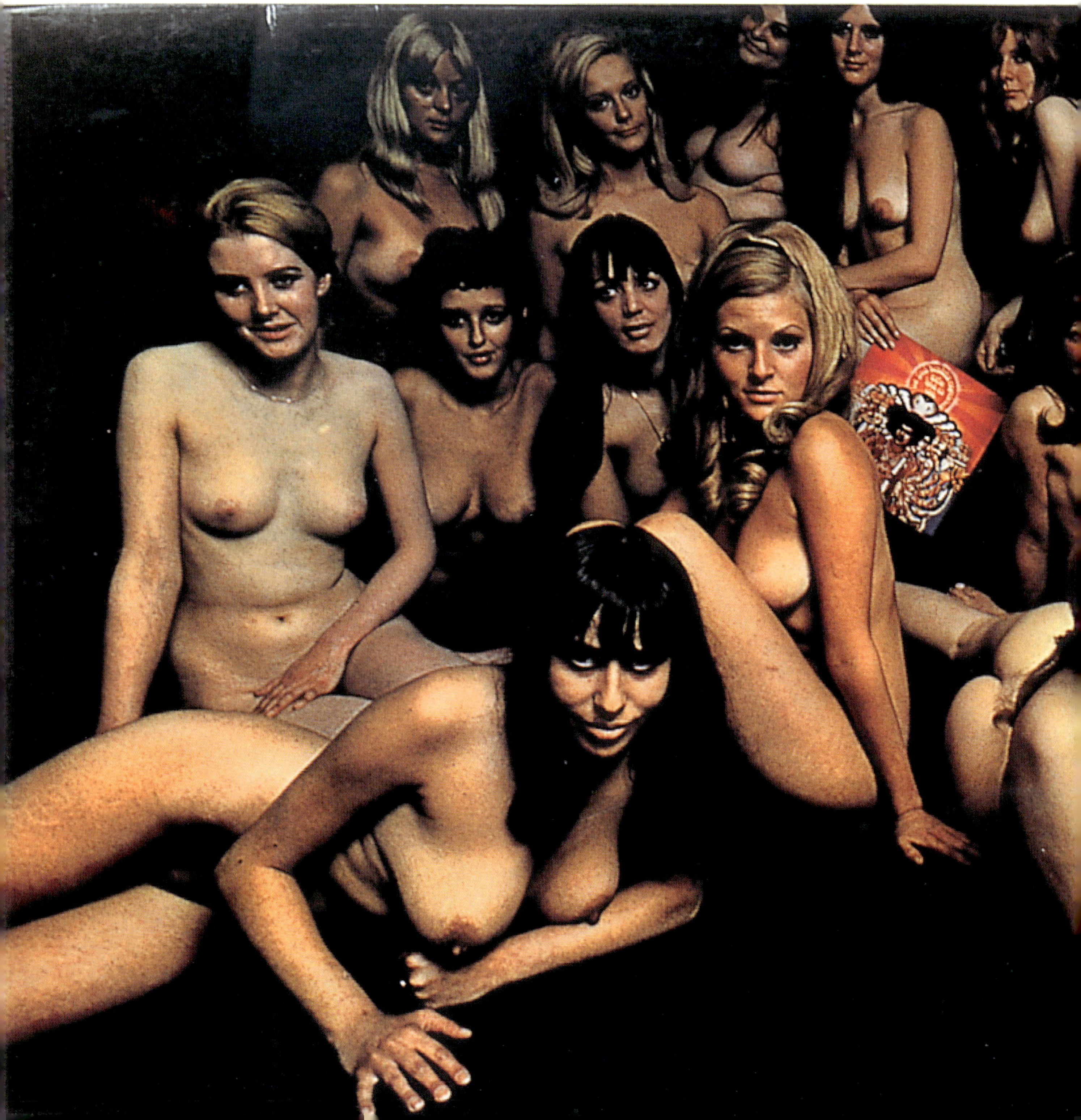

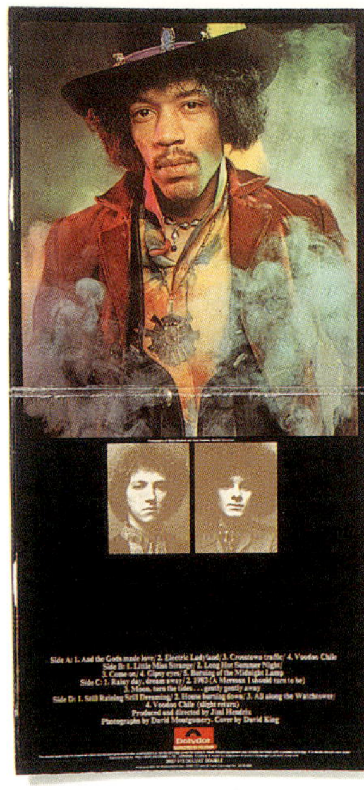

THE JIMI HENDRIX EXPERIENCE:ELECTRIC LADYLAND/
POLYDOR 2657012(1968) *front and back
Photographs by David Montgomery
Cover by David King

THE JIMI HENDRIX EXPERIENCE:
ELECTRIC LADYLAND/
POLYDOR 2657012 (1968) *inner

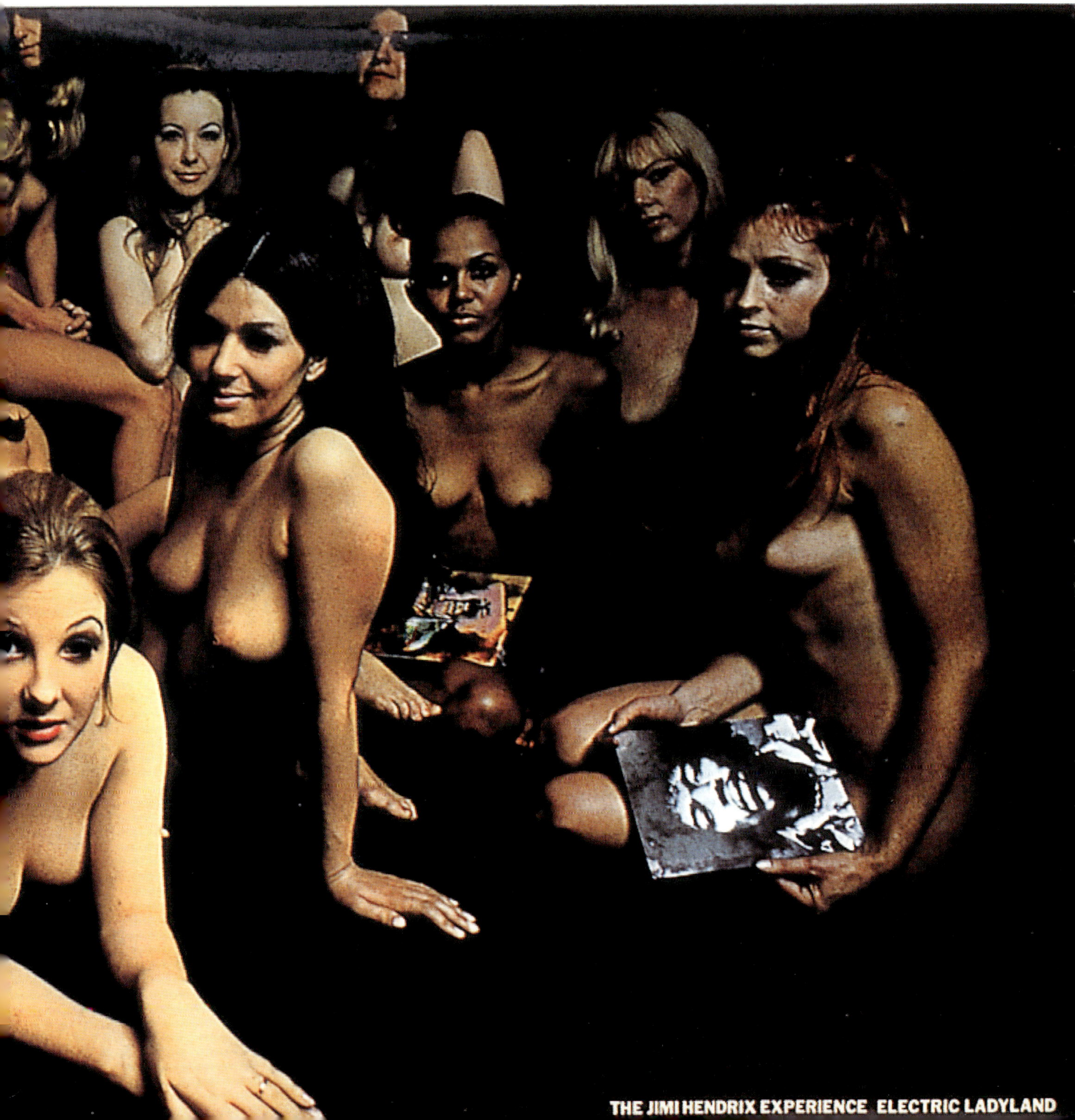

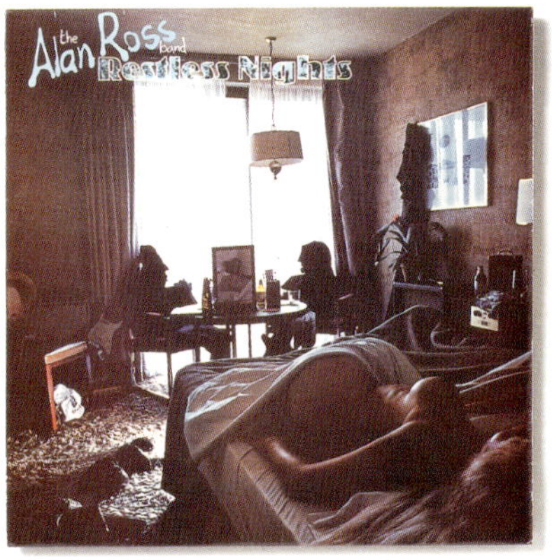

THE ALAN ROSS BAND:RESTLESS NIGHTS/
EBONY EBY1003(1978)*front
Sleeve Design and Photography/Bob Searles
Art Director/John Dyer

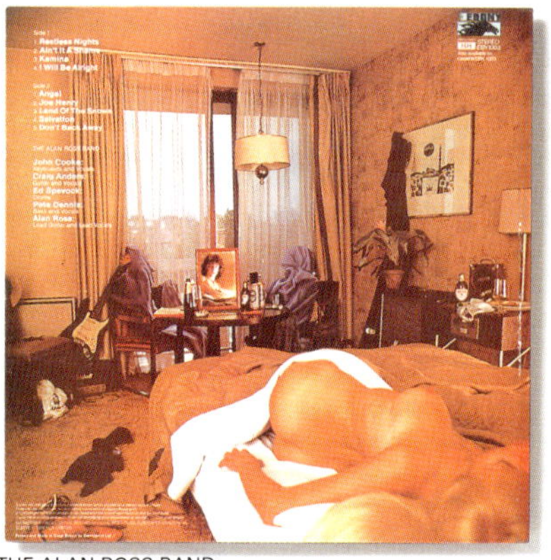

THE ALAN ROSS BAND:
RESTLESS NIGHTS/
EBONY EBY1003(1978)*back

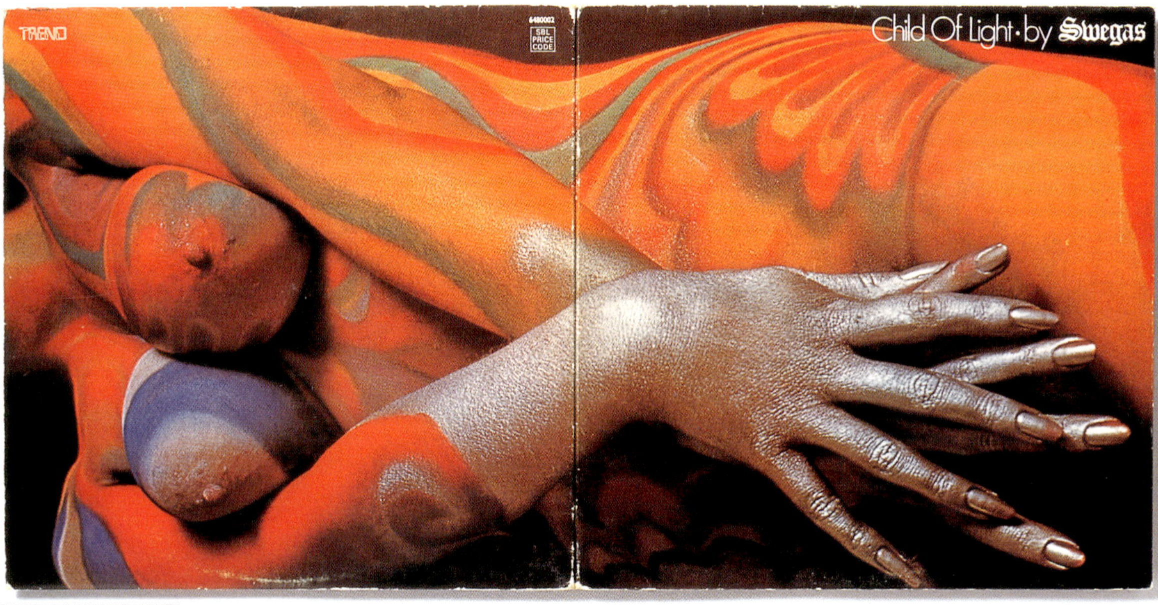

SWEGAS:CHILD OF LIGHT/
TREND 6480002() *front and back

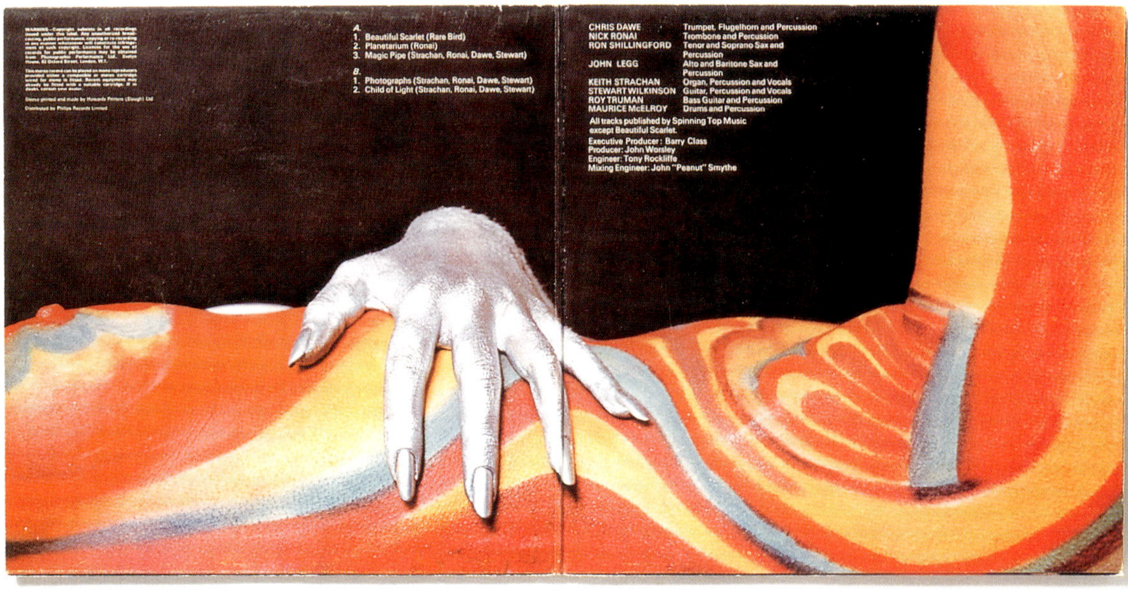

SWEGAS:CHILD OF LIGHT/
TREND 6480002() *inner

JONATHAN SWIFT:INTROVERT/
CBS 64412 (1971)

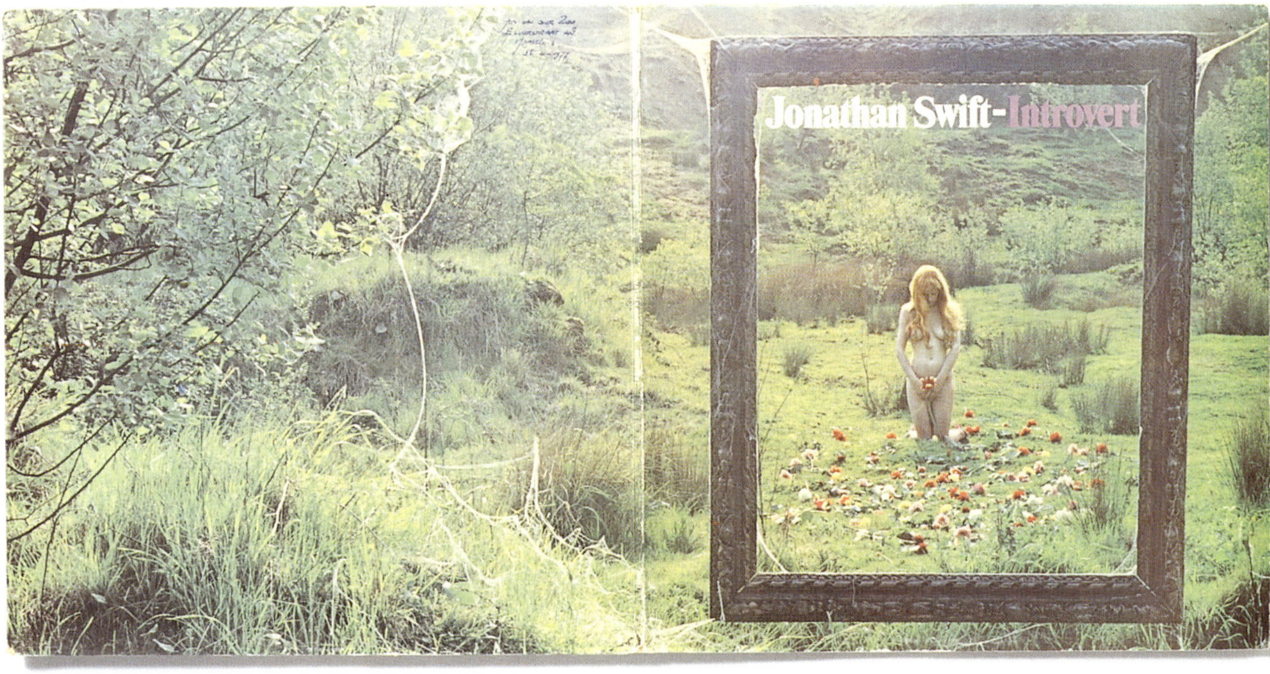

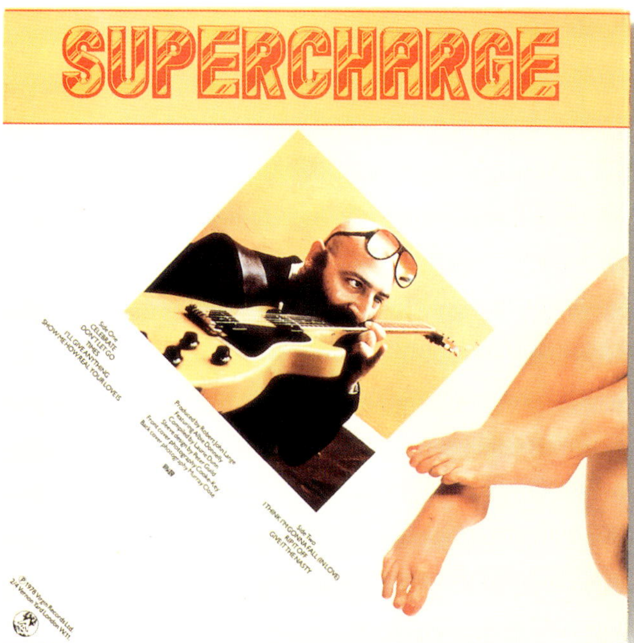

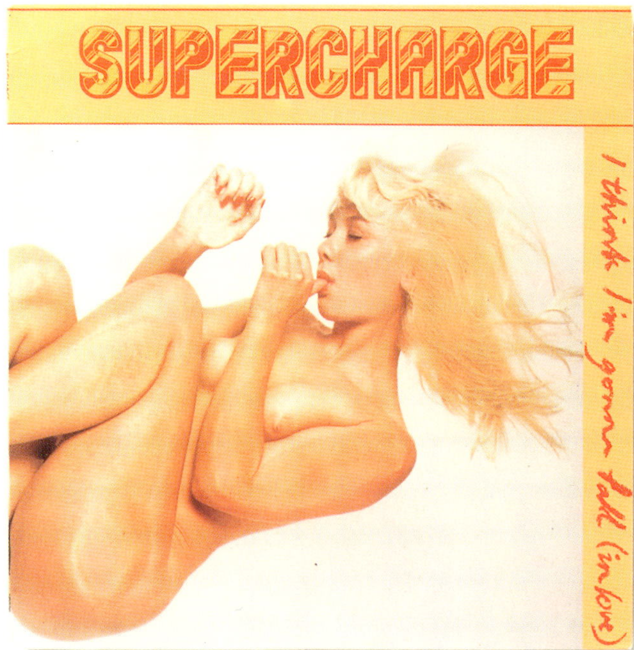

SUPERCHARGE:I THINK I'M GONNA FALL IN LOVE/
VIRGIN V2999(1978)*back

SUPERCHARGE:I THINK I'M GONNA FALL IN LOVE/
VIRGIN V2999(1978)*front
Sleeve Design by Peter Guild
Front Cover Photography/Cooke-key
Back Cover Photography by Murray Close

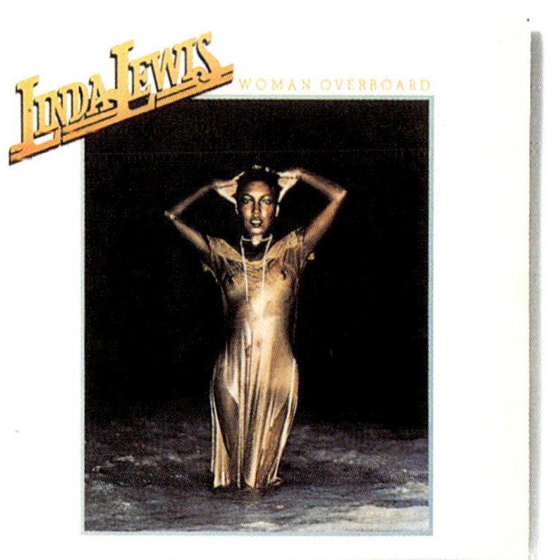

LINDA LEWIS:WOMAN OVER BOARD/SPARTY1003(1977)
Photo/James Wedge
Design/Ken Dolman
Art Direction/John Dyer

COCHISE:COCHISE/
UNITED ARTISTS UAS29117(1970)
Cover Design and Photos by Hipgnosis

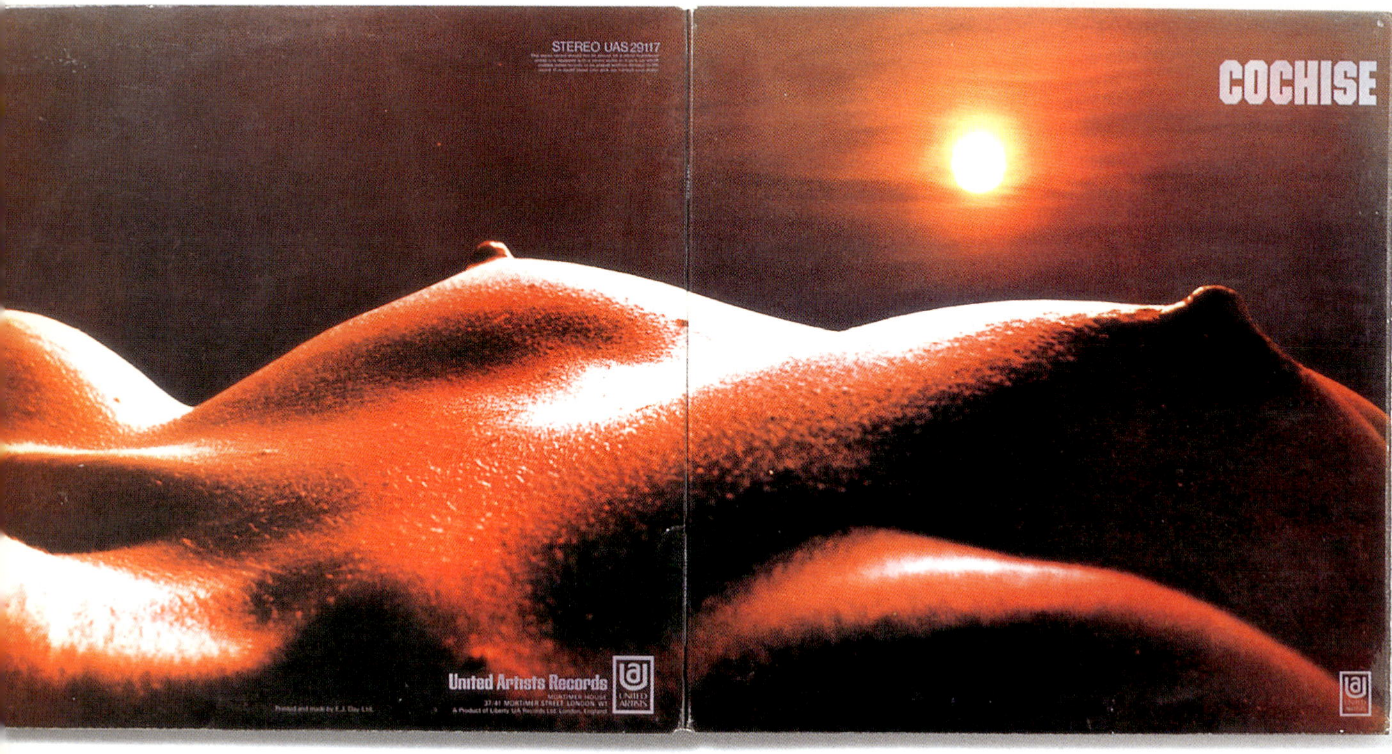

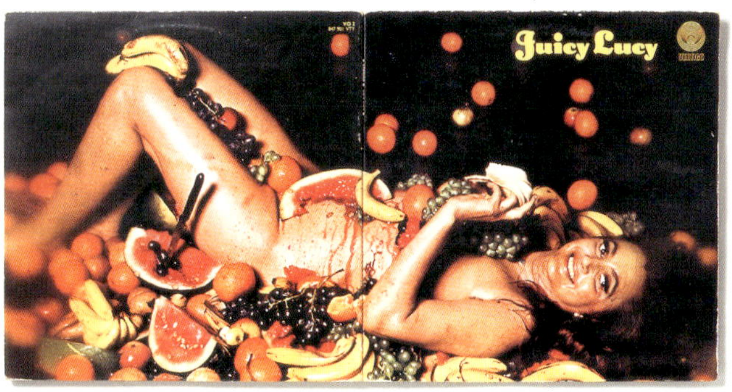

JUICY LUICY:JUICY LUCY/VERTIGO VO2(1969)
Cover Photograph Portrayed by Zelda Plum
Cover Design by Nigel Thomas,Glenn Campbell and Peter Smith
Photographs by Peter Smith

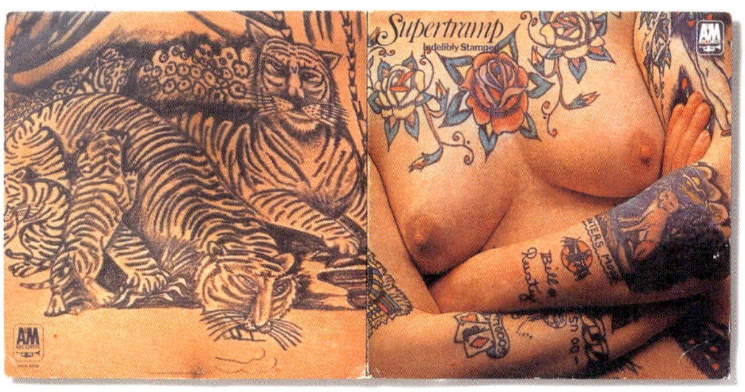

SUPERTRAMP:INDELIBLY STAMPED/A&M
AMLH64306(1971)
Art Direction&Sleeve Design/Bob Hook
Photographed by Keith Morris

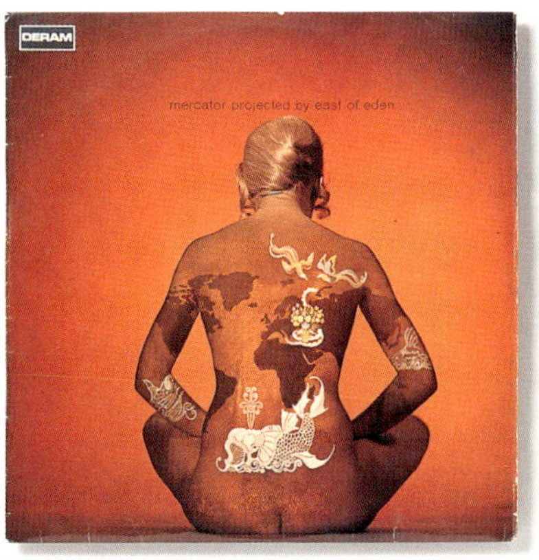

EAST OF EDEN:MERCATOR PROJECTED/
DERAM SML1038(1969)
Cover Photo/David Wedgbury
Sleeve Desgin/Decca Publicity Art Department

① GOLDEN EARRING:MOONTAN/
TRACK 2406 112(1973) *inner

② GOLDEN EARRING:MOONTAN/TRACK 2406 112(1973) *front and back

③ BAD FINGER:NO DICE/
APPLE SAPCOR16(1970) *front and back
Design by Gene Mahon and Richard DiLello,John Effort
Photographs/ Richard DiLello

④ BAD FINGER:NO DICE/
APPLE SAPCOR16(1970) *inner

①

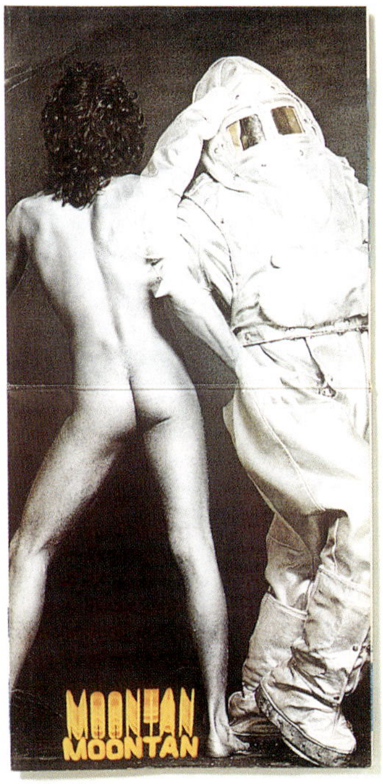

②

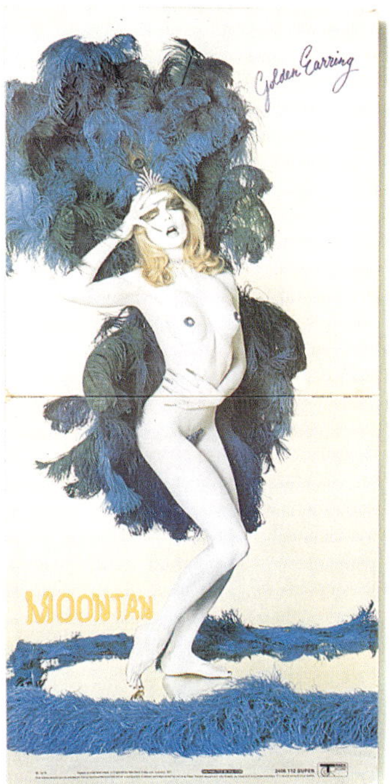

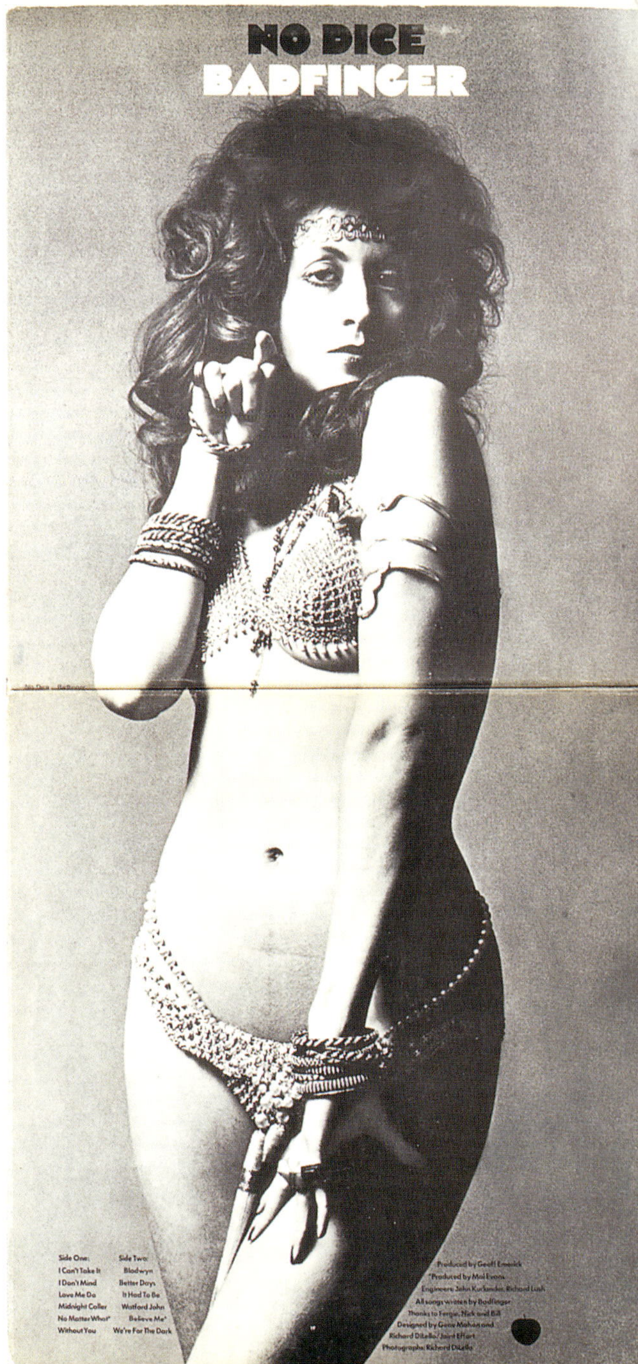

③

④

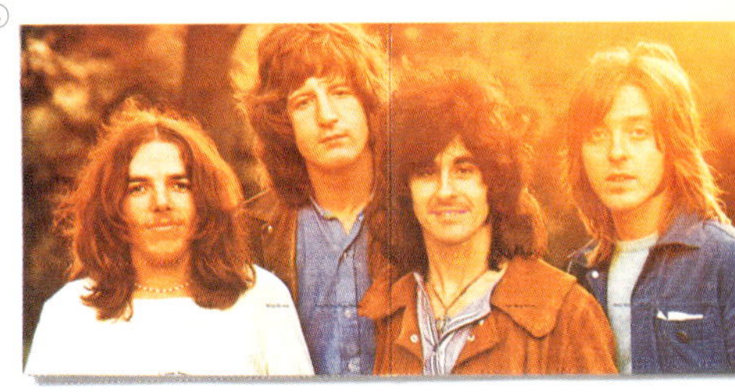

BOXER:BELOW THE BELT/
VIRGIN V2089(1975) *front and back
Album Cover Design and Concept/Nigel Thomas
Photography/Alex Henderson
Model/Stephanie Mariann
Graphics/Richard Evans

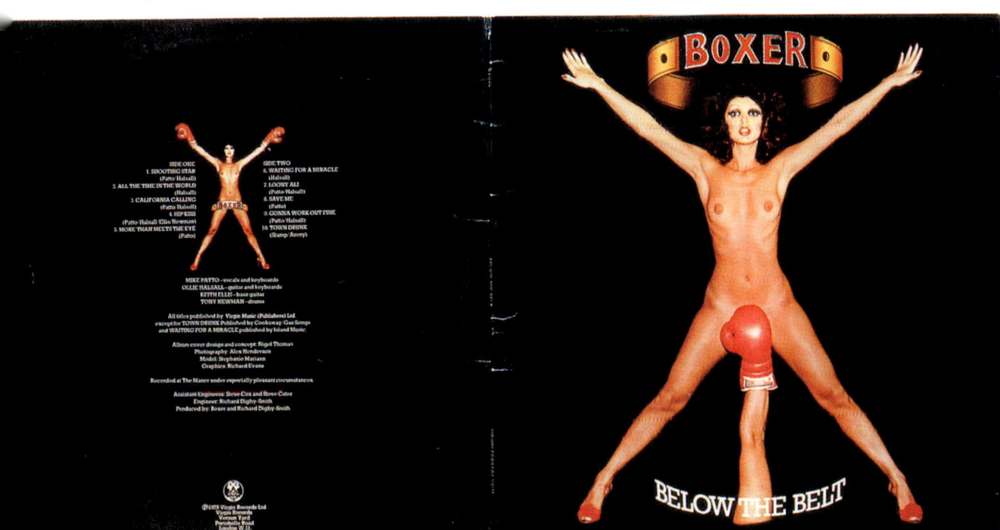

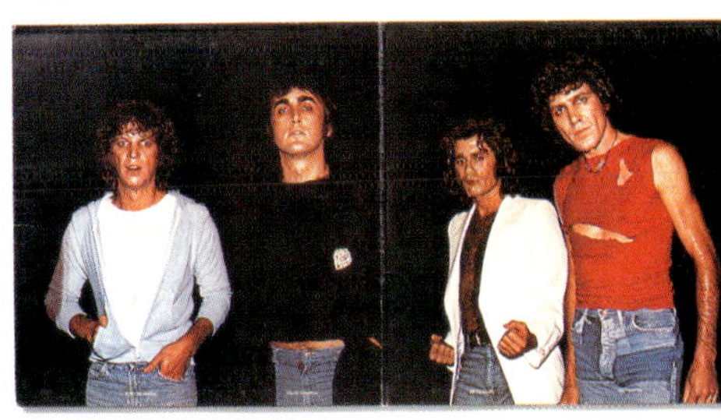

BOXER:BELOW THE BELT/
VIRGIN V2089(1975) *inner

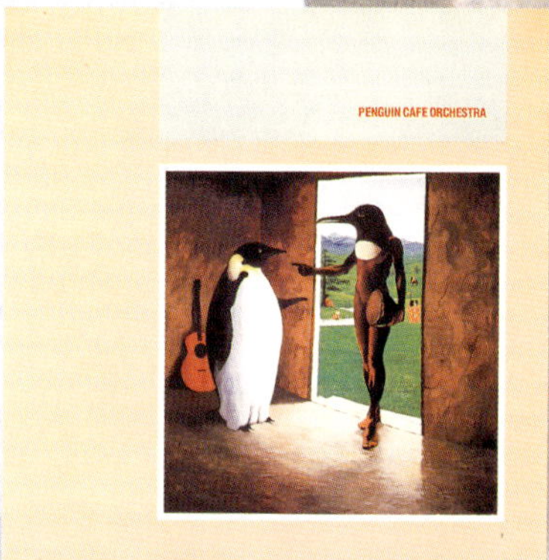

PENGUIN CAFE ORCHESTRA:
PENGUIN CAFE ORCHESTRA/EG EGED11(1981)
Cover Painting by Emily Young
Photography by Roger Whitaker
Design&Typography by HA HA HA Productions

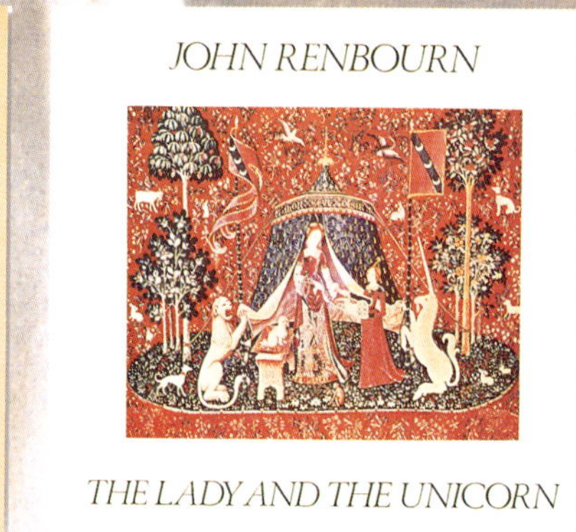

JOHN RENBOURN:THE LADY AND THE UNICORN/
TRANSATLANTIC TRA224(1970)

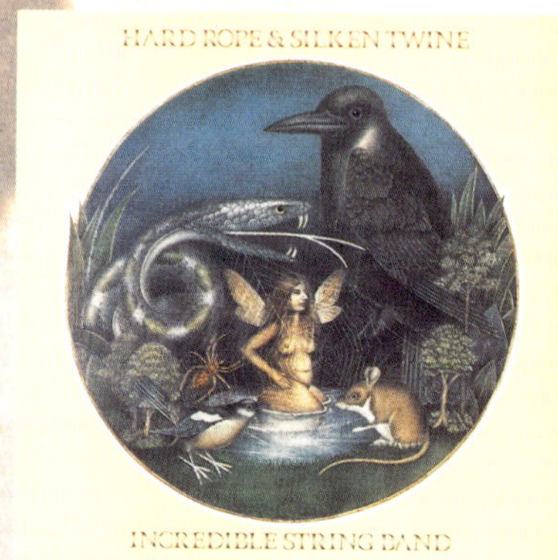

INCREDIBLE STRING BAND:
HARD ROPE&SILKEN TWINE/ISLAND ILPS9270(1973)
Illustration/Wayne Anderson

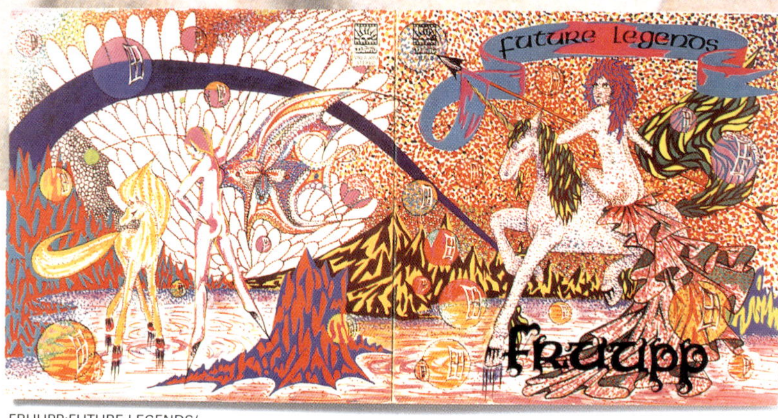

FRUUPP:FUTURE LEGENDS/
DAWN DNLS3053(1973)
Cover Painting/ Peter Farrelly
Cover Concept/ Paul Carles

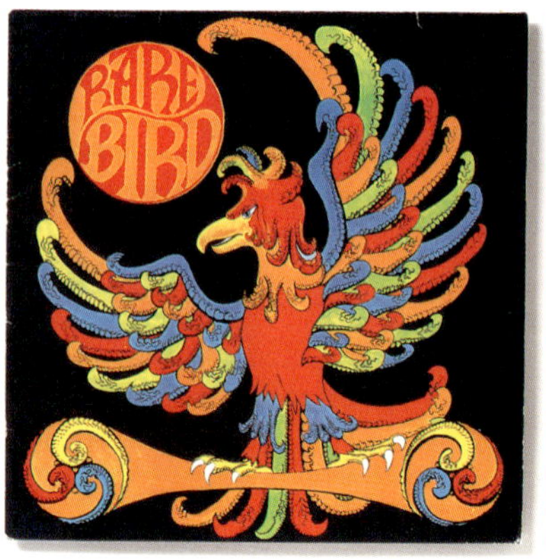

RARE BIRD:RARE BIRD/
CHARISMA CAS1005(1969)
Sleeve Design/Martin Davis

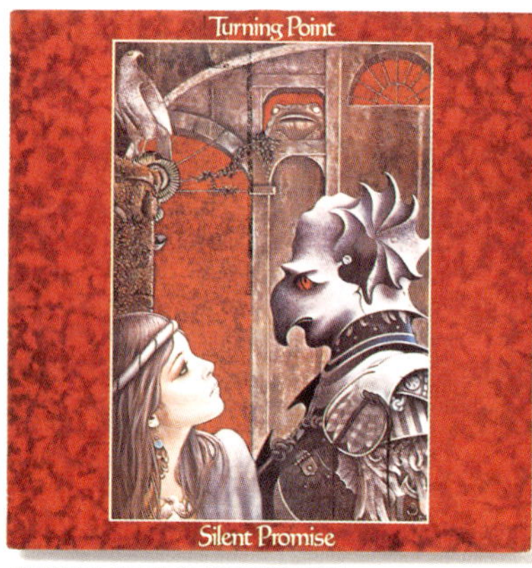

TURNING POINT:SILENT PROMISE/
GULL GULP1027(1978)
Illustration/Paul Monteagle
Sleeve Design/David Howells

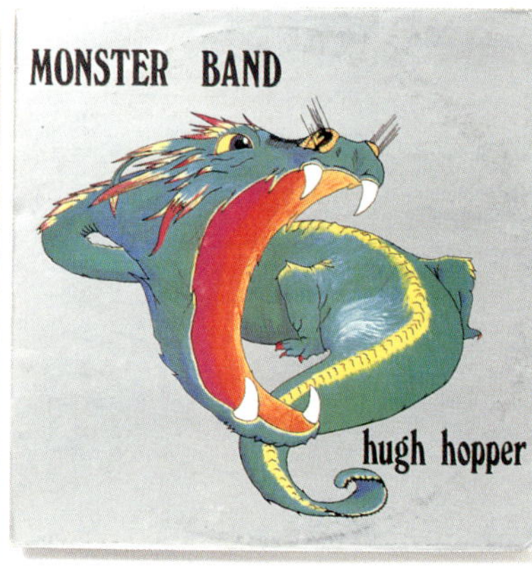

HUGH HOPPER:MONSTER BAND/
ATMOSPHERE IRI5003(1974)
Cover Design/Great Stour Publications

In Search of the Lost Record

animal history

animal history on cover arts
盤上の動物誌

animal history on cover arts

Imaginary Animals
空想動物

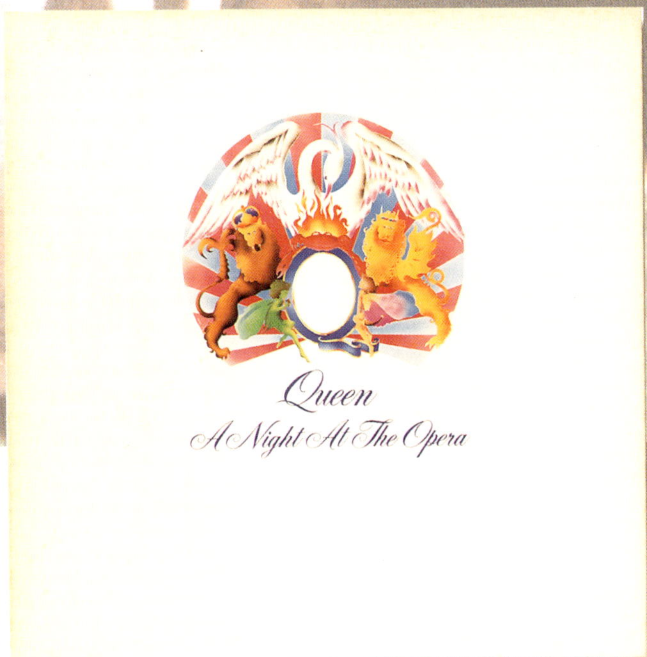

QUEEN:A NIGHT AT THE OPERA/EMI EMTC103(1975)
Art Direction/David Costa

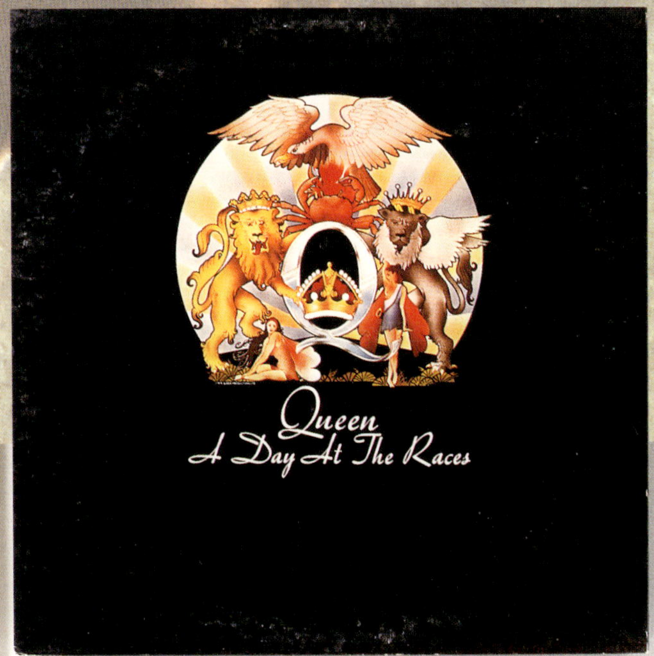

QUEEN:A DAY AT THE RACES/EMI EMTC104(1976)
Art Direction/David Costa

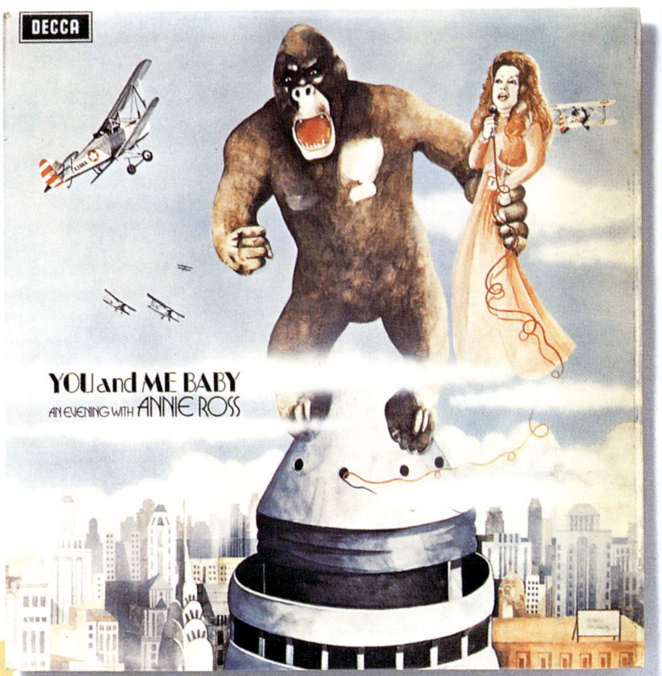

ANNIE ROSS:YOU AND ME BABY/DECCA SKL5099(1971)
Photograph/David Wedgbury
Sleeve Design by Decca Record Publicity Art Department

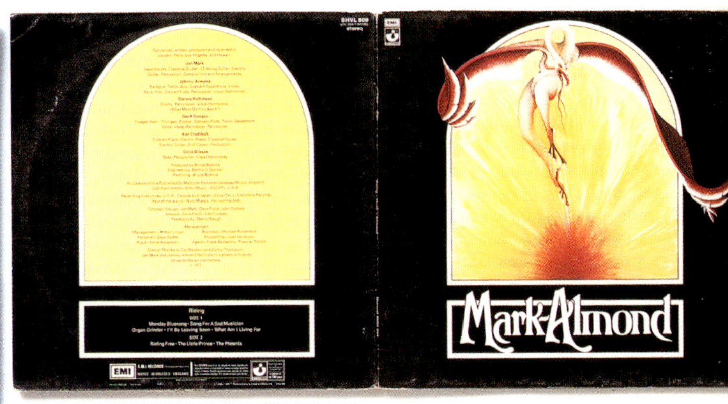

MARK ALMOND:RISING/HARVEST SHVL809(1972)
Artwork/Dave Field,John Corbett

cover arts

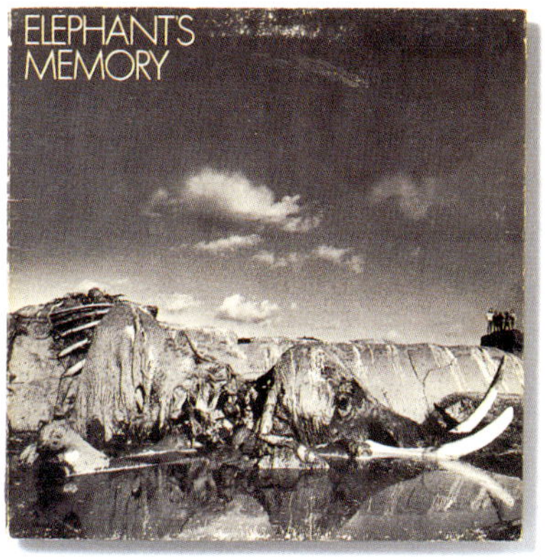

ELEPHANT'S MEMORY:ELEPHANT'S MEMORY/
APPLE SAPCOR22(1972)
Cover Photo/Peter Beard
Design/Michael Gross

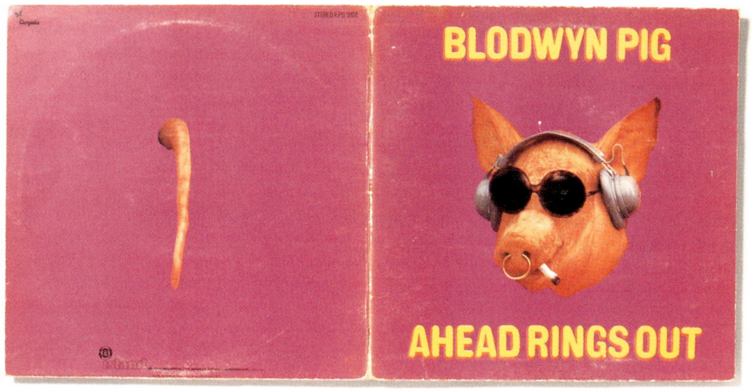

BLODWYN PIG:AHEAD RINGS OUT/
ISLAND ILPS9101(1969)
Photographs/Brian Ward
Design/John Williams

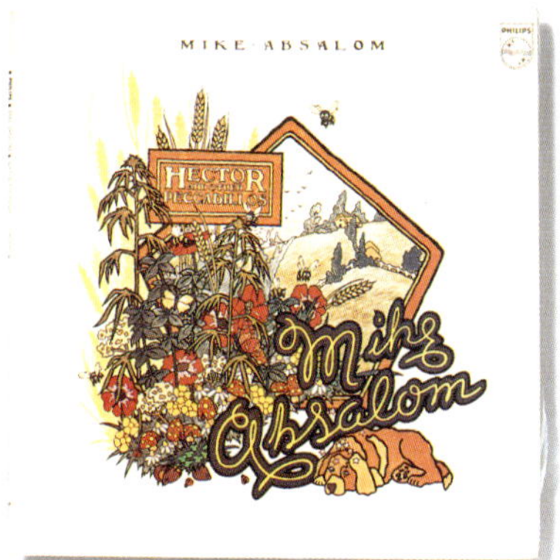

MIKE ABSALOM:HECTOR AND OTHER
PECCADILLOS/PHILIPS 6308 131(1972)
Illustalation and Design by Grahame Berney,
Dream Studios

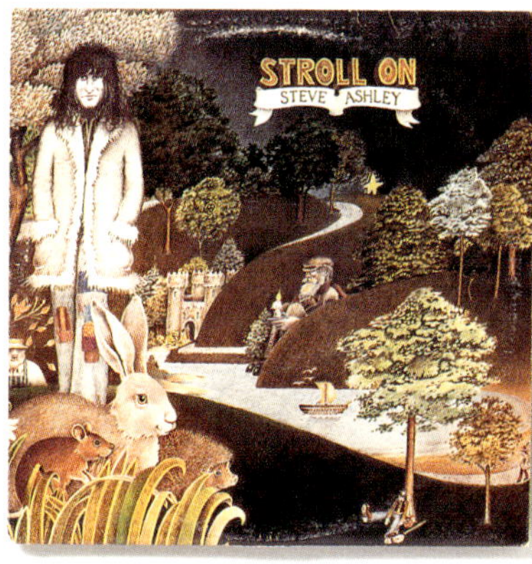

STEVE ASHLEY:STROLL ON/GULL GULP1003(1974)
Sleeve Illustration by Kenneth Laidlaw

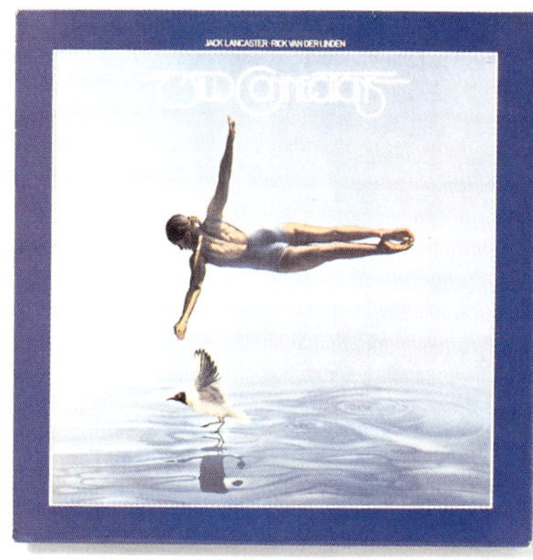

JACK LANCASTER,RICK VAN DER LINDEN:
WILD CONNECTIONS/ACROBAT ACRO2(1979)
Sleeve Concept/David Stewart
Cover Illustration/Mike Jaroszko
Photography/Andy Seymour
Design/Jonathan Dent

animal history on cover arts

Real Animals

実在の動物

In Search of the Lost Record

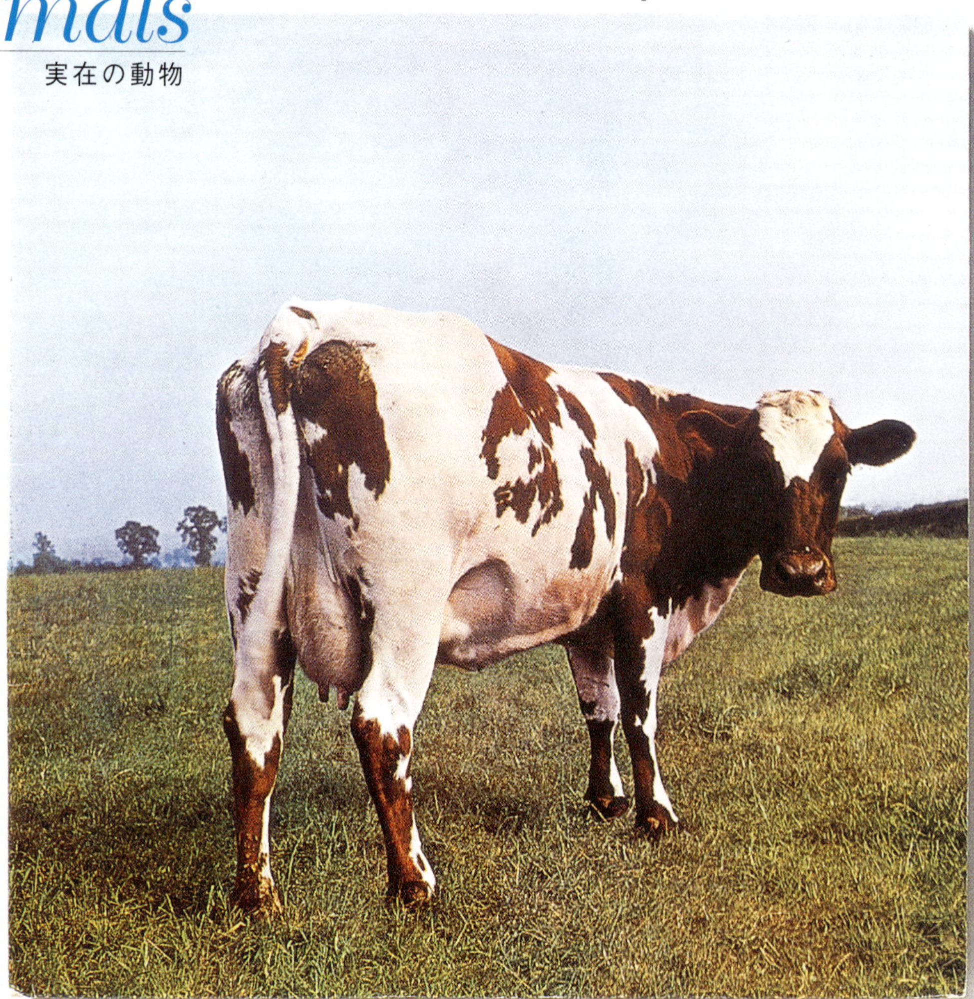

PINK FLOYD:ATOM HEART MOTHER/
HARVEST SHVL781(1970)
Cover Design&Photosby Hipgnosis

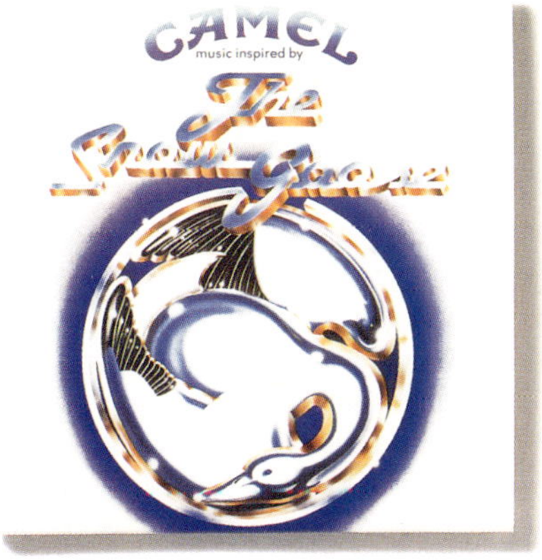

CAMEL:THE SNOW GOOSE/
DECCA SML-R5027(1975)
Sleeve Design by Modula

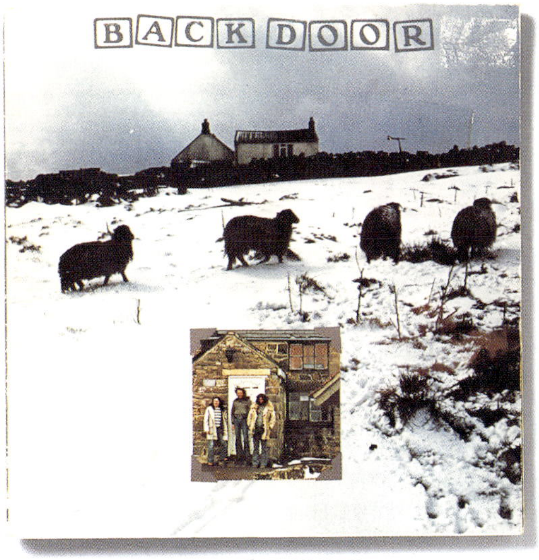

BACK DOOR:BACK DOOR/WARNER K46231(1973)
Art Direction/Seabrook,Graves,Aslett-Associates Ltd
Photography/Kevin McGowen

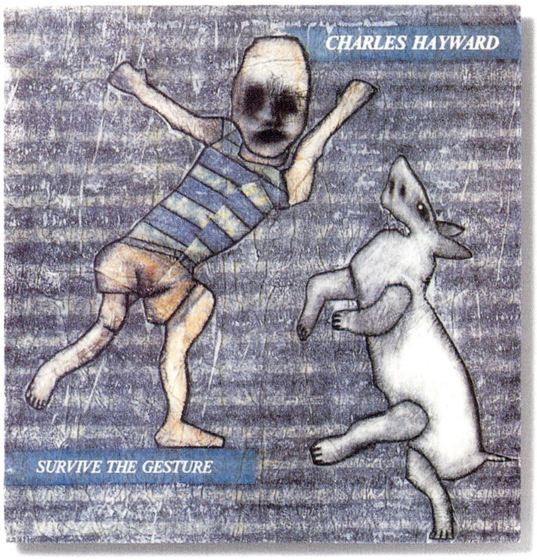

CHARLES HAYWARD:SURVIVE THE GESTURE/INK 31(1987)
Cover by Tony Hayward

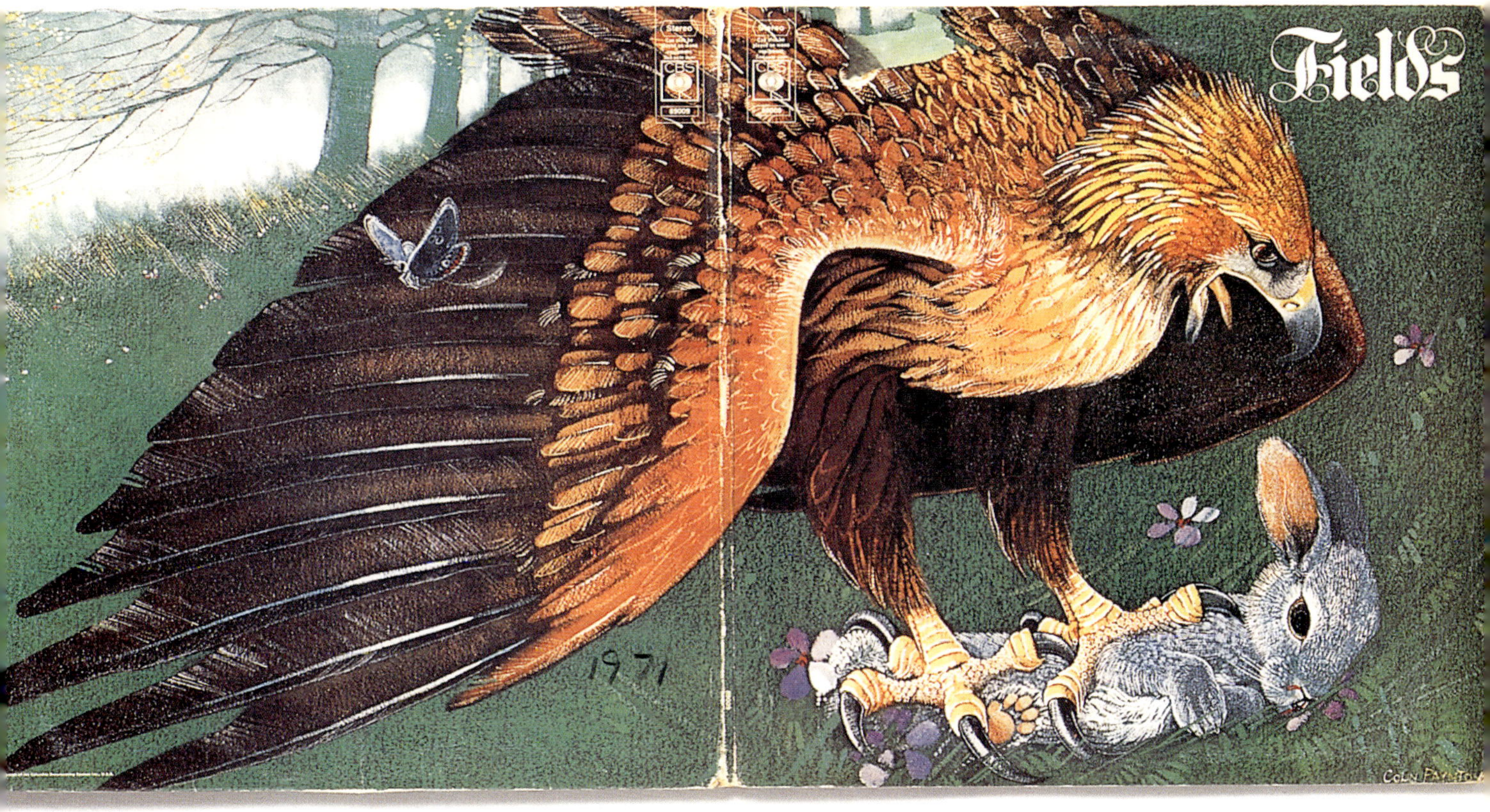

FIELDS:FIELDS/CBS 69009(1971)
Cover Design/Colin Paynton

アルバム・ジャケットのポートレートを、安易なパッケージ・デザインの代表とみなす考え方がある。事実、なんの工夫もないお気楽なポップ作品のなかに、そうしたジャケットが存在することはあるし、ヒプノシスやキーフといった実験精神あふれるデザイナーの登場も、そうした考え方にますます拍車をかける要因となっている。しかし、その一方で撮影対象の内面まで深く掘り下げ、ポートレートをただの宣伝材料からひとつの作品世界にまで高めた写真家の存在も見逃すことはできない。ブリティッシュ・ロックにおいてもっとも早い時期にそうした立場を確立させた写真家のひとりが、ゲルド・マンコヴィッツだ。

ゲルド・マンコヴィッツは46年ロンドン生まれの写真家。シナリオライターの父、精神分析医の母を両親にもつ彼は、カメラマンを目指しオランダに学んだ。その後、ロンドンに戻った彼は、ショウビジネスの世界と深く関わり、俳優など多くのポートレート写真を手がけている。レコードのジャケット写真に携わるきっかけとなったのは、チャド・アンド・ジェレミーの『イエスタデイズ・ゴーン』で、以後彼は、ローリング・ストーンズのオフィシャル・フォトグラファーとして彼らのステージ写真等を数多く手がけるとともに、スモール・フェイセス、P.P.アーノルド、ザ・ナイスなど、ストーンズと同じイミディエイト・レーベル所属ミュージシャンのアルバム・ジャケットあるいはジミ・ヘンドリクス、ザ・ヤードバーズ、ソフト・マシーンといった、彼らと同時代のアーティスト写真にもその才能を発揮した。若くして認められた彼は、同じ世代のミュージシャンたちと親密に交流し、そうした環境のなかで自らの特徴的な写真技法を完成させていったのだろう。70年代以降も彼は数多くのミュージシャンたちとコラボレートし、90年代に入ってからは、デザイナーのデヴィッド・コスタと組んでシルク・スクリーンの連作を手がけるなど、ますますその表現領域を広げつつある。

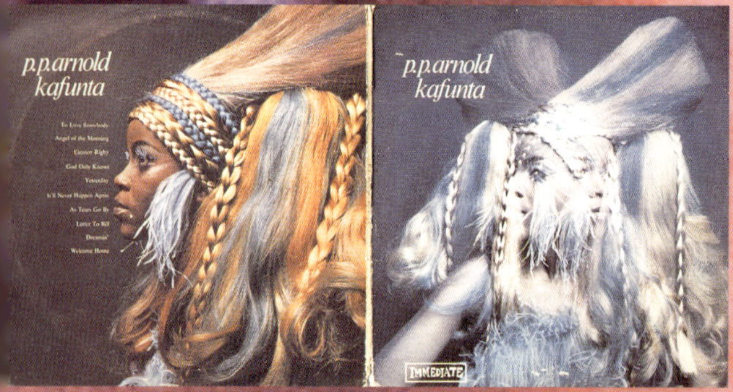

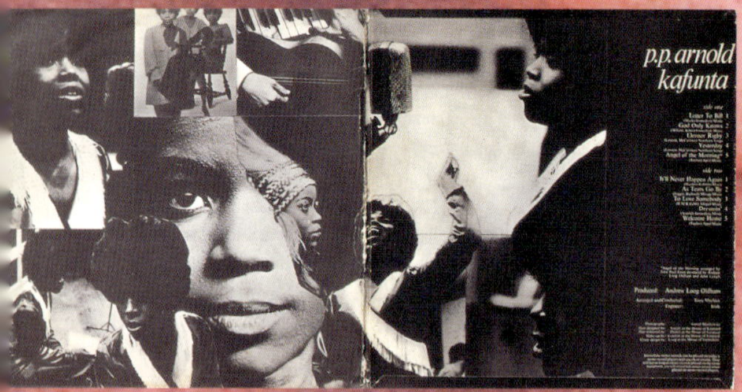

P.P.ARNOLD:KAFUNTA.IMMEDIATE IMPS 017(1968) *front and back
Photography/ Gered Mankowitz
Cover Design by Loog at the House ofImmediate

P.P.ARNOLD:KAFUNTA.IMMEDIATE IMPS 017(1968) *inner

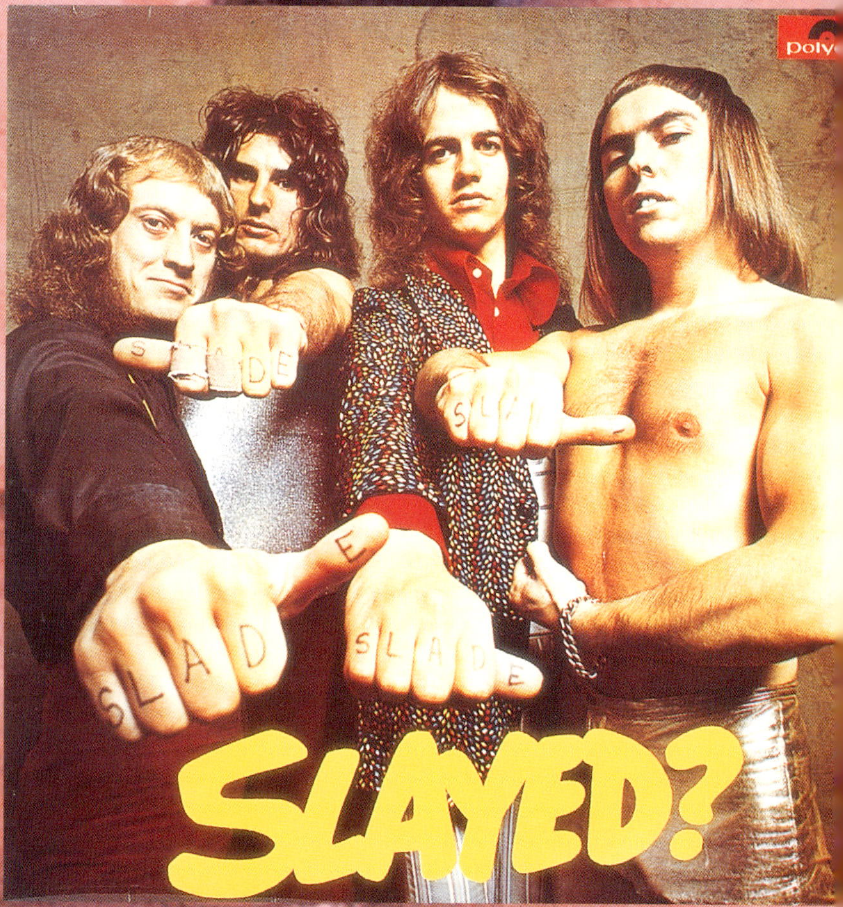

SLADE:SLAYED?/POLYDOR 2383 163(1972)
Cover Photograph Taken by Gered Mankowitz

portraits
ポートレート

portraits

Gered Mankowitz
ゲルド・マンコヴィッツ

For some, album cover photos were merely a part of package design and weren't seen as true artistic work. There are album covers such as this, care-free Pop album covers. The work of experimentalist artists, such as Hipgnosis and Keef, reinforced this attitude. However, we cannot overlook certain photographers who elevated the publicity photograph into an artistic creation by probing into the inner world of the subject. One such photographer of the British Rock world was Gered Mankowitz. He was born in London in 1946. His father was a script writer and his mother was a psychoanalyst. Mankowitz went to Holland to study photography under the famed Tom Blau. Shortly after returning to London, his long career taking innumerable portraits of actors began. His first album cover work was for Chad and Jeremy's "Yesterday's Gone". Then he became the official photographer for the Rolling Stones, documenting the band's many live performances. His other work includes albums by bands such as Small Faces, P. P. Arnold, The Nice, and others represented by the Immediate label, home of the Rolling Stones. Mankowitz also demonstrated his exquisite talent with photographs of Jimi Hendrix, The Yardbirds, Soft Machine and other bands and artists of the same generation. Receiving recognition while still relatively young, Mankowitz seemed to nurture his unique photography skills within the environment of his friendships and interaction with the artists who were his subjects. Mankowitz further continues to broaden his horizons. Presently, he collaborates with many musicians and among his recent notable projects there is a series of silkscreen images resulting from a collaboration with designer David Costa in the 90's.

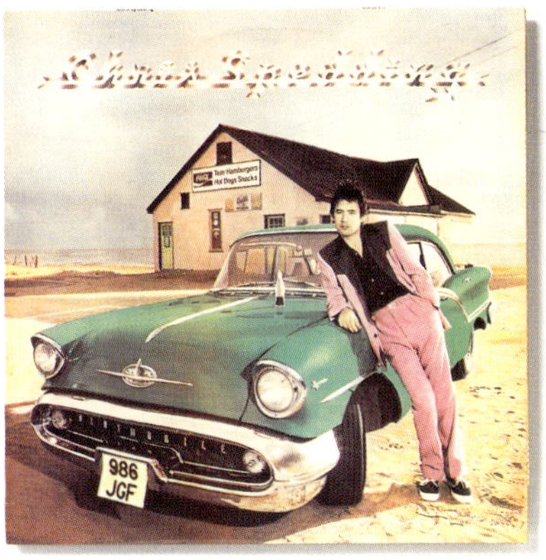

CHRIS SPEDDING:CHRIS SPEDDING/
RAK SRAK519(1976)
Cover Photography by Gered Mankowitz
Colour Tinting by Arthur Allen

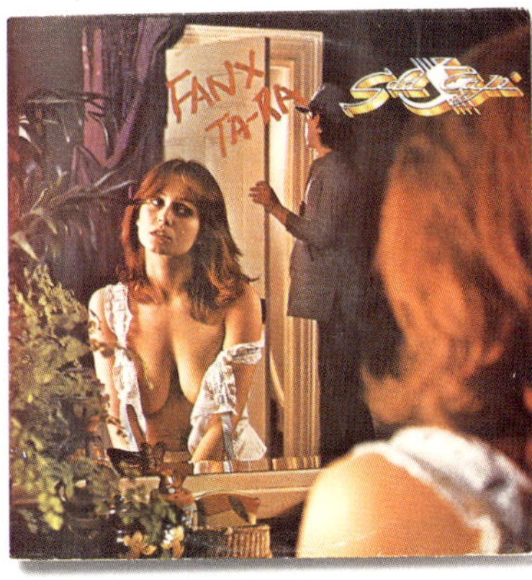

SAD CAFE:FANX TA-RA/ RCA PL 25101(1977)
Sleeve Art Direction and Design/ Graves Aslett ASSOC.LTD.(London)
Photography/ Gered Mankowitz

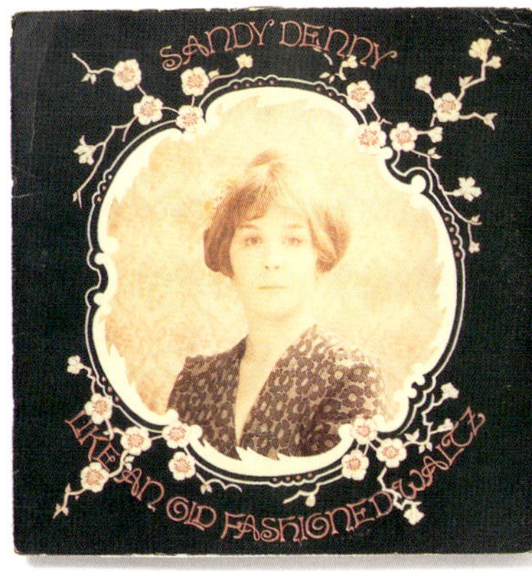

SANDY DENNY:LIKE AN OLD FASHONED WALTZ/
Island ILPS9258(1973)
Photograph by Gered Mankowitz
Design and Art Direction by Fabio Nicoli Associations

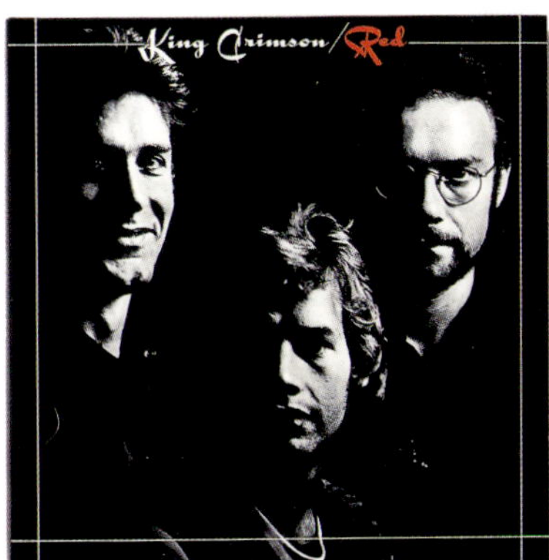

KING CRIMSON:RED/ Island ILPS9308(1974)
Cover by John Kosh
Photograph by Gered Mankowitz

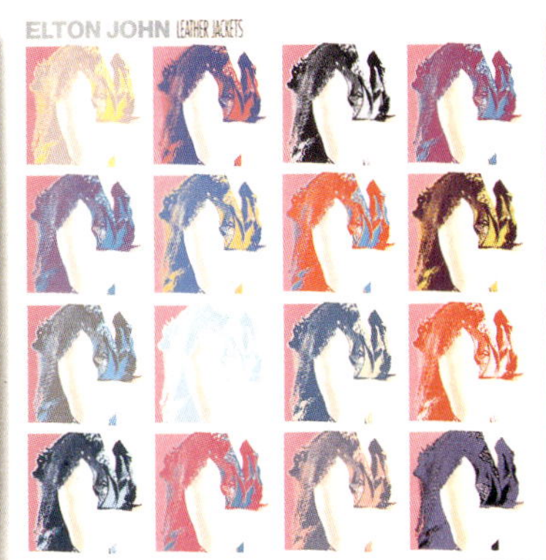

ELTON JOHN:LEATHER JACKETS/
ROCKET EJLP1(1986)
Art Direction/ David Costa
Photograpy/ Gered Mankowitz

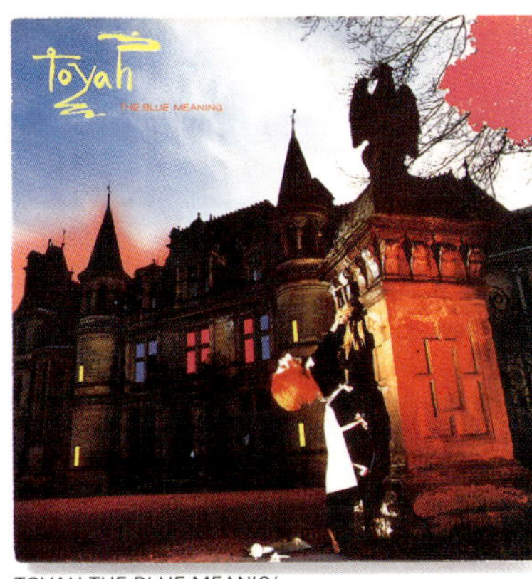

TOYAH:THE BLUE MEANIG/
SAFARI IEYA666(1980)
Cover by Bill Smith,Toyah, Gered Mankowitz

ts

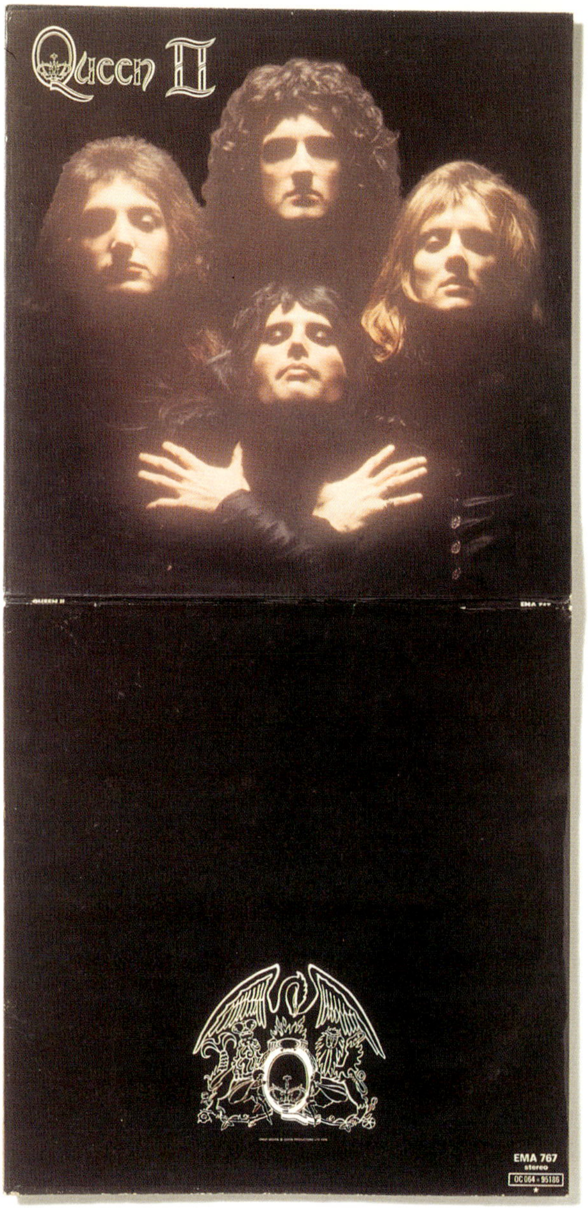

①

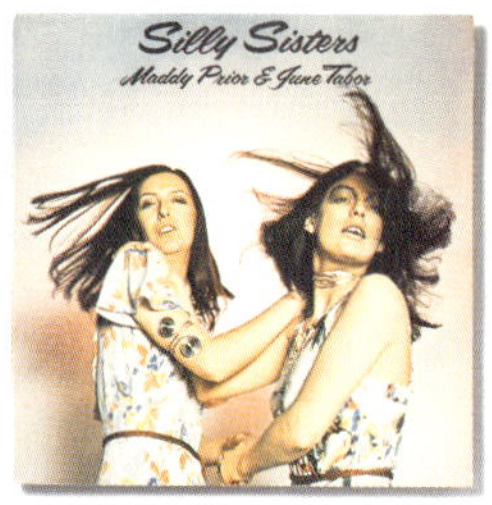

③

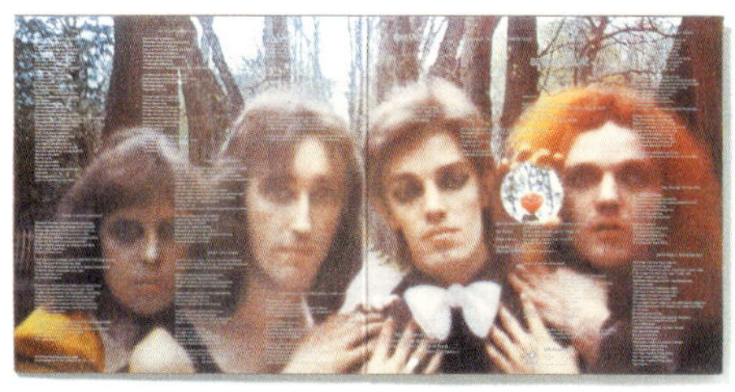

④

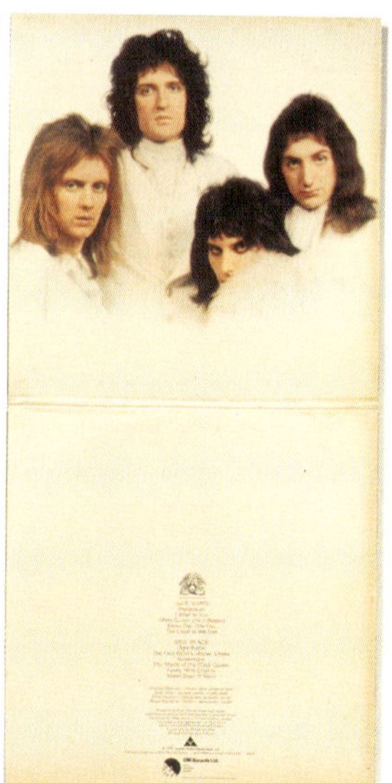

②

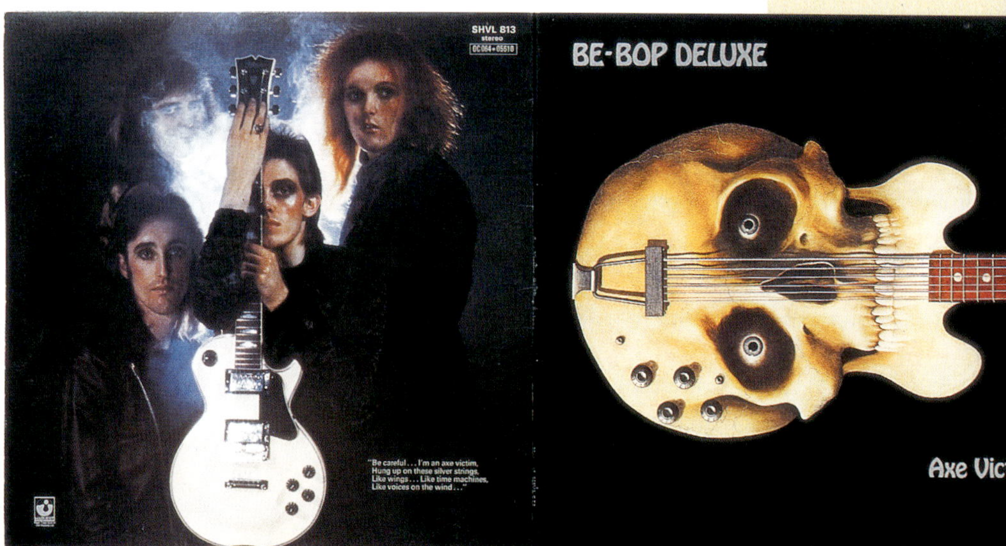

⑤

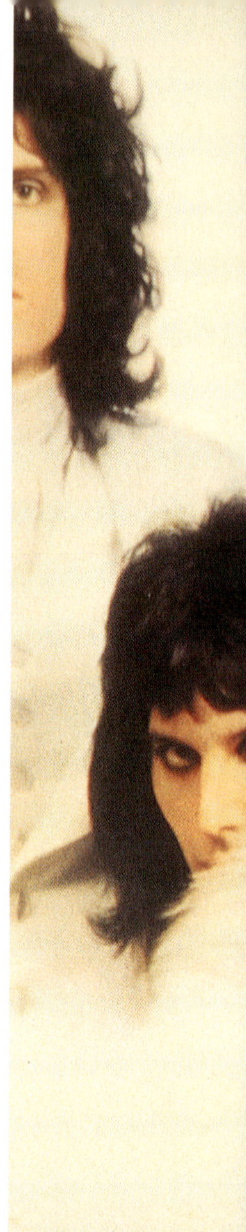

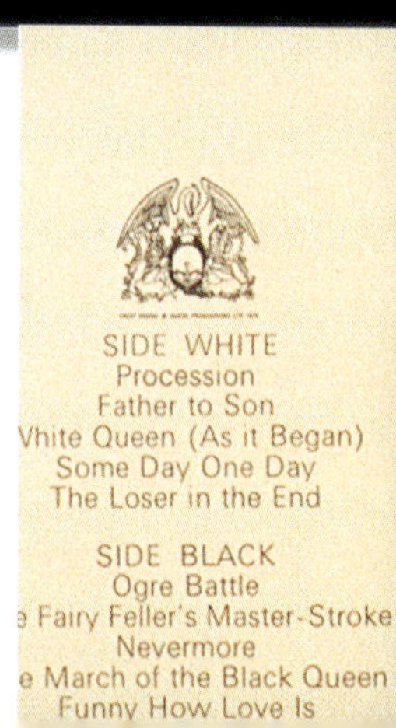

① QUEEN:QUEEN II /
EMI EMC3006(1973) *front and back
Photography and art direction by Mick Rock
Sleeve concept by Mick Rock and Queen

② QUEEN:QUEEN II / EMI EMC3006(1973) *Inner

③ MADDY PRIOR&JUNE TABOR:SILLY SISTERS/
CHRYSALIS CHR1101(1976)
Photography Mick Rock
Sleeve Design Edward Baker

④ BE-BOP DELUXE:AXE VICTIM/
HARVEST SHVL813(1974)*Inner

⑤ BE-BOP DELUXE:AXE VICTIM/
HARVEST SHVL813(1974)*front and back
Photography.etc/ Mick Rock

portraits

Mick Rock

ミック・ロック

アルバム・ジャケットにおける写真家の攻勢は、グラム・ロックやモダン・ポップの時代の到来とともに訪れた。その代表格はなんといってもミック・ロックだ。ミック・ロックは60年代末頃からミュージシャンのポートレートを撮り始め、クイーン、デヴィッド・ボウイ、コックニー・レベル、ルー・リードといったグラマラスなアーティストを数多く手がけ、後にはニューヨークに渡りトーキング・ヘッズ、ブロンディらとも濃密なコラボレーションを続けている。このほか紹介するのは、アルバム・ジャケットやアーティスト写真等を活躍の場にするフォトグラファーの、70年代以降の作品群。ミック・ロックほどの匂い立つ個性はないが、まるで音楽的傾向や被写体の異なる作品のなかにも、どこかに同じ時代の空気や確かな主張を感じさせているところは面白い。ジャック・キルビーはポップ系での仕事もあるが、圧倒的にイギリスのアヴァンギャルドなジャズ・ミュージシャンを撮ったものが多く、それ自体が貴重な資料となっている。

The boom in the number of album cover photographers coincided with the start of the age of Glam Rock and Modern Pop. Among such photographers, the most notable was Mick Rock. He started to take musician's portraits in the late 60's, working with big names such as Queen, David Bowie, Cockney Rebel, and Lou Reed. Later on he moved to New York and collaborated with bands like Talking Heads and Blondie. The other album covers presented here date from the 70's and are by photographers who were known for their work with album covers. Although there wasn't anyone who compared to Mick Rock's uniqueness, it is interesting to see that there was a commonality that runs through this generation of music photographers. Jak Kilby was involved with Pop music, but most of his works were associated with avant garde British Jazz musicians, which are considered to be very important documents.

portraits Fin Costello

フィン・コステロ

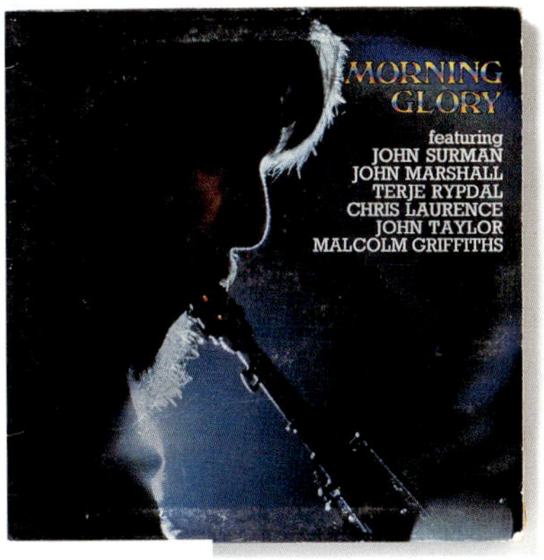

JOHN SURMAN:MORNING GLORY/
Island ILPS9237(1973)
Sleeve Design by Fabio Nikoli
Photography by Fin Costello

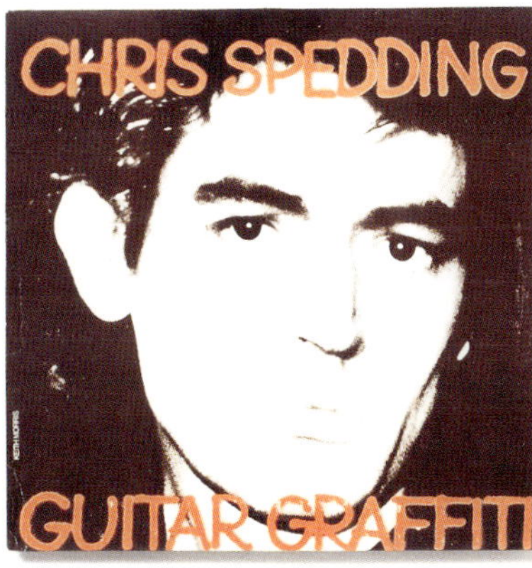

CHRIS SPEDDING:GUITAR GRAFFITI/
RAK SRAK534(1978)
Photography by FIn Costello
Art Director/ Dobney

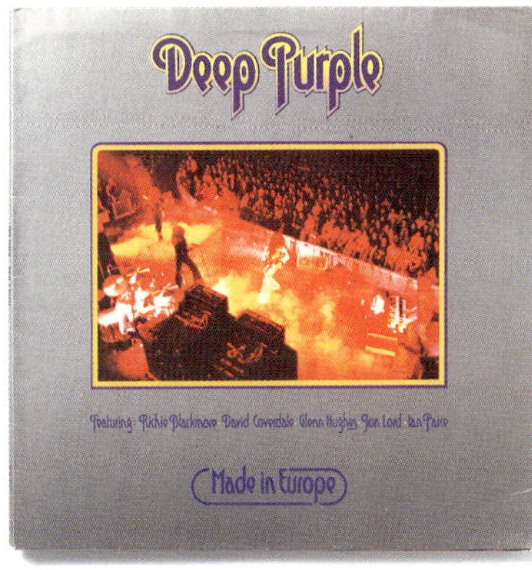

DEEP PURPLE:MADE IN EUROPE/
PURPLE TPSA7517(1976)
Cover Design/Phil Duffy,Cream
All Photos/Fin Costello

portraits Keith Morris

キース・モリス

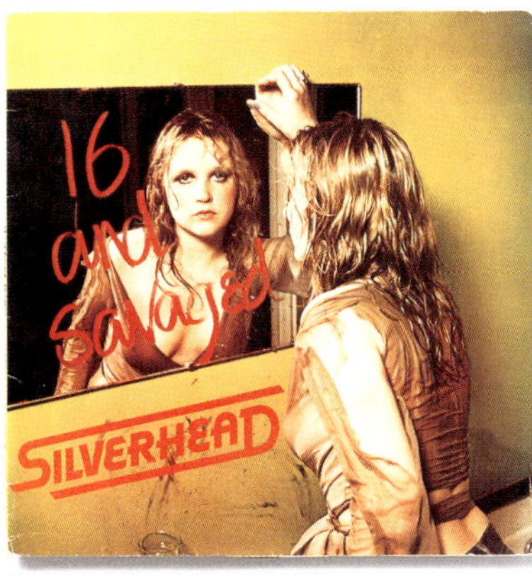

SILVER HEAD:16 AND SAVAGED/
PURPLE TPSA7511(1973)
All Photographs and Cover/ Keith Morris
Cover and Design/ Chelita Secunda

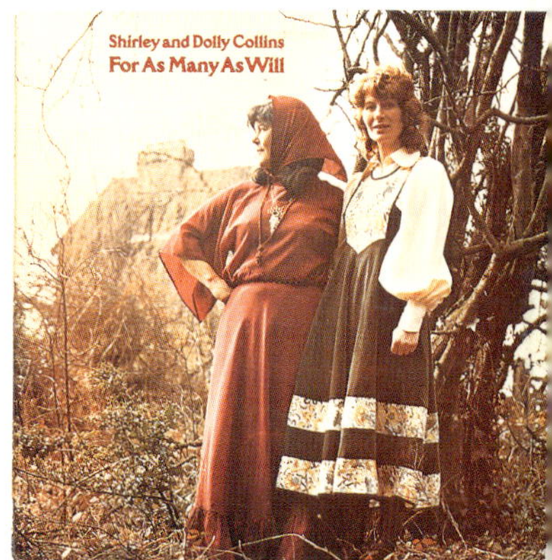

Shirley and Dolly Collins:For As Many As Will/
TOPIC 12TS380(1978)
Photographs by Keith Morris
Design by Tony Engle

① ②

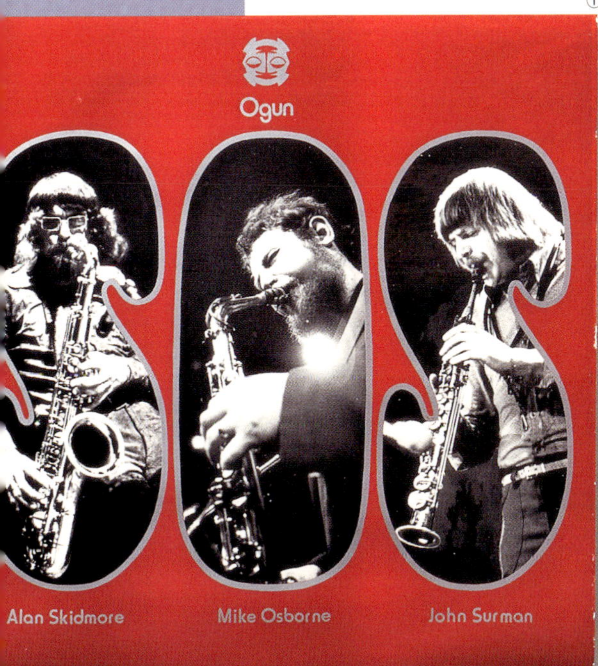

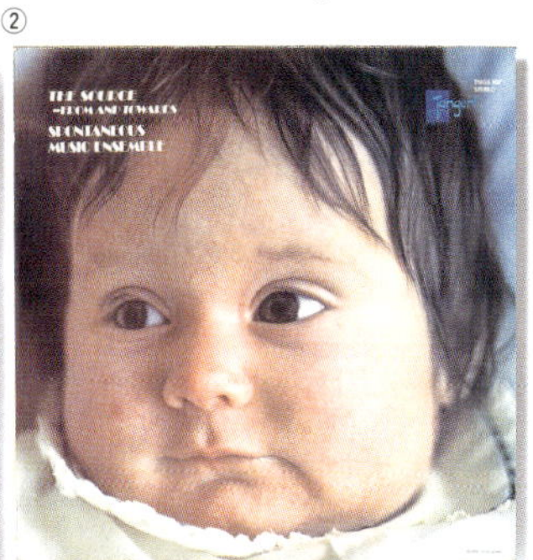

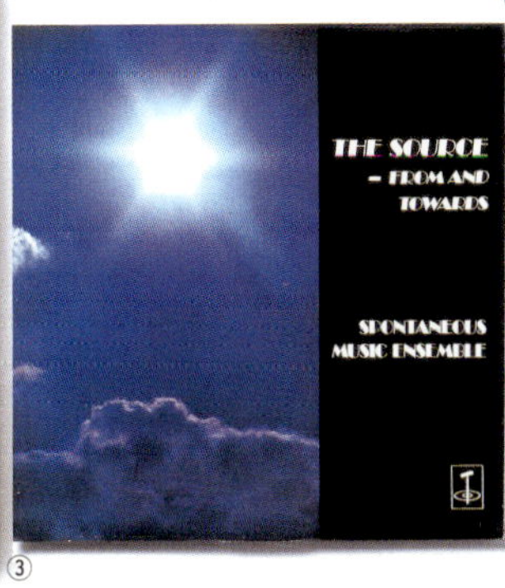

③

portraits Jak Kilby

ジャック・キルビー

① S.O.S.:S.O.S./ OGUN OG400(1975)
Front Cover Photographs by Jak Kilby
Cover Design by OGUN

② SPONTANEOUS MUSIC ENSEMBLE:
THE SOURCE-FROM AND TOWARDS/
TANGENT TNGS107(1971)*back

③ SPONTANEOUS MUSIC ENSEMBLE:
THE SOURCE-FROM AND TOWARDS/
TANGENT TNGS107(1971)*front
Photographs by Jak Kilby

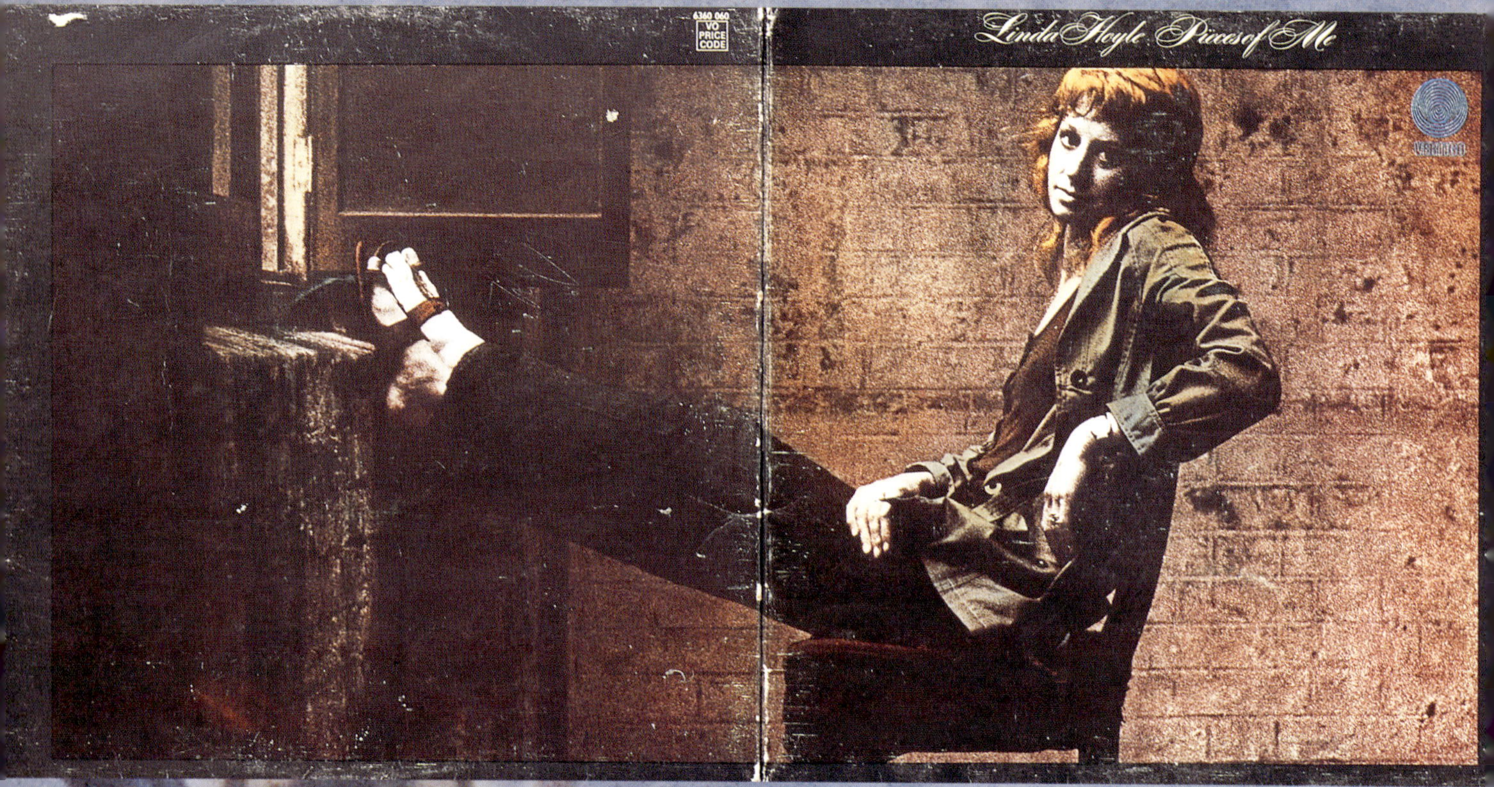

LINDA HOYLE:PIECES OF ME/
VERTIGO6360 060(1971)
Photography/ James Wedge

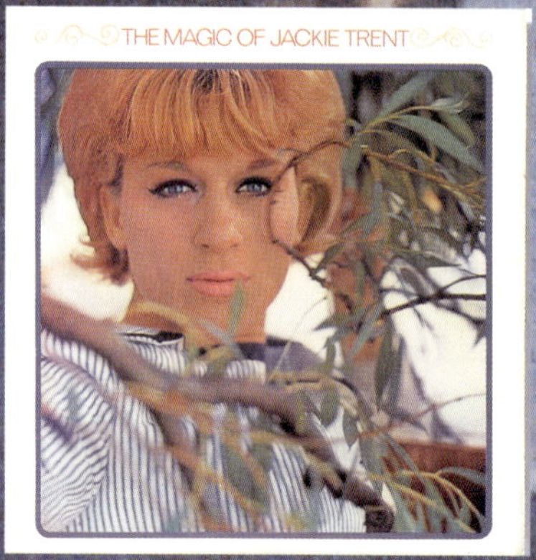

JACKIE TRENT:THE MAGIC OF JACKIE TRENT/
PYE NPL18125(1965)

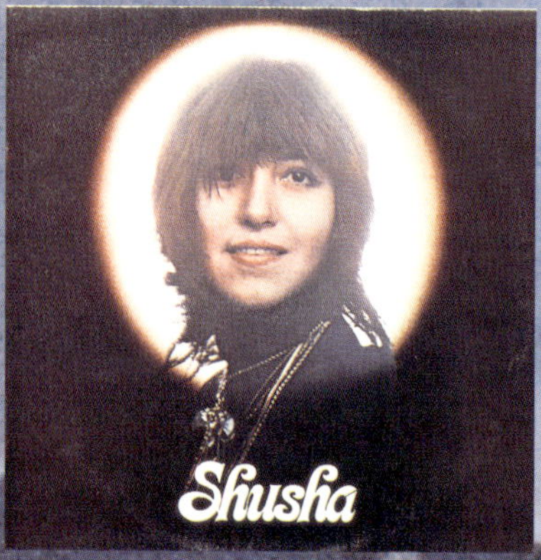

SHUSHA:SHUSHA/UNITED ARTISTS UAS29575(1974)

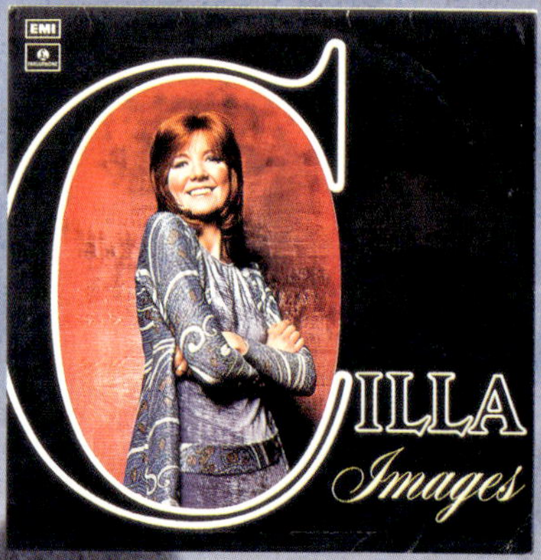

CILLA BLACK:IMAGES/PARLOPHONE PCS7128(1971)

In Search of the Lost Record

portraits

Women's Potraits

ポートレート女性編

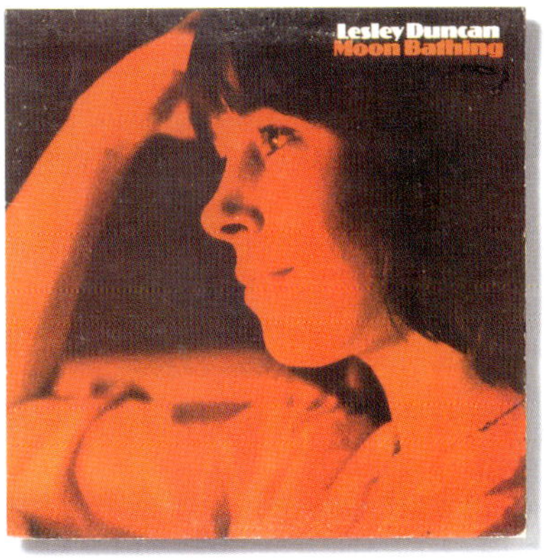

LESLEY DUNCAN:MOON BATHING/
GM GML1017(1975)
Pjptpgraphy/Peter Sanders
Sleeve Design/Will Robinson

CILLA BLACK:SURROUND YOURSELF WITH CILLA/PMC7079(1969)
Photo/Francis Loney

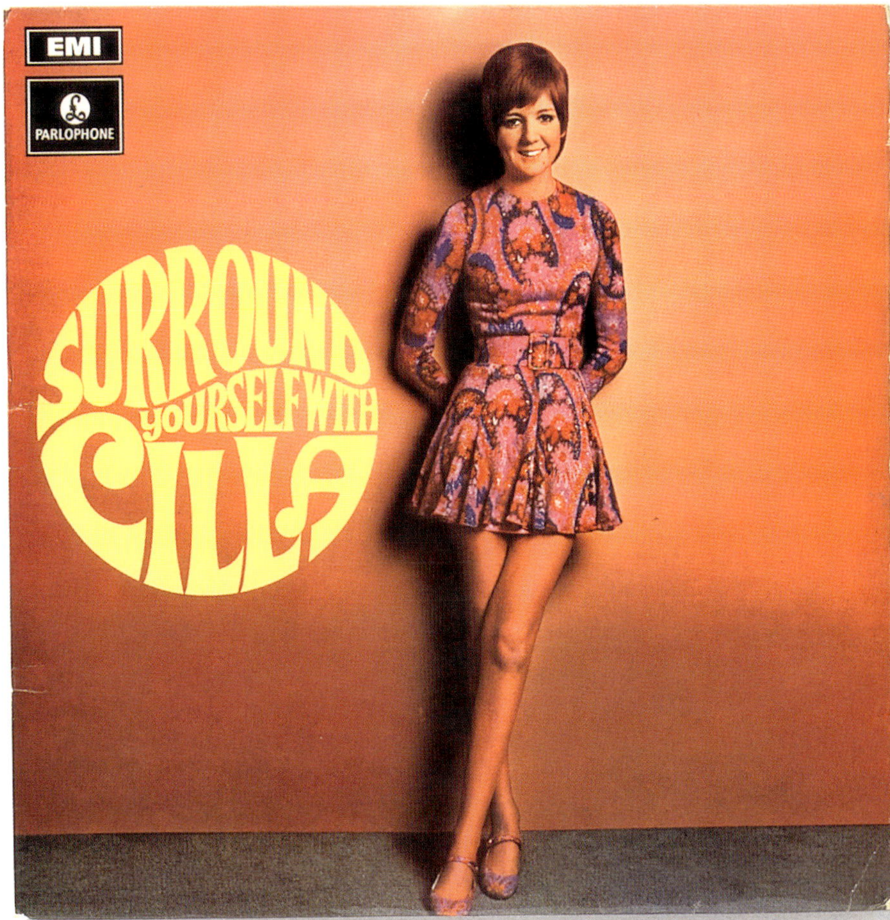

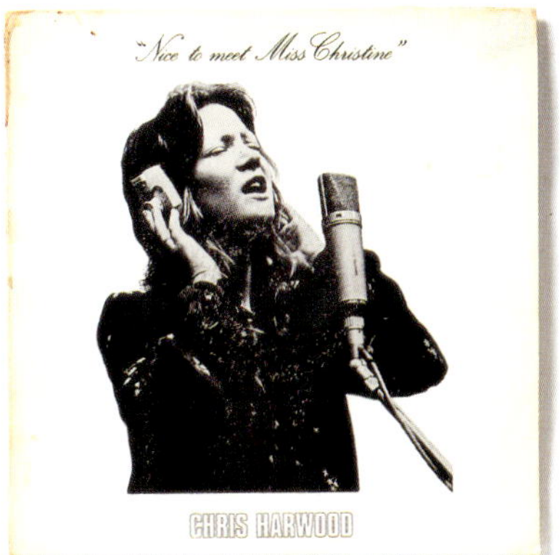

CHIRS HARWOOD:NICE TO MEET MISS CHRISTINE/
BIRTH RAB1
Photography/Barrie Wentzell

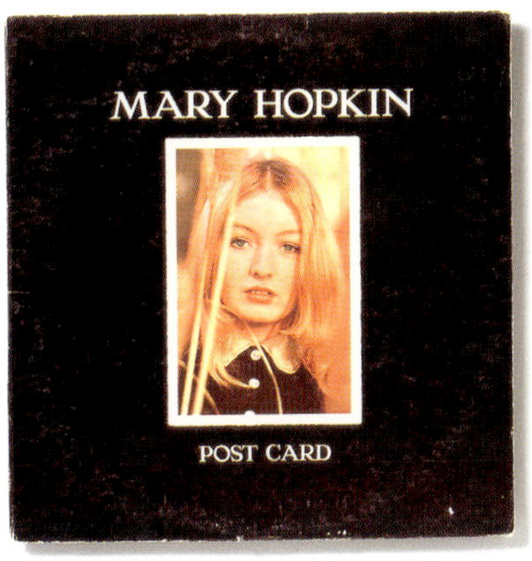

MARY HOPKIN:POST CARD/APPLE APCOR5(1969)
Photo/Linda

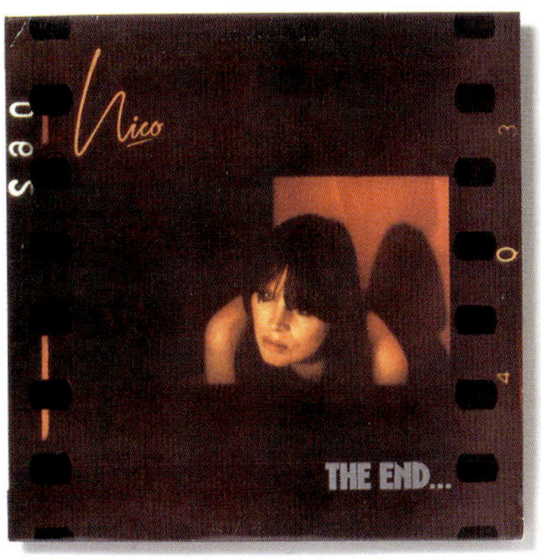

NICO:THE END.../ISLAND ILPS9311(1974)
Cover Photograpy Taken from the Film
'Les Hautes Solitudes'

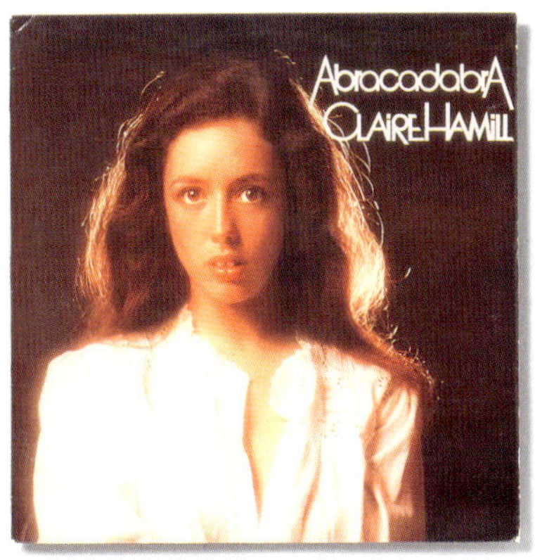

CLAIRE HAMILL:ABRACADABRA/KONK 104(1975)

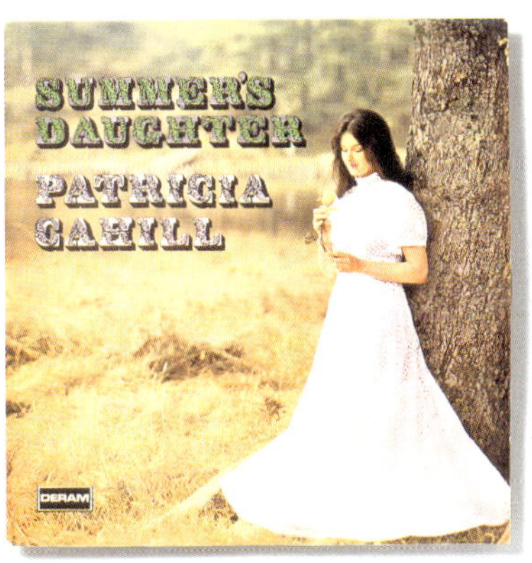

PATRICIA CAHILL:SUMMER'S DAUGHTER/
DERAM SDN22(1970)

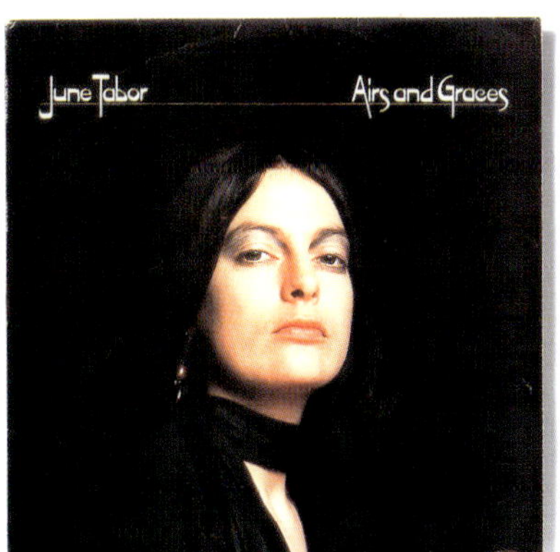

JUNE TABOR:AIRS AND GRACES:TOPIC 12TS298(1976)
Photography/June Tabor
Sleeve Design by Tony Engle

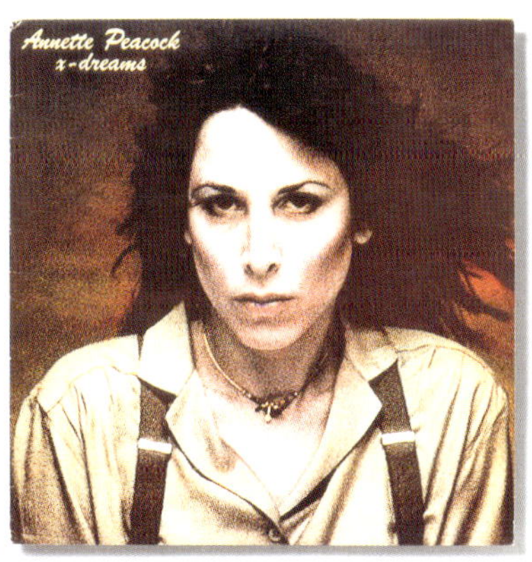

ANNETTE PEACOCK:X-DREAMS/AURA AUL702(1978)
Photography/Bob Carlos-Clarke

CLAIRE HAMILL:OCTOBER/
ISLAND ILPS9225(1973) *front and back
Photography/Patrick Litchfield
Sleeve Design/Chris Churchill Associates

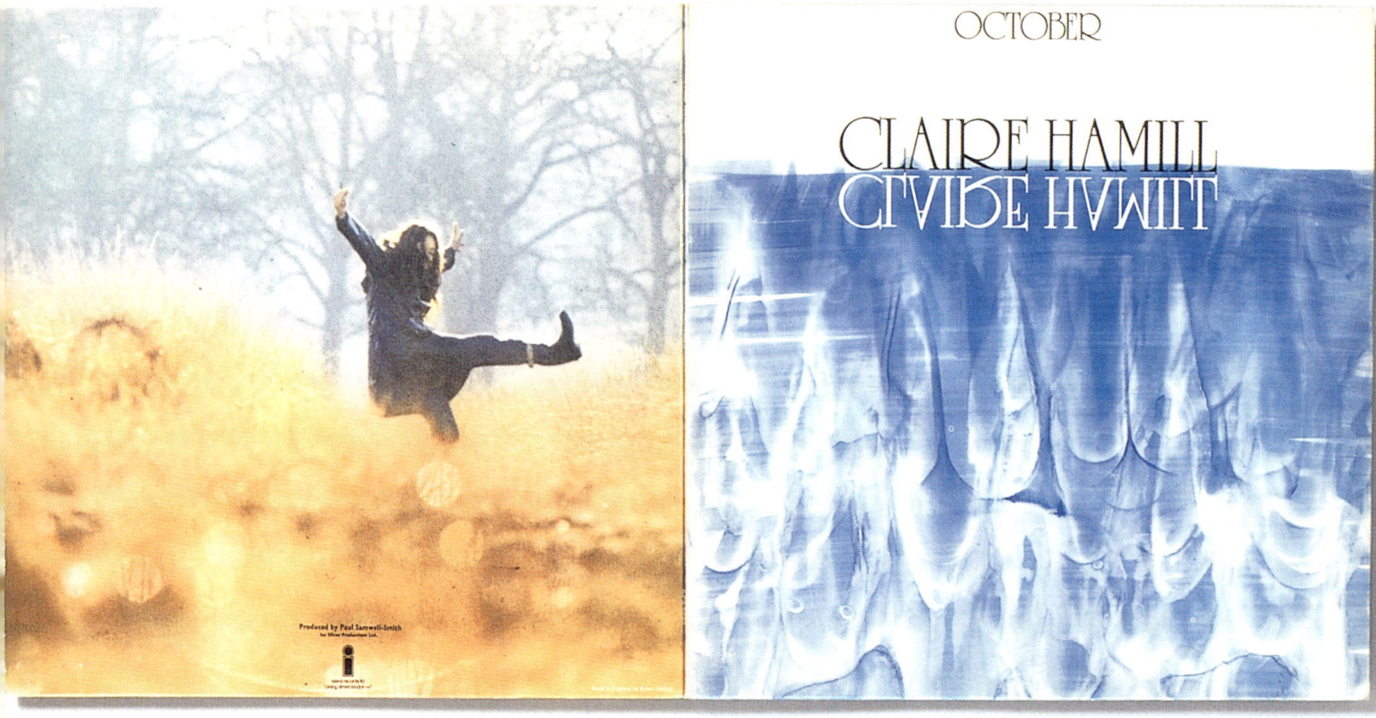

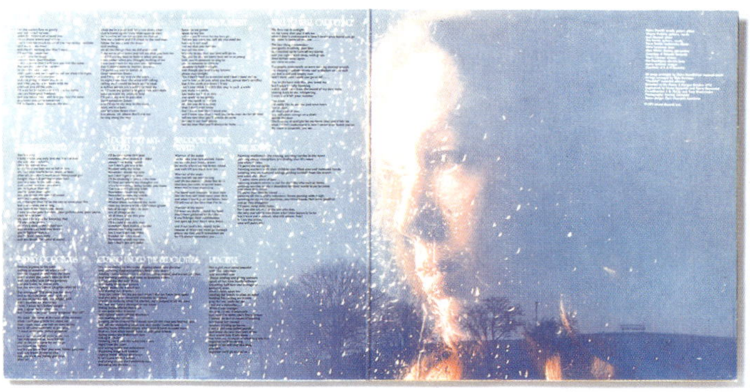

CLAIRE HAMILL:OCTOBER/ISLAND ILPS9225(1973) *inner

CONTRABAND:CONTRABAND/TRANSATLANTIC TRA278(1973)
Art Direction/Ann Sullivan
Co-ordination/Laurence Aston
Photography/Bruce Atkins
Design/Mick Brownfield,Chris Angell

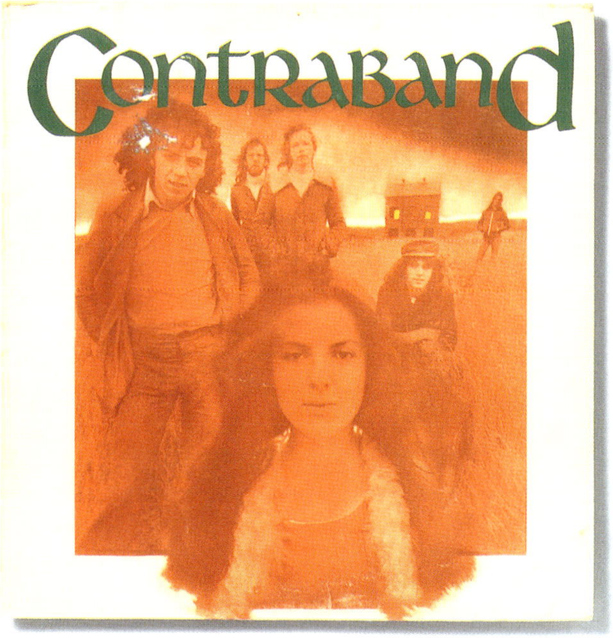

BRIDGET ST.JOHN:ASK ME NO QUESTIONS/
DANDELION 63750(1969)
Cover Design/ BRIDGET
Photo/ My dad(Cover)

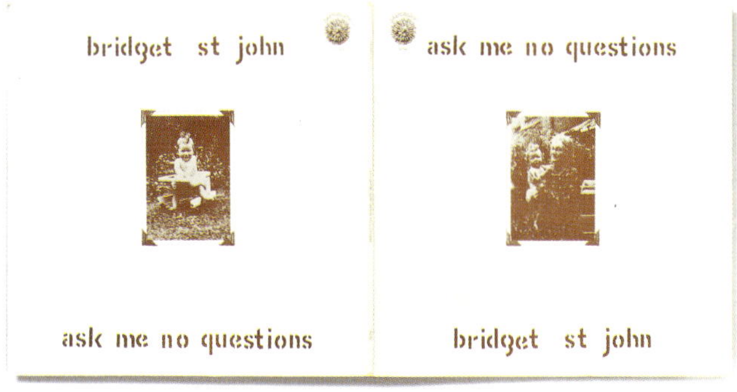

JULIE TIPPETTS:SUNSET GLOW/UTOPIA BULI1248(1975)*inner

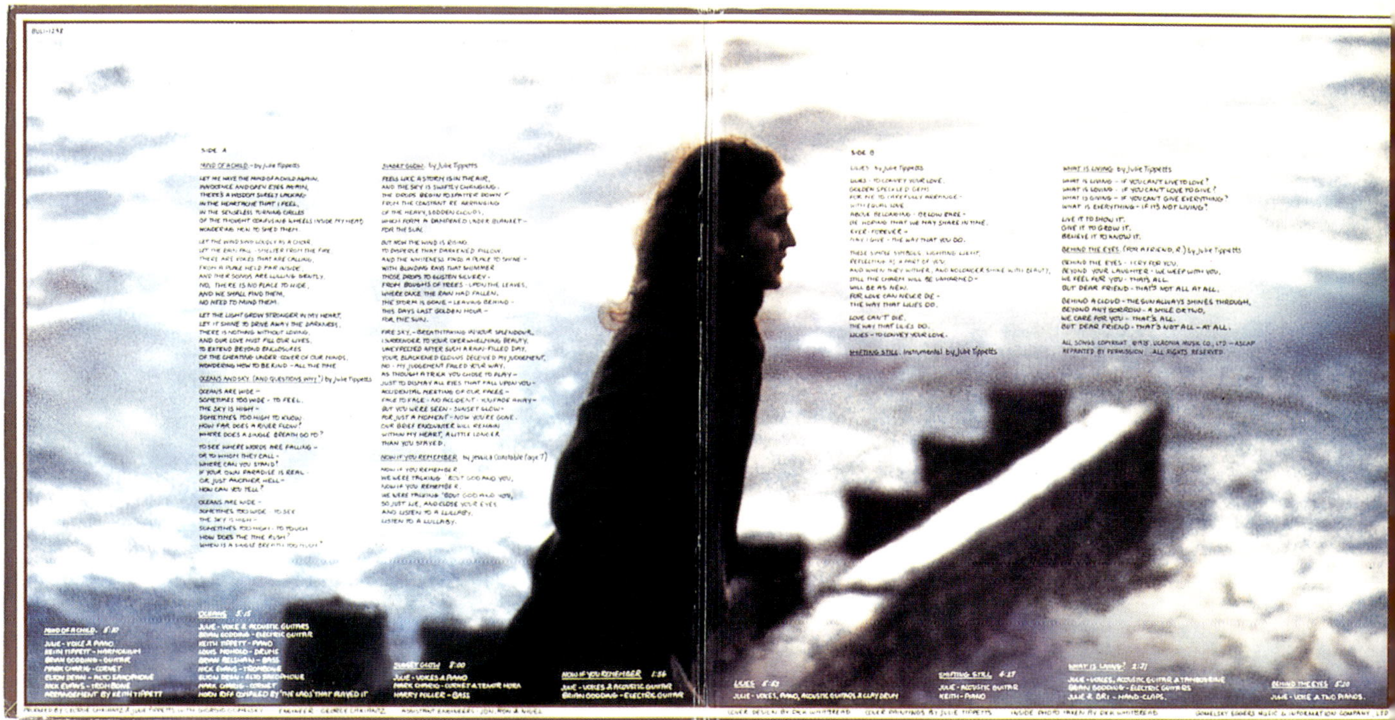

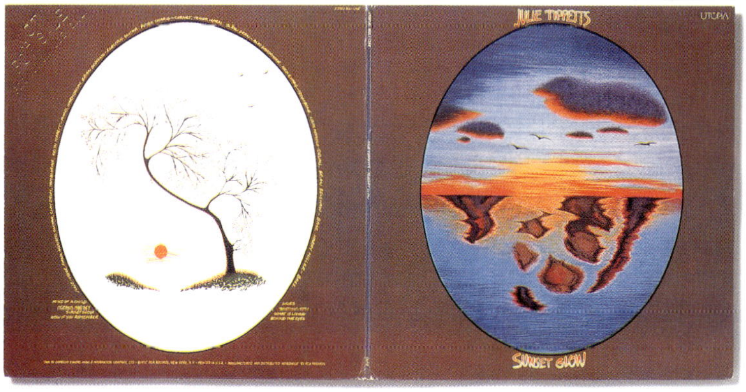

JULIE TIPPETTS:SUNSET GLOW/
UTOPIA BULI1248(1975) *front and back
Cover Design by Dick Whitebread
Cover Paintings by Julie Tippetts
Inside Photo Taken by Dick Whitebread

portraits

Men's Potraits

ポートレート男性編

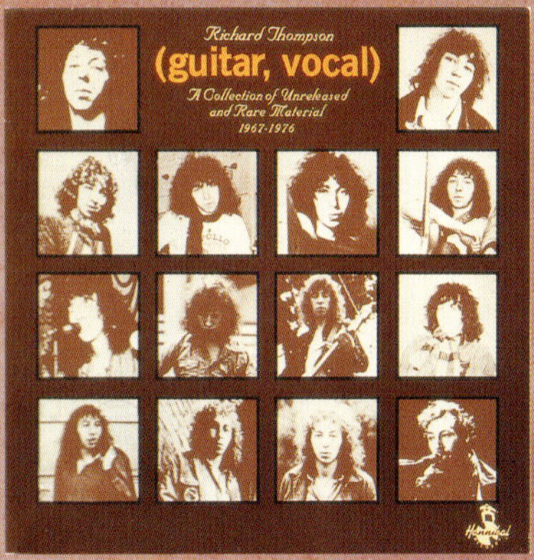

RICHARD THOMPSON:GUITAR,VOCAL/
HANNIBAL HNBL4801(1983)
Cover Concept/Richard Williams
Cover Design by Bloomfield,Travis

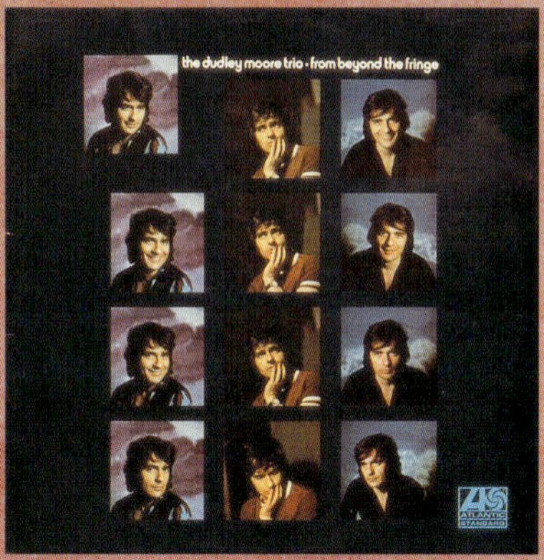

THE DUDLEY MOORE TRIO:
FROM 'BEYOND THE FRINGE'/ATRANTIC 2465 017()
Sleeve Design/Hamish&Gustav

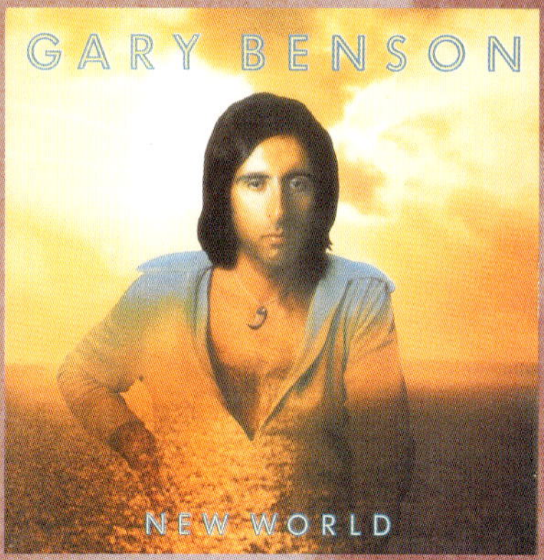

GARY BENSON:NEW WORLD/STATE ETAT10(1976)
Sleeve Design/Jo Mirowski
Photography/Martyn Goddard
Artwork/Wadewood

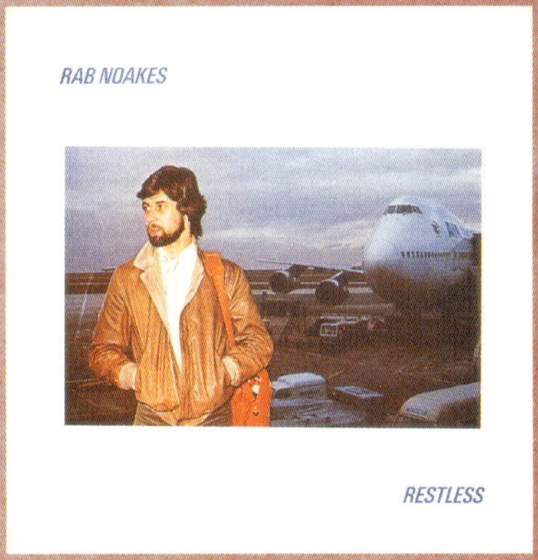

RAB NOAKES:RESTLESS/
RING O'RECORDS 2339 201(1978)

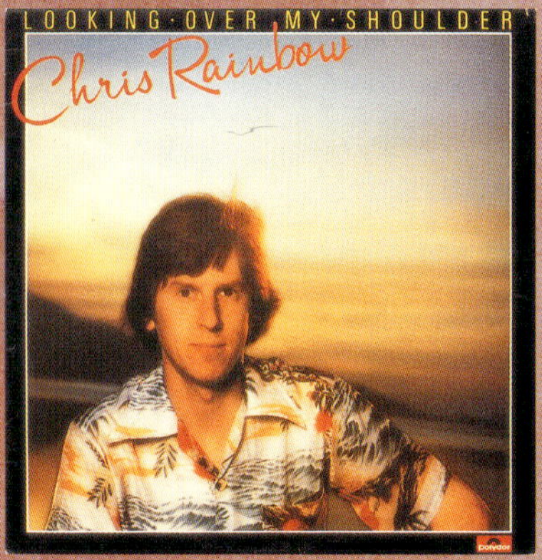

CHRIS RAINBOW:LOOKING OVER MY SHOULDER/
POLYDOR 2383 467(1976)
Design&Art Direction/Bill Smith
Photography/Martyn Goddard

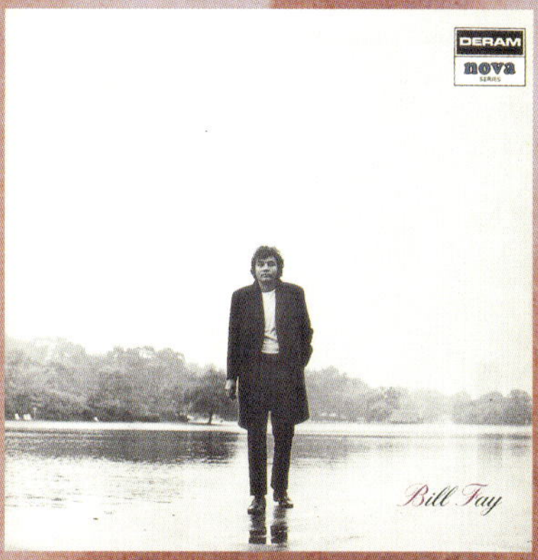

BILL FAY:BILL FAY/nova SDN12(1970)

In Search of the Lost Record

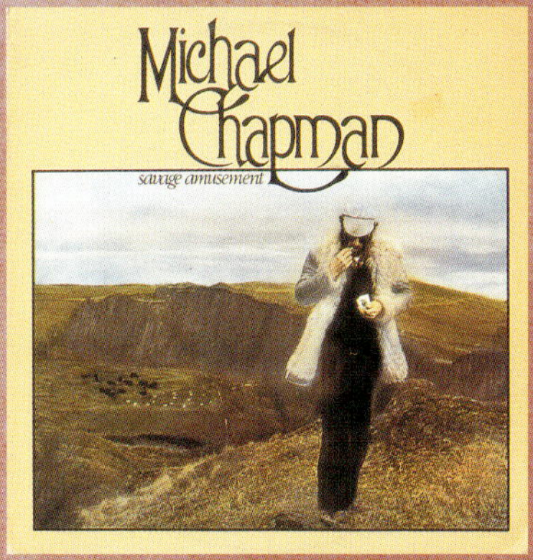

MICHAEL CHAPMAN:SAVAGE AMUSEMENT/
DECCA SKL-R5242(1976)
Sleeve Deisgn/Field
Cover Photographs/Michael Gimbut

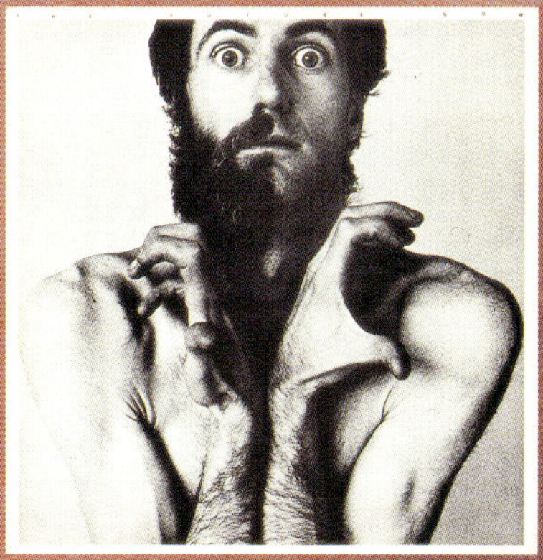

PETER HAMILL:AND CLOSE AS YOU THIS/
Photography by Anton Corbijn

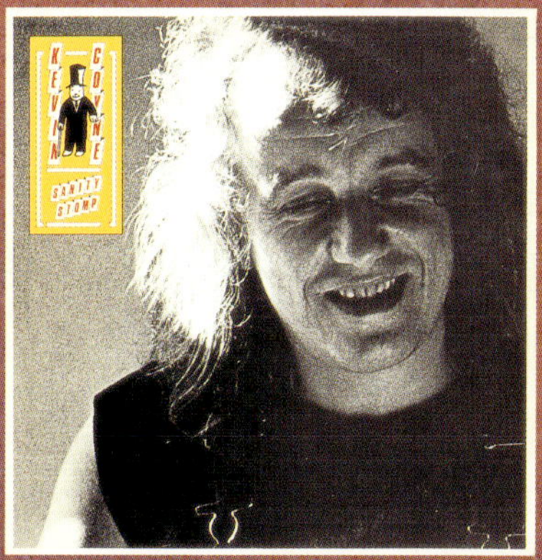

KEVIN COYNE:SANITY STOMP/
VIRGIN VGD3504(1980)
Front Cover Photo/ Rutter

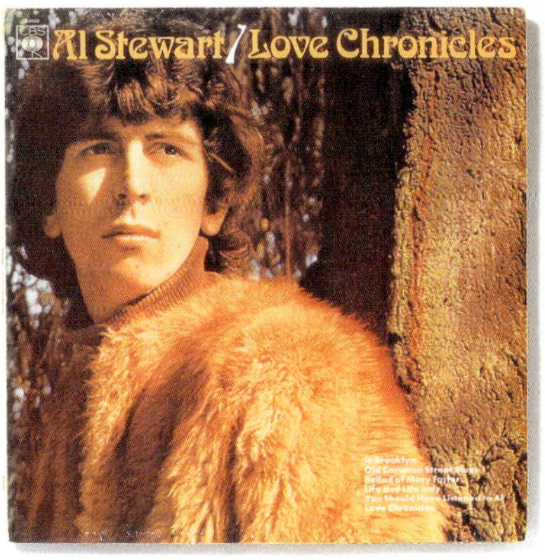

AL STEWART:LOVE CHRONICLES/
CBS 63460(1969)
Cover Photos/Sophie Litchfield
Album Design/John Hays

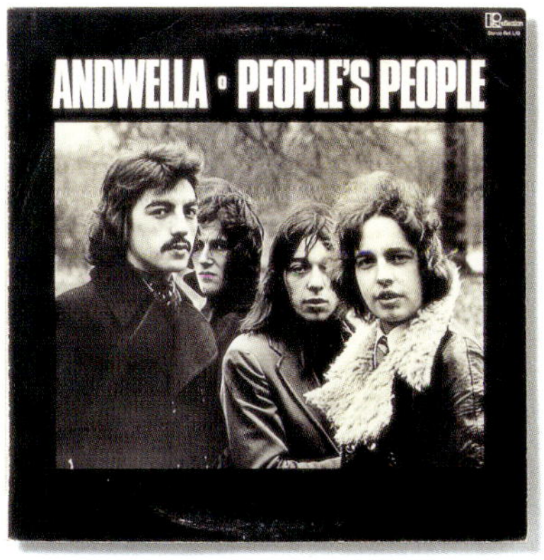

ANDWELLA:PEOPLE'S PEOPLE/
REFLECTION REFL10(1971)
Photography/Dezo Hoffman
Design/Ian Pedder

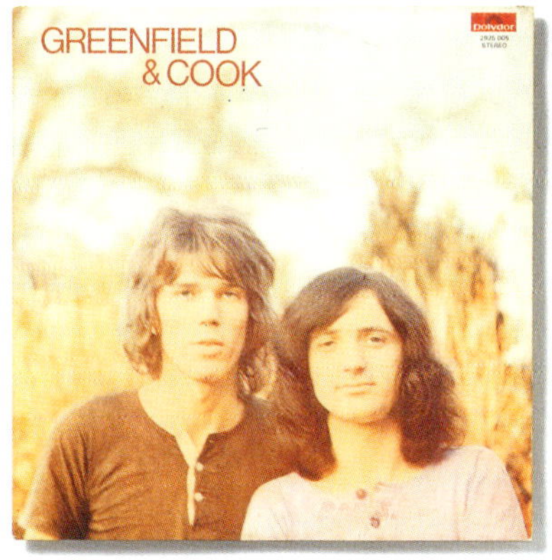

GREENFIELD&COOK:GREENFIELD&COOK/
POLYDOR 2925 005
Photos/Jaap Eggermont

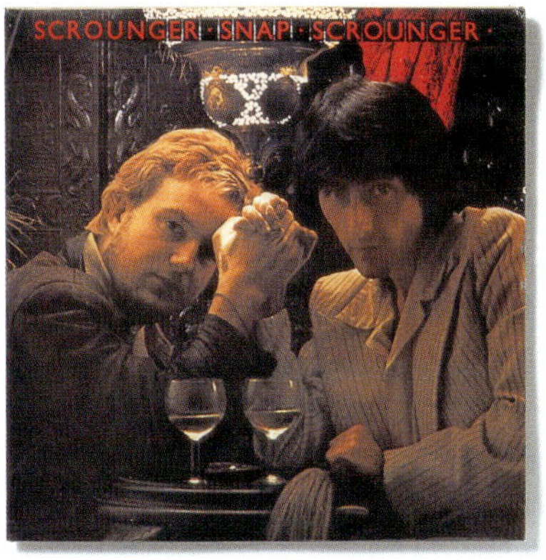

SCROUNGER:SNAP/ANCHOR ANCL2021(1976)
Sleeve Deisgn/Graves Aslett Associates
Sleeve Photo/Graves

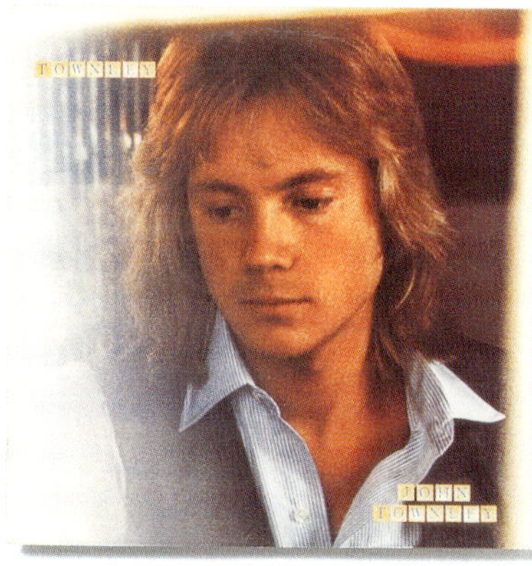
JOHN TOWNLEY:JOHN TOWNLEY/
EMI EMC3298(1979)
Sleeve Co-ordination/A.D.U.EMI,Paul Maxwell
Photography/David Tack

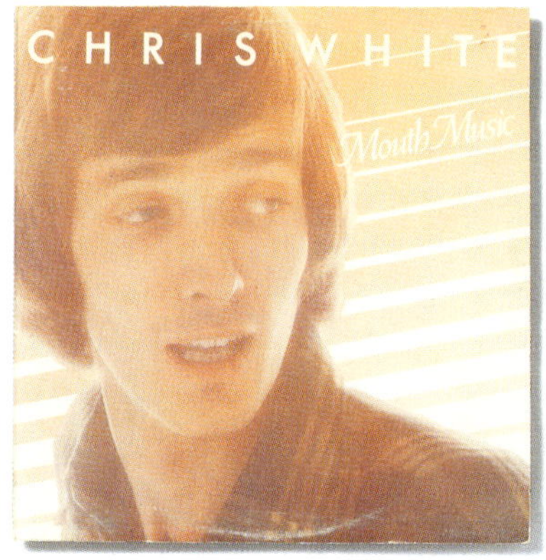

CHRIS WHITE:MOUTH MUSIC/CHARISMA CAS1118
Album Designed by Art Direction

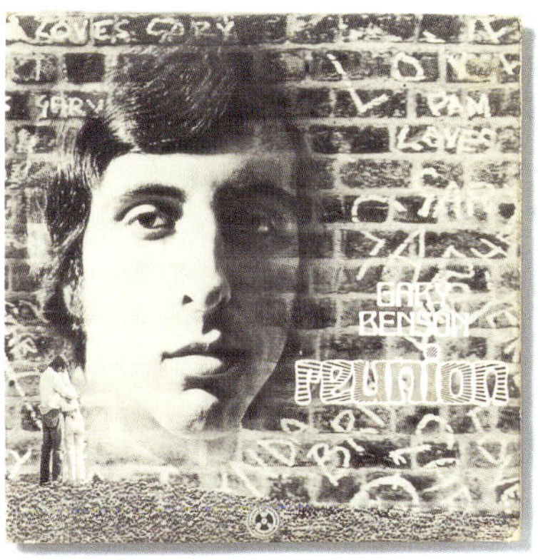

GARY BENSON:REUNION
/PENNY FARTHING PELS506
Sleeve Design by Drawing Board

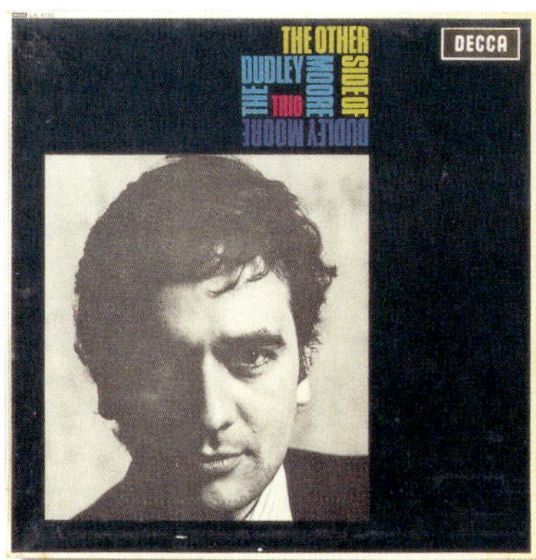

THE DUDLEY MOORE TRIO:
THE OTHER SIDE OF DUDLEY MOORE
/DECCA LK4732
Photograph/Lewis Morley

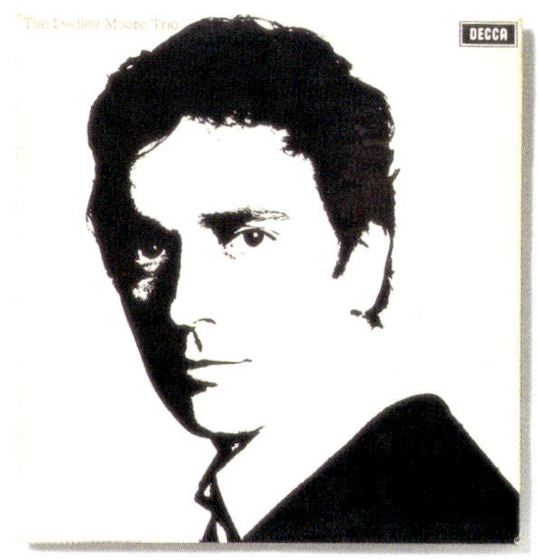

THE DUDLEY MOORE TRIO:THE DUDLEY MOORE TRIO/
DECCA SKL4976(1969)
Cover Photo/Barry Lategan

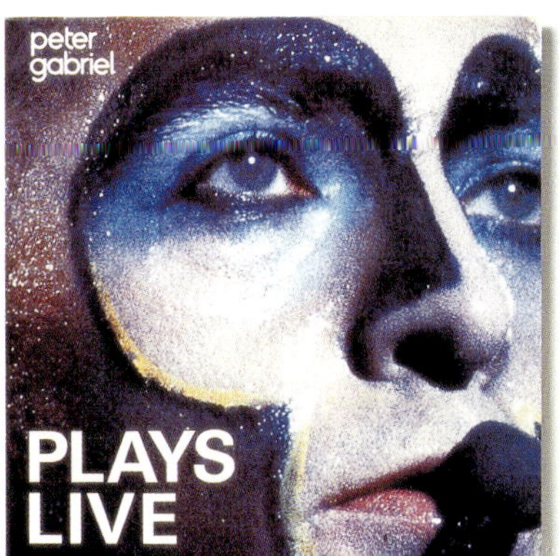

PETER GABRIEL:PLAYS LIVE/
CHARISMA PGDL1(1983)
Front Cover Photograph by Armand Gallo

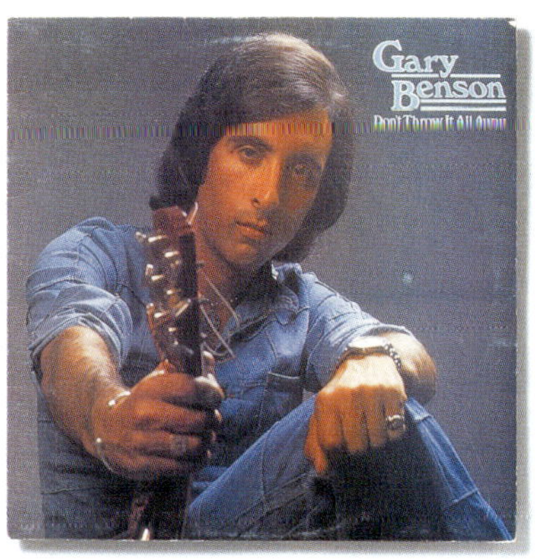

GARY BENSON:DON'T THROW IT ALL AWAY/
STATE ETAT3
Photography/Mike Leale
Art Direction/Paul Welch

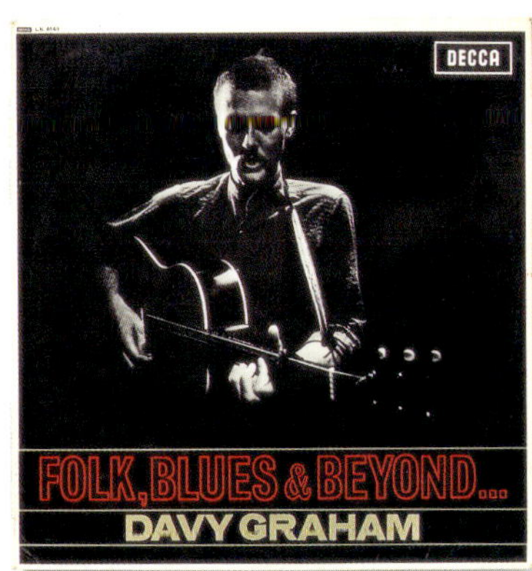

DAVY GRAHAM:FOLK,BLUES&BEYOND.../
DECCA LK4649(1964)
Cover Photography/Crispian Woodgate

ALAN PARKER:BAND OF ANGELS/
MCA MUPS471(1972)
Concept and Design/John Millerburg
Photography/Jim Jenkins

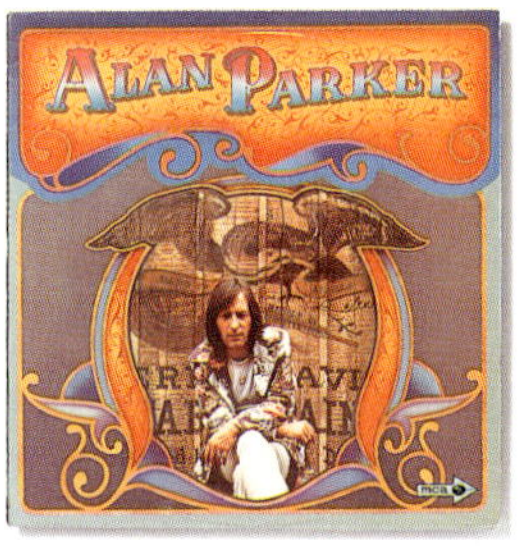

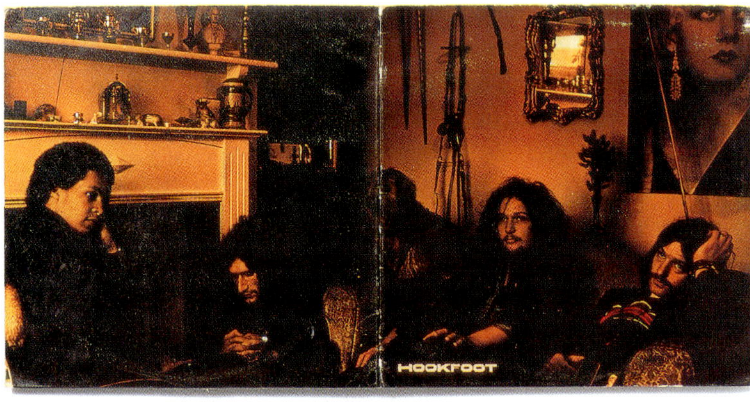

HOOKFOOT:HOOKFOOT/DJM DJLPS413(1971)
Cover Photograph by Ian Digby-Ovens
Sleeve Design and Liner Photograph by David Larkham

ALLAN TAYLOR:SOMETIMES/
LIBERTY LBG83483(1971) *front and back
Design and Produced by Art Direction
Photography by Mike Hasted

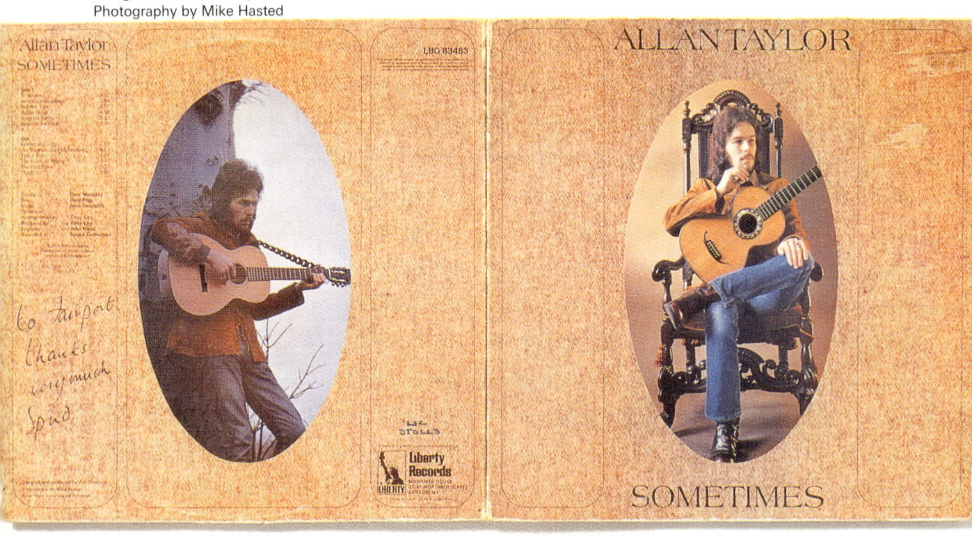

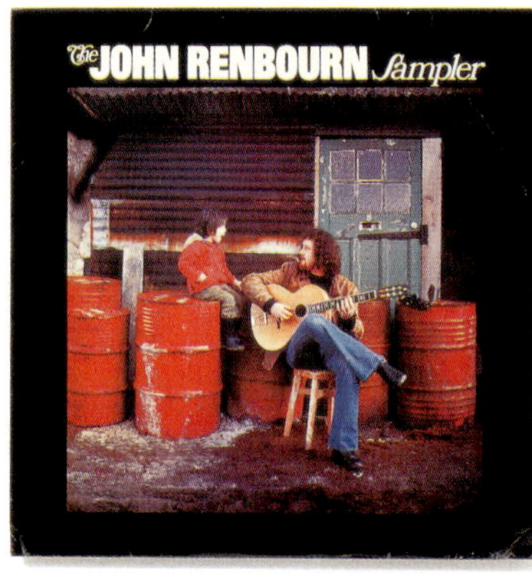

JOHN RENBOURN:THE JOHN RENBOURN SAMPLER/
TRANSATLANTIC TRA-SAM20(1971)
Photo & Cover Design/Shepard Sherbell

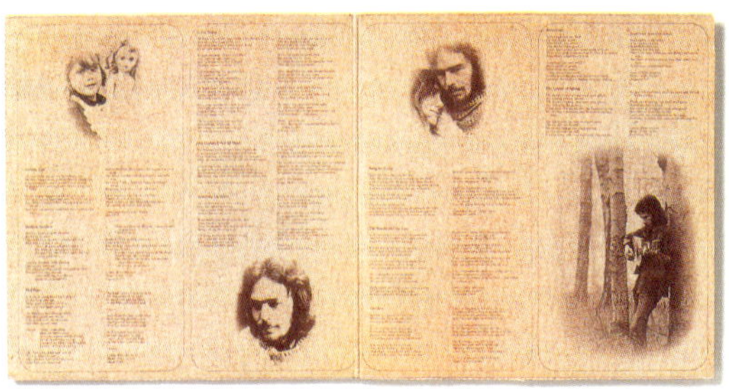

ALLAN TAYLOR:SOMETIMES/
LIBERTY LBG83483(1971) *inner

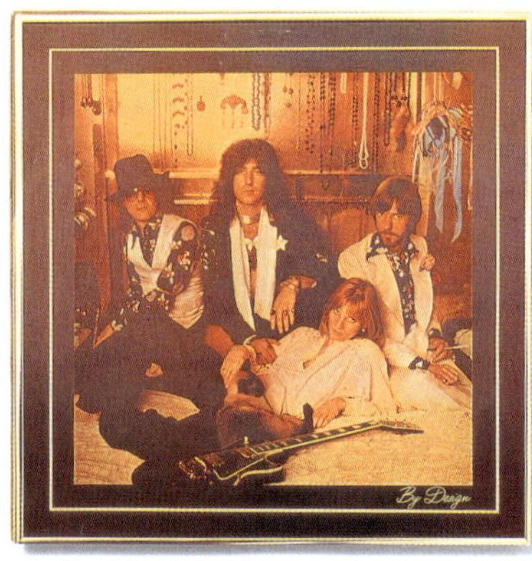

DESIGN:BY DESIGN/EMI EMC3113(1976)
Sleeve Design/Steve Newport For EMI Design
Photo/Mike Putland

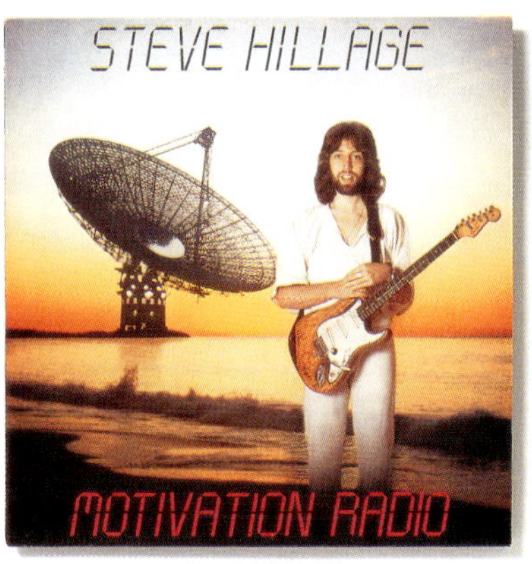

STEVE HILLAGE:MOTIVATION RADIO
/VIRGIN V2777(1977)

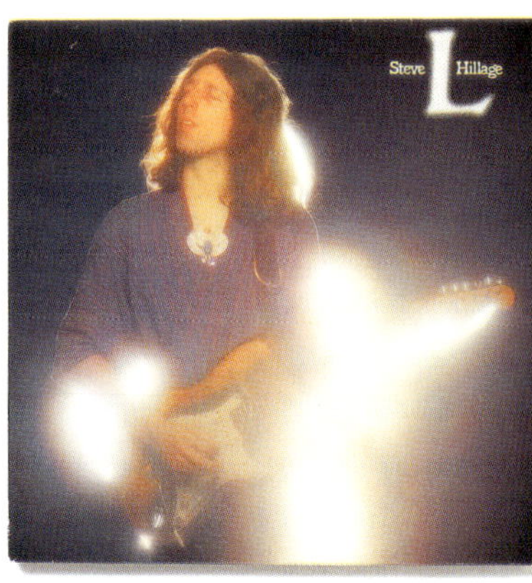

STEVE HILLAGE:L/VIRGIN V2066(1975)
Cover Design/Ken Dolman Cooke Key Associates
Cover Photography/Clayton Kenny

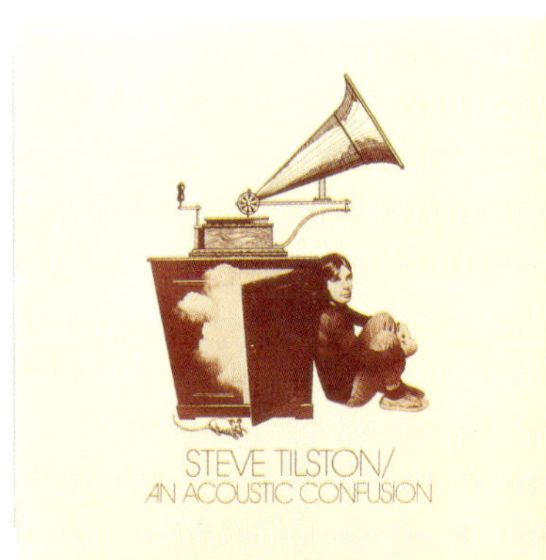

STEVE TILSTON:AN ACOUSTIC CONFUSION/
THE VILLAGE THING VTS5(1971)
Sleeve Front/Pete Jackson&Sam
Graphics/Plastic Dog

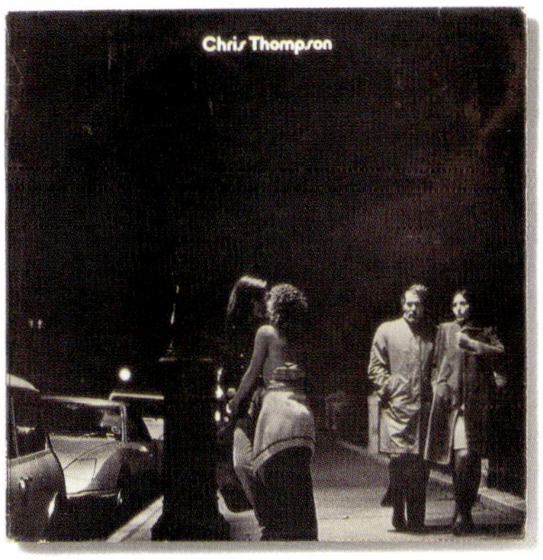

CHRIS THOMPSON:CHRIS THOMPSON/
THE VILLAGE THING VTS21
Front Photo/Monique Brossier
Graphics/Terry Brace,Plastic Dog

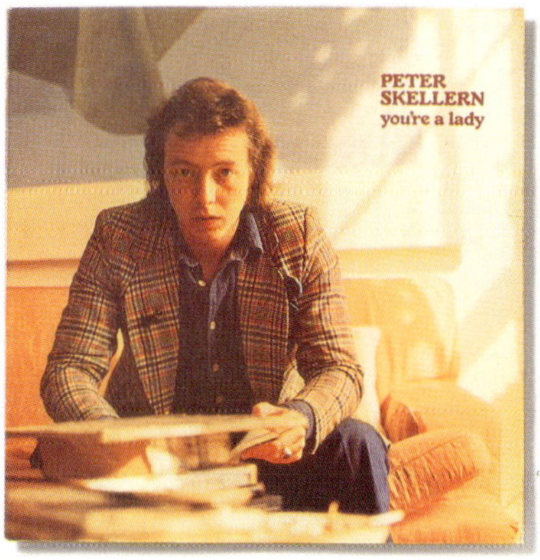

PETER SKELLERN:YOU'RE A LADY/
DECCA SKL5151(1972)
Cover Photographs/Marc Dimac

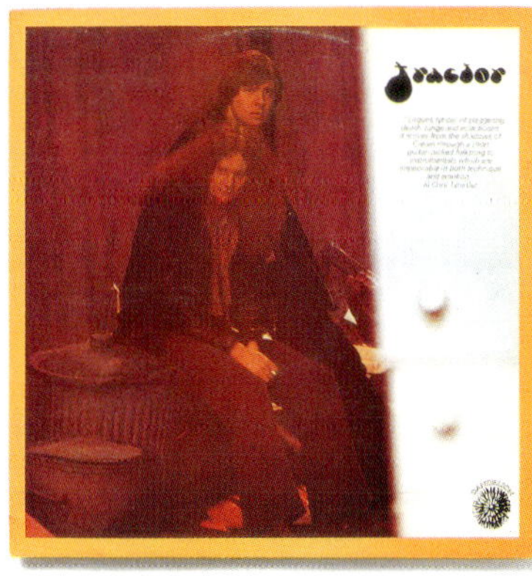

TRACTOR:TARCTOR/DANDELION 2310 217(1972)
Sleeve Design/Hamish Grimes
Photography/Alan Burgess

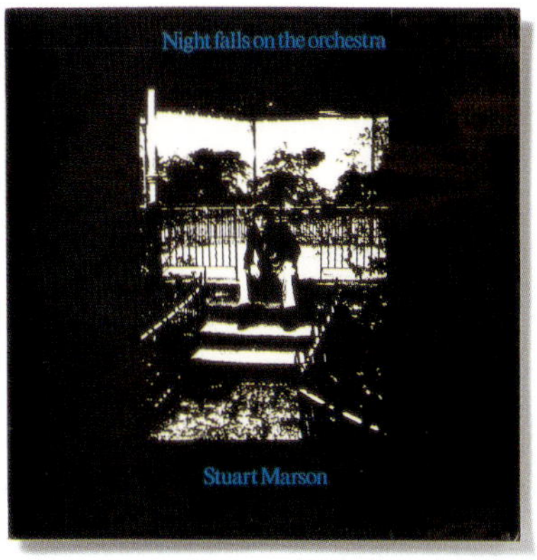

STUART MARSON:NIGHT FALLS ON THE ORCHESTRA/
SFA012
Sleeve Design/Tim Sellick

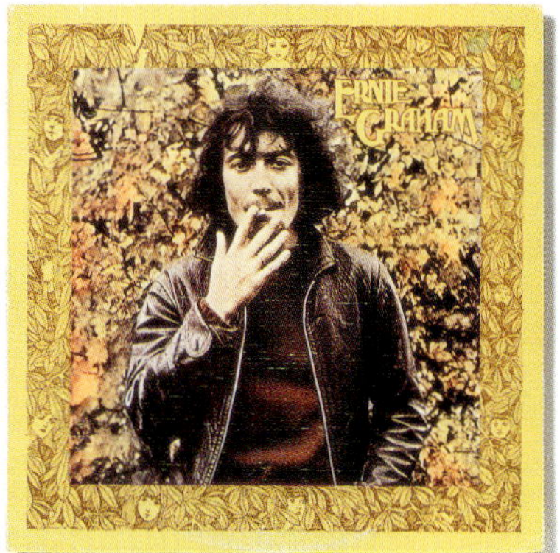

ERNIE GRAHAM:ERNIE GRAHAM/
LIBERTY LBS83485(1971)
Cover Design/Jeff Powell
Photography/ Chris Gabrin

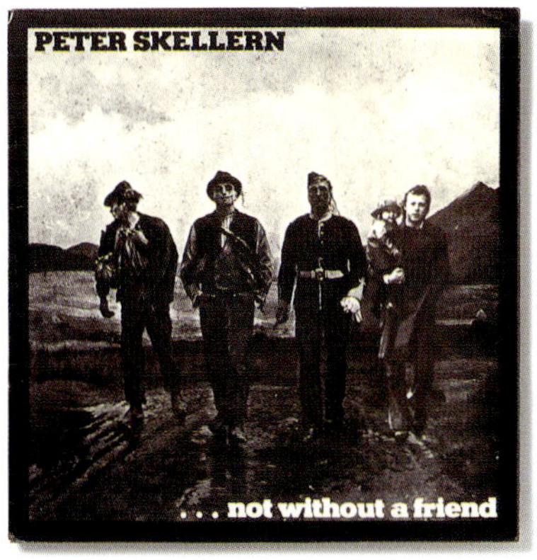

PETER SKELLERN:..NOT WITHOUT A FRIEND/
DECCA SKL5178(1973)
Cover Prepared by Jhon Kosh
Photography/Christopher Sykes

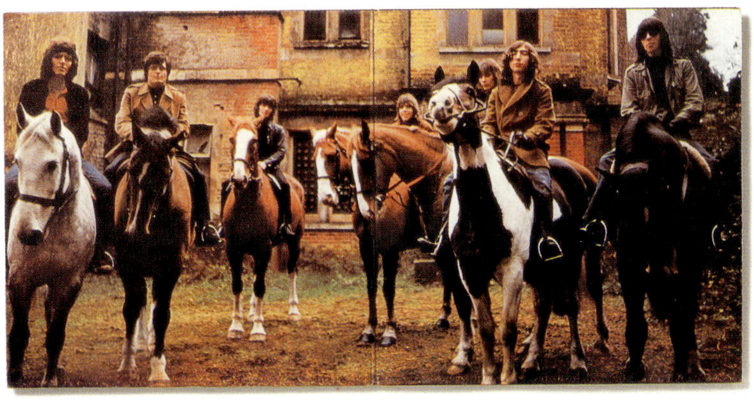

TRIFLE:FIRST MEETING/DAWN DNLS3017(1971)*inner

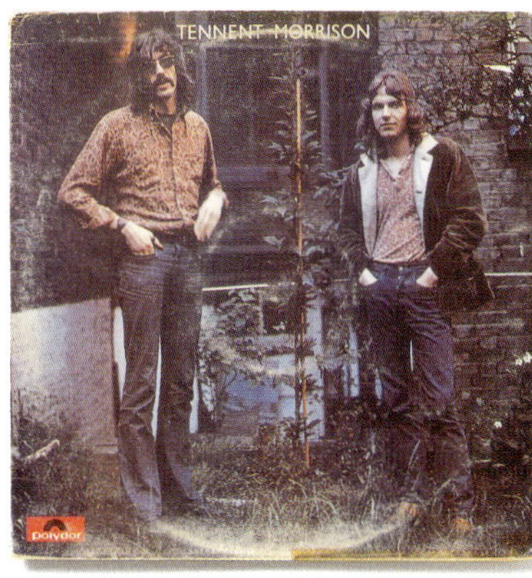

TENNENT MORRISON:TENNENT MORRISON/
POLYDOR 2383 152
Sleeve by Hipgnosis and John Blake

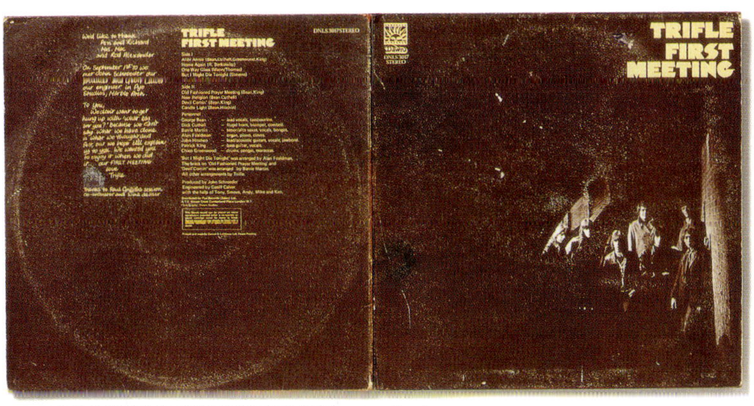

TRIFLE:FIRST MEETING/DAWN DNLS3017(1971)*front and back
Photograpy/Dawn Studios

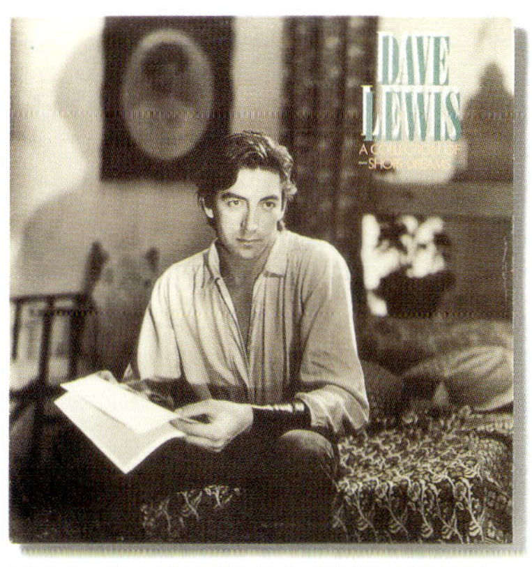

DAVE LEWIS:A COLLECTION OF-SHORT DREAMS-/
POLYDOR 2383 522(1978)
Photography/Peter Lavery
Concept/Dave Lewis&Bill Smith
Design&Art/Bill Smith

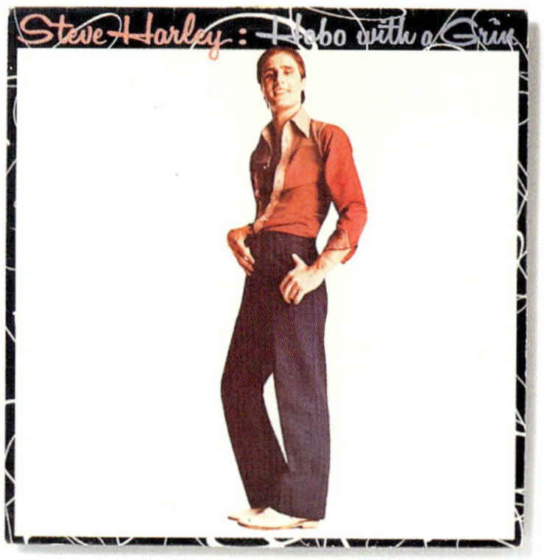

STEVE HARLEY:HOBO WITH A GRIN/
EMI EMC3254(1978)
Photo/Jim Shea
Design/Kosh

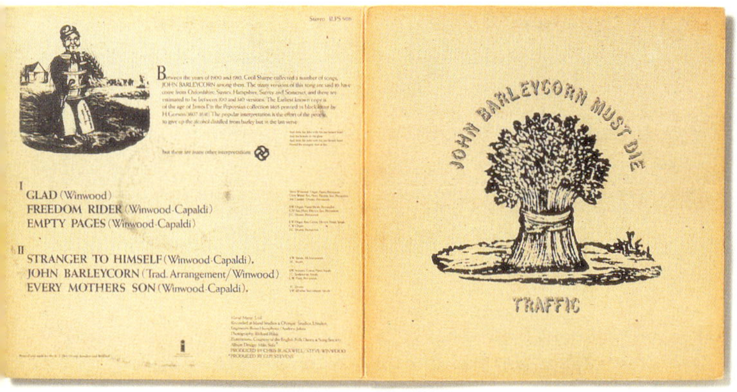

above: TARFFIC:JOHN BARLEYCORN MUST DIE/
ISLAND ILPS9116(1970) *front and back
Photography/Richard Polak
Illustarations/Courtesy of the English Folk Dance&Song Society
Album Design/Mike Sida

right: TARFFIC:JOHN BARLEYCORN MUST DIE/
ISLAND ILPS9116(1970) *inner

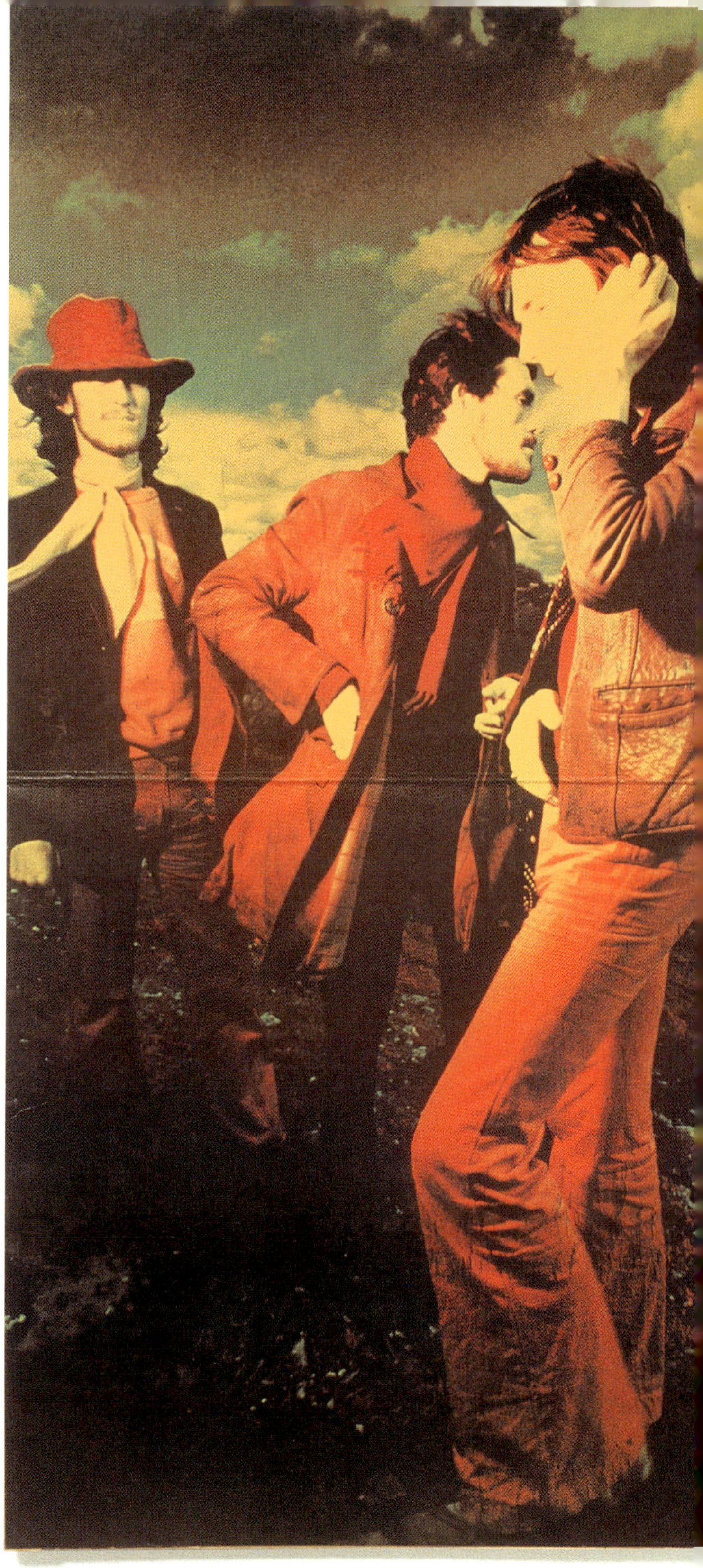

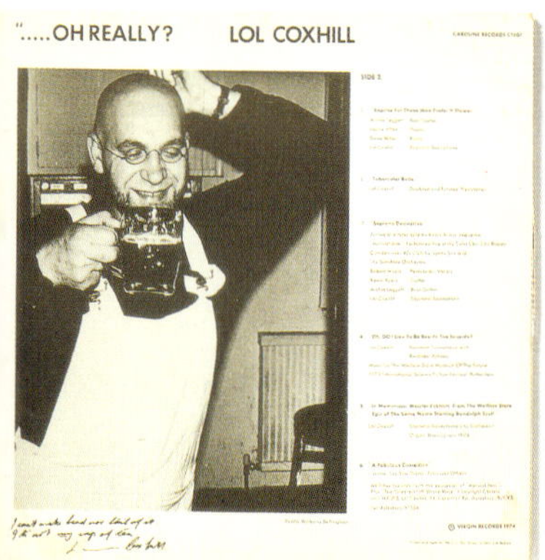

LOL COXHILL:OH REALLY?/
CAROLINE C1507(1974)
Photo/ Barbara Bellingham

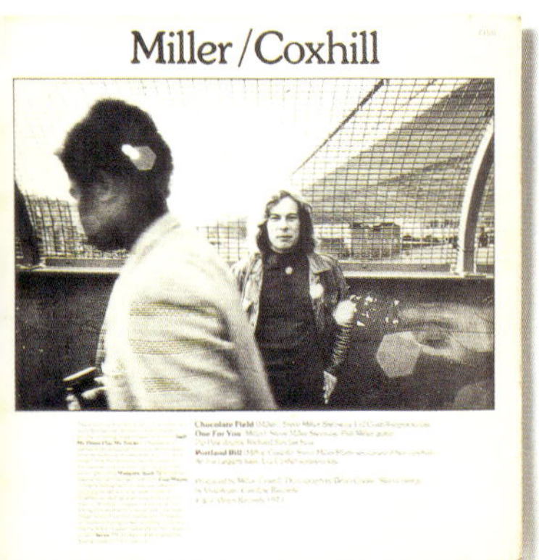

MILLER,COXHILL:MILLER COXHILL/
CAROLINE C1503(1973)
Photograph by Barbara Bellingham
Sleeve Design by Visualeyes

① MICHAEL DE ALBUQUERQUE:
WE MAY BE CATTLE BUT WE'VE ALL GOT NAMES/
RCA SF8383(1973)

② ROY HARPER:FLAT BAROQUE AND BERSERK/
HARVEST SHVL766(1970)
Photos by John McKenzie

③ DAVE LEWIS:FROM TIME TO TIME/
POLYDOR 2383 420(1976)
Photo/David Griffiths
Design/Wadewood

④ DESIGN:BY DESIGN/EMI EMC3113(1976)
Sleeve Design/Steve Newport For EMI Design
Photo/Mike Putland

⑤ PRINCIPAL EDWARDS MAGIC THEATRE:
SOUNDTRACK/
DANDELION 63752(1969)
Photo/ Duncan Flatman
Design/ Harry and Leslie

⑥ DAVE CARTWRIGHT:MASQUERADE/
DJM DJF20489(1976)
Front Cover Photograaphy/Donnelly-Burns-Davies

⑦ MIKE COOPER:DO I KNOW YOU?/
DAWN DNLS3005(1970)

⑧ PETER SKELLERN:KISSING IN THE
CACTUS/MERCURY 9109 700

⑨ NICK DRAKE:BRYTER LAYTER/
ISLAND ILPS9134(1970)
Sleeve Design and Front Cover Photograph/Nigel
Waymouth

⑩ KEVIN AYERS:
YES WE HAVE NO MANANAS SO GET YOUR
MANANAS TODAY/(1977)
Design/Peter Shepherd EMI Design
Cover Photo/Kevin Ayers by Peter Vernon

① 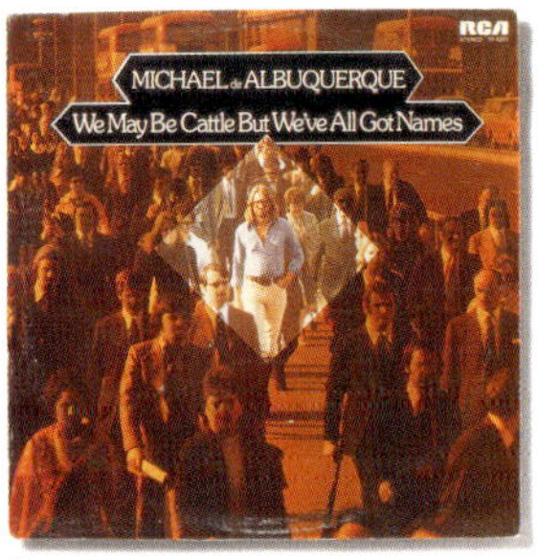

② 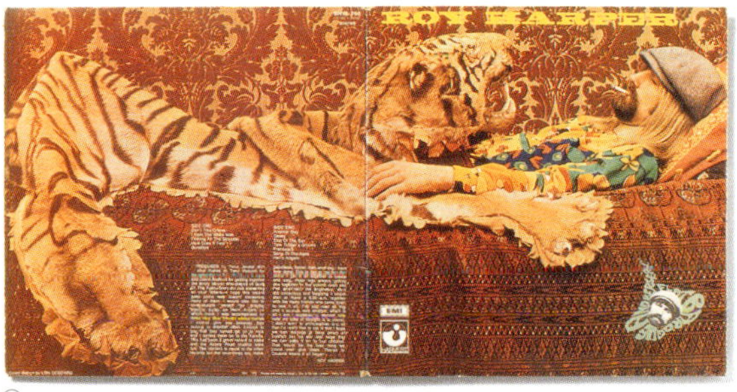

③ 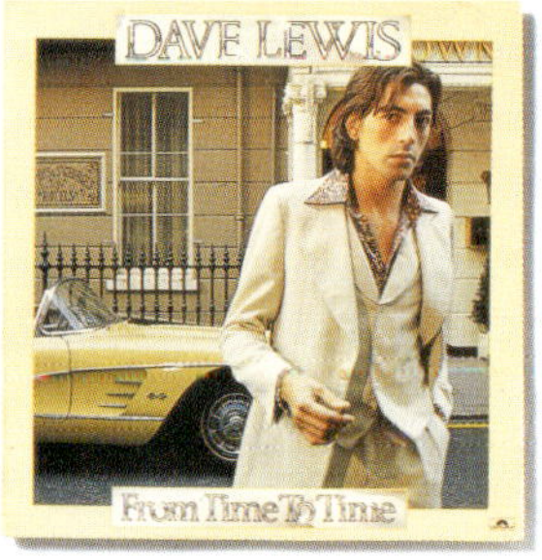

④ 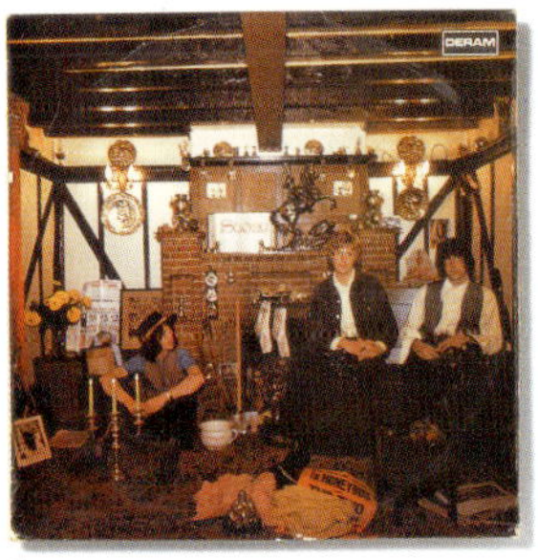

⑤ 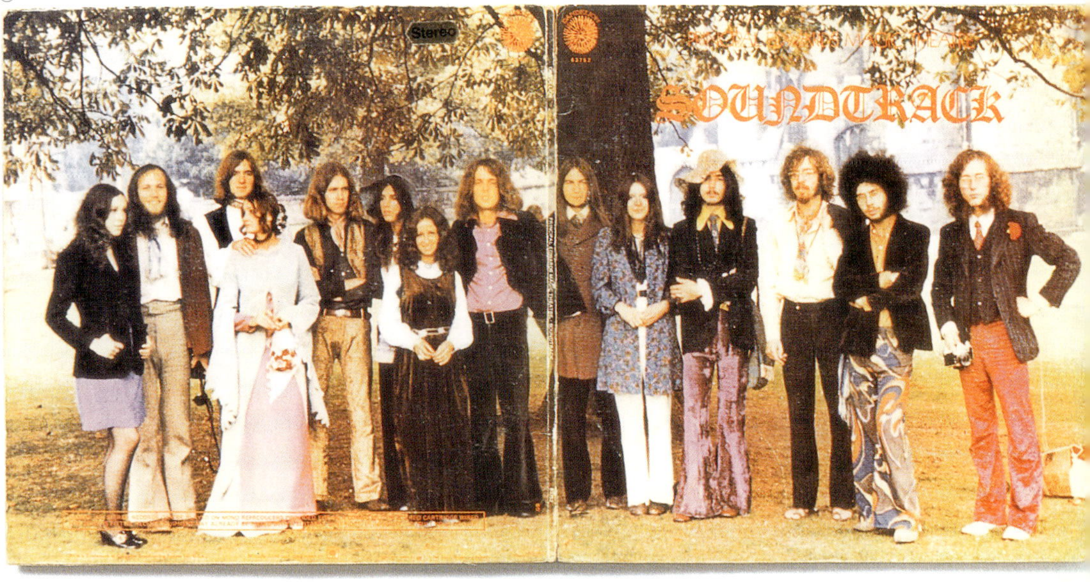

⑥ 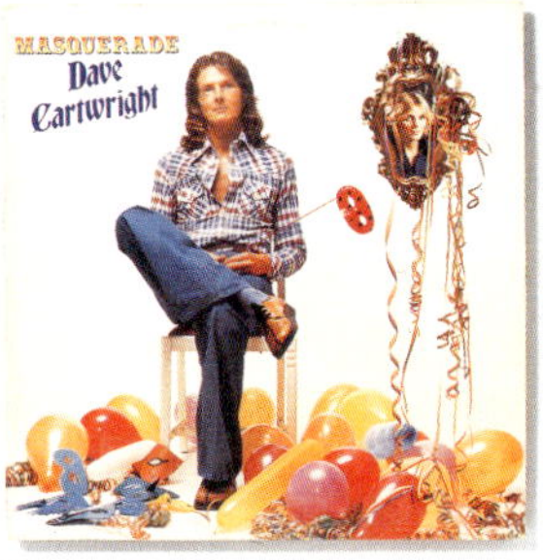

⑦ 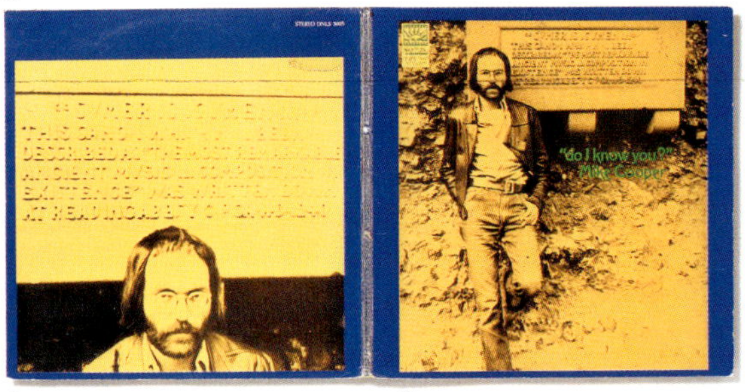

⑧ 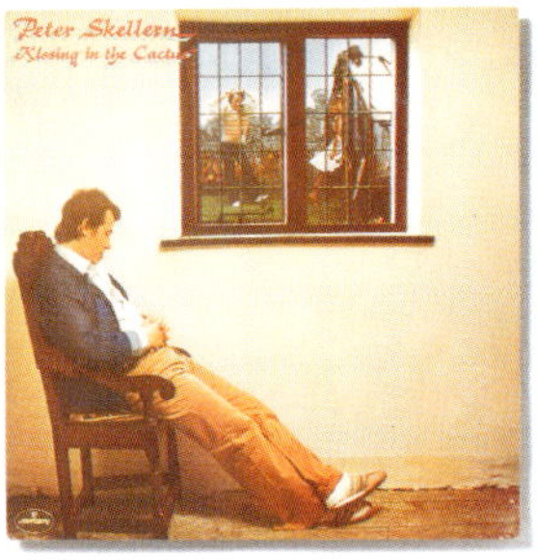

⑨ 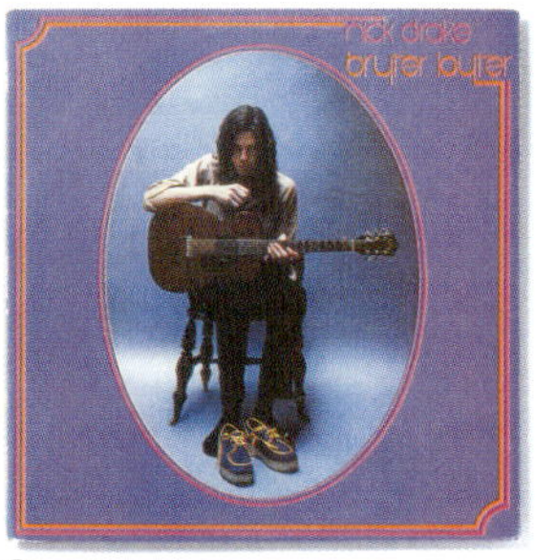

⑩ 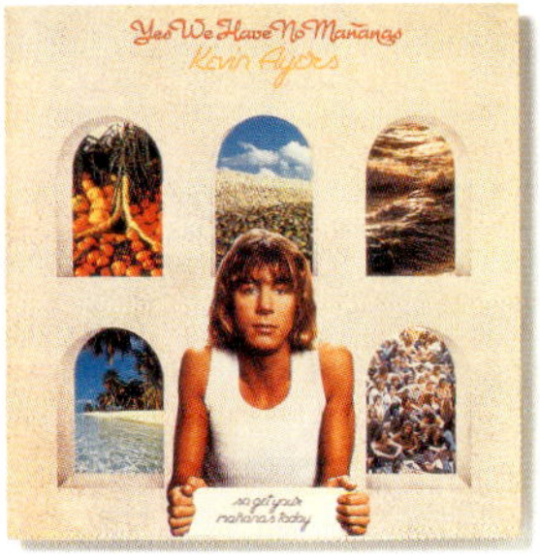

⑪ 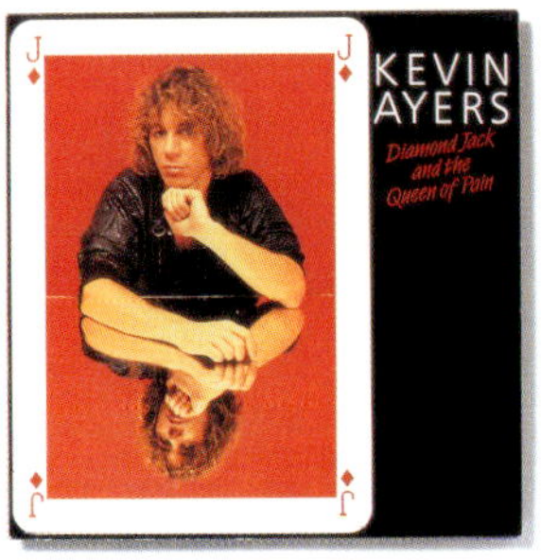

⑫ 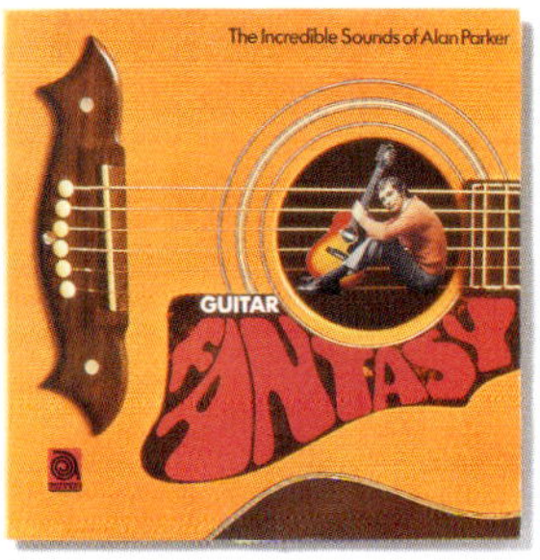

⑬ 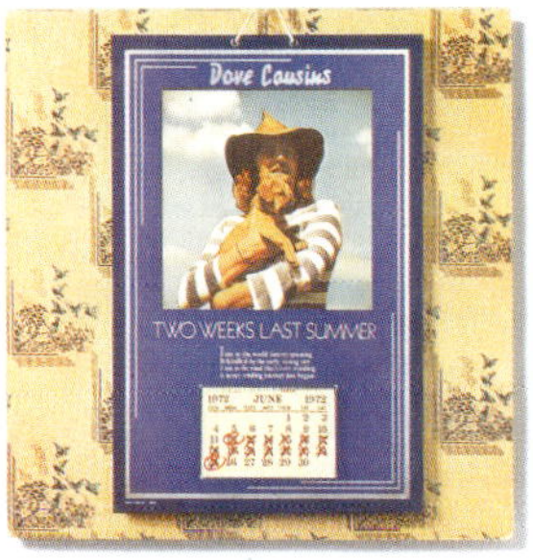

⑭ 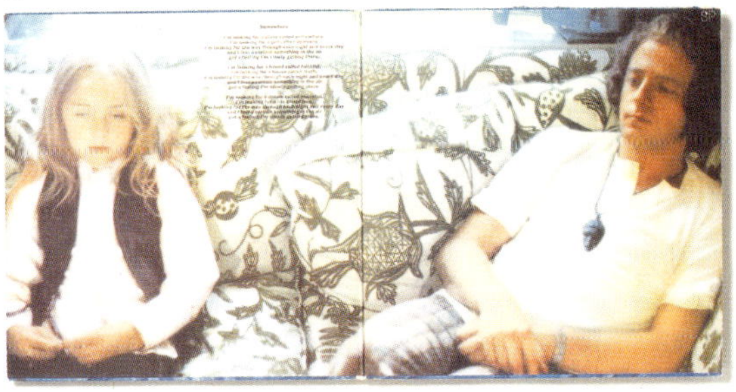

⑮ 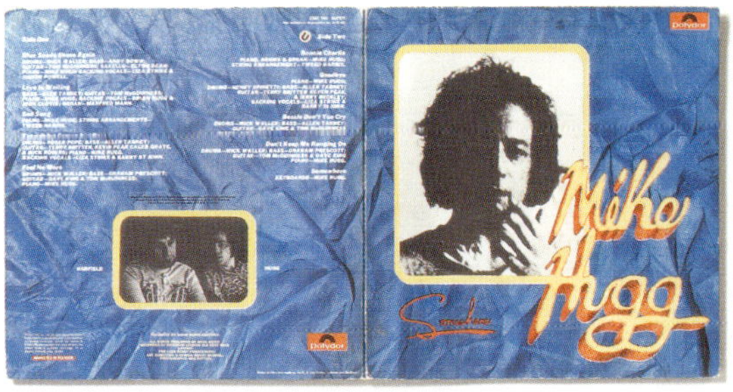

⑪ KEVIN AYERS:
DIAMOND JACK AND THE QUEEN OF PAIN/
CHARLY CR30224(1983)
Sleeve Design/Yeldham Muchmore

⑫ ALAN PARKER:GUITAR FANTASY/
ARISTOCRAT AR1022(1970)
Sleeve Design by Mike Grace
Photography by Alec Byrne

⑬ DAVE COUSINS:TWO WEEKS LAST SUMMER/
A&M AMLS68118(1972)
Art Direction/Mike Doud
Cover Designed by Mike Doud and John Kosh

⑭ MIKE HUGG:SOMEWHERE/
POLYDOR 2383 140(1972) *inner

⑮ MIKE HUGG:SOMEWHERE/
POLYDOR 2383 140(1972) *front and back
Art Direction&Design/Bunny Burnell
Photography/Bob Cotton

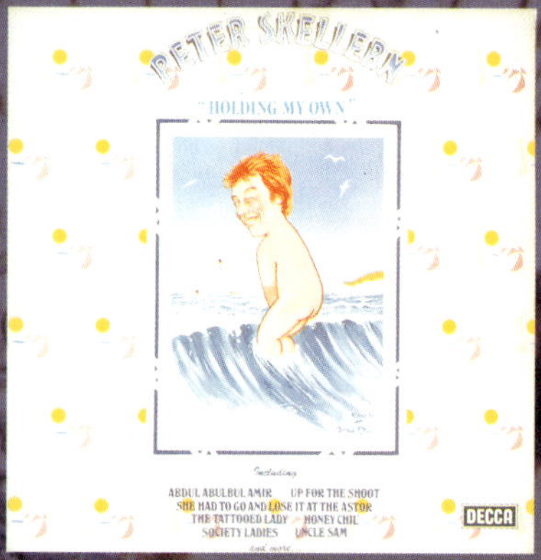

PETER SKELLERN:HOLDING MY OWN/
DECCA SKL5191(1974)
Illustration,Photography and Design/Michael Ross

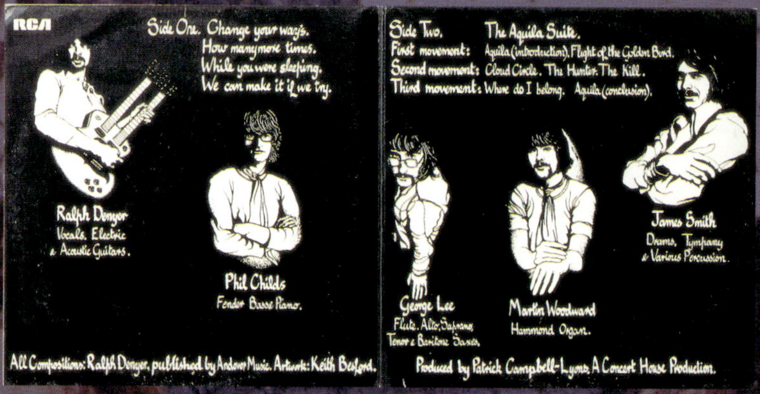

AQUILA:AQUILA/RCA SF8126(1970) *inner

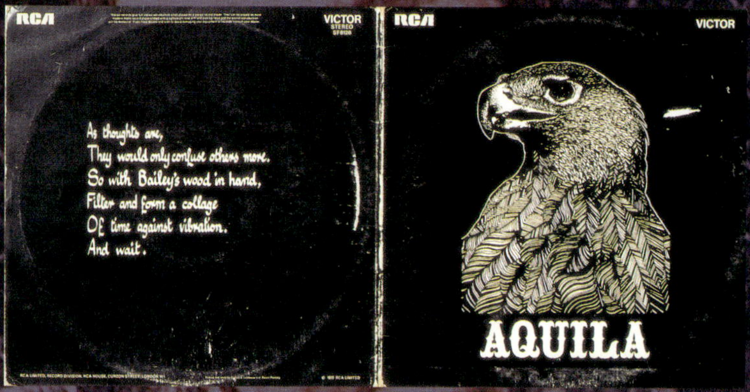

AQUILA:AQUILA/
RCA SF8126(1970) *front and back
Artwork/Keith Beslord

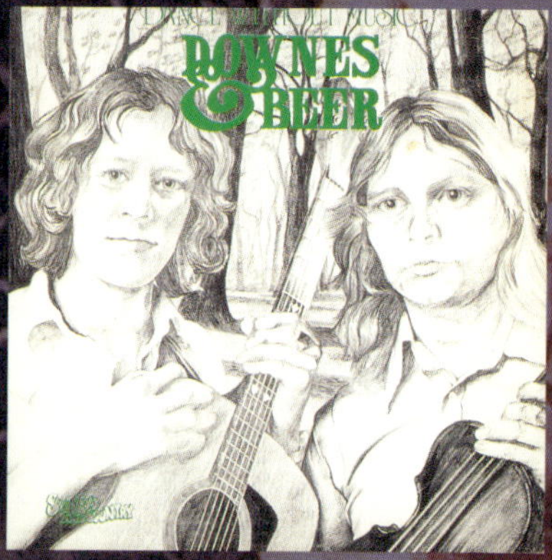

PAUL DOWNES,PHIL BEAR:DANCE WITHOUT
MUSIC/SFA 046()
Cover/Rob O'Conner

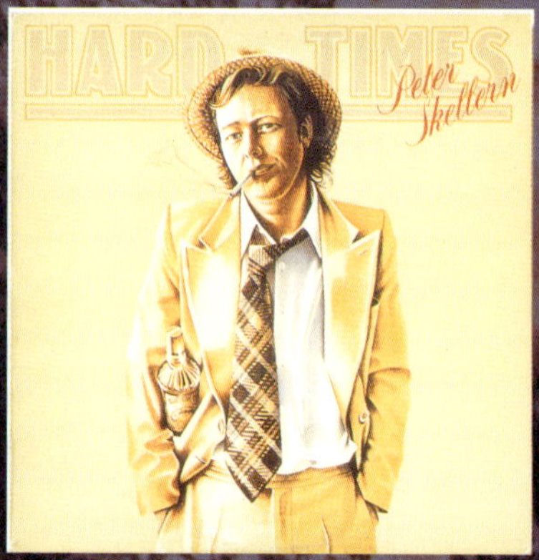

PETER SKELLERN:HARD TIMES/
ISLAND ILPS9352(1975)
Illustration/Tony Wright
Design/Eckford Stimpson

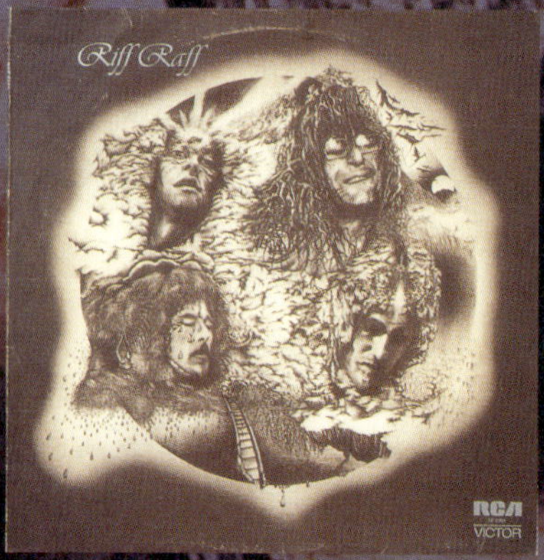

RIFF RAFF:RIFF RAFF/RCA SF8351(1973)
Sleeve/Dave Field

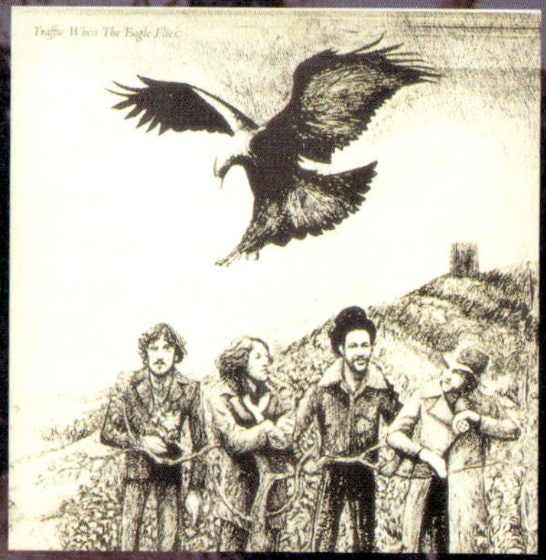
TRAFFIC:WHEN THE EAGLE FLIES/
ISLAND ILPS9273(1974)
Sleeve Design/Martin Hughes

portraits

Illustrated Portraits

ポートレート イラスト編

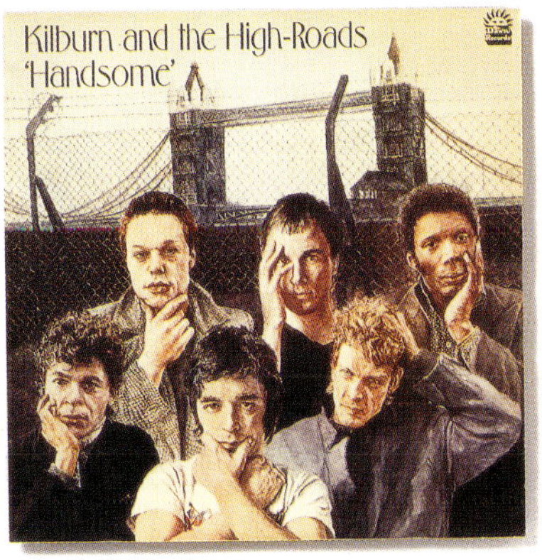

KILBURN AND THE HIGH-ROADS:HANDSOME/
DAWN DNLS3065(1975)
Painting/'The Kilburns Near Tower Bridge'
by Elizabeth Rathmell
Graphics/Gordon House

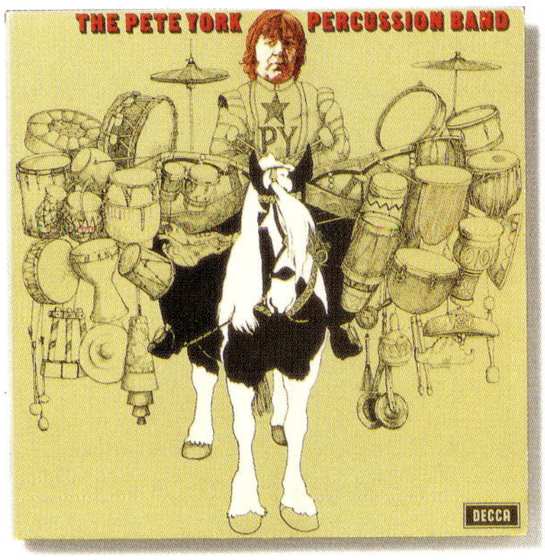

THE PETE YORK PERCUSSION BAND:
THE PETE YORK PERCUSSION BAND/DECCA
TXS109(1972)
Cover Painting/David Anstey

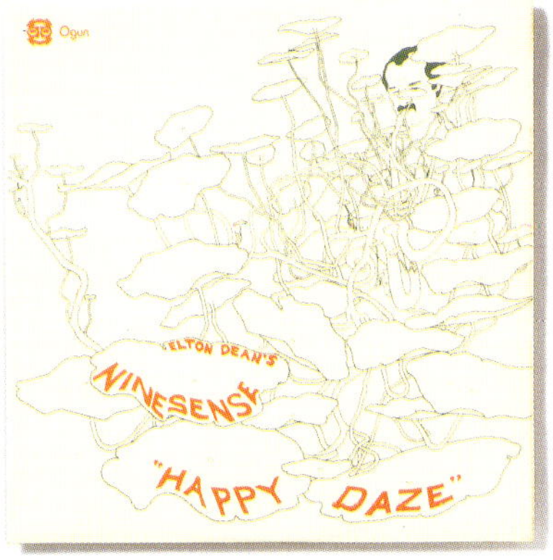

ELTON DEAN'S NINESENSE:
HAPPY DAZE/OGUN OG910(1977)

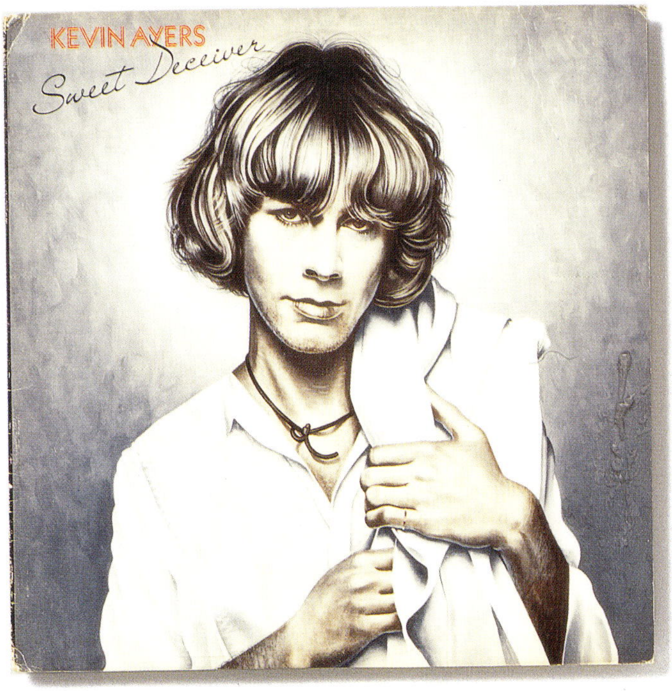

KEVIN AYERS:SWEET DECEIVER/
ISLAND ILPS9322(1975)
Illustration by Tony Wright
Cover Design/Eckford,Stimpson

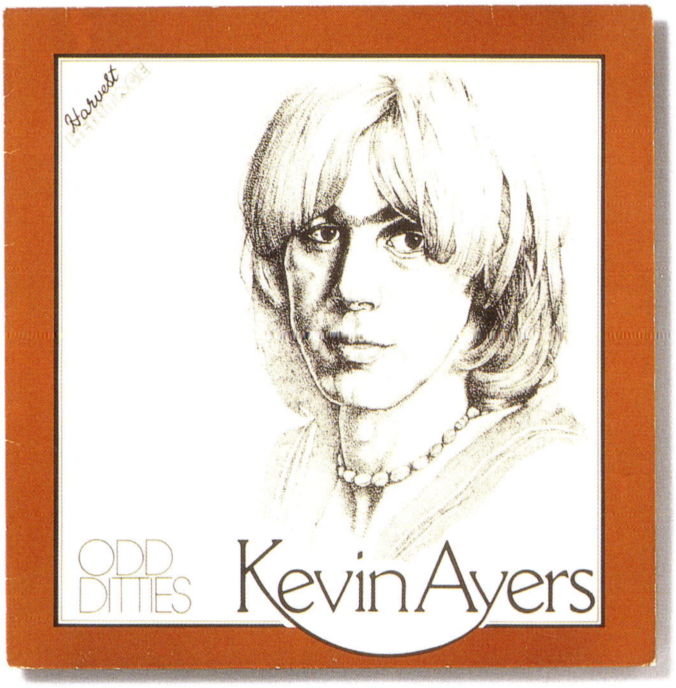

KEVIN AYERS:ODD DITTIES/
HARVEST SHSM2005(1975)
Cover Illustration/Ed Bishop
Sleeve Design/Rupert Ashmore

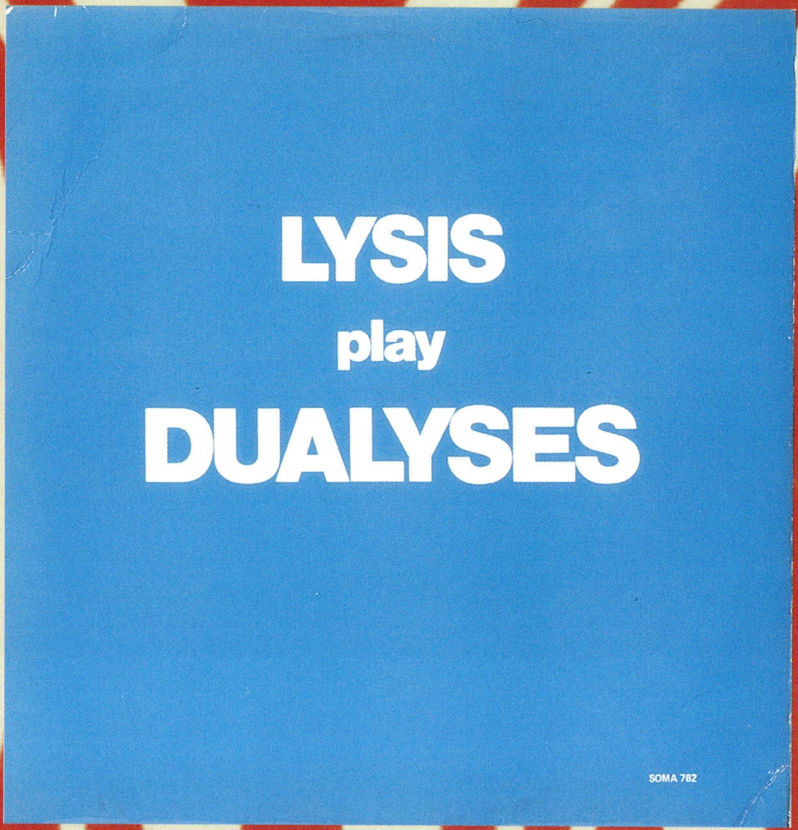

LYSIS:DUALYSES/SOMA 782(1978)

ROGER DEAN'S LYSIS:LYSIS LIVE/
MOSAIC GCM762(1976)

lettering
文字デザイン

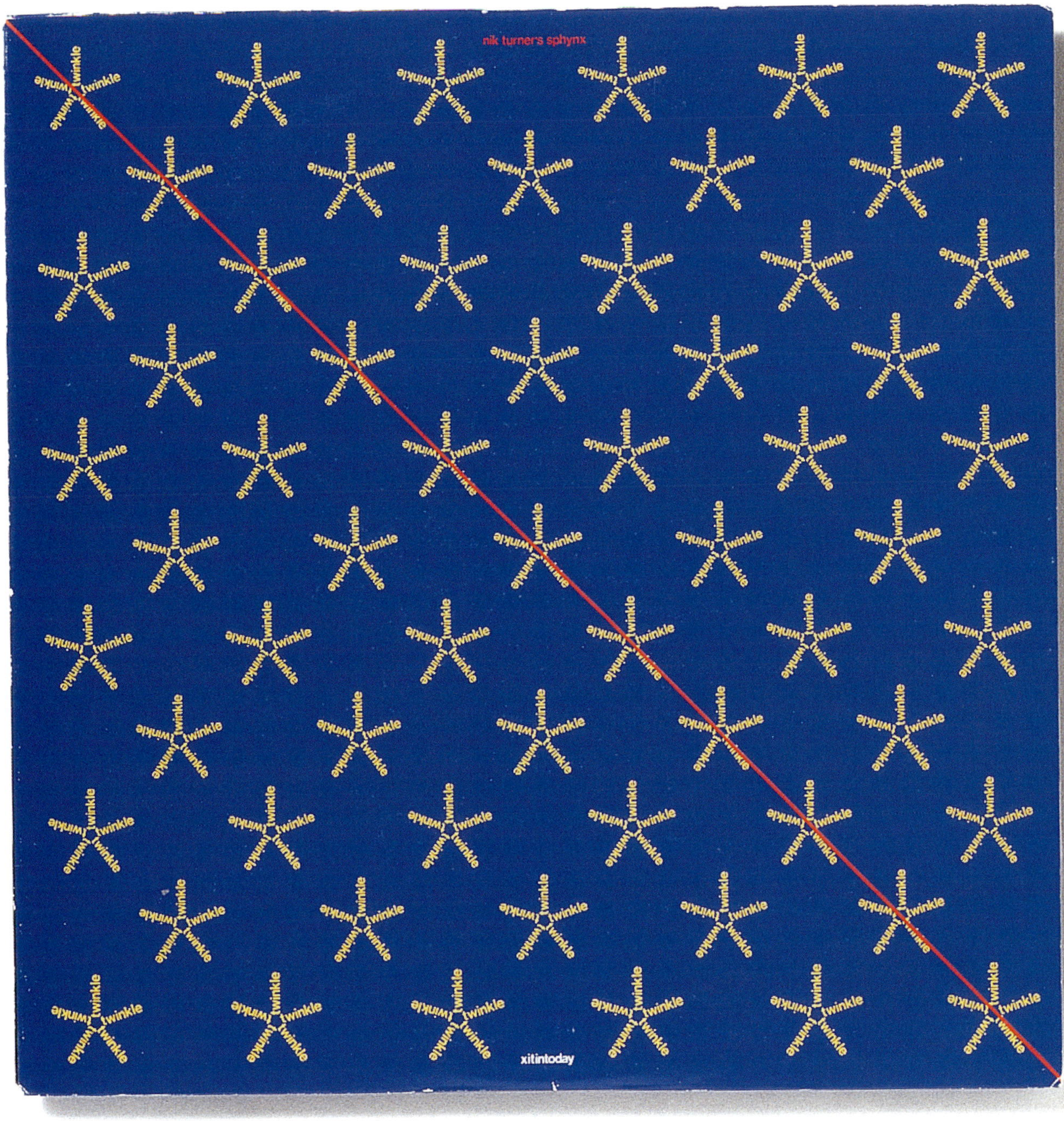

NIK TURNER'S SPHYNX:XITINTODAY/
CHARISMA CDS4011(1978)

一見手抜きのようにみえる文字だけが配されたアルバム・ジャケットも、アイデアを駆使することによって味のあるデザインに早変わりする。いや、文字だけイコール手抜きと考えるのはタイポグラフィーに関する認識が甘いだけのことだろう。もともと欧文表記の世界では、文字のかたち、色、置き方等を大胆にデザインすることで、活字そのものがひとつのアートの体をなすのである。たとえばp130ライシスLYSISの異なる二枚のジャケットは、シンプルな文字とバックに配した色使いの違いだけで無機的なイメージの統一と拡がりとを同時に表現しているし、ニック・ターナーズ・スフィンクス『xitintoday』は、「twinkle（キラキラ光る）」という文字を星形にパターン化させて配置することで、シャレを効かせながらSF風の効果もあげている。

At first glance, what seemed like an album cover simply decorated with letters could turn into a tasteful and pregnant design. To think of such design as corner-cutting demonstrated that there was little recognition of typography in album cover design. In Western orthography, daring designs in the shape, color, and positioning of letters made up an art form of it's own. For instance, the two versions of Lysis' album cover on page 130 featured a simple type treatment on a colored background, giving the work a unified, mechanical feel and an ever expanding image at the same time. On Nick Turner's Sphinx's "xitintoday", 'twinkle' was written in star-shaped letters effectively positioned in a certain pattern to give the whole work a science fiction-like image and played on words.

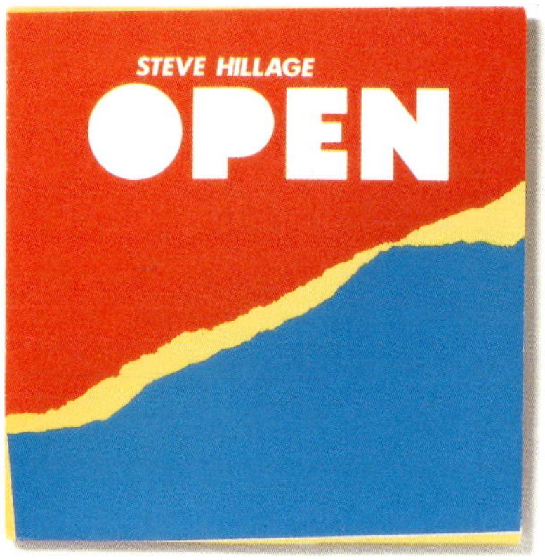

STEVE HILLAGE:OPEN/VIRGIN V 2135 (1979)
Design/Simon Ryan

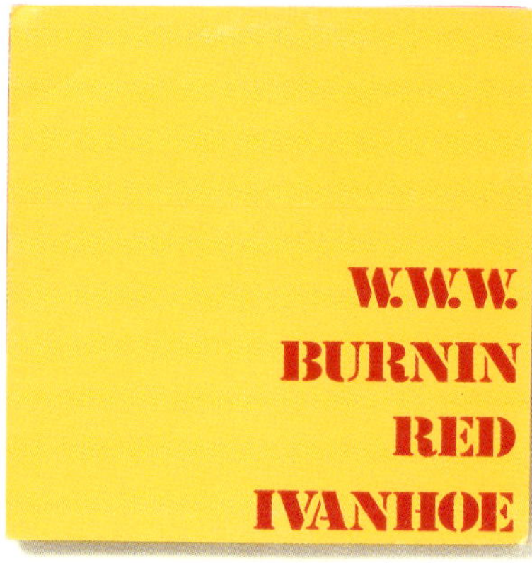

BURNIN RED IVANHOE:W.W.W./
DANDELION 2310 145(1971)
Cover Design/ BURNIN RED IVANHOE

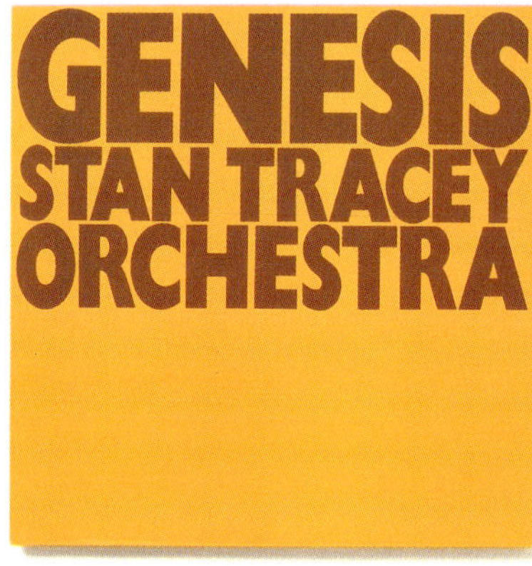

STAN TRACEY ORCHESTRA:GENESIS/
STEAM SJ114(1987)
Sleeve Design/Fiona Tracey

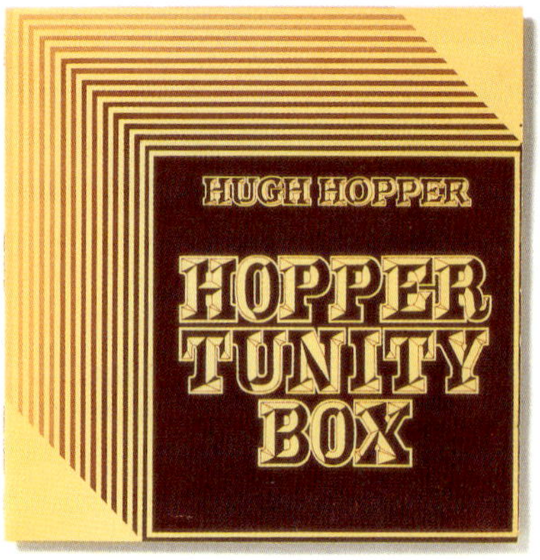

HUGH HOPPER:HOPPER TUNITY BOX/
COMPENDIUM FIDARDO7(1977)
Sleeve Design/Hugh Hopper&David Ace

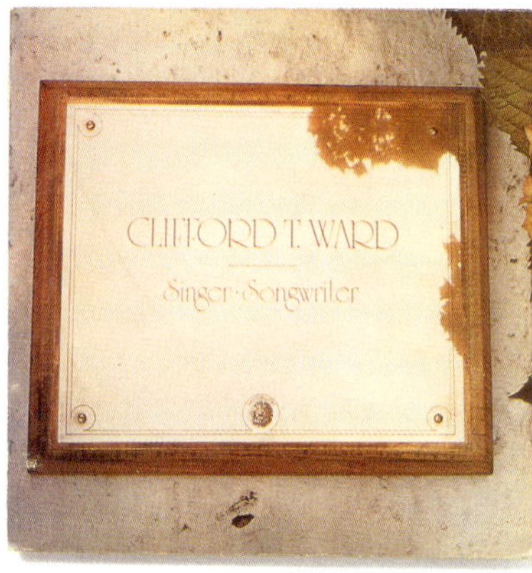

CLIFFORD T.WARD:SINGER SONGWRITER/
DANDELION 2310 216(1972)
Design/Hamish Grimes
Photography/Julian Hann

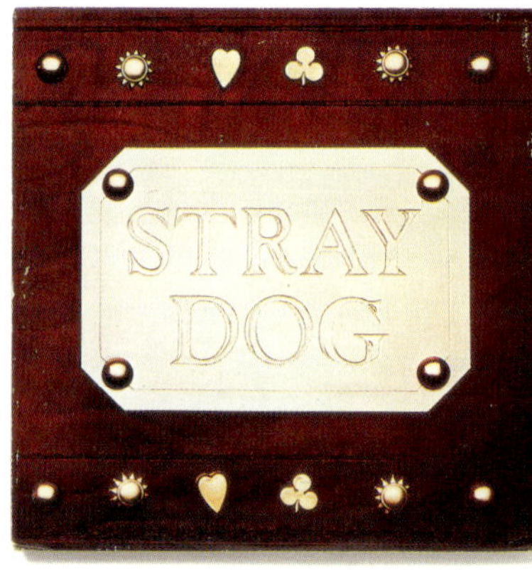

STRAYDOG:STRAYDOG/MANTICORE K43506(1973)
Sleeve Design/Fabio Nicoli Associates
Photography/Rosemary Adams
Art Direction/Fabio Nicoli

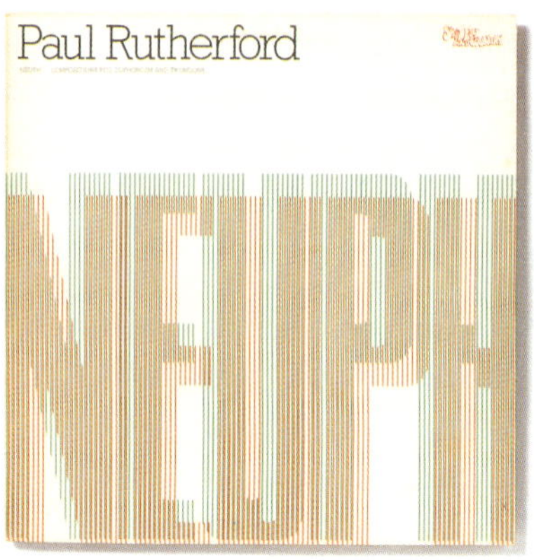

PAUL RUTHERFORD:NEUPH/
SHEET FOLK AND COUNTRY SFA092(1978)
Sleeve Design/Peter Bate

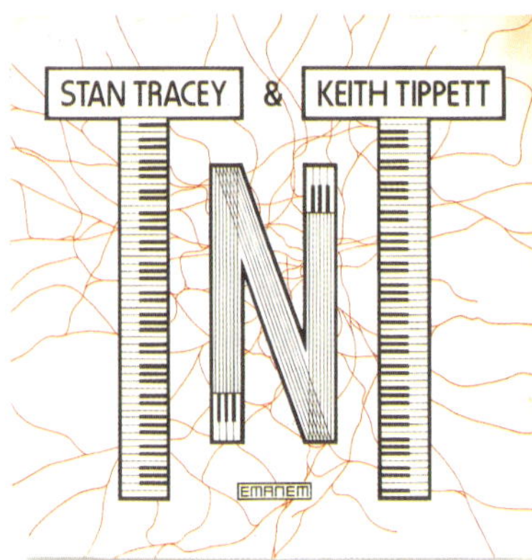

STAN TRACEY&KEITH TIPPETT:TNT/
EMANEM 3307(1976)

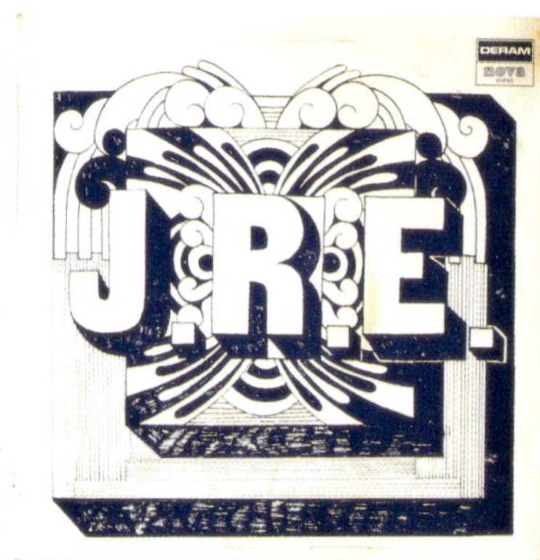

JAZZ ROCK EXPERIENCE:J.R.E./
DERAM nova SDN19(1970)

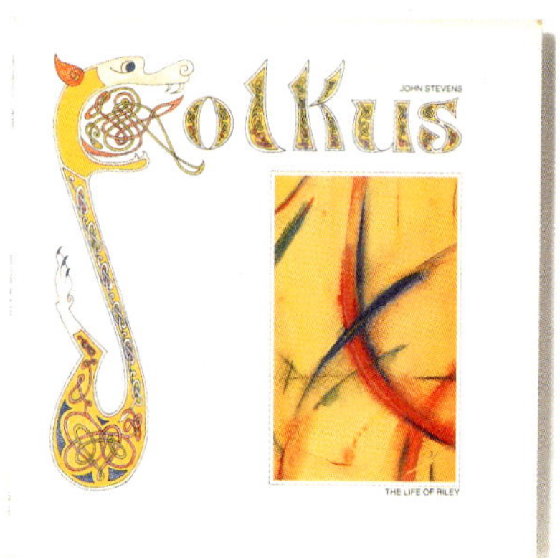

JOHN STEVENS-FOLKUS-:THE LIFE OF RILEY/
AFFNITY AFF130(1984)
Cover Artwork by Beth Moyse
Design/Liz Linda
Cover Painting/'The Life of Riley' by John Stevens

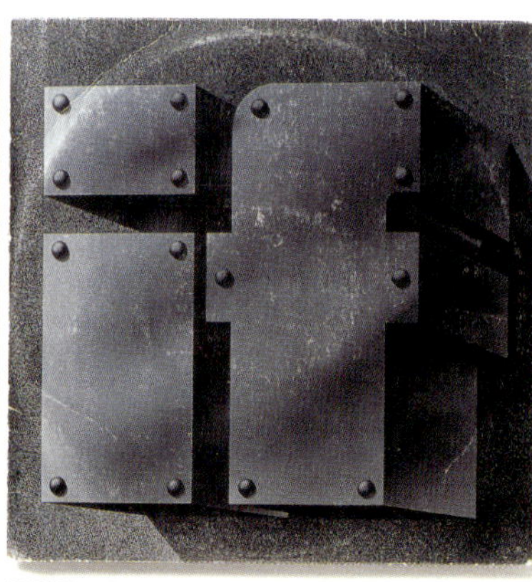

IF:IF/ISLAND ILPS9129(1970)
Cover Art/CCS Advertising Associates

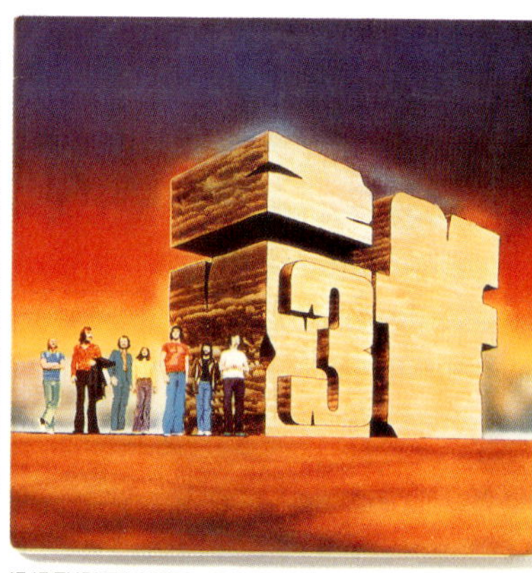

IF:IF THREE/UNITED ARTISTS UAG29158(1971)
Cover Art and Layout/Art Direction

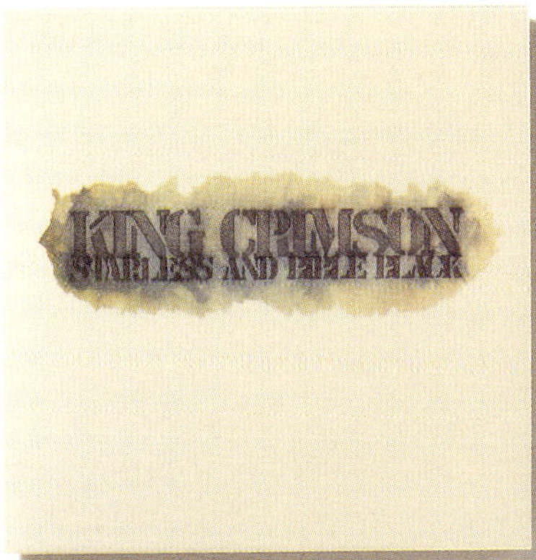

KING CRIMSON:STARLESS AND BIBLE BLACK/
ISLAND ILPS9275(1974)
Cover Design by Tom Phillips

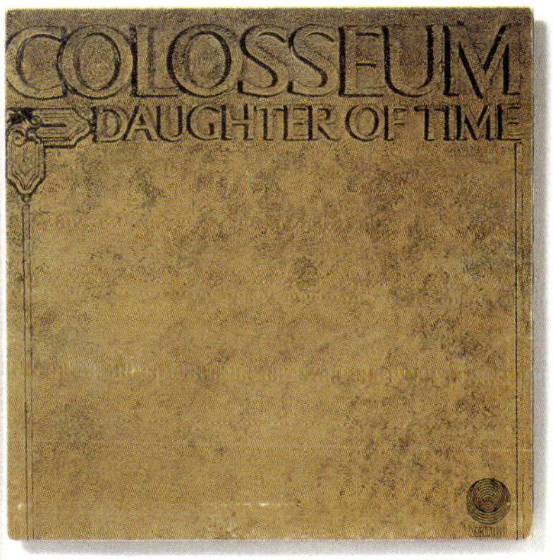

COLOSSEUM:DAUGHTER OF TIME/
VERTIGO 6360 017(1970)
Cover Design/Robin Nicoli(Design Machine)

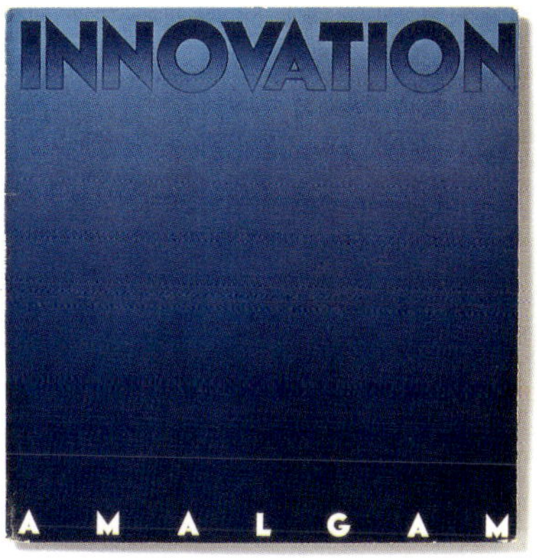

AMALGAM:INNOVATION/
TANGENT TGS121(I974)
Sleeve Design/Margaret Richards

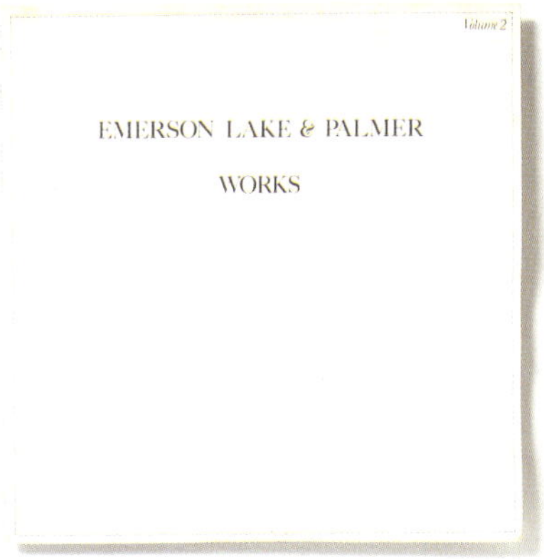

EMERSON,LAKE&PALMER:WORKS VOLUMES2/
ATLANTIC K50422(1977)

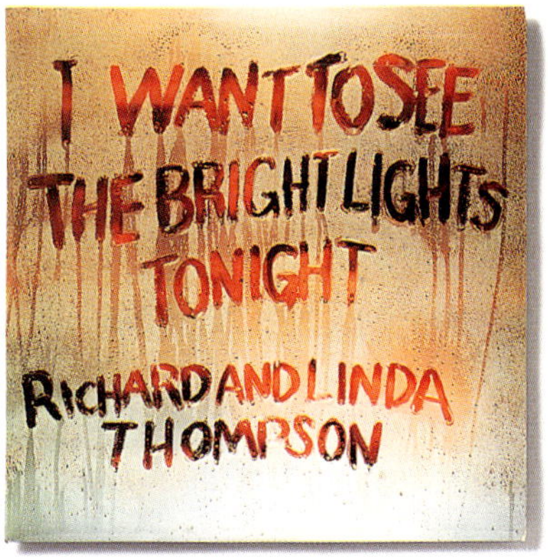

RICHARD AND LINDA THOMPSON:
I WANT TO SEE BRIGHT LIGHTS TONIGHT/
ISLAND ILPS9266(1973)

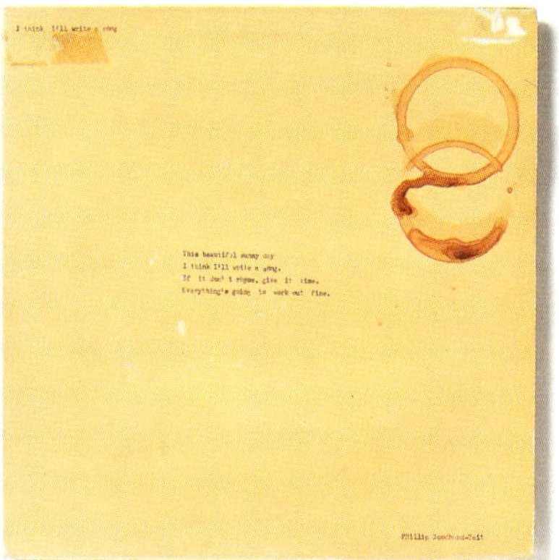

PHILLIP GOODHAND-TAIT:I THINK I'LL WRITE A SONG/
DJM DJLPS416(1971)
Sleeve Design by David Larkham

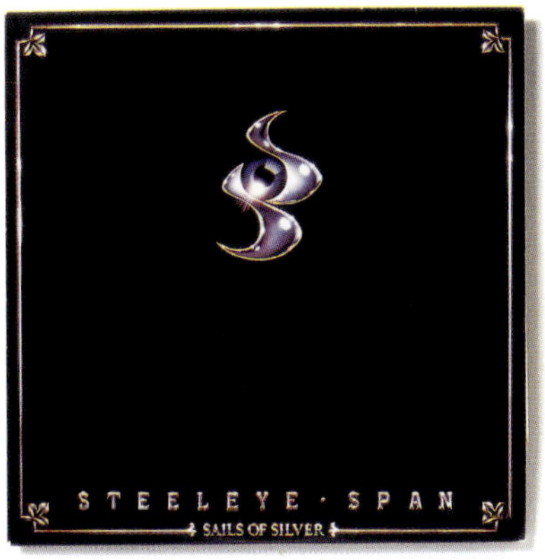

STEELEYE SPAN:SAILS OF SILVER/
CHRYSALIS CHR1304(1980)
Front Cover by Adrian Chesterman

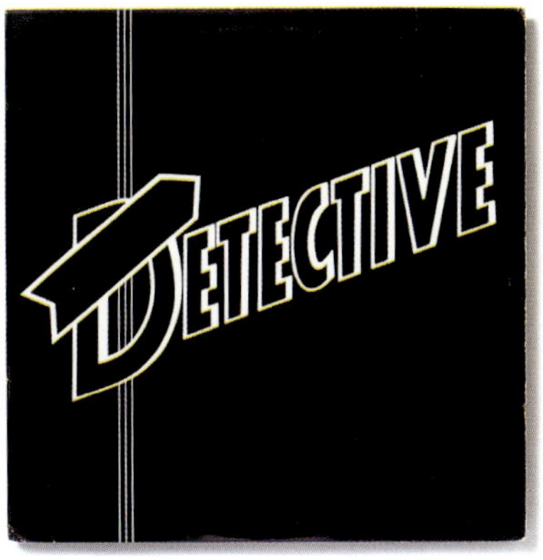

DETECTIVE:DETECTIVE/SWANSONG SSK59405(1977)
Design&Art Direction/Kosh

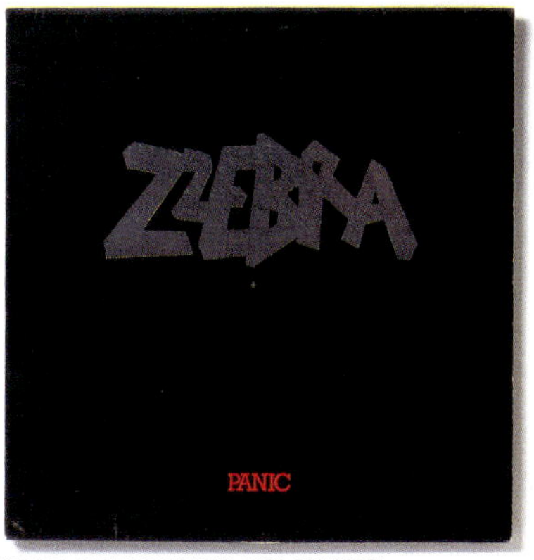

ZZEBRA:PANIC/POLYDOR 2383 326(1975)
Art Direction/Paul Welch
Logo Design/Marianne Landau

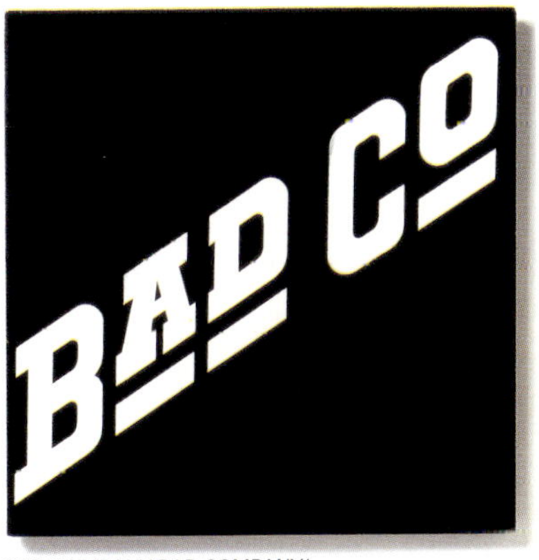

BAD COMPANY:BAD COMPANY/
ISLAND ILPS9279(1974)
Photo/Hipgnosis

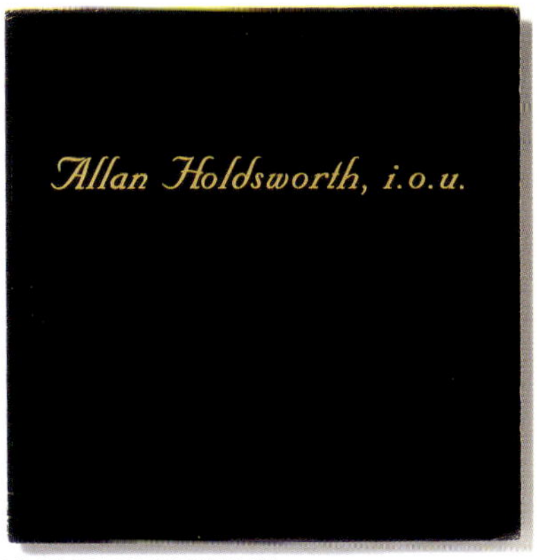

ALLAN HOLDSWORTH:I.O.U./
ENIGMA2031(1982)
Art Direction/Bret H.Linford

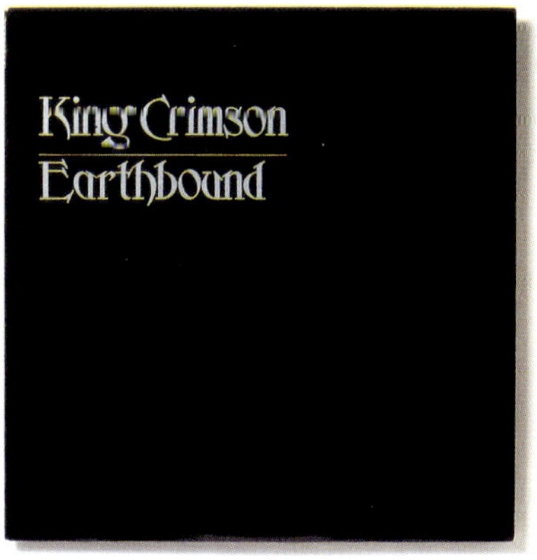

KING CRIMSON:EARTHBOUND/ISLAND HELP6(1972)

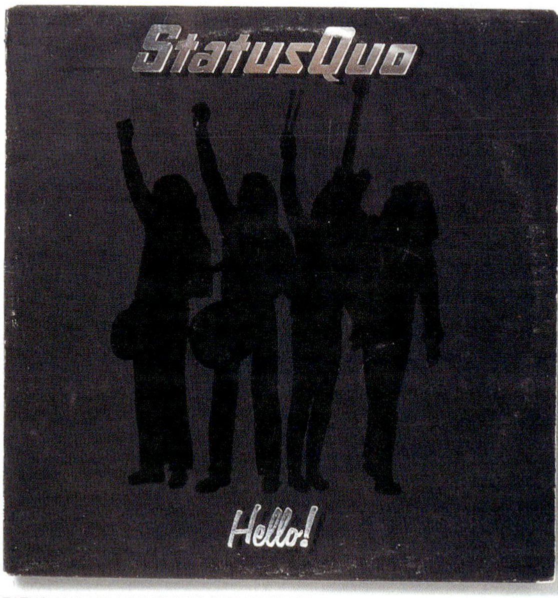

STATUS QUO:HELLO!/VERTIGO 6360 098(1973)

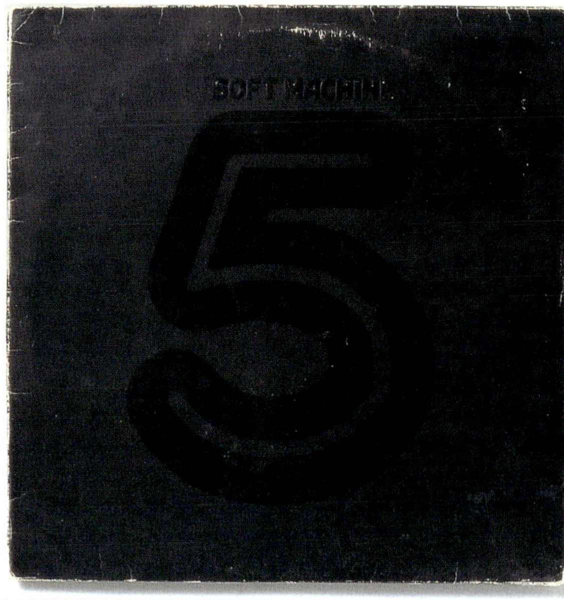

SOFT MACHINE:FIFTH/CBS 64806(1972)

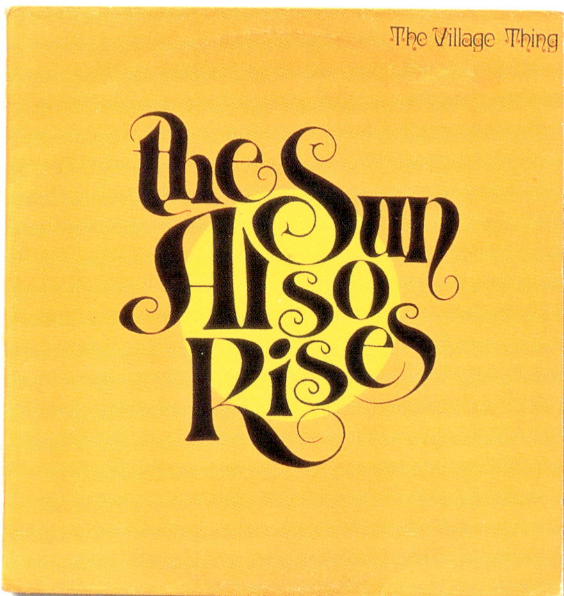

THE SUN ALSO RISES:THE SUN ALSO RISES/
THE VILLAGE THING VTS2(1970)
Sleeve Front by Andy Legett

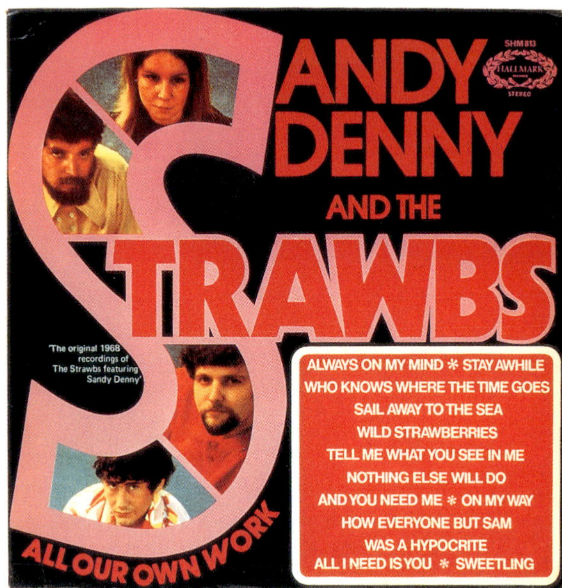

SANDY DENNY&THE STRAWBS:ALL OUR OWN WORK/
HALLMARK SHM813(1973)

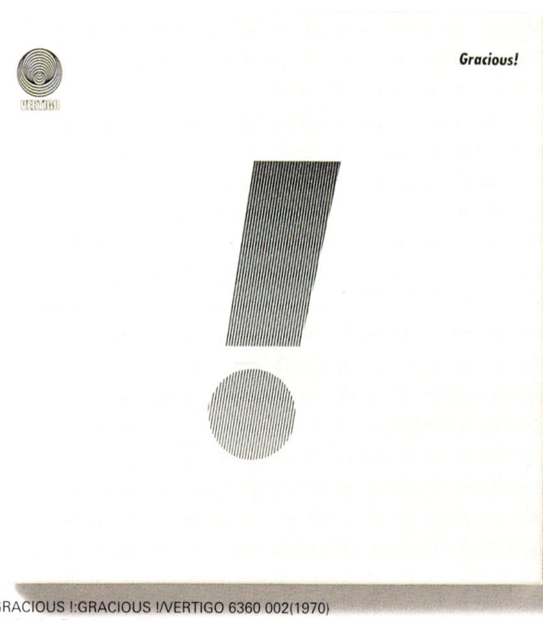

GRACIOUS !:GRACIOUS !/VERTIGO 6360 002(1970)
Design by Teenburger Designs

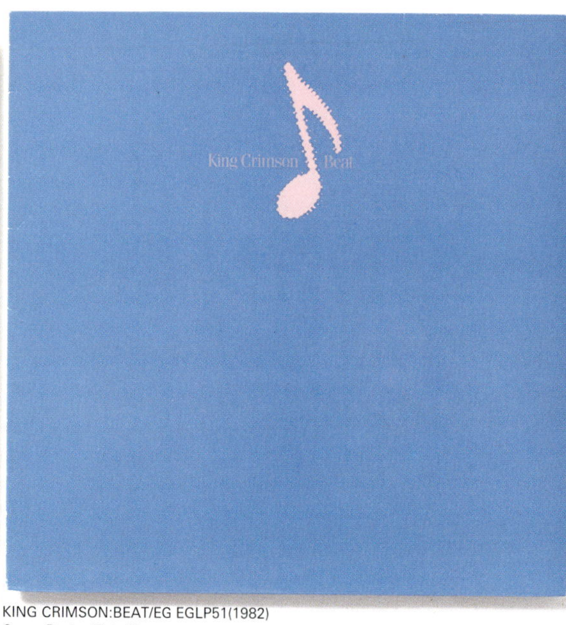

KING CRIMSON:BEAT/EG EGLP51(1982)
Cover Design/Rob O'connor

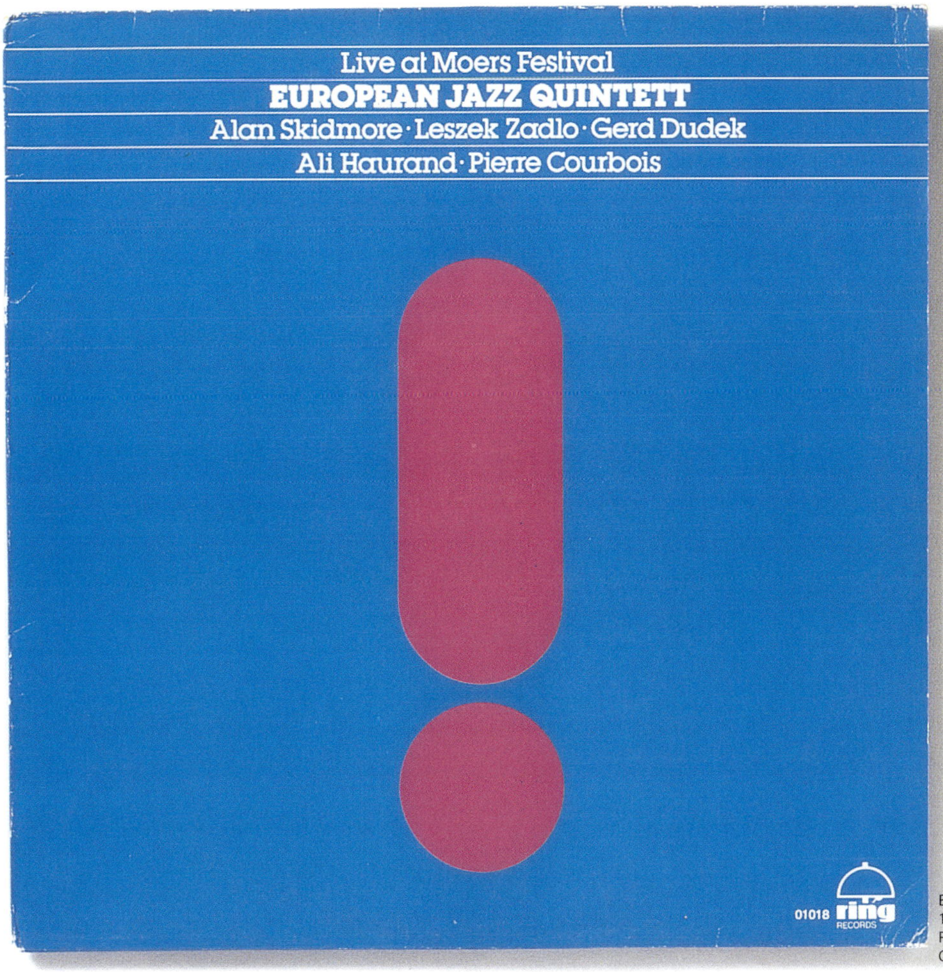

EUROPEAN JAZZ QUINTET:LIVE AT MOERS FESTIVAL/
101018
Photos/Norbert Gerdes
Cover Design/Otmar Klover

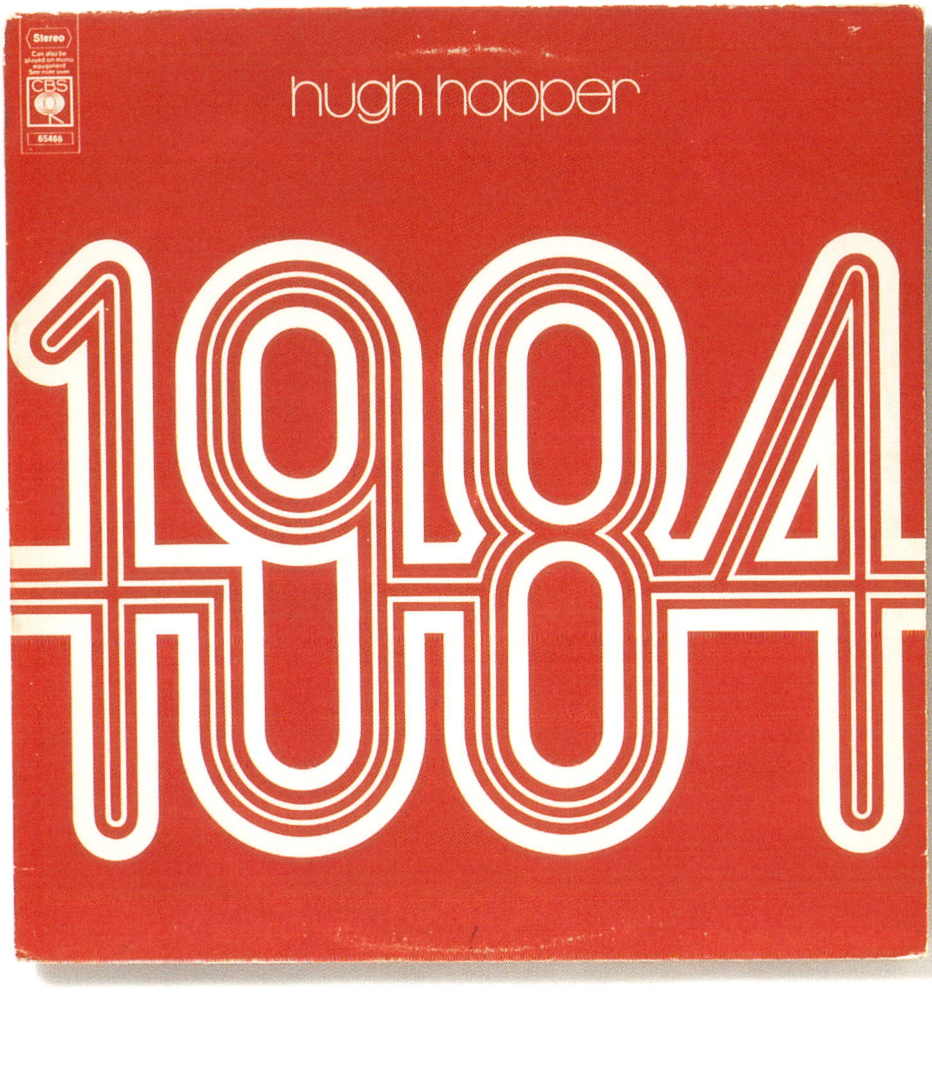

HUGH HOPPER:1984/CBS 65466(1973)

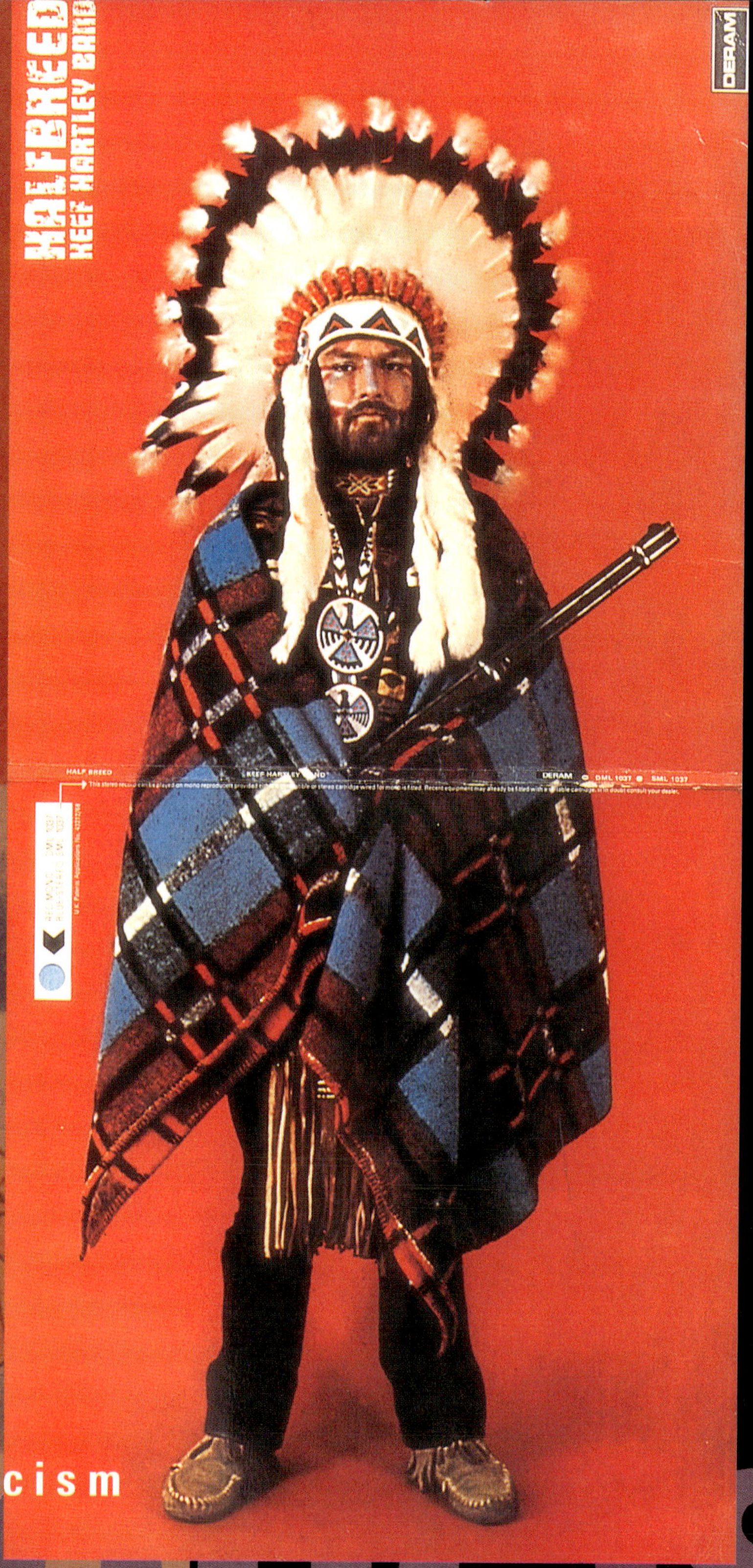

KEEF HARTLEY BAND:HALFBREED/
DERAM SML1037(1969)
Front Cover Photo/Bob Baker

exoticism, racism

エキゾチシズムとレイシズム

まずは、エキゾチシズム（異国情緒趣味）とレイシズム（民族主義）の語義を明確に分けておこう。前者はあくまでも趣味の問題であり、後者は切実な問題として示された政治的態度である。たとえば、旧英連邦・南アフリカのケープタウンに生まれ、その後イギリスに渡ったドラムス奏者ルイス・モホロが“VIVA-LA-BLACK”と叫ぶとき、そこに込められるメッセージはただひとつだ。一方、ブランドXで知られるパーカッション奏者モーリス・パートがサントレッダー名義で発表したアルバム『ZIN-ZIN』が、日本人の民族的優位性を訴えているとはとうてい思えない。もっとも、異国情緒趣味が悪いというわけでは全然ない。むしろ異国情緒趣味にはナンセンスな想像の飛躍があって、いつでもこちらの目を楽しませてくれる。印刷の仕上がりも美しいキーフ・ハートリー・バンドの『ハーフブリード』などは、ランカシャー生まれのドラムス奏者によるブルース・ロックで、決して北米原住民の民族的優位性を訴える政治的メッセージを主題としたものではないが、白人とネイティヴ・アメリカンの混血という意味で侮蔑的に使われる「ハーフブリード」を、自身の音楽的雑種性と重ね合わせている。エキゾチシズムともレイシズムともとれるジャケットのきわどいヒネリ加減には、なんともいえない効果がある。

To clarify the difference between exoticism and racism, I distinguish the former as a matter of personal taste and the latter as a political attitude. For example, when drummer Lewis Mohoro from Cape Town, South Africa (he later emmigrated to England), shouted "Viva La Black!", there was a salient political message in his song. Whereas, the solo release of "Zin Zin" by Brand X percussionist Maurice Part under the name 'Suntreader', wasn't considered a proclamation of the ethnic superiotity of the Japanese. I don't think less of trivial exoticism. In fact, their flights of fancy were always wonderfully amusing. "Half Breed", by the Keef Hartley Band, a Blues-Rock band lead by a drummer from Lancaster, was anything but a political message asserting the ethnic superiority of native North Americans. The album title refered to the their own hybrid identity as musicians rather than mixed races. This slightly risky game played on exoticism and politically incorrect messages and left quite an impression.

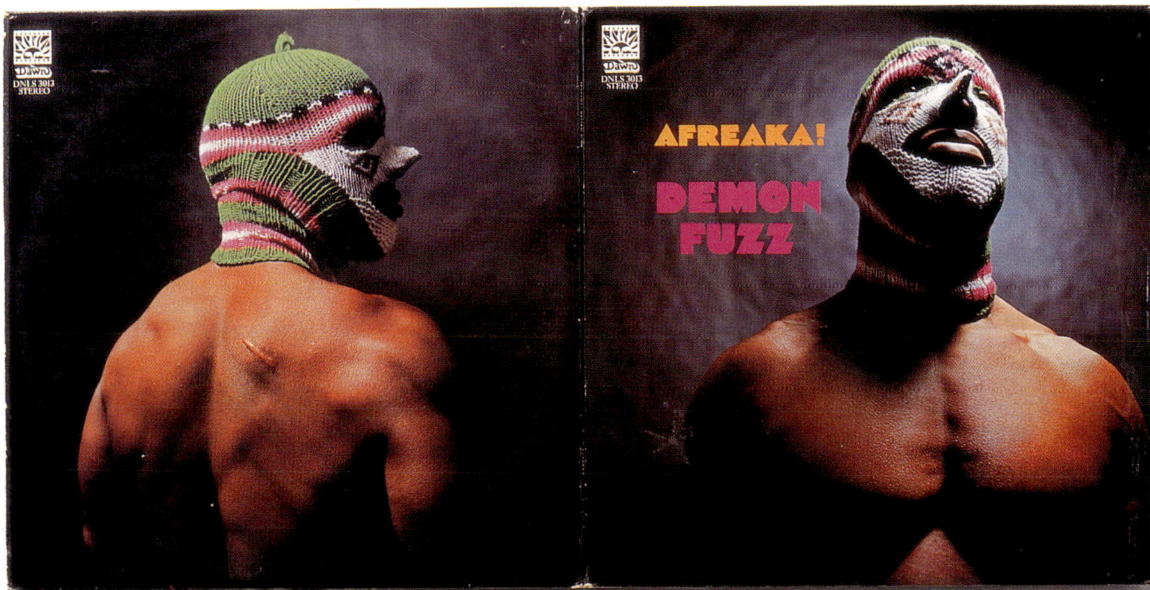

DEMON FUZZ:AFREAKA!/
DAWN DNLS3013(1971) *front and back

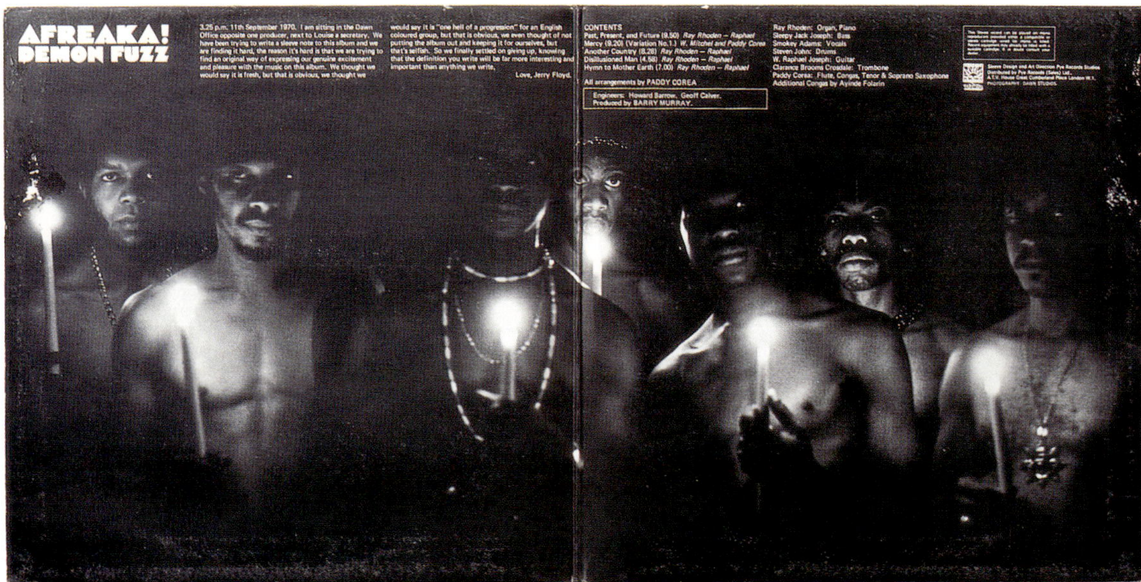

DEMON FUZZ:AFREAKA!/
DAWN DNLS3013(1971) *inner

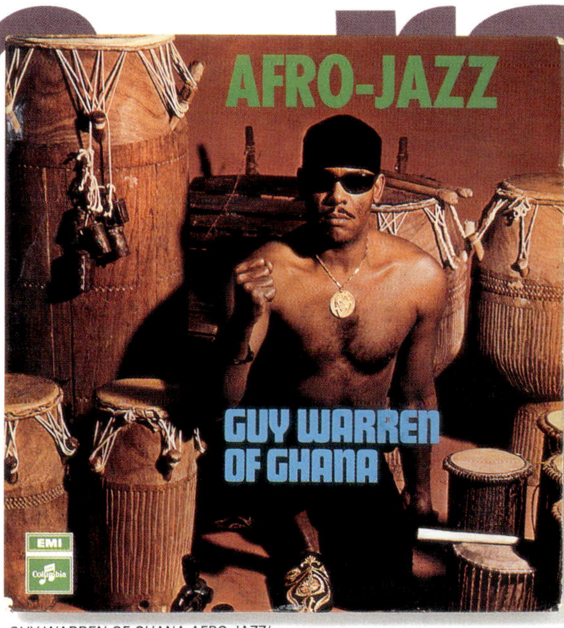

GUY WARREN OF GHANA:AFRO-JAZZ/
EMI SCX6340(1969)
Sleeve Design/Denis Preston
Photo/William Holden

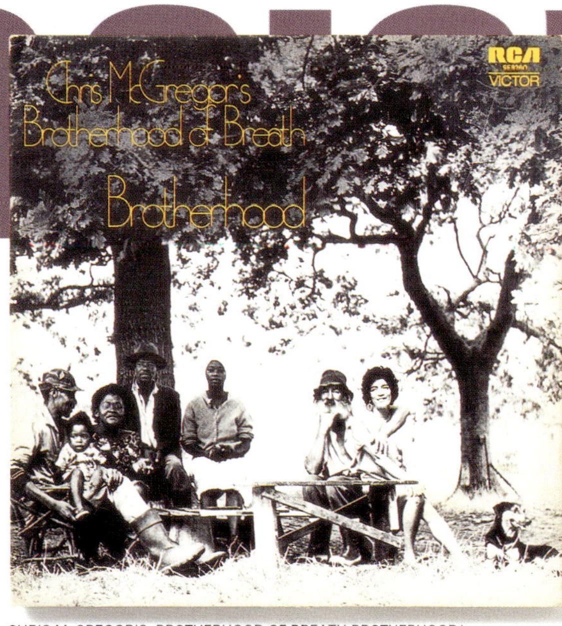

CHRIS McGREGOR'S BROTHERHOOD OF BREATH:BROTHERHOOD/
RCA SF8260(1972)
All Photographs by Courtesy of George Hallet

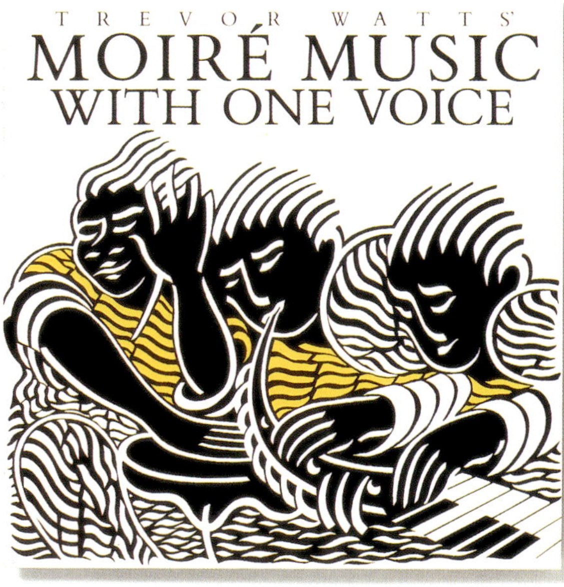

TREVOR WATTS' MOIRE MUSIC:WITH ONE VOICE/
ARC 03(1988)
Sleeve Design/Margaret Richards

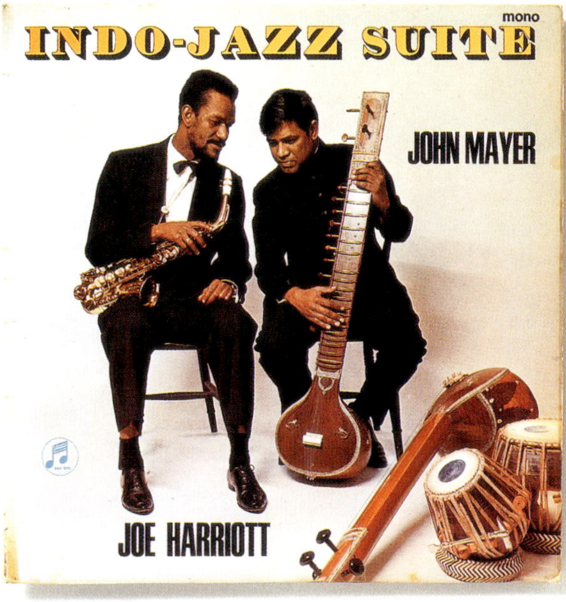

JOE HARRIOT DOUBLE QUINTET:INDO-JAZZ SUITE/
COLUMBIA SX6025(1966)
Sleeve Design/Denis Preston
Photography/Michael Joseph

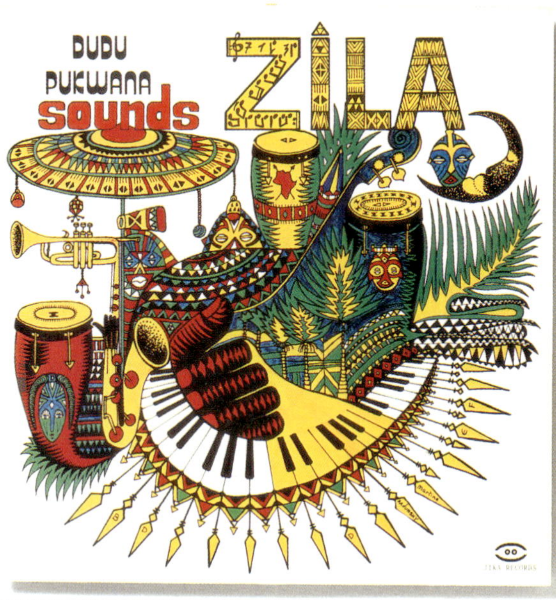

DU DU PUKWANA:SOUNDS ZILA/JIKA ZL1(1981)
Front Cover/Martine Radunsky
Cover Design and Photo/Jimi Matthews

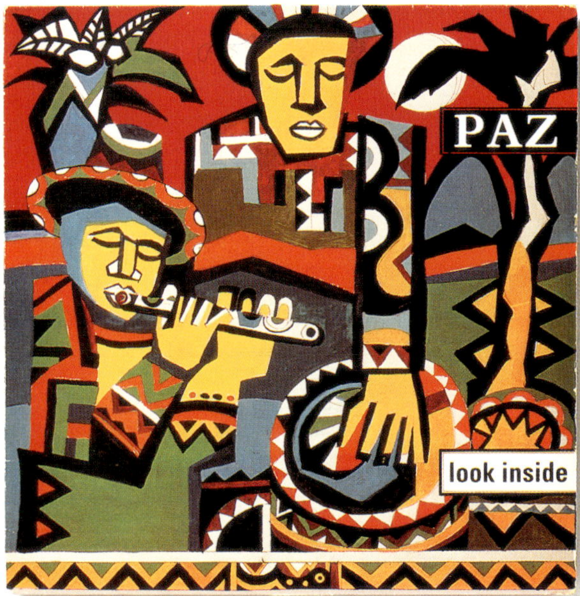

PAZ:LOOK INSIDE/PALADIN PALP001(1983)
Cover Painting/Peter Neal
Layout/Martyn Lambert
Typography/Cogent Phototypesetters

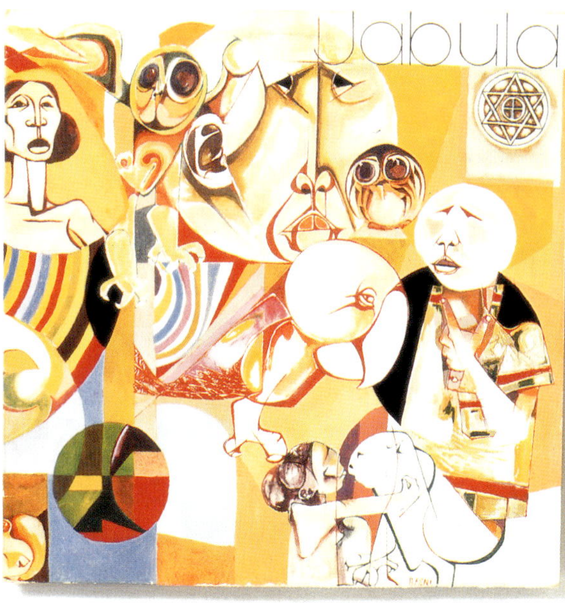

JABULA:JABULA/CAROLINE CA2004(1975)
Cover/Dumile Feni

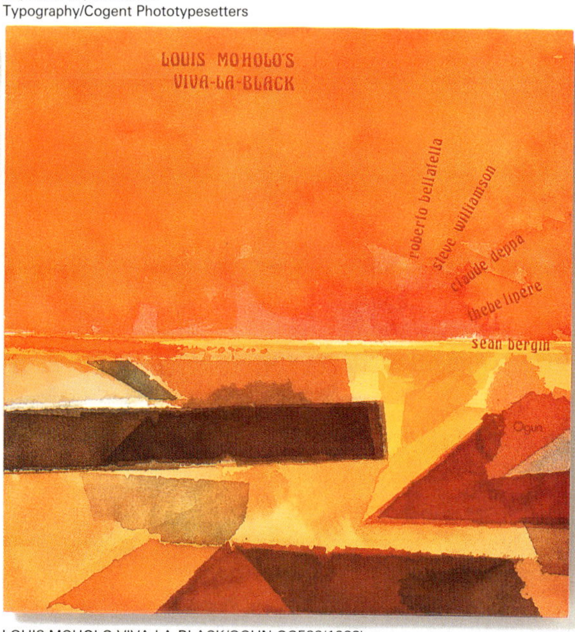

LOUIS MOHOLO:VIVA-LA-BLACK/OGUN OG533(1988)
Front Cover Painting by John Eaves
Sleeve Layout/Hazel Miller

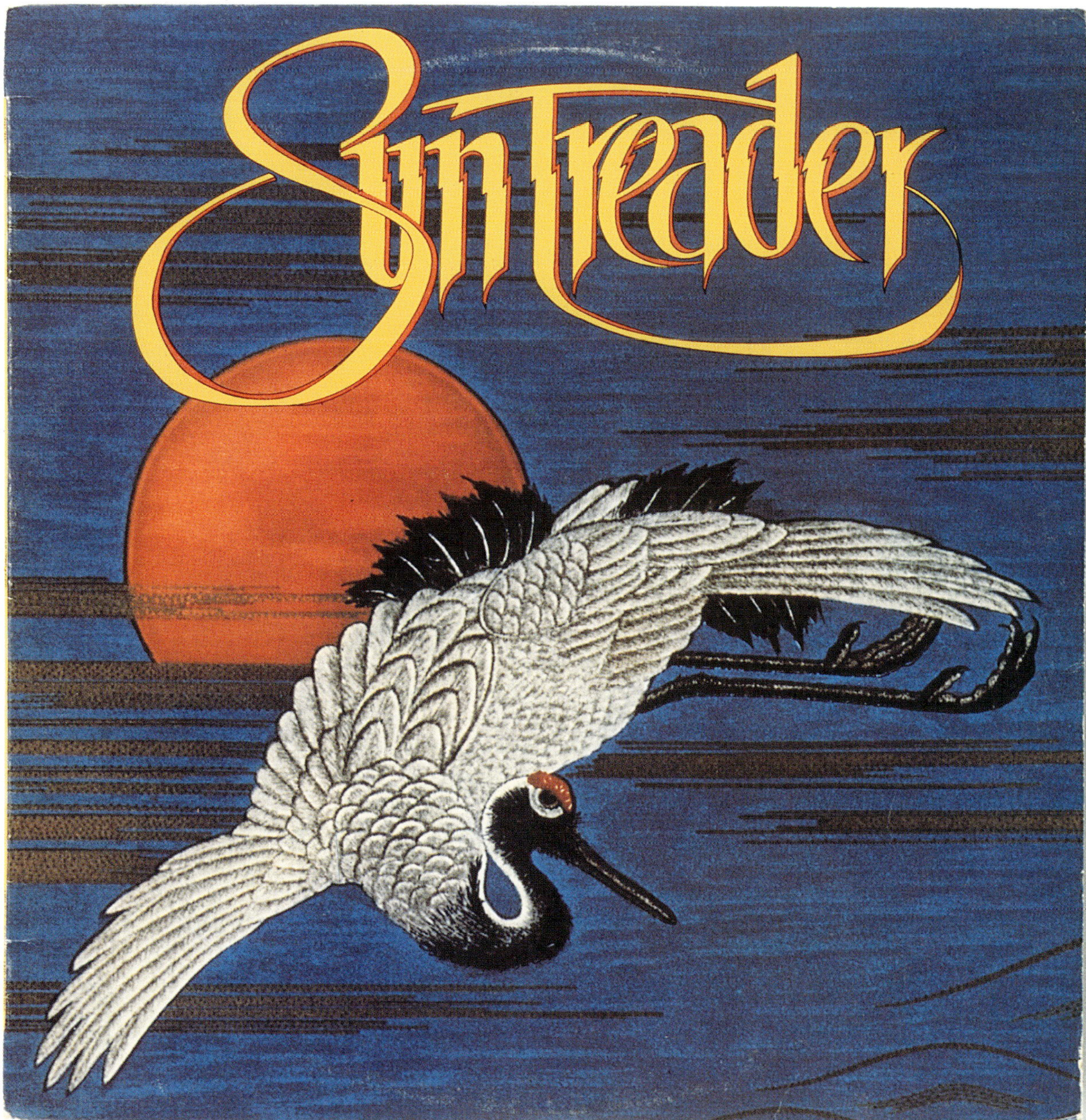

SUN TREADER:ZIN-ZIN/ISLAND HELP13(1973)
Cover Art/Yancy Studios

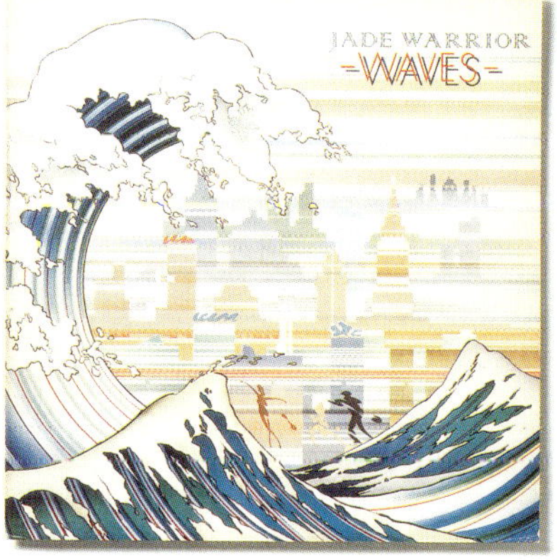

JADE WARRIOR:WAVES/ISLAND ILPS9318(1975)
Design&Illustration by Eckford/Stimpson

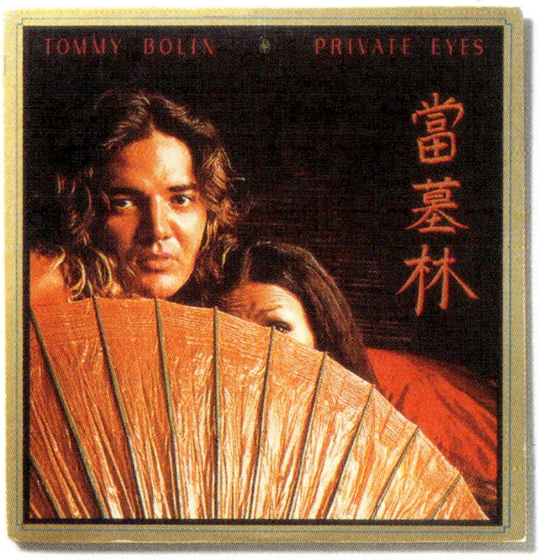

TOMMY BOLIN:PRIVATE EYES/CBS CBSB1612(1976)
Album Package by Jimmy Wachtel,Lorrie Sullivan

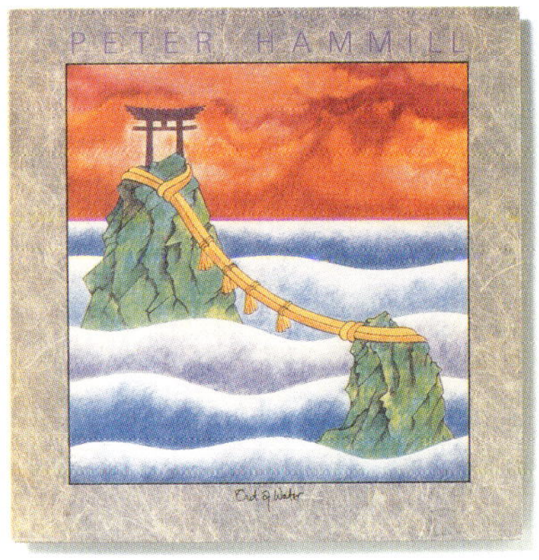

PETER HAMMILL:OUT OF WATER/
ENIGMA ENVLP1003(1990)
Cover by John Ellis

イギリスのジャズは、アメリカのジャズからさほど遅れを取ることなく、トラッド・ジャズ、ビバップ、モードといったメインストリームを形成させていった。そのため50年代まではアルバム・ジャケットのデザインにもアメリカ盤を踏襲したものが多かったが、やがてビートルズ誕生の一因ともなった英国独自のスキッフル・ブームとともに、イギリスのジャズが一気に多様化。それにつれてアルバム・カヴァー・デザインの方も、イギリス独自の色を帯び始めたように思える。60年代後半以降は、ロックをはじめとする他ジャンルとの錯綜もさらに激しくなり、音楽同様の実験色がデザインにも反映されるようになった。しかし、それらはかならずしもロックに寄り添ったものではなく、しっかりとジャズのアイデンティティを感じさせているからこそ魅力的なのだろう。
70年代以降もクロスオーヴァーやフリー・アヴァンギャルドといったシーンの拡がりから、アルバム・カヴァーにもいっそうの多様化がみられるようになったが、ジャズ独特のテイストが薄れていったことや、とくに70年代後半以降、マーケットの縮小からパッケージ・デザインとしてのアルバム・カヴァーにも廉価仕様が数多くみられるようになったことについては、残念というほかない。

jazz mode 1950's-1960's

50年代から60年代

jazz mode ジャズ・モード

JOHN STEVENS:THE SPONTANEOUS MUSIC ENSEMBLE/
MARMALADE 608 008(1969)
Sleeve Design by Paragon Publicity

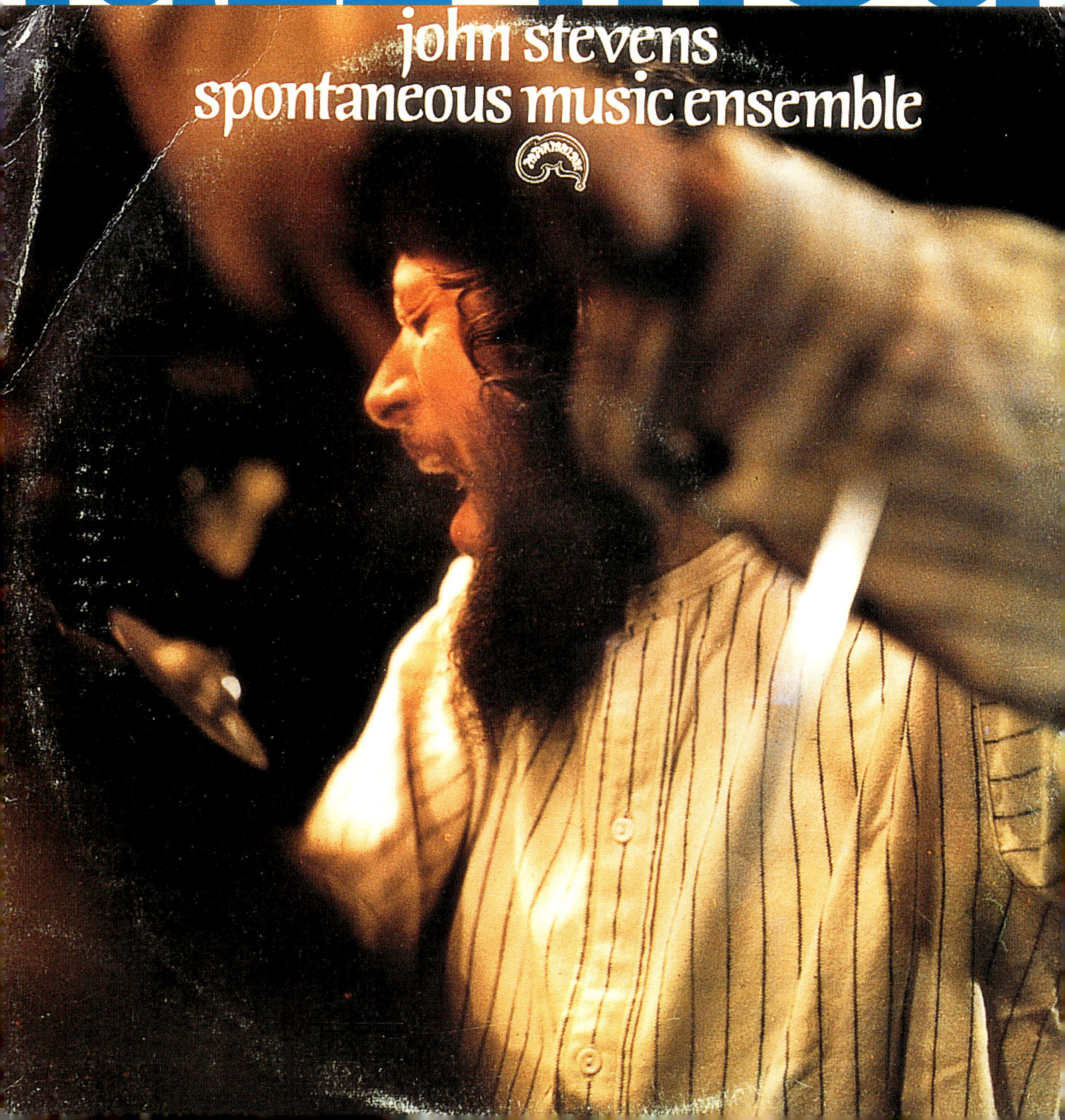

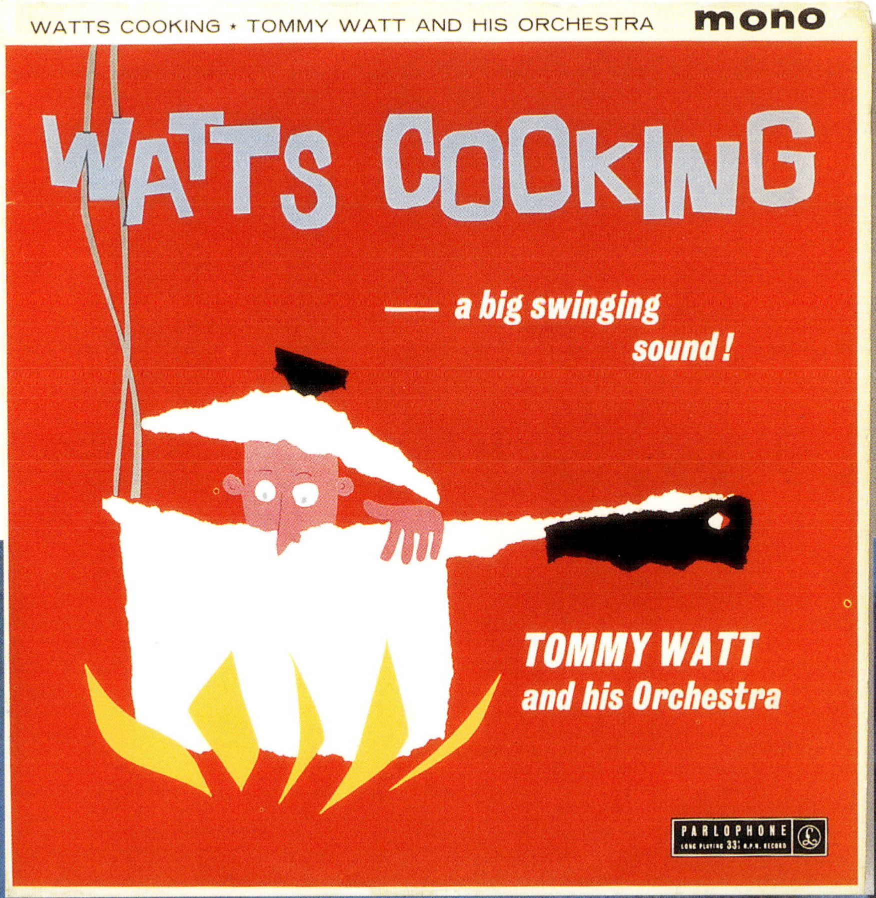

TOMMY WATT AND HIS ORCHESTRA/
WATT'S COKKING/PARLOPHONE PMC1107(1959)

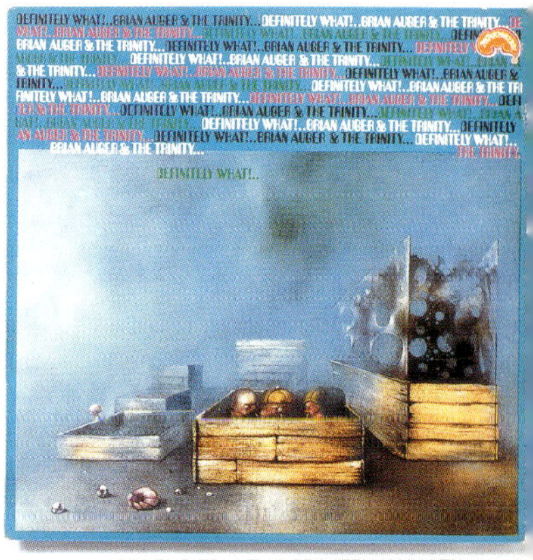

BRIAN AUGER&THE TRINITY:DEFINITELY WHAT!/
MARMALADE 607 003(1968)
Painting/ÅgThree MusiciansÅhby Jim Earp

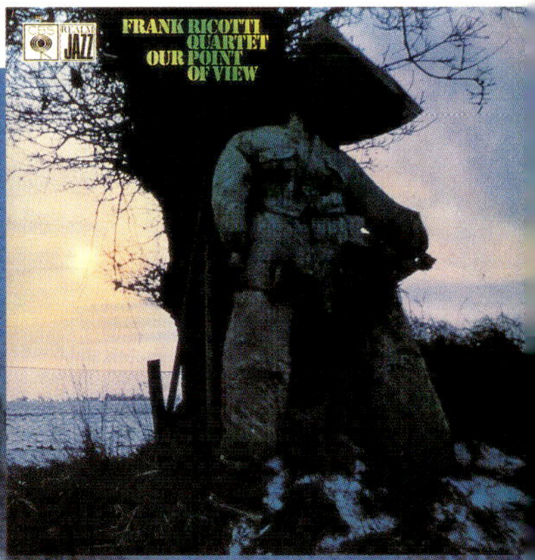

FRANK RICCOTTI QUARTET:
OUR POINT OF VIEW/
CBS 52668(1969)

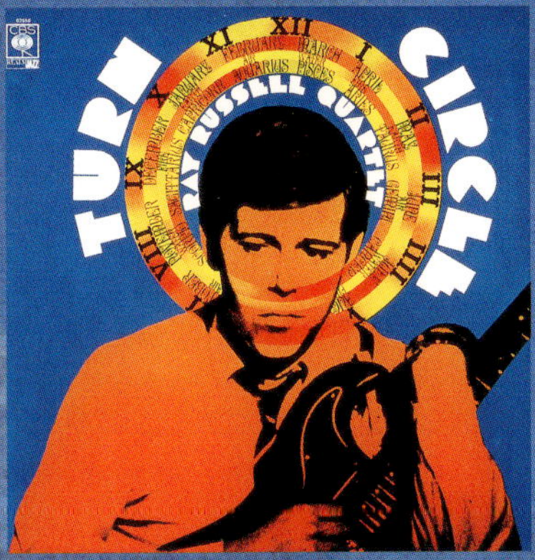

RAY RUSSELL QUARTET:TURN CIRCLE/
CBS 52586(1968)

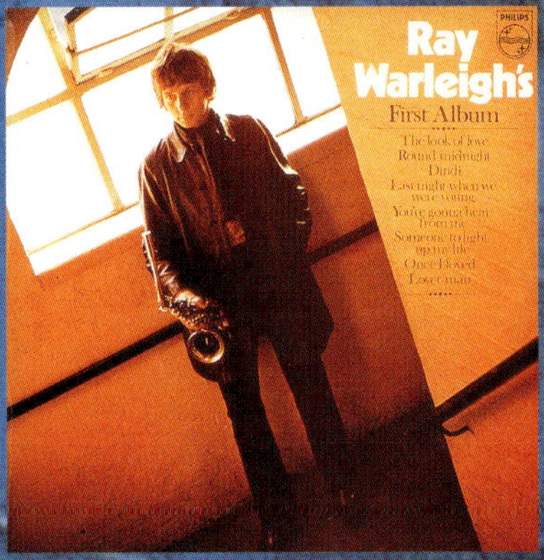

RAY WARLEIGH/RAY WARLEIGH'S FIRST ALBUM/
PHILIPS SBL7881(1969)

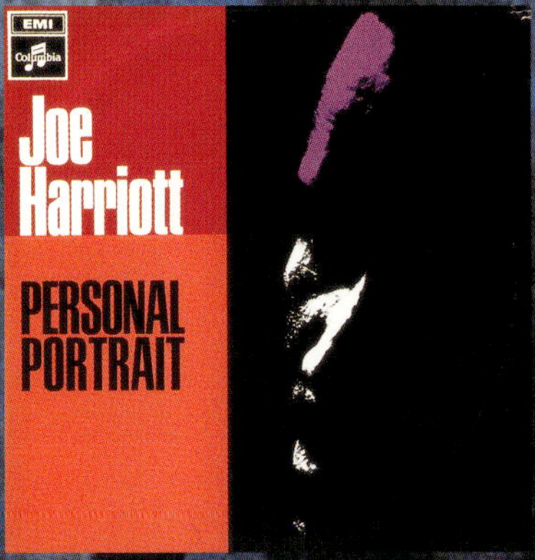

JOE HARRIOTT:PERSONAL PORTRAIT/
EMI SCX6249(1968)
Sleeve Design/Denis Preston
Photography/Stuart McIntyre

In Search of the Lost Record

The British Jazz scene did not lag behind that of America's. Trad Jazz, Be-Bop, Mode and all the other mainstream scenes had formed one after another in England. Therefore, up until the 50's album sleeves were derivative of those in America. But with the debut of Skiffle Boom, which, by the way, was a prelude to the appearance of the Beatles, the British jazz scene was infused with a flood of new and diversified scenes. Along with that came the distinctive "British" color of album sleeve design. From the late 60's, beginning with Rock, musical crossover become increasingly frequent, and this was reflected in the experiments in sleeve design. However, these crossovers were not always with Rock. In fact, the clear Jazz identity of the music made it appealing.

After the 70's there was further diversification in album cover sleeves paralleling the crossover, free, and avant garde music explored by more and more artists. It is a shame that the Jazz identity of cover design faded with time. This is particularly true of albums after the 70's, when cheaper, function-only versions of album covers became more common with the contraction of Jazz music market.

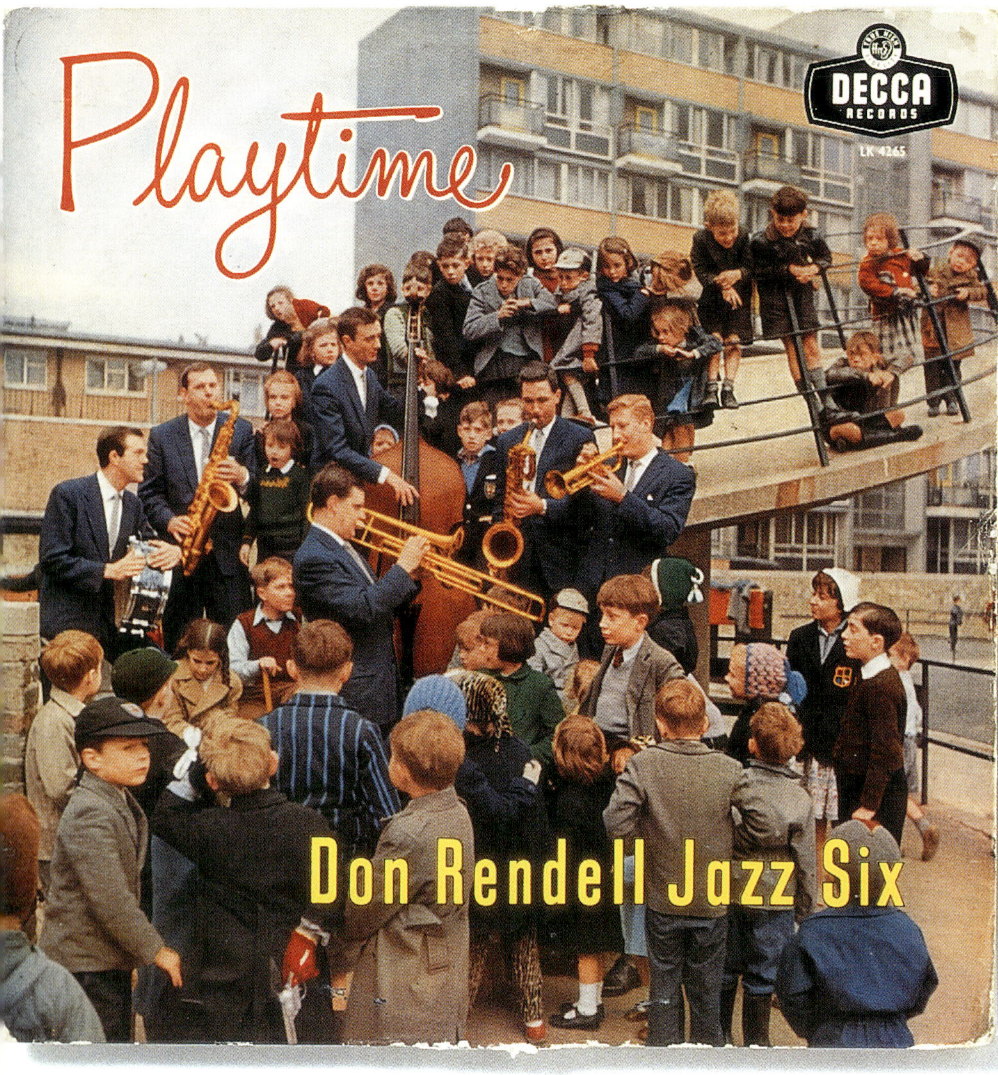

DON RENDELL JAZZ SIX:PLAYTIME/
DECCA LK4265(1958)
Cover Photo/Eric Jelly

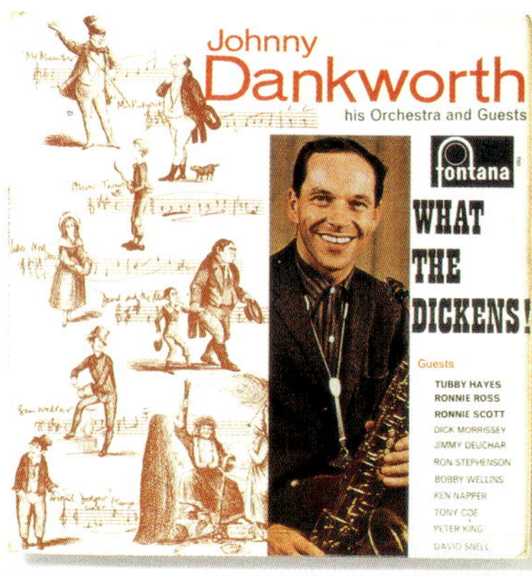

JOHNNY DANKWORTH:WHAT THE DICKENS!/
FONTANA STL5203(1963)

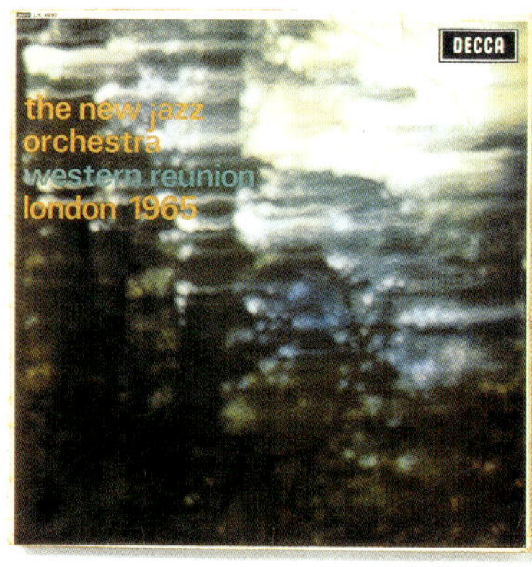

THE NEW JAZZ ORCHESTRA:WESTERN REUNION/
DECCA LK 4690(1965)

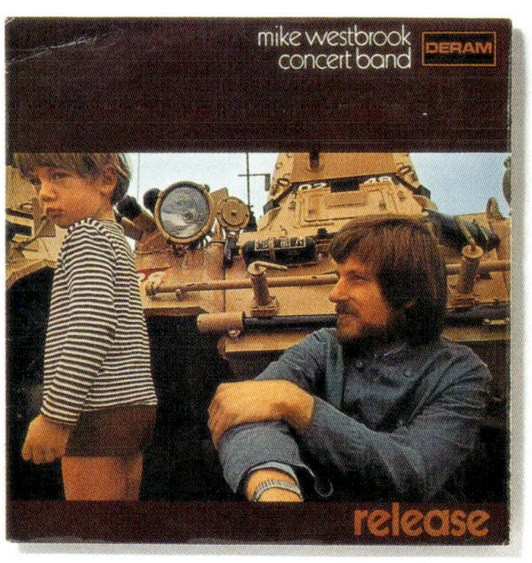

MIKE WESTBROOK CONCERT BAND:
RELEASE/DERAM SML1031(1968)
Sleeve Design/Mike Westbrook,Alan Jackson
Cover Photograph/Philip Stokes

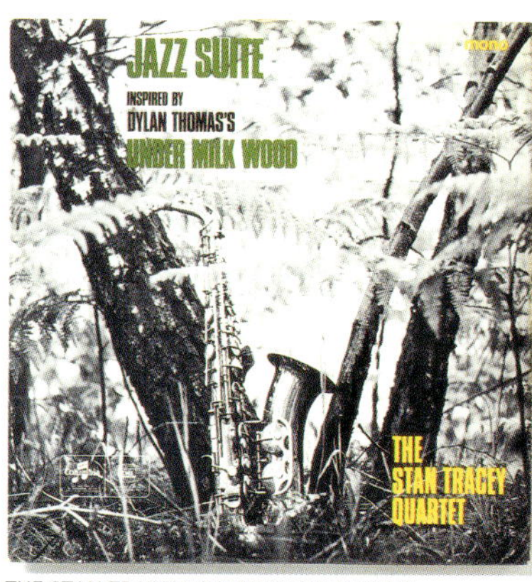

THE STAN TRACEY QUARTET:JAZZ SUITE/
COLUMBIA 33SX 1774(1965)
Sleeve Design/Denis Preston
Photograpy/Patrick Gwynn-Jones

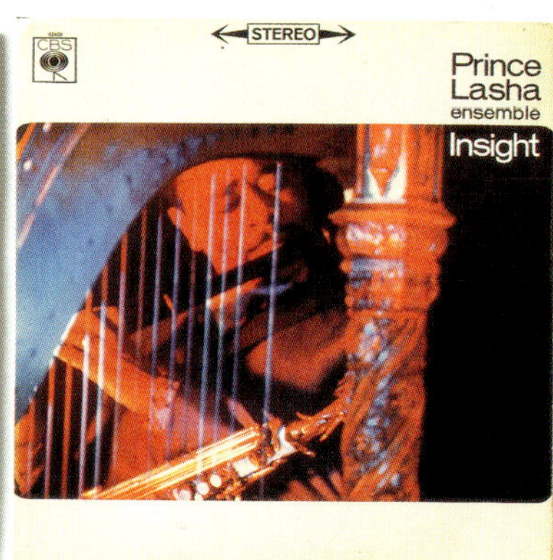

PRINCE LASHA ENSEMBLE:INSIGHT/
CBS SBPG62409(1966)
COver Art/Verity Graphics Arts
Cover Photo/Valery Allen

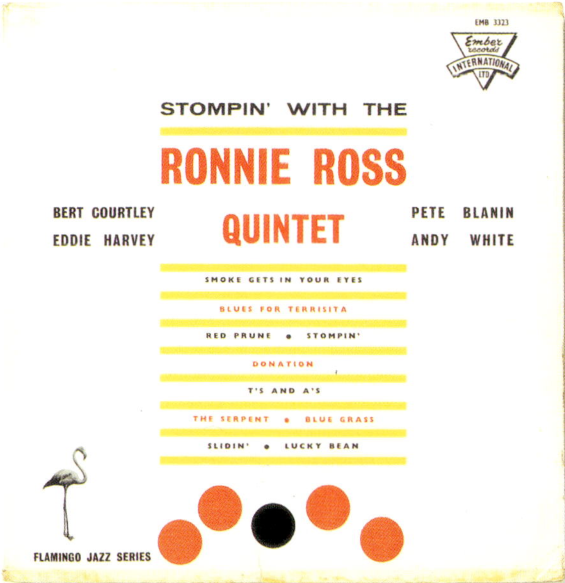

THE RONNIE ROSS QUINTET:
STOMPIN' WITH THE RONNIE ROSS QUINTET/
EMBER EMB3323(1961)

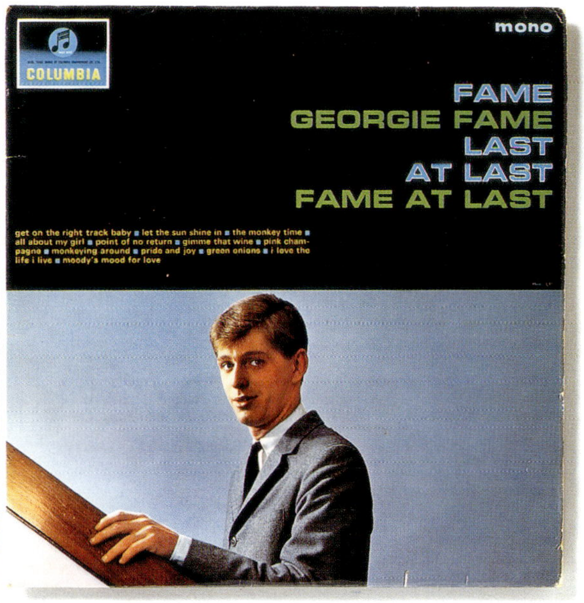

GEORGIE FAME:FAME AT LAST/
COLUMBIA 33SX 1638(1964)

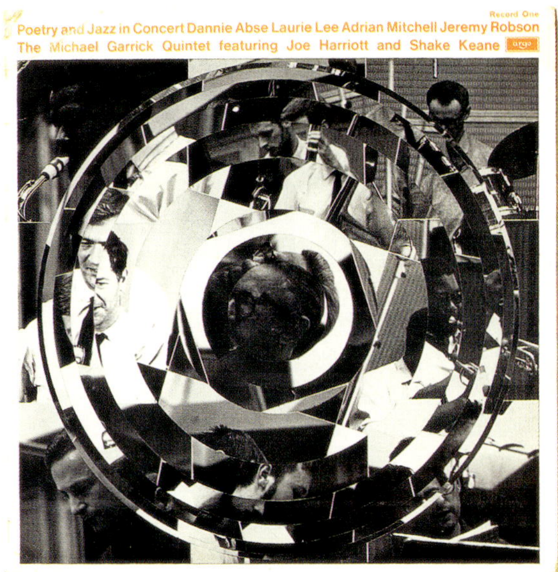

THE MICHAEL GARRICK QUINTET:
POETRY AND JAZZ IN CONCERT-1/
ARGO ZDA26(1963)

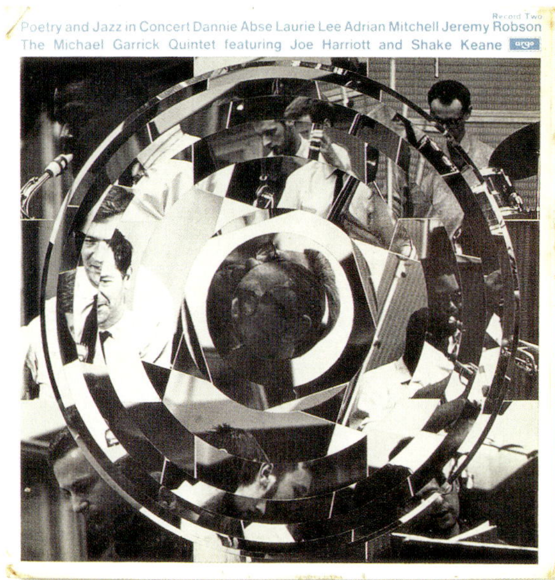

THE MICHAEL GARRICK QUINTET:
POETRY AND JAZZ IN CONCERT-2/
ARGO ZDA27(1963)

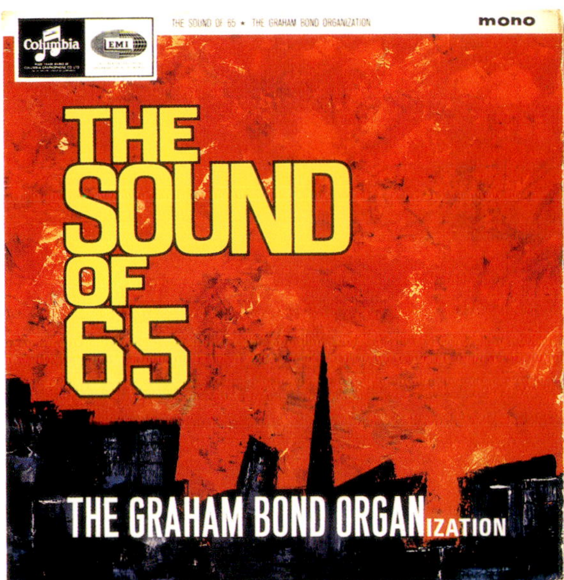

THE GRAHAM BOND ORGANIZATION:THE SOUND OF 65/
COLUMBIA 33SX 1711(1965)
Cover Design/Ginger Baker

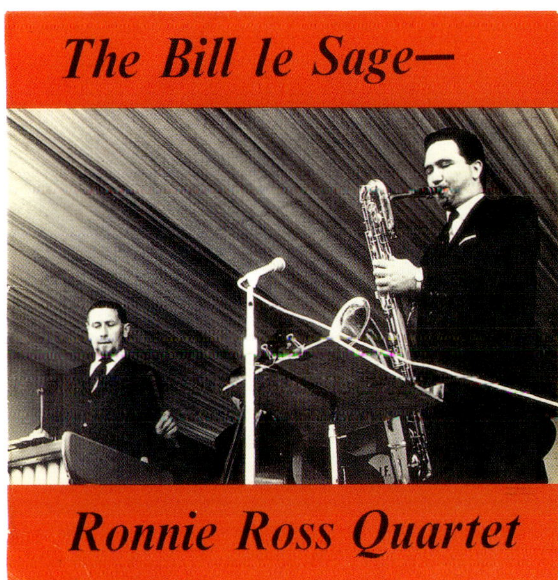

THE BILL LE SAGE-RONNIE ROSS QUARTET:
THE BILL LE SAGE-RONNIE ROSS QUARTET/
WORLD T346(1966)

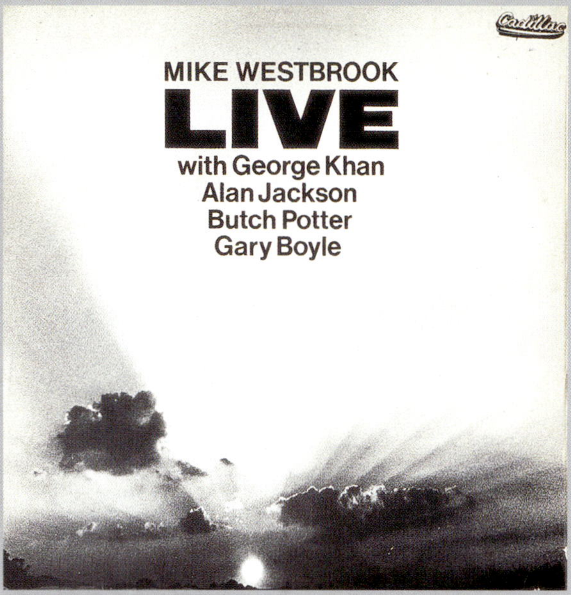

MIKE WESTBROOK:LIVE/CADILLAC SGC1001(1972)
Sleeve Design/Alan Jackson
Cover Photrograph/Roger Perry

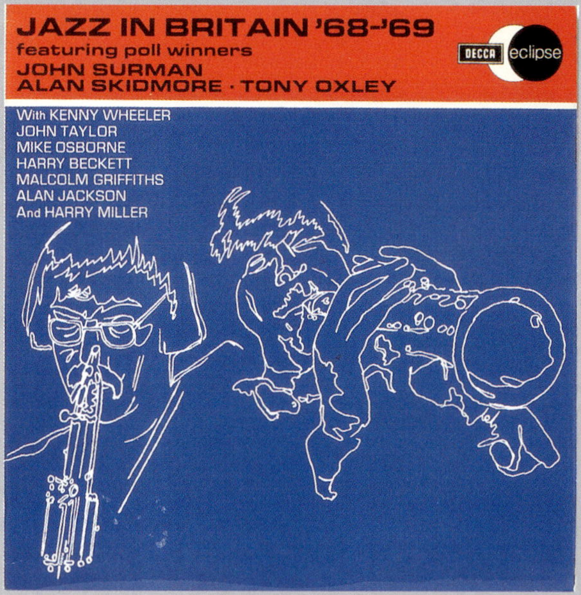

VARIOUS ARTISTS:JAZZ IN BRITAIN'68-'69/
DECCA ECS2114(1972)

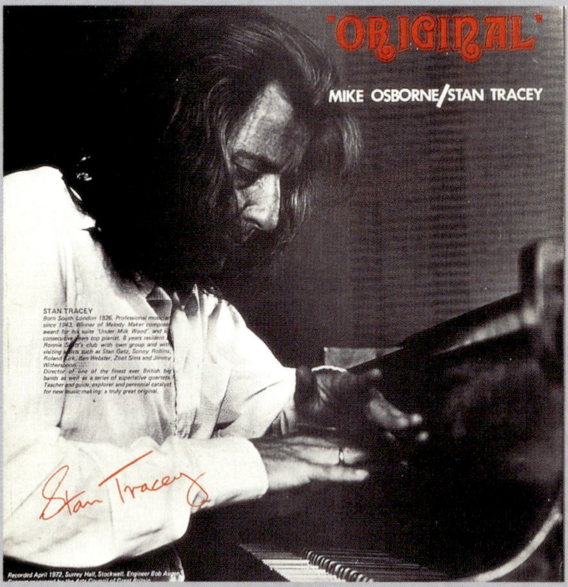

MIKE OSBORNE,STAN TRACEY:ORIGINAL/
CADILLAC SGC1002(1972) *back

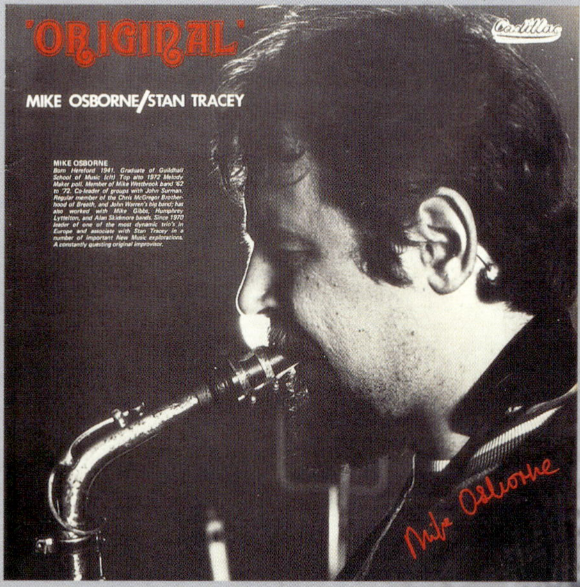

MIKE OSBORNE,STAN TRACEY:ORIGINAL/
CADILLAC SGC1002(1972) *front

1970's~ jazz mode

70年代以降

THE MIKE GIBBS BAND:JUST AHEAD/
POLYDOR 2683 011(1972) *front and back
Cover Design/Hamish Grimes
Photography/Mike Leale

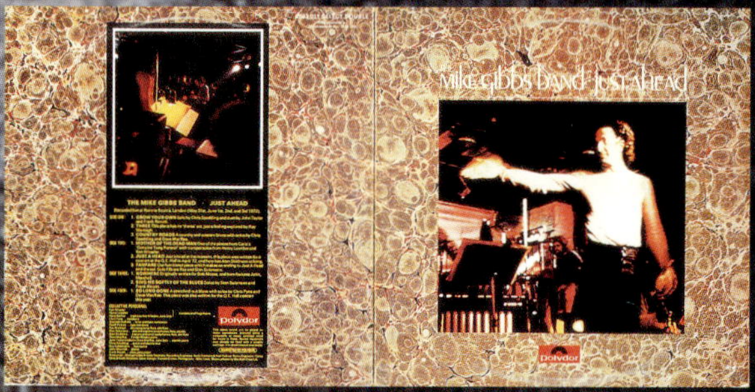

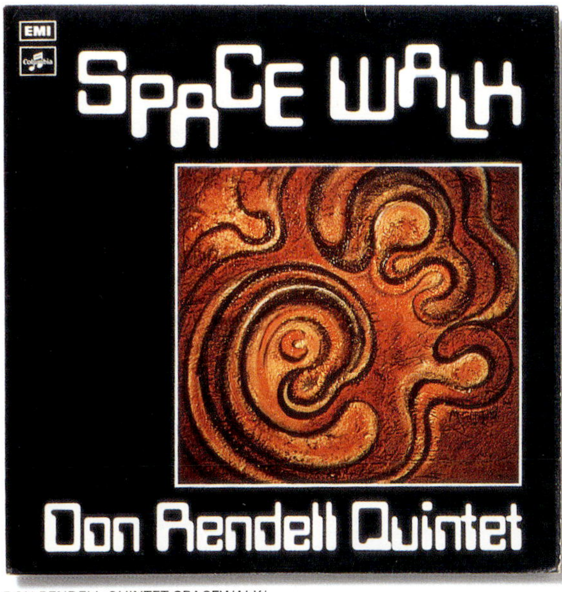

DON RENDELL QUINTET:SPACEWALK/
COLUMBIA SCX6491(1972)
Sleeve Design/Cecil McCartney

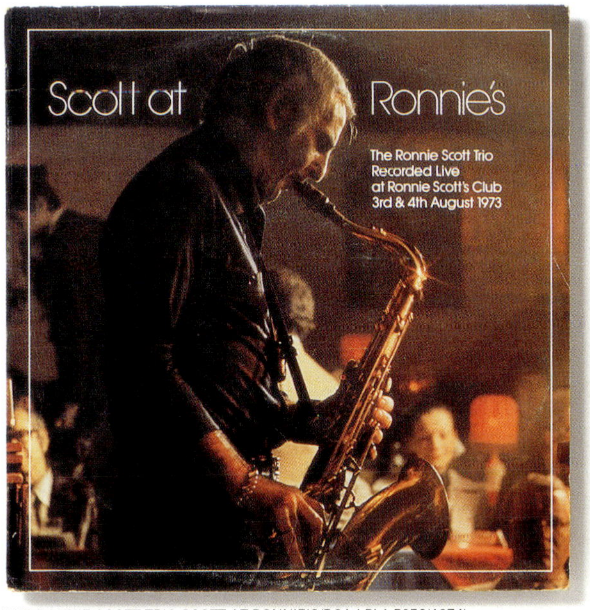

THE RONNIE SCOTT TRIO:SCOTT AT RONNIE'S/RCA LPL1 5056(1974)
Front Cover Photo/Martyn Adelman
Art Direction/John Dyer
Sleeve Design/Foster&Knowles

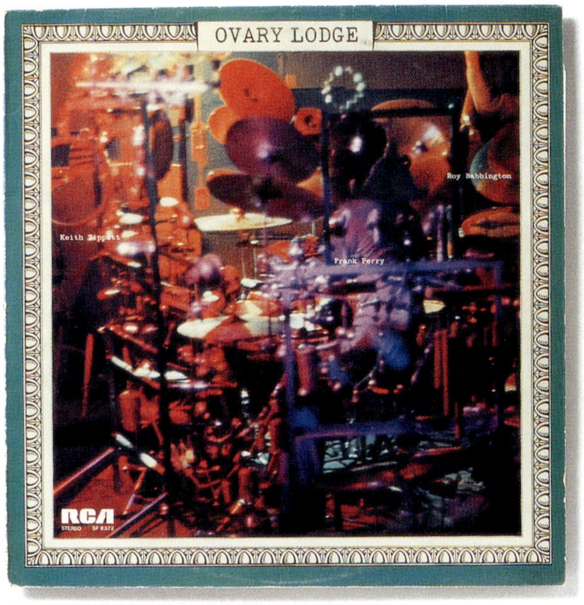

OVARY LODGE:OVARY LODGE/RCA SF8372(1973)
Photographer/Andy Burns

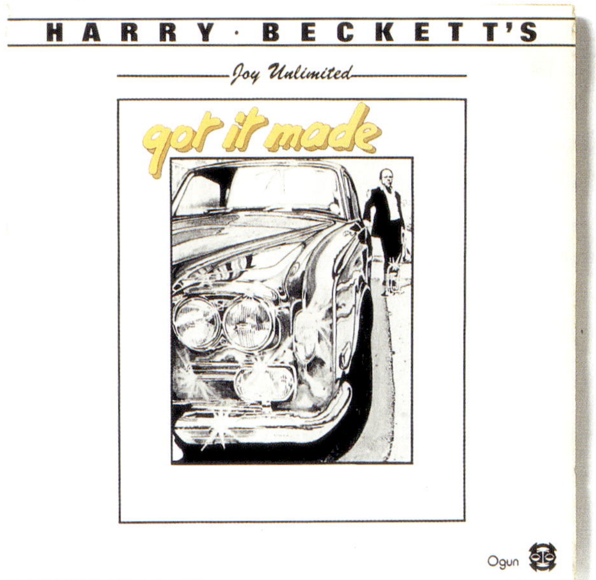

HARRY BECKETT'S JOY UNLIMITED:GOT IT MADE/
OGUN OG020(1977)
Sleeve Design by Penny and Steve Taylor
Photography by Fred Kavalier

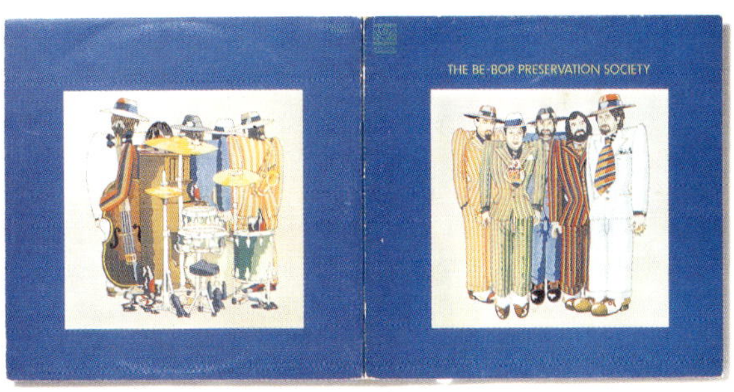

THE BE-BOP PRESERVATION SOCIETY:THE BE-BOP PRESERVATION SOCIETY/
DAWN DNLS 3027(1970) *front and back
Illustration and Inside Sleeve/Mick Wells

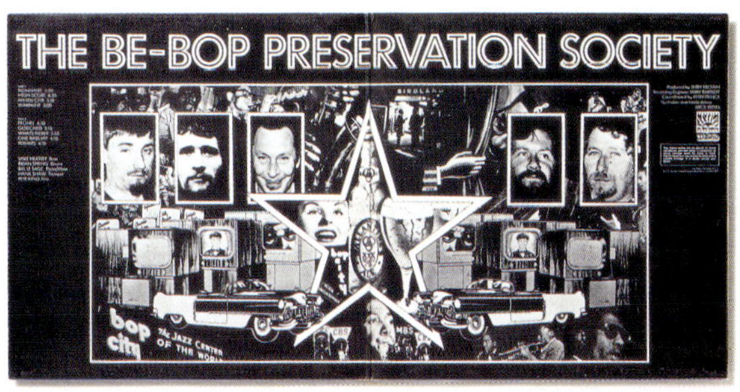

THE BE-BOP PRESERVATION SOCIETY:THE BE-BOP PRESERVATION SOCIETY/
DAWN DNLS 3027(1970)*inner

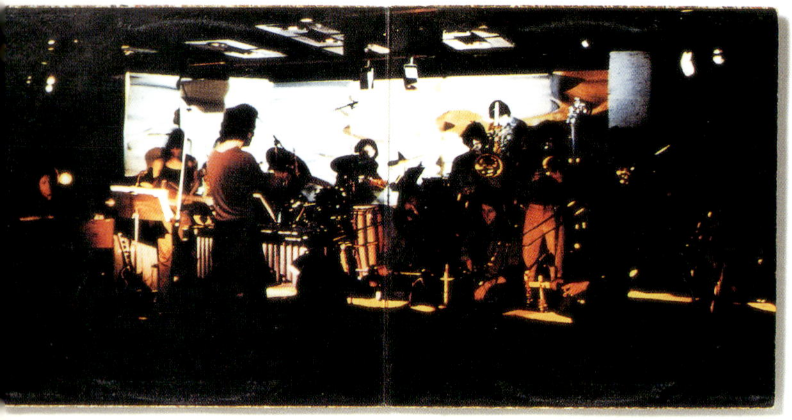

THE MIKE GIBBS BAND:JUST AHEAD/
POLYDOR 2683 011(1972) *inner

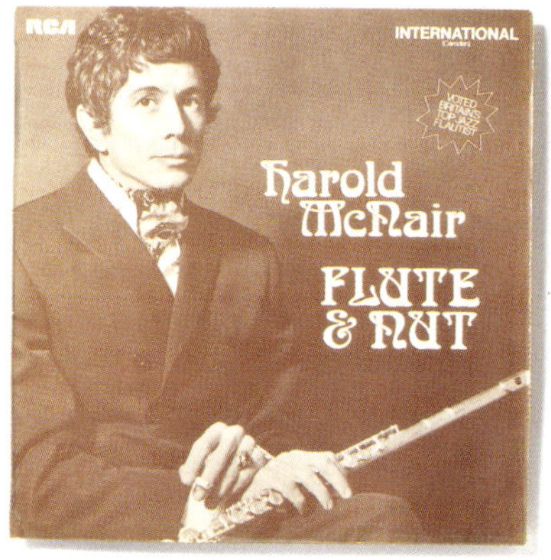

HAROLD McNAIR:FLUTE&NUT/RCA INTS1096(1970)
Cover Design/Royds London Ltd
Photography/Peter Mould

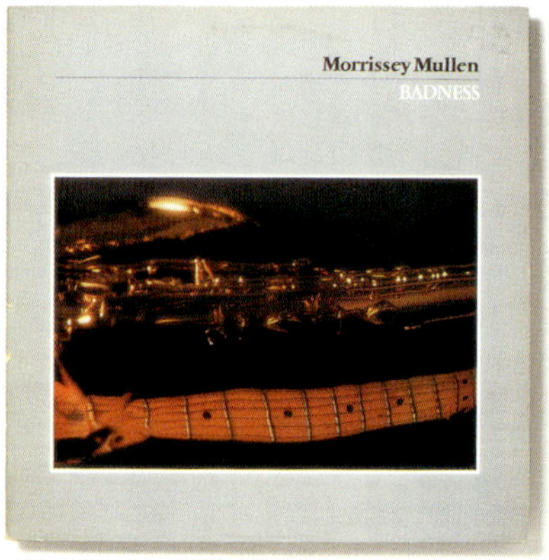

MORRISSEY MULLEN:BADNESS/
BEGGARS BANQUET BEGA27(1981)
Design/Citizen
Photo by The Lady Maclean

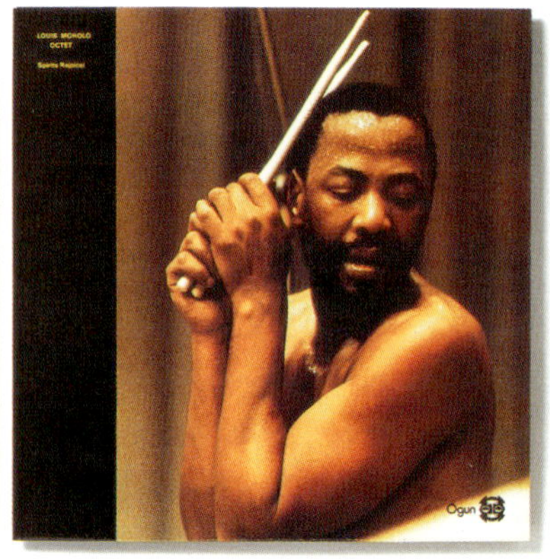

LOUIS MOHOLO OCTET:SPIRITS REJOICE!/
OGUN OG520(1978)
Photograph by Andreas Raggenbass

below: MIKE GIBBS:
THE ONLY CHROME-WATERFALL ORCHESTRA/
BRONZE ILPS9353(1975)

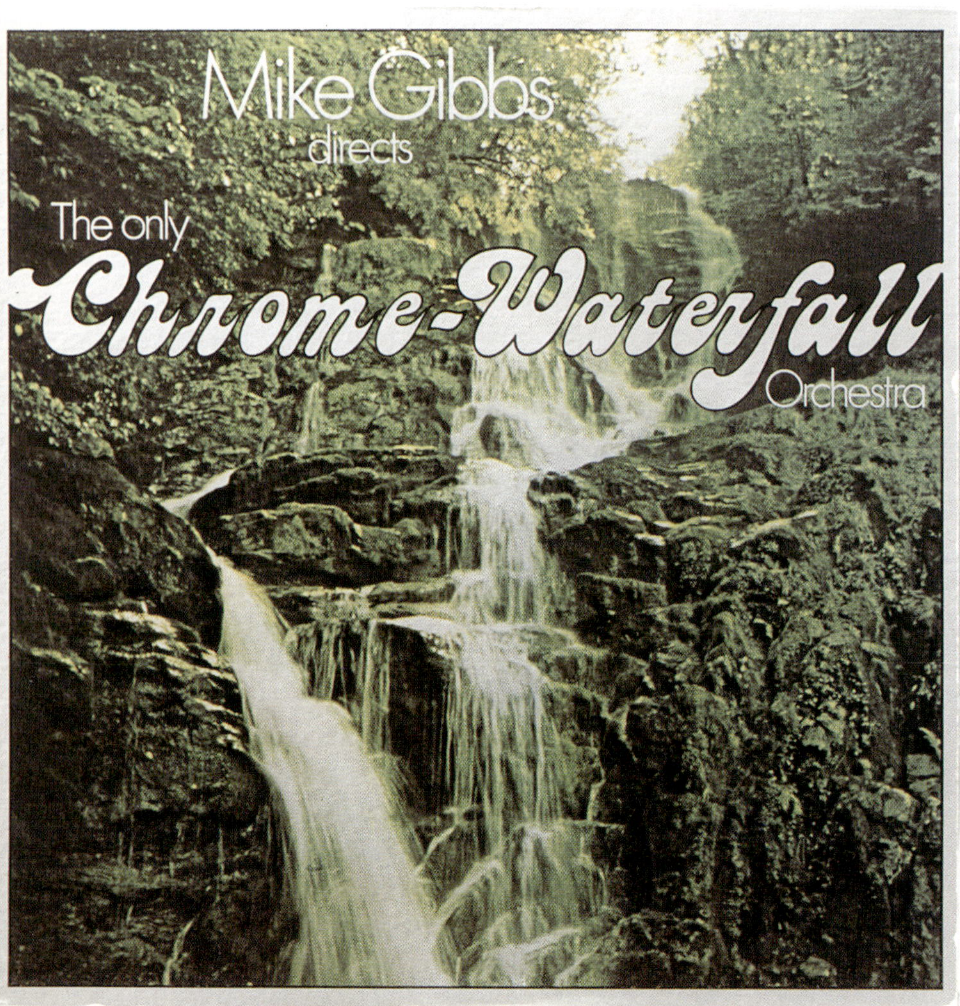

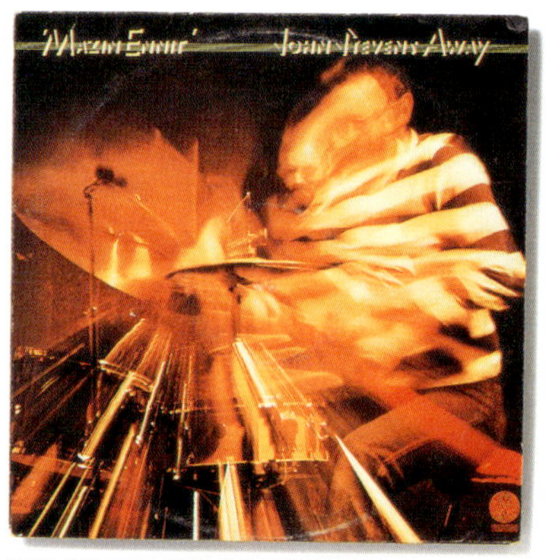

JOHN STEVEN'S AWAY:MAZIN ENNIT/V
ERTIGO 6360 141(1977)
Photography/Jerry Mason
Design/Martin Cropper at Design Machine

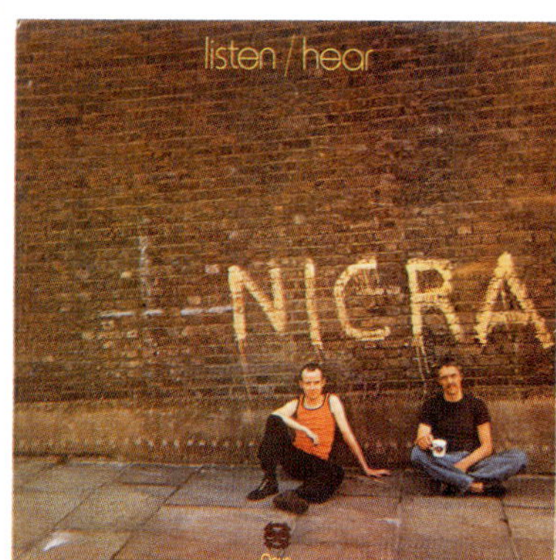

NICRA:LISTEN,HEAR/OGUN OG010(1977)
Sleeve Design by Stephen Taylor
Photograph by Lynne Richards

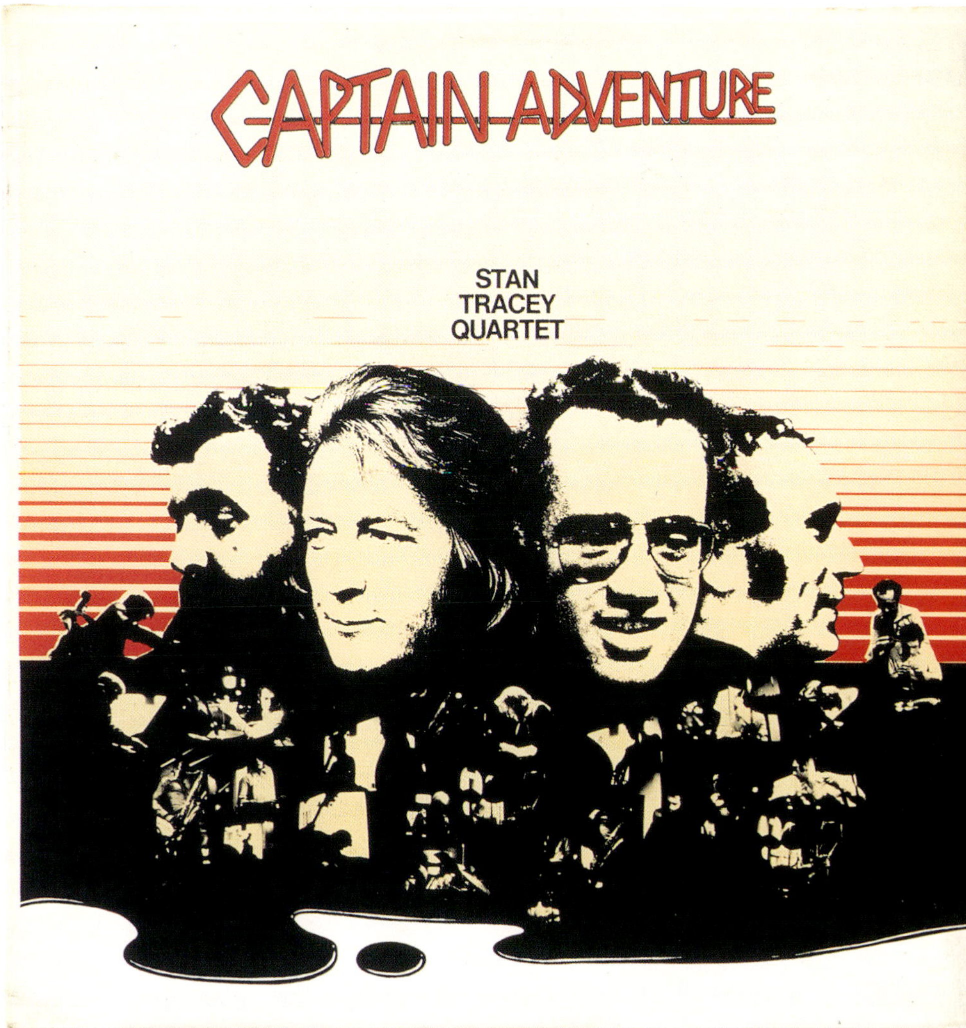

STAN TARACEY QUARTET/CAPTAIN ADVENTURE/STEAM SJ102(1975)
Sleeve Design/Dick Whitbread
Photograpy/Steve Berry&Dick Whitbread

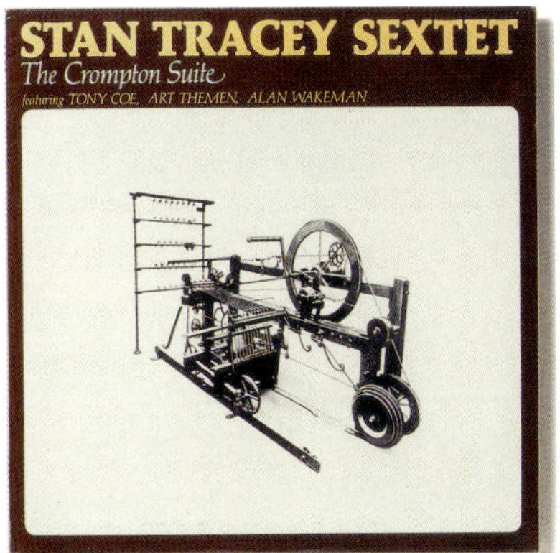

STAN TRACEY SEXTET:THE CROMPTON SUITE/
STEAM SJ109(1979)
Cover Photo Courtesy Bolton Museum
(Photograph by Jak Kilby)
Sleeve and Layout Liz Walton

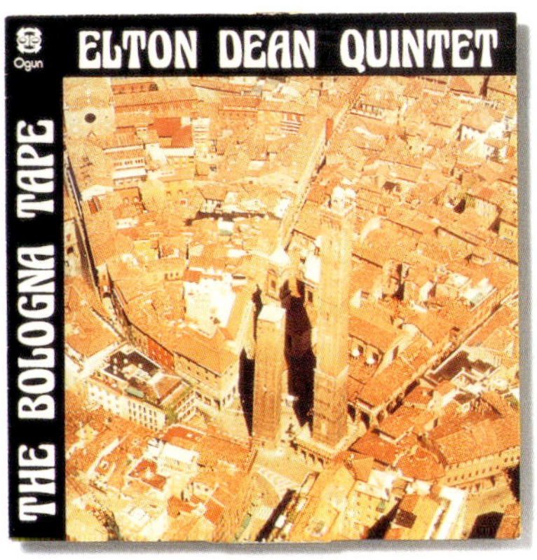

ELTON DEAN QUINTET:THE BOLOGNA TAPE/
OGUN OG530(1985)
Front Cover Photograph Loaned by Kind of
Permission of Pegasus Holidays
Cover Design and Layout by Hazel Miller,John Jack

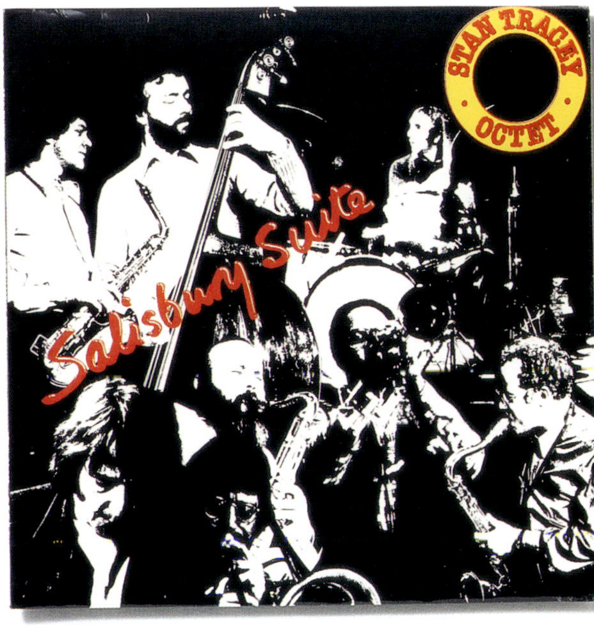

STAN TRACEY OCTET:THE SALISBURY SUITE/
STEAM SJ105(1978)
Sleeve Design&Photo by Dick Whithread

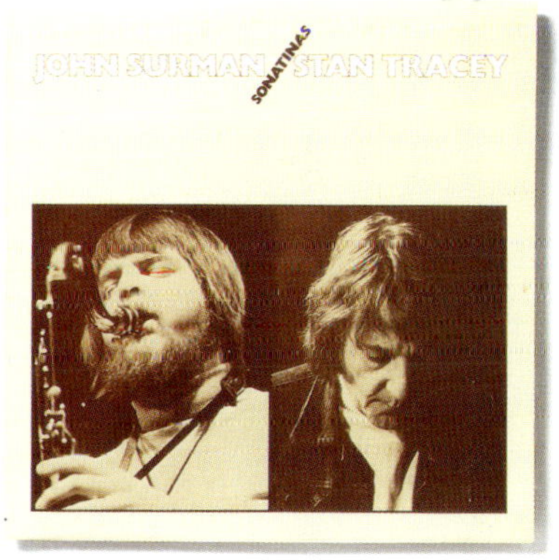

JOHN SURMAN&STAN TRACEY:SONATINAS/
STEAM SJ106(1978)
Photograph/Graham Ward
Sleeve Design/Dick Whitbread

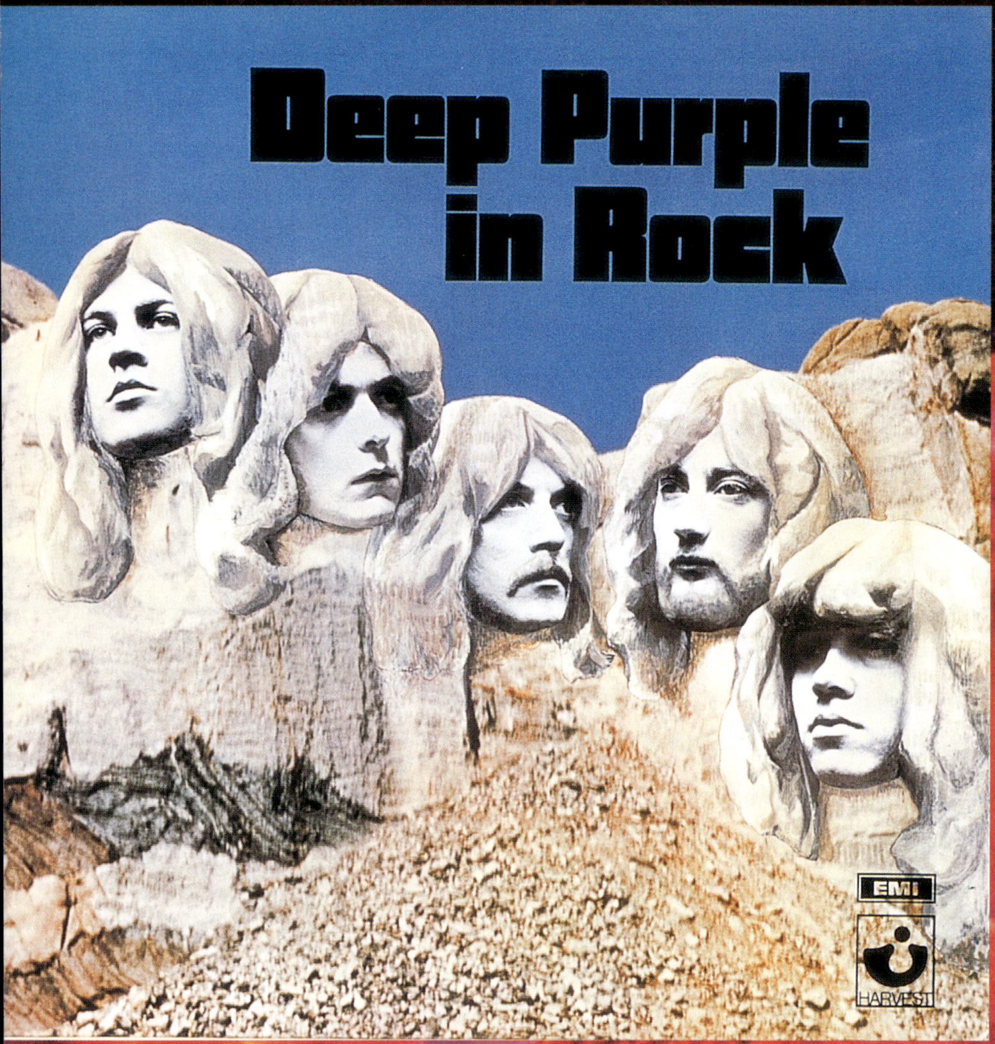

left: DEEP PURPLE:IN ROCK/
HARVEST SHVL777(1970) *UK version
Cover Design/Edwards Coletta Productions
Photography/Mike Brown, Alan Hall

below: DEEP PURPLE:IN ROCK *GERMAN version

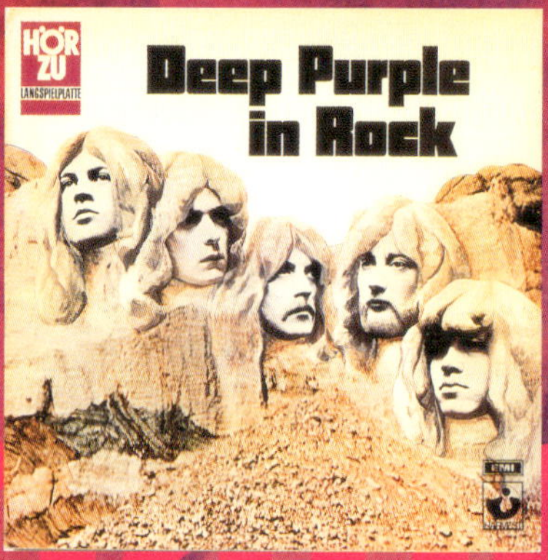

sleeve variations

デザイン違い

レコード・ジャケットのデザイン違いには、いくつかのパターンがある。まずひとつが、国ごとのデザイン違い。これをさらに細かく分けるなら、1、タイトル・ロゴやアーティスト名だけ母国語に変換したもの、2、その国のテイストに合わせて売り上げアップを図るため、すべてを別のデザインに差し替えたもの、3、あまりに卑わいなヴィジュアルのため、オリジナルのままでは発売できなかったもの、4、オリジナルを多少アレンジしたもの、等が挙げられる。そしてもうひとつのパターンが、セカンド・プレス以降、廉価仕様となってデザインが簡略化されたり、改良を加えられたりしたものだ。 p148-149には、一例としてディープ・パープルのデザイン違いジャケットを集めてみたが、『マシン・ヘッド』などは英国盤とスペイン盤とでどこが違うのかと思えば、たんに写真を裏焼きにして左右を入れ換えたくらいの違いでしかない。しかし、コレクターの多くは、たったそれだけの違いを発見しては狂喜し、血眼になってお目当てのレコードを探し求め続けるのである！ p150-151に掲載したジャケットのなかではキャラヴァンのファースト・アルバムが、イギリスとアメリカのお国柄を物語っているようで興味深い。パラディンのアメリカ盤に使われているデザインは、イギリス盤の内ジャケットに使われているものをそっくり流用してある。

There were several sleeve variations among album jackets. First of all, a jacket may have differed in version depending on the country where it was released. The variations generally followed a few patterns: the title logo and artist / band name were converted into a different language; for sales purposes, there was an entirely new design of the cover to match local tastes; images that may have been considered obsene in some countries were changed; or there was a slight re-arrangement of the original design. Another pattern of sleeve variation was the use of a different design for subsequent pressings of the album, which may have a different retail price. On pages 148 and 149, there is an example of Deep Purple's album sleeve variations. The only difference in the cover artwork between the UK and Spanish versions of "Machine Head" is that the cover photograph was turned upside-down and flopped. For record collectors, this sort of discovery would leave them wide-eyed and ecstatic, creating an endless frenzy of collectors on the hunt. On pages 150 and 151, you can see the variation between the UK and American versions of Caravan's first album cover, each interestingly expressing the two nation's different characters. The American version for the Paladin album cover design was exactly the same as the inner sleeve of the English version.

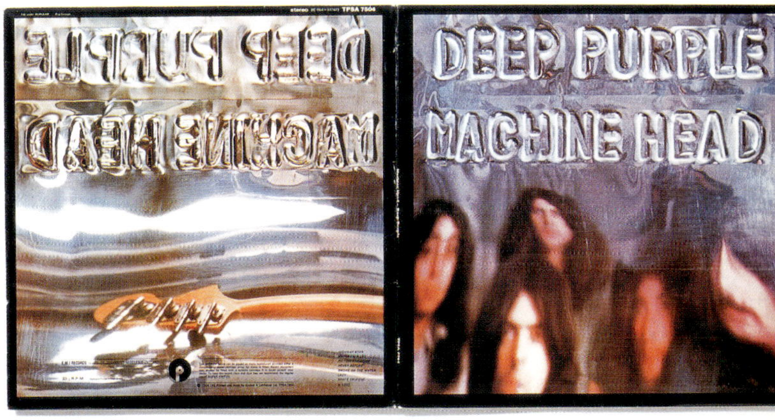

above: DEEP PURPLE:MACHINE HEAD/
PURPLE TPSA7504(1972)*UK version
Photography/Shepard Sherbell
Cover Design/R.Glover,J.Coletta

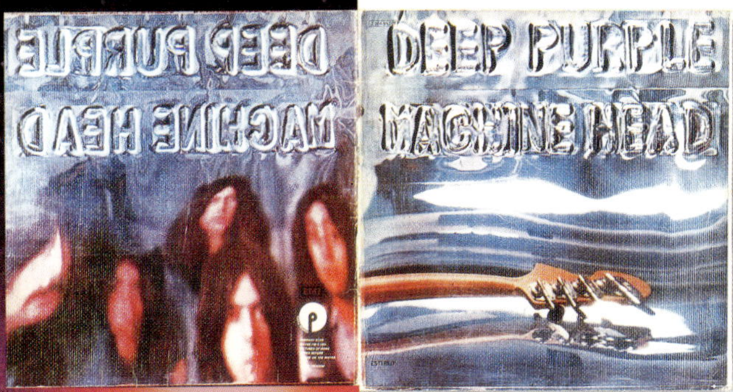

left: DEEP PURPLE:MACHINE HEAD *SPANISH version

DEEP PURPLE:
QUEMAR *"BURN" ARGENTINA version

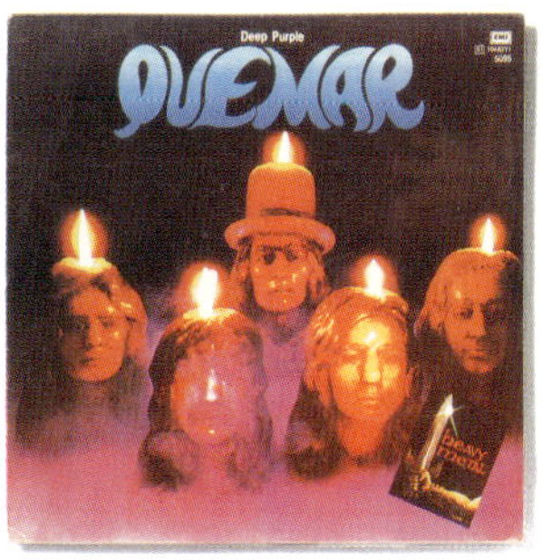

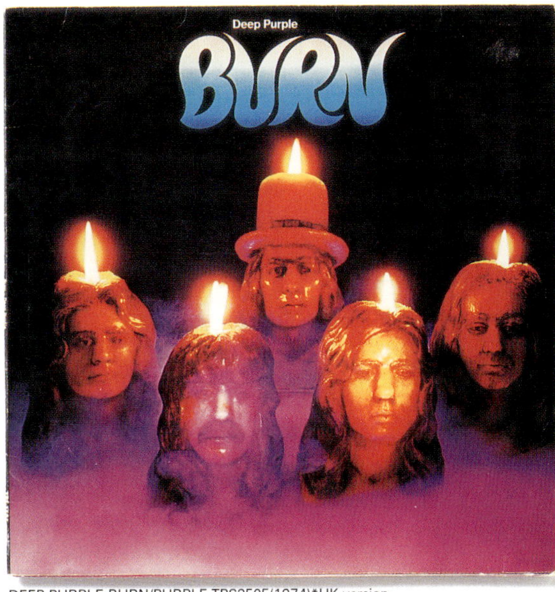

DEEP PURPLE:BURN/PURPLE TPS3505(1974)*UK version
Photography/Fin Costello

S

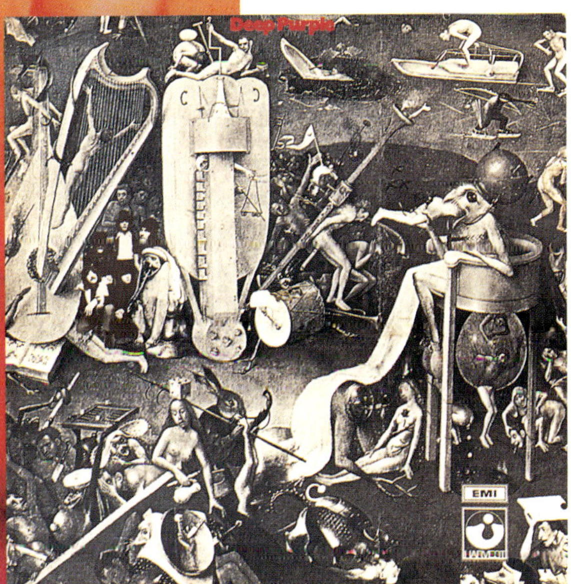

DEEP PURPLE:DEEP PURPLE/
HARVEST SHVL759(1969) *UK version

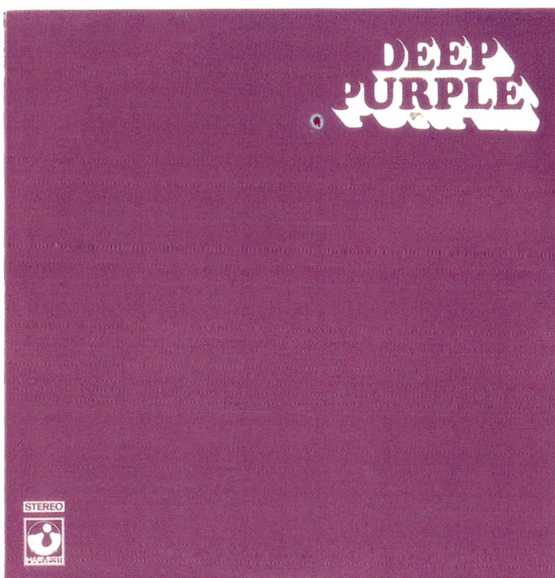

DEEP PURPLE:DEEP PURPLE/
HARVEST SHVL759 SERIES550(1969) *AUSTRALIA version

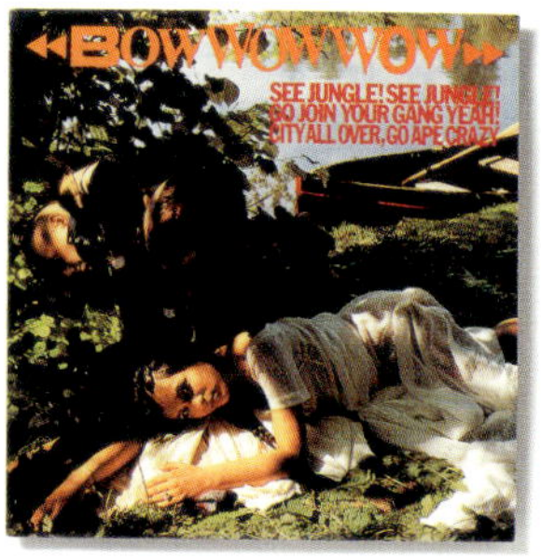

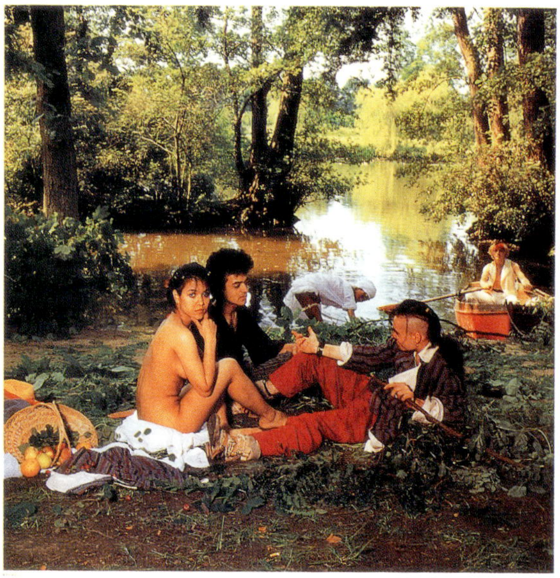

above: BOW WOW WOW:
SEE JUNGLE! SEE JUNGLE! GO JOIN YOUR GANG YEAH,CITY ALL OVER! GO APE CRAZY!
(1981)*USA version

right: BOW WOW WOW:
SEE JUNGLE! SEE JUNGLE! GO JOIN YOUR GANG YEAH,CITY ALL OVER! GO APE CRAZY!/
RCA RCALP3000(1981) *UK version

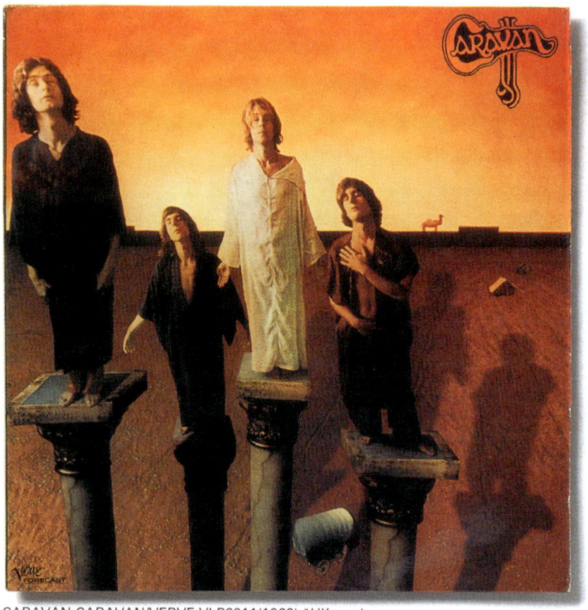

CARAVAN:CARAVAN/VERVE VLP6011(1969) *UK version
Sleeve Conception and Photography/Richard Bennett Zeff
Design and Graphics/Peter Dale

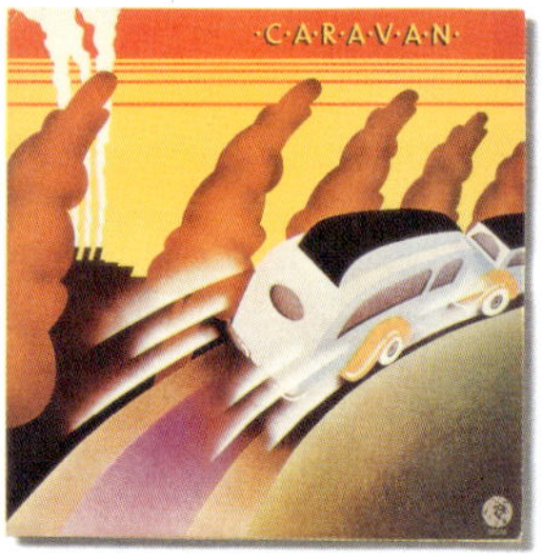

CARAVAN:CARAVAN(1969)
*USA Version

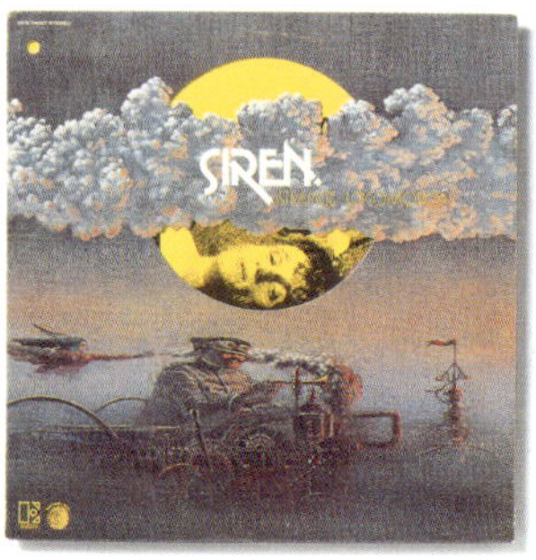

SIREN:STRANGE LOCOMOTION(1971)
*USA version

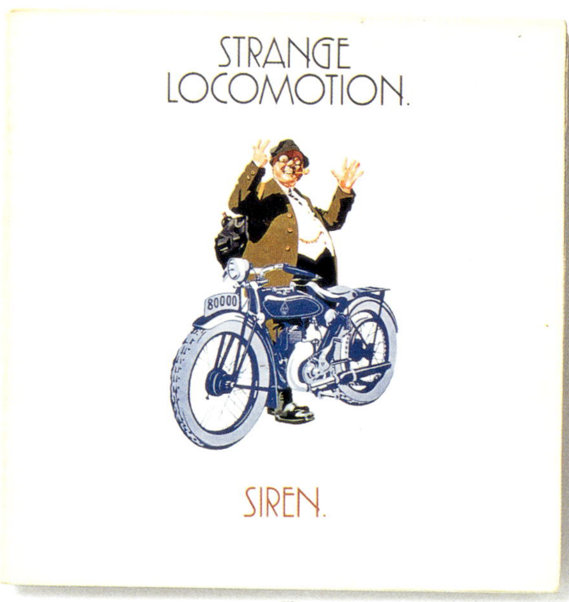

SIREN:STRANGE LOCOMOTION/
DANDELION DAN8001(1971)*UK version
Sleeve Design/Nick Cudworth,John Jonen
The Work of Ludwig Holwein

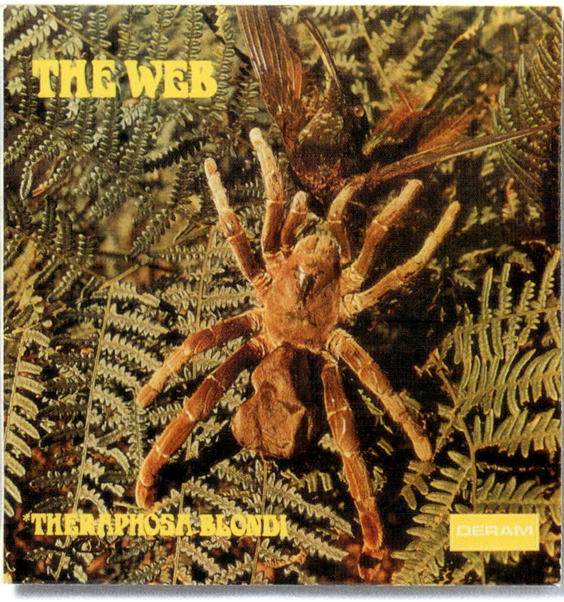

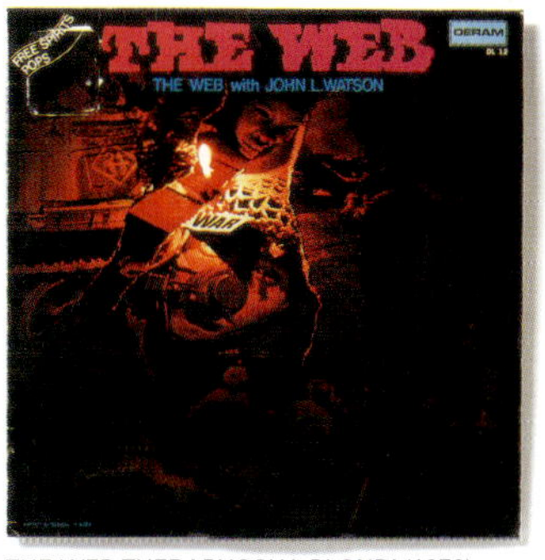

THE WEB:THERAPHOSHA BLONDI (1970)
*JAPANESE version

THE WEB:THERAPHOSHA BLONDI/
DERAM SML-R1058(1970) *UK version
Photography&Design/Terence Ibbott

PALADIN:PALADIN/ISLAND ILPS9150(1971) *UK version
Design/John Kosh
Photography/Tony May

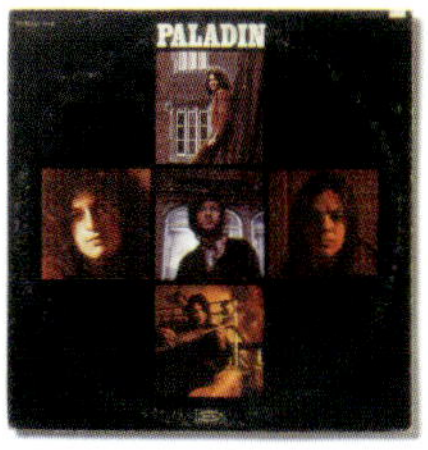

PALADIN:PALADIN(1971)
*USA Version

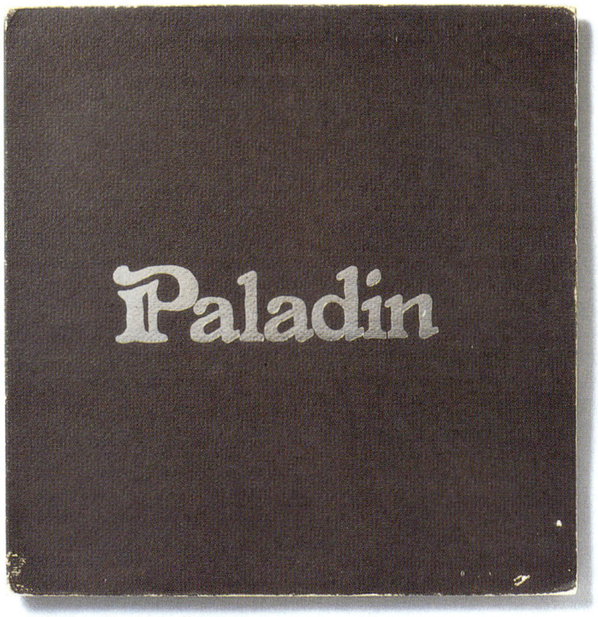

AL STEWART:MODERN TIMES/
CBS S80477(1975)*UK version
Sleeve Design and Photography by Hipgnosis

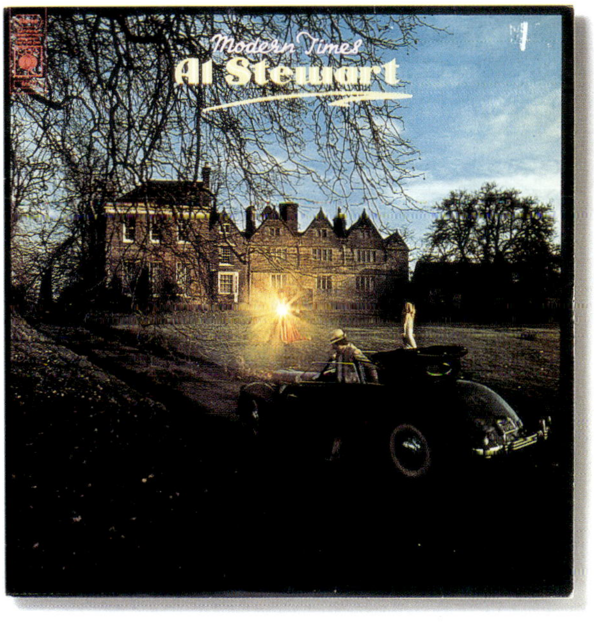

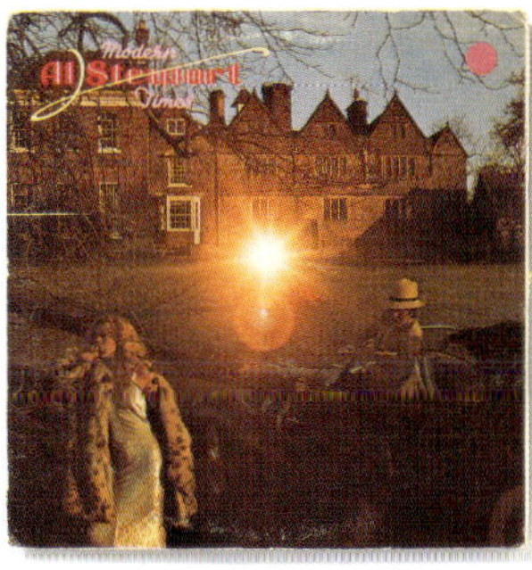

AL STEWART:MODERN TIMES(1975)
*USA version

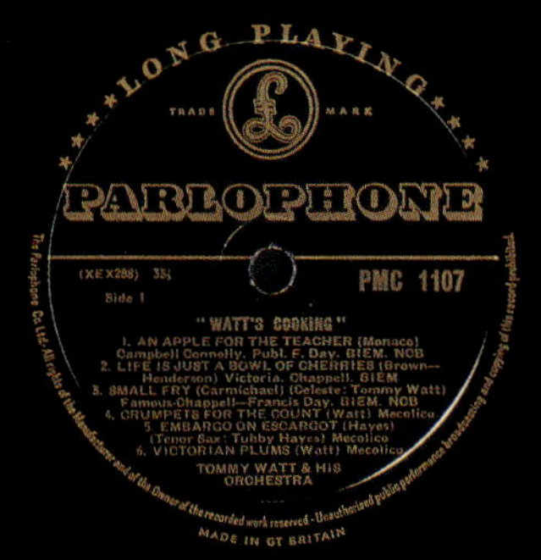

PARLOPHONE LABEL/GOLD LOGO

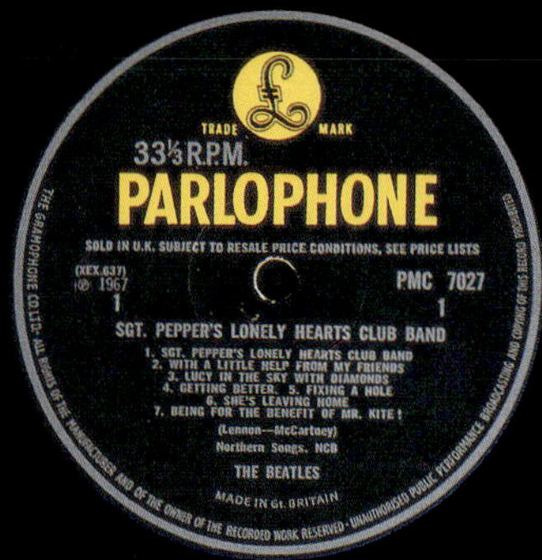

PARLOPHONE LABEL/YELLOW LOGO

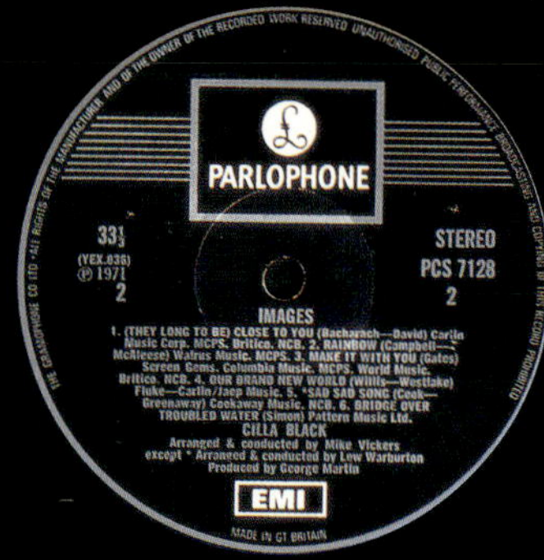

PARLOPHONE LABEL/WHITE LOGO

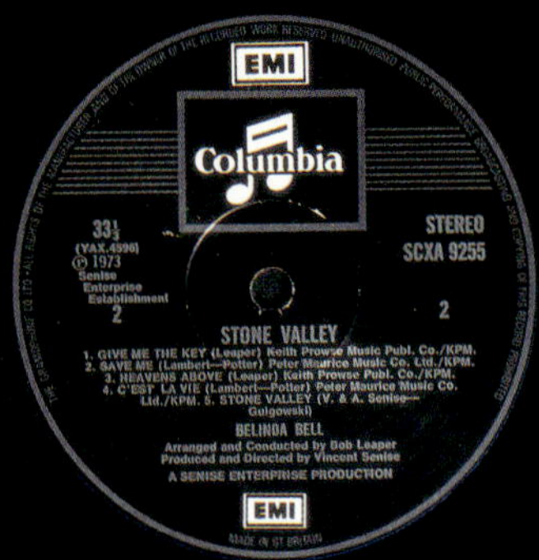

COLUMBIA LABEL/WHITE LOGO

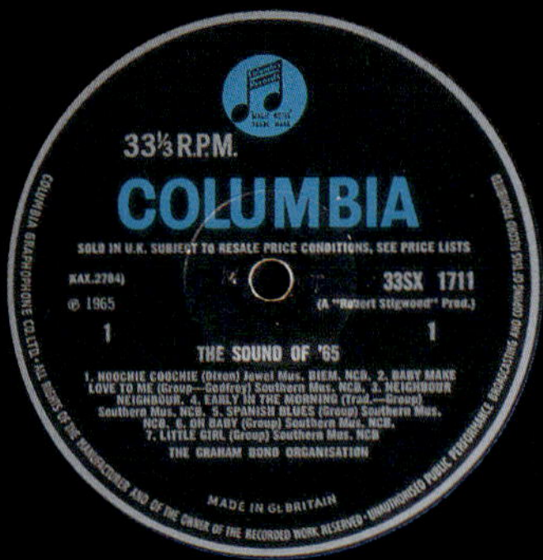

COLUMBIA LABEL/BLUE LOGO

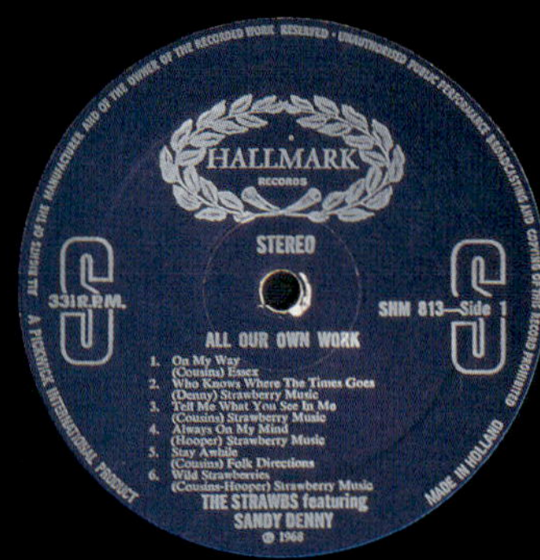

HALLMARK LABEL

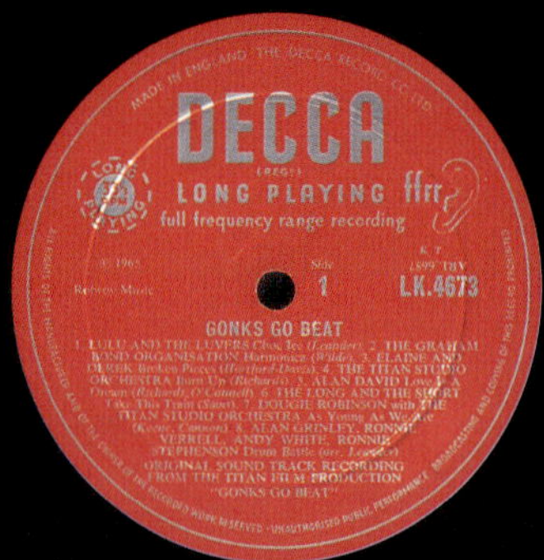

DECCA LABEL/RED

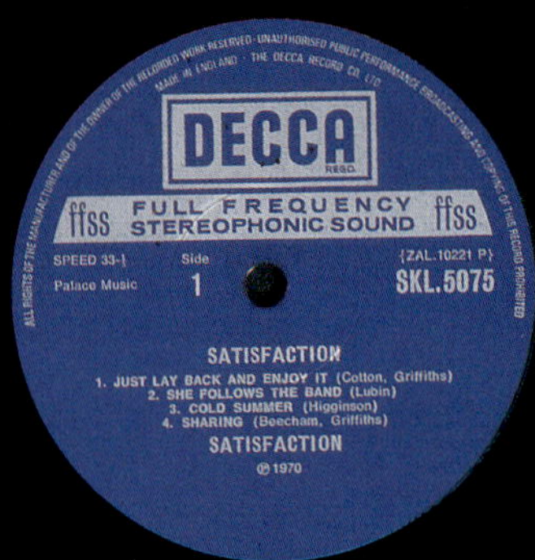

DECCA LABEL/BLUE

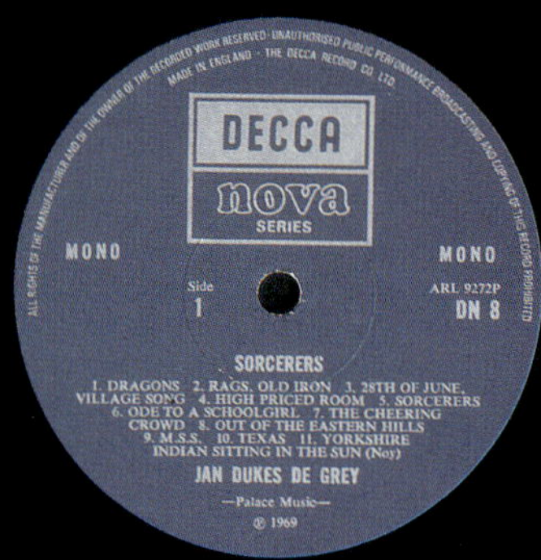

NOVA LABEL

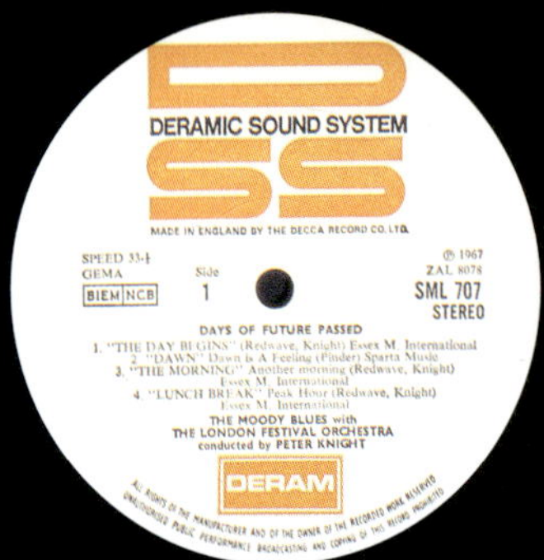

DERAM LABEL/DERAMIC SOUND SYSTEM

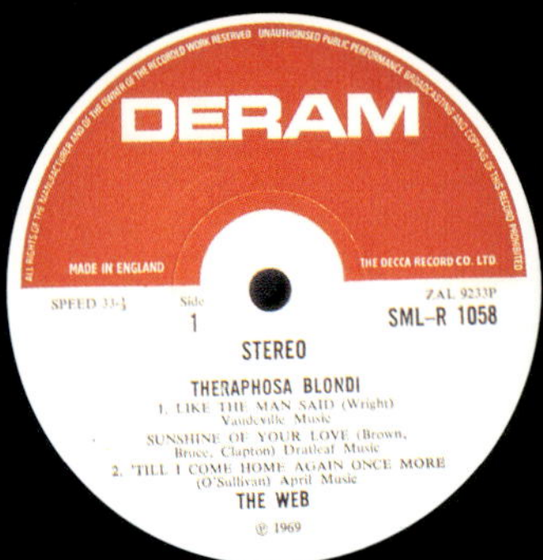

DERAM LABEL/RED

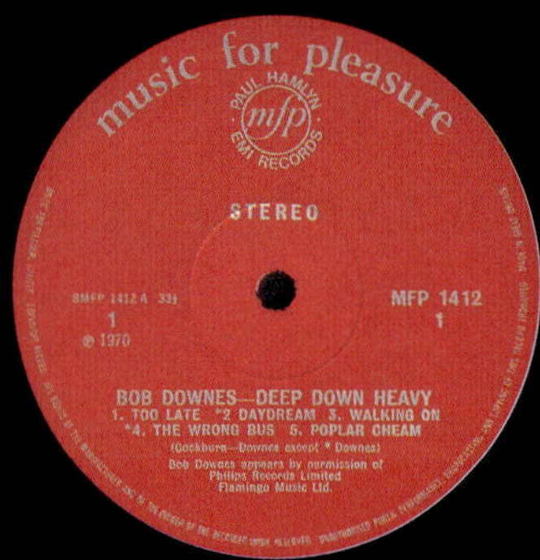

MFP LABEL

In Search of the Lost Record

record labels
レコード・レーベル

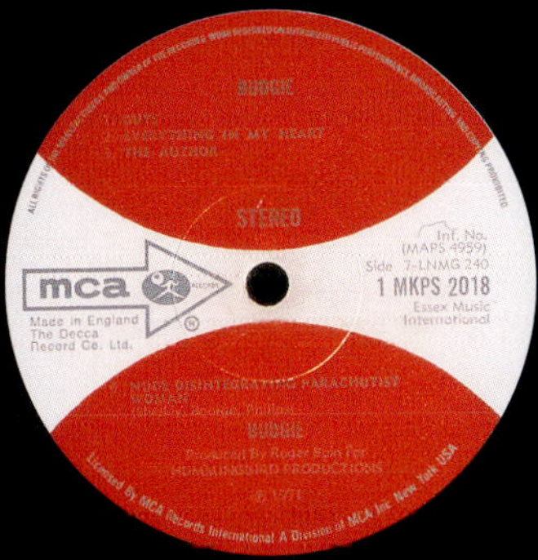

MCA LABEL

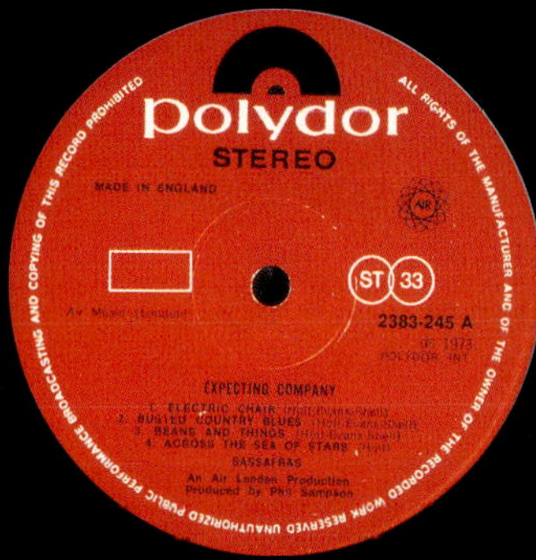

POLYDOR LABEL

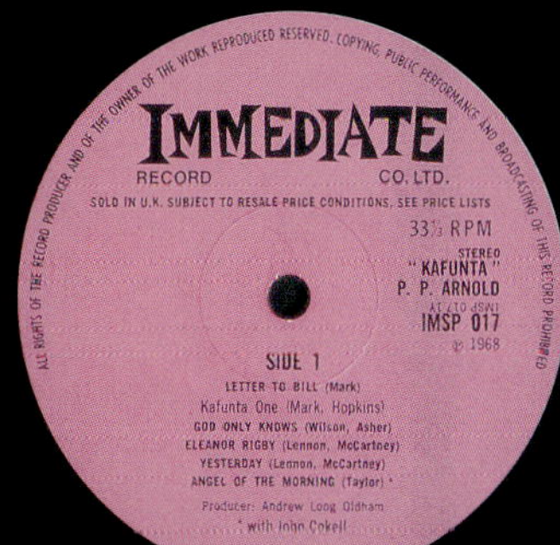

IMMEDIATE LABEL

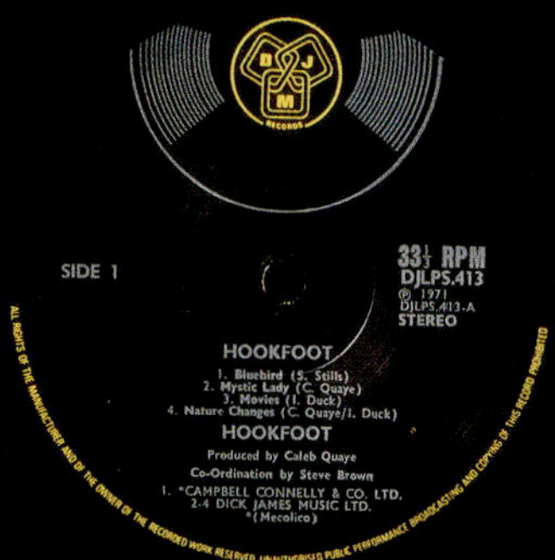

DJM LABEL

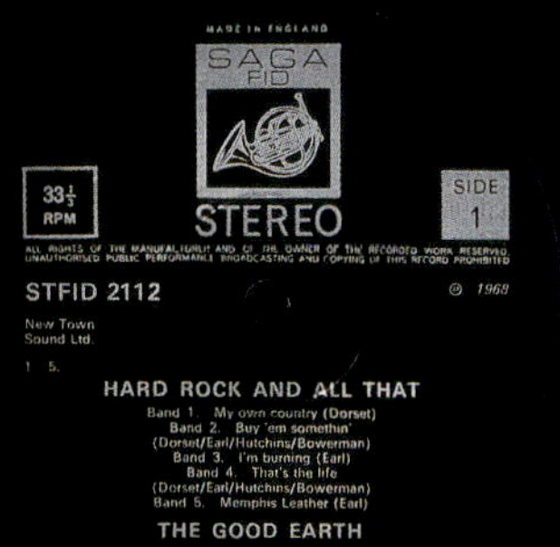

SAGA LABEL

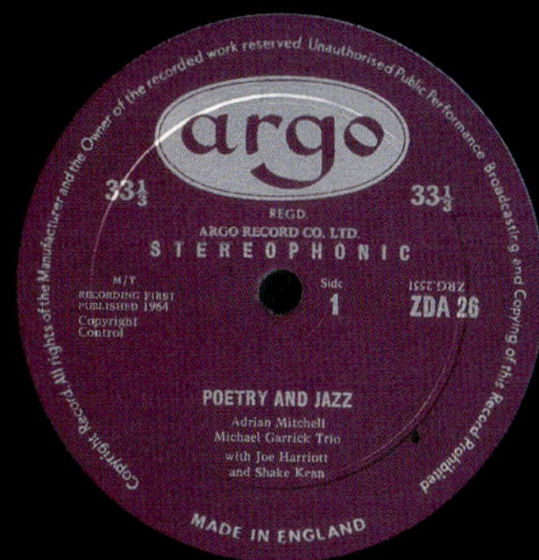

ARGO LABEL

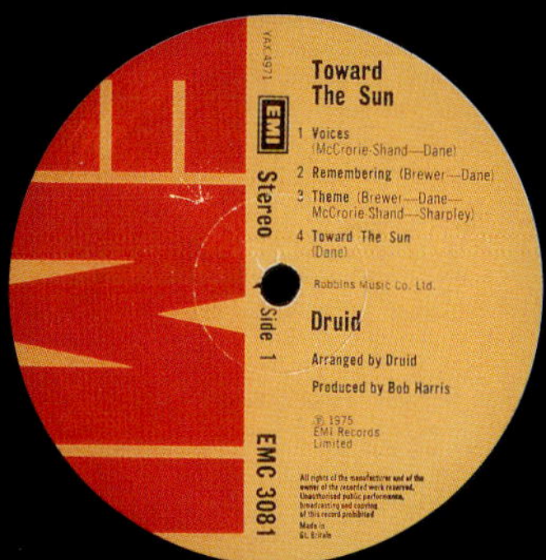

EMI LABEL

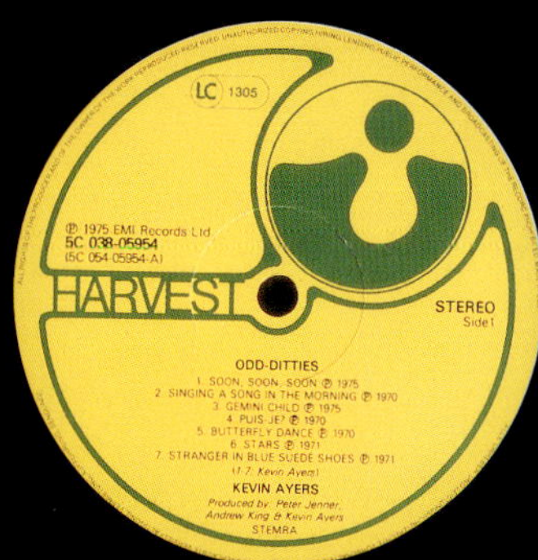

HARVEST LABEL

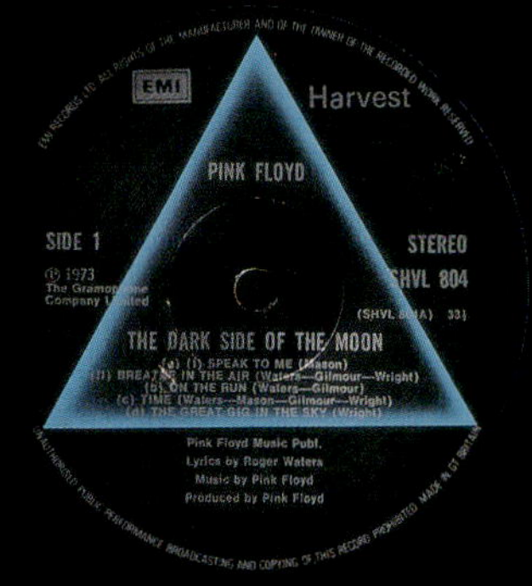

HARVEST LABEL/DARK SIDE OF THE MOON
(PINK FLOYD)

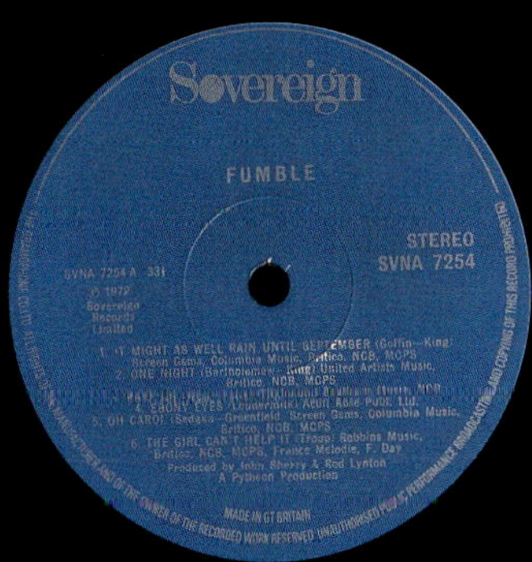

SOVEREIGN LABEL

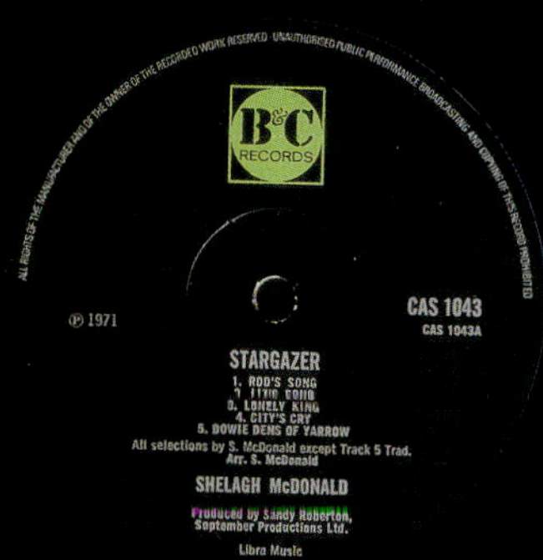

B&C LABEL

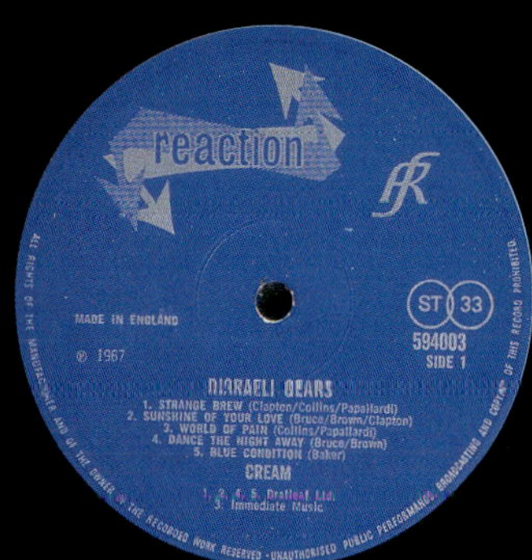

REACTION LABEL

In Search of the Lost Record

VERTIGO LABEL/SIDE 1(SPIRAL)

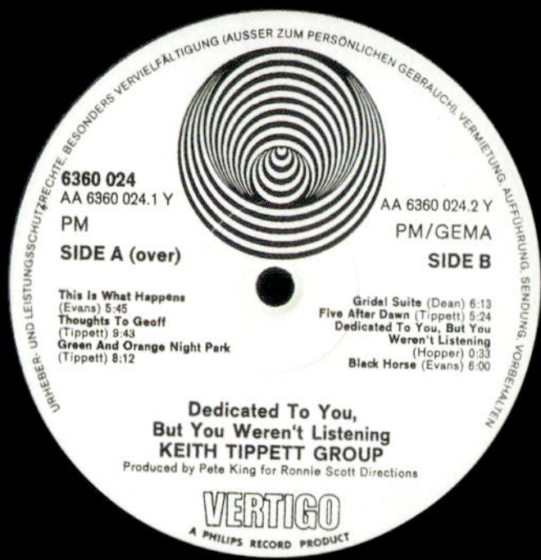

VERTIGO LABEL/SIDE 2

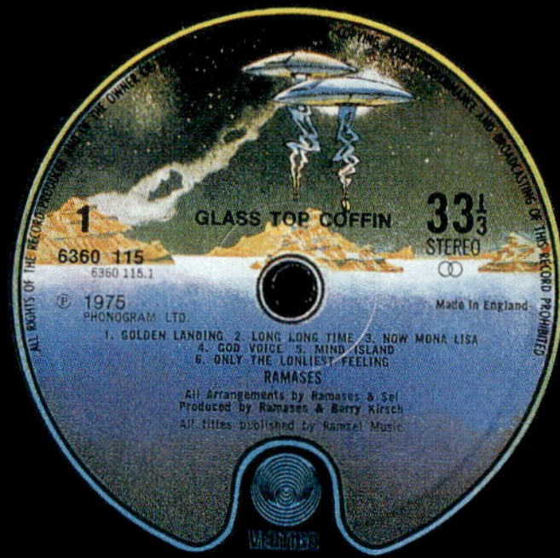

VERTIGO LABEL/SPACE SHIP

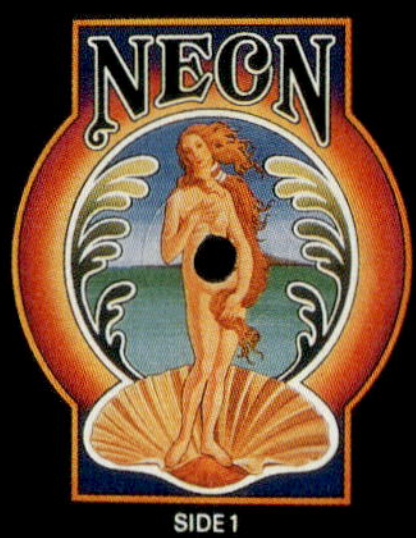

NEON LABEL/SIDE 1

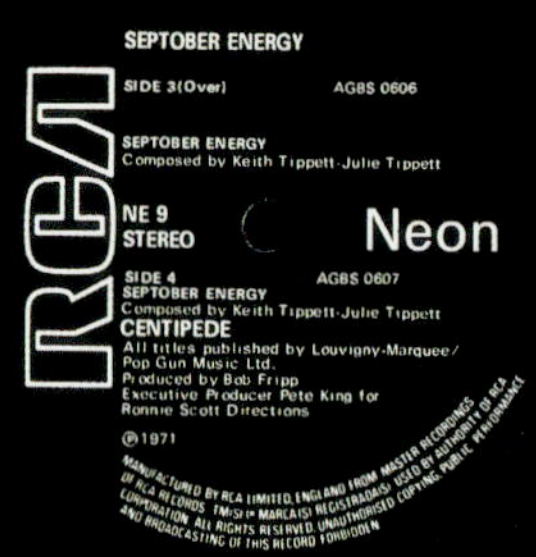

NEON LABEL/SIDE 2

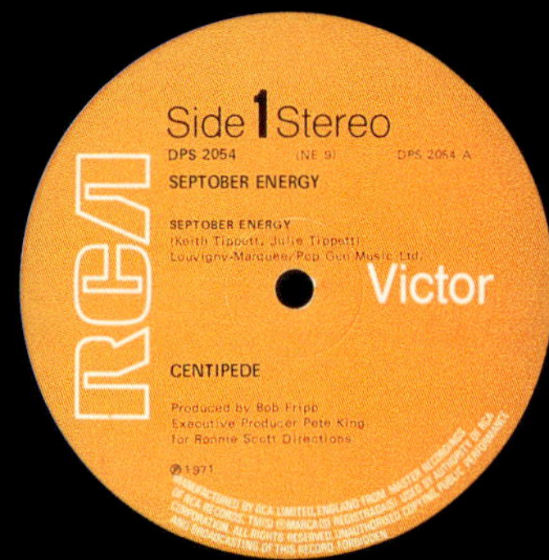

RCA LABEL

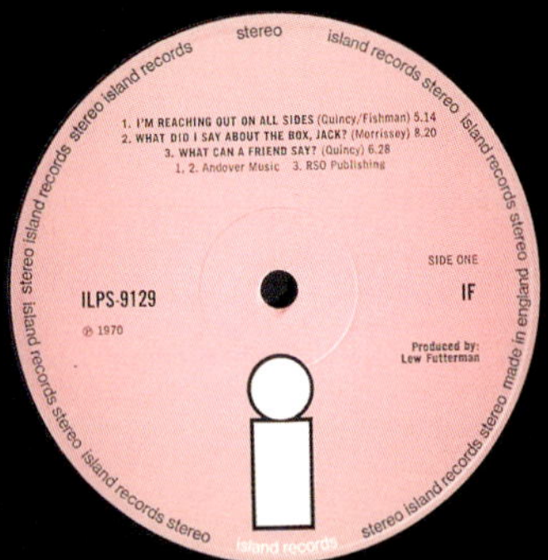

ISLAND LABEL/PINK

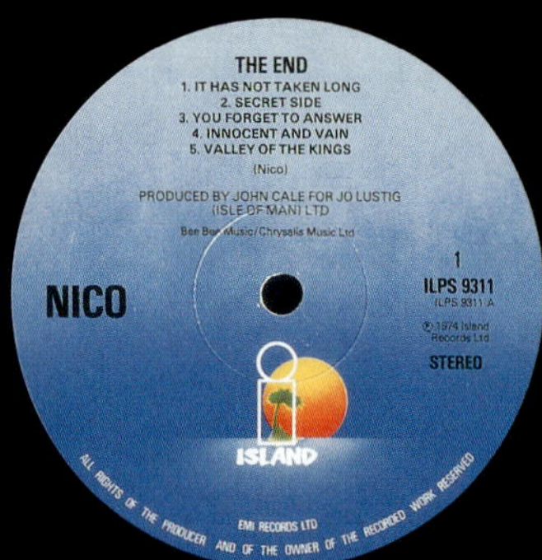

ISLAND LABEL/SUNSET ISLAND

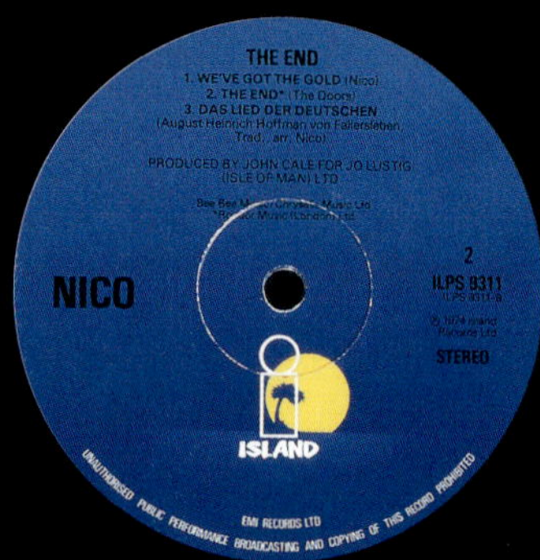

ISLAND LABEL/NIGHT PALM TREE

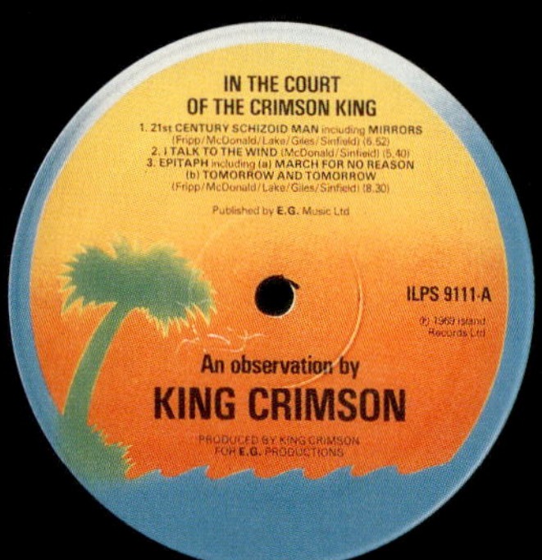

ISLAND LABEL/PALM TREE

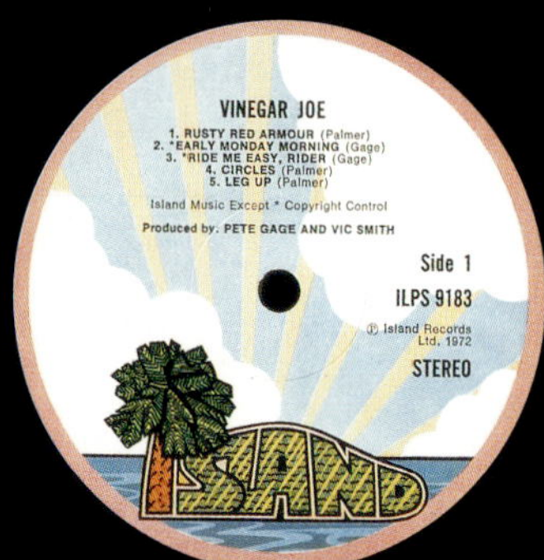

ISLAND LABEL/PINK RIM

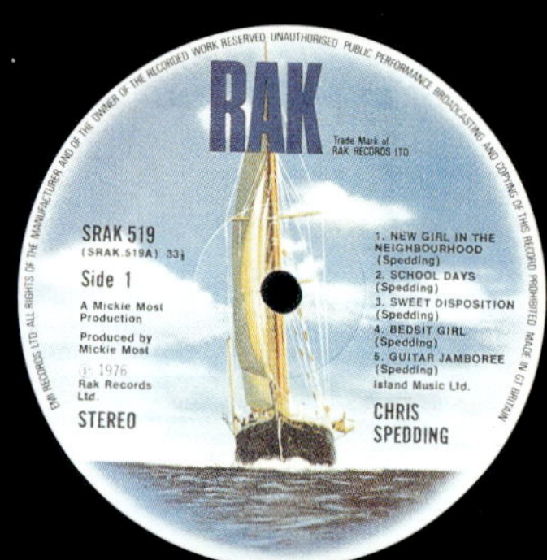

RAK LABEL

In Search of the Lost Record

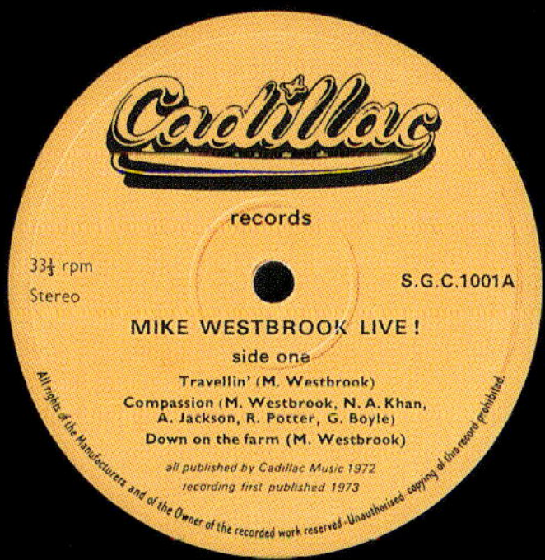

CADILLAC LABEL

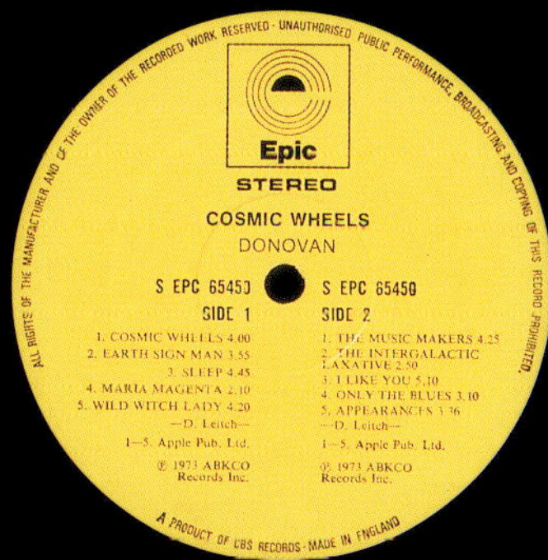

EPIC LABEL

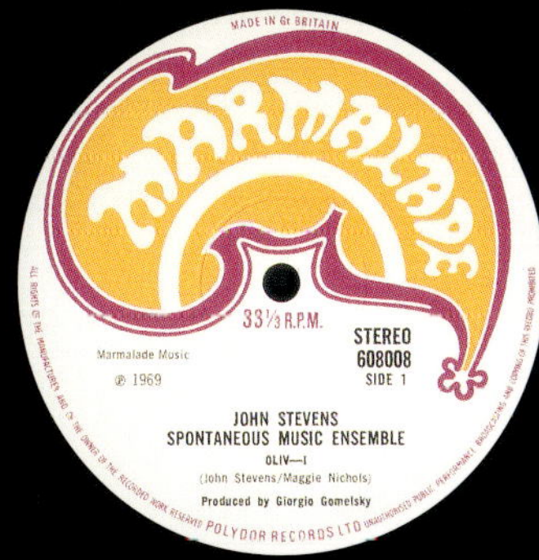

MARMALADE LABEL

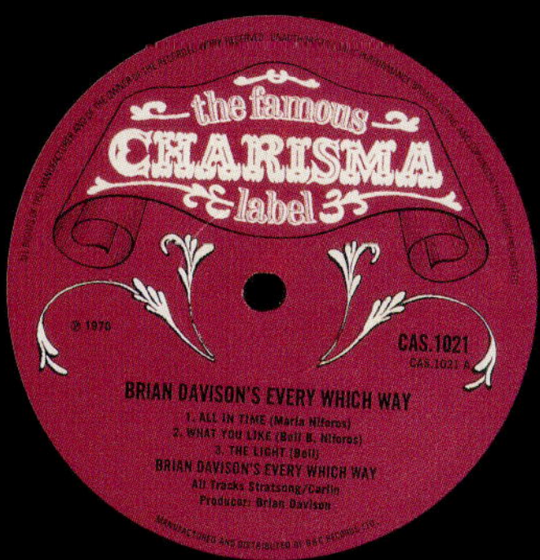

CHARISMA LABEL

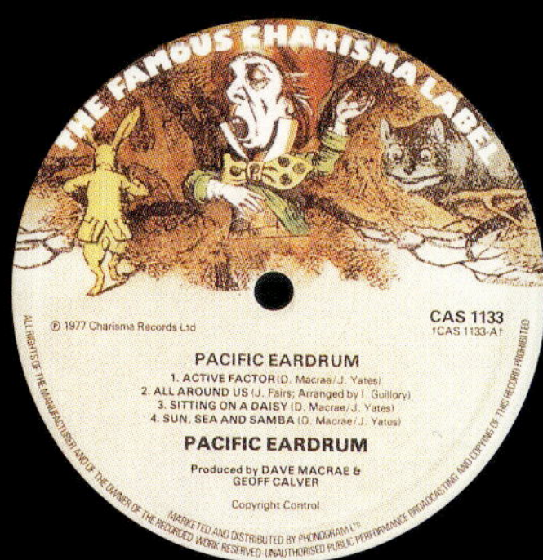

CHARISMA LABEL/MAD HATTER

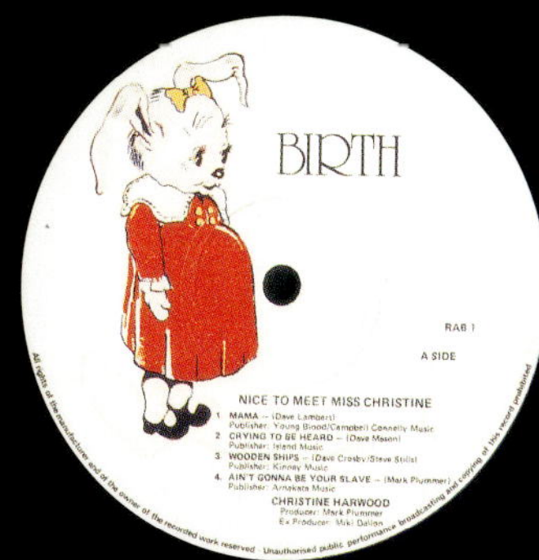

BIRTH LABEL

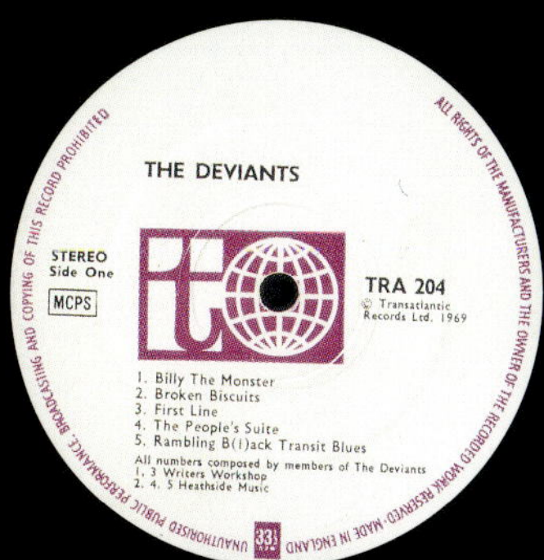

TRANSATLANTIC LABEL

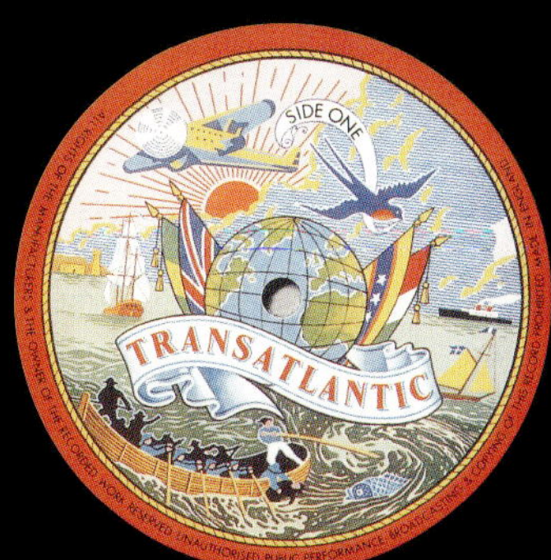

TRANSATLANTIC LABEL / PICTURE

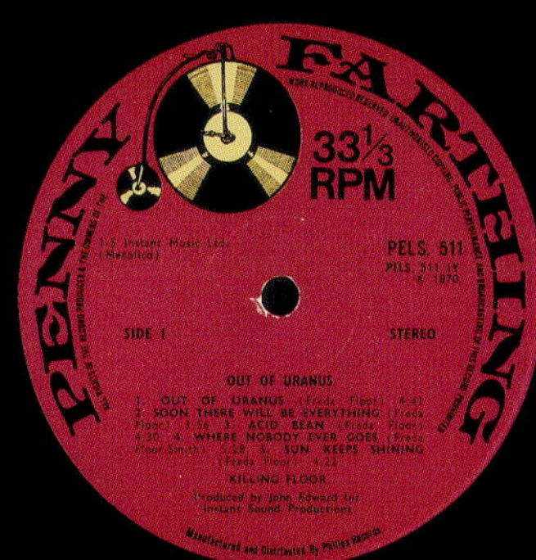

PENNY FARTHING LABEL

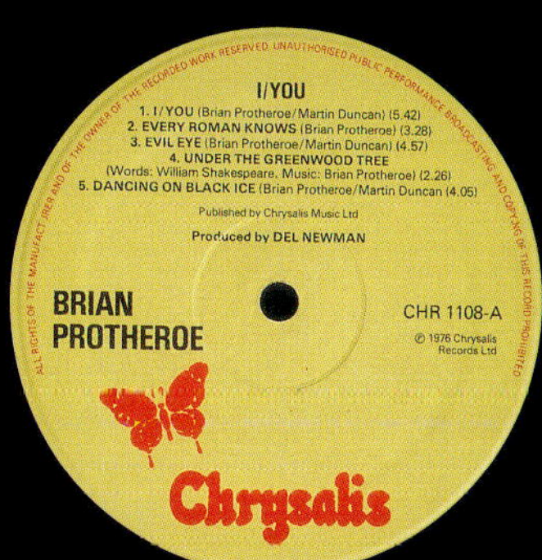

CHIRYSALIS LABEL

BELL LABEL

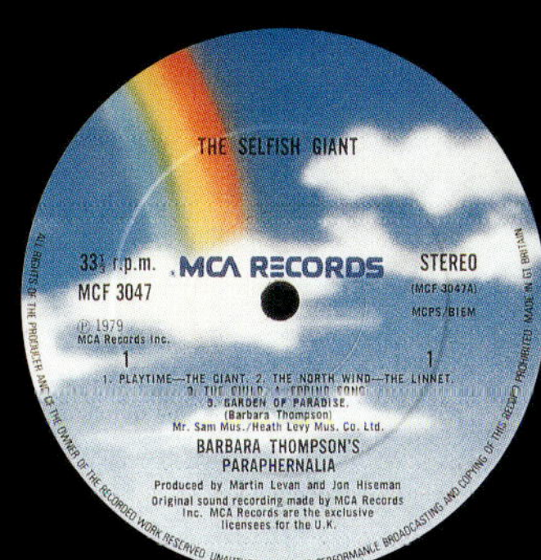

MCA LABEL/PICTURE

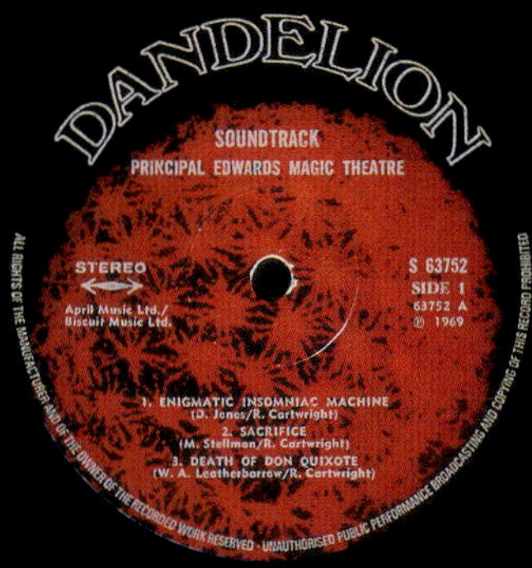

DANDELION LABEL/
DISTRIBUTED BY CBS

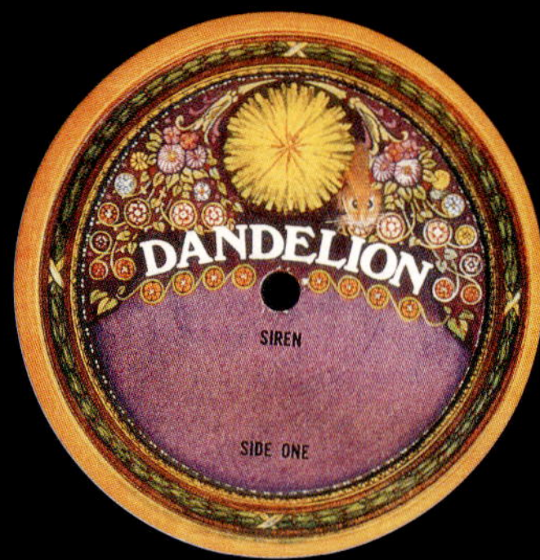

DANDELION LABEL/
DISTRIBUTED BY WARNER BROS.

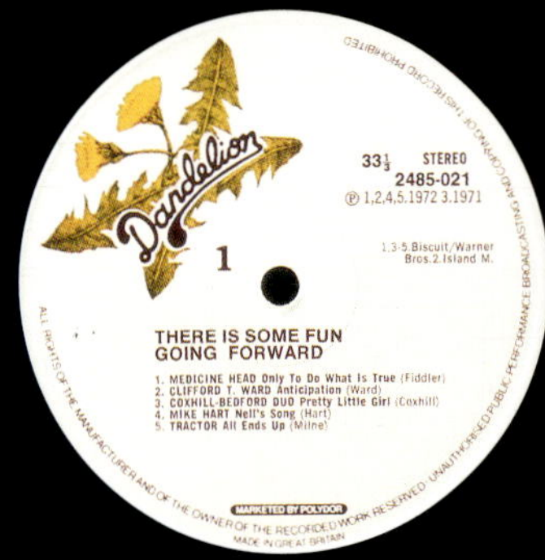

DANDELION LABEL/
DISTRIBUTED BY POLYDOR

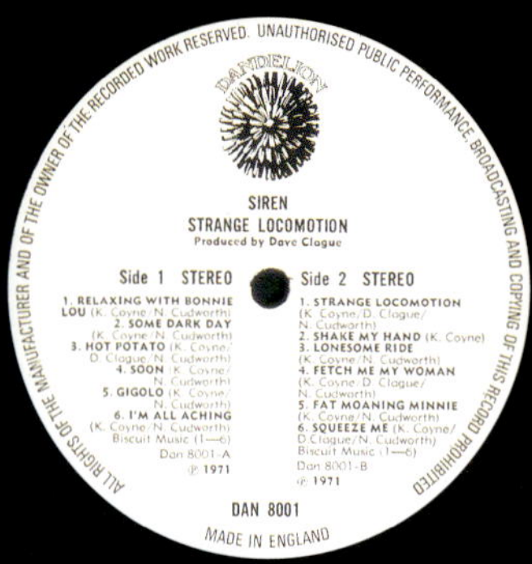

DANDELION LABEL/SIDE 2

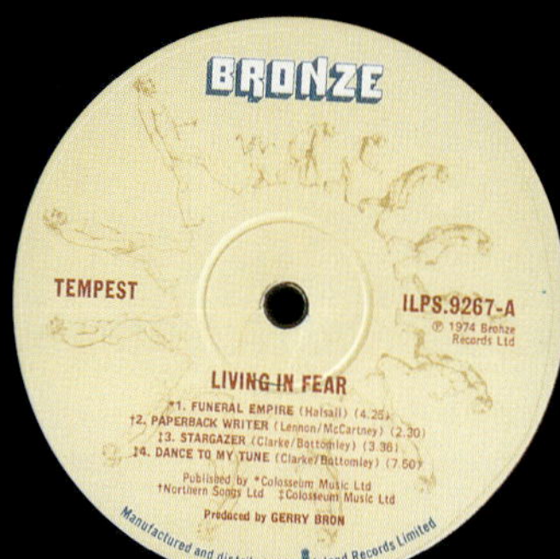

BRONZE LABEL

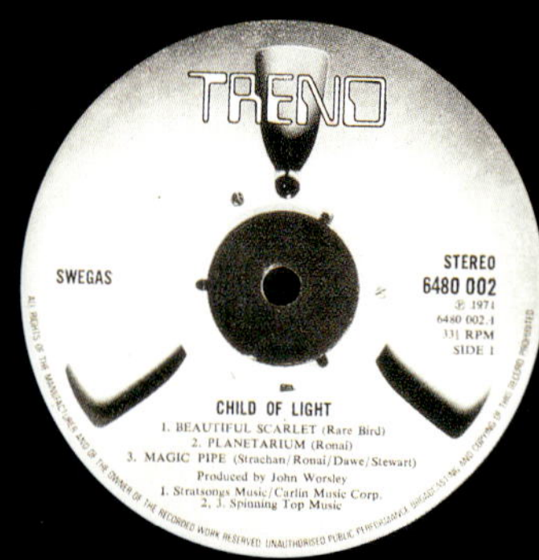

TRENTD LABEL

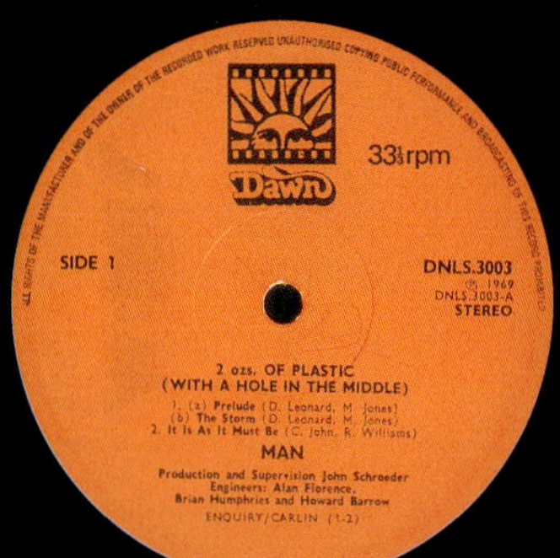

DAWN LABEL/ORANGE

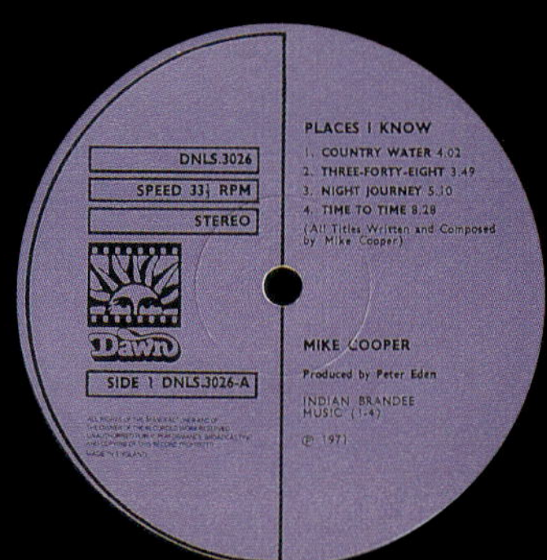

DAWN LABEL/PURPLE

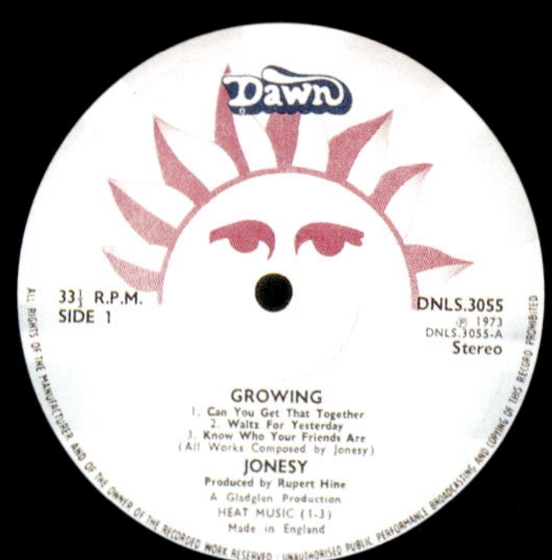

DAWN LABEL/

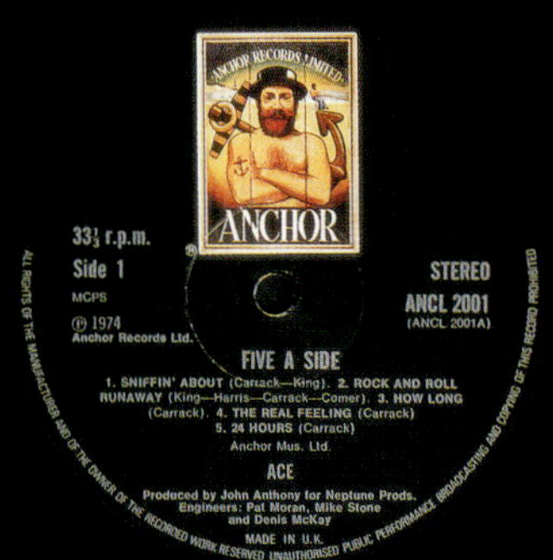

ANCHOR LABEL

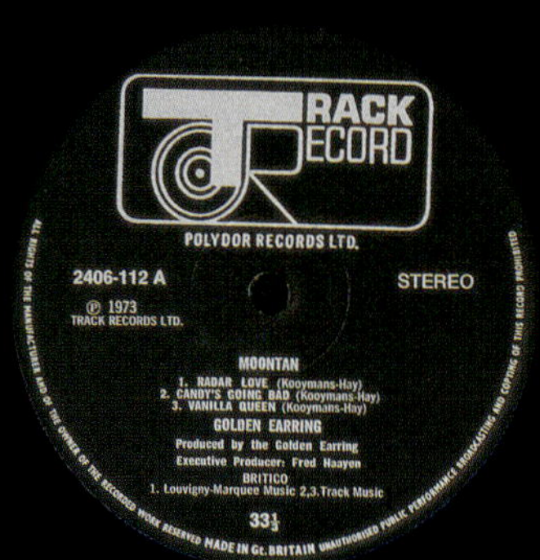

TRACK LABEL

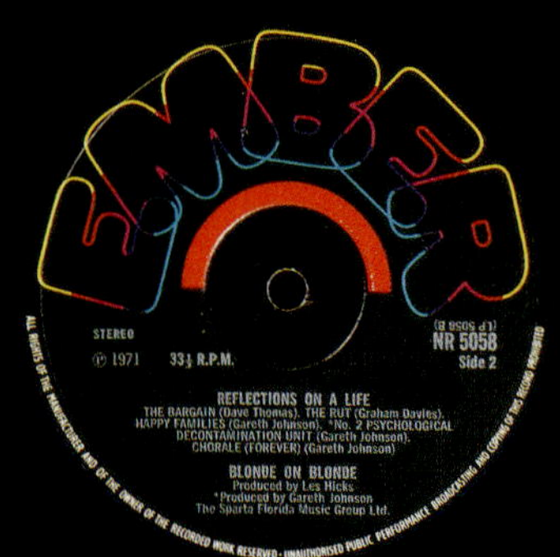

EMBER LABEL

In Search of the Lost Record

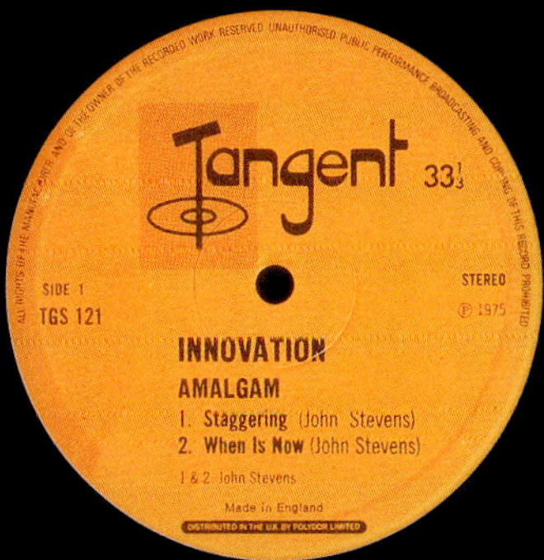

TANGENT LABEL

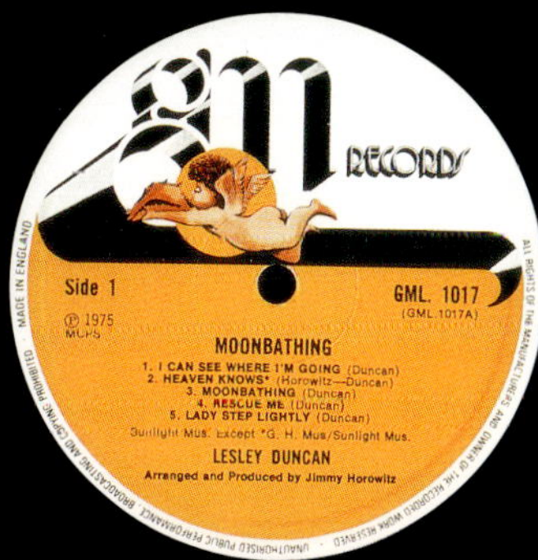

GM LABEL

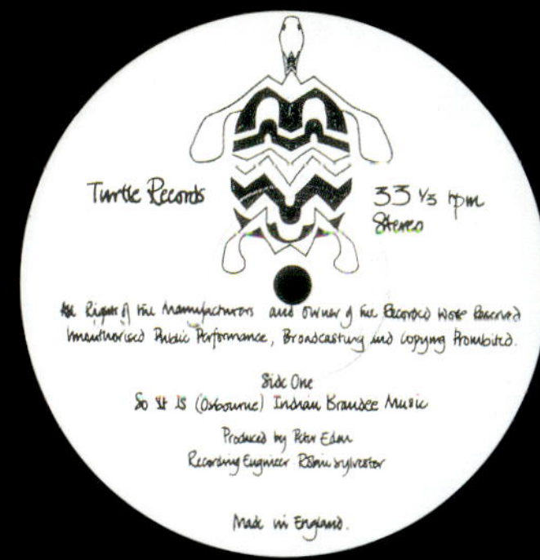

TURTLE LABEL

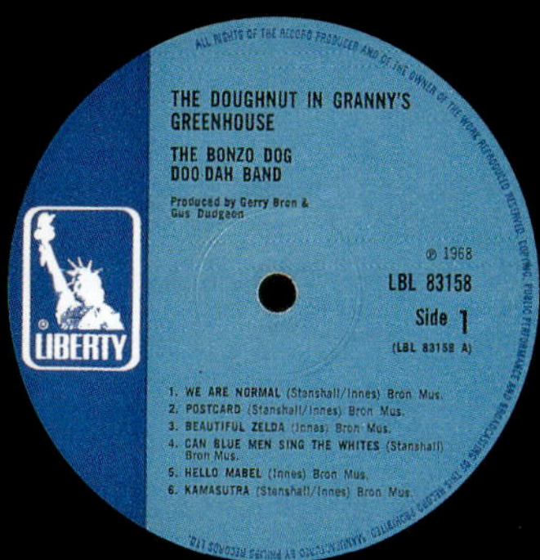

LIBERTY LABEL

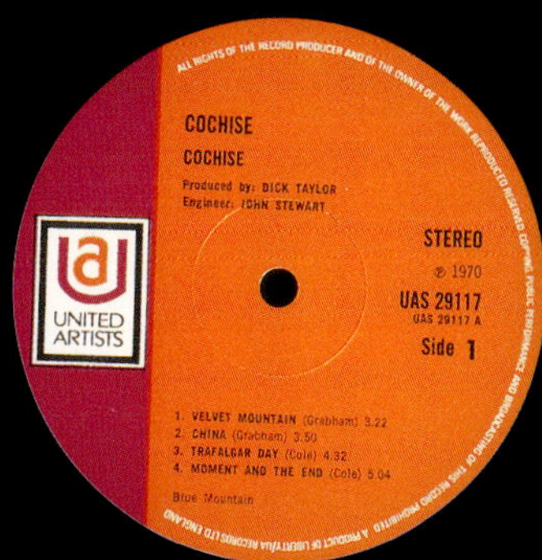

UNITED ARTISTS LABEL

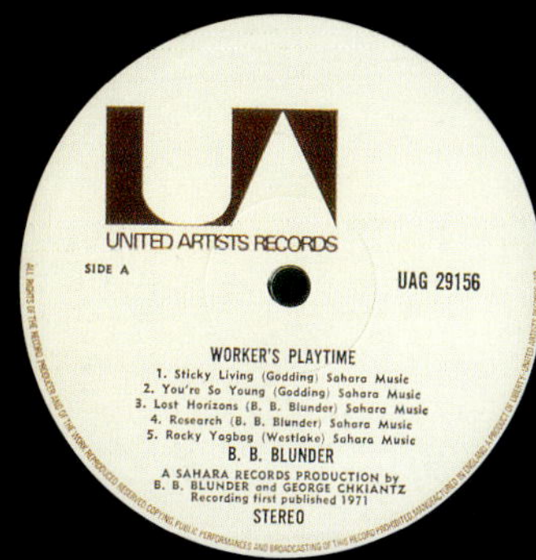

UNITED ARTISTS LABEL

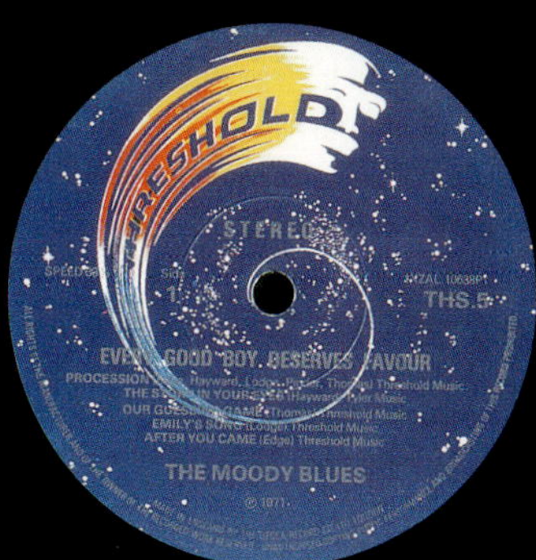

THRESHOLD LABEL

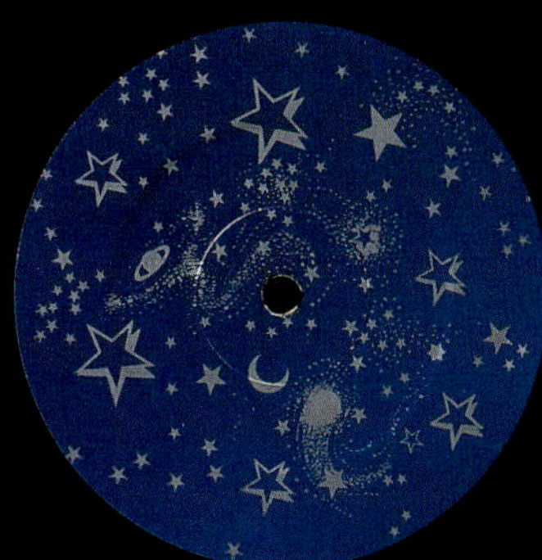
EPIC LABEL/COSMIC WHEELS(DONOVAN)

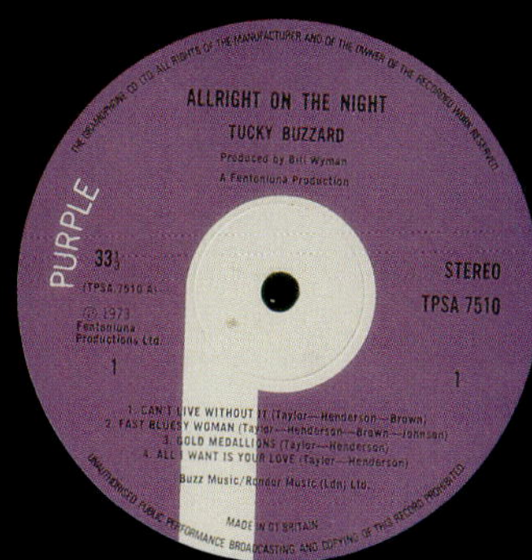

PURPLE LABEL

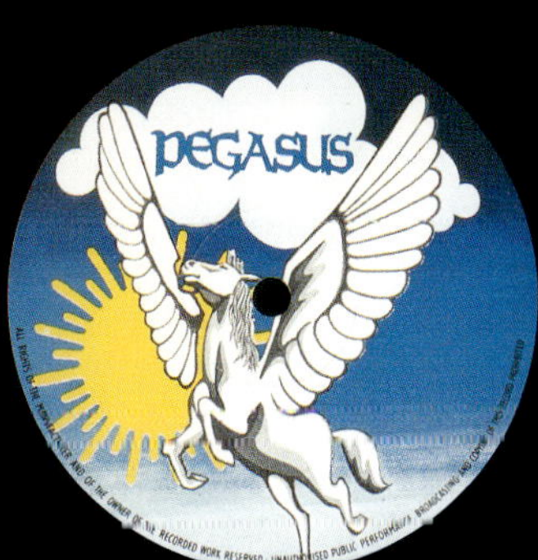

PEGASUS LABEL/SIDE 1

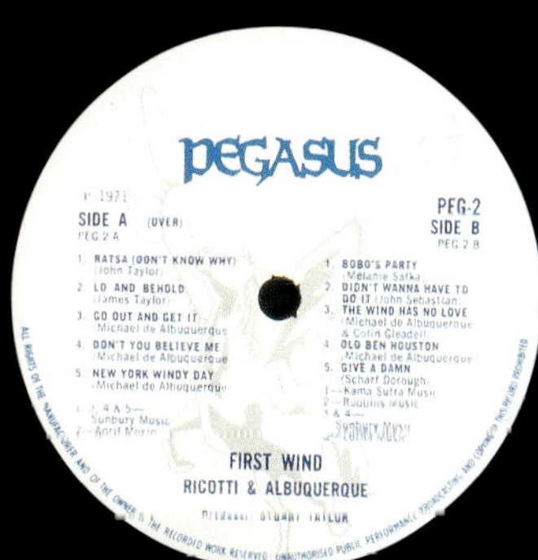

PEGASUS LABEL/SIDE 2

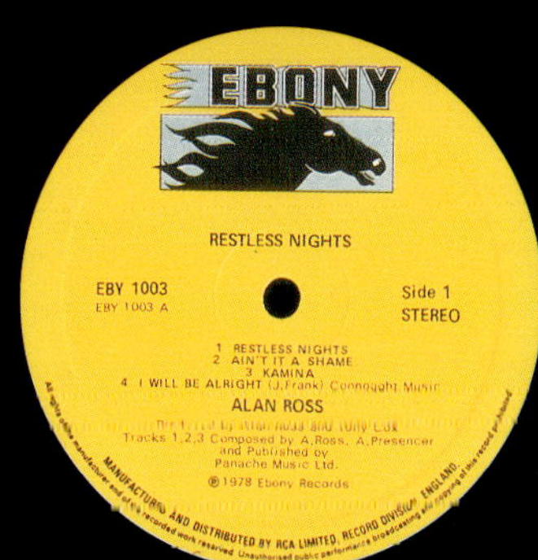

EBONY LABEL

In Search of the Lost Record

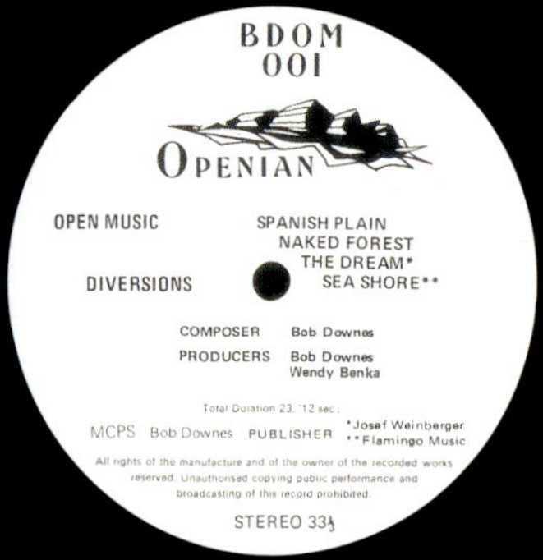

OPENIAN LABEL

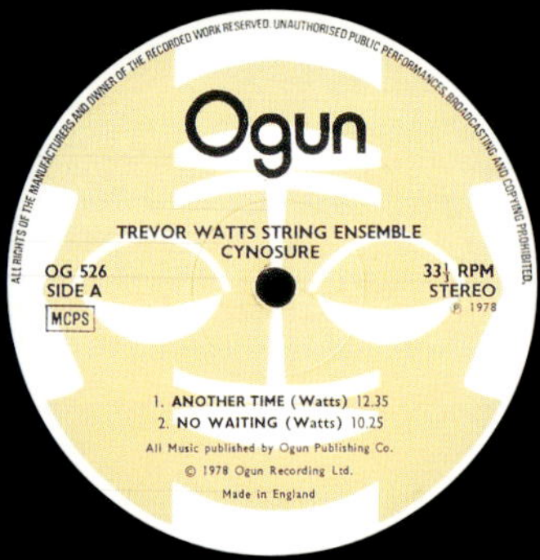

OGUN LABEL

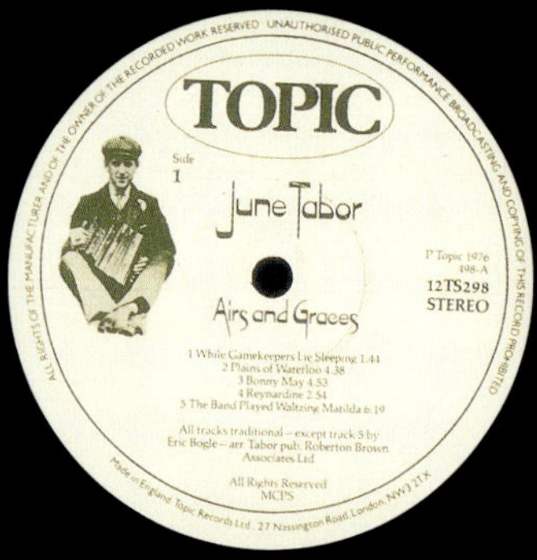

TOPIC LABEL

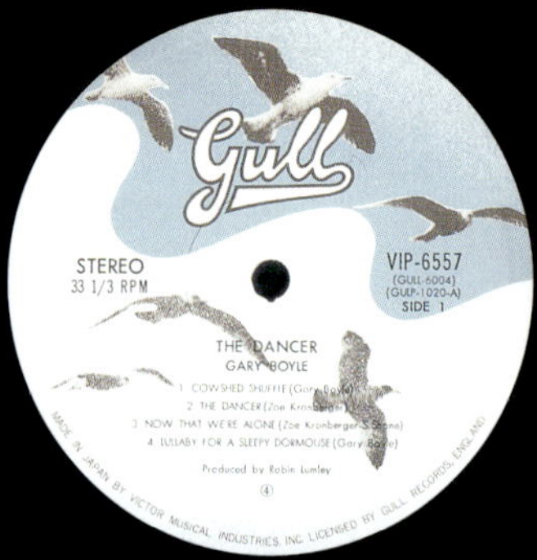

GULL LABEL

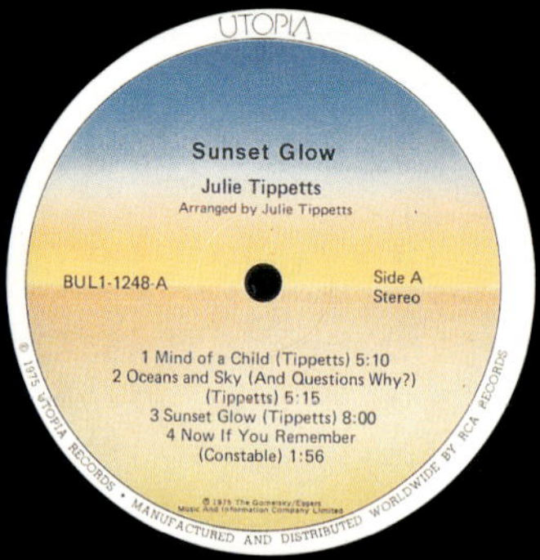

UTOPIA LABEL

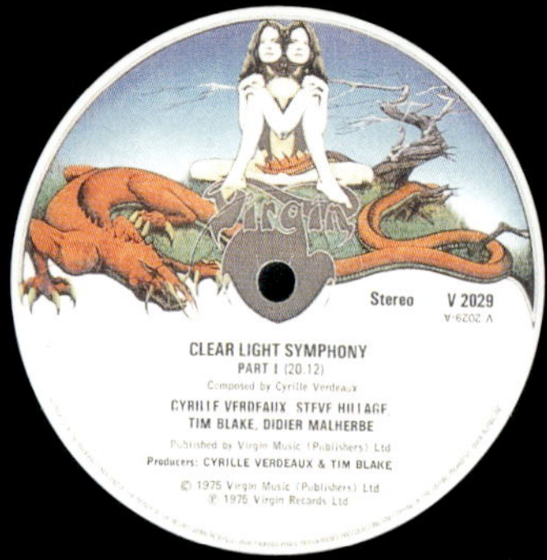

VIRGIN LABEL

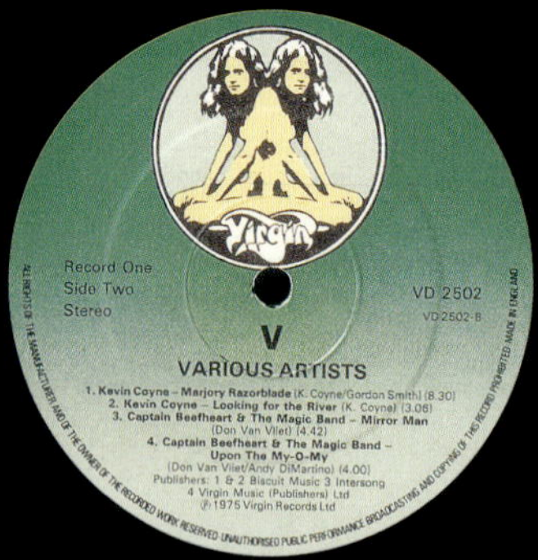

VIRGIN LABEL/LITTLE TWINS

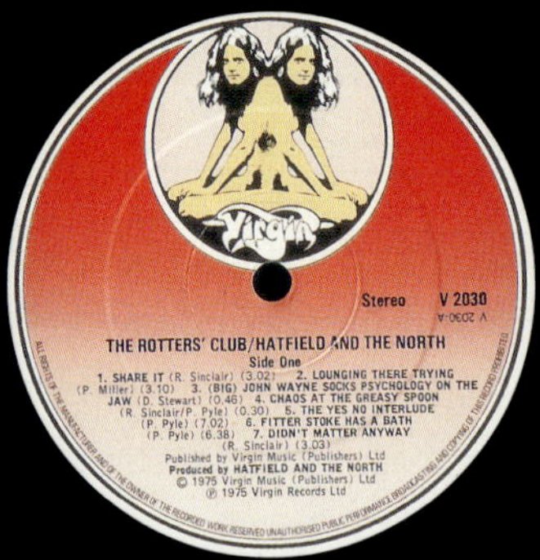

VIRGIN LABEL/TWINS

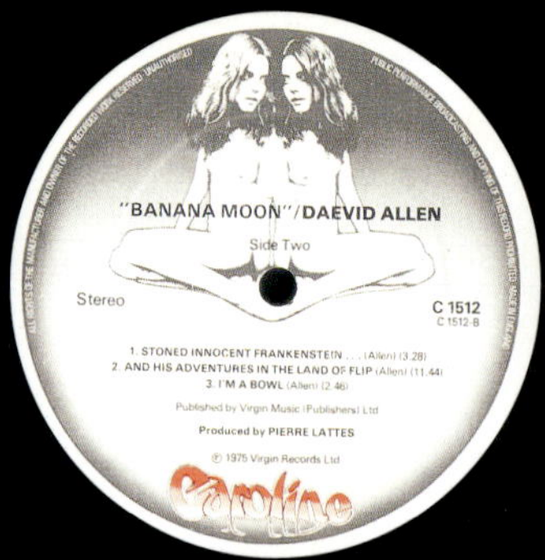

CAROLINE LABEL

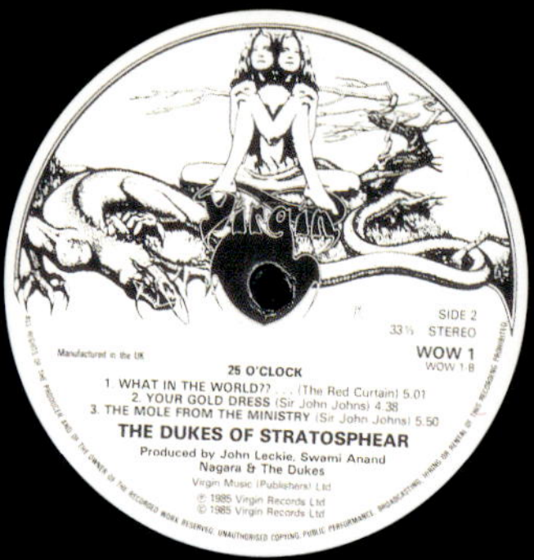

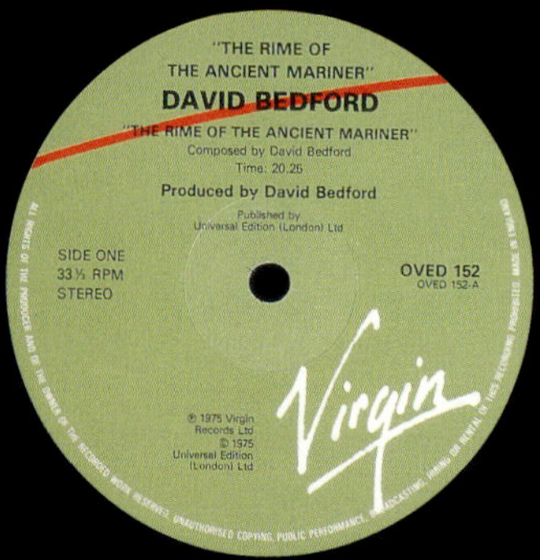

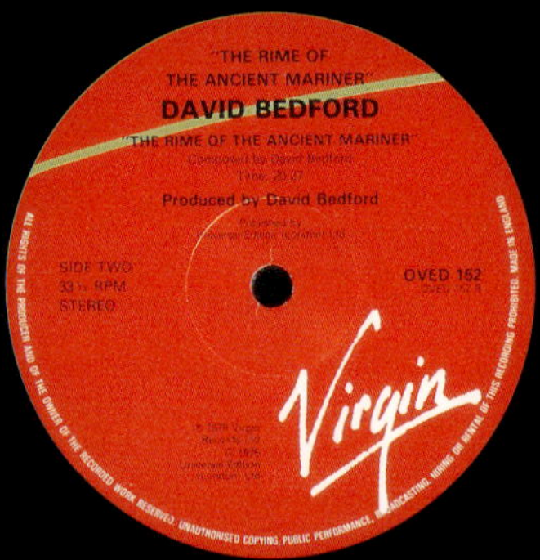

VIRGIN LABEL/MONOCROME

VIRGIN LABEL (SIDE 1/GREEN)

VIRGIN LABEL (SIDE 2/RED)

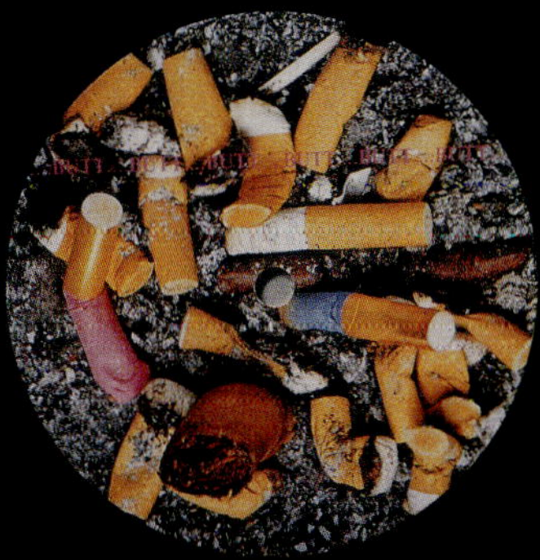

BUTT LABEL/ELECTRIC BANANA

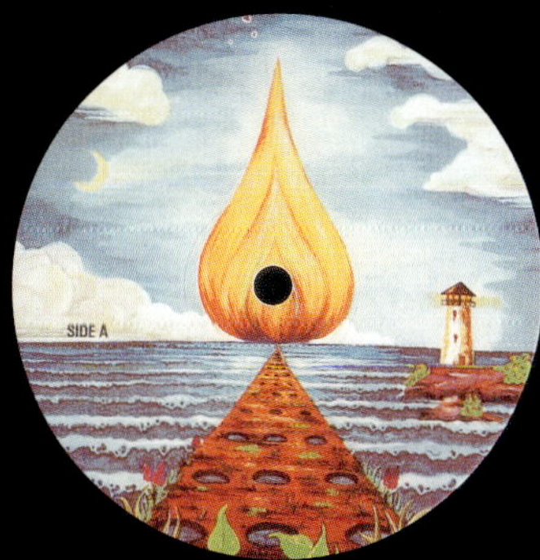

COMPENDIUM LABEL/SIDE 1

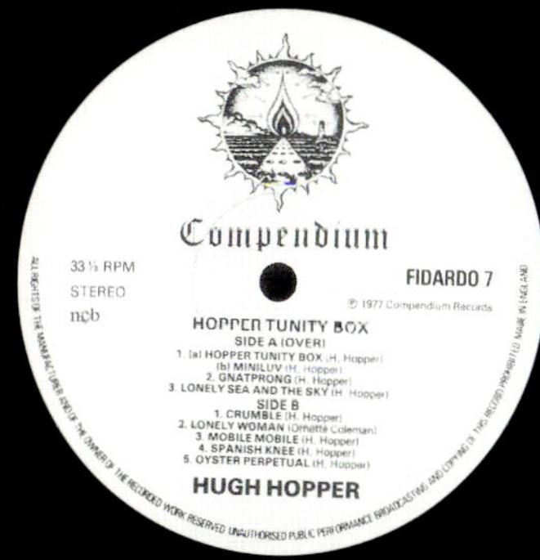

COMPENDIUM LABEL/SIDE 2

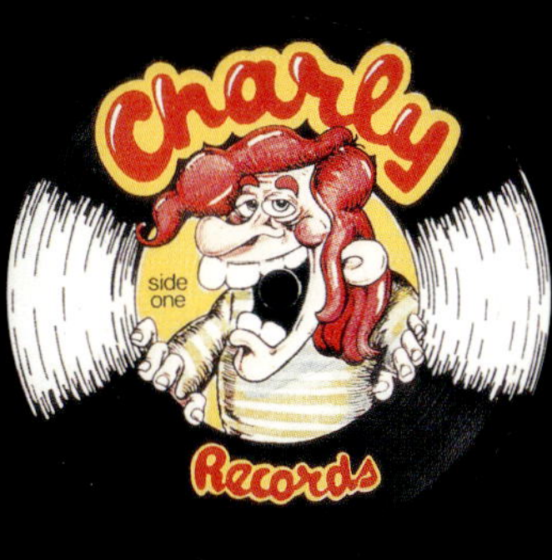

CHARLY LABEL/SIDE 1 (PICTURE LOGO)

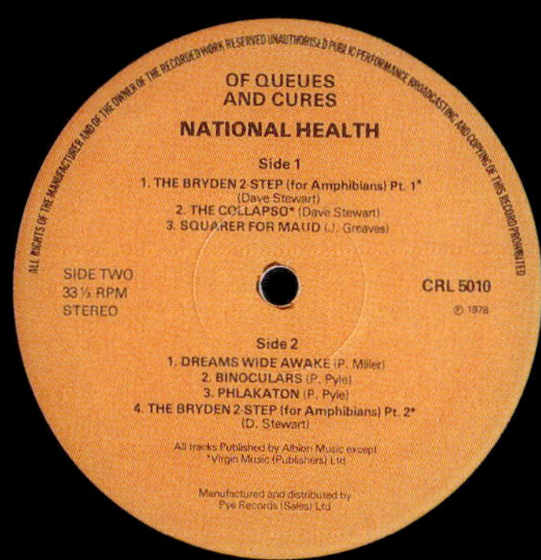

CHARLY LABEL/SIDE 2

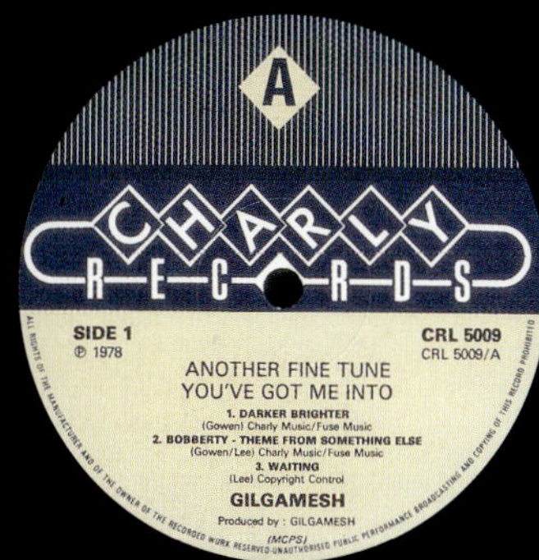

CHARLY LABEL

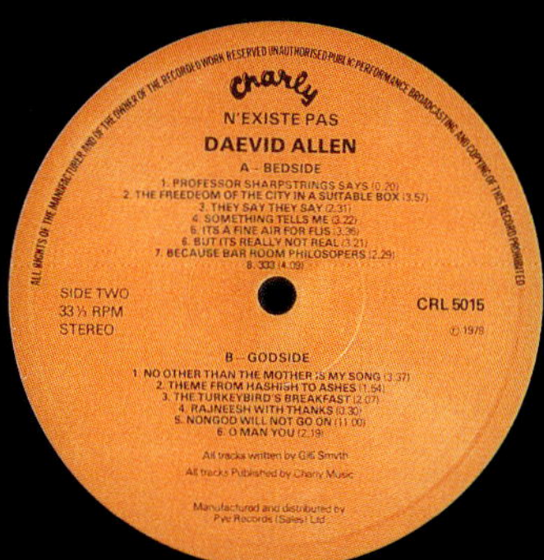

CHARLY LABEL/SIDE 2

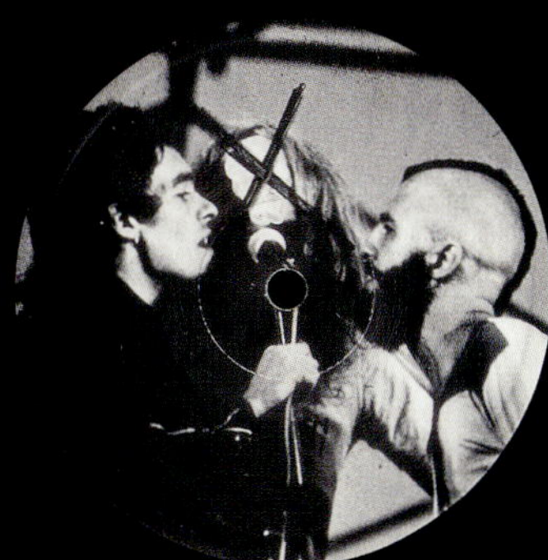

CHARLY LABEL/SIDE 1

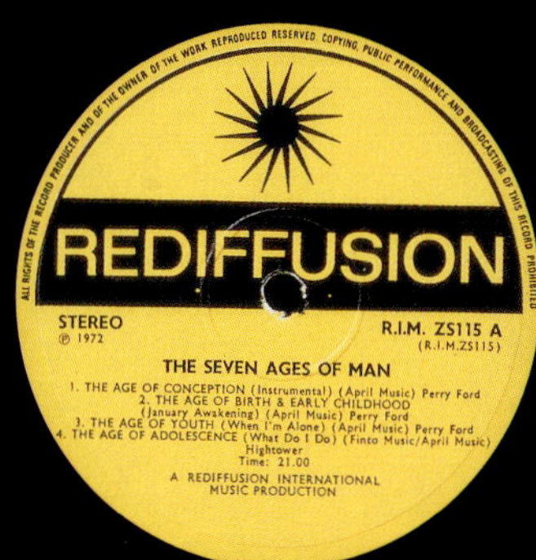

REDIFFUSION LABEL

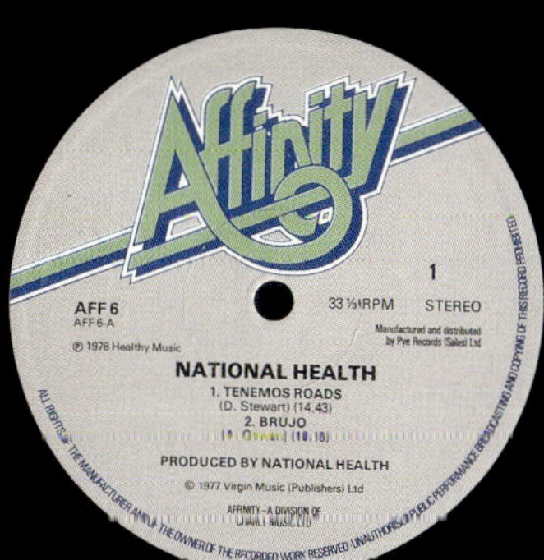

AFFINITY LABEL

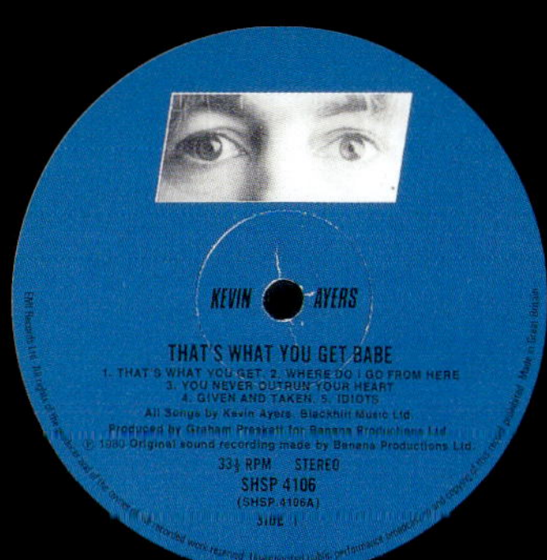

HARVEST LABEL/
THAT'S WHAT YOU GET BABE(SIDE 1)

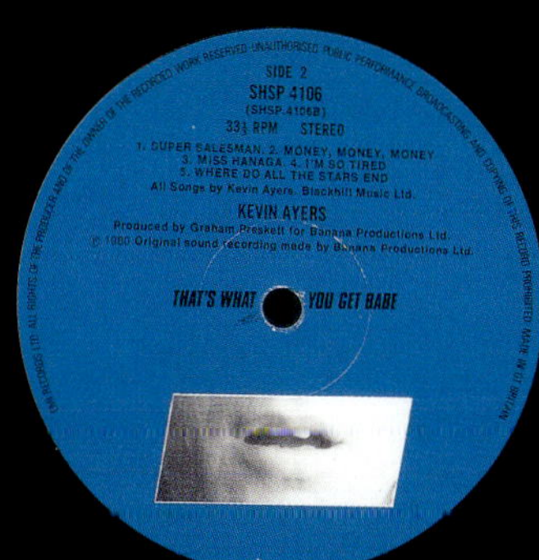

HARVEST LABEL/
THAT'S WHAT YOU GET BABE(SIDE 2)

STAFF

企画・構成・文	松井 巧
企画協力	村松千絵（レミントン社）
撮影	広瀬雅敏
デザイン	寺井恵司
編集	村松千絵
	浦田善浩（グラフィック社）
翻訳	吉田香織
	萩原裕美子
制作協力	TETSU

SPECIAL THANKS TO 浅井有／ 小山哲人／宮脇浩／横山茂（以上の各氏には、貴重なアナログ・レコードをお借りしました）

失われたレコードを求めて

2001年10月25日　初版第1刷発行

編著者　松井 巧

発行者　菅谷誠一
発行所　株式会社グラフィック社
〒102-0073 東京都千代田区九段北1-9-12
電話（03）3263-4318（代表）
URL＝http://www.graphicsha.co.jp

印刷・製本所　大日本印刷株式会社

ISBN4-7661-1268-7